COMMENTARIES AND INSIGHTS ON THE BOOK OF MORMON

1 NEPHI–ALMA 29

COMMENTARIES AND INSIGHTS ON THE BOOK OF MORMON

1 NEPHI–ALMA 29

ED J. PINEGAR AND RICHARD J. ALLEN

Covenant Communications Inc.

Covenant

Cover image *Lehi's Dream* © Greg Olsen, www.gregolsengallery.com
Cover design copyrighted 2007 by Covenant Communications, Inc.
Published by Covenant Communications, Inc.
American Fork, Utah

Printed in Canada
First Printing: October 2007

14 13 12 11 10 09 08 07 10 9 8 7 6 5 4 3 2 1

ISBN 10: 1-59811-461-1
ISBN 13: 978-1-59811-461-4

CONTENTS

PREFACE

Since the initial printing of the Book of Mormon in March, 1830—an edition of 5,000 copies prepared under the personal direction of the Prophet Joseph Smith and his brother Hyrum, working with the E. B. Grandin printing house in Palmyra, New York—this monumental work has attained a circulation of well over 100 million copies in multiple languages. It is by far the most compelling and effective missionary tool for spreading the gospel in the latter days. The coming forth of the Book of Mormon as a central dimension of the Restoration was foretold by the Lord's messengers. Isaiah spoke of a voice that would "whisper out of the dust" and be part of "a marvellous work and a wonder" that would transcend the wisdom and understanding of the world's prudent (Isaiah 29:4, 14). Ezekiel spoke of a record—the "stick of Ephraim" or, by extension, the stick of Joseph—that would be paired with the "stick of Judah" in the latter days as one unified message of truth (Ezekiel 37:16–17). John the Revelator proclaimed: "And I saw another angel fly in the midst of heaven, having the everlasting gospel to preach unto them that dwell on the earth, and to every nation, and kindred, and tongue, and people" (Revelation 14:6).

In our day, the Lord has made clear His purposes in bringing forth this gift of truth: "And [I] gave him [Joseph Smith] power from on high, by the means which were before prepared, to translate the Book of Mormon; Which contains a record of a fallen people, and the fulness of the gospel of Jesus Christ to the Gentiles and to the Jews also; Which was given by inspiration, and is confirmed to others by the ministering of angels, and is declared unto the world by them—Proving to the world that the holy scriptures are true, and that God does inspire men and call them to his holy work in this age and generation, as well as in generations of old; Thereby showing that he is the same God yesterday, today, and forever. Amen" (D&C 20:8–12).

The authors offer this work of commentary as an adjunct to the systematic process of acquiring more and more knowledge and understanding concerning the word of God—especially as it pertains to the Book of Mormon. The approach used is systematic and linear—"line upon line": "For behold, thus saith the Lord God: I will give unto the children of men line upon line, precept upon precept, here a little and there a little; and blessed are those who hearken unto my precepts, and lend an ear unto my counsel, for they shall learn wisdom; for unto him that receiveth I will give more" (2 Nephi 28:30). Each verse of the Book of Mormon is accounted for in this study, either verbatim—with accompanying discussion and cross-illumination through related sources and materials—or as part of a content summary for verses that can be readily navigated as a bridge to subsequent passages. In any case, the verses are always identified by number to the left of the text as it flows from beginning to end. All quotations from the scriptural text of the Book of Mormon are given in *italics* (except for those phrases that might be cited in the content summary bridges).

The commentary segments of the work include doctrinal explanations, applications for daily living, questions of conscience for the reader to ponder and consider, profiles of the principal personalities involved, supportive scriptural references from the other standard works, quotations from Church leaders and scholarly writers, historical notes, illustrations and reminiscences (introduced by the word "memories" when derived from the personal experiences of the authors), and "evidences" (cultural, linguistic, archaeological) of the authenticity of the Book of Mormon.

In this last regard, the authors express sincere gratitude to the Neal A. Maxwell Institute for Religious Scholarship at Brigham Young University for permission to include in this work summary segments adapted and derived from the publication *Echoes and Evidences of the Book of Mormon* (Provo, UT: FARMS, 2002), the general editors being Donald W. Parry, Daniel C. Peterson, and John W. Welch. The authors of this commentary acknowledge the non-exclusive nature of the permission to use this valuable information in the present work and recommend that readers consult *Echoes and Evidences of the Book of Mormon* as an authoritative source for establishing the authenticity of the Book of Mormon. These materials are introduced by the word "EVIDENCE" in the current volume.

In all of this, the authors have one purpose: to help readers "liken the scriptures" unto themselves, as Nephi counseled, "that ye may have hope" (1 Nephi 19:23, 24). The Book of Mormon is a repository of divine wisdom concerning the Redeemer of mankind. It is a "fountain of living waters" (1 Nephi 11:25) to refresh the soul thirsting for heavenly truths that can ennoble and exalt the individual through faith and obedience to the gospel plan. It is a source of doctrine representing "the fulness of the gospel of Jesus Christ to the Gentiles and to the Jews also" (D&C 20:9). On Sunday, November 28, 1841, the Prophet Joseph Smith, the instrument in the hands of the Lord in bringing forth the Book of Mormon in our time, spent the day conversing on "a variety of subjects," with the Apostles at Brigham Young's home. The Prophet chose to include in his journal only one of the themes discussed that day: "I told the brethren that the Book of Mormon was the most correct of any book on earth, and the keystone of our religion, and a man would get nearer to God by abiding by its precepts, than by any other book" (Joseph Smith, *History of The Church of Jesus Christ of Latter-day Saints,* comp. B. H. Roberts [Salt Lake City: The Church of Jesus Christ of Latter-day Saints, 1932–1951], 4:461). Thus came into being one of the most celebrated testimonies from the Prophet concerning the latter-day work he was divinely commissioned to perform.

To follow in the footsteps of the faithful personalities of the Book of Mormon is to cause the curtains of doubt to part and the veil covering our understanding to be lifted. When we proceed with a spirit of discovery and an attitude of humble openness to the message of the word of God, we find ourselves moving forward on a pathway of learning that is illuminated by the Spirit of the Lord. We can then partake of the fruit of Lehi's "tree of life," representing "the love of God" (1 Nephi 11:25), and hearken unto the final counsel of Moroni, the last in a long sequence of keepers of the sacred records:

> Yea, come unto Christ, and be perfected in him, and deny yourselves of all ungodliness; and if ye shall deny yourselves of all ungodliness, and love God with all your might, mind and strength, then is his grace sufficient for you, that by his grace ye may be perfect in Christ; and if by the grace of God ye are perfect in Christ, ye can in nowise deny the power of God. (Moroni 10:32)

The Prophet Joseph Smith completed the translation of the Book of Mormon by inspiration in less than three months' time, beginning on April 7, 1829. It was a monumental task. The careful reader of the book, looking back at the historical reality of how the book came to be in such an amazingly short period of time, is astonished to perceive that the nearly three hundred different personalities and thirty distinct groups of people referenced in the Book of Mormon are smoothly integrated throughout the pages of the text, with myriad cross-references, flashbacks, and forecasts of future events ("great views of that which is to come" [Mosiah 5:3])—all without the slightest degree of inconsistency or contradiction. It is a work of pure harmony, fully integrated as to doctrine and internal historical veracity. Truly the Book of Mormon is "Another Testament of Jesus Christ"—an irrefutable confirmation of the love of God and the majesty of His plan for our immortality and eternal life.

We give our sincere thanks to Kathryn Jenkins, Managing Editor of Covenant Communications, and to her colleagues for their devoted service in bringing this work to fruition. In addition we give thanks to our wives, Patricia Pinegar and Carol Lynn Allen, for their support and encouragement.

The Authors
Ed J. Pinegar
Richard J. Allen

ABBREVIATIONS

CR	Conference Report
Echoes	*Echoes and Evidences of the Book of Mormon,* ed. Donald W. Parry, Daniel C. Peterson, and John W. Welch (Provo, UT: FARMS, 2002).
HC	Joseph Smith, *History of The Church of Jesus Christ of Latter-day Saints,* 7 vols., comp. B. H. Roberts (Salt Lake City: Deseret Book, 1948–1950).
Nibley	Hugh Nibley, *Lehi in the Desert and the World of the Jaredites* (Salt Lake City: Bookcraft, 1952).
Sorenson	John L. Sorenson and Melvin J. Thorne, *Rediscovering the Book of Mormon* (Salt Lake City and Provo, UT: Deseret Book and FARMS, 1991).

THE BOOK OF MORMON

AN ACCOUNT WRITTEN BY THE HAND OF MORMON UPON PLATES TAKEN FROM THE PLATES OF NEPHI

Wherefore, it is an abridgment of the record of the people of Nephi, and also of the Lamanites—Written to the Lamanites, who are a remnant of the house of Israel; and also to Jew and Gentile—Written by way of commandment, and also by the spirit of prophecy and of revelation—Written and sealed up, and hid up unto the Lord, that they might not be destroyed—To come forth by the gift and power of God unto the interpretation thereof—Sealed by the hand of ***Moroni,*** *and hid up unto the Lord, to come forth in due time by way of the Gentile—The interpretation thereof by the gift of God.*

An abridgment taken from the Book of Ether also, which is a record of the people of Jared, who were scattered at the time the Lord confounded the language of the people, when they were building a tower to get to heaven— ***Which is to show*** *unto the remnant of the House of Israel what great things the Lord hath done for their fathers; and that they may know the covenants of the Lord, that they are not cast off forever—And also to the convincing of the Jew and Gentile that JESUS is the CHRIST, the ETERNAL GOD, manifesting himself unto all nations—And now, if there are faults they are the mistakes of men; wherefore, condemn not the things of God, that ye may be found spotless at the judgment-seat of Christ.*

TRANSLATED BY JOSEPH SMITH, JUN.

Moroni

Moroni, the son of Mormon and the last of the chosen record keepers commissioned to oversee the sacred work of preserving the word of God concerning the remnant of Joseph in the New World, is surely the author of this title page, for it contains the last of the words contributed in Moroni's day to the abridgment and compilation of the Book of Mormon, the material which was sealed up around A.D. 421 to await the dawning of the Restoration. The Prophet Joseph Smith declared:

> I wish to mention here that the title-page of the Book of Mormon is a literal translation, taken from the very last leaf on the left hand side of the collection or book of plates, which contained the record which has been translated, the language of the whole running the same as all Hebrew writing in general [that is, from right to left]; and that said title page is not by any means a modern composition, either of mine or of any other man who has lived or does live in this generation. (*HC* 1:71)

Which is to show

The title page is explicit concerning the purpose for the Book of Mormon: (1) to demonstrate and confirm unto the remnant of the house of Israel the goodness and mercy of God in having done such great things for the fathers of their lineage; (2) to reveal to them in this day the knowledge and operation of the sacred covenants of the Lord; (3) to comfort and persuade them that they are not "cast off forever"—that is, they are indeed part of the family of God and can look forward with an everlasting hope to a future heavenly reward of immortality and eternal life; and (4) to convince both Jew and Gentile of the divine mission of Jesus Christ, that He is verily the "Eternal God, manifesting himself unto all nations." The Book of Mormon then is "Another Testament of Jesus Christ"—as identified by the subtitle in modern editions of this sacred scripture. The word "testament" means essentially "covenant," or holy agreement between God and man. Through it we are granted the marvelous blessings of the redemption through the atoning grace of Father and Son according to our obedience and righteousness under the gospel plan. Nephi expressed it this way: "For we labor diligently to write, to persuade our children, and also our brethren, to believe in Christ, and to be reconciled to God; for we know that it is by grace that we are saved, after all we can do" (2 Nephi 25:23).

What are we to do when we receive the Book of Mormon? We are to accept with humble gratitude the blessings of the word of God given to us through this sacred record. Then, through the guidance of the Spirit of God, we are to follow its precepts and doctrines in order to "come unto Christ, and be perfected in him" (Moroni 10:32). We can apply the counsel of the title page as a four fold strategy for proceeding with this task:

FIRST, LET US REMEMBER TO BE GRATEFUL

Let us recognize the goodness of God throughout all generations past. We can remember His mercy in guiding Lehi and his group away from the destruction of ancient Jerusalem around 600 B.C., just prior to the Babylonian conquest. We can remember the Lord's kindness to Jared and his group some 1,500 years earlier in guiding them also to the promised land. We can follow the hand of the Lord in raising up prophets over the generations to provide the light of truth amidst the darkness of apostasy—Nephi, Jacob, Benjamin, Abinadi, Alma (father and son), Helaman, Samuel the Lamanite, the brother of Jared, Ether, and many others. We can remember the resurrected Lord and His healing influence upon the people, which led to two hundred years of peace and unity. In our daily lives, as we deal with adversity and challenges, we can remember that the Lord is a Lord of kindness. He does great things for His people. He remembers His sons and daughters and blesses them in His love. He will do that for us as well.

SECOND, LET US RECEIVE AND HONOR HIS COVENANTS NOW

Every time we read the Book of Mormon, we are renewed in the understanding and operation of our covenants with the Lord. As Alma the Elder stated at the Waters of Mormon: "Now I say unto you, if this be the desire of your hearts, what have you against being baptized in the name of the Lord, as a witness before him that ye have entered into a covenant with him, that ye will serve him and keep his commandments, that he may pour out his Spirit more abundantly upon you?" (Mosiah 18:10). Every time we study the words of this sacred text and participate weekly in the sacrament, we remember that our personal covenant with the Lord is the governing principle of our lives—today and always.

THIRD, LET US CULTIVATE AN ABIDING HOPE FOR THE FUTURE

The Book of Mormon is irrefutable evidence that we are not "cast off"—but belong to the fold of the Shepherd. The expression "cast off" or "cast out" occurs many times in the Book of Mormon. It is a kind of leitmotif of the human condition for those ancient people. Jacob said: "I have written according to the best of my knowledge, by saying that the time passed away with us, and also our lives passed away like as it were unto us a dream, we being a lonesome and a solemn people, wanderers, cast out from Jerusalem, born in tribulation, in a wilderness, and hated of our brethren, which caused wars and contentions; wherefore, we did mourn out our days" (Jacob 7:26). At the same time, their hearts were warmed by the assurance that after their mortal wanderings they would experience a sacred homecoming into the presence of the Father and the Son. Because of the Atonement and the plan of salvation, we are not "cast off" forever but are given the hope of immortality and eternal life.

Moroni was the last of the Nephites, left alone to fulfill his divine mission amidst universal warfare and wickedness. "And my father also was killed by them, and I even remain alone to write the sad tale of the destruction of my people. . . . And whether they will slay me, I know not" (Mormon 8:3). Under such trying circumstances what did Moroni write of? Hope! He preserved for us the words of his father Mormon: "And again, my beloved brethren, I would speak unto you concerning hope. How is it that you can attain unto faith, save ye shall have hope? And what is it that ye shall hope for? Behold I say unto you that ye shall have hope through the atonement of Christ and the power of his resurrection, to be raised unto life eternal, and this because of your faith in him according to the promise" (Moroni 7:40–41).

Finally, let us seek to acquire an enduring testimony

The uplifting knowledge that Jesus is the Christ, that He is the Creator and the Redeemer, the source and font of the power of the Redemption and the Atonement. If we do that, and endure to the end, we will become "children of the prophets" and "children of the covenant" (3 Nephi 20:25, 26), joint-heirs with Christ of all that the Father has (see Romans 8:17; D&C 84:38), and worthy to return to our heavenly home of glory, immortality, and eternal life. The Book of Mormon contains the "fulness of the gospel of Jesus Christ" (D&C 20:9) and is the key to a fulness of enduring joy—now and forever.

THE BOOK OF
FIRST NEPHI

An account of Lehi and his wife Sariah, and his four sons, being called, (beginning at the eldest) Laman, Lemuel, Sam, and Nephi. The Lord warns Lehi to depart out of the land of Jerusalem, because he prophesieth unto the people concerning their iniquity and they seek to destroy his life. He taketh three days' journey into the wilderness with his family. Nephi taketh his brethren and returneth to the land of Jerusalem after the record of the Jews. The account of their sufferings. They take the daughters of Ishmael to wife. They take their families and depart into the wilderness. Their sufferings and afflictions in the wilderness. The course of their travels. They come to the large waters. Nephi's brethren rebel against him. He confoundeth them, and buildeth a ship. They call the name of the place Bountiful. They cross the large waters into the promised land, and so forth. This is according to the account of Nephi; or in other words, I, Nephi, wrote this record. [Note: This preamble was included in the original edition of the Book of Mormon published in 1830.]

BOOK OVERVIEW

An account of God's dealings with the prophet Lehi and his family, including their exodus from Jerusalem into the wilderness, beginning around 600 B.C. and, ultimately, by way of an ocean journey, to the promised land in the Western Hemisphere. Their prophecies and visions, struggles and triumphs, lessons and preachments—all these are included for our edification and the strengthening of our testimony and conviction that Jesus is the Christ, the Son of God.

CHAPTER 1

OVERVIEW

Nephi establishes the context for his record and bears witness that it is true. The setting is his home city of Jerusalem around 600 B.C. He has been born of noble parentage and instructed in the ways of the Lord. Prophets have come among the people to call them to repentance. In vision, Nephi's father, Lehi, beholds many glorious things, including the Savior and the Twelve during their coming earthly ministry. As part of his vision, he reads in a book that Jerusalem will be destroyed. Lehi goes forth to warn the people. They reject his message and try to kill him. Nephi declares that the "tender mercies of the Lord" (verse 20) will deliver the righteous.

> *1 I, **NEPHI,** having been born of goodly **parents,** therefore I was taught somewhat in all the learning of my father; and having seen many afflictions in the course of my days, nevertheless, having been highly **favored** of the Lord in all my days; yea, having had a great knowledge of the goodness and the mysteries of God, therefore I make a record of my proceedings in my days.*

Nephi, Seer of Olden Time

Among the most recognized and admired of the Lord's prophet-servants, Nephi exemplifies faith, obedience, steadfastness, visionary leadership, and unflagging valor in cultivating and upholding the testimony of Jesus Christ as our Redeemer and Savior. As a younger contemporary of the prophet Jeremiah, peer of Daniel, and older contemporary of Ezekiel, Nephi is a firsthand observer of the cultural unrest and spiritual decline in the Holy Land on the eve of the destruction of Jerusalem around 587 B.C. at the hands of the invading Babylonians. Shortly before this upheaval, Lehi follows the command of the Lord and, having warned the recalcitrant people of the city with the voice of prophecy, takes his family and departs into the wilderness about 600 B.C.

The journey through the wilderness of what is now Saudi Arabia and then onward via ocean transit to the promised land of America is a chronicle of sacrifice and learning—sacrifice of worldly affluence in the pursuit of godly obedience, and learning anchored in the resolve to overcome tribulation and achieve happiness by following the counsel of God. The young Nephi rises in stature and wisdom through every step of this journey to become a leader with multiple missions: colonizer, nation-builder, historian, articulator and preserver of the word of God, teacher, spiritual leader, temple-builder, prophet, and family man.

Parents

Goodly parents teach their children concerning the goodness of God and the principles of the gospel of Jesus Christ.

Nephi conveys to his readers his gratitude for parental instruction and guidance within the family circle. It is a reminder of the solemn duty of parents to love and instruct their children.

In accordance with the pattern of heaven, parents have the fundamental mission of teaching their children the truths of salvation. The Lord himself gave this solemn instruction to Adam and Eve, who in turn made all things known unto their children, including the plan of redemption (see Moses 5:5–12). In our day the Lord has commanded anew that parents should teach their children righteousness: "And again, inasmuch as parents have children in Zion, or in any of her stakes which are organized, that teach them not to understand the doctrine of repentance, faith in Christ the Son of the living God, and of baptism and the gift of the Holy Ghost by the laying on of the hands, when eight years old, the sin be upon the heads of the parents. For this shall be a law unto the inhabitants of Zion, or in any of her stakes which are organized. . . . And they shall also teach their children to pray, and to walk uprightly before the Lord" (D&C 68:25–26, 28). "The Family: A Proclamation to the World" provides the most recent prophetic and apostolic articulation of this commandment.

Memories: Teaching by Example

Have you ever walked through a car lot, fingered a fender, kicked a tire, and turned to find your boy imitating you exactly—not even knowing why he was doing it? I have. It was a sobering moment. One day I had my two youngest sons in tow on a tour of a used car lot and did just that—kicked a tire. Brett, age five, came along behind me and was just withdrawing from a kick when Cory, age three, tested the tire in the identical manner. At first I laughed. Then I panicked as I realized how the game of follow-the-leader is very real in life. And it has to do with more than kicking tires. As parents we are teachers in word and in deed. In our lives there are teaching moments in family prayer, family scripture time, family home evening, family council, and family interviews—special times set aside to teach our children. Let us fully realize that we are teaching through who we are—every moment of every day. (Ed J. Pinegar)

Favored

Obedience brings the favor of the Lord. When we keep the commandments and submit to the will of our Heavenly Father, we enjoy the extraordinary blessing of having His Spirit with us always (see D&C 20:77, 79). Through obedience in heeding the promptings of the Spirit and honoring the covenant principles, we will be "favored of the Lord" (compare also 1 Nephi 3:16; Mosiah 10:13; Alma 48:20; Ether 1:34).

2 Yea, I make a record in the language of my father, which consists of the learning of the Jews and the language of the ***Egyptians.***

EVIDENCE: Egyptians

The text from which the Book of Mormon was translated was engraved on plates in a language Mormon refers to as "reformed Egyptian" (Mormon 9:32), a more succinct and space-saving form of expression than the native Hebrew.

The language of the Book of Mormon evolved as a blend of Egyptian (well known in the Palestine of Lehi's day) and Hebrew—much the same as modern English is a blend of multiple languages (see Nibley, 13–14). As Mormon explains, because "none other people knoweth our language, therefore he [the Lord] hath prepared means for the interpretation thereof" (Mormon 9:34). Thus Nephi's statement that the record he makes consists of both "the learning of the Jews and the language of the Egyptians" (1 Nephi 1:2) makes eminent sense, culturally.

> *3 And I know that the record which I make is **true;** and I make it with mine own hand; and I make it according to my knowledge.*

EVIDENCE: True—Colophon

The opening of 1 Nephi Chapter 1 (through verse 3) is similar to the opening of ancient Egyptian compositions, which typically include name of the author (the one actually writing the text), merits of the parents, confirmation of the truth of the writing, and a ceremonial closing, "and thus it is" (similar to Nephi's phrase "And thus it is, Amen," found in 1 Nephi 9:6; 14:30; 22:31; see Nibley, 17–18). This compositional structure is known as a "colophon," an Egyptian literary device well established in ancient times. The Greek word *colophon* means "finishing touch." In more recent times, the word *colophon* referred to an inscription (usually at the end of a book) giving the particulars about its publication, or to a publisher's emblem or trademark typically located on a title page.

> *4 For it came to pass in the commencement of the first year of the reign of Zedekiah, king of Judah, (my father, **Lehi,** having dwelt at Jerusalem in all his days); and in that same year there came many prophets, prophesying unto the people that they must repent, or the great city Jerusalem must be destroyed.*

Lehi, visionary guide to the promised land

Lehi, a descendant of Joseph through the lineage of Manasseh (see Alma 10:3), is a prophet figure we come to know—as if through personal acquaintance—by reading and rereading the rich and detailed account of his final years just before and after his departure from Jerusalem en route to the promised land around 600 B.C. Lehi is a model of many admirable qualities: worthiness to commune with the Lord and receive through revelation a prophetic view of the divine plan of happiness for mankind, a solemn witness of the divinity of the Messiah, a powerful teacher of gospel principles, a devoted father and patriarch in his family circle, a proponent and herald of the covenant of the Lord concerning the promised land, and an exemplar of personal repentance (when he murmured while in the depths of tribulation—see 1 Nephi 16:20, 25). We esteem Lehi as a visionary guide who alerts us to the destructive consequences of wickedness and pride, and who encourages us to gather our own families to the "promised land," the holy places of security and well-being—stakes, homes, and temples—appointed by God for the blessing of His sons and daughters.

> *5 Wherefore it came to pass that my father, Lehi, as he went forth* ***prayed*** *unto the Lord, yea, even with all his heart, in behalf of his people.*

PRAYED

This reference raises an important question of conscience for all: How often do we pray with real intent for the welfare of others? The faithful and penitent heart blossoms with charity toward others. Enos prayed without ceasing until he had obtained an assurance of forgiveness from the Lord, whereupon he experienced an overpowering concern for the welfare of others: "Now, it came to pass that when I had heard these words I began to feel a desire for the welfare of my brethren, the Nephites; wherefore, I did pour out my whole soul unto God for them" (Enos 1:9).

> *6 And it came to pass as he prayed unto the Lord, there came a pillar of fire and dwelt upon a rock before him; and he saw and heard much; and because of the things which he saw and heard he did quake and tremble exceedingly.*
> *7 And it came to pass that he returned to his own house at Jerusalem; and he cast himself upon his bed, being overcome with the Spirit and the things which he had seen.*
> *8 And being thus overcome with the Spirit, he was carried away in a vision, even that he saw the heavens open, and he thought he saw God sitting upon his throne, surrounded with numberless concourses of angels in the attitude of singing and praising their God.*
> *9 And it came to pass that he saw* ***One descending*** *out of the midst of heaven, and he beheld that his luster was above that of the sun at noon-day.*

1 Nephi 1:9–13

One descending

In his glorious vision, Lehi is privileged to observe the Messiah coming down among mortals. From the very beginning, the Book of Mormon chronicle is infused with the doctrine of the Atonement of Jesus Christ and His ministry of glory, grace, and truth.

EVIDENCE: Prophetic Call

The account describes the process by which Lehi is called to be a prophet of God through a visionary experience involving the divine council of heaven, with "God sitting upon his throne, surrounded with numberless concourses of angels" (verse 8). Lehi's experience with this heavenly council is analogous to references to such a council in many ancient Near Eastern texts. "In ancient conceptions, it is frequently the prophet's admission to this council as a mortal human being, and his knowledge of its decrees and secrets, that lends him authority as an earthly spokesman for God" (*Echoes,* 212). Even if Joseph Smith thoroughly studied the Bible before the translation of the Book of Mormon—which he apparently did not—he probably would not have noticed the complex patterns dealing with the calling of prophets. In the Book of Mormon, these patterns clearly appear, possibly even more clearly than in the Bible or any other ancient Near Eastern text.

10–12 Lehi is instructed in vision about the transcendent mission of the Messiah on behalf of God's children. Being filled with the Spirit, he is warned through the word of God about the impending destruction of Jerusalem resulting from chronic pride and wickedness.

> *13 And he read, saying: Wo, wo, unto Jerusalem, for I have seen thine abominations! Yea, and many things did my father read concerning* ***Jerusalem****—that it should be* ***destroyed,*** *and the inhabitants thereof; many should perish by the sword, and many should be carried away captive into Babylon.*

Jerusalem destroyed

Lehi's generation not only witnesses but also participates in the momentous happenings in the kingdoms of Israel and Judah.

Despite religious reforms by King Josiah (641 to 610 B.C.), the people are largely corrupt and idolatrous, and are led by wicked political and ecclesiastical leaders. Many prophets, including Jeremiah, have been empowered of the Lord to warn the people with clarity and sharpness. The message is clear: the people must repent or Jerusalem will be destroyed. Lehi, himself courageously active among the prophetic ranks, prays earnestly on behalf of his people. A vision is opened unto him concerning the coming of the Savior Jesus Christ and of the future destruction of Jerusalem. Many will be carried away captive into Babylon. Lehi preaches and prophesies to no avail. The people mock him and seek to take away his life. Therefore, the Lord commands him to take his family into the wilderness.

> *14 And it came to pass that when my father had read and seen many great and marvelous things, he did exclaim many things unto the Lord; such as: Great and marvelous are thy works, O Lord God Almighty! Thy throne is high in the heavens, and thy power, and goodness, and mercy are over all the inhabitants of the earth; and, because thou art merciful, thou wilt not suffer those who come unto thee that they shall perish!*
> *15 And after this manner was the language of my father in the* ***praising*** *of his God; for his soul did* ***rejoice,*** *and his whole heart was filled, because of the things which he had seen, yea, which the Lord had shown unto him.*

Praising, rejoice

The holy scriptures contain nearly a thousand references to thanksgiving, rejoicing, and praising—all manifestations of gratitude. Gratitude is a commandment of God. The scriptures counsel us to be grateful for five kinds of blessings: God and His goodness and greatness, the gospel of Jesus Christ and His atoning sacrifice, the goodness of people (from family members to neighbors to prophets and seers), the Gathering (into the Church and kingdom of God, with all its blessings, including stakes and temples), and the gifts of heaven (including the Holy Spirit and the gifts thereof). As Lehi emerges from his remarkable vision about the Redeemer and His mission of mercy, he is consumed with a sense of gratitude and praises the Lord.

In modern revelation the Lord reminds us of two things that offend God: "And in nothing doth man offend God, or against none is his wrath kindled, save those who confess not his hand in all things, and obey not his commandments" (D&C 59:21). To confess the Lord's hand in all things is to recognize His eternal goodness. We seal our gratitude before the Lord by keeping His commandments.

16–19 Nephi confirms that he gives only a partial account of his father's visions, prophesies, and writings. He reports that Lehi went forth among the people delivering to them the message he had received from the Lord, calling them to repentance, declaring the impending destruction of Jerusalem, and proclaiming the gospel of the Messiah. For this, Lehi was mocked and threatened.

20 And when the Jews heard these things they were angry with him; yea, even as with the prophets of old, whom they had cast out, and stoned, and slain; and they also sought his life, that they might take it away. But behold, I, Nephi, will show unto you that the ***tender mercies*** *of the Lord are over all those whom he hath chosen, because of their faith, to make them mighty even unto the power of deliverance.*

Tender mercies

Remember that the tender mercies of God are extended to all who act with faith, even unto deliverance. Nephi echoes the words of his father, who sounded this theme of mercy following his marvelous vision concerning the Savior (see 1 Nephi 1:14).

The Book of Mormon pervasively demonstrates the goodness and mercy of God, and Moroni asks that we ponder it in our hearts (see Moroni 10:3). In the title page, Moroni reminds us that the Book of Mormon will show the House of Israel what great things the Lord has done for them. Recognizing and remembering the goodness and mercy of God in our lives increases our love for God, helps us be humble, and fills our hearts with gratitude.

CHAPTER 2

OVERVIEW

The Lord commends Lehi for his obedience and commands him to take his family and depart into the wilderness. Abandoning his home and precious things, Lehi departs from Jerusalem. In a valley near the borders of the Red Sea, he builds an altar and offers a sacrifice of thanksgiving to the Lord. He counsels Laman and Lemuel against their murmurings and hard-heartedness. Through the Spirit, he confounds them into a state of obedience. Nephi prays for understanding and receives encouragement from the Lord, who promises him that in his faithfulness he will be a leader over Laman and Lemuel.

1 FOR behold, it came to pass that the Lord spake unto my father, yea, even in a dream, and said unto him: Blessed art thou Lehi, because of the things which thou hast done; and because thou hast been faithful and declared unto this people the things which I commanded thee, behold, they seek to take away thy life.
2 And it came to pass that the Lord commanded my father, even in a dream, that he should take his family and depart into the wilderness.

3 And it came to pass that he was ***obedient*** *unto the word of the Lord, wherefore he did as the Lord commanded him.*

Obedient

There is safety in following the Lord's counsel. A righteous branch of the house of Joseph must be established in the promised land; therefore, it is imperative that Lehi and his family heed the directive of the Lord to leave Jerusalem and journey toward the promised land.

The Lord is our refuge. We, like Lehi, experience moments of truth in our lives when we are prompted to seek refuge in the Lord. He will guide us to safety. He will nurture us and bless us according to our needs (see Alma 7:11–12).

Moreover, blessings await us as we follow the Lord's counsel: "I, the Lord, am bound when ye do what I say; but when ye do not what I say, ye have no promise" (D&C 82:10). If we devote ourselves to following the Lord, He will prepare the way for us to prosper and attain our spiritual potential.

President Gordon B. Hinckley confirms this principle as follows: "Prepare ye to follow the way of the Lord. That is what this church is all about—to help us to prepare to follow the way of the Lord, to walk in obedience to His commandments, to get into our lives the spirit of His work, to come to know Him and to love Him, and to seek to do His will. Prepare ye to follow the way of the Lord" (*Teachings of Gordon B. Hinckley* [Salt Lake City: Deseret Book, 1997], 471).

4 And it came to pass that he departed into the wilderness. And he left his house, and the land of his inheritance, and his gold, and his silver, and his precious things, and ***took nothing with him,*** *save it were his family, and provisions, and tents, and departed into the wilderness.*

Took nothing with him

A question of conscience: What would we willingly give by way of time and possessions in order to obey God? Sacrifice is a central principle of the gospel of Jesus Christ. It is closely connected with the development of faith, as the *Lectures on Faith* point out:

> Let us here observe, that a religion that does not require the sacrifice of all things never has power sufficient to produce the faith necessary unto life and salvation; for, from the first existence of man, the faith necessary unto the enjoyment of life and salvation never could be obtained without the sacrifice of all earthly things. . . .

> When a man has offered in sacrifice all that he has for the truth's sake, not even withholding his life, and believing before God that he has been called to make this sacrifice because he seeks to do his will, he does know, most assuredly, that God does and will accept his sacrifice and offering, and that he has not, nor will not seek his face in vain. Under these circumstances, then, he can obtain the faith necessary for him to lay hold on eternal life." (*Lectures on Faith* [Salt Lake City: Deseret Book, 1985], 6:7)

Memories: The Coat

I can recall my father telling me, as a young boy, the story about "the coat." He had been saving for some time to buy a heavy winter coat to protect my mother against the stark Canadian winters. Finally the coat fund was of sufficient size, and the time was at hand. As he sat with the family in sacrament meeting, he pondered the planned gift and thought of the joy it would bring to his wife.

As it turned out, the program that day centered on missionary work and the sacrifices that the Saints are called upon to make in order to carry the gospel message to others. My father's thoughts then shifted to a certain older couple in town who was preparing to go on a mission. They were struggling to gather sufficient resources for their mission, and the local church leaders had sent word requesting the support of local Saints. My father could not suppress an idea that came into his mind. He felt impressed to donate the coat funds (several hundred dollars—a goodly sum in those days) for the benefit of the missionary couple. He felt the need to follow the Spirit. After all, he had stated over and over again to his family that Nephi was one of his great scriptural heroes, and if Nephi had the faith to do as the Lord commanded (see 1 Nephi 3:7), then should he not exercise faith as well? He proceeded to donate the entire fund for the benefit of the missionary couple. Thus they were able to fulfill the Lord's errand. As part of their missionary service, the couple was called to preside over a branch of the Church that was struggling to achieve greater cohesion and unity. Their efforts succeeded, and the branch prospered under their leadership. My father later commented that it was a source of much satisfaction to him to know that the coat was having such a protective and benevolent influence in building the kingdom of God. As for my mother, the opportunity eventually presented itself to obtain a fine coat for her. (Richard J. Allen)

> *5 And he came down by the borders near the shore of the Red Sea; and he traveled in the wilderness in the borders which are nearer the Red Sea; and he did travel in the wilderness with his family, which consisted of my mother, Sariah, and my elder brothers, who were Laman, Lemuel, and Sam.*

*6 And it came to pass that when he had **traveled three days** in the wilderness, he pitched his tent in a valley by the side of a river of water.*

EVIDENCE: Traveled three days—Lehi's Journey to the First Camp

When Biblical characters fled Jerusalem or the surrounding areas, they almost always traveled to Egypt. Therefore, many scholars have taken issue with the idea that Lehi and his family traveled southeast from Jerusalem into Arabia. However, this route, which took Lehi's group to the end of the Red Sea, is congruent with recent evidence regarding travel in the sixth and seventh centuries B.C. (See *Echoes,* 56, 59.)

Zosimus

The Narrative of Zosimus was circulated in the first centuries A.D. but probably written before the birth of Christ. Zosimus tells of a righteous group of people leaving Jerusalem at the time of Jeremiah the prophet and then journeying across the ocean to a promised land. Many other details of the Narrative of Zosimus parallel the Book of Mormon account. Though we know nothing about Zosimus's life from historical accounts, in the narrative he prays, is visited by an angel, and sees a vision similar to Lehi's dream of the tree of life. (See *Echoes,* 135–138.)

*7 And it came to pass that he built an **altar of stones,** and made an offering unto the Lord, and gave thanks unto the Lord our God.*

EVIDENCE: Altar of Stones

From ancient times, Semitic (Hebrew and Arabic) sanctuaries featured an altar or pillar for the offering of sacrifices. A pile of stones often served this purpose, and Lehi's "altar of stones" would have complied with the ancient law specifying that the altar must be made of uncut stones. (See *Echoes,* 470.)

EVIDENCE: Sacrifices Offered by Lehi (see also 1 Nephi 5:9, 7:22)

According to Nephi, Lehi offers sacrifices on three occasions in the wilderness: when the travelers attain their first campsite, when Nephi and his brothers return with the brass plates, and when Nephi and his brothers arrive at the camp with Ishmael's family. The narrative explains that Lehi offers these sacrifices to thank the Lord for His blessings. In the Old Testament, the Lord requires such sacrifices ("peace offerings"—see Leviticus 3), and travelers make these offerings to seek the Lord's protection on their journeys (see Psalm 107).

1 Nephi 2:7–10

Nephi tells of two instances where his father's sacrifices are burnt offerings. Burnt offerings were required as a penance for sin rather than a symbol of gratitude. As we shall see, Lehi makes a burnt offering when Nephi, Sam, Laman, and Lemuel arrive at the first camp with the brass plates. Laman and Lemuel have assaulted Sam and Nephi, and Laban has been slain. Although the Lord had commanded Nephi to kill Laban, we can assume that Lehi did not want to take any chances. Furthermore, when his sons arrive with Ishmael's family, Lehi offers burnt offerings because Laman and Lemuel have tried to bind Nephi and leave him to die.

Joseph Smith could not have known which sacrifices and offerings the Mosaic Law required of travelers. (See *Echoes,* 62–64.)

> *8 And it came to pass that he called the name of the river, Laman, and it emptied into the Red Sea; and the valley was in the borders near the mouth thereof.*
> *9 And when my father saw that the waters of the river emptied into the fountain of the Red Sea, he spake unto Laman, saying: O that thou mightest be like unto this* ***river,*** *continually running into the fountain of all righteousness!*
> *10 And he also spake unto Lemuel: O that thou mightest be like unto this* ***valley,*** *firm and steadfast, and immovable in keeping the commandments of the Lord!*

EVIDENCE: River, Valley—Naming Geographical Features

Desert customs indicate that any water a Bedouin finds is named after him. In keeping with this tradition, at his first camp in the wilderness, Lehi named the river *Laman,* after his eldest son, and the valley *Lemuel,* after his second-eldest son. A valley and its water source could be known by several different names, each representing a different local tribe. (See *Echoes,* 466.)

EVIDENCE: Lehi's Poetry

Religious scholar Albert Bloch identified four types of verse in ancient desert poetry, and Lehi's *qasida* (see 1 Nephi 2:9–10) meets three of the types. This conformation to an ancient form of poetry is yet another proof of the authenticity of the Book of Mormon. (See *Echoes,* 461–462.)

EVIDENCE: Lehi's First Camp

In the narrative regarding Lehi's first camp in the wilderness, the most surprising statement is that there was a "continually running" stream of water in the area (verse 9). Most geographers would point out that Arabia is a desert where water flows only with the occasional heavy rain. However, Hugh Nibley reports that there is a point near the Gulf of Aqaba where a stream of water flows into the Red Sea. Students of Arabian culture and geography Lynne and Hope Hilton theorize that Lehi's first camp was at the oasis Al-Bad in Wadi al-Ifal—about seventy-five miles from Aqaba—where running water is seasonal but springs exist. (See *Echoes,* 60–61.)

> *11 Now this he spake because of the stiffneckedness of Laman and Lemuel; for behold they did murmur in many things against their father, because he was a visionary man, and had led them out of the land of Jerusalem, to leave the land of their inheritance, and their gold, and their silver, and their* ***precious things,*** *to perish in the wilderness. And this they said he had done because of the foolish imaginations of his heart.*

Precious things

From the record we know that Lehi is a man of means, having gold, silver, and precious things—at least in sufficient quantities to induce Laman and Lemuel to fret over the contrast between the comforts of their previous home life and the austere life in the wilderness. The word "inheritance" implies that the two older brothers covet the family property that would eventually have come into their possession. Being blind to the spiritual aspects of the family flight into the wilderness, they selfishly blame their father for the "foolish imaginations" (verse 11) that supposedly rob them of their worldly comforts.

Just how Lehi originally comes to be wealthy, we do not know. Some have supposed that he might have been a traveling tradesman or merchant with connections to Egypt (see, for example, Nibley, 32–33); to be sure, he seems to be familiar with caravan protocols and practices as he navigates the wilderness. From whatever source, his affluence provides ample framework for establishing, first, his trust in and loyalty to the Lord (having willingly given up all his worldly possessions for the cause of righteousness) and, second, the abundant record concerning the hard-heartedness, pride, and narrow-mindedness of Laman and Lemuel.

> *12 And thus* ***Laman*** *and* ***Lemuel,*** *being the eldest, did* ***murmur*** *against their father. And they did murmur because they knew not the dealings of that God who had created them.*

Laman, Arch-Murmurer

Few figures in the Book of Mormon teach as powerful a lesson as does Laman—not by exemplary and admirable deeds, but rather in the inevitable consequences of disobedience, rebellion, and evil. Laman is the archetype of dissension. He rejects the light of the gospel of Jesus Christ and is therefore subjected by choice to the ultimate penalty of being "cast off from the presence of the Lord" (1 Nephi 8:36).

What is the perilous agenda of Laman and the source of his discontent? When Lehi heeds the warnings of the Lord and takes his family into the wilderness around 600 B.C. to avoid the impending destruction of Jerusalem, Laman joins his brother Lemuel in accusing Lehi of being a "visionary man" who "had led them out of the land of Jerusalem, to leave the land of their inheritance, and their gold, and their silver, and their precious things, to perish in the wilderness. And this they said he had done because of the foolish imaginations of his heart" (1 Nephi 2:11). Thus Laman and his brother demonstrate a governing preference for earthly, rather than heavenly, treasures; for creature comforts rather than the challenges and opportunities of discipleship and spiritual growth. Moreover, they are jealous of the leadership role played by their younger brother Nephi: "We will not that our younger brother shall be a ruler over us" (1 Nephi 18:10). Consequently, they abuse Nephi and attempt to take his life, just as they have sought to kill their own father.

Laman casts a long, dark shadow across the landscape of the Book of Mormon. Whenever his descendants persist in following a philosophy of prideful jealousy, rage against spiritual authority, and rejection of the light of the gospel of Jesus Christ, they sink into a benighted state characterized by separation from God and a loathsome, warlike lifestyle.

We can learn from the negative example of Laman—and other dissenters and murmurers in the Book of Mormon—that happiness and joy flow only to those who "press their way forward, continually holding fast to the rod of iron" (1 Nephi 8:30) until they reach the tree of life and partake of the fruit thereof. The irony of the matter is that even the descendants of Nephi, when they eventually succumb to the devastating forces of pride, become cast off and lost, as Mormon mournfully observes at the end of the Book of Mormon: "Behold, the pride of this nation, or the people of the Nephites, hath proven their destruction" (Moroni 8:27).

Lemuel, the Arch-Conspirator

Lemuel, the second son of Lehi and Sariah, is virtually a mirror-image of his older brother, Laman. The two are perfectly harmonized in their murmurings, murderous plottings, and rebellions against the ways of the Lord. In terms of the hardness of their hearts and the recalcitrance of their spirits, they are identical twins.

Murmur

Murmuring is anchored in ignorance of spiritual truths. Murmuring against the Lord and the Lord's prophets is usually due to a lack of understanding of the dealings of God with His children.

Nephi confirms that his two older brothers are ignorant of the relationship between the Creator and His children. They have not aspired, apparently, to gain an appreciation of the eternal plan of happiness. Thus they murmur when confronted with eternal principles that run counter to their worldly philosophy. True conversion and the exercising of faith through prayer will lead one to praise God in trials and afflictions (see 1 Nephi 18:16).

Those who murmur against their fellows, in particular against the servants of God, forget a key factor: that they are in effect murmuring against God, who is all-powerful and all-knowing, and infinitely wiser than man. Elder Neal A. Maxwell has provided this counsel concerning murmuring:

> Murmuring against the Lord's anointed has been present in all dispensations. Sometimes that murmuring has been a virtual shout, while at other times it has consisted of murmurings of the heart. But even the latter are noticed. (See D&C 75:7).
>
> Nephi found favor with the Lord because he did not murmur as did his brothers, who murmured because they were sent back to Jerusalem for the plates, which was to them such "a hard thing." (1 Nephi 3:5). Laman and Lemuel felt imposed upon by what they thought, apparently, was not such a good idea—especially because of the personal risks involved. When prophets, like Nephi, are plain-speaking about such disobedience, some murmur the more at being found out and called down (2 Nephi 1:26).
>
> Murmuring (and it is usually against the prophets) can be a mere gripe and complaint or it may reflect a deep difference. But whatever the degree of dissent, it ought to be clear that though a particular leader is the ostensible object of the murmuring, as Moses told his complaining people, "your murmurings are not against us, but against the Lord" (Exodus 16:8). However, rocks can reach prophets, for they are proximate. But few are seen hurling stones skyward; they may have a grievance with God, but they also have had some experience with gravity.
>
> Just as the Jews murmured against Jesus because He told them who He was, so some murmur against His prophets today because of who they are (John 6:41). Even His disciples murmured on occasion at the strong doctrines of the Savior (John 6:61). Yet Jesus pointedly said, " My doctrine is not mine, but his that sent me" (John 7:16). Dissenters over doctrines today must face that same reality. . . .

> The failure to acknowledge God's omniscience is an enormous error that spreads through life and touches all our doings. For if we truly believe God to be what He says He is, then we can follow His prophets, His proctors in this mortal school, without resentment or murmuring. True, we will not always understand, nor will we find counsel easy to take—but the challenges will be manageable, when we have been humbled by knowing how great God is. This then makes us more manageable! And even though it is true that there must be an "opposition in all things," none of us has the personal obligation to provide that opposition. (*All These Things Shall Give Thee Experience* [Salt Lake City: Deseret Book, 1979], 106–107)

13–15 The two older sons, like the Jews of Jerusalem, do not believe the prophecy about the coming destruction of the city and are disposed (again, like their fellow Jewish citizens) to slay Lehi. Being filled with the Spirit, Lehi confounds Laman and Lemuel with his discourse so that they are shamed into obedience in the family camp, where, according to Nephi, "**my father dwelt in a tent**" (verse 15).

EVIDENCE: My father dwelt in a tent (1 Nephi 2:15)

One might wonder at Nephi's repeatedly telling us, "my father dwelt in a tent" (see also 1 Nephi 9:1; 10:16; 16:6). According to Hugh Nibley, Nephi's father's tent was the center of his universe. But to an Arab, the phrase "My father dwelt in a tent" tells us a great deal: Lehi and his family had taken on the Bedouin way of life for this journey. Because Nephi repeatedly mentions his father's living quarters, we learn that it is the center of authority and administration. It is apparent from many other statements in 1 Nephi that, as Nibley states, "Lehi's tent is the headquarters for all activities, all discussion and decisions." (See *Echoes,* 459–460.)

> *16 And it came to pass that I, Nephi, being exceedingly young, nevertheless being large in stature, and also having great desires to know of the mysteries of God, wherefore, I did cry unto the Lord; and behold he did visit me, and did* ***soften*** *my heart that I did believe all the words which had been spoken by my father; wherefore, I did not rebel against him like unto my brothers.*

Soften

Prayer softens hearts. The contrasting theme of the soft heart and the hard heart pervades the Book of Mormon. We can effectively plot the graph of spirituality in the Book of Mormon by reference to the hardness or softness of the hearts of the people at any given time. At the upper reaches of the chart is Nephi, whose petitions to the Lord result in a softening of his heart and a strengthening of his faith. At the lower reaches are Laman and Lemuel, who, because their hearts are insensitive and impenetrable, are devoid of faith and understanding. Where on this chart of spirituality does our heart register? Where prayerful desire is the driving force of one's life, the heart is softened and the mind is prepared to receive the blessings of the Lord.

The Lord reinforces this principle of the softened heart during His visit to the ancient Saints in America, the descendants of Lehi: "And ye shall offer for a sacrifice unto me a broken heart and a contrite spirit. And whoso cometh unto me with a broken heart and a contrite spirit, him will I baptize with fire and with the Holy Ghost, even as the Lamanites, because of their faith in me at the time of their conversion, were baptized with fire and with the Holy Ghost, and they knew it not" (3 Nephi 9:20). To bring before the Lord a softened heart is to demonstrate our deep and abiding love and respect for Him—our "fear of the Lord" as it is often stated in the scripture. "The fear of the LORD *is* the beginning of wisdom: and the knowledge of the holy *is* understanding" (Proverbs 9:10). Following the example of Nephi, let us seek to understand the things of the Lord.

> *17 And I spake unto* ***Sam,*** *making known unto him the things which the Lord had manifested unto me by his Holy Spirit. And it came to pass that he believed in my words.*
>
> *18 But, behold, Laman and Lemuel would not hearken unto my words; and being grieved because of the hardness of their hearts I cried unto the Lord for them.*

Sam

Nephi's next older brother provides a stark contrast to Laman and Lemuel, the oldest of Lehi's children. Nephi records: "And it came to pass that [Sam] believed in my words" (1 Nephi 2:17). This division of belief between Laman and Lemuel, on the one hand, and Nephi and Sam, on the other, continues from this time forward. It was to be confirmed to Lehi in his vision of the tree of life, for Sariah, Nephi, and Sam all partook of the fruit of the tree, but Laman and Lemuel refused to do so. Declared Lehi: "And behold, because of the thing which I have seen, I have reason to rejoice in the Lord because of Nephi and also of Sam; for I have reason to suppose that they, and also many of their seed, will be saved. But behold, Laman and Lemuel, I fear exceedingly because of you. . . ." (1 Nephi 8:3–4).

Just before passing beyond the veil, Lehi gives Sam a special blessing: "Blessed art thou, and thy seed; for thou shalt inherit the land like unto thy brother Nephi. And thy seed shall be numbered with his seed; and thou shalt be even like unto thy brother, and thy seed like unto his seed; and thou shalt be blessed in all thy days" (2 Nephi 4:11). After Lehi's death, Sam joins Nephi and his group when they separate themselves from their murderous older brothers (see 2 Nephi 5:6). After the separation, Sam and his posterity remain united with the posterity of Nephi according to the blessing pronounced by Lehi.

> *19 And it came to pass that the Lord spake unto me, saying: Blessed art thou, Nephi, because of thy **faith,** for thou hast sought me diligently, with lowliness of heart.*
> *20 And inasmuch as ye shall keep my commandments, ye shall **prosper,** and shall be led to a land of promise; yea, even a land which I have prepared for you; yea, a land which is choice above all other lands.*

FAITH, PROSPER

We are blessed through our faith. As we seek the Lord with lowliness of heart, He will cause us to prosper spiritually and temporally. All blessings come through faith in the Lord Jesus Christ. Without faith we can do nothing (see D&C 8:10), but with faith we can do all things (see Moroni 10:23).

21–24 Nephi is promised a position as leader and teacher over his brethren, based on his obedience. His brethren are to be cut off if they persist in their rebellion.

CHAPTER 3

OVERVIEW

The Lord commands Lehi in a dream to send his sons back to Jerusalem to obtain the brass plates from Laban. Laman and Lemuel complain, but Nephi confirms his willingness to obey the Lord and expresses his faith that a way will be prepared to accomplish the task.

> *1 AND it came to pass that I, Nephi, returned from speaking with the Lord, to the tent of my father.*
> *2 And it came to pass that he spake unto me, saying: Behold I have dreamed a dream, in the which the Lord hath commanded me that thou and thy brethren shall return to Jerusalem.*

*3 For behold, Laban hath the **record** of the Jews and also a genealogy of my forefathers, and they are engraven upon **plates of brass.***
4 Wherefore, the Lord hath commanded me that thou and thy brothers should go unto the house of Laban, and seek the records, and bring them down hither into the wilderness.

Record, plates of brass

During Lehi's time, the custodian of the priceless historical and scriptural chronicles of God's dealings with His people, preserved on plates of brass, has been an unscrupulous official in Jerusalem named Laban, a descendant of Joseph of Egypt (see 1 Nephi 5:16). It is according to the design of the Lord that these records have been preserved over time in written format. Furthermore, the Lord plans that Lehi should have possession of these records for the blessing of his posterity.

The scriptures are an indispensable road map for the journey of life. Lehi is commanded to obtain the brass plates before undertaking the journey to the promised land. It is essential that Lehi have the genealogy of his fathers, the written language of his forebears, and the recorded word of God—all of which are contained on the brass plates.

5 And now, behold thy brothers murmur, saying it is a hard thing which I have required of them; but behold I have not required it of them, but it is a commandment of the Lord.
6 Therefore go, my son, and thou shalt be favored of the Lord, because thou hast not murmured.
*7 And it came to pass that I, Nephi, said unto my father: I will **go and do** the things which the Lord hath commanded, for I know that the Lord giveth no commandments unto the children of men, save he shall **prepare a way** for them that they may accomplish the thing which he commandeth them.*

Go and do, prepare a way

These words of Nephi continue to echo down through time as an inspiration to all who follow the Lord. As we seek to do His will with an attitude of faith and trust, neither doubting nor murmuring, the Lord provides a way. Blessings that are withheld from those who murmur will flow unimpeded to the obedient. President Thomas S. Monson explains this: "I think of the decision of Laman and Lemuel, when they were commanded to go and obtain the plates of Laban. What does the record indicate that they did? They murmured and said, 'This is a hard thing which we have been commanded to do,' and they decided not to obey that commandment—and they lost the blessing. But Nephi, when he received that commandment, responded with that beautiful declaration: 'I will go and do the things which the Lord hath commanded,' and he did; and he received the coveted prize that comes through obedience" (*Be Your Best Self* [Salt Lake City: Deseret Book, 1979], 127).

8–18 Lehi rejoices in the faith and obedience of Nephi. The sons go again to "**the land of Jerusalem**" (verse 10), where Laman (who draws the primary lot in determining who should encounter Laban) is repelled by Laban and flees for his life. Laman is bent on having the team return to Lehi empty-handed.

EVIDENCE: THE LAND OF JERUSALEM (1 Nephi 3:10)

Nephi uses the expression "the land of Jerusalem" when referring to his homeland. However, several scriptural passages make it obvious that his home could not have been in or adjacent to the city of Jerusalem, though we're told that Lehi "dwelt at Jerusalem in all his days" (1 Nephi 1:4). While the usage of these terms seems contradictory, they actually reflect historical fact. In ancient Jewish documents, "the land of Jerusalem" is described as an area larger than the city of Jerusalem. The same documents reveal that in Palestine and Syria, a large area around a city would share the city's name, as would the inhabitants. According to Hugh Nibley, "This was a holdover from the time when the city and land were a single political unit, comprising a city-state; when this was absorbed into a larger empire, the original identity was preserved, though it had lost its original political significance" (*Echoes,* 456–457).

> *19 And behold, it is wisdom in God that we should obtain these records, that we may **preserve unto our children** the language of our fathers;*
> *20 And also that we may **preserve unto them** the words which have been spoken by the mouth of all the holy prophets, which have been delivered unto them by the Spirit and power of God, since the world began, even down unto this present time.*

PRESERVE UNTO OUR CHILDREN

Nephi persuades his brethren to stay the course, exercising faith, so that they might obtain the records for the sake of their posterity. Laman and Lemuel see only the pathway beneath their own feet; Nephi sees the pathway leading forward into the future where countless millions will derive spiritual strength unto deliverance from the word of God. For Nephi, this mission centers on the very souls that the coming Messiah refers to and blesses during His post-resurrection visit to

America: "And behold, ye are the children of the prophets; and ye are of the house of Israel; and ye are of the covenant which the Father made with your fathers, saying unto Abraham: And in thy seed shall all the kindreds of the earth be blessed. The Father having raised me up unto you first, and sent me to bless you in turning away every one of you from his iniquities; and this because ye are the children of the covenant—" (3 Nephi 20:25–26).

21–23 The brothers then go and retrieve their family treasures to use in bartering for the brass plates at the house of Laban.

> *24 And it came to pass that we went in unto Laban, and desired him that he would give unto us the records which were engraven upon the* ***plates of brass,*** *for which we would give unto him our gold, and our silver, and all our precious things.*

EVIDENCE: Plates of Brass

Here, an interesting Hebrew literary construction comes to light. "When one noun follows another in the English language—either in a descriptive or possessive phrase—we see constructs such as 'brass plates,' with 'brass' serving as an adjective. In Hebrew, this combination of terms would be 'plates brass.' In order for this construction to make sense in English, the word *of* is added, i.e. 'plates of brass.' Other examples of this Hebrew construction in the Book of Mormon include 'voice of the Spirit' (1 Nephi 4:18), instead of 'the Spirit's voice'; and 'skin of blackness' (2 Nephi 5:21), instead of 'black skin.'" (Sorenson, 79.)

25–30 The sons fail to persuade Laban to turn over the records. They flee for their lives, leaving behind the family treasures. Laman and Lemuel angrily beat Nephi and Sam—"and they did smite us even with a rod" (verse 28). An angel intervenes and restrains them.

EVIDENCE: Smiting with a Rod

According to Hugh Nibley, it is no surprise that Laman and Lemuel beat their younger brothers with a rod. In fact, Nibley says that "every free man in the East carries a stick, the immemorial badge of independence and authority, and every man asserts his authority over his inferiors by his stick." The use of a stick to show authority—whether by government officials, military officers, tax collectors, or schoolmasters—is very ancient. Laman and Lemuel obviously intend to show their usurped authority over Nephi, because the angel asks them why they smite their younger brother when the Lord has placed *him* as a ruler over *them.* (See *Echoes,* 460–461.)

31 And after the angel had departed, Laman and Lemuel again began to murmur, saying: How is it possible that the Lord will deliver Laban into our hands? Behold, he is a mighty man, and he can ***command fifty,*** *yea, even he can slay fifty; then why not us?*

EVIDENCE: Command Fifty—Number Usage

The Book of Mormon and the Old Testament are similar regarding number usage.

Biblical Hebrew employs cardinal numbers (one, two, three), ordinals (first, second, third), multiplicatives (double, sevenfold,) and fractions (half, third, tenth), avoiding complex numeric forms (those using *mono-, bi-, di-, uni-, tri-, multi-,* and *poly-*). Book of Mormon language follows this pattern as well.

Furthermore, in Hebrew, numbers are often used without the noun in constructions that seem to be missing something when translated into English. For example, Genesis 45:22 says that Joseph "gave three hundred of silver" to Benjamin, not qualifying exactly what the three hundred referred to. The King James translators added the word "pieces" to make the phrase sound more correct in English. In the Book of Mormon, the statement that Laban "can command fifty, yea, even he can slay fifty" (1 Nephi 3:31) does not specify what *fifty* refers to. As we read in *Echoes and Evidences,* fifty might refer to men, warriors, princes, or commanders of armies. Other Book of Mormon examples of this Hebrew usage pattern are found in 2 Nephi 11:3, Alma 57:19, and Alma 57:25.

In Hebrew, it is common practice to connect two or more numbers with "and." An example is found in 1 Kings 20:1, where we see "thirty and two kings" rather than "thirty-two kings." The Book of Mormon follows this usage pattern, as in "an army of forty and two thousand" (Mormon 2:9). (See *Echoes,* 174–175.)

CHAPTER 4

OVERVIEW

Nephi persuades his brothers to stay the course in the quest to obtain the brass plates. He returns and discovers Laban in a drunken state upon the street. Constrained by the Spirit, Nephi slays Laban and, in disguise, persuades Zoram, Laban's servant, to retrieve the brass plates. In his true identity, Nephi convinces the trembling Zoram to become part of the Lehi party and thus obtain his freedom. The group returns to Lehi's encampment.

1–5 Nephi persuades his brethren to return once again to the house of Laban, citing the power and example of Moses.

> *6 And I was* ***led by the Spirit,*** *not knowing beforehand the things which I should do.*

Led by the Spirit

This verse raises for each of us a fundamental question of conscience: Am I worthy to be led by the Spirit? Nephi is a supreme example of a servant of God who followed the Spirit in every thought and deed. He repeats again, at the end of his life, this eternal formula for spiritual success: "For behold, again I say unto you that if ye will enter in by the way, and receive the Holy Ghost, it will show unto you all things what ye should do" (2 Nephi 32:5). If we live by the Spirit, it will lead us in the pathways of truth and righteousness.

Memories: The Lord Is in Charge

In 1 Nephi 4:6, Nephi says, "And I was led by the Spirit, not knowing beforehand the things which I should do." This doesn't mean that Nephi hasn't studied or prayed or worked. He has already been righteous up to this point. But at this moment he doesn't know what to do. I often spoke with missionaries about this, saying to them:

> You will probably have the same thing happen to you out in the field. You'll say, "Oh Father," and at that moment when you pray, "What should I do?" then all of a sudden the words will come. You'll find yourself saying, "And by the power of the Spirit, I testify to you, Mr. Brown, that what I have said is true, and I know it's true because the Lord bore witness to me that it's true." You will bear your testimony with power, and then you'll wonder, "How did I do that?" Remember, the Lord is in charge! (Ed J. Pinegar)

> *7 Nevertheless I went forth, and as I came near unto the house of Laban I beheld a man, and he had fallen to the earth before me, for he was drunken with wine.*
> *8 And when I came to him I found that it was* ***Laban.***
> *9 And I beheld his sword, and I drew it forth from the sheath thereof; and the hilt thereof was of pure gold, and the workmanship thereof was exceedingly fine, and I saw that the blade thereof was of the most precious steel.*

1 Nephi 4:9–14

Laban, Keeper of the Records

Laban, a descendant of Joseph of Egypt, is living in Jerusalem at the time of Lehi's exodus (see 1 Nephi 5:16). Laban and his forefathers have kept the records of their progenitors on the plates of brass, beginning with the creation of the world and continuing through Adam, Moses, and the other holy prophets down to the time of Jeremiah, the contemporary of Zedekiah, at the time king of Judah (see 1 Nephi 5:10–16). It is therefore expedient that Lehi should have these records to take with him to the promised land in order to preserve the covenant truths of the gospel.

Laban represents a roadblock to the divine purposes of the Lord and must therefore be sacrificed for the sake of universal good. This doctrine has enduring validity. Even in modern times, the Lord makes clear the inexorable nature of the plan of salvation as it is administered by His servants, who will follow divine will with unfailing allegiance, or "others shall be planted in their stead" (D&C 64:40; compare D&C 93:50; 104:77). Concerning Joseph Smith, the Lord said: "And this ye shall know assuredly—that there is none other appointed unto you to receive commandments and revelations until he be taken, if he abide in me" (D&C 43:3). That condition—"if he abide in me"—is a standing law for all engaged in a divine stewardship. In the case of Laban, his commission was suspended because he did not abide in the Lord when ordered to relinquish the brass plates. Thus the plates were transferred to another—along with the commission to preserve and add to the records of—even to Lehi and to his successors in the thousand-year long chain of record keepers.

> *10 And it came to pass that I was constrained by the Spirit that I should kill Laban;*
> *but I said in my heart: Never at any time have I shed the blood of man. And I shrunk*
> *and would that I might not slay him.*
> *11 And the Spirit said unto me again: Behold the Lord hath delivered him into thy*
> *hands. Yea, and I also knew that he had sought to take away mine own life; yea, and*
> *he would not hearken unto the commandments of the Lord; and he also had taken*
> *away our property.*
> *12 And it came to pass that the Spirit said unto me again: Slay him, for the Lord hath*
> *delivered him into thy hands;*
> *13 Behold the Lord slayeth the wicked to bring forth his righteous purposes.* ***It is better that***
> ***one man should perish*** *than that a nation should dwindle and perish in unbelief.*
> *14 And now, when I, Nephi, had heard these words, I remembered the words of the*
> *Lord which he spake unto me in the wilderness, saying that: Inasmuch as thy seed shall*
> *keep my commandments, they shall prosper in the land of promise.*

It is better that one man should perish

Discipleship means a willing and consistent alignment with God's decrees. What does one do when commanded by God to pursue a course contrary to one's deepest values? Nephi learns the answer to this when he is constrained by the Spirit to kill Laban for the purpose of preserving the sacred record for an entire nation. He learns that the Spirit will direct us in all things. Sometimes a command is so difficult that we need to be taught by the Spirit concerning our specific instructions. Such was the case in regard to Nephi's taking the life of Laban. As Nephi faced the challenge of taking a human life by divine commandment, he must have come to an understanding of what the prophet Isaiah meant when he said: "For my thoughts are not your thoughts, neither are your ways my ways, saith the LORD. For as the heavens are higher than the earth, so are my ways higher than your ways, and my thoughts than your thoughts" (Isaiah 55:8–9).

The angelic instruction given to Nephi is a spiritual lesson in logic and its application (see 1 Nephi 4:11–17):

1. The Lord has delivered Laban into your hands.
2. Laban has sought to take your life.
3. Laban will not hearken to the commandments of the Lord.
4. Laban has taken away your property.
5. The Lord slays the wicked to bring forth his righteous purposes.
6. Better that one man should perish than an entire nation dwindle in unbelief.
7. If the descendants of Lehi keep the commandments, they shall prosper.
8. They can't keep the commandments if they don't obtain the law—and the law is engraved upon the records.

Having been taught, and having come to realize that the Lord truly has delivered Laban into his hands, Nephi proceeds to take Laban's life.

When we understand and appreciate a doctrine, principle, or commandment through the Spirit, it is easier to accept and live it.

EVIDENCE: It is better that one man should perish

Certain episodes in the Old Testament establish the legal precedent of justifying the sacrificing of one individual for the purpose of preserving an entire group of people. One example is the beheading of the traitor Sheba by the inhabitants of the city of Abel in order that the entire city might be spared destruction by David's army (see 2 Samuel 20). Another example, closer to the time of Lehi, is the deliverance of Jehoiakim, king of Judah, to the Babylonians by the Jewish counsel in order to defuse Nebuchadnezzar's threat that he will otherwise destroy the entire nation (see 2 Chronicles 36:6). Lehi is likely aware of this precedent of "one for many"—but Joseph Smith could not have been, since this rather obscure aspect of Jewish law was, as legal scholar John W. Welch has pointed out, not well known until quite recently. (See *Echoes,* 356–357.)

> *15 Yea, and I also thought that they could not keep the commandments of the Lord according to the law of Moses, save they should have the* ***law.***
> *16 And I also knew that the* ***law*** *was engraven upon the plates of brass.*
> *17 And again, I knew that the Lord had delivered Laban into my hands for this cause—that I might obtain the records according to his commandments.*

Law

The word of God is priceless, for it conveys the law that God would have us follow. Nephi's inward conviction about the essential nature of the scriptures points us forward several centuries to the time that King Benjamin, holding in his hands the very plates of brass brought by Nephi under commandment of the Lord, instructs his sons on these same principles:

> And he also taught them concerning the records which were engraven on the plates of brass, saying: My sons, I would that ye should remember that were it not for these plates, which contain these records and these commandments, we must have suffered in ignorance, even at this present time, not knowing the mysteries of God.
>
> For it were not possible that our father, Lehi, could have remembered all these things, to have taught them to his children, except it were for the help of these plates; for he having been taught in the language of the Egyptians therefore he could read these engravings, and teach them to his children, that thereby they could teach them to their children, and so fulfilling the commandments of God, even down to this present time.
>
> I say unto you, my sons, were it not for these things, which have been kept and preserved by the hand of God, that we might read and understand of his mysteries, and have his commandments always before our eyes, that even our fathers would have dwindled in unbelief, and we should have been like unto our brethren, the Lamanites, who know nothing concerning these things, or even do

> not believe them when they are taught them, because of the traditions of their fathers, which are not correct.
>
> O my sons, I would that ye should remember that these sayings are true, and also that these records are true. And behold, also the plates of Nephi, which contain the records and the sayings of our fathers from the time they left Jerusalem until now, and they are true; and we can know of their surety because we have them before our eyes.
>
> And now, my sons, I would that ye should remember to search them diligently, that ye may profit thereby; and I would that ye should keep the commandments of God, that ye may prosper in the land according to the promises which the Lord made unto our fathers (Mosiah 1:3–7).

14–31 Nephi realizes that the holy record is indispensable for the salvation of his family's posterity. Hence he obeys the Spirit, slays Laban, obtains the brass plates from Laban's servant by disguising himself as Laban, returns to reassure his terrified brethren, and then restrains the servant of Laban so that he cannot flee and disclose their clandestine activities to the city.

> *32 And it came to pass that I spake with him [Zoram], that if he would hearken unto my words,* ***as the Lord liveth,*** *and as I live, even so that if he would hearken unto our words, we would spare his life.*

EVIDENCE: As the Lord Liveth—Use of Oaths

To the ancient Semitic people, oaths were sacred and could not be violated. The most solemn oath would be by the life of a living thing. Nephi explains this as he restrains Zoram so that he cannot return to Jerusalem. Nephi's oath appeases the struggling Zoram, as he knows that no person would consider breaking such an oath." (See *Echoes,* 468.)

33–38 Nephi exacts an oath from Laban's servant, **Zoram,** that he will join their entourage, and the group sets off to return again to Lehi bearing the treasured plates of brass.

Zoram, Servant of Laban

Zoram is employed by Laban, a descendant of Joseph who has been keeper of the records in Jerusalem. When Nephi obeys the Spirit of the Lord and slays Laban in order to obtain the brass plates, Zoram is recruited as a member of the Lehi exodus (see 1 Nephi 4).

Later, Zoram marries the oldest daughter of Ishmael, who has also been persuaded by Nephi and his brethren to leave Jerusalem with his family (see 1 Nephi 16:7). When the aging Lehi blesses his sons after reaching the promised land, he includes Zoram, saying, "I know that thou art a true friend unto my son, Nephi, forever" (2 Nephi 1:30). Thereafter, Zoram maintains his allegiance to Nephi's group. When Nephi separates himself from his murderous older brothers, Laman and Lemuel, following the death of Lehi, Zoram is there to accompany him. In modern revelation, the name *Zoramites* is mentioned in association with the Nephite camp and the coming forth of the Book of Mormon (see D&C 3:16–20).

CHAPTER 5

OVERVIEW

Sariah is anxious about the well being of her sons. She murmurs against Lehi, who consoles her with assurances that they will be preserved by the Lord. The sons return safely, to the great relief of their parents. Lehi discovers that the brass plates contain the five books of Moses and the prophecies down to Lehi's time, including those of Jeremiah, his contemporary. The plates also contain a genealogy of Lehi's forebears, confirming that he is a descendant of Joseph of Egypt. Lehi is moved by the Spirit to prophecy concerning his seed.

> *1 AND it came to pass that after we had come down into the wilderness unto our father, behold, he was filled with joy, and also my mother,* ***Sariah,*** *was exceedingly glad, for she truly had mourned because of us.*
> *2 For she had supposed that we had perished in the wilderness; and she also had complained against my father, telling him that he was a visionary man; saying: Behold thou hast led us forth from the land of our inheritance, and my sons are no more, and we perish in the wilderness.*
> *3 And after this manner of language had my mother complained against my father.*

Sariah, Mother of Nations

Sariah is the wife of the prophet Lehi and the mother of Nephi and his siblings. Her small family circle—augmented by the addition of Zoram (the servant of Laban) and Ishmael and his family—becomes the foundation of entire nations in the new land. Sariah is thus destined to become the ancestral mother of millions, whose history, as recorded in the Book of Mormon, extends more than a thousand years into the future, and, in fact, continues even to this day. Despite severe tribulation occasioned by the hardships of the global journey, and despite her anguish over the rebellion of Laman and Lemuel, Sariah remains faithful to the commission given by the Lord. Though her worries about her children would, as on one occasion, cause her to murmur in agony (see 1 Nephi 5:2–3), she maintains her loyal support for her husband in his prophetic calling. Sariah stands as a noble and righteous woman, an exemplary daughter of God, and a fruitful matriarch, after the manner of her namesake, Sarah (or Sarai, wife of Abraham).

4–7 Lehi comforts Sariah and reminds her that the family would have perished had they remained in Jerusalem. The two parents rejoice when their sons return safely according to the promise of Lehi.

> *8 And she spake, saying: Now* ***I know of a surety*** *that the Lord hath commanded my husband to flee into the wilderness; yea, and I also know of a surety that the Lord hath protected my sons, and delivered them out of the hands of Laban, and given them power whereby they could accomplish the thing which the Lord hath commanded them. And after this manner of language did she speak.*

I know of a surety

Preserved for us in the Book of Mormon are the actual words of Sariah as she bears her testimony of their divine mission and the blessings of the Lord to her sons. Her action is a reminder of the principle of active gratitude. According to this principle, we step forward, when we discern the merciful hand of the Lord at work in our lives, and proclaim our witness of the same. In this way, others might be edified in the knowledge that we are firm in our covenant resolve. Active gratitude moves us beyond simply cultivating an inner conviction of the Lord's tender mercies; it empowers us to speak and act openly in praising the Lord for His blessings.

9–13 After the family thanks the Lord through sacrifice and burnt offerings, Lehi examines the brass plates and determines that they contain an account of all the Lord's dealings with His people from the Creation through the current day.

> *14 And it came to pass that my father, Lehi, also found upon the plates of brass a genealogy of his fathers; wherefore he knew that he was a descendant of* ***Joseph;*** *yea, even that Joseph who was the son of Jacob, who was sold into Egypt, and who was preserved*

by the hand of the Lord, that he might preserve his father, Jacob, and all his household from perishing with famine.
15 And they were also led out of captivity and out of the land of Egypt, by that same God who had preserved them.
16 And thus my father, Lehi, did discover the genealogy of his fathers. And Laban also was a descendant of ***Joseph,*** *wherefore he and his fathers had kept the records.*

Joseph

From this reference, we know that Lehi and his family have come from the Israelite line of Joseph of Egypt. From a later reference we learn specifically that Lehi is a "descendant of Manasseh, who was the son of Joseph who was sold into Egypt by the hands of his brethren" (Alma 10:3).

17–20 Lehi is moved by the Spirit to prophesy that the word of God contained in the brass plates will be preserved forever as a blessing to the people. Nephi rejoices that he and his family have obeyed God in obtaining the records.

21 And we had ***obtained the records*** *which the Lord had commanded us, and* ***searched them*** *and found that they were desirable; yea, even of great worth unto us, insomuch that we could preserve the commandments of the Lord unto our children.*
22 Wherefore, it was wisdom in the Lord that we should carry them with us, as we journeyed in the wilderness toward the land of promise.

Obtained the records; searched them

It is one thing to have access to the scriptures of God; it is quite another to search them actively and harvest the wisdom and truth preserved therein. In section 84 of the Doctrine and Covenants, the Lord reproves His people for having "treated lightly the things you have received" (D&C 84:54). He warns them that "they shall remain under this condemnation until they repent and remember the new covenant, even the Book of Mormon and the former commandments which I have given them, not only to say, but to do according to that which I have written—That they may bring forth fruit meet for their Father's kingdom. . . ." (D&C 84:57–58). Continually reading from the holy scriptures and applying with devotion the divine counsel contained therein will help us "bring forth fruit" meet for the kingdom of God.

CHAPTER 6

OVERVIEW

Nephi aspires to record and preserve the things of God, to the end that the readers will be persuaded to come unto God and be saved. The things of the world are not to be included in the record.

> *1 AND now I, Nephi, do not give the genealogy of my fathers in this part of my record; neither at any time shall I give it after upon these plates which I am writing; for it is given in the record which has been kept by my father; wherefore, I do not write it in this work.*
> *2 For it sufficeth me to say that we are descendants of Joseph.*
> *3 And it mattereth not to me that I am particular to give a full account of all the things of my father, for they cannot be written upon these plates, for I desire the room that I may write of the* ***things of God.***
> *4 For the fulness of mine intent is that I may persuade men to come unto the God of Abraham, and the God of Isaac, and the God of Jacob, and be saved.*
> *5 Wherefore, the things which are pleasing unto the world I do not write, but the things which are pleasing unto God and unto those who are not of the world.*

Things of God

Among God's greatest gifts to mankind is the gift of His word, granted as a loving endowment to build faith, secure obedience, and open the gateway to immortality and eternal life. The mission of prophets is to preserve this word and convey it to God's children. Nephi is commanded to make plates and to engrave thereon the record of his people and the record of his father—including Lehi's and Nephi's own prophecies—that he might persuade men to come unto Christ. All scriptures testify of Christ. They are testaments or witnesses of our Savior. We are to live by every word that proceeds from the mouth of God (see D&C 84:44). They are written to invite all to come unto Christ and be perfected in Him (see Moroni 10:32). Alma used the word of God to reclaim the Zoramites (see Alma 31:4–5), and we are to use the scriptures for similar purposes in our service to the Lord. We are to open our mouths (see D&C 33:8–10) and warn our neighbors (see D&C 88:81).

> *6 Wherefore, I shall give commandment unto my seed, that they shall not occupy these plates with things which are* ***not of worth*** *unto the children of men.*

Not of worth

What the prophets include in the sacred canon is of inestimable worth. From the beginning the Lord declared scripture to be the standard for human behavior and action: "And he humbled thee, and suffered thee to hunger, and fed thee with manna, which thou knewest not, neither did thy fathers know; that he might make thee know that man doth not live by bread only, but by every word that proceedeth out of the mouth of the Lord doth man live" (Deuteronomy 8:3).

CHAPTER 7

OVERVIEW

The Lord commands Lehi to send his sons back to Jerusalem to persuade Ishmael and his family to leave the city and join the group in the wilderness so that families can be established. Ishmael agrees; however, part of the group—Laman, Lemuel, two of the daughters of Ishmael, and his two sons with their families—rebel against Nephi on the return trip. Nephi counsels them to remember the Lord and to exercise faith, but they bind him and seek to take his life. Nephi supplicates the Lord for help, and his bands are loosed. Again, his older brothers threaten him, but finally desist in response to the pleading of one of the daughters and her mother, together with one of the sons. Nephi forgives his oppressors. The party arrives back at Lehi's encampment and offers thanks.

> *1 AND now I would that ye might know, that after my father, Lehi, had made an end of prophesying concerning his seed, it came to pass that the Lord spake unto him again, saying that it was not meet for him, Lehi, that he should take his family into the wilderness alone; but that his sons should take daughters to wife, that they might* ***raise up seed*** *unto the Lord in the land of promise.*

Raise up seed

The Lord commands Lehi to send his sons back to Jerusalem once again to seek a partnership with Ishmael's family for the journey to the promised land. Obedience gives Lehi's sons the opportunity to enter the pathway of vitality; this action will allow them to take Ishmael's daughters to wife that they may have a posterity.

*2 And it came to pass that the Lord commanded him that I, Nephi, and my brethren, should again return unto the land of Jerusalem, and bring down **Ishmael** and his family into the wilderness.*

Ishmael, Emigrant Father

Ishmael is a descendant of Ephraim (see *Journal of Discourses*, 23:184–185). He and his family live in Jerusalem at the time of Lehi's departure. Lehi is a descendant of Manasseh (see Alma 10:3). Thus both families are of the lineage of Joseph of Egypt through his two sons. Ishmael's family included his wife, five daughters, and two sons, "and their families" (1 Nephi 7:6). Presumably the two sons already had wives and children. With five daughters of marriageable age, the mathematical situation within Ishmael's family was conducive to an arrangement for marriages with the four sons of Lehi, plus Zoram, the latter receiving the oldest daughter as his wife (see 1 Nephi 16:7).

Ishmael does not live to complete the journey to the promised land. He dies in the wilderness "and [is] buried in the place called Nahom" (1 Nephi 16:34), but his family continues on to contribute to the founding of mighty nations.

3–5 Nephi and his brothers return to Jerusalem and persuade Ishmael, whose heart the Lord has softened, to bring his family forth and join with the Lehi group.

6 And it came to pass that as we journeyed in the wilderness, behold Laman and Lemuel, and two of the daughters of Ishmael, and the two sons of Ishmael and their families, did rebel against us; yea, against me, Nephi, and Sam, and their father, Ishmael, and his wife, and his three other daughters.
7 And it came to pass in the which rebellion, they were desirous to return unto the land of Jerusalem.
8 And now I, Nephi, being grieved for the hardness of their hearts, therefore I spake unto them, saying, yea, even unto Laman and unto Lemuel: Behold ye are mine elder brethren, and how is it that ye are so hard in your hearts, and so blind in your minds, that ye have need that I, your younger brother, should speak unto you, yea, and set an example for you?
9 How is it that ye have not hearkened unto the word of the Lord?
*10 How is it that ye have **forgotten** that ye have seen an angel of the Lord?*
*11 Yea, and how is it that ye have **forgotten** what great things the Lord hath done for us, in delivering us out of the hands of Laban, and also that we should obtain the record?*

1 Nephi 7:12–18

> *12 Yea, and how is it that ye have* ***forgotten*** *that the Lord is able to do all things according to his will, for the children of men, if it so be that they exercise faith in him? Wherefore, let us be faithful to him.*

Forgotten

It is sometimes hard to remember everything we should do. Sometimes in the hectic business of life we forget that which is most important in gaining eternal life—studying the scriptures, counting our blessings, and being faithful in keeping the commandments. Do we hearken to the word of God? Do we forget the blessings of the Lord in our lives?

13–14 Nephi prophesies to his associates of the impending destruction of Jerusalem for having rejected the prophets, including Jeremiah, and for having sought to slay Lehi.

> *15 Now behold, I say unto you that if ye will return unto Jerusalem* ***ye shall also perish with them.*** *And now, if ye have choice, go up to the land, and remember the words which I speak unto you, that if ye go ye will also perish; for thus the Spirit of the Lord constraineth me that I should speak.*

Ye shall also perish with them

Obedience is the pathway to life; murmuring is the pathway to death. The Lord's commandments are always given to enhance vitality, to edify the Saints as they seek to build the kingdom of God. Following His commandments is the key to life. In opposition to that, obeying reluctantly, or worse, allowing the spirit of dissention and murmuring to short-circuit obedience altogether is the sure pathway to decline and death.

> *16 And it came to pass that when I, Nephi, had spoken these words unto my brethren, they were angry with me. And it came to pass that they did lay their hands upon me, for behold, they were exceedingly wroth, and they did bind me with cords, for they sought to take away my life, that they might leave me in the wilderness to be devoured by wild beasts.*
> *17 But it came to pass that* ***I prayed unto the Lord,*** *saying: O Lord, according to my faith which is in thee, wilt thou deliver me from the hands of my brethren; yea, even give me strength that I may burst these bands with which I am bound.*
> *18 And it came to pass that when I had said these words, behold, the bands were loosed from off my hands and feet, and I stood before my brethren, and I spake unto them again.*

I prayed unto the Lord

Pray with faith and real intent—for the Lord will bless you and strengthen you along the pathway of mortality.

> *19 And it came to pass that they were angry with me again, and sought to lay hands upon me; but behold, one of the daughters of Ishmael, yea, and also her mother, and one of the sons of Ishmael, did* ***plead*** *with my brethren, insomuch that they did soften their hearts; and they did cease striving to take away my life.*

Plead

The act of pleading on behalf of the oppressed is a manifestation of charity. In the Book of Mormon, penitent Zeezrom intercedes on behalf of Alma and Amulek, who are imprisoned and abused without cause: "And it came to pass that he began to cry unto the people, saying: Behold, I am guilty, and these men are spotless before God. And he began to plead for them from that time forth . . ." (Alma 14:7). Similarly, King Lamoni agrees to assist in the release of Aaron and his companions from prison: "And he said unto Ammon: Come, I will go with thee down to the land of Middoni, and there I will plead with the king that he will cast thy brethren out of prison" (Alma 20:7).

The highest manifestation of pleading is administered by the Savior Himself, our Advocate with the Father: "I am Christ, and in mine own name, by the virtue of the blood which I have spilt, have I pleaded before the Father for them" (D&C 38:4). Again: "Listen to him who is the advocate with the Father, who is pleading your cause before him" (D&C 45:3; compare Moses 7:39). In our own day, the prophets have pled the cause of worthy brethren awaiting the blessings of the priesthood: "Witnessing the faithfulness of those from whom the priesthood has been withheld, we have pleaded long and earnestly in behalf of these, our faithful brethren, spending many hours in the Upper Room of the Temple supplicating the Lord for divine guidance" (Official Declaration—2).

> *20 And it came to pass that they were sorrowful, because of their wickedness, insomuch that they did bow down before me, and did plead with me that I would forgive them of the thing that they had done against me.*
> *21 And it came to pass that I did* ***frankly forgive*** *them all that they had done, and I did exhort them that they would pray unto the Lord their God for forgiveness. And it came to pass that they did so. And after they had done praying unto the Lord we did again travel on our journey toward the tent of our father.*

22 And it came to pass that we did come down unto the tent of our father. And after I and my brethren and all the house of Ishmael had come down unto the tent of my father, they did give thanks unto the Lord their God; and they did offer sacrifice and burnt offerings unto him.

Frankly forgive

Nephi repeatedly exhibits the quality of forgiveness when his brethren humble themselves and, for a time, display at least the beginnings of a penitent spirit. In this same context, Peter asks the Savior, "Then came Peter to him, and said, Lord, how oft shall my brother sin against me, and I forgive him? till seven times? Jesus saith unto him, I say not unto thee, Until seven times: but, Until seventy times seven" (Matthew 18:21–22).

CHAPTER 8

OVERVIEW

Lehi relates his remarkable vision of the tree of life to his family. Following the invitation of a man in a white robe, he traverses a dark and foreboding wasteland. Left alone, he prays for help and eventually reaches the tree of life, partakes of its fruit, and experiences great joy. He motions to Sariah, Sam, and Nephi to come forward to the tree and partake of its glorious fruit—which they do; however, to his great disappointment, Laman and Lemuel ignore his invitation. Lehi also beholds a rod of iron leading along the strait and narrow pathway toward the tree. In addition, he beholds a great and spacious building in which concourses of people deride those who seek to find their way along the path. Lehi also beholds mists of darkness that obscure the way, and he observes the quest of those who seek to reach the tree, many of whom fall by the wayside and are lost. Having related his vision, Lehi expresses great concern for his two older sons.

1 AND it came to pass that we had gathered together all manner of seeds of every kind, both of grain of every kind, and also of the seeds of fruit of every kind.
*2 And it came to pass that while my father tarried in the wilderness he spake unto us, saying: Behold, I have dreamed a dream; or, in other words, I have seen a **vision.***

Vision

What Lehi sees is a dynamic scene that instills in him two diametrically opposite emotions—one of joy on behalf of his righteous sons Sam and Nephi, and one of fear on behalf of Laman and Lemuel, whose attitudes and behavior are scarcely in keeping with divine mandate (see 1 Nephi 8:3–4). Lehi unfolds for his family the details of the vision that has become one of the most compelling statements of the gospel plan and of the consequences of mortal choice in all of holy writ. As we shall see, the tree of life vision encompasses a multiplicity of symbols that invite informed interpretation and greater understanding, based on the keys given in the scriptures themselves. This greater understanding leads to daily applications that promote increased goodness and righteousness in life.

3 And behold, because of the thing which I have seen, I have reason to rejoice in the
Lord because of Nephi and also of Sam; for I have reason to suppose that they, and also
many of their seed, will be saved.
4 But behold, Laman and Lemuel, I fear exceedingly because of you; for behold,
methought I saw in my dream, a dark and dreary wilderness.
5 And it came to pass that I saw a man, and he was dressed in a white robe; and he
came and stood before me.
6 And it came to pass that he spake unto me, and bade me follow him.
7 And it came to pass that as I followed him I beheld myself that I was in a ***dark and***
dreary waste.

Dark and dreary waste

This can be thought of as the environment of mortal man in today's world of temptation, doubt, and fear.

8 And after I had traveled for the space of many hours in darkness, I began to pray unto
the Lord that he would have mercy on me, according to the multitude of his tender
mercies.
9 And it came to pass after I had prayed unto the Lord I beheld a ***large and spacious***
field.

Large and spacious field

This represents the world.

1 Nephi 8:10–11

*10 And it came to pass that I beheld a **tree,** whose fruit was desirable to make one happy.*
*11 And it came to pass that I did go forth and partake of the **fruit** thereof; and I beheld that it was most sweet, above all that I ever before tasted. Yea, and I beheld that the fruit thereof was white, to exceed all the whiteness that I had ever seen.*

Tree, fruit

The tree and its fruit represent the love of God (see 1 Nephi 11:25). The fruit is desirable above all other things to make one happy. The love of God is expressed through the Lord Jesus Christ and His atoning sacrifice (see John 3:16). The ultimate gift from God through His Son is eternal life (see D&C 14:7)—where we dwell with God in a state of never-ending happiness (see Mosiah 2:41). We receive this love as we come unto Christ and partake of His atoning sacrifice through obedience to the doctrines and principles of His gospel.

EVIDENCE: Dark and dreary waste; large and spacious field; tree, fruit—desert imagery (1 Nephi 8:4–7, 10–12, 23; 11:8; 12:16; 15:17)

According to Hugh Nibley, Nephi's descriptions of Lehi's dreams provide "over a dozen vivid little snapshots or colored slides of the desert country that show that somebody who had a hand in the writing of the Book of Mormon actually lived there." Nibley explains that the first picture is of Lehi himself, a lone traveler in "a dark and dreary waste," and that this image—this nightmare—commonly haunted the early Arab poets. In Arabic poetry the "large and spacious field" symbolizes release from fear and oppression. The tree is such as one would find in the garden of kings. Records reveal that the Persian king and others had trees made of pure silver to represent the tree of life, and nowhere on earth is a living tree met with more reverence than in the deserts of Arabia. In fact, Nibley states that in Arabia, "certain trees are regarded as holy because of their life-giving propensities." These images, in addition to many others from Lehi's dream, portray a complete panorama of the Arabian desert country—a view which Joseph Smith had never seen. (See *Echoes,* 470–472.)

Orphic Gold Plates

In most cases, scholars and historians can easily identify the forgery of an ancient document if that document attempts to describe the intellectual, cultural, and social heritage of a specific civilization. This is accomplished by comparing the document with known information about the history that the document pretends to describe. Because the Book of Mormon sets forth a great deal of historical detail, if the book were fabricated by Joseph Smith, any forgery would be simple to expose.

In Orphism, a Greek religious movement that focused on purification of the soul, gold plates were buried with the dead. These plates were engraved with ritualistic writings designed to guide spirits in the afterlife. Orphics believed that a deceased person would find two paths, one of which would lead to a white cypress tree near a spring. Significantly, as Noel B. Reynolds states, "Egyptian ritualistic funerary texts also contain similar references to a 'tree growing by the fountain or spring of living water.'" (See *Echoes,* 138–140.)

12 And as I partook of the fruit thereof it filled my soul with exceedingly great joy; wherefore, I began to be desirous that my family should partake of it also; for I knew that it was desirable above all other fruit.
13 And as I cast my eyes round about, that perhaps I might discover my family also, I beheld a river of water; and it ran along, and it was near the tree of which I was partaking the fruit.
14 And I looked to behold from whence it came; and I saw the head thereof a little way off; and at the head thereof I beheld your mother Sariah, and Sam, and Nephi; and they stood as if they knew not whither they should go.
15 And it came to pass that I beckoned unto them; and I also did say unto them with a loud voice that they should come unto me, and partake of the fruit, which was desirable above all other fruit.
16 And it came to pass that they did come unto me and partake of the fruit also.
17 And it came to pass that I was desirous that Laman and Lemuel should come and partake of the fruit also; wherefore, I cast mine eyes toward the head of the river, that perhaps I might see them.
18 And it came to pass that I saw them, but they would not come unto me and partake of the fruit.
19 And I beheld a ***rod of iron,*** *and it extended along the bank of the river, and led to the tree by which I stood.*

Rod of iron

The word of God (see 1 Nephi 15:23–24).

20 And I also beheld a ***strait and narrow path,*** *which came along by the rod of iron, even to the tree by which I stood; and it also led by the head of the fountain, unto a large and spacious field, as if it had been a world.*

Strait and narrow path

The principles and ordinances of the everlasting gospel, which lead to life and exaltation (see 3 Nephi 14:14; D&C 132:22).

> *21 And I saw numberless concourses of people, many of whom were pressing forward, that they might obtain the path which led unto the tree by which I stood.*
> *22 And it came to pass that they did come forth, and commence in the path which led to the tree.*
> *23 And it came to pass that there arose a* ***mist of darkness;*** *yea, even an exceedingly great mist of darkness, insomuch that they who had commenced in the path did lose their way, that they wandered off and were lost.*

Mist of darkness

The temptations of the devil (see 1 Nephi 12:17).

> *24 And it came to pass that I beheld others pressing forward, and they came forth and caught hold of the end of the rod of iron; and they did press forward through the mist of darkness, clinging to the rod of iron, even until they did come forth and partake of the fruit of the tree.*
> *25 And after they had partaken of the fruit of the tree they did cast their eyes about as if they were ashamed.*
> *26 And I also cast my eyes round about, and beheld, on the other side of the river of water, a* ***great and spacious building;*** *and it stood as it were in the air, high above the earth.*

Great and spacious building

The pride, vain imaginations, and wisdom of the world (see 1 Nephi 11:35–36; 12:18).

> *27 And it was filled with people, both old and young, both male and female; and their manner of dress was exceedingly fine; and they were in the attitude of mocking and pointing their fingers toward those who had come at and were partaking of the fruit.*
> *28 And after they had tasted of the fruit they were ashamed, because of those that were scoffing at them; and they fell away into forbidden paths and were lost.*
> *29 And now I, Nephi, do not speak all the words of my father.*

30 But, to be short in writing, behold, he saw ***other multitudes*** *pressing forward;*
and they came and caught hold of the end of the rod of iron; and they did press their way forward, continually holding fast to the rod of iron, until they came forth and fell down and partook of the fruit of the tree.
31 And he also saw ***other multitudes*** *feeling their way toward that great and spacious building.*

Other multitudes

In seeking eternal life, one we are counseled to get on the strait and narrow path, to hold to the iron rod, and to press forward steadfastly. It takes great effort and perseverance to remain faithful and obedient and to avoid casting our lot with those fellow travelers who fail to reach out and grab hold of the iron rod, or who, having once chosen it, still fall by the wayside.

Lehi's vision of the tree of life was both an inspiring expression, in allegorical terms, of God's overarching plan of love and redemption, as well as a template for application in our immediate life. The tree of life is not an abstract model to be admired like a tapestry, but a road map that becomes all the more compelling to the extent we hold it up as a mirror in which to see ourselves in the very act of striving to gain that perfection which God has ordained our destiny.

In the vision we are granted a clear and unmistakable view of the types of people among the "other multitudes" ever present on the mortal landscape. Let us look at this fourfold typology of travelers and have the courage to discern in which type we might find ourselves:

Group 1. The Vagrants: Those who start but never get to the iron rod or are not faithful in holding to it and thus lose their way in the mists of darkness and wander off (see 1 Nephi 8:21–23). To avoid being part of this group, we must diligently search the scriptures and live according to every word that proceeds forth from the mouth of God.

Group 2. The Vacillators: Those who hold to the iron rod and start to enjoy the fruit of the tree, but when they find themselves mocked and ridiculed they are unable to withstand persecution and fall away (see 1 Nephi 8:24–28). One must always be willing to stand for truth and righteousness and live as Paul described: "For I am not ashamed of the gospel of Christ: for it is the power of God unto salvation to every one that believeth; to the Jew first, and also to the Greek" (Romans 1:16).

Group 3. The Vain: Those who feel their way to the spacious building and never get on the path to the tree of life. Wandering in strange roads, they become the mocking tenants of the spacious building (see 1 Nephi 8:31–33). This group represents the vast multitude of Heavenly Father's children who succumb to pride and vanity, and, like the others who stray from the pathway leading to truth, become separated from the things of God.

1 Nephi 8:31–38

Group 4. The Valiant: Those who hold to the iron rod, press forward with steadfastness, partake of the fruit of the tree, and remain faithful (see 1 Nephi 8:30).

32 And it came to pass that many were drowned in the depths of the ***fountain;*** *and many were lost from his view, wandering in strange roads.*

FOUNTAIN

This image is a representation of the depths of hell (see 1 Nephi 12:16).

33 And great was the multitude that did enter into that strange building. And after they did enter into that building they did point the finger of scorn at me and those that were partaking of the fruit also; but we heeded them not.
34 These are the words of my father: For as many as heeded them, had fallen away.
35 And Laman and Lemuel partook not of the fruit, said my father.
36 And it came to pass after my father had spoken all the words of his dream or vision, which were many, he said unto us, because of these things which he saw in a vision, he exceedingly feared for Laman and Lemuel; yea, he feared lest they should be cast off from the presence of the Lord.
37 And he did ***exhort them then with all the feeling of a tender parent,*** *that they would hearken to his words, that perhaps the Lord would be merciful to them, and not cast them off; yea, my father did preach unto them.*
38 And after he had preached unto them, and also prophesied unto them of many things, he bade them to keep the commandments of the Lord; and he did cease speaking unto them.

EXHORT THEM THEN WITH ALL THE FEELING OF A TENDER PARENT

Lehi's earnest appeal to his sons to follow the pathway to happiness is analogous to the Lord's appeal to all of His children to come unto Him and partake of eternal life.

MEMORIES: THE SPIRITUAL FOREST

The word "tree" is used 428 times in the scriptures. "Tree of life" itself occurs no fewer than twenty-nine times. Few images in the scriptures awaken in the hearts of truth-seekers more reverence and awe than the image of the noble tree, the unfailing emblem of enduring growth, timeless strength, and towering majesty. Jeremiah, Lehi's immediate contemporary, extended the image of the tree to the person directly: "Blessed *is* the man that trusteth in the LORD, and whose hope the LORD is. For he shall be as a tree planted by the waters, and *that* spreadeth out her roots by the river, and shall not see when heat cometh, but her leaf shall be green. . . ." (Jeremiah 17:7–8). Similarly, Lehi's younger contemporary, Ezekiel, wrote of his vision of the temple of God, which issues forth a stream of healing water to sustain trees and growth on either side (see Ezekiel 47:7–9), surely a further manifestation of God's spiritual nourishment of the Saints. A similar image is reflected by John in his vision of the tree of life in the midst of the paradise of God (see Revelation 2:7; 22:2, 14).

Again and again the image of the tree awakens in our souls a sense of spiritual potential. From the allegory of the olive trees as a likeness of Israel's unfolding and destiny (see Jacob 5) to the imagery of Zion's "branches" extending around the world to the very substance of Zion's organizational structure itself (i.e., poles and stakes of wood that support the canopy of spiritual refuge) to the very essence of the wooden cross of the Atonement. All of these tree-related emblems come back to one thing: the love of God manifested through the blessings of the gospel of Jesus Christ offered through grace to His sons and daughters as a means of bringing them home again.

All of us contribute, in our own way, to the growth of the spiritual forest. For all of us there are trees of significance somewhere in the record of our lives—some of which we may have planted and nourished personally. What are these trees, these personal trees of life? There is no dearth of models to reflect on. We come back to that sacred grove where the boy Joseph received the first messages about the Restoration and learned firsthand about the verity of the living Father and Son. We remember with admiration and respect the story of President Hinckley's venerated walnut tree that became, in effect, the podium for the new conference center from which emanates continual truth about the "tree of life" in the form of God's love.

My wife recounts her vivid childhood memory of a cherished willow tree, visible from her bedroom window, through whose limbs she could see in her mind's eye, season after season, the temple of God standing nearby as a symbol of everlasting life. For her, the willow tree was part of a spiritual forest that offers peace and hope. In our home today we still have on display a sculpture of the Holy Family beautifully carved from linden wood by an Austrian artist we met one year—a tree-based symbol of Christ's birth. A current neighbor of ours tells fondly of an ancient sycamore tree in their family homestead in the Northwest that contributed a towering stump upon which he erected a mechanical device that would swing his children on ropes in a great arc about the tree—a source of endless hours of family recreation and togetherness still talked about in family circles decades later. For him, the tree was part of the spiritual forest that symbolized the enduring family of God. And so it goes.

What are the trees in your life? There is value in walking through the spiritual forest of your life and in contemplating the blessings of God embodied in the imagery of those special trees that reflect His love and remind us of the promise: "To him that overcometh will I give to eat of the tree of life, which is in the midst of the paradise of God" (Revelation 2:7). [Richard J. Allen]

CHAPTER 9

OVERVIEW

Nephi reports that he is keeping two sets of records, each called the plates of Nephi. On the smaller ones he records the more sacred and spiritual things, and on the larger ones he records the secular history of the people.

1 AND all these things did my father see, and hear, and speak, as he dwelt in a tent, in the valley of Lemuel, and also a great many more things, which cannot be written upon these plates.
2 And now, as I have spoken concerning these plates, behold they are not the plates upon which I make a full account of the history of my people; for the plates upon which I make a full account of my people I have given the name of Nephi; wherefore, they are called the plates of Nephi, after mine own name; and these plates also are called the plates of Nephi.
3 Nevertheless, I have received a commandment of the Lord that I should make these plates, for the special purpose that there should be an account engraven of the ministry of my people.
4 Upon the other plates should be engraven an account of the reign of the kings, and the wars and contentions of my people; wherefore these plates are for the more part of the ministry; and the other plates are for the more part of the reign of the kings and the wars and contentions of my people.
5 Wherefore, the Lord hath commanded me to make these plates for a ***wise purpose*** *in him, which purpose I know not.*
6 But the Lord knoweth all things from the beginning; wherefore, he prepareth a way to accomplish all his works among the children of men; for behold, he hath all power unto the fulfilling of all his words. And thus it is. Amen.

Wise purpose

God is all-knowing and wise. The wise purpose that Nephi does not know about is that the first 116 pages of translation completed by the Prophet Joseph Smith from the Book of Lehi will be lost by Martin Harris—hence the need for Nephi's record, from which the prophet would then continue with his translation afresh.

CHAPTER 10

OVERVIEW

Nephi reports more concerning his father's prophecies: that Jerusalem will be destroyed and its people taken into captivity by the Babylonians, that they will be gathered back again in the Lord's due time, that the Messiah will be born 600 years after Lehi's departure from Jerusalem, that one [John the Baptist] will help to prepare the way and baptize Him. Nephi describes the Atonement, compares the House of Israel to the branches of an olive tree, and foretells of the Gentiles' receiving the fulness of the gospel. Nephi desires to behold the things his father has seen.

> *1 AND now I, Nephi, proceed to give an account upon these plates of my proceedings, and my reign and ministry; wherefore, to proceed with mine account, I must speak somewhat of the things of my father, and also of my brethren.*
> *2 For behold, it came to pass after my father had made an end of speaking the words of his dream, and also of exhorting them to all diligence, he spake unto them concerning the Jews—*
> *3 That after they should be destroyed, even that great city Jerusalem, and many be carried away captive into Babylon, according to the own due time of the Lord, they should return again, yea, even be brought back out of captivity; and after they should be brought back out of captivity they should possess again the land of their inheritance.*
> *4 Yea, even six hundred years from the time that my father left Jerusalem, a prophet would the Lord God raise up among the Jews—even a* **Messiah,** *or, in other words, a Savior of the world.*

Messiah

Lehi's remarkable prophesy concerning the coming of the Son of God (see 1 Nephi 10:4–17) confirms the consistent role of the Lord's chosen spokesmen to speak of the Redeemer of the world,

His life, Atonement, and Resurrection. All such pronouncements come by the power of the Holy Ghost, which power Lehi also received because of his faith on the Son of God.

> *5 And he also spake concerning the prophets, how great a number had testified of these things, concerning this Messiah, of whom he had spoken, or this Redeemer of the world.*
> *6 Wherefore, all mankind were in a lost and in a fallen state, and ever would be save they should* ***rely on this Redeemer.***

Rely on this Redeemer

As mortals we surely need to rely on the Lord in all things. Nephi, at the end of his ministry, gives the following formula for relying on the Redeemer:

> And now, my beloved brethren, after ye have gotten into this strait and narrow path, I would ask if all is done? Behold, I say unto you, Nay; for ye have not come thus far save it were by the word of Christ with unshaken faith in him, relying wholly upon the merits of him who is mighty to save.
>
> Wherefore, ye must press forward with a steadfastness in Christ, having a perfect brightness of hope, and a love of God and of all men. Wherefore, if ye shall press forward, feasting upon the word of Christ, and endure to the end, behold, thus saith the Father: Ye shall have eternal life (2 Nephi 31:19–21).

> *7 And he spake also concerning a prophet who should come before the Messiah, to prepare the way of the Lord—*
> *8 Yea, even he should go forth and cry in the wilderness:* ***Prepare ye the way*** *of the Lord, and make his paths straight; for there standeth one among you whom ye know not; and he is mightier than I, whose shoe's latchet I am not worthy to unloose. And much spake my father concerning this thing.*
> *9 And my father said he should baptize in Bethabara, beyond Jordan; and he also said he should baptize with water; even that he should baptize the Messiah with water.*
> *10 And after he had baptized the Messiah with water, he should behold and bear record that he had baptized the Lamb of God, who should take away the sins of the world.*

Prepare ye the way

John the Baptist proclaimed the preparatory gospel of repentance and obedience that would be fulfilled and completed through the mission of the Lamb of God, the "author of eternal salvation unto all them that obey him" (Hebrews 5:9). Through Jesus Christ and His atoning sacrifice, the gift of the Holy Ghost would be dispensed upon the faithful as the key to the remission of sins. Elder Bruce R. McConkie describes John's calling:

> John, who bore testimony of Jesus, did so for one reason and one reason only: he was seeking to persuade men to believe in Christ, to come unto him, to accept him as the Son of God, and to be saved by obedience to the laws and ordinances of his gospel. When John baptized for the remission of sins, he was not seeking disciples who would follow him, except as he guided them to the one who should come after. Indeed, the very remission of sins that he promised could not come until they received the Holy Ghost—the baptism of fire—which burns sin and evil out of a human soul as though by fire. John's whole purpose was to persuade his disciples to follow, not himself, but the Lord Jesus whose witness he was. (*The Mortal Messiah: From Bethlehem to Calvary,* 4 vols. [Salt Lake City: Deseret Book, 1979–1981], 1:438)

11–16 Lehi continues to speak to his sons concerning the gospel, the mission of the Savior, the scattering of Israel (such as to the promised land), and the gathering of Israel in the latter days.

> *17 And it came to pass after I, Nephi, having heard all the words of my father, concerning the things which he saw in a vision, and also the things which he spake by the power of the Holy Ghost, which* ***power*** *he received by* ***faith*** *on the Son of God—and the Son of God was the Messiah who should come—I, Nephi, was desirous also that I might see, and hear, and know of these things, by the power of the Holy Ghost, which is the gift of God unto all those who diligently seek him, as well in times of old as in the time that he should manifest himself unto the children of men.*

Power, faith

We must exercise faith and receive the blessings of the Holy Ghost to empower our lives unto repentance and good works.

> *18 For he is* ***the same yesterday, to-day, and forever;*** *and the way is prepared for all men from the foundation of the world, if it so be that they repent and come unto him.*
> *19 For he that diligently seeketh shall find; and the mysteries of God shall be unfolded unto them, by the power of the Holy Ghost, as well in these times as in times of old, and as well in times of old as in times to come; wherefore, the course of the Lord is one eternal round.*
> *20 Therefore remember, O man, for all thy doings thou shalt be brought into judgment.*
> *21 Wherefore, if ye have sought to do wickedly in the days of your probation, then ye are found unclean before the judgment-seat of God; and no unclean thing can dwell with God; wherefore, ye must be cast off forever.*
> *22 And the Holy Ghost giveth authority that I should speak these things, and deny them not.*

THE SAME YESTERDAY, TO-DAY, AND FOREVER

This statement concerning the unchangeable nature of God occurs several times in the Book of Mormon (see also 2 Nephi 2:4; Alma 31:17; Mormon 9:9; and Moroni 10:19). It occurs also in the Lord's own testimony about the divinity of His word as contained in the Book of Mormon:

> Proving to the world that the holy scriptures are true, and that God does inspire men and call them to his holy work in this age and generation, as well as in generations of old;
>
> Thereby showing that he is the same God yesterday, today, and forever. Amen" (D&C 20:11–12).

The Supreme Being exists as the "Unchanging One," or Jehovah, for that is the meaning of this name.

CHAPTER 11

OVERVIEW

Nephi ponders the things of the Lord and is caught away by the Spirit in vision. He beholds the tree of life, the virgin mother of the Lord, and the newly born Savior. He realizes that the tree represents the love of God, most desirable above all other things. Moreover, he beholds the ministry of the Savior and the preparatory work of John the Baptist. He then sees the Redeemer slain for all mankind and thereafter, the forces of the world, like a great and spacious building, that come against the twelve Apostles of the Lord until finally, it falls, even the pride of the world.

> *1 FOR it came to pass after I had desired to know the things that my father had seen, and believing that the Lord was able to make them known unto me, as I sat* ***pondering*** *in mine heart I was caught away in the Spirit of the Lord, yea, into an exceedingly high mountain, which I never had before seen, and upon which I never had before set my foot.*

Pondering

Pondering often opens our understanding to greater truths. Sometimes we feel that we must be "doing" something every minute, whereas nothing could be further from the truth. When we ponder before acting, we understand and appreciate principles more deeply, and this brings a higher degree of clarity to our thinking, thereby changing our attitudes and often our behavior. Pondering has a wonderful effect upon our very being. Is our desire to know the things of God great enough that we are willing to ponder and meditate upon them? (See D&C 138:1–11.)

Nephi's response to his father's prophetic ministry is an example of how pondering leads to knowledge and inspiration. It is a two-step process, as Nephi has discovered:

1. Cultivate a spiritual mode of inquiry.
    - Nephi has a great desire to know (see 1 Nephi 11:1).
    - He has faith in the principle that by seeking diligently he will find (see 1 Nephi 10:19).
    - He knows that God is the same yesterday, today, and forever (see 1 Nephi 10:18).
    - He cultivates the same mindset of faithful inquiry that the Apostle James commends: "If any of you lack wisdom, let him ask of God, that giveth to all men liberally, and upbraideth not; and it shall be given him" (James 1:5).
    - Nephi has a conviction that the mysteries of God will be revealed by the power of the Holy Ghost (see 1 Nephi 10:19).
2. Inquire of the Lord following humble meditation and pondering. The act of meditation and pondering means to contemplate, muse, or reflect upon things from the immediate

and present to the infinite and universal. It is something we should all do more often. Meditation and pondering provide the opportunity to sort things out, to create new concepts and ideas, to receive pure inspiration—even revelation—for our needs and concerns. The prophets have always pondered that they might know the things of God (see 1 Nephi 11:1; D&C 138:1).

Time to Reflect

President Gordon B. Hinckley explores the rewarding connection between regular pondering and meditating, on the one hand, and the advancement of the quality of our lives, on the other—as reflected in our inner peace, our relationships with family and colleagues, and our commitment to live by the word of God:

> We need the Spirit of the Lord in our lives more. . . . But there is hardly time to reflect and think and pause and meditate. I daresay that most of those in this room today have not taken an hour in the last year to just sit down quietly, each man to himself, as a son of God, reflecting upon his place in this world, upon his destiny, upon his capacity to do good, upon his mission to make some changes for good. We need to. I recall so vividly President McKay in his old age in a meeting with his counselors and the Twelve saying, "Brethren, we need to take more time to meditate, to think quietly." . . .
>
> I'm going to make a suggestion to each of you. On the next fast day, take occasion and arrange your affairs in such a way that you can be by yourself, maybe under a tree in the backyard, maybe in the locked bedroom of your home, where you can think. Read the scriptures and think of sacred things and think of yourself. Your attitude toward your wife—are you the kind of husband you ought to be, considerate, kind, generous, or are you a bully, an abuser? You cannot be a good servant of the Lord if there isn't peace in your heart concerning your companion. . . . Your attitude toward your children: Are you rearing them in an atmosphere of love, or are you the kind of man who thinks he has to deal out punishment all the time? I'm one who believes that it isn't necessary in rearing children to beat them. I'm one who believes that they will respond to love and appreciation. Think, under those circumstances, of your personal integrity—are you a man of honesty; are you a man who deals honestly with others? Say to yourselves, I must stand a little taller and be a little better. Try it, will you? Find a place where next fast day you can spend an hour with yourselves quietly

> thinking of what you can do to make yourselves more worthy of the sacred call which you have. (*Teachings of Gordon B. Hinckley* [Salt Lake City: Deseret Book, 1997], 334–335)

Learning the Will of God

Section 138 of the Doctrine and Covenants is a direct result of inspired pondering over the scriptures and the Atonement of our Savior Jesus Christ. President Joseph F. Smith gives us a remarkable illustration of this process:

> ON the third of October, in the year nineteen hundred and eighteen, I sat in my room pondering over the scriptures;
>
> And reflecting upon the great atoning sacrifice that was made by the Son of God, for the redemption of the world (D&C 138:1–2).

At the center of the prophet's attention was a statement from the New Testament concerning the mission of the resurrected Savior to preach "unto the spirits in prison" (1 Peter 3:19), including the reference: "For for this cause was the gospel preached also to them that are dead, that they might be judged according to men in the flesh, but live according to God in the spirit" (1 Peter 4:6). He then proceeds to give us the account of the heavenly plan of missionary work in the spirit realm for those who await deliverance and exaltation. How grateful we can be that prophetic pondering has enriched our lives with an expanded understanding of the mercy and love of the Father and the Son for their children. (Richard J. Allen)

> *2 And the Spirit said unto me: Behold, what desirest thou?*
>
> *3 And I said: I* ***desire to behold*** *the things which my father saw.*

Desire to behold

Nephi has a great desire to experience the remarkable spiritual manifestations his father has seen. Because of Nephi's righteousness and divine calling, he is given the privilege of receiving this vision wherein he is caught away by the Spirit and led by an angel into holy precincts. The angel instructs him, taking him through a series of inspired views regarding the future.

Each of us, if we are worthy and if there is a need, according to the will of the Lord, can receive angelic messengers. Certainly each of us, as well, can ponder the visions of the prophets and mingle our spiritual sensibility with theirs as we meditate upon the things of the Spirit.

1 Nephi 11:3

Reading the account of Nephi's vision in Chapters 11 through 14 of 1 Nephi is akin to taking a grand spiritual tour through the centuries of time. Through the eyes of Nephi, we are blessed with some two-dozen different sequential scenes of human history that are opened to us from a heavenly perspective. As we open our spiritual eyes, we see played out on the mortal stage the key events that form a continuum leading from Nephi's time to the final scenes of the world's history. During the early scenes, the familiar images from Lehi's vision of the tree of life are replayed for the young prophet Nephi and intermingled with the flow of history being portrayed in vision. Because the Lord has given us the Book of Mormon, we can relive again and again the inspiration from this angelic instruction unfolding before our eyes. The following chart may be helpful in covering the material in 1 Nephi 11–14:

Scenes from the Vision of Nephi

1 Nephi Chapters 11–14

Scene	Scripture	Presentation	No. of verses	Parallels with Lehi's dream (1 Nephi 8)
1.	11:8–11	The tree of life	4	The tree of life
2.	11:12–18	Jerusalem, Nazareth, virgin	7	
3.	11:19–23	Birth of Jesus	5	The tree of life = love of God
4.	11:24–25	Jesus going among the people	2	Rod of iron and fountain of living waters = love of God
5.	11:26–29	Baptism of Jesus by John; ministry of Jesus; 12 disciples	4	
6.	11:30	Angels descending and ministering	1	
7.	11:31	Savior heals the sick	1	
8.	11:32–34	Savior's crucifixion	3	

Scene	Scripture	Presentation	No. of verses	Parallels with Lehi's dream (1 Nephi 8)
9.	11:35–36	The world as a great and spacious building; fall of the building	2	great and spacious building = pride of world
10.	12:1–7	Lehi's generations in America; wars; time of destruction; visit of Savior	7	
11.	12:8–10	Twelve disciples as judges under twelve Apostles	3	
12.	12:11–13	Three+ generations of righteousness	3	
13.	12:14–15	Nephites and Lamanites gathered to battle	2	
14.	12:16–21	Fountain of filthy water; mists of darkness; broad roads of destruction; large and spacious building; terrible gulf; defeat of Nephites because of pride	6	fountain of filthy water = hell; mists of darkness = temptations that "hardeneth the heart" (v. 17); broad roads = false ways; large and spacious building = vain imaginations and pride; terrible gulf = justice of God
15.	12:22–23	Lamanites also dwindle in unbelief	2	
16.	13:1–4	Nations and kingdoms of Gentiles	4	
17.	13:5–9	Great church of the devil; yoke of iron (v. 5)	5	
18.	13:10	Many waters dividing Gentiles and Lamanites	1	
19.	13:11–22	Columbus and the inspired rise of the American Gentiles; Bible	12	
20.	13:23–37	Plain and precious things removed from Bible, causing people to stumble; hardens the heart (v. 27); prediction of coming forth of the Book of Mormon	15	

Scene	Scripture	Presentation	No. of verses	Parallels with Lehi's dream (1 Nephi 8)
21.	13:38–42	Other books come forth to restore the plain and precious things (Book of Mormon, D&C)	5	
22.	14:1–7	Gentiles urged to hearken to Lord and not harden their hearts (v. 1, 6); hardness as captivity (v. 7); Church of devil arrayed against Church of the Lamb of God; restoration proceeds as "a great and marvelous work" (v. 7)	7	
23.	14:8–17	Great and abominable church; two churches only (v. 10); mother of abominations gathered against the Saints; power of the Lamb of God descending upon the Saints; wrath of God upon the mother of harlots; wars; times of fulfilling of covenant	10	
24.	14:18–30	The remainder of the vision: John the Revelator; final chapters of world's history; Nephi forbidden to write it	13	

4–7 The Spirit commends Nephi for his faith and grants unto him the opportunity to view what Lehi had seen in vision, including the Son of God.

> *8 And it came to pass that the Spirit said unto me:* ***Look!*** *And I looked and beheld a tree; and it was like unto the tree which my father had seen; and the beauty thereof was far beyond, yea, exceeding of all beauty; and the whiteness thereof did exceed the whiteness of the driven snow.*

Look!

Through the power of the Spirit, Nephi's eyes are opened and he sees a panoramic display of divine truth unfolding before him in magnificent scenes—including the vision of the tree of life and the coming of the Messiah.

9–12 Nephi desires to know the interpretation of the tree of life.

*13 And it came to pass that I looked and beheld the great city of Jerusalem, and also
other cities. And I beheld the city of Nazareth; and in the city of Nazareth I beheld a
virgin, and she was exceedingly fair and white.*
*14 And it came to pass that I saw the heavens open; and an angel came down and stood
before me; and he said unto me: Nephi, what beholdest thou?*
15 And I said unto him: A virgin, most beautiful and fair above all other virgins.
16 And he said unto me: Knowest thou the ***condescension of God?***
*17 And I said unto him: I know that he loveth his children; nevertheless, I do not know
the meaning of all things.*

Condescension of God

In his grand vision, Nephi witnesses the birth of the Savior in the meridian of time by means of which the Redeemer, by choice, takes upon Himself mortality, an event referred to by the guiding angel as the "condescension of God" (1 Nephi 11:16, 26). The following passage by gospel scholar Kent P. Jackson may shed additional light on this doctrine:

> The condescension of God includes the condescension of Jehovah, Christ, the God of the world, who came down from his divine station to become flesh, to minister in mortality, and to suffer and die for the sins of the world. [He then quotes Mosiah 3:5, 7–9.] . . .
>
> Elder Bruce R. McConkie wrote: "The condescension of God (meaning the Son) consists in the fact that though he himself is the Lord Omnipotent, the very Being who created the earth and all things in it, yet being born of mortal woman, he submitted to all the trials of mortality, suffering 'temptations, and pain of body, hunger, thirst, and fatigue, even more than man can suffer, except it be unto death' (Mosiah 3:5–8), finally being put to death in a most ignominious manner." (Kent P. Jackson, ed., *Studies in Scripture, Vol. 7: 1 Nephi to Alma 29* [Salt Lake City: Deseret Book, 1987], 41)

*18 And he said unto me: Behold, the virgin whom thou seest is the mother of the Son
of God, after the manner of the flesh.*
*19 And it came to pass that I beheld that she was carried away in the Spirit; and after
she had been carried away in the Spirit for the space of a time the angel spake unto
me, saying: Look!*
20 And I looked and beheld the virgin again, bearing a child in her arms.

1 Nephi 11:21–25

21 And the angel said unto me: Behold the Lamb of God, yea, even the Son of the
Eternal Father! Knowest thou the meaning of the tree which thy father saw?
22 And I answered him, saying: Yea, it is the ***love of God,*** *which sheddeth itself abroad*
in the hearts of the children of men; wherefore, it is the most desirable above all things.
23 And he spake unto me, saying: Yea, and the most joyous to the soul.

Love of God

The love of God is expressed through Jesus Christ and His atoning sacrifice. This love can never fail—"for charity never faileth" (Moroni 7:46). If you build your life upon the Savior and are filled with this love, you will be like Him (see John 3:16; 2 Nephi 26:24; Helaman 5:12; Moroni 7:44–48). You will attain to the tree of life and partake of its precious fruit, "the most desirable above all things."

These passages of scripture raise another important question of conscience. The love of God is desirable above all other things to make one happy. Happiness is not only the design of our existence but what we cherish most. Do we have a deep desire and a plan to partake of the love of God (see also 1 Nephi 8:30; 11:25; Moroni 7:48)?

24 And after he had said these words, he said unto me: Look! And I looked, and I
beheld the Son of God going forth among the children of men; and I saw many fall
down at his feet and worship him.
25 And it came to pass that I beheld that the ***rod of iron,*** *which my father had seen,*
was the word of God, which led to the fountain of living waters, or to the ***tree of life;***
which waters are a representation of the love of God; and I also beheld that the tree of
life was a representation of the love of God.

Rod of iron

The symbolism of the rod of iron as the word of God is among the most memorable of all gospel metaphors. It is mentioned seven times in the Book of Mormon, but also occurs in other sacred scriptures, for example, in the book of Revelation: "And out of his mouth goeth a sharp sword, that with it he should smite the nations: and he shall rule them with a rod of iron: and he treadeth the winepress of the fierceness and wrath of Almighty God" (Revelation 19:15).

EVIDENCE: Tree of life; symbolism of the tree of life

The tree of life's appearance in the Book of Mormon is not surprising considering the Semitic background of the book. This ancient Near Eastern symbol is supported not just by Semitic evidences but by discoveries related to other ancient cultures in Mesopotamia and Egypt. While other cultures do not provide the meaning of the tree of life as clearly as does the Book of Mormon, occurrences of the symbol almost always include both a sacred tree and waters of life. (See *Echoes,* 397–398.)

26–36 Nephi sees the ministry of John the Baptist, who baptized the Savior. He sees the Savior going forth to preach to the people and bless and heal them. He witnesses the crucifixion and the subsequent battle between the forces of good and the forces of evil arrayed against the twelve Apostles. He also sees the eventual collapse of the great and spacious building, "the pride of the world" (verse 36).

CHAPTER 12

OVERVIEW

Nephi beholds the generations of inhabitants upon the land of promise, including their wars and contentions. He sees boundless destruction and upheavals upon the land just prior to the visit of the Lord among the people. The Lord chooses twelve disciples to judge the seed of Nephi, just as the twelve Apostles judge the twelve tribes of Israel. Nephi sees three generations pass away in righteousness because of the faith of the people. He then beholds the coming of contention and destruction through the incursion of pride and wickedness among his seed [the Nephites] and the seed of his brethren [the Lamanites]. Because of unbelief, the people slip into a loathsome state.

> *1 AND it came to pass that the angel said unto me: Look, and* ***behold thy seed,*** *and*
> *also the seed of thy brethren. And I looked and beheld the land of promise; and I beheld*
> *multitudes of people, yea, even as it were in number as many as the sand of the sea.*

Behold thy seed

From the vision of Nephi we find the truth confirmed that the mission and Atonement of the Savior serves as a beacon of hope and truth to guide generations through mortality. When a nation such as the Nephites honors the covenant promises, they prosper and blossom; but as they succumb to pride and worldliness, they decline and ultimately perish. That is the message and the warning of the Book of Mormon.

1 Nephi 12:1–23

Nephi and his circle of loved ones initially constitute but a handful of God's children. Yet in time they number in the millions. What a momentous view is given Nephi to see how this branch of Israel evolves and develops, ever unfolding or declining according to the willingness of the people to remain aligned with righteous principles—or to defect therefrom.

2–15 Nephi beholds the wars and contentions that will take place over the years leading up to the devastating upheavals in ancient America at the time of the Savior's death. He sees the appearance of the resurrected Lord among his people and the calling of the twelve disciples as ministers unto his seed. He beholds thereafter three subsequent generations of peace, and then the gradual lapse of spiritual vitality as the nations contend in the culminating battles of the era.

> *16 And the angel spake unto me, saying: Behold the* ***fountain of filthy water*** *which thy father saw; yea, even the river of which he spake; and the depths thereof are the depths of hell.*
> *17 And the* ***mists of darkness*** *are the temptations of the devil, which blindeth the eyes, and hardeneth the hearts of the children of men, and leadeth them away into broad roads, that they perish and are lost.*
> *18 And the* ***large and spacious building,*** *which thy father saw, is vain imaginations and the pride of the children of men. And a* ***great and a terrible gulf*** *divideth them; yea, even the word of the justice of the Eternal God, and the Messiah who is the Lamb of God, of whom the Holy Ghost beareth record, from the beginning of the world until this time, and from this time henceforth and forever.*

FOUNTAIN OF FILTHY WATER; MISTS OF DARKNESS; LARGE AND SPACIOUS BUILDING; GREAT AND TERRIBLE GULF

These symbolic expressions comprise the impressive range of metaphorical elements of evil and degeneracy depicted in Lehi's vision. Sin and its suffocating effects, pride and its delusional intoxication, exclusion from the presence of God—all of these are forceful and dramatic articulations of the destructive nature of wickedness and the consequences of losing one's grasp on the rod of iron.

19–23 Nephi beholds the extinction of his people because of pride and degeneracy.

CHAPTER 13

OVERVIEW

Nephi beholds the nations of the Gentiles, among whom a great and abominable church is established by the devil to contend against the Saints. Nephi beholds one (Christopher Columbus) who is directed by the Spirit to journey to the land of promise, followed by Gentiles seeking liberty under the guidance of the Spirit. He beholds the coming forth of the record of the Jews in its purity (the Bible), only to be defiled by the great and abominable church, which will remove from it many plain and precious parts, causing many to stumble. He sees the restoration of the fulness of the gospel, the bringing forth of "other books" (latter-day scriptures, including the Book of Mormon) that confirm the truths of the first (the Bible)—i.e., that the Savior is the Son of God and the Redeemer of the world.

1 AND it came to pass that the angel spake unto me, saying: Look! And I looked and
beheld many nations and kingdoms.
2 And the angel said unto me: What beholdest thou? And I said: I behold many nations
and kingdoms.
3 And he said unto me: These are the nations and kingdoms of the ***Gentiles.***

Gentiles

The word "Gentiles" has several meanings, depending upon the context in which it is used. Elder Bruce R. McConkie provides the following summary to aid in understanding this term:

> Various meanings have been attached to the name Gentiles in different ages, depending on the historical setting or the doctrinal teachings involved. Literally the meaning is, "of the same clan or race," and Biblical revisions frequently substitute the word nations in its place. . . .
>
> In the days of Abraham, the term was used to refer to those nations and peoples who had not descended from him, with the added assurance that all Gentiles who should receive the gospel would be adopted into the lineage of Abraham and be accounted his seed. (Abra. 2:9–11.) The Prophet taught that those so adopted became literally of the blood of Abraham. (Teachings, 149–150.) In the days of ancient Israel, those not of the lineage of Jacob were considered to be Gentiles, although the Arabs and other races of Semitic origin who traced their

lineage back to Abraham would not have been Gentiles in the strict Abrahamic use of the word.

After the Kingdom of Israel was destroyed and the Ten Tribes were led away into Assyrian captivity, those of the Kingdom of Judah called themselves Jews and designated all others as Gentiles. It is this concept that would have been taught to Lehi, Mulek and the other Jews who came to the Western Hemisphere to found the great Nephite and Lamanite civilizations. It is not surprising, therefore, to find the Book of Mormon repeatedly speaking of Jew and Gentile as though this phrase marked a division between all men; to find the United States described as a Gentile Nation (1 Ne. 13; 3 Ne. 21); and to find the promise that the Book of Mormon would come forth "by way of the Gentile." (Title page of Book of Mormon; D&C 20:9.)

Actually, of course, the house of Israel has been scattered among all nations, and Joseph Smith (through whom the Book of Mormon was revealed) was of the Tribe of Ephraim. At the same time the Prophet was of the Gentiles, meaning that he was a citizen of a Gentile Nation and also that he was not a Jew. Members of the Church in general are both of Israel and of the Gentiles. Indeed, the gospel has come forth in the last days in the times of the Gentiles and, in large measure, will not go to the Jews until the Gentile fulness comes in. (D&C 45:28–30.) (*Mormon Doctrine,* 2d ed. [Salt Lake City: Bookcraft, 1966], 310–311)

4–9 Nephi beholds the great and prideful church founded by the devil among the Gentiles.

10 And it came to pass that I looked and beheld many waters; and they divided the Gentiles from the seed of my brethren.
11 And it came to pass that the angel said unto me: Behold the wrath of God is upon the seed of thy brethren.
12 And I looked and beheld a man among the Gentiles, who was separated from the seed of my brethren by the many waters; and I beheld the ***Spirit of God, that it came down and wrought upon the man;*** *and he went forth upon the many waters, even unto the seed of my brethren, who were in the promised land.*

EVIDENCE: Spirit of God, that it came down and wrought upon the man

What motivated Columbus to discover the New World? According to recent Columbus scholarship, it was not primarily financial but spiritual. His *Libro de las Profecías* (*Book of Prophecies*), translated and published in 1991, demonstrates that Columbus was well-founded in the scriptures and was convinced that the Spirit of God was inspiring him in his quest for searching out new realms. One of his favorite scriptures was John 10:16: "And other sheep I have, which are not of this fold: them also I must bring, and they shall hear my voice; and there shall be one fold, and one shepherd." The resurrected Savior told the Saints in America: "And verily I say unto you, that ye are they of whom I said: Other sheep I have which are not of this fold" (3 Nephi 15:21). Joseph Smith could not have known about the deep spiritual motivation of Christopher Columbus. Only the inspiration of the Almighty could have placed in the text of the Book of Mormon the verity that the Spirit of God had come down and "wrought upon the man" to guide him in his travels. (See *Echoes,* 198–203.)

13–28 Nephi beholds the emergence of a Gentile people who are delivered from the oppression of their enemies by the power of God. The new nation prospers and benefits from receiving the record of the Jews (the Bible) to restore unto them the truths concerning the covenants of the Lord to the House of Israel. Among the Gentile nations Nephi sees the formation of the great and abominable church, founded by the devil. The desires of this church are to have the things of the world and to bring the Saints into captivity. It is this church that takes the plain and precious things away from the Bible, causing so many to stumble, insomuch that Satan gains power over them.

> *29 And after these **plain and precious things** were taken away it goeth forth unto all the nations of the Gentiles; and after it goeth forth unto all the nations of the Gentiles, yea, even across the many waters which thou hast seen with the Gentiles which have gone forth out of captivity, thou seest—because of the many plain and precious things which have been taken out of the book, which were plain unto the understanding of the children of men, according to the plainness which is in the Lamb of God—because of these things which are taken away out of the gospel of the Lamb, an exceedingly great many do stumble, yea, insomuch that Satan hath great power over them.*

Plain and Precious Things

Through the errors and misjudgments of men, many valuable truths were removed from the Bible. Because of this, many people stumble when depending on the Bible alone, and Satan can have power over them because of the plain and precious things that have been taken out of this book. Through the Book of Mormon the Lord has restored the fulness of the gospel in its pristine purity and plainness. This additional testament of Christ is indeed what the Prophet Joseph said it is: "I told the brethren that the Book of Mormon was the most correct of any book on earth and the keystone of our religion, and a man would get closer to God by abiding by its precepts, than by any other book" (Introduction to the Book of Mormon).

30–34 Nephi sees the Lord's design in blessing the Gentile nation upon the promised land—and also the remnant of the House of Israel in their midst—through His great mercy and loving-kindness in restoring the plain and precious truths left out of the record of the Jews.

> *35 For, behold, saith the Lamb: I will manifest myself unto thy seed, that they shall write many things which I shall minister unto them, which shall be plain and precious; and after thy seed shall be destroyed, and dwindle in unbelief, and also the seed of thy brethren, behold, these things shall be hid up, to come forth unto the Gentiles, by the gift and power of the Lamb.*
> *36 And in them shall be written my gospel, saith the Lamb, and my rock and my salvation.*
> *37 And blessed are they who shall seek to bring forth my Zion at that day, for they shall have the gift and the power of the Holy Ghost; and if they endure unto the end they shall be lifted up at the last day, and shall be saved in the everlasting kingdom of the Lamb; and whoso shall publish peace, yea,* ***tidings of great joy,*** *how beautiful upon the mountains shall they be.*

Tidings of Great Joy

Nephi is granted a view of the restoration of the word of God in the latter days. The word of God, in purity and fulness, gives to mankind the essential compass for navigating the perilous landscape of mortality. In a sense, we are all bound for a promised land, moving through uncharted seas but endowed with the dependable and steady lodestar of the restored gospel of Jesus Christ to guide our journey.

> *38 And it came to pass that I beheld the remnant of the seed of my brethren, and also the book of the Lamb of God, which had proceeded forth from the mouth of the Jew, that it came forth from the Gentiles unto the remnant of the seed of my brethren.*
> *39 And after it had come forth unto them I beheld other books, which came forth by the power of the Lamb, from the Gentiles unto them, unto the convincing of the Gentiles*

and the remnant of the seed of my brethren, and also the Jews who were scattered upon all the face of the earth, that the records of the prophets and of the twelve apostles of the Lamb are true.
40 And the angel spake unto me, saying: These last records, which thou hast seen among the Gentiles, shall establish the truth of the first, which are of the twelve apostles of the Lamb, and shall make known the plain and precious things which have been taken away from them; and shall make known to all kindreds, tongues, and people, that ***the Lamb of God*** *is* ***the Son of the Eternal Father,*** *and* ***the Savior*** *of the world; and that all men must come unto him, or they cannot be saved.*
41 And they must come according to the words which shall be established by the mouth of the Lamb; and the ***words of the Lamb*** *shall be made known in the records of thy seed, as well as in the records of the twelve apostles of the Lamb; wherefore they both shall be established in one; for there is one God and one Shepherd over all the earth.*

The Lamb of God; the Son of the Eternal Father; the Savior; Words of the Lamb

The angel continues to show Nephi the future. Nephi rejoices over the restoration of the gospel in latter days, including the coming forth of the Book of Mormon and other latter-day scriptures and the building up of Zion. Nephi sees that the Lord will remember the seed of his lineage and restore the missing plain and precious doctrines, which shall come forth to all people.

EVIDENCE: The Lamb of God; the Son of the Eternal Father; the Savior—Multiple Names of God

Many ancient religions gave their gods multiple names and titles. In fact, some Egyptian gods were bestowed with over one hundred. Likewise, the Old Testament ascribes dozens of names and titles to Deity, such as Redeemer, Savior, Lord, God, Jehovah, Shepherd, Prince of Peace, Everlasting Father, and many others. Similarly, the Book of Mormon contains a multitude of titles and names of deity, and scholar Susan Easton Black has identified 101 epithets for Christ therein. For example, in 1 Nephi 13:40 three of these names (the Lamb of God, the Son of the Eternal Father, the Savior of the world) are used in the same verse. Since nineteenth-century religious works did not tend to follow the ancient practice of giving numerous titles to deity, this is yet another proof of the Book of Mormon's authenticity. (See *Echoes,* 171–172.)

EVIDENCE: Words of the Lamb—Prophecy of the Lamb (1 Nephi 13:34, 41)
The wording of Lehi's prophecy in 1 Nephi 13, spoken by "the Lamb," might sound peculiar to some readers. However, modern scholars discovered an eighth-century Greek prophecy that predicts future destructions to be followed by the advent of a Messiah. This anciently popular prophecy was said to be uttered by the mouth of "the Lamb" (*pa-hib*). Obviously, as Hugh Nibley explains, Lehi's prophecy "is thus seen to be no anachronism, taken from Hellenistic or Christian times, as was once maintained." (See *Echoes,* 457.)

> *42 And the time cometh that he shall manifest himself unto all nations, both unto the Jews and also unto the Gentiles; and after he has manifested himself unto the Jews and also unto the Gentiles, then he shall manifest himself unto the Gentiles and also unto the Jews, and* ***the last shall be first, and the first shall be last.***

The last shall be first, and the first shall be last
In the purely historical sense, the Lord's covenant program commences with His chosen people, the House of Israel, who are dispersed as servants among the nations of the world to convey the good news of salvation and exaltation according to the Abrahamic commission. The Gentile peoples who are adopted into the fold, last of all, receive of the Lord's abundance, just as the first. Should the first fall short, they would be chastened, scattered, and gathered once more, at last, unto their reward. Thus the last would be first, and the first would be last.

In the sense of the Lord's grace and mercy, all are equally rewarded as they return home in obedience. Even those who come into the fold at the eleventh hour receive a reward equal to those who labored early in the Lord's vineyard—for the gift of eternal life is the Lord's to give. In the parable of the laborers (Matthew 20:1–16) the lord of the vineyard hires workers at the beginning of the day, agreeing to give them a penny for their labors. As it turns out, those whom he later hires at different stages of the day under the condition that "whatsoever is right, that shall ye receive" (Matthew 20:7) also receive their penny. When the first take issue with the outcome, thinking that they should have received more, the lord of the vineyard teaches them that he is the judge by asking,

> "Is it not lawful for me to do what I will with mine own? Is thine eye evil, because I am good? So the last shall be first, and the first last: for many be called, but few chosen" (Matthew 20:15–16).

CHAPTER 14

OVERVIEW

Nephi learns that the Gentiles, if they repent, will be numbered among the people of Israel. Nephi beholds the two churches in the earth: the widespread church of the devil and the much smaller church of the Lord. Upon the great church of the devil, which contends against the Saints of the Lord, the wrath of God is to be poured out without measure at the time the Lord renews His covenant with His people. Nephi beholds the Apostle John and sees what John sees concerning the end of the world. Nephi is restrained from recording those things.

> *1 AND it shall come to pass, that if the Gentiles shall hearken unto the Lamb of God in that day that* ***he shall manifest himself*** *unto them in word, and also in power, in very deed, unto the taking away of their stumbling blocks—*

He shall manifest himself

The Savior manifests himself in all things. To follow in His footprints with humility and devotion is to acknowledge His influence upon our life and the lives of our dear ones.

2–6 Nephi learns that the faithful among the Gentiles will be numbered among the house of Israel and become a blessed people in the promised land—provided they do not harden their hearts.

> *7 For the time cometh, saith the Lamb of God, that I will work* ***a great and a marvelous work*** *among the children of men; a work which shall be everlasting, either on the one hand or on the other—either to the convincing of them unto peace and life eternal, or unto the deliverance of them to the hardness of their hearts and the blindness of their minds unto their being brought down into captivity, and also into destruction, both temporally and spiritually, according to the captivity of the devil, of which I have spoken.*

A great and a marvelous work

The reference is to the restoration of the gospel of Jesus Christ in the latter days—an event of unprecedented scope and consequence, either to the eternal blessing of those who believe and obey, or to the eternal captivity of those who reject it. The prophet Isaiah anticipated this transcendent event in a vision received several generations before Nephi's vision: "Wherefore the Lord said, Forasmuch as this people draw near me with their mouth, and with their lips do honour me, but have removed their heart far from me, and their fear toward me is taught by the precept of men: Therefore, behold, I will proceed to do a marvellous work among this people, even a marvellous work and a wonder: for the wisdom of their wise men shall perish, and the understanding of their prudent men shall be hid" (Isaiah 29:13–14; compare 2 Nephi 25:17; 27:26).

> *8 And it came to pass that when the angel had spoken these words, he said unto me: Rememberest thou the covenants of the Father unto the house of Israel? I said unto him, Yea.*
> *9 And it came to pass that he said unto me: Look, and behold that great and abominable church, which is the mother of abominations, whose founder is the devil.*
> *10 And he said unto me: Behold there are save* ***two churches only;*** *the one is the church of the Lamb of God, and the other is the church of the devil; wherefore, whoso belongeth not to the church of the Lamb of God belongeth to that great church, which is the mother of abominations; and she is the whore of all the earth.*

Two churches only

Ultimately, an individual is either for God or against Him; either traveling the strait and narrow path or traveling some counterfeit route. Similarly, a church is organized either according to divine principles as inspired by the Lord or according to the precepts of men as inspired by the devil. God Almighty defined the threshold between the two possibilities in unmistakable terms on the occasion of the First Vision when Joseph Smith was commanded to join none of the creeds then extant, for "they draw near to me with their lips, but their hearts are far from me, they teach for doctrines the commandments of men, having a form of godliness, but they deny the power thereof" (JS—H 1:19). Outward allegiance without inner conviction lacks vitality. The angel explains to Nephi that forces antithetical to the Church of God will rise in contours of shallow greatness but eventually collapse under the weight of lifeless principles.

> *11 And it came to pass that I looked and beheld the whore of all the earth, and she sat upon many waters; and she had dominion over all the earth, among all nations, kindreds, tongues, and people.*
> *12 And it came to pass that I beheld the church of the Lamb of God, and* ***its numbers were few,*** *because of the wickedness and abominations of the whore who sat upon many waters; nevertheless, I beheld that the church of the Lamb, who were the saints of God, were also upon all the face of the earth; and their dominions upon the face of the earth were small, because of the wickedness of the great whore whom I saw.*

Its numbers were few

"For many are called, but few are chosen" (Matthew 22:14; compare Matthew 20:16; D&C 95:5; 121;34, 40). The reason some fall rather than rise is clear: "Because their hearts are set so much upon the things of this world, and aspire to the honors of men, that they do not learn this one lesson—That the rights of the priesthood are inseparably connected with the powers of heaven, and that the powers of heaven cannot be controlled nor handled only upon the principles of righteousness" (D&C 121:35–36). That applies within the priesthood of God as well as on the human stage of endeavor in general. Those who attach themselves to this church cannot control the powers of heaven or fulfill in any measure the commission to help bring about the immortality and eternal life of man (see Moses 1:39).

> *13 And it came to pass that I beheld that the great mother of abominations did gather together multitudes upon the face of all the earth, among all the nations of the Gentiles, to fight against the Lamb of God.*
> *14 And it came to pass that I, Nephi, beheld the* ***power of the Lamb of God,*** *that it descended upon the saints of the church of the Lamb, and upon the covenant people of the Lord, who were scattered upon all the face of the earth; and they were armed with righteousness and with the power of God in great glory.*

Power of the Lamb of God

Our Father in Heaven controls the destinies of nations as the course of human events moves inexorably toward the millennial reign. In all of God's laws there are consequences—both blessings and cursings. The Gentiles who hearken to the Lord will be blessed through His manifestations both in word and power. They will be numbered among the house of Israel. Those who seek to destroy (i.e., the adherents of the great and abominable church) shall fill the pit that they prepared for the destruction of others.

15–17 Nephi sees the culminating wars in which the wrath of God is poured out upon the great and abominable church—a sure sign that the work of the Restoration is about to commence.

18–28 Finally, Nephi sees the Apostle John, the one ordained by the Lord God to record the events pertaining to the end of the world. Nephi, like others called of God, is to see the things shown unto John, but not write them.

> *29 And I bear record that I saw the things which my father saw, and the angel of the Lord did make them known unto me.*
> *30 And now I make an end of speaking concerning the things which I saw while I was carried away in the spirit; and if all the things which I saw are not written,* ***the things which I have written are true.*** *And thus it is. Amen.*

The things which I have written are true

Nephi ends his report concerning the magnificent vision granted him through his prayer of faith by bearing testimony of its truth. Likewise, when we record our personal histories, with reference to the blessings bestowed upon us by a loving and merciful Lord, should we not also add the words of confirming witness that we know our report about the blessings of God unto His children to be true? Should we not expressly bear witness to our families and our posterity that our record is in accordance with the principles and teachings of the gospel of Jesus Christ?

Memories: A Message for the Multimedia Age

Some years ago my wife and I had the privilege of offering a Book of Mormon course for young single adults in our stake institute program. These were bright, eager, well-read young people with a keen desire to learn and follow true principles. It occurred to us early on that these young minds were trained in a peculiarly modern way to align themselves with the extraordinary imagery that characterizes the account of the visions of Lehi and Nephi in the opening chapters of the Book of Mormon. Of all the ages of mortality, our current generation—immersed as it is in an endless chain of multimedia experiences arising from the technological marvels of the day—should most readily understand and relate to the panorama of scenes that are so frequently projected onto our spiritual minds by the visionary prophets of God. What all of these holy men saw through the lens of spiritual truth—from Isaiah to John the Revelator, and from Lehi to Joseph Smith—was captured in powerful language and imagery.

With this understanding, one of the humble institute students in our class, following in the footsteps of a Lehi or a Nephi, was able to report: "The Book of Mormon is a compass for the future. It teaches us how to have a broken heart and a contrite spirit. We are strengthened as we intertwine our testimonies with the strong testimonies of others (just as Nephi blended his with Lehi's). . . . Above all things, we learn from the Book of Mormon to come unto Christ. I am so grateful when institute reminds me of this. We must not walk in our own light, but in the Savior's." (Richard J. Allen)

CONCLUDING THOUGHTS

How glorious was the vision granted to Nephi (1 Nephi 11–14)—to behold the divine plan of happiness as it unfolded for the blessing of God's children in all dispensations of time. Joseph Smith, the Prophet of the Restoration, was the instrument through whom the Lord blessed mankind with the vast spiritual wealth contained in the Book of Mormon—plus the Doctrine and Covenants, the Pearl of Great Price, and the inspired translation of the Bible. The process of scriptural restoration was characterized by the Lord in this magnificent phrase: "and the scriptures shall be given, even as they are in mine own bosom, to the salvation of mine own elect" (D&C 35:20). Indeed, the sanctuary for the word of the Lord is no less than the bosom of the Lord Himself, and it is from this holy and perfect source that all scripture flows to mankind.

Think of the process of conversion and sanctification—what King Benjamin's followers were to experience as "a mighty change" (Mosiah 5:2). What is this process if it is not to take into one's own bosom that which has come directly from the bosom of the Lord—even His word, conveyed by the Spirit of truth—and then to allow this light to burn within as the power of faith unto repentance and righteous action? By taking this manifestation of truth into our bosom, we can personally experience the mighty change that will carry us forward toward the tree of life where the love of God is granted in its fulness to the obedient and faithful travelers on the pathway of salvation.

CHAPTER 15

OVERVIEW

Nephi is grieved over the disputations of his older brothers, who are not able to understand the meaning the olive tree symbolism concerning the scattering and gathering of Israel. Nephi enjoins them to inquire of the Lord in faith over such things. He explains the coming forth of the gospel to the Gentiles and subsequently to the remnant of the seed of Lehi in fulfillment of the covenant promises of the Lord. Nephi interprets Lehi's vision for his brothers.

> *1 AND it came to pass that after I, Nephi, had been carried away in the spirit, and seen all these things, I returned to the tent of my father.*
> *2 And it came to pass that I beheld my brethren, and they were disputing one with another concerning the things which my father had spoken unto them.*

1 Nephi 15:3–11

> *3 For he truly spake many great things unto them, which were hard to be understood, save a man should* ***inquire of the Lord;*** *and they being hard in their hearts, therefore they did not look unto the Lord as they ought.*
> *4 And now I, Nephi, was grieved because of the hardness of their hearts, and also, because of the things which I had seen, and knew they must unavoidably come to pass because of the great wickedness of the children of men.*
> *5 And it came to pass that I was overcome because of my afflictions, for I considered that mine afflictions were great above all, because of the destruction of my people, for I had beheld their fall.*
> *6 And it came to pass that after I had received strength I spake unto my brethren, desiring to know of them the cause of their disputations.*
> *7 And they said: Behold, we cannot understand the words which our father hath spoken concerning the natural branches of the olive-tree, and also concerning the Gentiles.*
> *8 And I said unto them:* ***Have ye inquired*** *of the Lord?*
> *9 And they said unto me: We have not; for the Lord maketh no such thing known unto us.*

Inquire of the Lord—Have ye inquired?

Lack of understanding often fosters doubt and a weakening of desire. Even worse, however, is that growing unbelief can enter one's mind. Understanding comes through study and prayer—the same process that firms up one's testimony of true principles. If things are difficult to understand and accept, do you murmur or do you study things out in your mind and inquire of the Lord?

> *10 Behold, I said unto them: How is it that ye do not keep the commandments of the Lord? How is it that ye will perish, because of the hardness of your hearts?*
> *11 Do ye not remember the things which the Lord hath said?—If ye will not harden your hearts, and ask me in faith, believing that ye shall receive, with diligence in keeping my commandments, surely* ***these things shall be made known unto you.***

These things shall be made known unto you

If we keep the commandments and exercise our faith, God will answer our prayers. That is a fundamental principle of the gospel of Jesus Christ: "Ask, and it shall be given you; seek, and ye shall find; knock, and it shall be opened unto you" (Matthew 7:7; compare Luke 11:9; 3 Nephi 14:7; D&C 88:63).

12–13 Nephi explains the symbolism of the olive tree to his brethren: Following the mortal ministry of the Savior, the fulness of His gospel will, in the latter days, come unto the Gentiles, and from them once more unto the house of Israel (the Lehi colony being one of the natural branches broken off from the mother tree).

> *14 And at that day shall the remnant of our seed know that they are of the house of Israel, and that they are the covenant people of the Lord; and then shall they know and come to the knowledge of their forefathers, and also to the knowledge of the gospel of their Redeemer, which was ministered unto their fathers by him; wherefore, they shall come to the knowledge of their Redeemer and the very points of his doctrine, that they may know how to come unto him and be saved.*
> *15 And then at that day will they not rejoice and give praise unto their everlasting God, their rock and their salvation? Yea, at that day, will they not receive the strength and nourishment from the true vine? Yea, will they not come unto the true fold of God?*
> *16 Behold, I say unto you, Yea; they shall be remembered again among the house of Israel; they shall be grafted in, being a natural branch of the olive-tree, into the true olive-tree.*

17 Nephi continues his explanations to his brethren concerning the designs of the Lord through the Abrahamic covenant.

> *18 Wherefore, our father hath not spoken of our seed alone, but also of all the house of Israel, pointing to the covenant which should be fulfilled in the latter days; which covenant the Lord made to our father Abraham, saying:* ***In thy seed shall all the kindreds of the earth be blessed.***

IN THY SEED SHALL ALL THE KINDREDS OF THE EARTH BE BLESSED

The meaning and purpose of the Abrahamic covenant is made clear in the Pearl of Great Price:

> And I will make of thee [Abraham] a great nation, and I will bless thee above measure, and make thy name great among all nations, and thou shalt be a blessing unto thy seed after thee, that in their hands they shall bear this ministry and Priesthood unto all nations;

> And I will bless them through thy name; for as many as receive this gospel shall be called after thy name, and shall be accounted thy seed, and shall rise up and bless thee, as their father;
>
> And I will bless them that bless thee, and curse them that curse thee; and in thee (that is, in thy Priesthood) and in thy seed (that is, thy Priesthood), for I give unto thee a promise that this right shall continue in thee, and in thy seed after thee (that is to say, the literal seed, or the seed of the body) shall all the families of the earth be blessed, even with the blessings of the gospel, which are the blessings of salvation, even of life eternal. (Abraham 2:8–11; compare Genesis 17:1–9)

19–22 Continuing to answer their questions about the vision of the tree of life, Nephi speaks of the restoration of the Jews in the latter days.

> *23 And they said unto me: What meaneth the rod of iron which our father saw, that led to the tree?*
> *24 And I said unto them that it was the word of God; and whoso would* ***hearken unto the word of God,*** *and would hold fast unto it, they would never perish; neither could the temptations and the fiery darts of the adversary overpower them unto blindness, to lead them away to destruction.*

Hearken unto the word of God

Live by the word of God—and thus be able to avoid and resist temptation. The example of Laman and Lemuel is a principal illustration of the consequences of failing to search, ponder, and heed the word of God. By contrast, the example of Nephi and his faithful followers provides compelling evidence of the divine blessings that flow from a commitment to stay connected with the patterns of righteous living outlined in the holy scriptures.

25–35 Nephi concludes his pronouncements before his questioning older brothers, including an explanation of the watery gulf in Lehi's dream. Nephi explains that the essence of God's judgments is both temporal and spiritual in nature, for our temporal works will determine the spiritual outcome of our mortal probationary experience in the life hereafter. Those who die in wickedness cannot dwell with God.

36 Wherefore, the wicked are rejected from the righteous, and also from that tree of life, whose fruit is most precious and most desirable above all other fruits; yea, and it is the greatest of all the gifts of God. And thus I spake unto my brethren. Amen.

CHAPTER 16

OVERVIEW

Laman and Lemuel murmur because of the hardness of Nephi's words. He admonishes them to keep the commandments of the Lord so that the truth will not be painful to them. Lehi's sons and Zoram marry the daughters of Ishmael. The Lord commands Lehi and his group to journey farther into the wilderness in a south-southeasterly direction. The Liahona, or compass, guides their way according to their faith and diligence. Nephi breaks his bow, much to the dismay of his brothers. He constructs a new bow and follows the directions of the Liahona to find food. The group travels for many days. Ishmael dies and is buried in a place called Nahom. Many in the group murmur against Nephi and Lehi and desire to kill them. The voice of the Lord chastens and humbles the rebels.

1 AND now it came to pass that after I, Nephi, had made an end of speaking to my brethren, behold they said unto me: Thou hast declared unto us ***hard things, more than we are able to bear.***
2 And it came to pass that I said unto them that I knew that I had spoken hard things against the wicked, according to the truth; and the righteous have I justified, and testified that they should be lifted up at the last day; wherefore, the guilty taketh the truth to be hard, for it cutteth them to the very center.
3 And now my brethren, if ye were righteous and were willing to hearken to the truth, and give heed unto it, that ye might walk uprightly before God, then ye would not murmur because of the truth, and say: Thou speakest ***hard things*** *against us.*
4 And it came to pass that I, Nephi, did exhort my brethren, with all diligence, to keep the commandments of the Lord.
5 And it came to pass that they did humble themselves before the Lord; insomuch that I had joy and great hopes of them, that they would walk in the paths of righteousness.
6 Now, all these things were said and done as my father dwelt in a tent in the valley which he called Lemuel.

HARD THINGS; MORE THAN WE ARE ABLE TO BEAR

Nephi identifies a syndrome all too frequently encountered among dissenters from the truth: they judge the scriptures to be hard and painful—understandably so, since their behavior is at variance with the principles of righteousness unfolded in the scriptures. Such people are disposed to ignore the scriptures and thus anesthetize the pain of a guilty conscience. The correct action is to repent—in all humility and sincerity of heart; the resulting outcome is peace, comfort, and the hope of eternal life. President Gordon B. Hinckley emphasizes this point: "People ask me frequently what is my favorite verse of scripture. I have many and this is one of them, 'Be thou humble; and the Lord thy God shall lead thee by the hand, and give thee answer to thy prayers' (D&C 112:10). What a promise to those who walk without arrogance, to those who walk without conceit, to those who walk without egotism, to those who walk humbly. 'Be thou humble; and the Lord thy God shall lead thee by the hand, and give thee answer to thy prayers.' What a solid and wonderful promise that is" (*Teachings of Gordon B. Hinckley* [Salt Lake City: Deseret Book, 1997], 265).

> *7 And it came to pass that I, Nephi, took one of the daughters of Ishmael to* ***wife;*** *and also, my brethren took of the daughters of Ishmael to wife; and also Zoram took the eldest daughter of Ishmael to wife.*

WIFE OF NEPHI

Among those who rose in support of Nephi during the internal skirmish on the return trip from Jerusalem to bring Ishmael and his family to Lehi's camp is one of the daughters of Ishmael (see 1 Nephi 7:19). Could it be that Nephi chose as his wife the same young woman who sides with him during the conflict with his brothers and other members of Ishmael's family?

> *8 And thus my father had fulfilled all the commandments of the Lord which had been given unto him. And also, I, Nephi, had been blessed of the Lord exceedingly.*
> *9 And it came to pass that the voice of the Lord spake unto my father by night, and commanded him that on the morrow he should take his journey into the wilderness.*
> *10 And it came to pass that as my father arose in the morning, and went forth to the tent door, to his great astonishment he beheld upon the ground a* ***round ball of curious workmanship;*** *and it was of fine brass. And within the ball were two spindles; and the one pointed the way whither we should go into the wilderness.*

Round ball of curious workmanship

Imagine struggling to survive in the midst of an immense and hostile desert environment reflecting an ominous sameness in all directions. We are heeding the directive of God to attain a promised land of safety—but how far away and in which direction? Our provisions are strictly limited. Where do we turn meanwhile for nourishment and water? In His mercy and compassion, the Lord gives direction for Lehi's people by providing them with the Liahona—"the ball of curious workmanship" (1 Nephi 16:10). This miraculous device defines the direction they should travel according to the pointing of the spindles and also gives written instructions that appear on the ball. Alma compares the Liahona to the word of God as the source of guidance for daily living (see Alma 37:37–48).

President Harold B. Lee makes clear the nature and implications of the modern Liahona:

> Now the only safety we have as members of this church is to do exactly what the Lord said to the Church in that day when the Church was organized. We must learn to give heed to the words and commandments that the Lord shall give through his prophet, "as he receiveth them, walking in all holiness before me; . . . as if from mine own mouth, in all patience and faith" (D&C 21:4–5). There will be some things that take patience and faith. You may not like what comes from the authority of the Church. It may contradict your political views. . . . It may interfere with some of your social life. But if you listen to these things, as if from the mouth of the Lord Himself, with patience and faith, the promise is that "the gates of hell shall not prevail against you; yea, and the Lord God will disperse the powers of darkness from before you, and cause the heavens to shake for your good, and his name's glory" (D&C 21:6). . . . We are in the service of the Lord. We have the right to spiritual direction, if we live worthily. God grant that we may so live and study the scriptures, and let this be a reading habit that we indulge in daily, that we not fail of the high appointments for which we have been called in our Father's kingdom. (*The Teachings of Harold B. Lee,* ed. Clyde J. Williams [Salt Lake City: Bookcraft, 1996], 526, 152)

11–16 The small group of travelers crosses the river Laman and continues its journey for four days, reaching a place they name **Shazer** (verse 13–14), where they stop and replenish their food supply, as the record states, "**with our bows and our arrows and our stones and our slings**" (verse 15). They then continue in the same direction near the Red Sea for many days, following the guidance of the Liahona to more fertile areas of the land.

EVIDENCE: Shazer—Place name "Shazer" (1 Nephi 16:13–14)

Lehi's group, sometime after leaving their base camp, stops at a place they call *Shazer.* In Palestinian place-names, *shajer* is a common combination; the word means "trees," and many Arabs pronounce the word *shazher.* According to Nibley, the word *shajer* and related terms, such as *Shihor, Shaghur, Sajur, Saghir, Segor, Sozura, Shisur,* and *Shisar,* all refer either to seepage or to a clump of trees. Since Lehi and his family would only have stopped for any significant amount of time at a place that offered water and shade, they chose a perfect name for their stopping place. (See *Echoes,* 461.)

EVIDENCE: With our bows and our arrows and our stones and our slings—Nephi's Hunting Weapons

When hunting for food, Nephi and his brethren used bows and arrows, and slings and stones, rather than hunting weapons such as the sword, club, or javelin. Records show that early Hebrews used the same types of weapons as Nephi's party. Furthermore, ancient Arab writers claimed that the only wood suitable for creating a bow was the *nab* wood, which grew solely in the region where Nephi broke his bow. As Hugh Nibley states, "How many factors must be correctly conceived and correlated to make the apparently simple story of Nephi's bow ring true! The high mountain near the Red Sea at a considerable journey down the coast, the game on the peaks, hunting with a bow and sling, the finding of bow-wood viewed as something of a miracle by the party—what are the chances of reproducing such a situation by mere guesswork?" (See *Echoes,* 469–470).

> *17 And after we had* ***traveled for the space of many days,*** *we did pitch our tents for the space of a time, that we might again rest ourselves and obtain food for our families.*

EVIDENCE: Traveled for the space of many days—The Route

Due to a lack of accessible, accurate literature on the subject of ancient Arabia, Joseph Smith could not have known about the well-known "Incense Trail." This trail comprised a series of roads and trails that caravans used to transport frankincense and myrrh northward from southern Arabia. Lehi and his family may have picked up this route—traveling in the opposite direction of the incense-laden caravans—as they traveled south from Jerusalem and deeper into Arabia. While this well-established trail passed by wells and food sources, it also passed through large expanses of desert and over mountain passes. As Lehi's family journeyed, the Liahona guided them to areas where they could obtain food and water. Nevertheless, they often faced great afflictions (see 1 Nephi 17:1, 6), including famine, sickness, and disease (see Mosiah 1:17; Alma 9:22). Joseph

Smith would not have known of the specific hardships a traveling party would have faced as they traveled through Arabia (see *Echoes,* 83–86).

> *18 And it came to pass that as I, Nephi, went forth to slay food, behold, I did break my*
> ***bow,** which was made of fine steel; and after I did break my **bow,** behold, my brethren*
> *were angry with me because of the loss of my **bow,** for we did obtain no food.*
> *19 And it came to pass that we did return without food to our families, and being much*
> *fatigued, because of their journeying, they did suffer much for the want of food.*
> *20 And it came to pass that Laman and Lemuel and the sons of Ishmael did begin*
> *to murmur exceedingly, because of their sufferings and afflictions in the wilderness;*
> *and also my father began to murmur against the Lord his God; yea, and they were all*
> *exceedingly sorrowful, even that they did murmur against the Lord.*
> *21 Now it came to pass that I, Nephi, having been afflicted with my brethren because*
> *of the loss of my **bow,** and their **bows** having lost their springs, it began to be exceedingly*
> *difficult, yea, insomuch that we could obtain no food.*
> *22 And it came to pass that I, Nephi, did speak much unto my brethren, because they*
> *had hardened their hearts again, even unto complaining against the Lord their God.*
> *23 And it came to pass that I, Nephi, did make out of wood a **bow,** and out of a*
> *straight stick, an **arrow;** wherefore, I did arm myself with a **bow** and an **arrow,** with*
> *a sling and with stones. And I said unto my father: Whither shall I go to obtain food?*

EVIDENCE: Bow, arrow

What is the broader significance of the broken bow in Nephi's account, and why did he not simply use his original arrows with the new wooden bow he constructed? The following gives interesting insights into this issue:

> The symbolic message of the broken bow, first detected by Alan Goff, was highlighted in the March 1984 issue of the FARMS newsletter: "Bows were symbols of political power. One thinks of Odysseus bending the bow to prove himself. An overlord would break the bow of a disobedient vassal to symbolically put the rebel in his place" (see also Jeremiah 49:35; 51:56). That detail is significant in 1 Nephi 16. Nephi's bow broke, and the bows of Laman and Lemuel lost their springs, but when Nephi fashioned a new bow, making him the only one in camp with a bow, his brothers soon accused Nephi of having political ambitions (see 1 Nephi 16:37–38).

Once this point was detected, a further authentic detail about this particular account was soon noticed. It has to do with Nephi's arrows. Three times in his record, Nephi mentioned that he had broken his bow, but not once did he say that any of his arrows were damaged. Yet in 1 Nephi 16:23, Nephi says that he "did make out of wood a bow, and out of a straight stick, an arrow." Why would he need to make a new arrow if his old ones were still intact?

David S. Fox, in a letter to FARMS, suggests an answer:

"An examination of Nephi's account shows that whoever wrote that account was familiar in some detail with the field of archery." Consider what happens to an arrow at the instant the string is released: the full force of the drawn string is applied to the end of the arrow, trying to accelerate it, but also tending to bend or buckle the arrow. If the bow's draw weight and the arrow's stiffness are not perfectly matched, the arrow will stray off the intended course or fall short of the mark. An arrow that is too flexible will leave the bow with a vibration that can cause the arrow to behave erratically. On the other hand, an arrow that is too stiff is probably too heavy for the bow.

Nephi's steel bow likely used heavier, stiffer arrows than his simply fashioned wooden bow could handle. Nephi was physically large (see 1 Nephi 2:16; 4:31), and he would have had little reason to use a bow made from metal if he did not have considerable strength. The arrows to match the steel bow used by such a man would undoubtedly have been quite heavy in order for them to be of adequate stiffness. One experienced archer reports, "The arrows from the steel bow when shot from the wooden bow would be like shooting telephone poles." Hence, it is accurate that Nephi should mention, in one and the same breath, the fact that he made an arrow as well as a bow. Bow wood and arrow wood from the same tree or area could be matched as well.

One doubts that such information was known to Joseph Smith or to many, if any, of his contemporaries. Archery, as a means of self-defense or as a serious method of hunting or warfare, went out of vogue among Europeans many years before the time of Joseph Smith. On the other hand, archery as a sport did not emerge until the latter half of the nineteenth century.

David Fox concludes: "Nephi's statement that he made an arrow out of a straight stick is an additional subtle but significant example of internal consistency within the Book of Mormon. Anyone unfamiliar with the field of archery would have almost certainly omitted such a statement." Another bull's-eye for the Book of Mormon. (John W. Welch, ed., *Reexploring the Book of Mormon* [Salt Lake City and Provo: Deseret Book, Foundation for Ancient Research and Mormon Studies, 1992], 41–42)

24 And it came to pass that he did inquire of the Lord, for they had humbled themselves because of my words; for I did say many things unto them in the energy of my soul.
25 And it came to pass that the voice of the Lord came unto my father; and he was truly chastened because of his murmuring against the Lord, insomuch that he was brought down into the depths of sorrow.
26 And it came to pass that the voice of the Lord said unto him: Look upon the ball, and behold the things which are written.
27 And it came to pass that when my father beheld the things which were written upon the ball, he did fear and tremble exceedingly, and also my brethren and the sons of Ishmael and our wives.
28 And it came to pass that I, Nephi, beheld the pointers which were in the ball, that they did work according to the ***faith and diligence and heed*** *which we did give unto them.*

FAITH AND DILIGENCE AND HEED

Exercising faith, persevering in diligence, and giving heed to the word of the Lord brings into our lives certainty concerning the direction we should go. We see these ancient emigrants striving to measure up to the standards of faith, obedience, courage, and alignment with the scriptural truths that were decreed by God to be the central characteristics of His covenant relationship with Israel.

Throughout the Book of Mormon we see the rise and fall of the Nephite nation in accordance with their inclination either to give heed or set aside the principles embodied in the word of God and thus suffer the consequences of disobedience. Into a world where this dichotomy is so dramatically evident, the Lord, in His loving-kindness, has introduced an infallible guidance system. Our Liahona is the word of God (see Alma 37:37–47). As we hearken to the word and heed its divine message, we will walk uprightly before God.

29 And there was also written upon them a ***new writing,*** *which was plain to be read, which did give us understanding concerning the ways of the Lord; and it was*

> *written and changed from time to time, according to the faith and diligence which we gave unto it. And thus we see that by **small means** the Lord can bring about **great things.***

NEW WRITING; SMALL MEANS; GREAT THINGS

The Liahona was more than a compass. It was a revelatory instrument that provided understanding concerning spiritual matters, with writings that changed from time to time according to the faith and diligence given it. It was, in effect, a dynamic scripture source for the faithful. A small ball with great outcomes, the Liahona compares with our scriptures—small enough to hold in our hands but capable of producing an enormous influence in our lives. The language about small means leading to great outcomes also anticipates what Alma was to teach his son Helaman about the value of the scriptures:

> Behold I say unto you, that by small and simple things are great things brought to pass; and small means in many instances doth confound the wise.
>
> And the Lord God doth work by means to bring about his great and eternal purposes; and by very small means the Lord doth confound the wise and bringeth about the salvation of many souls.
>
> And now, it has hitherto been wisdom in God that these things should be preserved; for behold, they have enlarged the memory of this people, yea, and convinced many of the error of their ways, and brought them to the knowledge of their God unto the salvation of their souls" (Alma 37:6–8).

Alma then draws a comparison with the Liahona: "Nevertheless, because those miracles were worked by small means it did show unto them marvelous works. They were slothful, and forgot to exercise their faith and diligence and then those marvelous works ceased, and they did not progress in their journey" (Alma 37:41).

30–33 Nephi is able to follow the directions of the Liahona to obtain food for the camp, much to the joy and thanksgiving of the people. They continue their journey for many days before tarrying again for a period of time.

> *34 And it came to pass that Ishmael died, and was buried in the place which was called **Nahom.***

EVIDENCE: Nahom—Nahom's Location

The location of Nahom is basically settled from early inscriptions. However, the name *Nahom* is itself significant, especially the consonants *N, H,* and *M.* We can assume that when Lehi's family heard the Arabian name "Nihm," the word Nahom may have entered their minds. "Nahom" is used in the Old Testament and is derived from a Hebrew verb that means "to comfort" or "to console." We can assume that the name Nahom was significant to Lehi's and Ishmael's families, as this was the burial place of Ishmael (see *Echoes,* 81–83).

35–39 The daughters of Ishmael mourn for their father and complain about the afflictions of desert life. Laman and Lemuel incite the group to rise up and slay Lehi and Nephi, but the Lord chastens them unto repentance and again blesses the camp with food.

CHAPTER 17

OVERVIEW

The group journeys eastward until, after much tribulation—and through the guidance and sustaining hand of the Lord—they reach a fruitful seaside area which they call Bountiful. Nephi is commanded to build a ship. He constructs tools for the task. His brothers murmur against him and refuse to help. He reminds them of the blessings of God to Moses and the Israelites in delivering them from Egyptian bondage and in guiding them to the promised land. He urges his brothers to repent or be chastened of the Lord just as He chastened the Israelites when they failed to honor their covenants. The brothers seek to slay Nephi, but he commands them to desist or be consumed by touching him. The Lord shocks them to persuade them to obey.

> *1 AND it came to pass that we did again take our journey in the wilderness; and we did travel* ***nearly eastward*** *from that time forth. And we did travel and wade through much* ***affliction in the wilderness;*** *and our women did bear children in the wilderness.*

EVIDENCE: Nearly eastward—Lehi's Journey to Bountiful (see 1 Nephi 16:17–32, 39; 17:1, 4; Mosiah 1:1; Alma 9:10, 22; Alma 37:42; Omni 1:6)

Nephi describes events that happened at Nahom, then explains that the group traveled "nearly eastward from that time forth" (1 Nephi 17:1). No source—either modern or ancient—reveals that the existing Incense Trail turns east from the area where the Nihm tribe dwelt, i.e., where Nahom was located. Therefore, it would have been impossible for Joseph Smith, or anyone else who had not visited the area, to know this. But of course, Nephi knew this information, and his family traveled eastward until they reached the place they named Bountiful.

EVIDENCE: Affliction in the wilderness—Difficult Journey

This portion of travel for Lehi's group must have been challenging, as it comprises the greater part of the eight-year journey but is less than half the distance they had traveled from Jerusalem to Nahom. In this part of the route, Lehi could not have paralleled a road taken by incense caravans, since most of the caravans returning from the Mediterranean and Mesopotamia continued south from the Nahom area to the ancient seaport of Qana, rather than turning east. Lehi's family would have faced many difficulties in locating food and water and negotiating with the tribes east of Shabwah, the main staging area for caravans in the southern part of Arabia. Later in the Book of Mormon, Amaron and Alma write that the Lord saved Lehi and his family from their enemies (see Omni 1:6; Alma 9:10). Again, Joseph Smith would not have known details about the trails Lehi would have taken or the dangers and afflictions he and his family would have faced. (See *Echoes,* 88–92.)

EVIDENCE: Writings about Arabia

Writings about ancient Arabia were not available in Joseph Smith's area at the time he labored to translate the Book of Mormon. In fact, most of the classical writings about Arabia did not appear in libraries of accessible distance to Joseph until the early 1900s. (It should also be pointed out that very little detailed information on Arabia and its geography was provided by classical authors in the first place.) Therefore, the Prophet could not have obtained specific information about Arabia before or during the translation process, except what the Lord revealed to him. (See *Echoes,* 69–70.)

> *2 And so great were the blessings of the Lord upon us, that while we did live upon raw meat in the wilderness, our women did give plenty of suck for their children, and were strong, yea, even like unto the men; and they began to bear their journeyings without murmurings.*
> *3 And thus we see that the commandments of God must be fulfilled. And if it so be that the children of men keep the commandments of God he doth nourish them, and strengthen them, and provide* ***means whereby they can accomplish the thing which he has commanded them;*** *wherefore, he did provide means for us while we did sojourn in the wilderness.*

Means whereby they can accomplish the thing which he has commanded them

Keep the commandments and the Lord will provide. This is the sacred promise conveyed by the Book of Mormon and all of the holy prophets down through the generations.

> *4 And we did sojourn for the space of many years, yea, even eight years in the wilderness.*
> *5 And we did come to the land which we called* ***Bountiful,*** *because of its much fruit and also wild honey; and all these things were prepared of the Lord that we might not perish. And we beheld the sea, which we called Irreantum, which, being interpreted, is many waters.*
> *6 And it came to pass that we did pitch our tents by the seashore; and notwithstanding we had suffered many afflictions and much difficulty, yea, even so much that we cannot write them all, we were exceedingly rejoiced when we came to the seashore; and we called the place Bountiful, because of its much fruit.*

EVIDENCE: Bountiful—Details about Bountiful, Land of Fruit and Honey

(1 Nephi 17:5–6; 18:1–2, 6)

A vast majority of LDS scholars agree that the land of Bountiful was located in southern Oman, specifically in the Dhofar region. In fact, this is the only place on the southern portion of the Arabian Peninsula that fits Nephi's descriptions of Bountiful. The abundant fruit and wild honey that Nephi mentions could only be found in this area (see *Echoes,* 92–93).

> *7 And it came to pass that after I, Nephi, had been in the land of Bountiful for the space of many days, the voice of the Lord came unto me, saying: Arise, and get thee into the mountain. And it came to pass that I arose and went up into the mountain, and cried unto the Lord.*
> *8 And it came to pass that the Lord spake unto me, saying:* ***Thou shalt construct a ship,*** *after the manner which I shall show thee, that I may carry thy people across these waters.*

Thou shalt construct a ship

Obedience, based on faith, is the key to perfection. Nephi does whatsoever the Lord commands him to do because he exercises his faith in all diligence. We can emulate his example. The voice of the Lord tells Nephi to go up into the mountain, where Nephi calls upon the Lord. The Lord commands Nephi to build a ship according to the directions that will be given him. Laman and Lemuel doubt Nephi's ability and start to murmur. They complain about leaving Jerusalem and not being able to enjoy their wealth and about the difficulties that they've experienced over the years in traveling. They doubt—they lack faith. Throughout the Book of Mormon, the prophets, and in this case Nephi, attempt to show the doubting or wayward soul the goodness and mercy of God.

EVIDENCE: Wood for Shipbuilding

Many varieties of trees have grown in the Dhofar region for thousands of years. One writer states that the coast of southern Oman was "thickly wooded." Since most local species of trees would not be conducive to building a strong, seaworthy ship, it is possible that Nephi and his brothers obtained teak wood brought in from India. However, it is more probable that Nephi and his brothers cut several varieties of trees they found in the Dhofar area, using different woods for different sections of the ship. (See *Echoes,* 94–95.)

Ore

Many have wondered where Nephi would have located ore to fashion his shipbuilding tools. Ancient copper mines were over 600 miles from Lehi's family's campsite on the coast. Furthermore, Arabia is not known to contain significant iron deposits, nor are the neighboring regions. However, geologists from BYU recently found two large deposits of iron ore in the Dhofar area—both of which would have been only a few days walk from a seacoast campsite. Of course, Nephi did not need a large amount of ore to build his tools. (See *Echoes,* 96.)

9–12 The Lord directs Nephi to the place where he can find ore to make tools. Nephi constructs a bellows to manage the process.

> *13 And I will also be your light in the wilderness; and I will prepare the way before you, if it so be that ye shall keep my commandments; wherefore, inasmuch as ye shall keep my commandments ye shall be led toward the promised land; and ye shall know that it is by me that ye are led.*
> *14 Yea, and the Lord said also that: After ye have arrived in the promised land, ye shall know that I, the Lord, am God; and that I, the Lord, did deliver you from destruction; yea, that I did bring you out of the land of Jerusalem.*
> *15 Wherefore, I, Nephi, did strive to keep the commandments of the Lord, and I did exhort my brethren to* ***faithfulness and diligence.***

Faithfulness and diligence

We will have the strength and devotion to keep the commandments if we are faithful and diligent. We can serve others with charitable purpose if we are faithful and diligent. A lifestyle based on faith and diligence is the requirement of the Lord in all things. (See also 2 Corinthians 8:7; Hebrews 11:6; 2 Peter 1:5; 1 Nephi 2:19; Enos 1:12; Mosiah 4:6; Alma 32:40–43; D&C 6:20.)

16–40 As Nephi commences the monumental task of building a ship, his brothers revile and mock him, denying that he has been instructed of the Lord for this purpose and comparing him to Lehi and his "foolish imaginations" (verse 20). They characterize the people of Jerusalem as righteous, saying they kept the law of Moses. Nephi gives his brothers a history lesson: Moses was an instrument in the hands of the Lord in liberating the Israelites from Egyptian bondage and in granting them an inheritance in the land of promise. Although they hardened their hearts against the Lord, He enabled them to overcome the inhabitants of the land who were "ripe in iniquity" (verse 35).

> *40 And he loveth those who will have him to be their God. Behold, he loved our fathers, and he covenanted with them, yea, even Abraham, Isaac, and Jacob; and he remembered the covenants which he had made; wherefore, he did bring them* ***out of the land of Egypt.***
> *41 And he did straiten them in the wilderness with his rod; for they hardened their hearts, even as ye have; and the Lord straitened them because of their iniquity. He sent fiery flying serpents among them; and after they were bitten he prepared a way that they might be healed; and the labor which they had to perform was to look; and because of the simpleness of the way, or the easiness of it, there were many who perished.*

EVIDENCE: Out of the land of Egypt—Depth of Exodus Motif

Many similarities exist between the Israelites' biblical exodus from Egypt and the journey of Lehi's family from Jerusalem to the promised land. In fact, most modern Book of Mormon scholars believe that Nephi actually patterned his account after the exodus led by Moses hundreds of years previously.

Nephi, the son of a wealthy citizen of Jerusalem, would have been quite familiar with the story of the children of Israel and their flight from slavery. Many parallels are apparent between the two stories: both groups were led by prophets and departed from lands that had been condemned by God; both groups miraculously crossed immense water barriers to reach safety; both groups had a rebellious faction that murmured in the wilderness due to lack of food; both groups were commanded to "look" upon a metal object (the Liahona for the Lehites, a brazen serpent for the Israelites) in order to "live," and both groups were led by God to a promised land. Numerous other features of the stories attest to the conclusion that Nephi purposely modeled his account of his father's family's journey on the biblical exodus. Thus he could remind his recalcitrant older brothers that they were following a pathway not unlike their Israelite progenitors, who, despite enjoying the favor of the Lord's "matchless power" (verse 42), declined gradually in spiritual vitality. (See *Echoes,* 192–197.)

43 And now, after all these things, the time has come that they have become wicked, yea, nearly unto ripeness; and I know not but they are at this day about to be destroyed; for I know that the day must surely come that they must be destroyed, save a few only, who shall be led away into captivity.
44 Wherefore, the Lord commanded my father that he should depart into the wilderness; and the Jews also sought to take away his life; yea, and ye also have sought to take away his life; wherefore, ye are murderers in your hearts and ye are like unto them.
45 Ye are swift to do iniquity but slow to remember the Lord your God. Ye have seen an angel, and he spake unto you; yea, ye have heard his voice from time to time; and he hath spoken unto you in a still small voice, but ***ye were past feeling,*** *that ye could not feel his words; wherefore, he has spoken unto you like unto the voice of thunder, which did cause the earth to shake as if it were to divide asunder.*

Ye were past feeling

If our hearts are hardened, we cannot feel the Spirit. Conversely, if we come before the Lord with softened hearts ("a broken heart and a contrite spirit"—3 Nephi 9:20), then we are blessed to feel the Spirit and receive divine guidance for our lives.

Nephi reminds his brothers of the following: The Lord had led the Israelites out of Egypt to safety, the Egyptians were drowned in the Red sea, manna was provided for the Ishmaelites' food, water was given to them out of a rock, and the Lord led them day and night. The Israelites still hardened their hearts and reviled against Moses. The Israelites eventually became very wicked, and the Lord said that Jerusalem would be destroyed—hence the order that Lehi should leave Jerusalem. The Lord favors the righteous but will destroy the wicked. Nephi appeals to Laman and Lemuel to remember the Lord, but their hearts are "past feeling" (1 Nephi 17:45). This is surely a danger sign in the spiritual well-being of any person. If people cannot feel the promptings of the Spirit, they are left to their fallen state, unable to receive the blessings of the Lord.

46–52 Nephi calls upon his brethren to repent. They are angry and take steps to drown him in the sea. He repels them through the power of God so that they recoil in fear and dare not touch him for many days.

53 And it came to pass that the Lord said unto me: Stretch forth thine hand again unto thy brethren, and they shall not wither before thee, but ***I will shock them,*** *saith the Lord, and this will I do, that they may know that I am the Lord their God.*

I WILL SHOCK THEM

Nephi has great anguish for his brothers and is fearful they will be cast off forever. He bears fervent testimony of his faith and commitment to do all things the Lord commands him to do. Nephi confounds Laman and Lemuel and then, in response to the Lord's command, reaches out toward his brethren and shakes them through God's power.

54–55 After this observable event, Laman and Lemuel acknowledge the Lord and fall down to worship Nephi. He encourages them instead to worship the Lord and to honor their parents "that thy days may be long in the land which the Lord thy God shall give thee" (verse 55).

CHAPTER 18

OVERVIEW

Nephi and his brothers complete the ship. The Lord commands them to take provisions onto the ship and embark on the journey. Jacob and Joseph, Lehi's sons born in the wilderness, are mentioned. Laman and Lemuel and the sons of Ishmael and their wives are irreverent and boisterous during the journey. Nephi warns them to repent but is cruelly bound by his brothers. The Liahona ceases to operate during a violent tempest. The older brothers give no head to the anguished pleadings of Lehi, Sariah, Jacob, Joseph, and Nephi's wife and children. Fearful of impending destruction, the brothers finally release Nephi, who guides the ship once again by means of the Liahona. His prayers calm the sea. After many days, they arrive on the shores of the promised land and begin to till the soil and explore their new homeland.

1 AND it came to pass that they did worship the Lord, and did go forth with me; and we did work timbers of curious workmanship. And the Lord did show me from time to time after what manner I should work the timbers of the ship.
2 Now I, Nephi, did not work the timbers after the manner which was learned by men, neither did I ***build the ship*** *after the manner of men; but I did build it after the manner which the Lord had shown unto me; wherefore, it was not after the manner of men.*

1 Nephi 18:2–11

EVIDENCE: SHIPBUILDING

When Joseph Smith translated the Book of Mormon, most Americans knew relatively little about the Arabian Peninsula. If Americans thought anything of this region, they probably considered it a desert without the trees that could have been used to build a ship. However, recent evidence suggests that ancient Oman, where Bountiful was almost certainly located, boasted accomplished seamen and shipbuilders. Therefore, we know that the wood and other materials necessary for shipbuilding must have been obtainable in that region when Nephi and his family resided there. (See *Echoes,* 128–129.)

3–8 Nephi and his colleagues complete the ship. The Lord commands them to embark on the ocean journey.

> *9 And after we had been driven forth before the wind for the space of many days,*
> *behold, my brethren and the sons of Ishmael and also their wives began to make them-*
> *selves merry, insomuch that they began to dance, and to sing, and to speak with much*
> *rudeness, yea, even that they did forget by what power they had been brought thither;*
> *yea, they were lifted up unto exceeding rudeness.*
> *10 And I, Nephi, began to fear exceedingly lest the Lord should be angry with us, and*
> *smite us because of our iniquity, that we should be swallowed up in the depths of the sea;*
> *wherefore, I, Nephi, began to speak to them with much soberness; but behold they were*
> *angry with me, saying: We will not that our younger brother shall be a ruler over us.*
> *11 And it came to pass that Laman and Lemuel did take me and bind me with cords,*
> *and they did treat me with much harshness; nevertheless, the Lord did suffer it that*
> *he might* ***show forth his power,*** *unto the fulfilling of his word which he had spoken*
> *concerning the wicked.*

SHOW FORTH HIS POWER

It is instructive that the passengers on this journey reflect the qualities of both the hard-heartedness and softheartedness so pervasive throughout the Book of Mormon account. Laman and Lemuel—having lapsed, like the sons of Ishmael and their wives, into an attitude of rudeness, light-mindedness, and overweening pride—bind and torment Nephi for four days; "nevertheless, the Lord did suffer it that he might show forth his power, unto the fulfilling of his word which he had spoken concerning the wicked."

12–14 As the Liahona ceases to operate in the environment of rebellion and wickedness, a violent tempest arises, threatening to engulf the little party in a watery death. Nephi is bound for the space of four days.

> *15 And it came to pass that we were about to be swallowed up in the depths of the sea. And after we had been driven back upon the waters for the space of four days, my brethren began to see that the judgments of God were upon them, and that they must perish save that they should repent of their iniquities; wherefore, they came unto me, and loosed the bands which were upon my wrists, and behold they had swollen exceedingly; and also mine ankles were much swollen, and great was the soreness thereof.*
> *16 Nevertheless, I did look unto my God, and I did praise him all the day long; and I did not murmur against the Lord because of mine **afflictions.***

Afflictions

Afflictions can bring out the worst in us. Thoughts like "It's not fair," "Why me?" "What did I do to deserve this?" can pervade our minds. Do we seek to learn and grow from our afflictions, remembering that all of this is part of the test of mortality? How do we handle our afflictions? With resolve and faith in God? With patience and hope for the future? Nephi's example is one of Christlike perseverance and worshipful endurance.

Short though Bitter Was Their Pain, Everlasting Is Their Joy

The Latter-day Saints have experienced few periods of adversity that compare with the cruelty at the hands of the Missouri mobs during the formative years of the restored Church. As part of his journal entry for Monday, April 22, 1839, the Prophet Joseph Smith summarized the Saints' persecution by the Missouri mobs, gave thanks for the Lord's steadying hand, and called for civil redress. "The conduct of the Saints, under their accumulated wrongs and sufferings," said he, "has been praiseworthy; their courage in defending their brethren from the ravages of the mobs; their attachment to the cause of truth, under circumstances the most trying and distressing which humanity can possibly endure; their love to each other; their readiness to afford assistance to me and my brethren who were confined to a dungeon; their sacrifice in leaving Missouri, and assisting the poor widows and orphans, and securing them houses in a more hospitable land; all conspire to raise them in the estimation of all good and virtuous men, and has secured them the favor and approbation of Jehovah, and a name as imperishable as eternity. . . . Marvel not, then, if you are persecuted. . . . Afflictions, persecutions, imprisonments, and death, we must expect, according to the scriptures. . . ." (*HC* 3:329–331). As if to add a capstone to the monument of the Saints' endurance, the Prophet also quotes this verse as part of his narrative: "Short though bitter was their pain, everlasting is their joy" (330). (Richard J. Allen)

17–20 In the dire circumstances occasioned by the violent tempest, Lehi and Sariah, together with other family members, petition Laman and Lemuel to desist.

> *20 And there was nothing save it were the power of God, which threatened them with destruction, could soften their hearts; wherefore, when they saw that they were* ***about to be swallowed up*** *in the depths of the sea they repented of the thing which they had done, insomuch that they loosed me.*

Memories: About to Be Swallowed Up

One of the great teachings of life is that everyone is going to have afflictions, trials, and tribulations. Adversity is part of life. The righteous are not spared, for this is a testing time. Our test is how we respond to adversity. Adversity also allows God to show forth His power. Nephi did not murmur in his affliction—and neither should we. He praised God, and so should we. Again, since the hearts of Laman and Lemuel were not sensitive to the Lord, only external means could be used to effect a change: they were about to be swallowed up in the depths of the sea, so they repented. We learn a great lesson in regard to our spiritual wellness: Are we subject to the Spirit and the will of God by being easily entreated or do we too need external means to bring us to humility so as to bring about change? (Ed J. Pinegar)

21–25 The awful threat of destruction finally induces the older brothers to cease their persecutions. Nephi is released. Based on his faithfulness, the compass is again activated, and the emigrants from old Jerusalem soon become immigrants in a new and resource-rich land of promise.

CHAPTER 19

OVERVIEW

The Lord commands Nephi to make additional metal plates and record upon them the prophesies and sacred things pertaining to the people. On his other plates are to be recorded the more secular history of the people. According to the words of the angel, the Redeemer is to come 600 years from the time Lehi leaves Jerusalem. He is to be crucified for the sins of the world. The Jews are to be smitten and scattered—but gathered once again with the House of Israel when they no longer turn against their Lord. Nephi reads to his people the word of God from the brass plates and counsels them to liken these scriptures unto themselves.

1 AND it came to pass that the Lord commanded me, wherefore I did make ***plates*** *of ore that I might engraven upon them the record of my people. And upon the plates which I made I did engraven the record of my father, and also our journeyings in the wilderness, and the prophecies of my father; and also many of mine own prophecies have I engraven upon them.*

EVIDENCE: Plates—The Writings of Arabia

There is much evidence in the Middle East of writing being done on metal plates. The ancient Arabian peoples also often wrote on hard surfaces, such as stone or metal, so that their writings might be preserved. Nephi probably chose to write on gold plates because of his exposure to the brass plates, but perhaps also due to his experience in passing through southern Arabia. In addition, many of the characters on the Anthon transcript—a one-page document copied from the gold plates from which the Book of Mormon was translated—are similar to those of the Old North Arabian dialect. This dialect was used in northwest Arabia, the area where Lehi's family set up their first camp (see *Echoes,* 86–88).

2 And I knew not at the time when I made them that I should be commanded of the Lord to make these plates; wherefore, the record of my father, and the genealogy of his fathers, and the more part of all our proceedings in the wilderness are engraven upon those first plates of which I have spoken; wherefore, the things which transpired before I made these plates are, of a truth, more particularly made mention upon the first plates.
3 And after I had made these plates by way of commandment, I, Nephi, received a commandment that the ministry and the prophecies, the more plain and precious parts of them, should be written upon these plates; and that the things which were written should be kept for the instruction of my people, who should possess the land, and also for other ***wise purposes,*** *which purposes are known unto the Lord.*

Wise purposes

The Lord is all-knowing. His vision encompasses the entire destiny of mankind. He guides His prophets to act so as to maximize the spiritual harvest among the faithful and obedient. Elder

1 Nephi 19:3–9

Jeffrey R. Holland explains the nature of the "wise purposes" of the Lord in granting unto His sons and daughters "greater views" of the gospel:

> At least six times in the Book of Mormon, the phrase *for a wise purpose* is used in reference to the making, writing, and preserving of the small plates. One such wise purpose—the most obvious one—was to compensate for the future loss of 116 pages of manuscript translated by the Prophet Joseph Smith from the first part of Mormon's abridgment of the large plates of Nephi.
>
> But there is another "wise purpose" for the inclusion of these smaller plates in the highly edited material that would constitute the Book of Mormon. In Doctrine and Covenants 10:45 the Lord declared to Joseph Smith, "Behold, there are many things engraven upon the [small] plates of Nephi which do throw *greater views* upon my gospel."
>
> All the details and information contained in those first 116 pages of manuscript are not yet known. What *is* known is that most of the "greater views" of the gospel found in the teachings of the small plates of Nephi come from the personal declarations of these three great prophetic witnesses of the premortal Jesus Christ—Nephi, Jacob, and Isaiah. These three doctrinal and visionary voices make clear at the very outset of the Book of Mormon why it is "another testament of Jesus Christ."
>
> In declaring the special preparation these three had for receiving and teaching such "greater views" of the gospel, Nephi revealed the most persuasive qualification of all: They had seen the premortal Jesus Christ. (*Christ and the New Covenant: The Messianic Message of the Book of Mormon* [Salt Lake City: Deseret Book, 1997], 34–35)

4–7 Nephi reserves the smaller plates for recording the more sacred things concerning his people.

> *8 And behold he [the Messiah] cometh, according to the words of the angel, in* ***six hundred years*** *from the time my father left Jerusalem.*
> *9 And the world, because of their iniquity, shall judge him to be a thing of naught; wherefore they scourge him, and he suffereth it; and they smite him, and he suffereth it. Yea, they spit upon him, and he suffereth it, because of his loving-kindness and his long-suffering toward the children of men.*

SIX HUNDRED YEARS

The time of the Savior's first coming is fixed and confirmed for the people. Lehi had first made this fact known from his visionary experiences: "Yea, even six hundred years from the time that my father left Jerusalem, a prophet would the Lord God raise up among the Jews—even a Messiah, or, in other words, a Savior of the world" (1 Nephi 10:4).

10–16 Nephi describes the coming ministry of the Savior as conveyed in the words of the prophets Zenock, Neum, and Zenos (apparently given in the brass plates). The seismic dislocations in America at the time of the Savior's death are described. The Jews are to be scourged and scattered, but later gathered with the remnants of the house of Israel as the people return unto the Lord and He remembers His covenant promises.

> *17 Yea, and all the earth shall see the salvation of the Lord, saith the prophet; every nation, kindred, tongue and people shall be blessed.*
> *18 And I, Nephi, have written these things unto my people, that perhaps I might persuade them that they would* ***remember the Lord*** *their Redeemer.*

REMEMBER THE LORD

The purpose of the scriptures is to reveal the word of God, teach the truth, and testify of divine principles so that people might be persuaded to believe in Christ. The Book of Mormon offers insights into the lives of prophets of God, such as Nephi, who respond to the Lord's will by preserving for posterity the truths of salvation revealed to them through the Spirit.

Nephi records on the smaller plates that which he believes to be "sacred" (1 Nephi 19:6)—things that have a tendency to turn the hearts of the people toward the Savior, "that perhaps I might persuade them that they would remember the Lord their Redeemer" (1 Nephi 19:18).

> *19 Wherefore, I speak unto all the house of Israel, if it so be that they should obtain these things.*
> *20 For behold, I have workings in the spirit, which doth weary me even that all my joints are weak, for those who are at Jerusalem; for had not the Lord been merciful, to show unto me concerning them, even as he had prophets of old, I should have perished also.*
> *21 And he surely did show unto the prophets of old all things concerning them; and also he did show unto many concerning us; wherefore, it must needs be that we know concerning them for they are written upon the plates of brass.*

1 Nephi 19:22–24

> *22 Now it came to pass that I, Nephi, did teach my brethren these things; and it came*
> *to pass that I did read many things to them, which were engraven upon the plates of*
> *brass, that they might know concerning the doings of the Lord in other lands, among*
> *people of old.*
> *23 And I did read many things unto them which were written in the books of Moses;*
> *but that I might more fully persuade them to believe in the Lord their Redeemer I*
> *did read unto them that which was written by the prophet Isaiah; for I did* ***liken all***
> ***scriptures unto us,*** *that it might be for our profit and learning.*

Liken all scriptures unto us

As we read the scriptures, we can apply them to our lives in a sincere and purposeful way. The Lord will bless us with knowledge, wisdom, and guidance for our lives. When Nephi said, "I did liken all scriptures unto us, that it might be for our profit and learning," (1 Nephi 19:23), he was advising us, as Elder Russell M. Nelson states, "to weave the fiber of scriptural wisdom into the fabric of our own being" (*The Power within Us* [Salt Lake City: Deseret Book, 1988], 29). We learn in the beginning of the Book of Mormon that the test of mankind is always before us. Will we choose to obey the will of the Lord and receive the blessings of heaven or lose them through disobedience? The key is to learn vicariously from the scriptures.

> *24 Wherefore I spake unto them, saying: Hear ye the words of the prophet, ye who are*
> *a remnant of the house of Israel, a branch who have been broken off; hear ye the words*
> *of the prophet, which were written unto all the house of Israel, and* ***liken them unto***
> ***yourselves,*** *that ye may have hope as well as your brethren from whom ye have been*
> *broken off; for after this manner has the prophet written.*

How to Liken the Scriptures unto Ourselves

All scriptures are for our profit and learning—our compass for living. To obtain full value from them, we must take them personally and apply them to our lives. Here is a simple method for applying the word of God:

1. We must read the scriptures carefully.
2. We must ponder them as they relate to us.
3. We must write down each scripture reference and the main idea that is there.
4. We can write a personal statement on how we're going to live this scripture.

I will, I must, I shall, I can—these first-person commitment statements will make the scriptures live in our lives.

Take, for example, 1 Nephi 3:7: "And it came to pass that I, Nephi, said unto my father: I will go and do the things which the Lord hath commanded, for I know that the Lord giveth no commandments unto the children of men, save he shall prepare a way for them that they may accomplish the thing which he commandeth them."

Now apply it:

1. "I will keep the commandments because the Lord will help me by preparing a way."
2. "I will pray today" or "I will keep the commandment of the fast on Fast Sunday." These simple statements lead us to apply scripture directly to our lives.

Further example: "And I was led by the Spirit, not knowing beforehand the things which I should do" (1 Nephi 4:6).

APPLICATION

"I will live worthy of the Spirit that I might have direction in my life." Such a simple statement can have such a powerful effect upon one's life.

As a Book of Mormon teacher at BYU and at the Orem institute I had my students do applications with each reading assignment. It changed lives. Even to this day a student will tell me about their application booklet. One student did over 1,375 in one semester. Needless to say, the applications to life from the Book of Mormon gave inspiration and direction for their lives. (Ed J. Pinegar)

CHAPTER 20

OVERVIEW

Nephi quotes Isaiah 48 to his people.

1–22 From the beginning the Lord has declared the plan of salvation unto His people. They must be refined in the furnace of affliction as they remember to do His will. He calls upon all Israel to repent and be redeemed.

10 For, behold, I have refined thee, I have chosen thee ***in the furnace of affliction.***

In the furnace of affliction

This scripture from Isaiah has particular relevance for Nephi and his group. They've lost their home in Jerusalem, endured eight years of hardship in the wilderness, and finally completed a long ocean voyage to start life anew in a strange world. Being refined and chosen by the Lord through sore trials and adversity is a gospel theme that virtually all of God's children come to know through personal experience.

Through John the Revelator, the Lord confirmed this doctrine with a promise of eternal scope: "As many as I love, I rebuke and chasten: be zealous therefore, and repent. Behold, I stand at the door, and knock: if any man hear my voice, and open the door, I will come in to him, and will sup with him, and he with me. To him that overcometh will I grant to sit with me in my throne, even as I also overcame, and am set down with my Father in his throne" (Revelation 3:19–21).

From the walls of Zarahemla, Samuel the Lamanite proclaimed the same principle (see Helaman 15:3). And again in our day, the Lord has emphasized this doctrine once again in plainness and charity: "VERILY, thus saith the Lord unto you whom I love, and whom I love I also chasten that their sins may be forgiven, for with the chastisement I prepare a way for their deliverance in all things out of temptation, and I have loved you. . . ." (D&C 95:1).

The message of hope is this: If we find ourselves in the midst of sore affliction, we must turn to the Lord in full faith and devotion and know that He loves us and that He will deliver us in mercy and love, and multiply His blessings unto us in His own due time.

CHAPTER 21

OVERVIEW

Nephi quotes Isaiah 49.

1–12 The Messiah is called to bring Zion forth and to be a light unto the Gentiles. He is to liberate the captives and to gather the scattered of Israel with rejoicing.

> *13 Sing, O heavens; and be joyful, O earth; for the feet of those who are in the east shall be established; and break forth into singing, O mountains; for they shall be smitten no more; for* ***the Lord hath comforted his people,*** *and will have mercy upon his afflicted.*

The Lord hath comforted his people

Nephi's commitment is to teach his contemporaries and all future generations the principles of covenant righteousness so that they might enjoy the priceless blessings of the gospel of Jesus Christ. Thus he turns to the writings of Isaiah to support his fervent testimony, beginning with what we now call Isaiah 48 and 49. These chapters describe how the Lord's chosen people will be liberated and saved by the Messiah, who will gather them in once more from their scattered and chastened state with the help of the Gentile nations: "for the Lord hath comforted his people, and will have mercy upon his afflicted" (1 Nephi 21:13).

> *14 But, behold, Zion hath said: The Lord hath forsaken me, and my Lord hath forgotten me—but he will show that he hath not.*
> *15 For can a woman forget her sucking child, that she should not have compassion on the son of her womb? Yea, they may forget,* ***yet will I not forget thee,*** *O house of Israel.*

Yet will I not forget thee

Elder Jeffrey R. Holland reminds us of the unfailing devotion and compassion of the Lord toward His children as confirmed in the words of Isaiah:

> This poetic passage provides yet another reminder of Christ's saving role, that of protective, redeeming parent to Zion's children. He comforts his people and shows mercy when they are afflicted, as any loving father or mother would toward a child, but, as Nephi here reminds us through Isaiah, much more than any mortal father and mother could do. Although a mother may forget her sucking child (as unlikely as any parent might think that could be), Christ will not forget the children he has redeemed or the covenant he has made with them for salvation in Zion. The painful reminders of that watch care and covenant are the marks of the Roman nails graven upon the palms of his hands, a sign to his disciples in the Old World, his Nephite congregation in the New World, and to us in latter-day Zion that he is the Savior of the world and was wounded in the house of his friends. (*Christ and the New Covenant: The Messianic Message of the Book of Mormon* [Salt Lake City: Deseret Book, 1997], 84)

> *16 Behold, I have graven thee* ***upon the palms of my hands;*** *thy walls are continually before me.*

1 Nephi 21:16–23

UPON THE PALMS OF MY HANDS

To be engraved upon the palms of the Lord's hands is to be reminded symbolically that He gave His life for us and for all mankind—unto salvation for all of His children through the Resurrection. To have one's walls continually before the Lord is to be reminded that our homes and families are always before Him, and that His mission is one of eternal love toward us and toward our children through all generations.

17–21 The obedient are to be fruitful and enjoy the blessings of an abundant posterity.

> *22 Thus saith the Lord God: Behold, I will lift up mine hand to the Gentiles, and set up my standard to the people; and they shall bring thy sons in their arms, and thy daughters shall be carried upon their shoulders.*
>
> *23 And kings shall be thy **nursing fathers,** and their queens thy **nursing mothers;** they shall bow down to thee with their face toward the earth, and lick up the dust of thy feet; and thou shalt know that I am the Lord; for they shall not be ashamed that wait for me.*

MEMORIES: NURSING FATHERS, NURSING MOTHERS—AMERICA, A BLESSING UNTO THE WORLD

The Lord, in His infinite wisdom, knew that the gospel of liberty and truth could be restored to the earth only in an environment where the principles of liberty and truth were honored and constitutionally secured for each individual (see D&C Section 134; 98:5–6; 101:77, 80). He therefore prepared the seedbed of the Restoration by empowering an emerging segment of the Gentile flock who "did humble themselves before the Lord" (as Nephi saw it in vision—1 Nephi 13:16).

Because these enlightened Gentiles served the interests of the Almighty, they were blessed with the nurture of the gospel in all its fulness and with infinite blessings from God. Does this process continue even now? I heard an interesting answer to this question while serving a mission as a young elder in Germany. Ezra Taft Benson and his wife stopped by the mission home in Frankfurt for a visit around the Fourth of July 1959, and spoke with us informally about religious and political matters. At the time he was completing his eight-year term as secretary of agriculture in the Eisenhower administration. Elder Benson told us about his experiences with President Eisenhower and this man's spiritual power. He also said something that reminded me of the continuing role of the Gentiles (in particular the United States of America) in supporting God's design for the blessing of mankind. Elder Benson spoke to us about the government policy of providing foreign aid to many countries of the world and suggested that it was this policy, analogous to tithing, that was, in large measure, responsible for the prosperity of America. By blessing other nations, he said, America was being blessed by the Lord. This was a reminder to me that God's hand continues to be over this land "which is choice above all other lands" (1 Nephi 13:30). Thus the nursing fathers should continue to be nurtured, and the nursing mothers should continue to be blessed from on high. (Richard J. Allen)

24–26 The Lord is to fight the battles of His people and be their Redeemer and Savior, "and all flesh shall know that I, the Lord, am thy Savior and thy Redeemer, the Mighty One of Jacob."

CHAPTER 22

OVERVIEW

To his questioning brothers Nephi expounds themes from Isaiah. Israel will be scattered because of wickedness but gathered in the latter days through the administration and instrumentality of the Gentiles, among whom the Lord would bring about a "marvelous work," i.e., the restoration of the gospel according the covenant promises of old. The Lord will bless His people and Satan will be defeated.

1–19 Nephi reviews once again the doctrine of the scattering and gathering of Israel and the role of the Gentiles in the last days to act in support of the coming forth of the restored gospel, which restoration is to be a blessing to all the obedient and faithful as well as an instrumentality of judgment against all who strive against the work of God.

> *20 And the Lord will surely prepare a way for his people, unto the fulfilling of the words of Moses, which he spake, saying: A prophet shall the Lord your God raise up unto you, like unto me; him shall ye hear in all things whatsoever he shall say unto you. And it shall come to pass that all those who will not hear that prophet shall be cut off from among the people.*
> *21 And now I, Nephi, declare unto you, that this prophet of whom Moses spake was* ***the Holy One of Israel;*** *wherefore, he shall execute judgment in righteousness.*
> *22 And the righteous need not fear, for they are those who shall not be confounded. . . .*

The Holy One of Israel

The expression "The Holy One of Israel" is used some 70 times in the holy scriptures—particularly in the book of Isaiah, where it occurs no fewer than 26 times. The first two books of the Book of Mormon, 1 Nephi and 2 Nephi include this phrase 37 times.

23–24 Nephi looks into the future with prophetic vision and sees that the wicked and prideful are to be consumed as stubble at the time of the Second Coming when "the Holy One of Israel must reign in dominion, and might, and power, and great glory" (verse 24) and gather together His flock during the millennial period.

> *25 And he gathereth his children from the four quarters of the earth; and he numbereth his sheep, and they know him; and there shall be* ***one fold and one shepherd;*** *and he shall feed his sheep, and in him they shall find pasture.*

One fold and one shepherd

During His earthly ministry, the Lord declared: "And other sheep I have, which are not of this fold: them also I must bring, and they shall hear my voice; and there shall be one fold, and one shepherd" (John 10:16). The resurrected Lord reminded His flock in ancient America that they were, indeed, the ones of whom He spoke (see 3 Nephi 15:7, 21). Also, His other sheep of the scattered ten tribes are to be accounted within the fold (see 3 Nephi 16:3).

26–27 Nephi foresees that Satan will be bound during the millennial period and be rendered powerless because of the righteousness of the people.

> *28 But, behold, all nations, kindreds, tongues, and people shall* ***dwell safely*** *in the Holy One of Israel if it so be that they will repent.*
> *29 And now I, Nephi, make an end; for I durst not speak further as yet concerning these things.*

Dwell safely

What can we do to ensure that we will be safe during the latter-day period of turmoil and upheaval leading to the millennial reign? The key is given above: "*people shall* ***dwell safely*** *in the Holy One of Israel if it so be that they will repent*" (verse 28). Safety is a function of *where* we dwell—i.e., in the Holy One of Israel through righteous living.

30 Wherefore, my brethren, I would that ye should consider that the things which have been written upon the plates of brass are true; and they testify that a man must be ***obedient to the commandments*** *of God.*
31 Wherefore, ye need not suppose that I and my father are the only ones that have testified, and also taught them. Wherefore, if ye shall ***be obedient to the commandments, and endure to the end,*** *ye shall be saved at the last day. And thus it is. Amen.*

Be obedient to the commandments, and endure to the end

The principles of faith, obedience, courage, and following the counsel of the prophets are taught over and over in the Book of Mormon as basic tenets of the Lord's covenant with his chosen people and the blessings associated with it. Nephi chooses to conclude his first book with these words: "be obedient to the commandments, and endure to the end, ye shall be saved at the last day" (1 Nephi 22:31).

CONCLUDING THOUGHTS

Nephi, like his father Lehi before him, is privileged to view from a spiritual perspective the unfolding of the world's history from his day until the end of time. What these two prophets see and communicate to us is a guide for each of us. Many of the things Nephi's vision have already occurred, some in our day. Nephi clearly understood that there would be a sore battle raging between the church of the devil and the Church of the Lamb for the souls of men. We, as members of the Church, have various responsibilities in this battle: to stand for truth and righteousness as witnesses (see Mosiah 18:9); to warn our neighbor (see D&C 88:81); to build up the kingdom of God (see JST Matt 6:38); to be a light to the world and saviors to mankind (see D&C 103:9–10; Obadiah 1:21).

We have a prophet today who is led by the Lord Jesus Christ. We are well counseled to give heed to his words, for they are as if the Lord Himself gave them (see D&C 1:38; 3 Nephi 28:34–35).

THE BOOK OF
SECOND NEPHI

An account of the death of Lehi. Nephi's brethren rebel against him. The Lord warns Nephi to depart into the wilderness. His journeyings in the wilderness, and so forth. [Note: This preamble was included in the original edition of the Book of Mormon published in 1830.]

BOOK OVERVIEW

Lehi blesses his children and their posterity and then passes away. Nephi and his followers separate themselves from Laman and Lemuel and "live after the manner of happiness" (2 Nephi 5:27). Nephi and Jacob preach and expound the gospel of Jesus Christ and blend their testimonies with the words of Isaiah. Nephi comes to the end of his ministry and encourages everyone to learn of the doctrine of Christ and to practice its principles as they press forward steadfastly in the faith.

CHAPTER 1

OVERVIEW

Lehi reminds his sons of the great blessings that come through covenant obedience. Their posterity will prosper in the land of promise by remembering the Messiah, the Holy One of Israel—but disobedience will bring the wrath of God upon them and cause that another people will inherit the land. Lehi exhorts Laman and Lemuel with all the feeling of a loving parent to awake, arise, and remember the goodness of God and the blessings of righteousness. They are to honor their brother Nephi and recognize that his entreaties to them originate with the Holy Spirit. Lehi blesses his sons and gives them inspired promises that are conditioned on their obedience.

1 AND now it came to pass that after I, Nephi, had made an end of teaching my brethren, our father, Lehi, also ***spake many things unto them,*** *and rehearsed unto them, how great things the Lord had done for them in bringing them out of the land of Jerusalem.*

2 And he spake unto them concerning their rebellions upon the waters, and the mercies of God in sparing their lives, that they were not swallowed up in the sea.

3 And he also spake unto them concerning the land of promise, which they had obtained—how merciful the Lord had been in warning us that we should flee out of the land of Jerusalem.
4 For, behold, said he, I have seen a vision, in which I know that Jerusalem is destroyed; and had we remained in Jerusalem we should also have perished.
5 But, said he, notwithstanding our afflictions, we have obtained a land of promise, a land which is choice above all other lands; a land which the Lord God hath covenanted with me should be a land for the inheritance of my seed. Yea, the Lord hath covenanted this land unto me, and to my children forever, and also all those who should be led out of other countries by the hand of the Lord.

Spake many things unto them

Lehi's action on behalf of his children raises a question of conscience for us all: Do we consistently bless our children by teaching them to walk in the ways of truth? We all know and recognize that family is first and foremost in our lives. The plan of salvation and exaltation is centered in the family unit wherein are found the greatest work and joy in life. Let us therefore do what matters most for our families in the context of their temporal and spiritual security. According to Lehi, we should:

- Emphasize the blessings that flow from the Lord—despite our shortcomings and weaknesses.
- Confirm the truth of the word of God as a means of ensuring our safety and progress.
- Stress the covenant relationship we have with God.

6 Wherefore, I, Lehi, ***prophesy*** *according to the workings of the Spirit which is in me, that there shall none come into this land save they shall be brought by the hand of the Lord.*
7 Wherefore, this land is consecrated unto him whom he shall bring. And if it so be that they shall serve him according to the commandments which he hath given, it shall be a land of liberty unto them; wherefore, they shall never be brought down into captivity; if so, it shall be because of iniquity; for if iniquity shall abound cursed shall be the land for their sakes, but ***unto the righteous it shall be blessed forever.***
8 And behold, it is wisdom that this land should be kept as yet from the knowledge of other nations; for behold, many nations would overrun the land, that there would be no place for an inheritance.

9 Wherefore, I, Lehi, have obtained a promise, that inasmuch as those whom the Lord God shall bring out of the land of Jerusalem shall keep his commandments, they shall prosper upon the face of this land; and they shall be kept from all other nations, that they may possess this land unto themselves. And if it so be that they shall keep his commandments they shall be blessed upon the face of this land, and there shall be none to molest them, nor to take away the land of their inheritance; and they shall dwell safely forever.
10 But behold, when the time cometh that they shall dwindle in unbelief, after they have received so great blessings from the hand of the Lord—having a knowledge of the creation of the earth, and all men, knowing the great and marvelous works of the Lord from the creation of the world; having power given them to do all things by faith; having all the commandments from the beginning, and having been brought by his infinite goodness into this precious land of promise—behold, I say, if the day shall come that they will reject the Holy One of Israel, the true Messiah, their Redeemer and their God, behold, the judgments of him that is just shall rest upon them.
11 Yea, he will bring other nations unto them, and he will give unto them power, and he will take away from them the lands of their possessions, and he will cause them to be scattered and smitten.

Prophesy; unto the Righteous it shall be Blessed Forever

Lehi emphasizes one of the enduring themes of the Book of Mormon—that the promised land is an inheritance from the Lord that can be maintained only on principles of righteousness. If the people dwindle in unbelief and reject the Messiah, another people will receive their inheritance (compare 1 Nephi 2:20; 4:14; Mosiah 1:7; 2:27; Alma 48:25). The Jaredite nation learns this lesson the hard way. The last Jaredite king, Coriantumr, ignores the warning of the Lord (see Ether 13:21). Coriantumr, as sole survivor, lives to see the day when the Mulekites of Zarahemla, later absorbed into the Nephite nation, take over the inheritance of the promised land. Tragically, the Nephites eventually lose their gospel anchor through pride and wickedness and become extinct. Where is America today? What is the state of righteousness that prevails? Will the people of the land "reject the Holy One of Israel, the true Messiah, their Redeemer and their God"? If so, then "the judgments of him that is just shall rest upon them" and the Lord will "cause them to be scattered and smitten" (see 2 Nephi 1:10–11).

*12 Yea, as one generation passeth to another there shall be **bloodsheds, and great visitations** among them; wherefore, my sons, I would that ye would remember; yea, I would that ye would **hearken unto my words.***

EVIDENCE: Bloodsheds, and great visitations—Plural Amplification

Consider the grammatical construction used in this verse. The words *bloodshed* and *visitation* are rendered plural—in order to amplify the themes. In biblical Hebrew, a noun is often pluralized when one would expect a singular in order to amplify or emphasize the idea. However, the translators of the King James version changed these nouns to the singular. A few examples, with the correct Hebrew translation in brackets, include "and strength of salvation [salvations] . . ." (Isaiah 33:6), and "Thy brother's blood [bloods] crieth unto me from the ground" (Genesis 4:10). The Book of Mormon contains many such plural nouns, suggesting that its authors were familiar with the Hebrew writing style (see 1 Nephi 2:11, Jacob 4:7, Mormon 1:19, Alma 20:13). (See *Echoes,* 173.)

Hearken unto my words

The greatest legacy that parents can leave their children is to teach them the truths of salvation in clear and loving ways and to model these truths in a righteous lifestyle. What Lehi provides for his children is a pattern that all of us can follow. He emphasizes the goodness and mercy of the Lord but makes plain the consequences of failing to follow the principles of the gospel.

> *13 O that ye would* ***awake;*** *awake from a deep sleep, yea, even from the sleep of hell, and shake off the awful chains by which ye are bound, which are the chains which bind the children of men, that they are carried away captive down to the eternal gulf of misery and woe.*
> *14* ***Awake!*** *and* ***arise*** *from the dust, and hear the words of a trembling parent, whose limbs ye must soon lay down in the cold and silent grave,* ***from whence no traveler can return;*** *a few more days and I go the way of all the earth.*
> *15 But behold, the Lord hath redeemed my soul from hell; I have beheld his glory, and I am encircled about eternally in the arms of his love.*
> *16 And I desire that ye should* ***remember*** *to observe the statutes and the judgments of the Lord; behold, this hath been the anxiety of my soul from the beginning.*
> *17 My heart hath been weighed down with sorrow from time to time, for I have feared, lest for the hardness of your hearts the Lord your God should come out in the fulness of his wrath upon you, that ye be cut off and destroyed forever;*
> *18 Or, that a cursing should come upon you for the space of many generations; and ye are visited by sword, and by famine, and are hated, and are led according to the will and captivity of the devil.*

2 Nephi 1:19–23

> *19 O my sons, that these things might not come upon you, but that ye might be a choice and a favored people of the Lord. But behold, his will be done; for his ways are righteousness forever.*
> *20 And he hath said that: Inasmuch as ye shall keep my commandments ye shall prosper in the land; but inasmuch as ye will not keep my commandments ye shall be cut off from my presence.*
> *21 And now that my soul might have joy in you, and that my heart might leave this world with gladness because of you, that I might not be brought down with grief and sorrow to the grave,* ***arise*** *from the dust, my sons, and be men, and be determined in one mind and in one heart, united in all things, that ye may not come down into captivity;*
> *22 That ye may not be cursed with a sore cursing; and also, that ye may not incur the displeasure of a just God upon you, unto the destruction, yea, the eternal destruction of both soul and body.*
> *23* ***Awake,*** *my sons; put on the armor of righteousness. Shake off the chains with which ye are bound, and come forth out of obscurity, and* ***arise*** *from the dust.*

Awake, arise, remember

Lehi's impassioned plea to his rebellious sons, Laman and Lemuel, is a model of sincere parental counsel. What parent does not wish from the depths of the soul that his or her children will live the principles of the gospel and thereby avoid the destructive consequences of sin? What parent does not yearn for the joy and gladness that can come from children who "walk in truth" (3 John 1:4)? The anxiety of Lehi and Sariah for their children mirrors the anxiety of the Lord for all of His people. The awake-and-arise theme is sounded again by Moroni at the very end of the Book of Mormon:

> And again I would exhort you that ye would come unto Christ, and lay hold upon every good gift, and touch not the evil gift, nor the unclean thing.
>
> And awake, and arise from the dust, O Jerusalem; yea, and put on thy beautiful garments, O daughter of Zion; and strengthen thy stakes and enlarge thy borders forever, that thou mayest no more be confounded, that the covenants of the Eternal Father which he hath made unto thee, O house of Israel, may be fulfilled. (Moroni 10:30–31)

In latter-day scripture, the Lord again sounds the call to awake and arise in the context of the Second Coming: "Yea, let the cry go forth among all people: Awake and arise and go forth to meet the Bridegroom; behold and lo, the Bridegroom cometh; go ye out to meet him. Prepare yourselves for the great day of the Lord" (D&C 133:10).

EVIDENCE: From whence no traveler can return

Some critics of the Book of Mormon cite this verse (verse 14) as proof that the Book of Mormon is a compilation of plagiarized text. However, according to Hugh Nibley, "A recent study of Akkadian and Sumerian names for the world of the dead lists 'the hole, the earth, the land of no return, the path of no turning back, the road whose course never turns back, the distant land, etc.'" Lehi's phrase "from whence no traveler can return" fits perfectly with such terms (*Echoes,* 472).

24 Rebel no more against your brother, whose views have been glorious, and who hath kept the commandments from the time that we left Jerusalem; and who hath been an instrument in the hands of God, in bringing us forth into the land of promise; for were it not for him, we must have perished with hunger in the wilderness; nevertheless, ye sought to take away his life; yea, and he hath suffered much sorrow because of you.
25 And I exceedingly fear and tremble because of you, lest he shall suffer again; for behold, ye have accused him that he sought power and authority over you; but I know that he hath not sought for power nor authority over you, but ***he hath sought the glory of God, and your own eternal welfare.***
26 And ye have murmured because he hath been plain unto you. Ye say that he hath used sharpness; ye say that he hath been angry with you; but behold, his sharpness was the sharpness of the power of the word of God, which was in him; and that which ye call anger was the truth, according to that which is in God, which he could not restrain, manifesting boldly concerning your iniquities.
27 And it must needs be that the power of God must be with him, even unto his commanding you that ye must obey. But behold, it was not he, but ***it was the Spirit of the Lord which was in him,*** *which opened his mouth to utterance that he could not shut it.*

He hath sought the glory of God, and your own eternal welfare; it was the Spirit of the Lord which was in him

In character and action, Nephi is like the Jaredite prophet Ether, who "began to prophesy unto the people, for he could not be restrained because of the Spirit of the Lord which was in him" (Ether

12:2). Few accepted his teachings; most turned against him. Hardness of heart is a condition in which an individual misinterprets the well-intentioned outreach of one through whom the Spirit operates as being an act of aggression. Laman and Lemuel loathe their younger brother Nephi and conclude that he seeks unrighteous dominion over them. Lehi, as intermediary, attempts to persuade them that Nephi's actions are charitable—intended for their welfare. The situation is an instructive example of the correct operation of the priesthood. Nephi continually tries in patience and kindness to share with his brothers the insights of pure knowledge he has received through prayer and revelation—resorting to boldness only when moved upon by the Spirit. As the Lord declares in modern times: "No power or influence can or ought to be maintained by virtue of the priesthood, only by persuasion, by long-suffering, by gentleness and meekness, and by love unfeigned; By kindness, and pure knowledge, which shall greatly enlarge the soul without hypocrisy, and without guile—Reproving betimes [i.e., immediately] with sharpness, when moved upon by the Holy Ghost; and then showing forth afterwards an increase of love toward him whom thou hast reproved, lest he esteem thee to be his enemy" (D&C 121:41–43).

> *28 And now my son, Laman, and also Lemuel and Sam, and also my sons who are the sons of Ishmael, behold, if ye will hearken unto the voice of Nephi ye shall not perish. And if ye will hearken unto him I leave unto you a* ***blessing,*** *yea, even my first* ***blessing.***
> *29 But if ye will not hearken unto him I take away my first* ***blessing,*** *yea, even my* ***blessing,*** *and it shall rest upon him.*
> *30 And now, Zoram, I speak unto you: Behold, thou art the servant of Laban; nevertheless, thou hast been brought out of the land of Jerusalem, and I know that thou art a true friend unto my son, Nephi, forever.*
> *31 Wherefore, because thou hast been faithful thy seed shall be* ***blessed*** *with his seed, that they dwell in prosperity long upon the face of this land; and nothing, save it shall be iniquity among them, shall harm or disturb their prosperity upon the face of this land forever.*
> *32 Wherefore, if ye shall keep the commandments of the Lord, the Lord hath consecrated this land for the security of thy seed with the seed of my son.*

Blessing, blessed

Lehi bestows blessings upon his sons and members of his circle (such as Zoram, former servant of Laban) very much in keeping with the pattern reflected in the patriarchal blessings given by Jacob

(Israel) to his twelve sons and their posterity (see Genesis 49). In our day the Lord has called patriarchs to give blessings of personal revelation to worthy members of the Church. Those who seek such blessings learn thereby of their declared lineage in the house of Israel through which great blessings will flow. They are often informed of special gifts granted to them by Heavenly Father and given counsel and warnings about proper conduct. In addition, a worthy father can give a father's blessing to his sons and daughters at important milestones of their lives, calling forth upon their heads special blessings and gifts that will guide their footsteps. (See Ed J. Pinegar and Richard J. Allen, *Your Patriarchal Blessing* [American Fork, UT: Covenant Communications, 2005].)

Memories: A Father's Blessing

Many years ago, on the eve of getting married and starting a family of my own, I asked my father to give me a father's blessing. He fasted and prayed and then bestowed upon me a wonderful blessing of personal encouragement and counsel, somewhat in the spirit of Lehi's famous dream. At the conclusion of the blessing, he stated something that can be readily shared with others because of its universal application: "And now my beloved son as you journey forth into the uncertain world, reach up your hands to the lap of God. And if you will do this He will lead you, He will guide you, save and exalt you in the Eternal Worlds."

This image of reaching up one's hands to the lap of God has a story behind it that may encourage other fathers who receive a request for a father's blessing. In a conversation with my father contemporaneous with the bestowal of the blessing, which he had written down and memorized before giving, he told me that my request to receive this blessing had caused him much concern and effort. He wanted to be in tune with the Spirit to carry out this task well. In praying about it one night, he saw in his mind the image of a child kneeling before God and reaching his hands up to the lap of God in humility and devotion, as if to seek guidance and support. This image was then carried into the blessing as the seal of counsel. I have pondered countless times over the years how well this image reflects a true spirit of meekness and humility so essential to devoted discipleship.

Often truth is conveyed more readily in the form of imagery or stories with symbolic power. Just as the prophet Lehi received wisdom from on high in the form of a panoramic vision intended for the blessing of all mankind, so my own father received inspiration to give counsel to his own son in a unique and effective way. Similarly, fathers and mothers can tell uplifting stories to their children and grandchildren. As they seek inspiration from on high, they will find the most effective imagery for expressing true principles in a way that the rising generation will understand and use more readily in making choices that bless and enlighten. (Richard J. Allen)

CHAPTER 2

OVERVIEW

Lehi gives an inspired discourse to Jacob and his other sons concerning the plan of salvation and the Atonement of Jesus Christ. Through the "merits, and mercy, and grace of the Holy Messiah" (verse 8), all of God's children are given the gift of the resurrection and, based on their obedience, can look forward to eternal life in the hereafter. Lehi explains the principle of agency in the context of the reality of opposition in all things, and recounts the fall of man as a gateway to joy. He enjoins his sons to choose everlasting life rather than eternal death.

1 AND now, Jacob, I speak unto you: Thou art my first-born in the days of my tribulation in the wilderness. And behold, in thy childhood thou hast suffered ***afflictions*** *and much sorrow, because of the rudeness of thy brethren.*
2 Nevertheless, Jacob, my first-born in the wilderness, thou knowest the ***greatness of God;*** *and he shall consecrate thine afflictions for thy gain.*

Afflictions; greatness of God

Lehi, as a loving parent, teaches Jacob and his other sons the plan of redemption so that they might understand and appreciate the goodness of God and His grace toward His children. Lehi's goal is to guide his sons to choose liberty and eternal life over captivity and damnation. We, as loving parents, should teach our children likewise. We have the privilege of testifying that redemption comes through the Atonement of our Savior Jesus Christ as we seek after righteousness and covenant to be faithful and obedient. We should all teach that opposition is part of the plan and is necessary for our growth. Without trials, tribulation, and adversity, we cannot become perfected. As we come to recognize the law of opposition in all things we can see that our choices—the use of our agency—determine our course and our blessings here on earth and in the eternities to come.

3 Wherefore, thy soul shall be blessed, and thou shalt dwell safely with thy brother, Nephi; and thy days shall be spent in the service of thy God. Wherefore, I know that thou art redeemed, because of the righteousness of thy Redeemer; for thou hast beheld that in the fulness of time he cometh to bring salvation unto men.
4 And thou hast beheld in thy youth his glory; wherefore, thou art blessed even as they unto whom he shall minister in the flesh; for the Spirit is the same, yesterday, today, and forever. And the way is prepared from the fall of man, and salvation is free.

5 And men are ***instructed sufficiently*** *that they know good from evil. And the law is given unto men. And* ***by the law no flesh is justified;*** *or, by the law men are cut off. Yea, by the temporal law they were cut off; and also, by the spiritual law they perish from that which is good, and become miserable forever.*
6 Wherefore, redemption cometh in and through the ***Holy Messiah;*** *for he is full of grace and truth.*

Instructed sufficiently; by the law no flesh is justified; Holy Messiah

Heavenly Father makes known His plan of salvation and exaltation in sufficient detail to enable us, through obedience, to come home to Him and His Son once again. From the days of Adam onward this has been the case: "And thus the Gospel began to be preached, from the beginning, being declared by holy angels sent forth from the presence of God, and by his own voice, and by the gift of the Holy Ghost" (Moses 5:58). However, even though we are instructed sufficiently concerning the heavenly commandments and the laws of God, and even though we strive in all sincerity to live up to these commandments and laws, we are imperfect. By our mortal nature we fall short of the mark. It takes more than what we can bring to bear on our own. It takes a Redeemer, full of grace and truth, to be our Advocate. It takes the Atonement of the Lamb of God to lift us beyond our mortal capabilities, that we might be "perfect in Christ" (Moroni 10:32). Redemption comes only through our Savior Jesus Christ. Those who believe in Him and who come forth with a broken heart and contrite spirit and repent, enduring to the end, will be saved.

Let us, like Lehi, teach our children and posterity more about the Atonement. Clearly, it is instructive that Lehi focuses on the subject of the Atonement in his final discourse and exhortation to Jacob and his brothers.

7 Behold, he offereth himself a sacrifice for sin, to answer the ends of the law, unto all those who have ***a broken heart and a contrite spirit;*** *and unto none else can the ends of the law be answered.*

A broken heart and a contrite spirit

Nephi trusts in the Lord and acknowledged humbly his own personal weakness and total dependence upon the Lord. As we submit our will to that of the Father and cultivate "a broken heart and a contrite spirit" (2 Nephi 2:7; compare 2 Nephi 4:32. Ether 4:15, D&C 20:37), we too are supported and strengthened by the Lord. On the other hand, when we harden our hearts and rebel against the prophets, we fail to trust in the Lord and subject ourselves to the ultimate consequence of sin—separation from God.

> *8 Wherefore, how great the importance to make these things known unto the inhabitants of the earth, that they may know that there is no flesh that can dwell in the presence of God, save it be through the* ***merits, and mercy, and grace of the Holy Messiah,*** *who layeth down his life according to the flesh, and taketh it again by the power of the Spirit, that he may bring to pass the resurrection of the dead, being the first that should rise.*
>
> *9 Wherefore, he is the firstfruits unto God, inasmuch as he shall make intercession for all the children of men; and they that believe in him shall be saved.*
>
> *10 And because of the intercession for all, all men come unto God; wherefore, they stand in the presence of him, to be judged of him according to the truth and holiness which is in him. Wherefore, the ends of the law which the Holy One hath given, unto the inflicting of the punishment which is affixed, which punishment that is affixed is in opposition to that of the happiness which is affixed, to answer the ends of the* ***atonement—***

Merits, and mercy, and grace of the Holy Messiah; atonement

This wonderful passage (verse 8) is the only one in all of holy writ where the three key words *merits*, *mercy*, and *grace* are used together in relationship to the Atonement. Joseph Fielding Smith has summarized the dual blessings of the Atonement succinctly: "The atonement of our Savior is twofold in its benefits to mankind through the shedding of his blood. First, all mankind are redeemed from death and will receive the resurrection. This is the free gift of God. Second, it gives to all those who will repent of all their sins, redemption from their sins if they will accept and obey his gospel and endure to the end" (*Answers to Gospel Questions,* 5 vols. [Salt Lake City: Deseret Book, 1957–1966], 1:182).

Let us seek to understand and appreciate more fully the Atonement of Christ and share our understanding and thanksgiving with others. Gratitude will draw us closer to the Lord. This acts as a catalyst that brings about within us a change of attitude, leading to improved actions.

Memories: The Gap

Lehi, in his discourse to his son Jacob concerning the Atonement, states that "the law is given unto men. And by the law no flesh is justified . . ." (2 Nephi 2:5). The implication is inescapable: no mortal can ever live the law of God perfectly. Hence no mortal can ever be justified to return to

God's presence on the basis of a perfect record in abiding by the law. That is beyond mortal reach. Some may be more faithful than others in keeping the commandments, but none can do it perfectly. There will always be a gap in performance that must be bridged.

Over the years as a teacher I have observed with great interest when students have grappled with this paradox—which Lehi used effectively to cause Jacob and his other sons to focus on understanding the need for the Atonement. I will customarily draw two parallel, horizontal lines on the chalkboard, labeling the lower one mortality and the upper one perfection. Then I will ask the students to locate themselves in the blank space between the lines. "Where are you now in the process of perfection?" is the question. The dots will be placed at various points in the space defined by the two lines, but never will a dot be placed as high as the top line—perfection. There is always a gap between the highest dot and the top line. "So it appears that none of us can return to the presence of the Lord purely on the basis of being justified by the law, that is, through total obedience to the law. Correct?" They will always agree.

Then we read together the stirring testimony of Lehi concerning the Atonement as given in 2 Nephi 2:7–9. Lehi defines the way to bridge the "gap" through the "merits, and mercy, and grace of the Holy Messiah" (verse 8). How plain and simple is the logic. How persuasive is the doctrine. How beautiful is the message of hope and salvation. How exquisite is the text as a means of defining "grace." To conclude the exercise, I then write the name of the Savior on the chalkboard at the very place in the chart where the gap must be closed. In this way, we understand better how we are, in effect, beneficiaries of the grace of the Savior, who closes the gap for each individual, after all we can do. It is at that point that the meaning of being "perfect in Christ" (Moroni 10:32) becomes apparent. (Richard J. Allen)

> *11 For it must needs be, that there is an* ***opposition in all things.*** *If not so, my first-born in the wilderness, righteousness could not be brought to pass, neither wickedness, neither holiness nor misery, neither good nor bad. Wherefore, all things must needs be a compound in one; wherefore, if it should be one body it must needs remain as dead, having no life neither death, nor corruption nor incorruption, happiness nor misery, neither sense nor insensibility.*

Opposition in all things

Afflictions and challenges are part of the plan—a necessary element of our probationary test in mortality (see Abraham 3:25; D&C 29:39). They help us to grow and are ultimately for our good (see D&C 122:7).

How can we view opposition and adversity in a heavenly light and explain these things to others? Lehi skillfully teaches the doctrine of opposition in all things as eternal truth—a law upon which man is allowed to fulfill his destiny. The essence of mortality is that we are meant to face trials, tribulations, affliction, and adversity. Without such trials, there can be no joy. Growth and joy come from overcoming opposition with honor and courage. Just as afflictions are essential, so also are choices. There are inevitable consequences and blessings in all things as a result of our choices. The choices we make determine our destiny.

> *12 Wherefore, it must needs have been created for a thing of naught; wherefore there would have been* ***no purpose in the end of its creation.*** *Wherefore, this thing must needs destroy the wisdom of God and his eternal purposes, and also the power, and the mercy, and the justice of God.*

No purpose in the end of its creation

Elder Jeffrey R. Holland explains that goodness, holiness, and life would be dissolved in the absence of their opposites: wickedness, misery, and death. Opposition in all things brings illumination and meaning to the highest aspirations of mankind:

> A related principle Lehi introduced as another backdrop to the eternal drama of the Fall and the Atonement is that of opposition, of contending enticements, a concept closely linked with choice and agency. If choice is to exist and agency is to have any meaning, alternatives must be presented. As Lehi phrased it, "It must needs be, that there is an opposition in all things." [2 Nephi 2:11.] His reasoning and his vocabulary are clear and to the point. Righteousness has no meaning without the possibility of wickedness. Holiness would hold no delight unless we realized the pain of misery. Good could have no moral meaning if nothing could be considered bad. Even life—the nature and eternal possibilities of which are the subject of the plan of salvation and Lehi's discourse about it—would have no meaning if we knew nothing of the nature and limitations of death.
>
> In short, without opposites and alternatives, "there would have been no purpose in the . . . creation [of human life]." [2 Nephi 2:12.] All experiences in time and eternity would have been common, lifeless, indistinguishable—"a compound in one." [2 Nephi 2:11.] At the end of this sequence would be the

> worst realization of all. There could be no happiness because there was no sorrow, and there could be no righteousness because there was no sin. But fortunately, there are happiness, righteousness, eternal life, and God, even as Lehi stresses that those blessings come only at the risk of confronting misery, wickedness, death, and the devil. (*Christ and the New Covenant: The Messianic Message of the Book of Mormon* [Salt Lake City: Deseret Book, 1997], 202)

Memories: When Stumbling Blocks Are Stepping Stones

Opposition is here to stay. The attitude one has toward this "growth" requirement is essential to progress and happiness. A simple story concerning my friend John Covey teaches this principle beautifully. I went to the office of my friend for a little visit. We talked about our families and our callings in one of the BYU stakes. We continued and I asked how things were going? He responded, "Ed, I have this big problem I'm facing—but I'm really excited because when I achieve my goal I will have grown so much." I stood in awe of my friend. We must face life with a positive and hopeful attitude regardless of the situation. He taught me a wonderful lesson—that stumbling blocks are not problems; they are stepping stones for growth. (Ed J. Pinegar)

Memories: A Staircase of Tribulation

Several years ago it was my privilege to serve in a branch presidency at the Missionary Training Center in Provo, Utah. On one occasion, Elder Richard G. Scott was scheduled to speak at the general devotional services. He approached his assignment in an unusual way by inviting questions from the audience of several thousand new missionaries. One young elder asked the Apostle what to do when one came upon walls in life that seemed to act as barriers to progress. Elder Scott's thoughtful response was, in effect, that walls, when viewed from the right perspective, are not walls at all, but the vertical part of a step upward. Thus our attitude toward opposition in life can influence how we respond to adversity, and what might at first glance seem to be a barrier can turn out to be a step toward advancement. What positive and inspiring counsel!

As we rise above adversity through the help of the Lord, we advance another step upward. It is all in how you look at it and how you respond. "Know thou, my son, that all these things shall give thee experience, and shall be for thy good" is how the Lord answered the pleas of the suffering Joseph Smith (see D&C 122:7). And furthermore: "For after much tribulation come the blessings. Wherefore the day cometh that ye shall be crowned with much glory; the hour is not yet, but is nigh at hand" (D&C 58:4). A staircase of tribulation, when seen this way, is one that we would all be well advised to climb—in full faith and devotion. (Richard J. Allen)

13 Lehi continues with his discourse on opposition, explaining that any philosophy dispensing with the dimension of opposition would, in the end, bring about the dissolution of reality itself, including the reality of God.

> *14 And now, my sons, I speak unto you these things for your profit and learning; for there is a God, and he hath created all things, both the heavens and the earth, and all things that in them are,* ***both things to act and things to be acted upon.***
> *15 And to bring about his eternal purposes in the end of man, after he had created our first parents, and the beasts of the field and the fowls of the air, and in fine, all things which are created, it must needs be that there was an opposition; even the forbidden fruit in opposition to the tree of life; the one being sweet and the other bitter.*
> *16 Wherefore, the Lord God gave unto man that he should* ***act for himself.*** *Wherefore, man could not act for himself save it should be that he was enticed by the one or the other.*

BOTH THINGS TO ACT AND THINGS TO BE ACTED UPON; ACT FOR HIMSELF

Agency is a gift. The right to choose is necessary for our growth. We are a result of the use of our agency. Our choices determine the consequences of our actions. Agency can operate because there is (1) opposition in all things, (2) knowledge of good and evil, (3) laws and commandments given by God, and (4) the freedom to choose. This gift is better referred to as moral agency, which connotes responsibility and accountability in regard to choices (see Articles of Faith 1:2) You are free to choose liberty and eternal life or captivity and death (see 2 Nephi. 2:27).

Brigham Young gave inspired counsel concerning moral agency, its effects, and its blessings:

> All rational beings have an agency of their own; and according to their own choice they will be saved or damned. . . .
>
> The volition of the creature is free; this is a law of their existence and the Lord cannot violate his own law; were he to do that, he would cease to be God. He has placed life and death before his children, and it is for them to choose. If they choose life, they receive the blessing of life; if they choose death, they must abide the penalty. This is a law which has always existed from all eternity, and will continue to exist throughout all the eternities to come. Every intelligent being must have the power of choice, and God brings forth the results of the acts of his creatures to promote his Kingdom and subserve his purposes in the salvation and exaltation of his children. . . .

> He has given them the privilege of choosing for themselves, whether it be good or evil; but the result of our choice is still in his hand. All his children have the right of making a path for themselves of walking to the right or to the left, of telling the truth or that which is not true. This right God has given to all people who dwell on the earth, and they can legislate and act as they please; but God holds them in his hands, and he will bring forth the results of his glory, and for the benefit of those who love and serve him, and he will make the wrath of men to praise him. All of us are in the hands of that God. (*Discourses of Brigham Young*, comp. John A. Widtsoe [Salt Lake City: Deseret Book, 1954], 62)

Refusing to choose is also a choice, for passive neutrality also leads to consequences—often of a destructive nature. Let us cultivate the courage to make decisions based on eternal principles and act upon our righteous values.

17–21 Lehi recounts the fall of Lucifer from heaven and the creation of Adam and Eve, who partook of the forbidden fruit and brought about the fall of mankind.

> *21 And the days of the children of men were prolonged, according to the will of God, that they might repent while in the flesh; wherefore, their state* ***became a state of probation,*** *and their time was lengthened, according to the commandments which the Lord God gave unto the children of men. For he gave commandment that all men must repent; for he showed unto all men that they were lost, because of the transgression of their parents.*

Became a state of probation

Mortality is a time appointed for testing and probation, a time to prepare to meet God (see Alma 12:24). We prepare to meet God by keeping the commandments and taking upon ourselves the divine nature of Jesus Christ (see 2 Peter 1:3–10; Moroni 7:48; D&C 4). Let us remember that the work of Heavenly Father and our Savior Jesus Christ is to bring to pass our immortality and eternal life (see Moses 1:39).

In likening the words of Lehi to our own lives, we should remember that our mortal state is essentially a time to repent and keep the commandments.

> *22 And now, behold, if Adam had not transgressed he would not have fallen, but he would have remained in the garden of Eden. And all things which were created must*

have remained in the same state in which they were after they were created; and they
must have remained forever, and had no end.
23 And they would have had no children; wherefore they would have remained in a
state of innocence, having no joy, for they knew no misery; doing no good, for they
knew no sin.
24 But behold, all things have been done in the wisdom of him who knoweth all things.
25 ***Adam fell that men might be; and men are, that they might have joy.***

Adam fell that men might be; and men are, that they might have joy

Lehi was no stranger to adversity, tribulations, and challenges. He understood firsthand the goodness of God and the evils of Satan. Within Lehi's own family, there were great dichotomies: humility versus pride, spirituality versus selfishness, obedience versus rebellion. It is no wonder that the aging patriarch, in his parting discourse to his sons, sounded the eternal theme: "For it must needs be, that there is an opposition in all things. . . ." (2 Nephi 2:11). He could see with utter clarity that Laman and Lemuel and their followers, should they not change their prevailing lifestyle, would harvest a miserable destiny of darkness and death. Conversely, Nephi and his circle would enjoy untold blessings of the Lord based on their faithfulness and obedience. For Nephi, and all like him, there would be welcome meaning to the profound maxim uttered by Lehi: "Adam fell that men might be; and men are, that they might have joy" (2 Nephi 2:25).

EVIDENCE: The Role of Eve

Many modern religious scholars do not believe that Mother Eve used logic to convince Adam to partake of the forbidden fruit. Rather, they see her as using her feminine wiles to achieve her goal. But the Book of Mormon depicts an Eve that understands the consequences of *not* partaking of the forbidden fruit, an intelligent Eve who is a *helpmeet,* not a weak and subservient *helpmate.* The Hebrew word *ezer* ("help") is used in Genesis 2:18: "I will make him an help meet for him." Donald Parry declares that *ezer* generally applies to the Lord, and says that the divine connotation of the term shows that "Eve is emulating God himself when she becomes a help. She is working with Adam in a work that becomes a help. Certainly the term 'help' does not denote a lesser status or subordinating role, but an equal, or perhaps even superior, role." Similarly, in *Paradise Lost,* John Milton's Eve offers a compelling explanation to Adam as to why they should partake of the fruit and enter mortality. When he translated the Book of Mormon, Joseph Smith would have been familiar with biblical views on Eve, but probably not with Milton's uncommon views nor with the Hebrew meaning of her name. (See *Echoes,* 442–445.)

26 And the Messiah cometh in the fulness of time, that he may redeem the children of men from the fall. And because that they are redeemed from the fall they have become free forever, knowing good from evil; to act for themselves and not to be acted upon, save it be by the punishment of the law at the great and last day, according to the commandments which God hath given.
27 Wherefore, men are free according to the flesh; and all things are given them which are expedient unto man. And they are ***free to choose*** *liberty and eternal life, through the great Mediator of all men, or to choose captivity and death, according to the captivity and power of the devil; for he seeketh that all men might be miserable like unto himself.*

Free to Choose

This passage, along with Joshua's "choose you this day" (Joshua 24:15), is one of the most celebrated scriptures on moral agency. It raises an important question of conscience: Do our choices lead us to eternal life? Moral agency was given that all mankind would be accountable for their own actions (see D&C 101:78). Every choice has an impact in determining our destiny.

There Are Two Roads

David O. McKay explained the principle of agency using the following illustration:

> God is standing in the shadow of eternity, it seems to me, deploring the inevitable results of the follies, the transgressions and the sins of His wayward children, but we cannot blame Him for these any more than we can blame a father who might say to his son, "There are two roads, my son, one leading to the right, one leading to the left. If you take the one to the right it will lead you to success and to happiness. If you take the one to the left it will bring upon you misery and unhappiness and perhaps death, but you choose which you will. You must choose; I will not force either upon you." The young man starts out and, seeing the allurements and the attractiveness of the road to the left and thinking it a short cut to his happiness, he concludes to take it. The father knows what will become of him; he knows that not far from that flowery path there is a mire hole into which the boy will fall; he knows that after he struggles out of that mire hole he will come to a slough into which he will flounder. He sees others who have chosen that path in that same slough, and he knows that in their struggles to

> get on dry land there will be fighting. He could see it long before the boy reached that condition, and he could, therefore, foretell it. The father loves the boy just the same, and would still continue to warn him and plead for him to return to the right path.
>
> God, too, has shown the world, through His prophets in ages gone by, that many of His people, individuals as well as nations, would choose the path that leads to misery and to death, and He foretold it, but the responsibility is upon those who would not heed God's message, not upon God. (*Pathways to Happiness* [Salt Lake City: Bookcraft, 1957], 93–94)

Memories: Just Be Good . . . Just Be Good

A wayward child is not the sign of a failing parent. A failing parent is one who has not taught his or her children. We are not perfect, and the Lord is surely aware of that, but we are required to try with all our heart, might, mind, and strength to teach our children the gospel of Jesus Christ (see D&C 68:25–28). As parents we must never give in . . . never give out . . . and never give up. Life is fragile and filled with adversity.

My father passed away on Mother's Day 1947. I was the youngest in our family—a twelve-year-old deacon. I tried to be a good boy. I remember my angel mother when I would ask her what she wanted for her birthday, Mother's Day, and Christmas. The answer was always the same: "Oh Ed, I have everything one would need. I don't need anything." I would implore her, "Mom, I want to give you a present." Her answer for many years was the same, " Ed, just be good . . . just be good." This was from the heart of a loving, caring, and pleading mother. All she ever wanted for her children was for them to be good. Nothing else really mattered.

I know our joy and rejoicing is in our family—even as is our Heavenly Father's joy (see Moses 1:39). Having said all this, I know there are times when, after we have done all, our children may choose for a time to turn away from the truth. What do we do? We pray unceasingly (see Mosiah 27:14). We plead and exhort when moved upon by the Spirit (see D&C 100:5–6; D&C 121:41–44). We seek help from others. The goodness of God will then give us a sense of peace, knowing we have done all. Heavenly Father has done all in perfectness, and yet even in His infinite wisdom and power some of His children chose to disobey and follow Lucifer. Our lot is to humbly follow the Lord's advice: "Therefore, dearly beloved brethren, let us cheerfully do all things that lie in our power; and then may we stand still, with the utmost assurance, to see the salvation of God, and for his arm to be revealed" (D&C 123:17). (Ed J. Pinegar)

28 And now, my sons, I would that ye should look to ***the great Mediator,*** *and hearken unto his great commandments; and be faithful unto his words, and choose eternal life, according to the will of his Holy Spirit;*
29 And not choose eternal death, according to the will of the flesh and the evil which is therein, which giveth the spirit of the devil power to captivate, to bring you down to hell, that he may reign over you in his own kingdom.

The great Mediator

Elder Bruce R. McConkie shares this insight concerning the process of divine mediation:

> "Look to the great Mediator," Lehi said, "and hearken unto his great commandments; and be faithful unto his words, and choose eternal life, according to the will of his Holy Spirit." (2 Nephi 2:28). Our Lord's mission was to bring to pass "the great mediation of all men," meaning that in his capacity as Mediator he had power to intervene between God and man and effect a reconciliation. This mediation or reconciliation was affected through his atoning sacrifice, a sacrifice by means of which sinful men—by the proper use of agency—can wash away their guilt and place themselves in harmony with God. Men "are free to choose liberty and eternal life, through the great mediation of all men, or to choose captivity and death, according to the captivity and power of the devil." (2 Ne. 2:27.) Those choosing obedience receive the Holy Ghost, are reconciled to God in this world, and continue in his presence in the world to come. (*Mormon Doctrine*, 2nd ed., 472; *Doctrinal New Testament Commentary*, 3 vols. [Salt Lake City: Bookcraft, 1965–1973], 3:79)

30 I have spoken these few words unto you all, my sons, in the last days of my probation; and I have chosen the good part, according to the words of the prophet. And I have ***none other object*** *save it be the everlasting welfare of your souls. Amen.*

None other object

Both Lehi and Sariah are admirable examples of parents with a pure motivation for the eternal happiness and joy of their children. Thus, Lehi closes his mortal ministry with a plea to his children in which he lays out choices and the consequences of these choices with clarity and parental love, having no other object "save it be the everlasting welfare" of their souls (see 2 Nephi 2:30). His final loving exhortation to his children is the same counsel we should convey to our own families:

"Look to the great Mediator, and hearken unto his great commandments: and be faithful unto his words, and choose eternal life, according to the will of his Holy Spirit; And not choose eternal death, according to the will of the flesh and the evil which is therein, which giveth the spirit of the devil power to captivate" (2 Nephi 2:28–29).

CHAPTER 3

OVERVIEW

Lehi blesses his youngest son, Joseph. He teaches him about his heritage as a descendant of Joseph of Egypt and a partaker, with his posterity, of the glorious covenant blessings bestowed upon the house of Israel by the Lord. Lehi prophesies of a coming prophet, also named Joseph, who will be instrumental in restoring the gospel in the latter days.

1–5 Lehi blesses his last-born, **Joseph,** who is born in the wilderness. Lehi promises Joseph that his seed, if faithful, will endure and enjoy the security of the land of promise. Lehi identifies himself as a descendant of Joseph of Egypt, who foresaw in vision the unfolding of the history of the house of Israel, including Lehi's day and the latter-day restoration in which the Messiah would again manifest Himself and deliver the people from darkness.

Joseph, Son of Lehi

Joseph is the youngest of the sons of Lehi and Sariah, having been born in the wilderness like his older brother Jacob (see 1 Nephi 18:7). The experiences of his family are defined by severe contrasts: on the one hand, the honorable example of righteous parents and the nobility of brothers Nephi, Sam, and Jacob, and on the other hand, the rebellious and cruel behavior of Laman and Lemuel. Joseph is therefore exposed to constant heartache (see 1 Nephi 18:18–19).

As if to add comforting balance to a life of burden, Lehi gives Joseph a father's blessing in which the promises of the ancient patriarch, Joseph of Egypt, as preserved on the brass plates of Laban, are referenced to give hope and encouragement to the boy: Lehi promises young Joseph that he will participate in the Lord's design, as foretold by Joseph of old, to raise up a righteous branch of Israel that will preserve the word of God, that it might come forth in the latter days as a further confirmation of the divine mission of the Redeemer.

Joseph remembers the words of Lehi. He is to accompany Nephi and his righteous circle as they separate themselves from the wickedness of Laman and Lemuel (see 2 Nephi 5:6) and establishes a secure place where they can "live after the manner of happiness" (2 Nephi 5:27). Jacob and Joseph are both later consecrated as priests and teachers by the hand of Nephi (see Jacob 1:18) and they devote their energies and services to building up the kingdom of God all their days.

> *6 For Joseph truly testified, saying:* ***A seer*** *shall the Lord my God raise up, who shall be* ***a choice seer*** *unto the fruit of my loins.*
>
> *7 Yea, Joseph truly said: Thus saith the Lord unto me:* ***A choice seer*** *will I raise up out of the fruit of thy loins; and he shall be esteemed highly among the fruit of thy loins. And unto him will I give commandment that he shall do a work for the fruit of thy loins, his brethren, which shall be of great worth unto them, even to the bringing of them to the knowledge of the covenants which I have made with thy fathers.*
>
> *8 And I will give unto him a commandment that he shall do none other work, save the work which I shall command him. And I will make him great in mine eyes; for he shall do my work.*
>
> *9 And he shall be great* ***like unto Moses,*** *whom I have said I would raise up unto you, to deliver my people, O house of Israel.*
>
> *10 And Moses will I raise up, to deliver thy people out of the land of Egypt.*
>
> *11 But* ***a seer*** *will I raise up out of the fruit of thy loins; and unto him will I give power to bring forth my word unto the seed of thy loins—and not to the bringing forth my word only, saith the Lord, but to the convincing them of my word, which shall have already gone forth among them.*

A SEER, A CHOICE SEER

Lehi, who is separated from his unrighteous countrymen in Jerusalem by command of the Lord, has a special kinship with Joseph of Egypt, also a prophet of separation in the days of his father, Jacob, known as Israel (see Genesis 32:28). Lehi gives a benedictory patriarchal blessing to his youngest son, a namesake of the ancient Joseph, promising him, in effect, that he will also prevail with God in righteousness. As part of this blessing, Lehi cites passages from Joseph of Egypt, his direct ancestor, concerning a coming prophet, like unto Moses, who will do a great work in renewing the covenant promises of the Lord in the latter days. The reference is to Joseph Smith, the great Prophet of the Restoration. Joseph of Egypt, whose words are preserved on the brass plates of Laban, had looked forward in time to behold the ministry of his namesake, Joseph Smith.

EVIDENCE: LIKE UNTO MOSES—PROPHECY BY JOSEPH OF OLD (2 Nephi 3:5–15)
In the standard account in Genesis chapter 50, Joseph says to his brethren from his deathbed in Egypt, "God will surely visit you, and bring you out of this land," but reveals nothing about the Hebrews' future enslavement by the Egyptians. In 2 Nephi we read that Joseph in Egypt prophesied that God would send a prophet called Moses to deliver His people from Egyptian bondage. That this story is ancient is corroborated by Jewish tradition, particularly in a second-century translation of the Bible into Aramaic. In *Targum Neofiti,* we read of Joseph's interpretation of the butler's dream: "The three branches are the three fathers of the world: namely; Abraham, Isaac, and Jacob, the sons of whose sons are to be enslaved in the slavery of the hand of Egypt."

It should be noted that Joseph Smith's translation of the Bible contains the patriarch Joseph's prophecy that his people would be enslaved by the Egyptians (see *Echoes,* 238–240).

12–15 Lehi cites the prophecy of Joseph of Egypt that the writings of his posterity will one day be blended with the writings of the Jews (the Bible) in order to establish peace and renew the knowledge of sacred covenants. Unto this end, a modern seer will be raised up and blessed to prevail in his ministry.

> *15 And his name shall be* ***called after me;*** *and it shall be after the name of his father. And he shall be like unto me; for the thing, which the Lord shall bring forth by his hand, by the power of the Lord shall bring my people unto salvation.*

CALLED AFTER ME
In a remarkable concurrence of names, Lehi instructs his son Joseph concerning Joseph of Egypt, who foresaw the work of Joseph Smith Jr., son of Joseph Smith Sr.

Brigham Young, successor to the martyred Prophet, stated:

> I honor and revere the name of Joseph Smith. I delight to hear it; I love it. I love his doctrine. . . . I feel like shouting Hallelujah, all the time, when I think that I ever knew Joseph Smith, the Prophet whom the Lord raised up and ordained, and to whom he gave keys and power to build up the kingdom of God on earth and sustain it. These keys are committed to this people, and we have power to continue the work that Joseph commenced, until everything is prepared for the coming of the Son of Man. This is the business of the Latter-day Saints, and it is all the business we have on hand. (*Discourses of Brigham Young,* comp. John A. Widtsoe [Salt Lake City: Deseret Book, 1954], 458).

16–21 Lehi continues his quotations from Joseph of Egypt, who has prophesied that the Lord will one day bring forth the writings of his seed even as "from the dust" (verse 19)—namely the Book of Mormon, translated by Joseph Smith through the power of God.

The Grand Design

It has often amused me to note the incredulity of those unfamiliar with the Church when they learn that the founder was a young man of little formal education who arose from obscurity to claim that he was called of God and supported in his ministry by angelic messengers. "How could a credible work come from a nobody?" "How could a divine movement stem from such backward and accidental circumstances?" Such is the essence of their attitude concerning Joseph Smith.

Accident indeed! As Joseph made clear a few weeks before his martyrdom, he believed that his calling was premortal in nature: "Every man who has a calling to minister to the inhabitants of the world was ordained to that very purpose in the Grand Council of heaven before this world was. I suppose that I was ordained to this very office in that Grand Council. It is the testimony that I want that I am God's servant, and this people His people" (*HC,* 6:364).

We learn from Joseph of Egypt that the future Prophet, a man who "shall be great like unto Moses" (2 Nephi 3:9), would be called "after the name of his father." And indeed, there was a Joseph Smith Sr., who was born in 1773, about as many years *after* the birth of Christ as Joseph of Egypt was born *before* Christ.

The grand design of heaven came full circle on September 21, 1823, when the young Joseph Smith was retiring for the night in his family's log home at Manchester, New York. Let us look in on the scene: He prays earnestly for forgiveness of his sins and with patient confidence that his prayer will be answered seeks a divine manifestation to know his standing before the Lord. While yet in prayer he receives a heavenly visitation from a glorious angel, known anciently as Moroni, who informs Joseph that God had a work for him to do, and that his name "should be had for good and evil among all nations, kindreds, and tongues, or that it should be both good and evil spoken of among all people" (*HC,* 1:11–12). Moroni tells Joseph of the existence of a book "written upon gold plates, giving an account of the former inhabitants of this continent," containing "the fulness of the everlasting Gospel" (12). He quotes prophecies of Malachi that are about to be fulfilled and tells Joseph of his role in their fulfillment. Moroni repeats his visitation twice during the night, adding more knowledge each time. After the third visit Joseph hears the cock crow, announcing a new day and confirming the dawning of a new dispensation of the gospel—the dispensation of the fulness of times and the restoration of all things. The following morning Joseph is again visited by Moroni and allowed to see the gold plates for the first time—uncovered from their burial spot in nearby Hill Cumorah. Thus was laid the foundation of the young man's prophetic calling in bringing forth "a book that is sealed" (Isaiah 29:11), constituting an important part of the Lord's "marvellous work and a wonder," long foretold (see Isaiah 29:14). What Joseph of Egypt had foreseen was taking place not by accident, but according to the grand design of heaven established from before the foundations of the earth for the salvation and exaltation of mankind. (Richard J. Allen)

22–25 Lehi concludes his remarks to his youngest son, Joseph, reminding him that his future namesake will perform mighty miracles on behalf of the covenants of the Lord. Lehi encourages his son to hearken unto the words of his older brother, Nephi, and look forward to a fulfillment of the glorious promises of the Lord.

Memories: A Prophet's Testimony of Joseph

Many years ago we lived next door to Ernie Wilkins and his wonderful family. Ernie was married to Maurine Lee, the daughter of president Harold B. Lee. President Lee would often come down to visit. One day when I was going out to get the mail, I noticed President Lee standing in the front yard of their home. I had met him before but was still nervous in going over and saying hello and striking up a conversation. Fear fled and I girded up my courage and went over and said hello. We visited and I asked him some questions and said that I sustained him with all my heart.

As I started to leave he said, "Wait, Brother Pinegar. I want to tell you something about the Prophet Joseph." He said, "You mentioned that you sustain me as a prophet today and I am grateful for your faith and prayers. I want you to know how I love and sustain the prophet of the dispensation of the fulness of times—the Prophet Joseph. Yes, I am a prophet today, but Joseph—he was the prophet of the Restoration. I love and revere the Prophet Joseph." I felt the depth of his love for the Prophet Joseph and the sincerity of his heart. I shall never forget the testimony of a prophet of God of the Prophet Joseph Smith. (Ed J. Pinegar)

CONCLUDING THOUGHTS

The words of John Taylor, incorporated into the Doctrine and Covenants as Section 135, include this praise for the Prophet, whose martyrdom he witnessed:

> Joseph Smith, the Prophet and Seer of the Lord, has done more, save Jesus only, for the salvation of men in this world, than any other man that ever lived in it. In the short space of twenty years, he has brought forth the Book of Mormon, which

> he translated by the gift and power of God, and has been the means of publishing it on two continents; has sent the fulness of the everlasting gospel, which it contained, to the four quarters of the earth; has brought forth the revelations and commandments which compose this book of Doctrine and Covenants, and many other wise documents and instructions for the benefit of the children of men; gathered many thousands of the Latter-day Saints, founded a great city, and left a fame and name that cannot be slain. He lived great, and he died great in the eyes of God and his people; and like most of the Lord's anointed in ancient times, has sealed his mission and his works with his own blood; and so has his brother Hyrum. In life they were not divided, and in death they were not separated! (D&C 135:3)

CHAPTER 4

OVERVIEW

Nephi comments on the prophecies of Joseph of Egypt pertaining to his posterity. Lehi blesses his grandchildren and counsels them to be righteous. He passes away and is buried. Nephi expresses his deepest thoughts about life—rejoicing in the goodness of God and praising Him for the blessings that flow to us through His love and mercy.

> *1 AND now, I, Nephi, speak concerning the prophecies of which my father hath spoken,*
> *concerning Joseph, who was carried into Egypt.*
> *2 For behold, he truly prophesied concerning all his seed. And the prophecies which he*
> *wrote, there are not many greater. And he prophesied concerning us, and our future*
> *generations; and they are* ***written upon the plates of brass.***

Written upon the plates of brass

It was Nephi who, at the peril of his life, retrieved the brass plates of Laban according to the commandments of God. Surely Nephi must have rejoiced to witness the power of the scriptural message from his ancestor, Joseph, as cited by Lehi. Nephi now comments on the promises of God concerning Lehi's posterity conveyed through Joseph's prophesies. Those in the latter days who are of the lineage of Joseph, through Ephraim and Manasseh, can also rejoice to know the origin of the covenant blessings to which they have access by the goodness and mercy of a loving Father in

Heaven. That is one of the key benefits for students of the Book of Mormon, according to Moroni's preface, "that they may know the covenants of the Lord."

> *3 Wherefore, after my father had made an end of speaking concerning the prophecies of Joseph, he called* ***the children*** *of Laman, his sons, and his daughters, and said unto them: Behold, my sons, and my daughters, who are the sons and the daughters of my first-born, I would that ye should give ear unto my words.*
> *4 For the Lord God hath said that: Inasmuch as ye shall keep my commandments ye shall prosper in the land; and inasmuch as ye will not keep my commandments ye shall be cut off from my presence.*
> *5 But behold, my sons and my daughters, I cannot go down to my grave save I should leave a blessing upon you; for behold, I know that if ye are* ***brought up in the way*** *ye should go ye will not depart from it.*

The children; brought up in the way

Lehi comes to the end of a long and productive life. Just as Jacob of old had done, Lehi offers patriarchal exhortations to his sons.

But Lehi does not stop there. He gathers his grandchildren about him to impress upon them his principal patriarchal message: obey and prosper or disobey and be cast off. He reminds them that if they are "brought up in the way [they] should go," they will not depart from it.

Parents today are anxiously concerned about the welfare and spiritual growth of their children and grandchildren. For those, like Lehi and Sariah, who observe that some of their children are falling by the wayside, the encouraging words of John Taylor come to mind, for he gave assurances that "Your Sons and Daughters Will Be Saved":

> God has fulfilled His promises to us, and our prospects are grand and glorious. Yes, in the next life we will have . . . our sons and daughters. If we do not get them all at once, we will have them some time. . . . You that are mourning about your children straying away will have your sons and your daughters. If you succeed in passing through these trials and afflictions and receive a resurrection, you will, by the power of the priesthood, work and labor, as the Son of God has, until you get all your sons and daughters in the path of exaltation and glory. This is just as sure as that the sun rose this morning over yonder mountains. Therefore, mourn not because all your sons and daughters do not follow in the path that you have

marked out to them, or give heed to your counsels. Inasmuch as we succeed in securing eternal glory, and stand as saviors, and as kings and priests to our God, we will save our posterity. (*Millennial Star,* 22 January 1894, 51–52)

Two Levels of Love

What special message would you have for your children and other family members if you knew your time was drawing nigh? There are in the scriptures detailed accounts of several occasions where prophets have provided remarkable benedictory pronouncements on their children: the blessings that Jacob (Israel) gave to his sons (see Genesis 49), the blessings of Lehi for his sons and their families (see 2 Nephi 1–4); and the counsel of Alma for his sons Helaman, Shiblon, and Corianton (see Alma 36–42). Under similar circumstances, during the stressful Liberty Jail episode, the Prophet Joseph Smith provided his family with tender communications that demonstrated his love and concern for his wife and children.

In a letter dated March 21, 1839, to Emma, with the salutation "Affectionate Wife," the Prophet Joseph wrote: "I have sent an Epistle to the church directed to you because I wanted you to have the first reading of it and then I want Father and Mother to have a copy of it. Keep the original yourself as I dictated the matter myself and shall send another as soon as possible" (*The Personal Writings of Joseph Smith*, comp. Dean C. Jessee [Salt Lake City: Deseret Book, 1984], 408; text modernized in some places). By "Epistle" he means his inspired composition dated March 20, 1839, that contains the material subsequently excerpted as Sections 121, 122, and 123 of the Doctrine and Covenants (see *HC,* 3:289–305).

It is instructive that he wanted Emma to be the first to read this extraordinary document, and then to have his parents be the next ones to read it. That shows two levels of love on the part of the Prophet—charity, or "the pure love of Christ" (Moroni 7:47), and familial love, or the deep and abiding affection between husband and wife and within the larger family circle. By sharing the inspiring and edifying epistle, the Prophet wanted to bestow on Emma and his parents the hope, courage, faith, and love that are inseparable elements of a "godly walk and conversation" (D&C 20:69), even at times of extreme adversity. By wanting Emma and his parents to be the first to read the document, the Prophet was extending a warm and affectionate personal privilege to those closest to him in the world. (Richard J. Allen)

6–10 Lehi completes his blessings to his grandchildren and also the sons of Ishmael and all of his household.

> *11 And after he had made an end of speaking unto them, he spake unto Sam, saying: Blessed art thou, and thy seed; for thou shalt inherit the land like unto thy brother Nephi. And thy seed shall be numbered with his seed; and thou shalt be* ***even like unto thy brother,*** *and thy seed like unto his seed; and thou shalt be* ***blessed in all thy days.***

Even like unto thy brother; blessed in all thy days

Sam, the third son of Lehi and Sariah, is given a special blessing by his father, including the prophecy that he will be like Nephi and that his posterity will be like Nephi's posterity. What more encouraging promise could there be for a son than to be like the paragon of obedience and spiritual purity represented by a brother such as Nephi? And what more glorious forecast for one's life could there be than to be "blessed in all thy days"? Lehi's vision enables him to foresee the persisting goodness of his son over the years.

> *12 And it came to pass after my father, Lehi, had spoken unto all his household, according to the feelings of his heart and the Spirit of the Lord which was in him, he waxed old. And it came to pass that* ***he died, and was buried.***

He died, and was buried

With Lehi's passing, we see the transition into the spiritual realm of a man who has played two eternal roles: that of a loving and exemplary parent, and that of a prophet or servant of God. All parents in Zion play these two roles—for all have the opportunity to be guardians of, and counselors to, their families while at the same time all have callings of various kinds in the Church and kingdom of heaven. That raises an important question of conscience for us all: Do we infuse our dual roles with optimum balance and devotion, as did Lehi? Do we blend our service to God and family in such a way that the Spirit can guide us to be effective on both fronts?

> *13* ***And it came to pass*** *that not many days after his death, Laman and Lemuel and the sons of Ishmael were angry with me because of the admonitions of the Lord.*

EVIDENCE: And It Came to Pass

And it came to pass is the translation of a Hebrew expression often used in scripture. Though the Hebrew form is found over 1,200 times in the Bible, it is translated just 727 times as "and it came to pass" in the King James Version, probably because the translators considered the expression repetitive. Often the translators simply left the phrase out or translated it as "and it was," "and it became," or "and." Because of the Book of Mormon's Semitic origin, and because the book comprises histories and chronologies similar to those in the Old Testament, we would expect the phrase *and it came to pass* to be an integral feature of the book—and it is. (See *Echoes,* 163–164.)

Memories: Grand Miracles

While I was serving as bishop in a ward in Maryland many years ago, a young student called me on the phone with a request. Claiming to be doing a report on the Mormon Church for one of her classes, she wanted to know if I could tell her how many times it says "and it came to pass" in the Book of Mormon. I told her that the phrase does indeed occur rather frequently in the book—perhaps as often as it says in the Bible "verily, verily I say unto you"—but I was not certain of the exact total. So I told her something of the spiritual nature of the book and suggested that she read it and keep track of the count. From her attitude I could discern that her interest was to discredit, rather than to learn, the truth.

I have often thought of this incident as an example of how people overlook the miraculous nature of the Book of Mormon. Here is a lengthy and complex chronicle of God's dealings with covenant peoples in America that was brought forth by the gift and power of God in less than three months of actual working time, with no significant changes after the fact, beyond the correction of a few printing errors and subsequent divisions into chapter and verse. The Book of Mormon has been a compass of spiritual guidance and inspiration for countless millions of people since its appearance in 1830 as a text that has since been subtitled "Another Testament of Jesus Christ."

No less a miracle than the book itself is the means by which it is distributed and witnessed in the world through more than 50,000 missionaries serving at their own expense for one to two years in hundreds of missions throughout the world. In addition, a further miracle in the stakes and wards of the Church allows hundreds of thousands of converts to receive fellowship and strengthen their testimonies of the truthfulness of the Book of Mormon and the restored gospel.

The young girl who coyly asked about the phrase "and it came to pass" would be well counseled to prayerfully read the volume with a sincere desire to learn. The result of such a quest would be this: a marvelous miracle would "come to pass" in her own life. (Richard J. Allen)

> *14 For I, Nephi, was constrained to speak unto them, according to his word; for I had spoken many things unto them, and also my father, before his death; many of which sayings are written upon mine other plates; for a more history part are written upon mine other plates.*

2 Nephi 4:15–17

> *15 And upon these I write the things of my soul, and many of the scriptures which are engraven upon the plates of brass. For* ***my soul delighteth in the scriptures,*** *and my heart pondereth them, and writeth them for the learning and the profit of my children.*
> *16 Behold, my soul* ***delighteth*** *in the things of the Lord; and my heart* ***pondereth*** *continually upon the things which I have seen and heard.*

My soul delighteth in the scriptures

How do we feel about the scriptures? Do we delight in them? Do we ponder them? The scriptures, the word of God, are given that we might increase our faith and know how to live a Christlike life. We are counseled to feast upon the word of God (see 2 Nephi 32:3) and live by every word that comes forth of God (see D&C 84:43–46). Remember, the word of God is the rod of iron that leads to the tree of life.

> *17 Nevertheless, notwithstanding the great goodness of the Lord, in showing me his great and marvelous works,* ***my heart exclaimeth:*** *O wretched man that I am! Yea, my heart sorroweth because of my flesh; my soul grieveth because of mine iniquities.*

My heart exclaimeth

It is natural and appropriate that every follower of Christ should seek to express feelings about the gospel and the Savior in the most humble and yet eloquent terms of praise and love possible. Nephi's psalm, which begins with verse 17 and extends through verse 35, is a memorable example of this kind of spiritual utterance.

Consider what Nephi has gone through: As a young man he is uprooted with little warning from his native environment to spend eight years in the desert, enduring adversity of all kinds, including life-threatening torment at the hands of his older brothers. Then he completes a sometimes perilous sea journey to a strange new land where every manner of challenge has to be met. His father, the spiritual anchor of the family, has just passed away, and the older brothers again take up their aggressive assault against him, which soon forces him and his immediate circle, upon divine warning, to again flee into the wilderness and start anew. Amid such uncertainties and despite his tribulations, Nephi expresses gratitude for divine guidance and heartfelt love for the Lord.

The Psalm of Nephi (see 2 Nephi 4:17–35) creates a bond between Nephi and all of us. We all struggle with sin and temptation, and we all have deep feelings of gratitude for the gospel plan and the Atonement. We, like Nephi, know that we must trust in the Lord, receive His love with thanksgiving, and recognize His gifts to us in all things. As we read and re-read the Psalm of Nephi, we can let his words resonate within us and then ponder what thoughts and utterances we might wish to generate as an expression of our own personal situation before God and our gratitude for His love and mercy. We can let the "Psalm of [our own names]" become a mirror of our own devotion and reverence for the Lord and a testimony of our own certainty in the blessings of the Atonement.

The Psalm of Nephi—Plight and Joy of our Earthly Existence

18 I am encompassed about, because of the temptations and the sins which do so easily beset me.

19 And when I desire to rejoice, ***my heart groaneth because of my sins;*** *nevertheless, I know in whom I have trusted.*

20 My God hath been my support; he hath led me through mine afflictions in the wilderness; and he hath preserved me upon the waters of the great deep.

21 He hath filled me with his love, even unto the consuming of my flesh.

22 He hath confounded mine enemies, unto the causing of them to quake before me.

23 Behold, he hath heard my cry by day, and he hath given me knowledge by visions in the night-time.

24 And by day have I waxed bold in mighty prayer before him; yea, my voice have I sent up on high; and angels came down and ministered unto me.

25 And upon the wings of his Spirit hath my body been carried away upon exceedingly high mountains. And ***mine eyes have beheld great things,*** *yea, even too great for man; therefore I was bidden that I should not write them.*

26 O then, if I have seen so great things, if the Lord in his condescension unto the children of men hath visited men in so much mercy, why should my heart weep and my soul linger in the valley of sorrow, and my flesh waste away, and my strength slacken, because of mine afflictions?

27 And why should I yield to sin, because of my flesh? Yea, why should I give way to temptations, that the evil one have place in my heart to destroy my peace and afflict my soul? Why am I angry because of mine enemy?

28 ***Awake, my soul! No longer droop in sin.*** *Rejoice, O my heart, and give place no more for the enemy of my soul.*

29 Do not anger again because of mine enemies. Do not slacken my strength because of mine afflictions.

*30 **Rejoice, O my heart,** and cry unto the Lord, and say: O Lord, I will praise thee*
forever; yea, my soul will rejoice in thee, my God, and the rock of my salvation.
31 O Lord, wilt thou redeem my soul? Wilt thou deliver me out of the hands of mine
enemies? Wilt thou make me that I may shake at the appearance of sin?
32 May the gates of hell be shut continually before me, because that my heart is broken and
my spirit is contrite! O Lord, wilt thou not shut the gates of thy righteousness before me,
that I may walk in the path of the low valley, that I may be strict in the plain road!
*33 O Lord, wilt thou **encircle me around in the robe of thy righteousness!** O Lord,*
wilt thou make a way for mine escape before mine enemies! Wilt thou make my path
straight before me! Wilt thou not place a stumbling block in my way—but that thou
wouldst clear my way before me, and hedge not up my way, but the ways of mine enemy.
*34 O Lord, I have trusted in thee, and **I will trust in thee forever.** I will not put my*
trust in the arm of flesh; for I know that cursed is he that putteth his trust in the arm
of flesh. Yea, cursed is he that putteth his trust in man or maketh flesh his arm.
35 Yea, I know that God will give liberally to him that asketh. Yea, my God will give
me, if I ask not amiss; therefore I will lift up my voice unto thee; yea, I will cry unto
thee, my God, the rock of my righteousness. Behold, my voice shall forever ascend up
*unto thee, **my rock and mine everlasting God.** Amen.*

My Heart Groaneth Because of My Sins; Mine Eyes Have Beheld Great Things; Awake, My Soul! No Longer Droop in Sin; Rejoice, O My Heart; Encircle Me Around in the Robe of Thy Righteousness; I Will Trust in Thee Forever; My Rock and Mine Everlasting God

These themes of grandeur flow with persuasive power and touch our hearts. Much like the psalms of David, the psalm of Nephi is a summary of the life of a prophet of God and his triumph in breaking through the challenges of mortality and emerging into the dawn of the eternal light of the Lord.

A Psalm for Us All

Nephi's psalm can relate to all of us. Nephi, in his humble and self-effacing psalm, helps all of us in our trials and tribulations here upon the earth. It seems that each of us has experienced feelings similar to those of Nephi. Thus we can understand that the psalm becomes one of the great applications to life in the Book of Mormon to help us and give us hope.

1. He recognizes the goodness of God—as should we.
2. He laments and has sorrow for sin—as should we.
3. He struggles with temptation and sin—as do we.
4. He seeks joy and trusts in the Lord despite sorrows—as should we.
5. He acknowledges the support of the Lord—as should we.
6. He is filled with the love of the Lord—and we can be too.
7. His enemies are confounded—and ours can be too.
8. His prayers are answered—and ours can be too.
9. He is filled with the Spirit—and we can be too.
10. He is blessed by the condescension of the Lord—and so are we.
11. He recognizes with all these blessings that there is a choice to make: Why does he linger in sorrow, slacken because of his afflictions, yield to sin, give way to temptations, and become angry because of his enemies? Stop, he says, and start anew: We are to awaken our souls (get up and get going and be positive about life), because we can rejoice in the Lord and praise Him forever because He is the rock of our salvation.
12. He pleads with the Lord to redeem his soul—as should we.
13. He seeks help to overcome his enemies—as should we.
14. He seeks help to shake at the very appearance of sin (to abhor sin)—as should we.
15. He seeks that the gates of hell will be closed because of his broken heart and contrite spirit—and we can qualify too.
16. He wants to walk in the low valley (walk with the Lord . . . be obedient)—as should we.
17. He pleads with the Lord for the robe of righteousness, a way to escape, a straight path, and help against his enemies—and so can we.
18. He trusts in the Lord in all things and not in the arm of flesh—and so must we.
19. He has faith that the Lord would give to him what he asks for so long as he does not ask amiss—as must we.
20. He will continue to pray and depend upon the rock of his righteousness—and so must we.

The Psalm of Nephi can help us in all that we do. (Ed J. Pinegar)

2 Nephi 4:35

Memories: Where Is the Poetry?

While serving as a young missionary in Germany, I recall speaking with a highly educated and very articulate older woman concerning the Book of Mormon. It was encouraging when she agreed to read the Book of Mormon, especially since we had testified of its divine source (something that not infrequently dissuaded the self-satisfied to look no further). Upon one of our return visits, I asked her for her impressions of the book. Her response was instructive. She said that she was very conversant with the Bible, especially with the poetic sections of the Old Testament, such as the Psalms, which she read regularly with much benefit. The Book of Mormon was interesting, she reported, but it contained no uplifting poetry such as she admired in the Bible.

To this we could only respond by drawing her attention to the plain and precious gospel truths contained in the Book of Mormon, often expressed with directness and clarity so that they could not be misunderstood. Although we encouraged her to continue with her reading, we could tell that she was not looking at this material in the context of scripture, but rather out of an aesthetic interest. She wanted to be lifted poetically rather than spiritually. Thus we eventually moved on to others more open to the message of the restored gospel.

Over the years I have thought about this woman, wishing that I had asked her at the time to pay particular attention to certain passages from the Book of Mormon, especially 2 Nephi Chapter 4, which contains what is often called the "Psalm of Nephi" (see 2 Nephi 4:17–35). This magnificent outpouring of Nephi's personal witness about truth and the commitment to righteous living is a poetic testament to God's goodness and the need of man to rise above human weakness and trust implicitly in the Lord.

While it is true that the Book of Mormon does not contain an abundance of psalmic literature such as that found in the Old Testament, it does contain many passages of unsurpassed beauty. Besides the Psalm of Nephi, one can point to Mormon's lament concerning his grief over the demise of the great Nephite nation (see Mormon 6:16–22), beginning "And my soul was rent with anguish" (Mormon 6:16). There is also Jacob's soaring statement that begins, "Behold, great and marvelous are the works of the Lord" (Jacob 4:8–10), or King Limhi's metaphoric expression about the frailties of men—"Yea, they are as a wild flock" (Mosiah 8:21), or Ammon's extraordinary statements about the "Lord of the Harvest" (Alma 26:5–8), or Zenos' expressive treatment about prayer (see Alma 33:3–11), or Alma on cultivating faith as a seed (see Alma 32) and his memorable admonition to his son Helaman to counsel with the Lord (see Alma 37:35–37). Such passages provide ample confirmation that prophets other than those of ancient Israel could express spiritual truth in language of power and beauty.

In the final analysis, however, it is not the words, but rather the Word, that makes the difference. It is not the beauty of language, per se, but the confirmation of the Spirit of God that prophetic utterance, being the key to repentance and salvation, can change lives for the better and draw people closer to the Master. (Richard J. Allen)

CONCLUDING THOUGHTS

We can rejoice in the blessings of the covenant. We can seek, like Lehi and Sariah, to guide our families in the way of truth and light. We can be consoled by the Psalm of Nephi. We can trust in our God, who has given us living prophets to guide and direct us here upon the earth. Our task is to follow them as if the words they speak were given by our Savior Himself.

CHAPTER 5

OVERVIEW

Out of jealousy and anger, Laman and Lemuel seek to kill Nephi. Nephi follows the Lord's counsel and flees with his circle of followers into the wilderness. Thus Laman and his followers are separated from the anchor of the gospel and the Nephites and Lamanites become two separate nations.

> *The Nephites separate themselves from the Lamanites, keep the law of Moses, and build a temple—Because of their unbelief, the Lamanites are cursed, receive a skin of blackness, and become a scourge unto the Nephites. About 588–559 B.C.*

1–4 Nephi cries unto the Lord because of the anger of Laman and Lemuel, who seek to take away his life because he has usurped (they claim) their rightful power of leadership.

> *5 And it came to pass that the Lord did warn me, that I, Nephi, should depart from them and* ***flee into the wilderness,*** *and all those who would go with me.*
> *6 Wherefore, it came to pass that I, Nephi, did take my family, and also Zoram and his family, and Sam, mine elder brother and his family, and Jacob and Joseph, my younger brethren, and also my sisters, and all those who would go with me. And all those who would go with me were those who believed in the warnings and the revelations of God; wherefore, they did hearken unto my words.*

2 Nephi 5:7–10

> *7 And we did take our tents and whatsoever things were possible for us, and did* ***journey in the wilderness*** *for the space of many days. And after we had journeyed for the space of many days we did pitch our tents.*

FLEE INTO THE WILDERNESS; JOURNEY IN THE WILDERNESS

Following the death of Lehi, the older sons, Laman and Lemuel, resume their rebelliousness. When their murmuring turns to murderous design, Nephi is warned of the Lord to flee, and he and his righteous associates separate themselves so that they might "live after the manner of happiness" (2 Nephi 5:27). With Nephi's departure, Laman and Lemuel lose the anchor of gospel strength. They are in effect separated from God, which is the ultimate consequence of sin. We separate ourselves from God, in effect, when we reject His word and fail to follow the living prophet.

Thus the Nephites and the Lamanites become separate nations. The latter embrace idleness and wickedness; the former establish a Christ-centered lifestyle based on industry, self-reliance, and temple worship.

8–9 The followers of Nephi call their new venue "Nephi" and refer to themselves as "the people of Nephi."

> *10 And we did observe to keep* ***the judgments,*** *and* ***the statutes,*** *and* ***the commandments*** *of the Lord in all things, according to* ***the law*** *of Moses.*

EVIDENCE: THE JUDGMENTS, THE STATUTES, THE COMMANDMENTS, THE LAW—REPETITION OF "THE"

In English, a writer or speaker can introduce a list of nouns with a single article such as *the.* However, in Hebrew, the article is repeated before each noun. For example, in 2 Nephi 5:10, we read: "We did observe to keep the judgments, and the statutes, and the commandments of the Lord." If Joseph Smith had written the Book of Mormon rather than translating it by the power of God, he would have probably worded this sentence in a more modern way, i.e., "We did observe to keep the judgments, statutes, and commandments of the Lord." But he did not do so, and thus left for us yet another footprint of the divine influence upon the record called the Book of Mormon. (See *Echoes,* 176.)

EVIDENCE: HEBREW TERMS: JUDGMENTS, STATUTES, COMMANDMENT, LAW

Upon reading this passage in 2 Nephi, one might wonder why Nephi did not simply state that his people were "strict to observe the law." Instead, he explains that they observed the *law, statutes, judgments,* and *commandments* of the Lord. The Hebrew language uses several words to imply different semantic aspects and subtle nuances of the English word *law.* One example is the word *mishpat*, which means "judgment" or passing a verdict; this concept embraces most phases of a legal trial. Another example is the word *torah,* a word that connotes more than just "the law" in the modern sense. *Torah* is derived from the verb yarah, meaning "to show, to instruct, to teach." Joseph Smith, untrained in the Hebraic language when he translated the Book of Mormon, could not have understood the innate complexities of Nephi's phrase (see *Echoes,* 353–56).

11 And the Lord was with us; and we did ***prosper*** *exceedingly; for we did* ***sow*** *seed, and we did* ***reap*** *again in abundance. And we began to* ***raise flocks,*** *and herds, and animals of every kind.*
12 And I, Nephi, had also ***brought the records*** *which were engraven upon the plates of brass; and also the ball, or compass, which was prepared for my father by the hand of the Lord, according to that which is written.*
13 And it came to pass that we began to ***prosper*** *exceedingly, and to* ***multiply*** *in the land.*
14 And I, Nephi, did take the sword of Laban, and after the manner of it did make ***many swords,*** *lest by any means the people who were now called Lamanites should come upon us and destroy us; for I knew their hatred toward me and my children and those who were called my people.*
15 And I did teach my people to ***build buildings,*** *and to work in all manner of wood, and of iron, and of copper, and of brass, and of steel, and of gold, and of silver, and of precious ores, which were in great abundance.*

Prosper; raise flocks; brought the records; multiply; many swords; build buildings

Nephi is the prototype of the enlightened leader who leads his people toward prosperity and productivity. Industry, learning, self-sufficiency, family growth, defense, community expansion, construction—all of these actions promote prosperity and well-being for a people. At the heart of this philosophy is the written word of God, which Nephi has brought with him and applied on behalf of his people. How can we better apply the example of Nephi for the security and happiness of our own families and communities? How can we better combine practical learning, spirituality, and leadership to bless our children and the coming generations?

EVIDENCE: BUILD BUILDINGS—COGNATE ACCUSATIVE

In the grammatical construction referred to as the cognate accusative, a noun is used with a same-root verb, as in Genesis 37:5, where we learn that Joseph "dreamed a dream." In English, we would normally phrase this as "Joseph had a dream." Many examples of the cognate accusative exist in the Hebrew Bible, though this form is not apparent in most translations. The Book of Mormon includes many uses of the cognate accusative, such as "I will work a great and a marvelous work" (1 Nephi 14:7), "This was the desire which I desired of him (Enos 1:13), "build buildings" (2 Nephi 5:15, Mosiah 23:5), "succor those that stand in need of your succor" (Mosiah 4:16), and "judge righteous judgment" (Mosiah 29:29, 43). Again we perceive the footprint of divine influence in the wording used in the Book of Mormon (see *Echoes,* 177).

> *16 And I, Nephi, did build a* ***temple;*** *and I did construct it after the manner of the temple of Solomon save it were not built of so many precious things; for they were not to be found upon the land, wherefore, it could not be built like unto Solomon's temple. But the manner of the construction was like unto the temple of Solomon; and the workmanship thereof was exceedingly fine.*

EVIDENCE: TEMPLE

Nephi aspires to provide the highest spiritual blessings for his people by erecting a temple in their midst. How unusual is this? Critics of the Book of Mormon have cited Nephi's building of a temple in Mesoamerica as an evidence that the book was a fraud, stating that no real Jew would desire to have a temple outside of Jerusalem. However, on papyri discovered in 1954, we learn of a large group of Jews who had fled from the land of Jerusalem—perhaps at the time the city was destroyed—and who resided far up the Nile. These Jews developed a program to build a temple in their new location. (See *Echoes,* 474.)

Commenting on one of the smaller temples built in areas some distance from Jerusalem at the time of Lehi, an Israeli archaeologist, Avraham Negev, has stated: "The most remarkable discovery at Arad [an ancient city located in the Negev, some 30 kilometers northeast of Be'er Sheva] is the temple which occupied the north-western corner of the citadel. . . . Its orientation, general plan and contents, especially the tabernacle, are similar to the Temple of Solomon" (*Echoes,* 130). Joseph Smith could not have known of the practice of erecting smaller temples away from Jerusalem at the time of Lehi's exodus and relocation to the promised land—but Nephi did, and he acted on this knowledge in his new location away from the original colony.

17–18 Nephi causes his people to be industrious and serves as their devoted leader while declining to be their king.

> *19 And behold, the words of the Lord had been fulfilled unto my brethren, which he spake concerning them, that I should be their ruler and their teacher. Wherefore, I had been their ruler and their teacher, according to the* ***commandments of the Lord,*** *until the time they sought to take away my life.*

EVIDENCE: Commandments of the Lord—"Construct State"

In biblical Hebrew, we often see two or more nouns strung together in a chain, referred to by linguists as the "construct state." When a Hebraic double noun is translated into English, the word *of* is often inserted between the nouns to indicate the relationship. For example, the Hebrew version of "stone tables" is rendered "tables of stone" (Exodus 24:12) in English, and "the Lord's word" becomes "the word of the Lord" (Genesis 15:4). The Book of Mormon frequently uses the construct state, in instances such as "plates of brass" (1 Nephi 3:24), "rod of iron" (1 Nephi 8:19), "sword of Laban" (2 Nephi 5:14), and "commandments of the Lord" (2 Nephi 5:19). According to T. W. Brookbank, the term *Lord's* is found only twice in the entire Book of Mormon, while *Lord* is used in possessive constructions over 300 times in phrases like "commandments of the Lord" or "name of the Lord." (See *Echoes,* 175–176; T. W. Brookbank, "Hebrew Idioms and Analogies in the Book of Mormon," *Improvement Era,* September 1914, 1062.)

> *20 Wherefore, the word of the Lord was fulfilled which he spake unto me, saying that: Inasmuch as they will not hearken unto thy words they shall be* ***cut off from the presence of the Lord.*** *And behold, they were cut off from his presence.*

Cut off from the presence of the Lord

Because they will not hearken to the commandments of the Lord and follow the righteous leadership of Nephi, Laman and Lemuel and their followers are cut off from the presence of the Lord. Nephi is taken from their midst—a repetition of the process through which Lehi was removed from the doomed city of Jerusalem. The application is inescapable: Let us hearken to our living prophets as they speak the word of the Lord—or else we choose to separate ourselves from the Lord (see 3 Nephi 28:34–35).

The Choice

The gospel of Jesus Christ is based on agency. Joshua said it well: "Choose you this day whom ye will serve; . . . but as for me and my house, we will serve the Lord" (Joshua 24:15). Lehi confirmed the same principle: "Wherefore, men are free . . . to choose liberty and eternal life, through the great Mediator of all men, or to choose captivity and death, according to the captivity and power of the devil . . ." (2 Nephi 2:27). The consequences of choice are very clear: the faithful and obedient remain within the fold of the Lord; the rebellious and wicked suffer separation from the fold and thus relinquish the blessings associated with being close to the Lord. A stark illustration of this pattern was the separation that occurred between the Lamanites and the Nephites shortly after the death of Lehi. Because of the persistent, murderous designs of the older brothers, Nephi was commanded by the Lord to flee, thus leaving the rebellious band outside the circle of divine blessings (see 2 Nephi 5:20).

In the larger gospel context, the doctrine of separation is the ultimate punishment for unrepentant sin. There can be no more devastating verdict than this: "Where God and Christ dwell they cannot come" (D&C 76:112). By contrast, what could be more welcome than to hear, "Well done, thou good and faithful servant: thou hast been faithful over a few things, I will make thee ruler over many things: enter thou into the joy of thy lord" (Matthew 25:21). (Richard J. Allen)

21–25 The Lord brings a curse of darkness upon the Lamanites because of their iniquity—and to ensure their separation from the Nephites. They become an idle and devious people whose role is to be a "scourge" unto the Nephite to cause them to remember the Lord (verse 25).

> *26 And it came to pass that I, Nephi, did consecrate Jacob and Joseph, that they should be priests and teachers over the land of my people.*
> *27 And it came to pass that* ***we lived after the manner of happiness.***

We lived after the manner of happiness

Nephi organizes administrative officers—his younger brothers Jacob and Joseph—to care for the spiritual needs of the people. In the framework of industry, cooperation, and spiritual enlightenment, the Nephites—by way of contrast with their Lamanite brothers—live "after the manner of happiness."

28–34 Some thirty years after the exodus from Jerusalem, the Lord commands Nephi to make "other plates" upon which to engrave things "which are good in my sight, for the profit of thy people" (verse 30). Thus two sets of plates are perpetuated, one set for spiritual matters and one for historical events.

CHAPTER 6

OVERVIEW

Jacob proceeds to perform his labors in righteousness on behalf of the people. He cites the prophet Isaiah and discourses on the crucifixion of the Savior and on the scattering and gathering of Israel. In the latter days the Lord will again recover those who believe in Him.

> *1 THE words of Jacob, the brother of Nephi, which he spake unto the people of Nephi:*
> *2 Behold, my beloved brethren, I, Jacob, having been* ***called of God,*** *and* ***ordained*** *after the manner of his holy order, and having been* ***consecrated*** *by my brother Nephi, unto whom ye look as a king or a protector, and on whom ye depend for safety, behold ye know that I have spoken unto you exceedingly many things.*
> *3 Nevertheless, I speak unto you again; for I am* ***desirous for the welfare of your souls.*** *Yea, mine anxiety is great for you; and ye yourselves know that it ever has been. For I have exhorted you with all diligence; and I have taught you the* ***words of my father;*** *and I have spoken unto you concerning* ***all things which are written,*** *from the creation of the world.*
> *4 And now, behold, I would speak unto you concerning* ***things which are, and which are to come;*** *wherefore, I will read you the words of Isaiah. And they are the words which my brother has desired that I should speak unto you. And I speak unto you for your sakes, that ye may* ***learn and glorify the name of your God.***

CALLED OF GOD; ORDAINED; CONSECRATED; DESIROUS FOR THE WELFARE OF YOUR SOULS; WORDS OF MY FATHER; ALL THINGS WHICH ARE WRITTEN; THINGS WHICH ARE, AND WHICH ARE TO COME; LEARN AND GLORIFY THE NAME OF YOUR GOD

These key words identify the pattern by which Jacob fulfills his spiritual mission among the people. He is an authorized servant of God who is motivated by a pure desire to bless lives through conveying the words of the prophets—both present and past. He desires that others have the opportunity of enhancing their spiritual awareness and coming to know and glorify God. What a useful checklist for us as "fellowcitizens with the saints, and of the household of God" (Ephesians 2:19). What is our calling? What is our motivation? What tools do we use? What is the objective of our service? In the space of just three verses we have a road map of how to fulfill our mission on earth.

5 And now, the words which I shall read are they which Isaiah spake concerning all the house of Israel; wherefore, they may be ***likened unto you,*** *for ye are of the house of Israel. And there are many things which have been spoken by Isaiah which may be* ***likened unto you,*** *because ye are of the house of Israel.*

LIKENED UNTO YOU

Jacob follows the example of his brother Nephi by citing words from Isaiah as found in the brass plates. Jacob uses the same expression—"liken"—that his brother has used earlier when exhorting his people to apply the scriptures to their own situations and conditions (see 1 Nephi 19:23–24).

6 And now, these are the words: Thus saith the Lord God: Behold, I will lift up mine hand to the Gentiles, and set up my standard to the people; and they shall bring thy sons in their arms, and thy daughters shall be carried upon their shoulders.
7 And kings shall be thy nursing fathers, and their queens thy nursing mothers; they shall bow down to thee with their faces toward the earth, and lick up the dust of thy feet; and thou shalt know that I am the Lord; for they shall not be ashamed that wait for me.
8 And now I, Jacob, would speak somewhat concerning these words. For behold, the Lord has shown me that those who were at Jerusalem, from whence we came, have been ***slain and carried away captive.***
9 Nevertheless, the Lord has shown unto me that they should ***return again.*** *And he also has shown unto me that the Lord God, the Holy One of Israel, should manifest himself unto them in the flesh; and after he should manifest himself they should scourge him and crucify him, according to the words of the angel who spake it unto me.*
10 And after they have hardened their hearts and stiffened their necks against the Holy One of Israel, behold, the judgments of the Holy One of Israel shall come upon them. And the day cometh that they shall be smitten and afflicted.
11 Wherefore, after they are driven to and fro, for thus saith the angel, many shall be afflicted in the flesh, and shall not be suffered to perish, because of the prayers of the faithful; they shall be ***scattered, and smitten, and hated;*** *nevertheless, the Lord will be merciful unto them, that when they shall come to the knowledge of their Redeemer, they shall be* ***gathered together*** *again to the lands of their inheritance.*

SLAIN AND CARRIED AWAY CAPTIVE; RETURN AGAIN; SCATTERED, AND SMITTEN, AND HATED; GATHERED TOGETHER

Jacob is inspired by the words of Isaiah (see Isaiah 49:22–23) to discourse on the principle of the scattering and gathering of the house of Israel. Isaiah had prophesied some 200 years earlier concerning the coming of the Messiah and the eventual fulfillment of God's covenant with His chosen people, who would be scattered and then gathered in the last days. As a prophet in his own right, Jacob is shown by the Lord that Jerusalem has been destroyed and its inhabitants scattered (i.e., through the Babylonian conquest around 587 B.C.).

Jacob is aware because of his own experience that divine scattering occurs both as a punishment and as a protection—a punishment for the wicked who ignore the warnings of the Lord (as in the case of his own brothers, Laman and Lemuel) and a preservation for the righteous (as in the case of his own community under the leadership of Nephi).

In addition, scattering by way of persecution supports the fulfillment of the Abrahamic covenant whereby the gospel is delivered abroad by spokespersons for the Lord, as in the Pauline persecution during the first century B.C. ("Therefore they that were scattered abroad went every where preaching the word"—Acts 8:4). In our day, "scattering" sends missionaries to convey the good news of the Restoration and invite all to come to Christ. Similarly, divine gathering in the dispensation of the fulness of times brings together countless faithful Saints into the protection of the stakes of Zion where all the blessings of the priesthood, including temple ordinances, are available.

12–17 Jacob perceives that the Gentile nations will be favored of the Lord in the last days when the Lord again begins to gather His people. He will defeat the enemies of Israel with the manifestation of great power. Jacob cites Isaiah 49:16–18, but interpolates for us a phrase that is apparently included on the brass plates but not in our King James version—"for the Mighty God shall deliver his covenant people" (see 2 Nephi 6:17; compare Isaiah 49:17). The people will know in those future times that the Lord is their Savior and Redeemer.

CHAPTER 7

OVERVIEW

Jacob reads to his people Isaiah chapter 50, which is included in the text of the Book of Mormon.

1–11 The Lord inquires of His people: "Have I **cast thee off forever**?" (verse 1). The truth is that the people have sold themselves—separated themselves from God—through iniquity. He confirms that He has power from on high to redeem them. He has the ability to reach them with His word and to hear of their needs as a Redeemer. He shall endure suffering on their behalf—"I gave my back to the smiter . . ." (verse 6). Empowered of God, He [the Son] will prevail. Those who think to sustain themselves on their own light will sorrow.

Cast thee off forever.

This expression has particular relevance to the people in the Book of Mormon. Moroni states in his preface that one purpose of the record is to assure the people "that they are not cast off forever" and to have hope in Christ. Some eighteen times in subsequent passages the phrase "cast off"—in the sense of spiritual separation from God through wickedness—is used in the Book of Mormon. Nephi, Jacob, and their future descendants are sensitive to the additional meaning of being "cast off," since they constitute a branch of Israel separated from their homeland of Jerusalem and are required to live as "wanderers in a strange land" (Alma 26:36). They must continue their quest to one day be worthy of a place in the heavenly home above, where they will be integrated with their fathers in the presence of the Lord. Thus the words of Isaiah resonate with the Nephites—just as they have meaning for modern-day readers who rejoice in the Atonement and give thanks for the plan of happiness as a means to prevent being "cast off forever."

Isaiah Chapters Included in the Book of Mormon	
1 Nephi 20	Isaiah 48
1 Nephi 21	Isaiah 49
2 Nephi 7	Isaiah 50
2 Nephi 8	Isaiah 51
2 Nephi 12	Isaiah 2
2 Nephi 13	Isaiah 3
2 Nephi 14	Isaiah 4
2 Nephi 15	Isaiah 5
2 Nephi 16	Isaiah 6
2 Nephi 17	Isaiah 7
2 Nephi 18	Isaiah 8
2 Nephi 19	Isaiah 9
2 Nephi 20	Isaiah 10
2 Nephi 21	Isaiah 11

Isaiah Chapters Included in the Book of Mormon (cont.)	
2 Nephi 22	Isaiah 12
2 Nephi 23	Isaiah 13
2 Nephi 24	Isaiah 14
2 Nephi 27	Isaiah 29
Mosiah 14	Isaiah 53
Mosiah 15; 3 Nephi 20	Isaiah 52 (parts)
3 Nephi 22	Isaiah 54

Memories: Isaiah and the Arches of Time

Some twenty complete chapters from Isaiah—plus large portions of one additional chapter and many scattered references—are included in the Book of Mormon (see sidebar chart). Readers sometimes come upon the frequent passages from Isaiah in the Book of Mormon as if encountering a daunting cliff. These passages are clearly there for a divine purpose—not to serve as perplexing obstacles (as Laman and Lemuel perceived them—see 1 Nephi 22:1), but rather as the means of ascending to a loftier perspective of gospel insight from which vital covenant truths can be confirmed. How can teachers and parents apply Isaiah's lofty themes and poetic language to everyday living? Here is one idea I have used over the years in my teaching.

Many of us remember watching our television screens on July 20, 1969, spellbound as Neil Armstrong stepped from the Eagle lunar module onto the surface of the moon, uttering the now historic phrase: "That's one small step for man, one giant leap for mankind." The spectacular color imagery of the earth's orb taken on that Apollo 11 mission and on other space flights allowed men their first recorded glimpses of their magnificent blue-green, cloud-shrouded home from a heavenly perspective. But these views of earth were not the first to be discerned by mortals. As Moses was being instructed of the Lord millennia before, he "cast his eyes and beheld the earth, yea, even all of it; and there was not a particle of it which he did not behold, discerning it by the spirit of God" (Moses 1:27). Similarly, with a spiritual eye, Moroni saw his future readership—one and all: "Behold, I speak unto you as if ye were present, and yet ye are not. But behold, Jesus Christ hath shown you unto me, and I know your doing" (Mormon 8:35).

Of all the ages of mankind, we are the first generation to cultivate a firsthand sense of space travel and a truly universal perspective. Our modern telescopes can see farther into the reaches of the universe than ever before, even detecting, for the first time, planets such as ours circulating around distant stars. Thus we should understand better than any other generation what is hinted at in the Lord's statement that "all things are present with me, for I know them all" (Moses 1:6).

What is continually before the Lord is shared freely with His sons and daughters through His Spirit, at least "all things that are expedient for them" (D&C 75:10; compare 2 Nephi 3:19). Thus Nephi was able to experience and share his magnificent panoramic vision of the unfolding of Israel's destiny, stretching in great arches of time from his day even to the Second Coming (see 1 Nephi 11–14). How carefully he must have selected thereafter his themes and illustrations for the small plates of sacred engravings so that precisely the right message would be conveyed to future generations, in precisely the right way. How keenly he must have felt the need to help his audience understand the scriptures, especially Isaiah, and "liken them unto yourselves" (1 Nephi 19:24).

What a harmonious kinship Nephi must have felt for his predecessor Isaiah. Isaiah, of all the Lord's prophets, was perhaps the consummate navigator of the grand arches of time that interlock the human experience from beginning to end, and one of most accomplished in articulating what he saw with power and urgency. Isaiah, as the Lord's prophet, could crisscross the milestones of history from the foundations of the earth to the meridian of time and on to the millennial reign and back again.

Here is the analogy: Once you have seen the extraordinary images of the earth as perceived from the moon, you will never again ponder the earth in the same way; once you have read Isaiah with the guidance of the Spirit, you will never again ponder God's plan of salvation and Israel's covenant calling in the same way. You will have been lifted to a higher level of understanding and enlightenment from one of the greatest of God's anointed.

Like Nephi, we can integrate the words of Isaiah into our thoughts and aspirations. We can then rise spiritually far above Babylon into the freer atmosphere where "greater views" (D&C 10:45) of our destiny and calling are imparted by our Lord. (Richard J. Allen)

CHAPTER 8

OVERVIEW

Jacob reads Isaiah 51 and 52:1–2 to his people. This material is included in the text of the Book of Mormon.

1–25 The Lord directs His people to discern their royal heritage and realize their position in the grand design of His plan of happiness. He promises them comfort, joy, and abundance in place of suffering and oppression. He will be their light and their salvation. While earthly kingdoms will vanish, His kingdom will endure forever. He will gather the redeemed to Zion and inspire them to awaken, put on their beautiful garments, and be lifted to the stature of their divine potential.

> *3 For the Lord shall **comfort** Zion, he will **comfort** all her waste places; and he will make her wilderness like Eden, and her desert like **the garden of the Lord. Joy and gladness** shall be found therein, **thanksgiving** and the voice of **melody. . . .***
> *11 Therefore, the redeemed of the Lord shall return, and come with **singing** unto Zion; and **everlasting joy** and holiness shall be upon their heads; and they shall obtain **gladness and joy;** sorrow and mourning shall flee away.*

Comfort, the garden of the Lord, everlasting joy, gladness, thanksgiving, singing, melody

These uplifting thoughts are presented by Jacob to his fellow citizens who have been separated from their original homeland and from their murderous brothers to eke out an isolated existence in the wilderness of their afflictions. We can liken these passages to ourselves. Do we find joy and gladness in our mortal sojourn—despite the tribulation we might face? Do we raise our voices in thanksgiving to the Lord—despite every reversal we might encounter? Do we testify that the message of Isaiah is true—that the Lord, the Almighty, the Redeemer, is the enduring source of our joy and happiness—not the perishable and transitory things of this world? Do we rejoice that the gospel of Jesus Christ is the only dependable and lasting source of comfort and vitality?

> *9 **Awake, awake!** Put on strength, O arm of the Lord; **awake as in the ancient days.** Art thou not he that hath cut Rahab, and wounded the dragon?*

Awake! awake as in the ancient days

The oppressed people are heard raising their voices in supplication to the Lord that He might come in might on their behalf as He did in ancient days when He overcame Rahab (Egypt) and wounded the dragon (Satan).

> *19 These **two sons** are come unto thee, who shall be sorry for thee—thy desolation and destruction, and the famine and the sword—and by whom shall I comfort thee?*
> *20 Thy **sons** have fainted, save these **two;** they lie at the head of all the streets; as a wild bull in a net, they are full of the fury of the Lord, the rebuke of thy God.*

Two sons

This reference is apparently to two prophets in the last days who shall come on behalf of the Jews at a time of oppression (compare Revelation 11:1–17; also Zechariah 4:11–14). Latter-day revelation provides additional knowledge concerning this matter: "Q. What is to be understood by the two witnesses, in the eleventh chapter of Revelation? A. They are two prophets that are to be raised up to the Jewish nation in the last days, at the time of the Restoration, and to prophesy to the Jews after they are gathered and have built the city of Jerusalem in the land of their fathers" (D&C 77:15). In its present form, Isaiah 51:17–20 refers to "sons" but not "two sons" as does the comparable section in 2 Nephi 8:17–20.

> *24* ***Awake, awake, put on thy strength, O Zion;*** *put on thy* ***beautiful garments,***
> *O Jerusalem, the holy city; for henceforth there shall no more come into thee the uncircumcised and the unclean.*
> *25 Shake thyself from the dust;* ***arise,*** *sit down, O Jerusalem; loose thyself from the*
> *bands of thy neck, O captive daughter of Zion.*

Awake, awake, put on thy strength, O Zion; beautiful garments; arise

These thoughts are also conveyed in the instructions of the resurrected Savior to His assembled Saints in the New World (see 3 Nephi 20:36) and in the parting words of Moroni (see Moroni 10:31). The Prophet Joseph Smith explained: "What is meant by the command in Isaiah, 52d chapter, 1st verse, which saith: Put on thy strength, O Zion—and what people had Isaiah reference to? He had reference to those whom God should call in the last days, who should hold the power of priesthood to bring again Zion, and the redemption of Israel; and to put on her strength is to put on the authority of the priesthood, which she, Zion, has a right to by lineage; also to return to that power which she had lost" (D&C 113:7–8). Thus the symbolism of putting on garments of strength and beauty refers to the endowment of priesthood blessings upon the faithful, empowering and enabling them to rise in majesty as joint-heirs with Christ. (Note that 2 Nephi 8:24–25 is parallel to Isaiah 52:1–2, which really belongs at the end of Isaiah 51, as the Book of Mormon confirms.)

I Thought of the Old Prophet

We have witnessed through history the fulfilling of the prophecies of Isaiah. In our day we have been given the keys of gathering from the prophet Moses, and Elias restored the blessings of Abraham through which all nations will be blessed (see D&C 110:11–12). We are part of this great latter-day work where we become the very individuals who help fulfill Isaiah's prophecies. Wilford Woodruff describes this doctrine in terms of an experience he had as a young boy:

When I was a boy, there was an old man who used to visit at my father's house. His name was Robert Mason, and I heard teachings from him from the time that I was eight years old and upwards, and they were teachings that I shall ever remember. And he taught my father's household many important truths concerning the church and kingdom of God, and told them many things in relation to the prophets and the things that were coming upon the earth. But his teachings were received by but few. They were unpopular with the Christian world, but nearly all who did receive his teachings have joined the Latter-day Saints.

Prophets were not popular in that day any more than now, and I have often thought of many things which the old man taught me in the days of my youth since I received the fulness of the gospel and became a member of the Church of Christ.

He said, "When you read the Bible, do you ever think that what you read there is going to be fulfilled? The teachers of the day," said he, "spiritualize the Bible, but when you read in the Bible about the dreams, visions, revelations and predictions of Ezekiel, Isaiah, Jeremiah, or any other of the prophets or apostles, relative to the gathering of Israel and the building up of Zion, . . . you may understand that it means just what it says, and that it will be fulfilled upon the earth in the last days. And when you read of men laying hands upon the sick and healing them, and casting out devils and working miracles in the name of Jesus Christ, it means what it says." And he further said, "The church of Christ and Kingdom of God is not upon the earth, but it has been taken from the children of men through unbelief and because they have taken away from the gospel some of its most sacred ordinances, and have instituted in their stead forms and ceremonies without the power of God, and have turned from the truth unto fables; but," said he, "it will soon be restored again unto the children of men upon the earth, with its ancient gifts and powers, for the scriptures cannot be fulfilled without it. I shall not live to see it, but," said he to me, "you will live to see that day, and you will become a conspicuous actor in that kingdom, and when you see that day, then that which the prophets have spoken will be fulfilled."

I did not join any church, believing that the church of Christ in its true organization did not exist upon the earth. But when the principles of the everlasting gospel were first proclaimed unto me, I believed it with all my heart, and was

> baptized the first sermon I heard, for the Spirit of God bore testimony to me in power that it was true.
>
> And I believe that I should never have joined any church had I not heard the fulness of the gospel. I was greatly blessed in receiving it, and was filled with joy unspeakable, and I have never been sorry but I have rejoiced all the day long. . . . I thought of the teaching and words of the old prophet Mason, for he came the nearest to being a true prophet of God in his predictions and works of any man I ever saw, until I saw men administering in the Holy Priesthood. (*Journal of Discourses,* 4:99–100; see Jack M. Lyon, Jay A. Parry, and Linda R. Gundry, eds., *Best-Loved Stories of the LDS People,* vol. 2 [Salt Lake City: Deseret Book, 1999], 305–306)

Memories: How Far Can You See?

When my children were very small I used to enjoy placing them one at a time on top of the refrigerator, their little legs hanging down and their eyes wide open with anticipation. They seemed to enjoy having for a short time a new vista across the full extent of the room. When they had built up enough courage, they would jump down into my waiting arms and enjoy a dizzying ride around and around before being gently dropped to their feet on the floor. This same practice has been continued with the small grandchildren, who invariably insist that the activity be repeated over and over.

Life is an endless flow of opportunities to find new vistas that afford the privilege of seeing farther into the distance. In my youth, my father would often take us fishing in the high Canadian Rockies where, from the tops of the ridges, we could see astonishing views across the entire mountain range in all directions. Similarly, air travelers always find captivating the view of the earth below. Moreover, now that space travel is a reality, we can see, for the first time in history, the entire earth hanging in space.

Reading the words of Isaiah, for me, is not unlike those experiences of flight and high altitude. Of all the prophets, Isaiah seemed to have an especially keen gift of transporting us with eloquent wisdom to high places from which to view the panorama of God's creation and plan of redemption from beginning to end.

It is up to Isaiah and other prophets of God to help us comprehend the divine influence at work on our behalf, to discern the Lord's hand in the creation and forward movement of the grand design of heaven for God's children. When Jacob, Nephi's younger brother, needed corroborating testimony to support his theme of the destiny of Israel and the ultimate consummation of the covenant promises, to whom did he turn? Like his brother Nephi, he turned to Isaiah. (See 2 Nephi 6–8; compare Isaiah 49–52).

Note the breathtaking expanse and variety of Isaiah's vision within these verses, extending as they did:

- to the latter-day *Restoration*: "I will lift up mine hand to the Gentiles, and set up my standard to the people . . ." (2 Nephi 6:6);
- to the *Exodus*: "Behold, at my rebuke I dry up the sea . . ." (2 Nephi 7:2);
- to the *ministry of the Savior*: "I hid not my face from shame and spitting" (2 Nephi 7:6);
- to the *gainsayers and self-righteous* in all generations: "ye shall lie down in sorrow" (2 Nephi 7:11);
- to the *ancient prophets of the covenant*: "Look unto Abraham, your father . . ." (2 Nephi 8:2);
- from the *Garden of Eden* to the *millennial kingdom* in the same verse: "he will make her wilderness like Eden, and her desert like the garden of the Lord . . ." (2 Nephi 8:3);
- to the *day of judgment*: "my salvation is gone forth, and mine arm shall judge the people . . ." (2 Nephi 8:5);
- to the renewal of the earth at the *Second Coming*: "Lift up your eyes to the heavens, and look upon the earth beneath; for the heavens shall vanish away like smoke, and the earth shall wax old like a garment . . ." (2 Nephi 8:6);
- from the *Old Testament days* to the *Restoration* in one verse: "Awake, awake! Put on strength, O arm of the Lord; awake as in the ancient days . . ." (2 Nephi 8:9);
- to the *latter-day gathering*: "Therefore, the redeemed of the Lord shall return, and come with singing unto Zion . . ." (2 Nephi 8:11);
- from the *Creation* to Israel's *everyday struggles of oppression*: "And forgettest the Lord thy maker, that hath stretched forth the heavens, and laid the foundation of the earth, and hast feared continually every day, because of the fury of the oppressor . . ." (2 Nephi 8:13);
- to the *travail of Judah* in the final days of the world: "Thy sons have fainted, save these two; they lie at the head of all the streets . . ." (2 Nephi 8:20);
- and finally to the *latter-day and millennial deliverance*: "Shake thyself from the dust; arise, sit down, O Jerusalem; loose thyself from the bands of thy neck, O captive daughter of Zion" (2 Nephi 8:25).

Returning from an experience with Isaiah is analogous, in a way, to a homecoming from a hike through the high mountains, or the safe landing of an aircraft after a long journey, or the return of the space shuttle to earth. In a more domestic comparison, just as the grandchildren repeatedly jump with trust from the top of the fridge into the arms of the waiting grandfather below, we can, in like measure, "mount up with wings of eagles" (Isaiah 40:31) to the upper reaches of spiritual insight through the visions of Isaiah, and then return with greater understanding into the arms of the Savior, who is ready to say, "Welcome home." (Richard J. Allen)

CHAPTER 9

OVERVIEW

Jacob delivers a masterful discourse on the plan of happiness and the Atonement of Jesus Christ. Each step of man's existence is covered: the premortal realm, the Creation, the Fall, birth into mortality, the mortal experience itself, death, the spirit world, the Resurrection, the Judgment, and the ultimate state of the children of God (depending on their obedience and faithfulness). Jacob shows the intersecting pathways traced by the Savior, by Lucifer, and by different types of mortals (depending on their circumstances and actions).

> *1 AND now, my beloved brethren, I have read these things [the words of Isaiah] that*
> *ye might know concerning the* ***covenants of the Lord*** *that he has covenanted with all*
> *the house of Israel—*
> *2 That he has spoken unto the Jews, by the mouth of his holy prophets, even from the*
> *beginning down, from generation to generation, until the time comes that they shall be*
> *restored to the true church and fold of God; when they shall be gathered home to the*
> *lands of their inheritance, and shall be established in all their lands of promise.*
> *3 Behold, my beloved brethren, I speak unto you these things that ye may* ***rejoice,*** *and*
> *lift up your heads forever, because of the blessings which the Lord God shall bestow*
> *upon your children.*
> *4 For I know that ye have searched much, many of you, to know of things to come;*
> *wherefore I know that ye know that our flesh must waste away and die; nevertheless,*
> *in our bodies* ***we shall see God.***

Covenants of the Lord; rejoice; we shall see God

Through the Atonement of Christ all will be resurrected, and those who honor their covenant agreements with the Lord will rejoice and return home again into His presence.

The Doctrine of the Atonement

> Nothing in the entire plan of salvation compares in any way in importance with that most transcendent of all events, the atoning sacrifice of our Lord. It is the most important single thing that has ever occurred in the entire history of created things; it is the rock foundation upon which the gospel and all other things rest. Indeed, all "things which pertain to our religion are only appendages to it," the Prophet said. (*Teachings*, 121.)
>
> The doctrine of the atonement embraces, sustains, supports, and gives life and force to all other gospel doctrines. It is the foundation upon which all truth rests, and all things grow out of it and come because of it. Indeed, the atonement is the gospel. In recording the Vision, the Prophet wrote: "And this is the gospel, the glad tidings, which the voice out of the heavens bore record unto us—That he came into the world, even Jesus, to be crucified for the world, and to bear the sins of the world, and to sanctify the world, and to cleanse it from all unrighteousness; That through him all might be saved whom the Father had put into his power and made by him." (D&C 76:40–42.) To the Nephites the resurrected Lord spoke similarly: "Behold I have given unto you my gospel, and this is the gospel which I have given unto you—that I came into the world to do the will of my Father, because my Father sent me. And my Father sent me that I might be lifted up upon the cross." (3 Ne. 27:13–14.)
>
> Salvation comes because of the atonement. Without it the whole plan of salvation would be frustrated and the whole purpose behind the creating and populating of the earth would come to naught. With it the eternal purposes of the Father will roll forth, the purpose of creation be preserved, the plan of salvation made efficacious, and men will be assured of a hope of the highest exaltation hereafter. (*Doctrines of Salvation*, vol. 1, 121–138.) . . . .
>
> A knowledge of two great truths is essential to an understanding of the doctrine of the atonement: 1. The fall of Adam; and 2. The divine Sonship of our Lord.

Adam's fall brought spiritual and temporal death into the world. Spiritual death is to be cast out of the presence of the Lord (2 Ne. 9:6) and to die as pertaining to things of righteousness, or in other words things of the Spirit. (Helaman 14:15–18.) Temporal death or natural death is the separation of body and spirit, the body going back to the dust from which it was created and the spirit to a world of waiting spirits to await the day of the resurrection.

To atone is to ransom, reconcile, expiate, redeem, reclaim, absolve, propitiate, make amends, pay the penalty. Thus the atonement of Christ is designed to ransom men from the effects of the fall of Adam in that both spiritual and temporal death are conquered; their lasting effect is nullified. The spiritual death of the fall is replaced by the spiritual life of the atonement, in that all who believe and obey the gospel law gain spiritual or eternal life—life in the presence of God where those who enjoy it are alive to things of righteousness or things of the Spirit. The temporal death of the fall is replaced by the state of immortality which comes because of the atonement and resurrection of our Lord. The body and spirit which separated, incident to what men call the natural death, are reunited in immortality, in an inseparable connection that never again will permit the mortal body to see corruption. (Alma 11:37–45; 12:16 18.) Immortality comes as a free gift, by the grace of God alone, without works of righteousness. Eternal life is the reward for "obedience to the laws and ordinances of the Gospel." (Third Article of Faith.) (Bruce R. McConkie, *Mormon Doctrine,* 2d ed. [Salt Lake City: Bookcraft, 1966], 60–62)

5 Yea, I know that ye know that in the body he shall show himself unto those at Jerusalem, from whence we came; for it is expedient that it should be among them; for it behooveth the great Creator that he suffereth himself to become subject unto man in the flesh, and die for all men, that all men might become subject unto him.
6 For as death hath passed upon all men, to fulfil the merciful plan of the great Creator, there must needs be a ***power of resurrection,*** *and the resurrection must needs come unto man by reason of the fall; and the fall came by reason of transgression; and because man became fallen they were cut off from the presence of the Lord.*

Power of resurrection

There must needs be an infinite Atonement to overcome the Fall and bring about the Resurrection in fulfillment of the merciful plan of redemption. Through the Atonement we are liberated from the bands of death: "For as in Adam all die, even so in Christ shall all be made alive" (1 Corinthians 15:22).

> *7 Wherefore, it must needs be an **infinite atonement**—save it should be an **infinite atonement** this corruption could not put on incorruption. Wherefore, the first judgment which came upon man must needs have remained to an endless duration. And if so, this flesh must have laid down to rot and to crumble to its mother earth, to rise no more.*

Infinite atonement

Intercession on behalf of mankind had to occur at the Creator's level. Only the application of infinite power, infinite love, infinite grace, infinite mercy could have rendered death powerless for all mankind and opened the gateway for all to "work out [their] own salvation with fear and trembling" (Philippians 2:12; compare Moroni 9:27).

> *8 O the wisdom of God, his mercy and grace! For behold, if the flesh should rise no more our spirits must become subject to that angel who **fell from before** the presence of the Eternal God, and became the devil, to rise no more.*

EVIDENCE: Fell from before—Compound Prepositions

A characteristic feature of Hebrew grammar is compound prepositions. Some examples from English translations of the Old Testament include *from before*, *from behind*, and *to behind*. With its Hebrew roots, it is not surprising that the Book of Mormon also includes compound prepositions. For example, in addition to its appearance in 2 Nephi 9:8, we see the use of the compound preposition *from before* in Mosiah 17:4, Alma 44:12, and 3 Nephi 4:12. (See *Echoes*, 172–173.)

> *9 And our spirits must have become like unto him, and we become devils, angels to a devil, to be shut out from the presence of our God, and to **remain with the father of lies,** in misery, like unto himself; yea, to that being who beguiled our first parents, who transformeth himself nigh unto an angel of light, and stirreth up the children of men unto secret combinations of murder and all manner of secret works of darkness.*

Remain with the father of lies

The Atonement protects us from being subject to the devil. How grateful we should be for Christ's Atonement—which acts as a barrier of security that protects us from the influence of the devil, provided we act in accordance with the principles of righteousness.

10–14 Jacob rejoices that the Atonement will cause temporal death to deliver up its dead and spiritual death its captives. All mankind are to be restored to a state of immortality, becoming living souls with a perfect knowledge and remembrance of their thoughts and deeds in mortality—whether in anguish for wickedness or rejoicing for righteousness.

> *15 And it shall come to pass that when all men shall have passed from this first death unto life, insomuch as they have become immortal, they must appear before the* ***judgment-seat of the Holy One of Israel;*** *and then cometh the* ***judgment,*** *and then must they be judged according to the holy judgment of God.*
> *16 And assuredly, as the Lord liveth, for the Lord God hath spoken it, and it is his eternal word, which cannot pass away, that they who are righteous shall be righteous still, and they who are filthy shall be filthy still; wherefore, they who are filthy are the devil and his angels; and they shall go away into everlasting fire, prepared for them; and their torment is as a lake of fire and brimstone, whose flame ascendeth up forever and ever and has no end.*

Judgment-seat of the Holy One of Israel; judgment

Jacob assures us that we shall have a perfect recollection of our guilt or righteousness. We come before the judgment-seat of Christ to be judged according to our works and are restored according to our deeds, works, and the desires of our hearts (see Alma 5:15; 33:22; 41:3). We shall be judged out of the books according to that which is written (see 2 Nephi 29:11; 3 Nephi 27:26).

> *17 O the* ***greatness and the justice of our God!*** *For he executeth all his words, and they have gone forth out of his mouth, and his law must be fulfilled.*
> *18 But, behold, the righteous, the saints of the Holy One of Israel, they who have believed in the Holy One of Israel, they who have endured the crosses of the world, and despised the shame of it, they shall inherit the kingdom of God, which was prepared for them from the foundation of the world, and their joy shall be full forever.*

19 O the greatness of the ***mercy*** *of our God, the Holy One of Israel! For he delivereth his saints from that awful monster the devil, and death, and hell, and that lake of fire and brimstone, which is endless torment.*

Greatness and the justice of our God; mercy of our God

Our hearts should be continually filled with gratitude and praise in recognizing the goodness and mercy of God.

20 O how great the holiness of our God! For ***he knoweth all things,*** *and there is not anything save he knows it.*

He knoweth all things

God is omniscient: He knows all things (see D&C 38:1–2; 88:7–13). God is omnipotent: He has power and wisdom to do all things (see Mosiah 4:9; Alma 26:35). God is omnipresent: He is above, in, and through all things through the extension of His divine influence and the reach of His Holy Spirit (see D&C 88:41). Knowing this, we find that our confidence, faith, and trust in God are increased, our love for Him magnified.

The Greatest Knowledge We Can Have: The Atonement—Power unto Immortality and Eternal Life

Understanding the Atonement of Christ and its relationship to our eternal existence is the greatest knowledge we can have in our quest to return to God, our Eternal Father. The Atonement is the center of the gospel of Jesus Christ. When we diligently apply its principles to our lives through the covenant process—through faith unto repentance, baptism, and receiving the gift of the Holy Ghost—we become liberated from our fallen state. We become free through Christ by obedience (see Galatians 5:1). Yet "it is by (the) grace (of God) that we are saved, after all we can do" (2 Nephi 25:23). We apply the Atonement to our lives through the gospel and through priesthood authority in The Church of Jesus Christ of Latter-day Saints. It is this knowledge of the Atonement and Christ's role in our lives that will motivate and cause us to change.

This is why the Book of Mormon was given to us as another witness and testament that Jesus is the Christ. The Lord said, "Behold I have given unto you my gospel, and this is the gospel which I have given unto you—that I came into the world to do the will of my Father, because my Father sent me. And my Father sent me that I might be lifted up upon the cross; and after that I had been lifted up upon the cross, that I might draw all men unto me . . ." (3 Nephi 27:13–14).

It is by such means that the Atonement will draw us to the Lord. The reality of the Atonement demonstrates the tender mercy and the goodness of God: "For God so loved the world, that he gave his only begotten Son, that whosoever believeth in him should not perish, but have everlasting life" (John 3:16).

This gift becomes the key—the difference in our lives. When we understand this doctrine, when we appreciate it and apply it to our lives, we change. We become converted. And converted people are different people. They act differently. They are grateful. They feel indebted to the Lord their God for their very lives. (Ed J. Pinegar)

> *21 And he cometh into the world that he may save all men if they will hearken unto his voice; for behold,* ***he suffereth the pains of all men,*** *yea, the pains of every living creature, both men, women, and children, who belong to the family of Adam.*

He suffereth the pains of all men

The suffering of our Savior Jesus Christ not only encompasses the power of reconciliation and atonement, but also enables Him to nurture us in times of trials and adversity, understanding as He does our mortal condition (see D&C 19:15–18; Alma 7:11–12). Elder Henry B. Eyring explains the suffering Christ:

> Now, for me, at the right moment, I can begin to feel the pain the Savior felt for sins, yours and mine. His groan within himself came after he had paid the price for us, after the Atonement. His being troubled was not some abstract grief for our sins and those of the house of Israel. His was real pain, recently felt, as he took upon him the sins of the world. I can't experience that, but I can sense it enough to have sorrow for what I have added to it. I can resolve to add no more. And I can feel determination that I will help offer the full blessings of the Atonement to as many as I can, because that passage helps me feel, in a small way, what taking upon him the sins of all mankind cost the Savior. (*To Draw Closer to God: A Collection of Discourses* [Salt Lake City: Deseret Book, 1997], 69–70)

Receiving the blessings of the Atonement in our lives requires living by faith unto repentance, receiving the life-saving ordinances, and continually pressing forward with steadfastness in Christ. The Savior has done His part, having suffered the pains of all men. Now we must do ours.

Jacob's remarkable sermon on the Atonement calls for a pattern of behavior that will bring us closer to the Savior and generate a condition in which joy and peace can abound. King Benjamin put the truth in plain terms: "And now, if you believe all these things see that ye do them" (Mosiah 4:10).

> *22 And he suffereth this that the resurrection might pass upon all men, that all might*
> *stand before him at the great and judgment day.*
> *23 And he commandeth all men that they must* ***repent,*** *and be baptized in his name,*
> *having perfect faith in the Holy One of Israel, or they cannot be saved in the kingdom*
> *of God.*
> *24 And if they will not* ***repent*** *and believe in his name, and be baptized in his name,*
> *and endure to the end, they must be damned; for the Lord God, the Holy One of Israel,*
> *has spoken it.*

Repent

The Atonement is love expressed in infinite terms. When we feel this love, it will motivate us to righteousness. Repentance based on faith is the greatest thing we can do to be saved. Let us realize that to make the Atonement totally efficacious in our lives we must apply the doctrine of Christ through obedience to the principles and ordinances of the gospel—faith, repentance, baptism, and the gift of the Holy Ghost, plus enduring to the end (see Articles of Faith 1:4; 2 Nephi 31; D&C 20:37).

> *25 Wherefore,* ***he has given a law;*** *and where there is no law given there is no punish-*
> *ment; and where there is no punishment there is no condemnation; and where there is*
> *no condemnation the mercies of the Holy One of Israel have claim upon them, because*
> *of the atonement; for they are delivered by the power of him.*
> *26 For the atonement satisfieth the demands of his justice upon all those who have not*
> *the law given to them, that they are delivered from that awful monster, death and hell,*
> *and the devil, and the lake of fire and brimstone, which is endless torment; and they*
> *are restored to that God who gave them breath, which is the Holy One of Israel.*
> *27* ***But wo unto him that has the law given,*** *yea, that has all the commandments*
> *of God, like unto us, and that transgresseth them, and* ***that wasteth the days of his***
> ***probation,*** *for awful is his state!*

2 Nephi 9:27

He has given a law; But wo unto him that has the law given that wasteth the days of his probation

The words of Jacob raise a question for those who consider carefully their place in the design of the Almighty. Where no law is given, the mercies of the Holy One prevail unto deliverance. But we have been given the commandments from God in order to achieve happiness through obedience (see Mosiah 2:41). Every day consists of twenty-four hours that sometimes flee away into oblivion because we fail to organize every needful thing (see D&C 88:119; 109:8, 15). Thus, the questions of conscience become, Do we take the time to plan and make happiness our pursuit (see Alma 27:18)? How do we use our time? Are our priorities in keeping the commandments of God?

EVIDENCE: Wo unto him—Prophetic Speech Formulas

Many phrases or formulaic expressions distinguish the prophetic speech of the Old Testament. These expressions are often used at the beginning of a prophecy or revelation with the purpose of introducing important, sacred information. Not surprisingly, these speech patterns also appear in the Book of Mormon. The following are examples from both volumes:

- **The woe oracle**—"Woe unto . . ." (Isaiah 5:8, 11, 20; Habakkuk 2:0, 12, 15; 1 Nephi 1:13; 2 Nephi 9:27; 15:21). This formula is found approximately forty times in the Book of Mormon.
- **The messenger formula**—"Thus saith the Lord" (Amos 1:3, 6; 1 Nephi 20:17; Mosiah 3:24; Alma 8:17).
- **The proclamation formula**—"Hear the word of the Lord" (1 Kings 22:19; Amos 7:16; Isaiah 49:1); "hearken to the word of the Lord" (Jacob 2:27); "hear the words of Jesus" (3 Nephi 30:1); and "hearken unto the words which the Lord saith" (Helaman 13:21).
- **The oath formula**—"The Lord God hath sworn . . ." (Amos 4:2, 8:7) or "as the Lord liveth (Judges 8:19, Ruth 3:13, 1 Nephi 3:15, 4:32).
- **The revelation formula**—"The word of the Lord came to . . ." (1 Samuel 15:10; Zechariah 7:1); "the voice of the Lord came unto him" (Helaman 13:3; Jacob 2:11; Alma 43:24).

A writer attempting to imitate the Bible would probably have either overlooked these formulas or used them incorrectly. Not so with the Prophet Joseph Smith, whose inspired translation of the Book of Mormon includes authentic prophetic speech formulas reflecting the antiquity of the text (see *Echoes,* 169–170).

28 O that cunning plan of the evil one! O the vainness, and the frailties, and the foolishness of men! When they are learned they think they are wise, and they hearken not unto the counsel of God, for they set it aside, supposing they know of themselves, wherefore, their wisdom is foolishness and it profiteth them not. And they shall perish.
29 ***But to be learned is good if they hearken unto the counsels of God.***

But to be learned is good if they hearken unto the counsels of God

This famous quotation reminds us of a truth all too frequently forgotten: When we hearken to the counsels of God, we are blessed in our learning and progress. However, the learning of man cannot save us. The learning gained in the world is good only as far as we counsel with God in all things. Gospel knowledge is the only knowledge that will lead us to eternal life.

30 But wo unto the rich, who are rich as to the things of the world. For ***because they are rich they despise the poor,*** *and they persecute the meek, and their hearts are upon their treasures; wherefore, their treasure is their god. And behold, their treasure shall perish with them also.*

Because they are rich they despise the poor

A warning is given concerning those who have riches and make them their treasure to the exclusion of charity, for their riches will perish with them. Remember that all things are the Lord's. We show gratitude through charity.

31–38 Jacob identifies an array of transgressions that lead to destruction and separation from God.

39 O, my beloved brethren, remember the awfulness in transgressing against that Holy God, and also the awfulness of yielding to the enticings of that cunning one. Remember, ***to be carnally-minded is death, and to be spiritually-minded is life eternal.***

To be carnally-minded is death, and to be spiritually-minded is life eternal

This celebrated maxim captures the essence of the dichotomy between the telestial and the celestial manner of living. Jacob must surely have remembered the words of his father Lehi:

> Wherefore, men are free according to the flesh; and all things are given them which are expedient unto man. And they are free to choose liberty and eternal life,

> through the great Mediator of all men, or to choose captivity and death, according to the captivity and power of the devil; for he seeketh that all men might be miserable like unto himself.
>
> And now, my sons, I would that ye should look to the great Mediator, and hearken unto his great commandments; and be faithful unto his words, and choose eternal life, according to the will of his Holy Spirit;
>
> And not choose eternal death, according to the will of the flesh and the evil which is therein, which giveth the spirit of the devil power to captivate, to bring you down to hell, that he may reign over you in his own kingdom. (2 Nephi 2:27–29)

The lesson is plain and clear: Think good thoughts, do good deeds, love God, and keep the commandments.

> *40 O, my beloved brethren, give ear to my words. Remember the greatness of the Holy One of Israel. Do not say that I have spoken hard things against you; for if ye do, ye will revile against the truth; for I have spoken the words of your Maker. I know that the words of truth are hard against all uncleanness; but the righteous fear them not, for* ***they love the truth*** *and are not shaken.*

They love the truth

The faithful and obedient do not take offense at the truth. Those who love the truth—the word of God—discover in themselves an authentic sign of righteousness.

> *41 O then, my beloved brethren, come unto the Lord, the Holy One. Remember that his paths are righteous. Behold, the way for man is narrow, but it lieth in a straight course before him, and* ***the keeper of the gate is the Holy One of Israel;*** *and he employeth no servant there; and there is none other way save it be by the gate; for he cannot be deceived, for the Lord God is his name.*

The keeper of the gate is the Holy One of Israel

We are loved by Heavenly Father and our Savior Jesus Christ. Everything They do is for the immortality and eternal life of mankind. The Lord gave His life because He loved us (see 2 Nephi 26:24). He continually speaks of His love for us (see John 13:34–35). An important question of conscience is this: How would we feel regarding our life if we had to face our Savior today? Alma expressed the horror of it when he was not fully repentant (see Alma 36:14–17)—and the joy of being in the presence of the Lord after his forgiveness (see Alma 36:19–22). The Savior employs no servant at the holy gate. Let us remember that we are to come before our Savior face to face—and thereby experience either joy or sorrow, depending upon the nature of our thoughts, desires, and deeds in this life.

Memories: The Keeper of the Gate

Several years ago a colleague in my high priests group recounted a story about an event that had recently taken place in the local temple where he was serving as a temple worker. Two young women had come to the recommend desk at the front of the temple to be admitted. They were greeted warmly by the official stationed there, who requested to see their recommends. As he described it, for some reason a feeling of uneasiness came over him. He examined the first recommend, glancing at the authorizing signatures and then back into the eyes of the young woman. He felt impressed to say, "This is not the signature of your stake president, is it?" Chagrined, the young woman confessed that it was not. The official then counseled the two, in a kind but firm way, to leave and return again when they were worthy to do so, and they would be welcome in the House of the Lord.

The event is a reminder to us all that the temples of the Most High are sacred precincts reserved for those with a broken heart and a contrite spirit—those who are sincerely striving to keep all of the commandments and abide by the standards of temple-worthy Saints. The temple experience is in many respects a type pointing to our eventual return to the home from whence we have come. Jacob made clear that the process of admittance into our Heavenly Father's presence is by way of a very special gate keeper—the Holy One of Israel, who "cannot be deceived, for the Lord God is his name" (2 Nephi 9:41). (Richard J. Allen)

42 And whoso knocketh, to him will he open; and the wise, and the learned, and they that are rich, who are puffed up because of their learning, and their wisdom, and their riches—yea, ***they are they whom he despiseth;*** *and save they shall cast these things away, and consider themselves fools before God, and come down in the depths of humility, he will not open unto them.*
43 But the things of the wise and the prudent shall be hid from them forever—yea, that happiness which is prepared for the saints.

They are they whom he despiseth

The Lord turns away from the proud and the haughty. They fall short of the state of happiness. Seek to be humble—for humility is an exalting virtue.

44–45 Jacob pleads with his listeners to repent and come unto the Rock of their Salvation. They are fully responsible for the outcome of their lives.

> *46 **Prepare your souls for that glorious day** when justice shall be administered unto the righteous, even the day of judgment, that ye may not shrink with awful fear; that ye may not remember your awful guilt in perfectness, and be constrained to exclaim: Holy, holy are thy judgments, O Lord God Almighty—but I know my guilt; I transgressed thy law, and my transgressions are mine; and the devil hath obtained me, that I am a prey to his awful misery.*

Prepare your souls for that glorious day

How does one look forward in confidence to the Day of Judgment? In a word, by being righteous.

47–49 Jacob is constrained to teach his followers about the consequences of sin.

> *50 Come, my brethren, every one that thirsteth, come ye to the waters; and he that hath no money, come buy and eat; yea, come **buy wine and milk without money** and without price.*
> *51 Wherefore, do not spend money for that which is of no worth, nor your labor for that which cannot satisfy. Hearken diligently unto me, and remember the words which I have spoken; and come unto the Holy One of Israel, and feast upon that which perisheth not, neither can be corrupted, and **let your soul delight in fatness.***

Buy wine and milk without money; let your soul delight in fatness

The theme of gospel blessings being free is found elsewhere in the scriptures. In this instance, Jacob is quoting Isaiah 55:1–2. Compare also 2 Nephi 26:25 and Alma 1:20. The Savior dispenses His atoning blessings without charge, requiring only a broken heart and a contrite spirit (see 3 Nephi 9:20). As an extension of this thought, we remind ourselves that this life is the time to prepare to meet God (see Alma 5:28; 12:24; 34:32). We need time to rest and relax. We need a plan on how to use our time and our temporal assets. We need not live a life of guilt wondering if we have done enough. The bottom-line question of conscience is this: Do we spend our time and money on what matters most? Do we invest our hearts and souls in the things of the Lord—which He dispenses free of charge to the faithful and obedient of Zion?

> 52 *Behold, my beloved brethren,* ***remember the words of your God; pray unto him continually by day, and give thanks unto his holy name by night.*** *Let your hearts rejoice.*

Remember the Words of Your God

If the words of this prophet of former times resonate in our hearts, then his message becomes current, timely, and authoritative. We remember the words of God by pondering them, praying continually in humility and thanksgiving, and by keeping the commandments.

EVIDENCE: Pray unto him continually by day, and give thanks unto his holy name by night

This construct is an example of what is called a "synonymous parallelism"—where the substance of one line is repeated or echoed with a variation in the second. This kind of poetic construct appears frequently in the Old Testament and was first articulated in 1898 by E. W. Bullinger, a clergyman and biblical scholar. Types of parallelisms include synonymous, synthetic, antithetic, alternate, repeated alternate, extended alternate, and chiasmus. Donald W. Parry points out that "the Book of Mormon contains numerous examples of each of the seven types of parallelism presented in Bullinger's work" (*Echoes,* 160–161). The fact that no one had articulated the various types of parallelisms at the time the Book of Mormon was translated is yet another witness to the book's authenticity. (See other examples in 1 Nephi 17:45 and 2 Nephi 25:2; see also *Echoes,* 106–161.)

> 53 *And behold* ***how great the covenants of the Lord,*** *and how great his condescensions unto the children of men; and because of his greatness, and his grace and mercy, he has promised unto us that our seed shall not utterly be destroyed, according to the flesh, but that he would preserve them; and in future generations they shall become a righteous branch unto the house of Israel.*
>
> 54 *And now, my brethren, I would speak unto you more; but on the morrow I will declare unto you the remainder of my words. Amen.*

2 Nephi 9:54

How great the covenants of the Lord

Jacob's discourse on covenant integrity and honor centers on the Atonement of Jesus Christ.

Applying the Atonement in Our Lives

The word is clear on how we apply the Atonement to our lives. In this chapter Jacob counsels us on things to beware of that would prevent us from receiving the blessings of the Atonement in our lives. Here are a few:

1. Transgressing the laws and failing to repent (see 2 Nephi 9:27). Unrepentant sins separate us from the Lord and leave us exposed to the whole law (see D&C 19:15–19).
2. Wasting away our lives through idleness (see 2 Nephi 9:27). How often is idleness the gateway to transgression!
3. Holding to the learning of man and failing to take the counsel of God (see 2 Nephi 9:28–29). Some of God's children become enamored by their secular learning. The learning of man ever changes with the passage of time. God's knowledge is eternal—and absolute. Jacob said it best, "But to be learned is good if they hearken unto the counsels of God" (2 Nephi 9:29). God is omniscient, having unlimited knowledge (see 2 Nephi 9:20; D&C 38:1–2; 88:7–13); possesses "a fulness of truth, yea, even of all truth" (D&C 93:26); "has all power, all wisdom, and all understanding" (Alma 26:35); is infinite in understanding (see Psalm 147:4–5); and comprehends all things (see Alma 26:35; D&C 88:41).
4. Letting riches become our treasure (see 2 Nephi 9:30). If our hearts are set upon our earthly treasures, we often forget the poor and the needy. If we seek to do good with our wealth, we are blessed (see Jacob 2:19).
5. Being unwilling to hear the word of God (see 2 Nephi 9:31). We live by every word that proceedeth forth from the mouth of God (see D&C 84:43–46). In the tree of life vision, those who did not hold to the iron rod wandered off in strange paths and ended up in the spacious building or perished in the depths of the river (hell).
6. Being unwilling to see (see 2 Nephi 9:32). If we fail to have an eye single to the glory of God, we will be full of darkness; by way of contrast, we can be filled with light and comprehend all things (see D&C 88:67).

7. Having not made a covenant or yielded our hearts to the Lord, having an uncircumcised heart (see 2 Nephi 9:33). Until we yield our heart to the Lord we will never be purified or sanctified (see Helaman 3:35).
8. Lying (see 2 Nephi 9:34). To lie is to bear false witness. In this circumstance, we are dishonest with our fellowmen. We are no longer worthy of entrance into the temple of our God.
9. Murdering (see 2 Nephi 9:35). "Thou shalt do no murder" (Matthew 19:18). Elder Bruce R. McConkie expounded on the sin of murder:

> Murder, the unlawful killing of a human being with malice aforethought or under such circumstances of criminality that the malice is presumed, "is a sin unto death" (1 John 5:16–17), a sin for which there is "no forgiveness" (D&C. 42:79), meaning that a murderer can never gain salvation. "No murderer hath eternal life abiding in him" (1 John 3:15). He cannot join the Church by baptism; he is outside the pale of redeeming grace. . . . Murderers are forgiven eventually—but only in the sense that all sins are forgiven except the sin against the Holy Ghost; they are not forgiven in the sense that celestial salvation is made available to them. (Matt. 12:31–32; *Teachings*, 356–357.) After they have paid the full penalty for their crime, they shall go on to a telestial inheritance. (See Rev. 22:15.) (*Mormon Doctrine,* 2d ed. [Salt Lake City: Bookcraft, 1966], 520)

10. Committing whoredoms (see 2 Nephi 9:36). Living an unchaste life (sexual transgressions) is committing whoredoms, yet is forgivable through repentance.
11. Worshipping false gods (idols) (see 2 Nephi 9:37). There are many idols we can worship. Anything that is not of God should be avoided. We are to have no other gods before us (see Exodus 20:3).
12. Remaining unrepentant (see 2 Nephi 9:38). Those who die in their sins—will remain in their sins when they behold His face. There is hope for their growth and repentance in the hereafter (see D&C 138).
13. Being carnally minded (see Nephi 9:39). Those who are carnally minded love Satan more than God (see Moses 5:13). They become a natural man—an unrepentant man (see Mosiah 2:38; Mosiah 3:19)

Jacob reminds us that to be spiritually minded is life eternal. This glorious chapter can change lives. I had my gospel students read this chapter for thirty straight days. It changed their lives, and it will make a difference in the life of anyone who does this. (Ed J. Pinegar)

CONCLUDING THOUGHTS

The plan of happiness is dependent upon the Atonement, the centerpiece of the gospel and the empowering element of the plan of salvation. Our very lives are dependent upon the infinite and eternal sacrifice of our Lord and Savior Jesus Christ. President Gordon B. Hinckley testifies:

> I sense in a measure the meaning of His atonement. I cannot comprehend it all. It is so vast in its reach and yet so intimate in its effect that it defies comprehension. When all is said and done, when all of history is examined, when the deepest depths of the human mind have been explored, there is nothing so wonderful, so majestic, so tremendous as this act of grace when the Son of the Almighty, the prince of His Father's royal household, . . . gave His life in ignominy and pain so that all of the sons and daughters of God, of all generations of time, every one of whom must die, might walk again and live eternally." (*Teachings of Gordon B. Hinckley* [Salt Lake City: Deseret Book, 1997], 28)

CHAPTER 10

OVERVIEW

Jacob recaptures the essence of his message to the people: the Lord will remember His covenant promises to the house of Israel; the Jews who will crucify their Lord will be scattered and smitten but later gathered and restored to their inheritance as they return to the worship of the true Savior; the Gentile nations will foster the Restoration and receive grand blessings of liberty as they turn to the Lord. Jacob exhorts the people to be reconciled cheerfully to God through obedience and thus enjoy the blessings of eternal grace bestowed through the Atonement of Jesus Christ.

> *1 AND now I, Jacob, speak unto you again, my beloved brethren, concerning this*
> ***righteous branch** of which I have spoken.*
> *2 For behold, the **promises** which we have obtained are **promises** unto us according*
> *to the flesh; wherefore, as it has been shown unto me that many of our children shall*

perish in the flesh because of unbelief, nevertheless, God will be ***merciful*** *unto many; and* ***our children shall be restored,*** *that they may come to that which will give them* ***the true knowledge of their Redeemer.***

Righteous branch; promises; merciful; our children shall be restored; the true knowledge of their Redeemer

Jacob's prophetic view of the future of the house of Israel assures us that God is in charge, that the principles of mercy and truth will prevail, and that many children among his posterity—though they will surely pass through tribulation and trial—will eventually be restored. Like Lehi and Nephi before him, Jacob knows of the catastrophes that await the future generation of Nephites because of pride and wickedness, but he also knows that God will restore the righteous seed of Israel to their covenant blessings in the latter days. Do we have the same degree of faith in God's mercy and love for our own children and grandchildren? Though they might pass through sore tribulation and reversal, do we believe in the power of God's deliverance to the degree that we can say, with Jacob, that these future generations can look forward to the full measure of God's blessings—based on their righteousness and covenant valor?

3 Wherefore, as I said unto you, it must needs be expedient that ***Christ****—for in the last night the angel spake unto me that this should be his name—should come among the Jews, among those who are the more wicked part of the world; and they shall crucify him—for thus it behooveth our God, and* ***there is none other nation on earth that would crucify their God.***
4 For should the mighty miracles be wrought among other nations they would repent, and know that he be their God.
5 But ***because of priestcrafts and iniquities,*** *they at Jerusalem will stiffen their necks against him, that he be crucified.*

EVIDENCE: Christ. Foreknowledge of Christ's Advent (see 2 Nephi 10:3, Alma 7:10–12; Mosiah 3:5–10; Helaman 8:13–20)

Long before the birth of the Savior, prophets in the Book of Mormon testified of His coming and described important events in His life. In fact, in this book aptly subtitled "Another Testament of Jesus Christ," we read prophecies about His birth, His mother's name, His baptism, His teachings, His miraculous healings, His casting out of devils, His temptations and suffering, His crucifixion, and, finally, His resurrection. The Book of Mormon also declares that many prophets in the Old World knew and prophesied about details in Christ's life many years before his birth. Critics of the Book of Mormon state that the specifics of Christ's life could not possibly have been known before he was born, but we learn from ancient documents that early Christians believed otherwise. For example, in the twelfth chapter of the *Epistle of Barnabas,* we read that Moses knew that the Messiah would be named Jesus. (See *Echoes,* 242–246.)

There is none other nation on earth that would crucify their God; because of priestcrafts and iniquities

In general, the people among whom the Savior ministered during His mortal sojourn accepted Him and were inclined to regard Him in a prophetic light—though a true understanding of the coming Messiah as the Redeemer and Son of God had been lost over the preceding generations. It was the ecclesiastical leadership of the Jewish culture that turned on the Savior with vengeance and caused Him to be put to death. Caiaphas, the high priest, one of the Sadducees, presided over the council in which the Savior was falsely accused and condemned (see Matthew 26:3; 57).

> *6 Wherefore, because of their iniquities, destructions, famines, pestilences, and bloodshed shall come upon them; and they who shall not be* ***destroyed*** *shall be* ***scattered*** *among all nations.*
> *7 But behold, thus saith the Lord God: When the day cometh that they shall* ***believe in me,*** *that I am Christ, then have I covenanted with their fathers that they shall be* ***restored*** *in the flesh, upon the earth, unto the lands of their inheritance.*
> *8 And it shall come to pass that they shall be* ***gathered*** *in from their long dispersion, from the isles of the sea, and from the four parts of the earth; and the nations of the Gentiles shall be great in the eyes of me, saith God, in carrying them forth to the lands of their inheritance.*

Destroyed; scattered; believe in me; restored; gathered

The Lord will remember His covenant promises to His people. When they again turn to Him, He will restore their blessings and their inheritance. It is instructive that the establishment of the modern state of Israel was proclaimed on May 14, 1948, with the help of Great Britain (a "Gentile" nation). Israel was admitted as a member of the United Nations a year later, on May 11, 1949. The United States, another "Gentile" nation, has been a staunch supporter of Israel since the beginning of its modern-day existence. The rancor and conflict between Israel and her Arab neighbors continues to this day. Eventually, at the time of the Second Coming, the Jewish people will remember who their true Savior is:

> And then shall the Jews look upon me and say: What are these wounds in thine hands and in thy feet?
>
> Then shall they know that I am the Lord; for I will say unto them: These wounds are the wounds with which I was wounded in the house of my friends. I am he who was lifted up. I am Jesus that was crucified. I am the Son of God.
>
> And then shall they weep because of their iniquities; then shall they lament because they persecuted their king (D&C 45:51–53).

The Lord will remember His covenant people and will gather them in. We, too, belong to the covenant fold. Will we remember our covenants regarding the seed of Abraham—that we may assist in the gathering of Israel and that through us and our seed all mankind may be blessed (see D&C 110:11–16).

> *9 Yea, the kings of the **Gentiles** shall be nursing fathers unto them, and their queens shall become nursing mothers; wherefore, the promises of the Lord are great unto the **Gentiles,** for he hath spoken it, and who can dispute?*
> *10 But behold, this land, said God, shall be a land of thine inheritance, and the **Gentiles shall be blessed** upon the land.*
> *11 And this land shall be **a land of liberty unto the Gentiles,** and there shall be no kings upon the land, who shall raise up unto the Gentiles.*
> *12 And I will fortify this land against all other nations.*
> *13 And he that fighteth against Zion shall perish, saith God.*
> *14 For he that raiseth up a king against me shall perish, for I, the Lord, the king of heaven, will be their king, and **I will be a light unto them forever,** that hear my words.*

A Land of Liberty unto the Gentiles; Gentiles Shall Be Blessed; I Will Be a Light unto Them Forever

The Lord will remember the Gentiles of the promised land and bless them with liberty as they come unto Him. President Spencer W. Kimball recalls this promise in the context of the dangers of worldwide conflict:

> Victory and defeat alike leave countries devastated and the conqueror and the conquered reduced. Wickedness brings war and war vomits destruction and suffering, hate, and bloodshed upon the guilty and the innocent alike.

> This book [Book of Mormon] should convince of the futility of war and the hazards of unrighteousness. A few prophets swimming in a sea of barbarism find it difficult to prevent the crumbling and final collapse of corrupt peoples. There is a great but conditional promise:
>
> "And this land shall be a land of liberty unto the Gentiles, and there shall be no kings upon the land. . . .
>
> "And I will fortify this land against all other nations. . . .
>
> "I, the Lord, the king of heaven, will be their king, and I will be a light unto them forever, that hear my words." (2 Nephi 10:11–12, 14.) (*Faith Precedes the Miracle* [Salt Lake City: Deseret Book, 1972], 332–334)

15–22 Jacob summarizes the essence of his message: that the Lord will remember His covenant people, protect them from their enemies, and gather them again in the latter days through the auspices of the Gentile nations. Jacob entreats his people—who have been led away from their homeland to one of the "isles" of the sea (verses 20–21)—to be righteous and obedient and thus harvest the blessings of heaven.

> *23 Therefore,* ***cheer up your hearts,*** *and remember that ye are free to act for yourselves—to choose the way of everlasting death or the way of eternal life.*
>
> *24 Wherefore, my beloved brethren,* ***reconcile yourselves to the will of God,*** *and not to the will of the devil and the flesh; and remember, after ye are reconciled unto God, that it is only in and* ***through the grace of God*** *that ye are saved.*

Cheer up your hearts; reconcile yourselves to the will of God; through the grace of God

Jacob's tenor is one of cheer and rejoicing in the opportunity we have to align ourselves with the principles of heaven and enjoy the blessings of grace. The counsel of Jacob applies to us as well as to his listeners in ancient America. We are to reconcile ourselves to the will of God and remember that we are saved through His grace. Therefore, let us seek the will of God in all things and act on the words of Nephi: "For we labor diligently to write, to persuade our children, and also our brethren, to believe in Christ, and to be reconciled to God; for we know that it is by grace that we are saved, after all we can do" (2 Nephi 25:23).

> *25 Wherefore, may God raise you from death by the power of the resurrection, and also from everlasting death by the* ***power of the atonement,*** *that ye may be received into the eternal kingdom of God, that ye may praise him through grace divine. Amen.*

Power of the atonement

Jacob invokes a priestly blessing upon his listeners (and his modern readers) regarding the power of the Atonement. It is only in and through the Atonement of Jesus Christ that we have hope of being reconciled to God and gathered into the fold of the Lord to complete our preparations for returning to our heavenly home.

CHAPTER 11

OVERVIEW

Nephi speaks of the power of witnesses to establish the divinity of the Savior's mission and provide guidance for the obedient. He blends his own testimony with that of Isaiah and Jacob for the good of his posterity. All three have seen God, who will send "more witnesses" (verse 3) to prove His word. Nephi delights in confirming the truths of the gospel. He records many of the words of Isaiah so that others can liken these words to their own lives and rejoice.

> *1 AND now, Jacob spake many more things to my people at that time; nevertheless only these things have I caused to be written, for the things which I have written sufficeth me.*
> *2 And now I, Nephi, write more of* ***the words of Isaiah,*** *for my soul delighteth in his words. For* ***I will liken his words unto my people,*** *and I will send them forth unto all my children, for* ***he verily saw my Redeemer, even as I have seen him.***

The words of Isaiah; I will liken his words unto my people; he verily saw my Redeemer, even as I have seen him

Prophets of God are witnesses of the reality and mission of the Savior. They confirm for us the truthfulness of His gospel and of divine principles. Nephi has deep admiration and respect for the words of Isaiah, who ministered a scant century and a half before him. Both have seen God and convey to their listeners and readers the glorious message of redemption and reconciliation—plus a compelling warning for mortals to relinquish worldly pursuits and come unto Christ.

3 And my brother, Jacob, also has seen him as I have seen him; wherefore, ***I will send their words forth unto my children*** *to prove unto them that my words are true. Wherefore, by* ***the words of three,*** *God hath said, I will establish my word. Nevertheless,* ***God sendeth more witnesses,*** *and he proveth all his words.*

I will send their words forth unto my children; the words of three; God sendeth more witnesses

Nephi is moved by the spirit of prophecy to bear witness to the truthfulness of the gospel before his people. He pours out his soul in the expression of joy over the things that delight him most—the words and testimony of the prophets—Isaiah and Jacob, in this case—which prove that all of the words of God are true. Nephi finds spiritual fulfillment in the opportunity to confirm the divinity of Christ's mission and the power of the Atonement, based on grace, justice, mercy, and love. In all of this, Nephi chooses to blend his witness with that of his brother Jacob and, especially, with the prophet Isaiah, declaring that "by the words of three, God hath said, I will establish my word. Nevertheless, God sendeth more witnesses, and he proveth all his words" (verse 3).

Memories: The Cords of Testimony

All of us have been edified by experiences in testimony meetings of being able to blend together the witnesses of many individuals concerning the truthfulness of the gospel. The Book of Mormon, "Another Testament of Jesus Christ," is a sacred compilation of testimonies from a long sequence of prophets. It is a kind of tapestry of recorded witnesses, the strands or cords of which are the individual testimonies of inspired men of God speaking under the influence of the Spirit.

When the Savior appeared to the ancient Nephites following His resurrection, He taught them with such power and authority that peace prevailed among them for some 200 years. Among the scriptural references He cited was this statement from Isaiah: "Enlarge the place of thy tent, and let them stretch forth the curtains of thy habitations; spare not, lengthen thy cords and strengthen thy stakes" (3 Nephi 22:2; compare Isaiah 54:2). The reference to cords is interesting. The word *cord* in the scriptures sometimes has a negative connotation, as in "cords of death" (D&C 121:44) or cords of confinement and restriction. In the image from Isaiah, however, the word *cords* refers to the means of supporting the tent of Zion, or the canopy of the expanding kingdom of God on the earth. Thus the stakes anchor the cords, and the cords (acting with the tent poles) support the curtains or tent fabric. In an earlier reference from Isaiah, the word *cords* is used in a similar way: "Look upon Zion, the city of our solemnities: thine eyes shall see Jerusalem a quiet habitation, a tabernacle *that* shall not be taken down; not one of the stakes thereof shall ever be removed, neither shall any of the cords thereof be broken" (Isaiah 33:20).

If the word *stake* has reference to a community of Saints joined in a mutual cause to build up the tent of Zion or the kingdom of God, what does the word *cord* imply? In general, it shares with the word *stake* the same symbolic meaning. "Elder Joseph Fielding Smith informs us that . . . Zion is the tent, the settlements surrounding her, are the cords and stakes." (*Essentials in Church History*, 146–147.) (Roy W. Doxey, *The Doctrine and Covenants Speaks* [Salt Lake City: Deseret Book, 1964], 2:205–206)

However, one could make the case that the word *cord* could imply something more specific. The strength of the communities of God resides in the character and Christlike attributes of the Saints who live there. These attributes are evidenced by their words and deeds while engaged in a "godly walk and conversation" (D&C 20:69) according to patterns prescribed by the gospel of Jesus Christ. In that sense, the word *cord* might be taken, therefore, to imply the living testimony of the Saints. It is the strength of that testimony, born of the Spirit, that supports the tent of Zion.

One of the themes of the Book of Mormon is the extraordinary leverage that is gained when testimonies of righteous people are intertwined. Just as a cord is made stronger by braiding together individual strands, so is the witness of truth strengthened when individual testimonies are interwoven to support each other.

This process of intertwining testimonies was encapsulated perfectly by Nephi when he said that he was going to send forth to his children the words of Isaiah and Jacob concerning the Redeemer "to prove unto them that my words are true. Wherefore, by the words of three [in this case Nephi, Jacob, and Isaiah], God hath said, I will establish my word. Nevertheless, God sendeth more witnesses, and he proveth all his words. Behold, my soul delighteth in proving unto my people the truth of the coming of Christ. . . ." (2 Nephi 11:3–4).

The process of sending "more witnesses" is ongoing and ever operational. The greatest miracle in this whole process occurs when the individual reader of the Book of Mormon intertwines his or her own testimony with that of the authors and compilers of the work in the form of steady spiritual growth and increased righteousness—all through a process of lengthening the cords of Zion and extending the kingdom of God on the earth. (Richard J. Allen)

EVIDENCE: The words of three—The Witnesses

Contrary to some skeptics, Joseph Smith was not the only person to see the gold plates from which he translated the Book of Mormon. Eleven others bore witness that they saw the plates, and the honesty and consistency of these men is evident in surviving documents written by or about them (see *Echoes*, 203–210).

4 Behold, ***my soul delighteth*** *in proving unto my people the truth of the coming of*
Christ; for, for this end hath the law of Moses been given; and all things which have been
given of God from the beginning of the world, unto man, are the typifying of him.
5 And also ***my soul delighteth*** *in the covenants of the Lord which he hath made to*
our fathers; yea, ***my soul delighteth*** *in his grace, and in his justice, and power, and*
mercy in the great and eternal plan of deliverance from death.
6 And ***my soul delighteth*** *in proving unto my people that save Christ should come all*
men must perish.
7 For if there be no Christ there be no God; and if there be no God we are not, for there
could have been no creation. But ***there is a God,*** *and he is Christ, and he cometh in*
the fulness of his own time.

My soul delighteth; there is a God

There is deep and abiding joy in having a testimony of the gospel and sharing it with others in the spirit of truth and love. In fact, such joy exceeds that which derives from any other source, as the Lord makes clear:

> And if it so be that you should labor all your days in crying repentance unto this people, and bring, save it be one soul unto me, how great shall be your joy with him in the kingdom of my Father!
>
> And now, if your joy will be great with one soul that you have brought unto me into the kingdom of my Father, how great will be your joy if you should bring many souls unto me!" (D&C 18:15–16)

Let us remember that we are totally dependent upon God for all things. Let us remember also, to express our thanksgiving to our Heavenly Father and His Only Begotten Son by sharing the gospel message with others.

8 And now I write some of the words of Isaiah, that whoso of my people shall see these
words may lift up their hearts and rejoice for all men. Now these are the words, and ye
may liken them unto you and unto all men.

The Manner of Prophesying Among the Jews

The words of Isaiah teach us of the mission and divinity of Jesus Christ (see Isaiah 7:14; 9:6–7;

53:1–2), the destiny of the house of Israel (see Isaiah 2:1–5; 27:12–13; 43:1–7; 49:5–17), and the things we need to do to be worthy of the blessings of God (see Isaiah 58:1–14; 5:8–24).

Isaiah is quoted extensively in the New Testament. As already mentioned, some twenty complete chapters (and parts of one additional chapter) from Isaiah are found in the Book of Mormon. Familiar phrases of Isaiah are also found in the Doctrine and Covenants. This should not be surprising. All scriptures are the words of Christ. They resonate with one another. The doctrine is His. He is the one who gave the words.

To understand the words of Isaiah and the manner of prophesying among the Jews (see 2 Nephi 25:1), we can tune our ear to the following kinds of constructions:

- Dualism: Language and words with dual meanings can be best understood in terms of the cultural and religious background of the people of that day.
- Historical Setting: Understanding cultural and historical patterns, including details of the Mosaic Law, can often bring clarity to the reading of the ancient prophets and enable us to liken their words more readily to our own circumstances.
- Geographical Setting: Knowing the location of cities and surrounding areas brings more meaning to certain passages (see Isaiah 10:28–32, for example).
- Figurative Language: Certain figures of speech common in that day were used with regularity, sometimes making it difficult for us to understand specific passages unless we become familiar with the patterns used. Isaiah used graphic imagery to portray meanings so that the depth of understanding would increase. For example, using Sodom and Gomorrah as an example portrays not just wickedness, but gross wickedness worthy of destruction.
- Spirit of Prophecy: Nephi was to give us this counsel at a future time: "Wherefore, hearken, O my people, which are of the house of Israel, and give ear unto my words; for because the words of Isaiah are not plain unto you, nevertheless they are plain unto all those that are filled with the spirit of prophecy. But I give unto you a prophecy, according to the spirit which is in me; wherefore I shall prophesy according to the plainness which hath been with me from the time that I came out from Jerusalem with my father; for behold, my soul delighteth in plainness unto my people, that they may learn" (2 Nephi 25:4). Nephi makes clear to us that to understand Isaiah we need the spirit of prophecy. The spirit of prophecy is a gift of the Spirit (see D&C 46:22). Knowing that Jesus Christ is the Savior of the world comes by the spirit of prophecy. This is the gift that the sons of Mosiah possessed (see

Alma 17:3). This gift requires great effort on our part to be worthy. One cannot simply ask without putting forth effort as the example of Oliver Cowdery has demonstrated (see D&C 9:7–8). (Ed J. Pinegar and Richard J. Allen)

CHAPTER 12

OVERVIEW

Nephi quotes Isaiah 2. In the latter days the temple of the Lord will be erected in a lofty place. Nations will flow unto Zion to be instructed of the Lord and walk in His paths. Haughtiness, pride, and evil will be defeated at the Second Coming. Peace will prevail during the millennial reign of the Lord. The wicked will recoil in fear at His presence.

1 THE word that ***Isaiah,*** *the son of Amoz,* ***saw*** *concerning Judah and Jerusalem:*

Saw

The Hebrew word from which "saw" is translated in the King James edition is *khazah,* which means "envisioned." Thus the inference is that Isaiah received the word (or message from the Lord) through a vision. (See footnote 2b for Isaiah 2:1 in the LDS edition of the Bible.)

Isaiah, Prophet of God

Isaiah plays a profound role in the Book of Mormon. His inspired word accompanies Lehi and his family upon the plates of brass obtained from Laban, and it continues to travel to all points of the globe in the pages of the Book of Mormon, a modern witness for Christ. The Savior's commandment with reference to Isaiah still rings with great force: "AND now, behold, I say unto you, that ye ought to search these things. Yea, a commandment I give unto you that ye search these things diligently; for great are the words of Isaiah. For surely he spake as touching all things concerning my people which are of the house of Israel; therefore it must needs be that he must speak also to the Gentiles. And all things that he spake have been and shall be, even according to the words which he spake" (3 Nephi 23:1–3).

The style of Isaiah is unique. The Lord gave him a profound gift to express with resounding power the message of the visions accorded him as the spokesperson for the Lord in his day. His humble response to the call of the Lord is recorded in Isaiah 6 (see 2 Nephi 16). He wrote in the period 740 B.C. to 701 B.C. at a time when Israel had incurred the anger of the Lord to an especially high degree through her wanton behavior, pride, and idolatry. Isaiah intermingles references to events of his own day with those of coming events, often within the same passage. His is the age-old prophetic message that "wickedness never was happiness" (see Alma 41:10), that Israel will suffer by persisting in her prideful and ungodly walk, and that good will eventually triumph in the last days as the faithful are gathered together in holy places of refuge.

Isaiah continually reminds us of our covenant obligations before the Lord. If the Book of Mormon is a "Another Testament of Jesus Christ," then Isaiah is the bridge that helps to unite the voice of the Old Testament and the voice of the New Testament (in which Isaiah is quoted more than any other prophet) and then, in turn, the voices of prophets from the Book of Mormon. We can be grateful that Isaiah is so often cited in the Book of Mormon, which serves a greater role in interpreting and unfolding the words of Isaiah than any other book.

> *2 And it shall come to pass in the last days, when* ***the mountain of the Lord's house*** *shall be established in the top of the mountains, and shall be exalted above the hills, and* ***all nations shall flow unto it.***

The mountain of the Lord's house; all nations shall flow unto it

Isaiah sees our day: the temple, the gathering of Israel, and the establishment of Zion. Nephi is also favored to view the latter days in prophetic vision, as are most certainly all the prophets in all dispensations. Among the first initiatives undertaken by the Nephites upon separating themselves from the Lamanites is to construct a temple, patterned after the great temple of Solomon. Clearly Nephi has a keen sense of covenant history and a commitment to align his growing branch of Israel with the practices of a Zion people (see 2 Nephi 5:16).

> This great prophecy [2 Nephi 12:2–3], as is often the case, is subject to the law of multiple fulfillment. 1. In Salt Lake City and other mountain locations temples, in the full and true sense of the word, have been erected, and representatives of all nations are flowing unto them to learn of God and his ways. In this connection and as part of the general fulfillment of Isaiah's prophecy, is the fact that one of the world's greatest genealogical societies has been established in Salt Lake City—a society to which people of all nations come to do the ancestral research which must precede the performance of vicarious temple ordinances. 2. But the day is yet future when the Lord's house is to be built on that "Mount Zion" which is "the city of New Jerusalem" in Jackson County, Missouri. (D&C 84:2–4.) Mount Zion, itself,

> will be the mountain of the Lord's house in the day when that glorious temple is erected. 3. When the Jews flee unto Jerusalem, it will be "unto the mountains of the Lord's house" (D&C 133:13), for a holy temple to be built there also as part of the work of the great era of restoration. (Ezek. 37:24–28.)" (Bruce R. McConkie, *Mormon Doctrine,* 2d ed. [Salt Lake City: Bookcraft, 1966], 518)

How do these grand concepts apply to each of us and our families today? As the seed of Abraham, we have a great responsibility to participate in bringing the saving and exalting truths of the gospel to all quarters of the earth and promoting and sustaining the gathering of the Lord's elect to Zion.

> *3 And many people shall go and say, Come ye, and let us go up to the mountain of the Lord, to the house of the God of Jacob; and he will teach us of his ways, and we will walk in his paths; for* ***out of Zion shall go forth the law, and the word of the Lord from Jerusalem.***

Out of Zion shall go forth the law, and the word of the Lord from Jerusalem

These words from verse 3 celebrate the flow of divine blessings from the two priesthood centers of the Lord's ministry (New Jerusalem and Old Jerusalem) on behalf of His sons and daughters in the latter days. Does this phrase from the writings of Isaiah represent a reinforcement of the same concept—expressed twice in different formulations for emphasis, or does it represent two related concepts (law and word), each with a separate meaning? Perhaps the following illustration will help to answer this question.

Memories: Both Law and Truth

My wife and I were living in the East during the construction of the Washington D.C. Temple. After that magnificent six-spired edifice was completed, we went one day to the top of the Washington Monument to enjoy the panoramic view. From that high perspective, we could view the great "temples of constitutional government"—the Lincoln Memorial to the west, the Jefferson Monument to the south, and the U.S. Capitol to the east. However, we were thrilled to view another imposing edifice to the north. It was the noble temple of the Lord rising against the horizon—an apt reminder that the Restoration was inaugurated soon after the Lord brought about the establishment of a system of laws in America that would foster the inalienable rights and agency of man: "And for this purpose have I established the Constitution of this land, by the hands of wise men whom I raised up unto this very purpose, and redeemed the land by the shedding of blood" (D&C 101:80).

In the millennial government of the Messiah, there are to be two grand centers of gathering: the New Jerusalem on the American continent and the Old Jerusalem (as renewed) in the Holy Land. Isaiah makes prophetic reference to this future establishment: "And many people shall go and say, Come ye, and let us go up to the mountain of the LORD, to the house of the God of Jacob; and he will teach us of his ways, and we will walk in his paths: for out of Zion shall go forth the law, and the word of the LORD from Jerusalem" (Isaiah 2:3; compare Micah 4:2). It is noteworthy that this same passage is also quoted by Jacob (see 2 Nephi 12:3), for his ministry among the emigrant remnants of Israel, like that of his older brother Nephi, took place in the New World, which was ordained of God to be the gathering place for Joseph and his seed (see Ether 13:8).

The phrase "for out of Zion shall go forth the law" was explained by President Harold B. Lee as follows:

> I have often wondered what the expression meant, that out of Zion shall go forth the law. Years ago I went with the brethren to the Idaho Falls Temple, and I heard in that inspired prayer of the First Presidency a definition of the meaning of that term "out of Zion shall go forth the law." Note what they said: "We thank thee that thou hast revealed to us that those who gave us our constitutional form of government were men wise in thy sight and that thou didst raise them up for the very purpose of putting forth that sacred document [as revealed in Doctrine and Covenants section 101]. . . . We pray that kings and rulers and the peoples of all nations under heaven may be persuaded of the blessings enjoyed by the people of this land by reason of their freedom and under thy guidance and be constrained to adopt similar governmental systems, thus to fulfill the ancient prophecy of Isaiah and Micah that . . . 'out of Zion shall go forth the law and the word of the Lord from Jerusalem'" (*Improvement Era,* October 1945, 564.)" (Donald W. Parry, Jay A. Parry, and Tina M. Peterson, *Understanding Isaiah* [Salt Lake City: Deseret Book, 1998], 27)

Isaiah must have foreseen the day when a great Gentile nation would arise based on laws that were consonant with celestial principles—a seedbed for the Restoration and the establishment of Zion and the New Jerusalem. Hence the phrase: "out of Zion shall go forth the law." From Jerusalem, the birthplace of the Savior, the eternal influence of the Word of God would flow forever. Such might be the inference of the phrase "and the word of the Lord from Jerusalem."

In the confluence of the two—the everlasting principles of celestial law and the redeeming word of truth—are met all of the essential powers and precepts leading to immortality and eternal life. (Richard J. Allen)

4 And he shall judge among the nations, and shall rebuke many people: and they shall
beat their swords into plow-shares, *and their spears into pruning-hooks—nation*
shall not lift up sword against nation, neither shall they learn war any more.
5 O house of Jacob, come ye and ***let us walk in the light of the Lord;*** *yea, come, for*
ye have all gone astray, every one to his wicked ways.

Beat their swords into plow-shares; let us walk in the light of the Lord

Isaiah foresees the time when the Lord will return to judge the people and restore peace to the world. Transforming swords and spears into the instruments of life-sustaining production—plow-shares (i.e. the shearing blades of the plow) and pruning hooks—is a memorable symbol of the transition from war to peace-time enterprises (compare Joel 10:9; Micah 4:3). With the dawning of His millennial reign, the Lord brings effulgent light to a world previously dominated by darkness and evil. His sons and daughters savor the opportunity to walk in His light and abandon the patterns of their former wickedness.

6–16 Isaiah perceives the epic conflict between the proud people of the world and the humble people who follow the ways of the Lord in His majesty. Pride will be brought down and haughtiness will be eliminated through the power of the Almighty.

17 And ***the loftiness of man shall be bowed down,*** *and the haughtiness of men shall*
be made low; and the Lord alone shall be exalted in that day.
18 And the idols he shall utterly abolish.
19 And ***they shall go into the holes of the rocks, and into the caves of the earth,***
for the fear of the Lord shall come upon them and the glory of his majesty shall smite
them, when he ariseth to shake terribly the earth.
20 In that day a man shall cast his idols of silver, and his idols of gold, which he hath
made for himself to worship, to the moles and to the bats;
21 To go into ***the clefts of the rocks,*** *and into* ***the tops of the ragged rocks,*** *for the*
fear of the Lord shall come upon them and the majesty of his glory shall smite them,
when he ariseth to shake terribly the earth.

> *22* ***Cease ye from man,*** *whose breath is in his nostrils; for wherein is he to be accounted of?*

THE LOFTINESS OF MAN SHALL BE BOWED DOWN; THEY SHALL GO INTO THE HOLES OF THE ROCKS, AND INTO THE CAVES OF THE EARTH; THE CLEFTS OF THE ROCKS; THE TOPS OF THE RAGGED ROCKS; CEASE YE FROM MAN

Isaiah's imagery of the anguish and self-consciousness of the haughty and wicked in the face of the Lord's presence is powerful motivation for all of us to avoid this state of affairs. The wicked find no shield and protection from the consuming glance of the eye of Deity—not in holes of the rocks, not in caves, not in ragged summits of stone. In contrast, the righteous find comfort and solace when charity dominates their lives and virtue garnishes their thoughts: "then shall thy confidence wax strong in the presence of God; and the doctrine of the priesthood shall distil upon thy soul as the dews from heaven. The Holy Ghost shall be thy constant companion, and thy scepter an unchanging scepter of righteousness and truth; and thy dominion shall be an everlasting dominion, and without compulsory means it shall flow unto thee forever and ever" (D&C 121:45-46).

CHAPTER 13

OVERVIEW

Nephi quotes Isaiah 3.

1–26 The wickedness of Judah will bring forth the judgments of the Lord. The people are brought into pathways of error because of misguided leadership. The Lord pleads for repentance and righteousness. The daughters of Zion have given themselves over to pride and superficiality. There shall be mourning for the men of war who are lost.

> *12 And my people, children are their oppressors, and women rule over them. O my people,* ***they who lead thee cause thee to err*** *and destroy the way of thy paths.*

THEY WHO LEAD THEE CAUSE THEE TO ERR

Nephi is favored with a prophetic view of the destiny of the people of Lehi. The visions that Nephi beholds when caught away in the Spirit (see 1 Nephi 11–14) give him a comprehensive view of the unfolding history of the remnant of the house of Israel in the New World. Jacob, his brother, is given a similar inspired view of the future. What they behold is often marked with the painful consequences of pride and wickedness. As it turns out, the Lamanites, in general, pursue the paths of wickedness because of the misguided traditions of their fathers. Only occasionally do they penetrate the darkness of their upbringing to emerge into the light of gospel truth. Later, despite periods of great spiritual abundance and prosperity, the Nephite nation itself eventually becomes extinct through the effects of consuming pride and wickedness. We would therefore do well, in our day, to pay strict attention to the warning of Isaiah that "they who lead thee cause thee to err"—and take steps to ensure that our own personal leadership in family, Church, and community is on track and in alignment with the values and principles of the gospel of Jesus Christ.

CHAPTER 14

OVERVIEW

Nephi quotes Isaiah chapter 4.

1–6 During the millennial reign of the Lord, glory and beauty shall prevail. Holiness will abound among the Saints of Zion when the Lord cleanses Zion and her daughters of all filth. The glory of the Lord will rest upon the dwelling places of the Lord's elect.

> *5 And the Lord will create upon every dwelling-place of mount Zion, and upon her assemblies,* ***a cloud and smoke by day and the shining of a flaming fire by night;*** *for upon all the glory of Zion shall be a defence.*
> *6 And there shall be a tabernacle for a shadow in the daytime from the heat, and for* ***a place of refuge, and a covert from storm and from rain.***

A CLOUD AND SMOKE BY DAY AND THE SHINING OF A FLAMING FIRE BY NIGHT

During the exodus following the deliverance of the Israelites from Egyptian bondage, the Lord marked the place of holiness and the pathway for progress by means of unmistakable signs: "For the cloud of the LORD *was* upon the tabernacle by day, and fire was on it by night, in the sight of all the house of Israel, throughout all their journeys" (Exodus 40:38; compare Numbers 9:15–20). In the celestial realm, this same glory will be the central source of enduring light: "And there shall be no night there; and they need no candle, neither light of the sun; for the Lord God giveth them light: and they shall reign for ever and ever" (Revelation 22:5). In the meantime, the dwelling places of Zion are to be repositories of light and truth as the Saints teach and live the principles of the gospel in their families. To the degree that families of Zion are righteous and obedient, they radiate the light of the truth in their countenances—and their homes therefore begin to display, however modestly, the "flaming fire" of the gospel. Could it be that our homes in Zion—like the temples of the Lord—will some day literally receive the visual "flaming fire" of God's blessings to be upon them as we proceed toward that time when the glory of the Father and the Son will supplant all other light? Concerning this theme, Elder Orson Pratt offered the following words on June 15, 1873:

> I do not see any cloud covering this house [the Salt Lake Tabernacle], or the congregation that is before me. What is the reason? The time has not yet come. The time is to come when God will meet with all the congregation of his Saints, and to show his approval, and that he does love them, he will work a miracle by covering them in the cloud of his glory. I do not mean something that is invisible, but I mean that same order of things which once existed on the earth so far as the tabernacle of Moses was concerned, which was carried in the midst of the children of Israel as they journeyed in the wilderness. Did God manifest himself in that tabernacle that was built according to the pattern which he gave unto his servant Moses? He did. In what way? In the day time a cloud filled that tabernacle. The Lord intended his people to be covered with the cloud continually, and he intended to reveal himself unto them, and to show forth his glory more fully amongst them; but they sinned so much in his sight that he declared—"My presence shall not go up with this people, lest I should break forth upon them in my fury and consume them in a moment." Because of their wickedness he withdrew his presence, and his glory in a great measure was taken from them; but still Moses was permitted to enter the tabernacle, and to behold the glory of God, and it is said that he talked with the Lord face to face—a blessing which God did intend to bestow upon all Israel had they kept his law and had not hardened their hearts against him. But in the latter days there will be a people so pure in Mount Zion, with a house established upon the tops of the mountains, that God will manifest himself, not only in their Temple and upon all their assemblies, with a visible cloud during the day, but when the night shall come, if they shall be assembled for worship, God will meet with them by his pillar of fire; and when they retire to their habitations, behold each habitation will be lighted up by the

> glory of God—a pillar of flaming fire by night. (*Journal of Discourses,* 26 vols. [London: Latter-day Saints' Book Depot, 1854–1886], 16:82–83)

A PLACE OF REFUGE, AND A COVERT FROM STORM AND FROM RAIN

In latter-day scripture, the Lord has proclaimed: "Behold, it is my will, that all they who call on my name, and worship me according to mine everlasting gospel, should gather together, and stand in holy places" (D&C 101:22). That gathering ensures for the faithful and obedient a continuing access to light and truth—as well as to safety and security: "And that the gathering together upon the land of Zion, and upon her stakes, may be for a defense, and for a refuge from the storm, and from wrath when it shall be poured out without mixture upon the whole earth." (D&C 115:6). Elder Boyd K. Packer has explained this concept:

> Each stake is a defense and a refuge and a standard. A stake is self-contained with all that is needed for the salvation and exaltation of those who would come within its influence, and temples are ever closer. . . .
>
> We speak of the Church as our refuge, our defense. There is safety and protection in the Church. It centers in the gospel of Jesus Christ. Latter-day Saints learn to look within themselves to see the redeeming power of the Savior of all mankind. The principles of the gospel taught in the Church and learned from the scriptures become a guide for each of us individually and for our families.
>
> We know that the homes we establish, and those of our descendants, will be the refuge spoken of in the revelations—the "light," the "standard," the "ensign" for all nations, and the "refuge" against the gathering storms (see D&C 115:5–6; Isaiah 11:12; 2 Nephi 21:12).
>
> The ensign to which all of us are to rally is Jesus Christ, the Son of God, the Only Begotten of the Father, whose Church this is and whose name we bear and whose authority we carry. ("A Defense and a Refuge," *Ensign*, Nov. 2006, 87–88)

These passages from Isaiah invoke a special set of questions of conscience for us all: Do we express often enough in our family circles our gratitude to God that such circles of comfort and safety are possible only as a blessing from heaven? Do we recognize the privilege of assembling in congregations of worship where the Spirit can be dispensed liberally for our edification? Do we look to the temples of God as sanctuaries where the gathering is promoted with no restrictions of time and date, where the promises of eternity are fulfilled for all of God's children of all generations?

How do we liken these passages from Isaiah to our daily lives? Here is a short checklist of ideas to aid us in worshipping the Lord in courage and truth, thereby showing our worthiness to receive the protecting hand of the Lord:

- Strive to become and remain part of the Lord's fold—the pure in heart (see D&C 97:21).
- Stand in holy places (see D&C 101:22).
- Maintain a perspective that is long-suffering and patient, for things work out in the due time of the Lord, and the trials of life are for our ultimate good.
- Remember that the protecting hand of the Lord comes to those who do their part.
- Operate on faith, with hope in the comfort and security of the Lord's care.

Memories: A Covert from Storm and from Rain

My wife, Carol Lynn, and I were privileged a few years ago to study the Book of Mormon with a group of young singles enrolled in a stake institute course. We presented the material in the context of its being an inspired road map to guide our footsteps in the latter days, just as President Ezra Taft Benson had counseled: "We must make the Book of Mormon a center focus of study [as] it was written for our day. The Nephites never had the book; neither did the Lamanites of ancient times. It was meant for us. Mormon wrote near the end of the Nephite civilization. Under the inspiration of God, who sees all things from the beginning, he abridged centuries of records, choosing the stories, speeches, and events that would be most helpful to us. . . . If they saw our day and chose those things which would be of greatest worth to us, is not that how we should study the Book of Mormon? We should constantly ask ourselves, 'Why did the Lord inspire Mormon (or Moroni or Alma) to include that in his record? What lesson can I learn from that to help me live in this day and age?'" (*Ensign*, Nov. 1986, 4).

That question was answered for us dramatically by an event that occurred shortly after the commencement of the institute class that year—the terror attack of September 11, 2001. Like everyone in the nation, we were shocked by the devastating upheaval wrought upon our way of life by evil forces. Could there be any security and peace after such a revolutionary shift in the status quo? And then we read together from the words of Isaiah that Nephi had included in his record: "And the Lord will create upon every dwelling-place of mount Zion, and upon her assemblies, a cloud and smoke by day and the shining of a flaming fire by night; for upon all the glory of Zion shall be a defence. And there shall be a tabernacle for a shadow in the daytime from the heat, and for a place of refuge, and a covert from storm and from rain" (2 Nephi 14:5–6, compare Isaiah 4:5–6).

One of the students later wrote to us expressing how the Book of Mormon, and specifically that passage from Isaiah, had been a blessing and a guide at a time of challenge: "When I consider 2 Nephi 14:5–6, I can't help but think of our nation's recent events. In a time when evil is so apparent and terror so present, I have asked myself where I might find refuge or safety. Right now I live far from the 'Holy Places' of my youth, namely my family and dear friends. But even so far away, I can find refuge in many places, like institute. After a hectic day at work, where my attention is distracted by so many busy, yet less important things, I am glad to have institute as a refuge, a place to associate with other saints, to feel the Spirit, and to study the word of God. It has truly been a blessing, 'a covert from storm and from rain.'" (Richard J. Allen)

CHAPTER 15

OVERVIEW

Nephi quotes Isaiah chapter 15 for his people and their posterity.

1–30 Isaiah presents an interesting simile in which the house of Israel is compared to a vineyard. The master of the vineyard does all in his power to obtain an abundant harvest, but the vineyard brings forth wild fruit. The analogy illustrates the Israelites turning their backs on the Lord and His principles. They shall be brought low, for "they have cast away the law of the Lord of Hosts, and despised the word of the Holy One of Israel" (verse 24). The Lord will raise an ensign to gather the worthy to the cause of righteousness.

Historical Framework

Nephi, in his fledgling but prospering circle of saints in the promised land, must have a feeling of dispersal, of being scattered—considering how far he is from his native Jerusalem, and the fact that he is now separated from his older brothers because of their rejection of righteousness. Is it any wonder that he is attracted to the writings of Isaiah, one of whose major themes is the scattering and eventual gathering of Israel? How Nephi must yearn for the security of his people, for their adherence to the principles of covenant integrity so that they might be gathered and preserved as a community of faithful servants unto the Lord. How he must anguish over the visionary views given him of his people's future apostasy and decline. How much he must rejoice to view the latter-day Restoration and gathering in of the remnants of his lineage as confirmed by Isaiah: "The remnant shall return, yea, even the remnant of Jacob, unto the mighty God" (2 Nephi 20:21). Nephi clearly perceives, like Isaiah, the coming "times of refreshing" (Acts 3:19) when the Lord will raise up an ensign to signal the ushering in of the last days: "And the Lord will set his hand again the second time to restore his people from their lost and fallen state. Wherefore, he will proceed to do a marvelous work and a wonder among the children of men" (2 Nephi 25:17; compare Isaiah 29:14). Thus Nephi lays out plainly the design of the Lord in preserving these very records for the blessing of coming generations: "Wherefore, he shall bring forth his words unto them, which words shall judge them at the last day, for they shall be given them for the purpose of convincing them of the true Messiah" (2 Nephi 25:18).

> *4* ***What could have been done more*** *to my vineyard that I have not done in it? Wherefore, when I looked that it should bring forth grapes it brought forth wild grapes.*

What could have been done more?

The language in Isaiah's simile anticipates the words of Zenos included in the allegory of the olive trees preserved by Jacob from the brass plates (see Jacob 5:41, 47, 49). We sense the anxiety and pain of the Lord of the Vineyard as he observes the shortcomings of His children—despite His everlasting love and ever-enduring patience. We remember the report of Enoch cited in the Pearl of Great Price:

> And it came to pass that the God of heaven looked upon the residue of the people, and he wept; and Enoch bore record of it, saying: How is it that the heavens weep, and shed forth their tears as the rain upon the mountains?
>
> And Enoch said unto the Lord: How is it that thou canst weep, seeing thou art holy, and from all eternity to all eternity?
>
> And were it possible that man could number the particles of the earth, yea, millions of earths like this, it would not be a beginning to the number of thy creations; and thy curtains are stretched out still; and yet thou art there, and thy bosom is there; and also thou art just; thou art merciful and kind forever;
>
> And thou hast taken Zion to thine own bosom, from all thy creations, from all eternity to all eternity; and naught but peace, justice, and truth is the habitation of thy throne; and mercy shall go before thy face and have no end; how is it thou canst weep?
>
> The Lord said unto Enoch: Behold these thy brethren; they are the workmanship of mine own hands, and I gave unto them their knowledge, in the day I created them; and in the Garden of Eden, gave I unto man his agency;

> And unto thy brethren have I said, and also given commandment, that they should love one another, and that they should choose me, their Father; but behold, they are without affection, and they hate their own blood;
>
> And the fire of mine indignation is kindled against them; and in my hot displeasure will I send in the floods upon them, for my fierce anger is kindled against them.
>
> Behold, I am God; Man of Holiness is my name; Man of Counsel is my name; and Endless and Eternal is my name, also. (Moses 7:28–35)

*18 **Wo unto them that draw iniquity with cords of vanity,** and **sin** as it were with **a cart rope;***
19 That say: Let him make speed, hasten his work, that we may see it; and let the counsel of the Holy One of Israel draw nigh and come, that we may know it.
*20 Wo unto them that **call evil good, and good evil,** that put darkness for light, and light for darkness, that put bitter for sweet, and sweet for bitter!*
21 Wo unto the wise in their own eyes and prudent in their own sight!

WO UNTO THEM THAT DRAW INIQUITY WITH CORDS OF VANITY; SIN WITH A CART ROPE; CALL EVIL GOOD, AND GOOD EVIL

Isaiah enumerates some of the failings of the Israelites that bring the wrath of God down upon them. Note the metaphor of "drawing" (enticing, pulling, attracting, embracing) iniquity with cords or ropes of vanity and pride. The phrase anticipates what King Benjamin says concerning the wise strategy for overcoming the carnal man by yielding "to the enticings of the Holy Spirit" (Mosiah 3:19). Isaiah warns of the opposite—yielding to the enticings of iniquity by drawing evil deeds to the individual by way of a cord. Furthermore, the people are warned against sinning "with a cart rope"—as if they were tethered to unrighteousness by a rope that binds them to the sinful load or burden they are dragging behind them down the pathway of life. The reference to those who "call evil good, and good evil" is an appropriate characterization of our modern culture of relative morals and abandoned principles.

*26 And he will **lift up an ensign** to the nations from far, and will hiss unto them from the end of the earth; and behold, they shall come with speed swiftly; none shall be weary nor stumble among them.*
*27 **None shall slumber nor sleep;** neither shall the girdle of their loins be loosed, nor the latchet of their shoes be broken;*

28 Whose arrows shall be sharp, and all their bows bent, and their horses' hoofs shall be counted like flint, and their wheels like a whirlwind, their roaring like a lion.
29 ***They shall roar like young lions;*** *yea, they shall roar, and lay hold of the prey, and shall carry away safe, and none shall deliver.*
30 And in that day they shall roar against them like the roaring of the sea; and if they look unto the land, behold, darkness and sorrow, and the light is darkened in the heavens thereof.

Lift up an ensign; none shall slumber nor sleep; they shall roar like young lions

The Lord will raise an ensign to the nations in the latter days and many people will flow unto it to be fed spiritual truth (compare Isaiah 11:10, 12; 18:3; Zechariah 9:16; 2 Nephi 21:10, 12; D&C 64:42; 105:39). We are participating in that process today. The ensign is the restored gospel of Jesus Christ in its fulness, with blessings of salvation for all mankind and exaltation for the faithful and elect. The work goes on inexorably, without interruption, as the Prophet Joseph Smith confirmed from the squalor of Liberty Jail. "How long can rolling waters remain impure? What power shall stay the heavens? As well might man stretch forth his puny arm to stop the Missouri river in its decreed course, or to turn it up stream, as to hinder the Almighty from pouring down knowledge from heaven upon the heads of the Latter-day Saints" (D&C 121:33).

CHAPTER 16

OVERVIEW

Nephi quotes Isaiah chapter 6 for his people and the coming generations.

1–13 Isaiah receives his calling as the mouthpiece of the Lord. He is humbled through a sense of his own imperfections and unworthiness. A seraphim (angel) carries out a ritualistic purification of Isaiah's lips to remove his iniquity. The Lord asks whom He should send to the people and Isaiah responds "Here am I; send me" (verse 8). The Lord gives Isaiah the commission to call the people to repentance, for they see not the way of salvation and hear not the eternal truth. Some, however, will respond and return to the Lord.

8 Also I heard the voice of the Lord, saying: ***Whom shall I send,*** *and who will go for us? Then I said:* ***Here am I; send me.***

Whom shall I send? Here am I; send me.

These words are reminiscent of the defining event in the premortal existence where the Savior is chosen to be the Redeemer according the plan of the Father: "And the Lord said: Whom shall I send? And one answered like unto the Son of Man: Here am I, send me. And another answered and said: Here am I, send me. And the Lord said: I will send the first" (Abraham 3:27). Isaiah follows the pattern set by the Son of God, in that he is a willing servant of the Lord, committed to following the principles of truth and light. As an application of this principle, we should take care (1) that we are accepting of the will of the Lord in regard to our various callings and assignments in the kingdom, and (2) that we perform our labors in keeping with the will of the Lord and His pattern of righteousness, rather than succumbing to the prideful and usurping pattern of Lucifer, who wanted to retain God's honor unto himself.

My Grace Is Sufficient

It is instructing that Isaiah, among all of the ancient prophets unsurpassed in mastery of his prophetic language, responded with contrition and meekness to his calling: "Then said I, woe is me! for I am undone [i.e., overwhelmed by a sense of inadequacy]; because I am a man of unclean lips, and I dwell in the midst of a people of unclean lips: for mine eyes have seen the King, the Lord of hosts" (Isaiah 6:5). Then in the continuing heavenly vision the Lord dispatches one of his angels to reassure the newly called prophet: "thine iniquity is taken away, and thy sin purged" (verse 7), whereupon Isaiah responds with humble words reminiscent of the Savior's own response in the premortal realm: "Here am I; send me" (verse 8; compare Abraham 3:27). This pattern of meekness in the face of a divine calling is not unlike the attitude of Moses on the mount: "Who am I, that I should go unto Pharaoh," says Moses to the Lord, "and that I should bring forth the children of Israel out of Egypt?" (Exodus 3:11). Whereupon the Lord responds with reassurance, "Certainly I will be with thee. . . ." (Exodus 3:12). But Moses persists: "O my Lord, I am not eloquent, neither heretofore, nor since thou hast spoken unto thy servant: but I am slow of speech, and of a slow tongue" (Exodus 4:10). Now the Lord comes back with this unassailable logic: "Who hath made man's mouth? or who maketh the dumb, or deaf, or the seeing, or the blind? have not I the Lord? Now therefore go, and I will be with thy mouth, and teach thee what thou shalt say" (Exodus 4:11–12).

In a similar way, Jeremiah had to overcome deep feelings of inadequacy when he was called as prophet: "Then said I, Ah, Lord God! behold, I cannot speak: for I am a child" (Jeremiah 1:6). Then the reassuring words of the Lord came to him: "Say not, I am a child; for thou shalt go to all that I shall send thee, and whatsoever I command thee thou shalt speak. Be not afraid of their faces: for I am with thee to deliver thee, saith the Lord. Then the Lord put forth his hand, and touched my mouth. And the Lord said unto me, Behold, I have put my words in thy mouth" (Jeremiah 1:7–8).

In ancient America, Moroni too expressed feelings of incompetence: "Lord, the Gentiles will mock at these things, because of our weakness in writing. . . . And thou hast made us that we could write but little, because of the awkwardness of our hands. . . ." (Ether 12:23–24). But the Lord's response to this sense of inadequacy is the same as the response to Moses, Jeremiah, Isaiah, and all leaders called to serve: "If men come unto me I will show unto them their weakness. I give unto men weakness that they may be humble; and my grace is sufficient for all men that humble themselves before me; for if they will humble themselves before me, and have faith in me, then will I make weak things become strong unto them" (Ether 12:27).

Thus the ancient records plainly teach the key to service and the answer to feelings of inadequacy on the part of anyone called on the Lord's errand: His grace is sufficient to lift us above our weakness and infuse our souls with the strength and the vision to succeed. When the Lord extends a calling, He provides the grace, the power, and the ability to make us equal to the task. He reminds us: "With men it is impossible, but not with God: for with God all things are possible" (Mark 10:27). (Richard J. Allen)

CHAPTER 17

OVERVIEW

Nephi quotes Isaiah chapter 7 to his people and the coming generation.

1–25 Ephraim and Syria enter a confederacy and come up against Judah to do battle. The Lord sends Isaiah to warn Ahaz, king of Judah, about the peril, but gives assurance that the alliance "shall not stand" (verse 7) because the days of Ephraim as a nation are numbered. When the Lord asks Ahaz to request a sign, the king demurs, but the Lord gives him a sign: the announcement of the coming of Immanuel, to be born of a virgin. The Lord alludes to the coming Assyrian conquest that will result in the ten tribes (Ephraim) being carried away [which event occurs in the year 721 B.C.].

> *14 Therefore, the Lord himself shall give you a sign—Behold, a virgin shall conceive, and shall bear a son, and shall call his name* ***Immanuel.***

IMMANUEL

Nephi sees in vision the coming of the Savior, born of "a virgin, most beautiful and fair above all other virgins" (1 Nephi 11:15). How Nephi must rejoice over this passage from Isaiah that confirmed his own spiritual witness concerning the Lamb of God, who will come to earth out of eternal love for God's children. The Book of Mormon, like the Old Testament, is a handbook of prophetic utterances foretelling the atoning mission of the Redeemer, Jesus Christ (see, for example, Isaiah 9:6; Hosea 13:14; Micah 5:2; Zechariah 9:9; 1 Nephi 10:11; 2 Nephi 17:14; Mosiah 13:33; Alma 7:7–13; Helaman 14:2). Chapter 7 of Isaiah deals with the first level of meaning as to the historical events of the day and as to the prediction that the alliance of Ephraim and Syria would not stand against Judah; but the higher implication of the message is that no earthly kingdom will stand against the kingdom of God to be established by the Son of God Himself during His earthly ministry.

> *20 In the same day shall the Lord shave with a razor that is hired, by them beyond the river, by the king of Assyria, the head, and the hair of the feet; and it shall also consume the* ***beard.*** *(Compare Isaiah 7:20, the source for this passage.)*

EVIDENCE: BEARD—VIEWS OF THE NATIVES (2 Nephi 17:20; Mosiah 11:8; Mormon 9:32; Ether 6:7; Moroni 8:8)

Around the time of the Book of Mormon's first publication, several other books were published that reflected the thinking of the times. These include Abner Cole's satire of the Book of Mormon titled *Book of Pukei,* Reverend Spaulding's *Manuscript Story,* and Ethan Smith's *View of the Hebrews.* In the *Book of Pukei,* we read of Native Americans dressed in Egyptian raiment and wearing long beards but also using items such as blankets, moccasins, and bark canoes. As he obviously mocks the Book of Mormon's origins, Cole also mistakenly gives the ancient Americans traits of contemporary Native Americans in upstate New York. In fact, in the Book of Mormon, we find no references to blankets, footwear, or beards, except in references to the Old World or to older scripture (such as the writings of Isaiah, cited above). Furthermore, Book of Mormon watercraft are called "barges," "vessels," or "ships," and they are made of unspecified materials (see *Echoes,* 318–323).

CHAPTER 18

OVERVIEW

Nephi quotes Isaiah chapter 8.

1–22 Isaiah conveys the word of the Lord—which predicts the defeat of earthly confederations such as that established by Ephraim and Syria against Judah. Assyria will pass through them as a great river. Fear not such alliances, but fear the Lord and keep His commandments. Watch for His coming. Those who reject Him "shall be driven to darkness" (verse 22), having no light.

> *13* ***Sanctify the Lord*** *of Hosts himself, and* ***let him be your fear,*** *and let him be your dread.*
> *14 And he shall be for a sanctuary; but for* ***a stone of stumbling,*** *and for a rock of offense to both the houses of Israel, for a gin and a snare to the inhabitants of Jerusalem.*
> *15 And many among them shall stumble and fall, and be broken, and be snared, and be taken.*
> *16* ***Bind up the testimony, seal the law among my disciples.***
> *17 And* ***I will wait upon the Lord,*** *that hideth his face from the house of Jacob, and I will look for him.*

Sanctify the Lord; let him be your fear a stone of stumbling; bind up the testimony; seal the law among my disciples; I will wait upon the Lord

These Messianic pronouncements give a preview of the Lord's ministry. He will indeed be a stumbling block for all who will not accept Him as the Messiah but remain calcified in empty rituals. His disciples will instead follow His law and keep his testimonies (i.e., commandments—see 2 Chronicles 34:31; Psalm 25:10; 78:56; 119:22, 168).

> *18 Behold, I and the children whom the Lord hath given me are for* ***signs and for wonders in Israel*** *from the Lord of Hosts, which dwelleth in Mount Zion.*

Signs and for wonders in Israel

The prophet Isaiah has two sons, both of which bear symbolic names that correspond to the predicted outcome of God's designs for His people:

- Maher-shalal-hash-baz (see 2 Nephi 18:1, 3; compare Isaiah 8:1, 3) in Hebrew means, approximately, "hurrying to the spoil hastens the plunder" (alluding to the misguided alliance of Ephraim and Syria which was defeated with the Assyrian invasion of 721 B.C.—and by extension to the eventual defeat of all earthly kingdoms rising up in alliance against the kingdom of God).

- Shearjashub (see 2 Nephi 17:3; compare Isaiah 7:3) in Hebrew means "a remnant shall return" (alluding to the eventual restoration of Israel in the latter days according to the design of God).

Thus the names of these two sons constitute a prophetic statement about the scattering and gathering of Israel according to the judgment and mercy of the Almighty.

CHAPTER 19

OVERVIEW

Nephi quotes Isaiah chapter 9.

1–21 The people who walk in darkness are to see a great light—even the coming of the Messiah. "For unto us a child is born" (verse 6) who shall fulfill grand and supernal offices of divine service for all the people. Despite the grievous misdeeds of the house of Israel, the Lord's hand is continually stretched out to them.

> *6* ***For unto us a child is born, unto us a son is given;*** *and the government shall be upon his shoulder; and his name shall be called, Wonderful, Counselor, The Mighty God, The Everlasting Father, The Prince of Peace.*
> *7 Of the increase of government and peace there is no end, upon the throne of David, and upon his kingdom to order it, and to establish it with judgment and with justice from henceforth, even forever.*

For unto us a child is born, unto us a son is given

This majestic portrait of the Lamb of God, who comes as Redeemer and Savior of the world, is among the most beloved statements in all of the holy scriptures. The musical setting for this passage in Handel's *Messiah* is justifiably admired around the globe. President Gordon B. Hinckley has stated:

> Jesus was in very deed the great Jehovah of the Old Testament, who left His Father's royal courts on high and condescended to come to earth as a babe born in the most humble of circumstances. His birth was foretold centuries earlier by Isaiah, who declared prophetically, "For unto us a child is born, unto us a

son is given: and the government shall be upon his shoulder: and his name shall be called Wonderful, Counsellor, The mighty God, The everlasting Father, The Prince of Peace" (Isa. 9:6).

This Jesus Christ of whom we solemnly testify is, as John the Revelator declared, "the faithful witness, and the first begotten of the dead, and the prince of the kings of the earth." He "loved us, and washed us from our sins in his own blood, and hath made us kings and priests unto God and his Father; to him be glory and dominion for ever and ever" (Rev. 1:5–6). ("A Testimony of the Son of God," *Liahona,* December 2002, 3)

CHAPTER 20

OVERVIEW

Nephi quotes Isaiah chapter 10 to his people and future readership.

1–34 Isaiah speaks the words of the Lord: The people of Zion need not fear earthly powers such as Assyria. The Lord will use such powers for His own purposes and then remove from Zion the burden of the boastful and aggressive Assyrians and gather His remaining faithful of the remnant of Jacob. Such will also be the case at the time of the Second Coming when the enemies of the Lord's people will be overthrown and the obedient of Zion recovered.

> *20 And it shall come to pass in that day, that the remnant of Israel, and such as are escaped of the house of Jacob, shall no more again stay upon him that smote them, but shall* ***stay upon the Lord, the Holy One of Israel, in truth.***
> *21* ***The remnant shall return,*** *yea, even the remnant of Jacob, unto the mighty God.*

Stay upon the Lord, the Holy One of Israel, in truth; the remnant shall return

The message is clear: Those who depend upon the Lord and keep His commandments need not fear worldly influences and oppression, for the people of Zion shall be delivered by the hand of God and be gathered once again in safety. The Lord may use earthly powers to further His designs, but men need not boast of their own strength, for the Lord is in charge and will fight the battles of Zion.

CHAPTER 21

OVERVIEW

Nephi quotes Isaiah chapter 11 for the benefit of his listeners and his posterity.

1–26 The Stem of Jesse (Jesus Christ) shall come forth endowed with the Spirit of the Almighty and judge the people in righteousness. During the millennial reign of Christ, enmity among creatures will vanish and the earth will be filled with the knowledge of the Lord. The Lord shall raise an ensign to gather the scattered of the house of Israel for the second and final time.

> *1 AND there shall come forth a rod out of* ***the stem of Jesse,*** *and a branch shall grow out of his roots.*
> *2 And the Spirit of the Lord shall rest upon him, the spirit of* ***wisdom*** *and* ***understanding,*** *the spirit of counsel and might, the spirit of knowledge and of the fear of the Lord;*
> *3 And shall make him of quick* ***understanding*** *in the fear of the Lord; and he shall not judge after the sight of his eyes, neither reprove after the hearing of his ears.*
> *4 But with* ***righteousness*** *shall he judge the poor, and reprove with equity for the meek of the earth; and he shall smite the earth with* ***the rod of his mouth,*** *and with the breath of his lips shall he slay the wicked.*
> *5 And* ***righteousness*** *shall be the girdle of his loins, and* ***faithfulness*** *the girdle of his reins.*

THE STEM OF JESSE; RIGHTEOUSNESS; WISDOM; UNDERSTANDING; FAITHFULNESS; THE ROD OF HIS MOUTH

Modern-day revelation has unfolded the meaning of these verses: "WHO is the Stem of Jesse spoken of in the 1st, 2d, 3d, 4th, and 5th verses of the 11th chapter of Isaiah? Verily thus saith the Lord: It is Christ" (D&C 113:1–2). Elder Bruce R. McConkie elaborates as follows: "Christ is the Stem of Jesse (Isa. 11:1–5; D&C 113:1–2), by which is meant that our Lord came as a descendant of that noble Israelite who sired David the King (Ruth 4:17)" (*Mormon Doctrine,* 2d ed. [Salt Lake City: Bookcraft, 1966], 766). When the angel Moroni appeared to the young Joseph Smith on the night of September 21, 1823, he quoted, among many other scriptures, the eleventh chapter of Isaiah, "saying that it was about to be fulfilled" (JS—H 1:40). This event underscores the importance of Isaiah chapter 11 in the process of the Restoration.

*6 **The wolf also shall dwell with the lamb,** and the leopard shall lie down with the*
kid, and the calf and the young lion and fatling together; and a little child shall lead
them.
7 And the cow and the bear shall feed; their young ones shall lie down together; and
the lion shall eat straw like the ox.
8 And the sucking child shall play on the hole of the asp, and the weaned child shall
put his hand on the cockatrice's den.
9 They shall not hurt nor destroy in all my holy mountain, for the earth shall be full of
the knowledge of the Lord, as the waters cover the sea.

The wolf also shall dwell with the lamb

This view of the peace that will prevail during the millennium shows how malice, enmity, and any natural animosity between creatures will vanish. Opposites are to be blended in harmony one with another. The Spirit of the Lord will prevail throughout the realm and dissipate darkness and hatred.

*10 And in that day there shall be **a root of Jesse, which shall stand for an ensign** of*
the people; to it shall the Gentiles seek; and his rest shall be glorious.

A root of Jesse, which shall stand for an ensign

Modern-day revelation explains this verse as follows: "What is the root of Jesse spoken of in the 10th verse of the 11th chapter? Behold, thus saith the Lord, it is a descendant of Jesse, as well as of Joseph, unto whom rightly belongs the priesthood, and the keys of the kingdom, for an ensign, and for the gathering of my people in the last days" (D&C 113:5–6). In a related topic, Elder Bruce R. McConkie states also: "Christ is the Root of David. (Rev. 5:5; 22:16.) This designation signifies that he who was the Son of David was also before David, was pre-eminent above him, and was the root or source from which the great king in Israel gained his kingdom and power" (*Mormon Doctrine,* 2d ed. [Salt Lake City: Bookcraft, 1966], 657).

Consider also the expression "a rod out of the stem of Jesse" (2 Nephi 21:1; Isaiah 11:1) in terms of this additional statement from modern-day revelation: "What is the rod spoken of in the first verse of the 11th chapter of Isaiah, that should come of the Stem of Jesse? Behold, thus saith the Lord: It is a servant in the hands of Christ, who is partly a descendant of Jesse as well as of Ephraim, or of the house of Joseph, on whom there is laid much power" (D&C 113:3–4).

> *11 And it shall come to pass in that day that the Lord shall set his hand again the second time to* ***recover the remnant*** *of his people which shall be left, from Assyria, and from Egypt, and from Pathros, and from Cush, and from Elam, and from Shinar, and from Hamath, and from the islands of the sea.*
> *12 And he shall* ***set up an ensign for the nations,*** *and shall assemble the outcasts of Israel, and gather together the dispersed of Judah from the four corners of the earth.*

Recover the remnant; set up an ensign for the nations

To Isaiah, as to Nephi and all of the Lord's chosen prophets, the vision of the Lord's ultimate design for His people is made manifest. The final gathering proceeds under the aegis of a mighty ensign raised in the latter days to invite all to come unto Christ. This ensign is the banner of the gospel of Jesus Christ, with all of its saving and exalting principles, doctrines, ordinances, and programs.

How do these matters apply to us today? We are part of the ensign—the Church, the kingdom, the stakes of Zion, the temples of the Almighty, the homes of the families of God. It is our duty to spread the gospel to the peoples of the earth, to raise our families in the spirit of love and righteousness, and to accomplish the sacred work of the temples (see D&C 138:53–47; Jacob 5:70–77).

CHAPTER 22

OVERVIEW

Nephi quotes Isaiah chapter 12.

1–6 In this short and exultant expression of praise and worship, Isaiah perceives the state of mind of the Lord's flock in the millennial period: They are comforted in the knowledge that God is their salvation. They trust in the Lord. They are thankful and full of joy. The bear witness of His goodness as He dwells among them.

> *1 AND in that day thou shalt say: O Lord, I will* ***praise*** *thee; though thou wast angry with me thine anger is turned away, and thou* ***comfort****edest me.*
> *2 Behold,* ***God is my salvation;*** *I will* ***trust,*** *and not be afraid; for the Lord JEHOVAH is* ***my strength and my song;*** *he also has become my salvation.*

3 Therefore, with ***joy*** *shall ye draw water out of the wells of* ***salvation.***
4 And in that day shall ye say: Praise the Lord, call upon his name, ***declare his doings***
among the people, make mention that his name is exalted.
5 ***Sing unto the Lord;*** *for he hath done excellent things; this is known in all the*
earth.
6 Cry out and shout, thou inhabitant of Zion; for ***great is the Holy One of Israel***
in the midst of thee.

Praise; comfort; God is my salvation; trust; my strength and my song; joy; salvation; declare his doings; sing unto the Lord; great is the Holy One of Israel

This hymn of praise from Isaiah is a poetic masterpiece of worship and reverence before the Lord. Nephi, who preserves for us one of his own psalms of praise (see 2 Nephi 4:15–35), must have been touched by this moving pronouncement from Isaiah. Among other popular LDS hymns, "The Lord is My Light" (no. 89), was inspired by this chapter of Isaiah.

CHAPTER 23

OVERVIEW

Nephi quotes Isaiah chapter 13 for the instruction of his people and their posterity.

1–22 Just as the ancient kingdom of Babylon was to rise and fall in the unfolding of the course history, the future kingdom of worldly power—the kingdom of the devil (see D&C 1:16) or the "mother of abominations . . . the whore of all the earth" (1 Nephi 14:10), will be destroyed at the time of the Second Coming. Isaiah shares what he has seen and heard in vision concerning this unprecedented calamity.

22 I will be ***merciful*** *unto my people, but the* ***wicked shall perish.***

Merciful; wicked shall perish

This sentence is the most appropriate condensation of the essence of Isaiah chapter 13.

CHAPTER 24

OVERVIEW

Nephi quotes Isaiah chapter 14 for the good of his listeners and future readership.

1–32 Israel, the Lord's chosen people, will in the last days be restored and gathered to the lands of their inheritance. They will be liberated from captivity and given rest and peace. Babylon—both the historical kingdom as well as the symbolic kingdom representing the world of pride and wickedness—will be defeated through the judgments of God. Just as Lucifer was cast down from heaven for rebellion, he and his dominion will be cast down to the pit as part of the final judgment of the Lord. What will be the news upon the earth in that day? "That the Lord hath founded Zion, and the poor of his people shall trust in it" (verse 32).

> *1 FOR* ***the Lord will have mercy on Jacob,*** *and will yet choose Israel, and set them in their own land; and the strangers shall be joined with them, and they shall cleave to the house of Jacob.*
> *2 And the people shall take them and bring them to their place; yea, from far unto the ends of the earth; and* ***they shall return to their lands of promise.*** *And the house of Israel shall possess them, and the land of the Lord shall be for servants and handmaids; and they shall take them captives unto whom they were captives; and they shall rule over their oppressors.*
> *3 And it shall come to pass in that day that* ***the Lord shall give thee rest,*** *from thy sorrow, and from thy fear, and from the hard bondage wherein thou wast made to serve.*

The Lord will have mercy on Jacob; they shall return to their lands of promise; the Lord shall give thee rest

Isaiah relates the joy that will be associated with that future time when Israel will be restored. Remember that Nephi and his people are perpetually conscious of being strangers and wanderers in a foreign land (see 1 Nephi 17:23; Alma 13:23; 26:36), constantly embattled on all sides by their enemies, dreaming of a better world in the light of the glory of God. How uplifting must the words of Isaiah must be to these people, a branch of Israel broken off and yearning for reunion in the arms of the Lord.

> *12 How art thou* ***fallen from heaven, O Lucifer,*** *son of the morning! Art thou cut down to the ground, which did weaken the nations!*

13 For thou hast said in thy heart: I will ascend into heaven, I will exalt my throne above the stars of God; I will sit also upon the mount of the congregation, in the sides of the north;
*14 I will ascend above the heights of the clouds; **I will be like the Most High.***
*15 Yet thou shalt be **brought down to hell,** to the sides of the pit.*

Fallen from heaven, O Lucifer; I will be like the Most High; brought down to hell

The name Lucifer (meaning "light bearer") is used in the scriptures only three times: in the Isaiah reference just cited (see Isaiah 14:12 and 2 Nephi 24:12), plus a third time in modern scripture:

> And this we saw also, and bear record, that an angel of God who was in authority in the presence of God, who rebelled against the Only Begotten Son whom the Father loved and who was in the bosom of the Father, was thrust down from the presence of God and the Son,
>
> And was called Perdition, for the heavens wept over him—he was Lucifer, a son of the morning.
>
> And we beheld, and lo, he is fallen! is fallen, even a son of the morning! (D&C 76:25–27; see also the references in 2 Nephi 2:17; Moses 4:3–4)

The fall of Lucifer, the devil, from the premortal courts of heaven signifies his ultimate downfall—along with all worldly institutions of pride and evil that follow his pattern of wickedness—during the final scenes of the earth's history. We can profitably apply this lesson to our own lives by meticulously avoiding the example of Lucifer.

*24 The Lord of Hosts hath sworn, saying: Surely as I have thought, so shall it come to pass; and **as I have purposed, so shall it stand—***
25 That I will bring the Assyrian in my land, and upon my mountains tread him under foot; then shall his yoke depart from off them, and his burden depart from off their shoulders.
26 This is the purpose that is purposed upon the whole earth; and this is the hand that is stretched out upon all nations.
*27 For the Lord of Hosts hath purposed, and who shall disannul? **And his hand is stretched out, and who shall turn it back?***

As I have purposed, so shall it stand; and his hand is stretched out, and who shall turn it back?

Our faith in the Almighty is anchored in the certainty that His word will be fulfilled. He keeps all of His promises—in justice and mercy. Abraham confirmed that "there is nothing that the Lord thy God shall take in his heart to do but what he will do it" (Abraham 3:17).

CHAPTER 25

OVERVIEW

Nephi confirms that many who are not conversant with the manner of prophesying of the Jews find Isaiah's words difficult to comprehend. Nevertheless, those filled with the spirit of prophesy will understand Isaiah's words, for his words speak of the judgments of God to come upon all nations. In the day of the fulfillment of these prophesies, the people will understand. For now, Nephi prophesies in plainness to the people. He traces the history of the Jewish nation, including the destruction by the Babylonians, the return from exile, the coming of the Messiah, His crucifixion and resurrection, and the further scattering and persecution of the Jews for generations to come. In the latter days the Lord will bring about a marvelous work and a wonder in restoring His word to convince the Jews and all the world of the truthfulness of the gospel. Nephi records his testimony of the divinity of Christ, which testimony will be preserved by the hand of the Lord and come forth in the due time of the Lord.

> *1 NOW I, Nephi, do speak somewhat concerning the words which I have written, which have been spoken by the mouth of Isaiah. For behold, Isaiah spake many things which were* ***hard for many of my people to understand;*** *for they know not concerning the manner of prophesying among the Jews.*
> *2 For I, Nephi, have not taught them many things concerning the manner of the Jews; for their works were works of darkness, and their doings were doings of abominations.*
> *3 Wherefore,* ***I write unto my people,*** *unto all those that shall receive hereafter these things which I write, that they may know the judgments of God, that they come upon all nations, according to the word which he hath spoken.*

Hard for many of my people to understand; I write unto my people

After recording many chapters of Isaiah on the small plates for his posterity, Nephi comments on the selected quotations. This is among the most insightful explanations of the message of Isaiah available from any source. As an introduction, Nephi recaptures the essence of his Isaiah citations in one phrase: "that they may know the judgments of God, that they come upon all nations, according to the word which he hath spoken" (verse 3). Having, through the grace and kindness of God, escaped with his family from the predicted destruction of Jerusalem, Nephi learns firsthand the utter certitude of God's word with respect to the impending judgments that must come upon the generations of the wicked should they reject the warnings of Isaiah and the other prophets.

> *4 Wherefore, hearken, O my people, which are of the house of Israel, and give ear unto my words; for because the words of Isaiah are not plain unto you, nevertheless they are* ***plain unto all those that are filled with the spirit of prophecy.*** *But I give unto you a prophecy, according to the spirit which is in me; wherefore I shall prophesy according to the plainness which hath been with me from the time that I came out from Jerusalem with my father; for behold, my soul delighteth in plainness unto my people, that they may learn.*

Plain unto all those that are filled with the spirit of prophecy

Nephi, a native of Jerusalem, understands the manner and customs of the Jewish people. Not only does Nephi know from personal experience the lands and conditions that Isaiah describes, but he is also blessed with a prophetic view of the unfolding of Israel's future experiences—including the birth and crucifixion of the Redeemer at the hands of the wicked. He has experienced the same visionary view of God's dealings with the covenant people that Isaiah has witnessed. Thus, Nephi is able to identify the key to interpreting Isaiah's writings: "they are plain unto all those that are filled with the spirit of prophecy" (2 Nephi 25:4). Like the sons of Mosiah, who give themselves to much study, fasting, and prayer to obtain "the spirit of prophecy, and the spirit of revelation" (Alma 17:3), we too can come to understand more fully the words of Isaiah and those of all of God's prophets through diligent study and faith.

5–19 Nephi has not taught his people after the manner of prophesying of the Jews, but has instead spoken to them plainly of that which is to come. He now sets forth his own prophecies in plainness so that "no man can err" (verse 7). The Lord always forewarns the people when destruction is nigh. Jerusalem has been destroyed by the Babylonians, according to the word of prophecy. But the survivors will be gathered back again. Nevertheless, they will dwindle in unbelief and crucify the Messiah when He comes among them 600 years from the time Lehi has left Jerusalem. After the resurrection of the Lord, Jerusalem will again be destroyed and the Jews will be scattered and smitten for generations.

They will be gathered again at a future time when they come to believe in Jesus Christ, the only true Messiah.

Thus, Nephi issues his confirmation of God's design with respect to the geopolitical flow of history: No nation, no people, no generation can escape the judgments of God. The scattering and gathering will proceed on the basis of God's purposes for mankind, according to their responsiveness to the word of truth as proclaimed by God's emissaries.

> *20 And now, my brethren, I have spoken plainly that ye cannot err. And as the Lord God liveth that brought Israel up out of the land of Egypt, and gave unto Moses power that he should heal the nations after they had been bitten by the poisonous serpents, if they would cast their eyes unto the serpent which he did raise up before them, and also gave him power that he should smite the rock and the water should come forth; yea, behold I say unto you, that as these things are true, and as the Lord God liveth, there is* ***none other name given under heaven save it be this Jesus Christ,*** *of which I have spoken, whereby man can be saved.*
> *21 Wherefore, for this cause hath the Lord God promised unto me that* ***these things which I write shall be kept and preserved,*** *and handed down unto my seed, from generation to generation, that the promise may be fulfilled unto Joseph, that his seed should never perish as long as the earth should stand.*
> *22 Wherefore, these things shall go from generation to generation as long as the earth shall stand; and they shall go according to the will and pleasure of God; and the nations who shall possess them shall be* ***judged of them*** *according to the words which are written.*

None other name given under heaven save it be this Jesus Christ; these things which I write shall be kept and preserved; judged of them

Nephi speaks in plainness of the central truth of the gospel—that Jesus Christ is the only name given under heaven whereby mankind can be saved. He blends his testimony with that of Isaiah ("Yea, and my soul delighteth in the words of Isaiah . . ."—2 Nephi 25:5). The Lord promises Nephi that his testimony of these things will be preserved and come forth at a future time unto the seed of Joseph, that the covenant blessings might be preserved. The avenue for the coming forth of this witness of Jesus Christ is the Book of Mormon.

> *23 For we labor diligently to write, to persuade our children, and also our brethren, to believe in Christ, and to be reconciled to God; for we know that* ***it is by grace that we are saved, after all we can do.***

It is by grace that we are saved, after all we can do

We are saved by the grace of God after we have done all in our power to demonstrate our faithful obedience to His commandments and our enduring commitment to live as He would have us live. We cannot be saved without the help of our Savior Jesus Christ—just as God the Father ordained it to be in the plan of redemption. Elder Bruce R. McConkie illuminates this central principle of the gospel.

> Let us now come to the matter of whether we must do something to gain the blessings of the Atonement in our lives. And we find the answer written in words of fire and emblazoned across the whole heavens; we hear a voice speaking with the sound of ten thousand trumpets; the very heavens and the earth are moved out of their place, so powerful is the word that goes forth. It is a message that neither men nor angels nor the Gods themselves can proclaim with an undue emphasis.
>
> This is the word: Man cannot be saved by grace alone; as the Lord lives, man must keep the commandments (Eccl. 12:13; Matt. 19:17; 1 Ne. 22:31; D&C 93:20); he must work the works of righteousness (Matt. 7:21; James 2:18–26; D&C 78:5–7); he must work out his salvation with fear and trembling before the Lord (Philip. 2:12); he must have faith like the ancients—the faith that brings with it gifts and signs and miracles.
>
> Does it suffice to believe and be baptized without more? The answer is no, in every language and tongue. Rather, after belief, after repentance, after baptism, "Ye must press forward with a steadfastness in Christ, having a perfect brightness of hope, and a love of God and of all men. Wherefore, if ye shall press forward, feasting upon the word of Christ, and endure to the end, behold, thus saith the Father: Ye shall have eternal life. And now, behold, . . . this is the way; and there is none other way nor name given under heaven whereby man can be saved in the kingdom of God." (2 Ne. 31:20–21.) (*Sermons and Writings of Bruce R. McConkie* [Salt Lake City: Bookcraft, 1998], 76–77)

This passage (2 Nephi 25:23) raises a question of conscience for us all. Are we persuading our children to come unto Christ and recognize that it is only through Jesus Christ that they can have remission of their sins?

24 And, notwithstanding we believe in Christ, ***we keep the law of Moses,*** *and look forward with steadfastness unto Christ, until the law shall be fulfilled.*
25 For, for this end was the law given; wherefore the law hath become dead unto us, and ***we are made alive in Christ*** *because of our faith; yet we keep the law because of the commandments.*

We keep the law of Moses; we are made alive in Christ

Nephi gives a succinct explanation of the connection between the law of Moses and the power of the Atonement: of itself, the law is dead, but in Christ those who are obedient to the law are made alive through their faith.

26 And we talk of Christ, we rejoice in Christ, we preach of Christ, we prophesy of Christ, and we write according to our prophecies, ***that our children may know*** *to what source they may look for a remission of their sins.*

That our children may know

With the full energy of his soul, Nephi proclaims the central motivation for his actions and those of his followers: to bless the lives of their children through the truth and power of the word of God. With overwhelming desire, they want their children to look to Christ in all things, to understand that Christ is the Author of our salvation and exaltation (see Hebrews 5:8–9). We too are to teach these truths to the coming generations.

27–30 Nephi reemphasizes the need to look beyond the law of Moses to the living gospel of the Jesus Christ. He has spoken plainly to his people so that no one can misunderstand. They are to believe in Christ as the Holy One of Israel. The counsel Nephi gives to them (and to us) is to worship Him with "all your might, mind, and strength, and your whole soul; and if ye do this ye shall in nowise be cast out" (verse 29).

CHAPTER 26

OVERVIEW

Nephi prophecies of the coming of Christ to His Saints in America after His resurrection. Signs will identify His birth and great upheavals will occur at the time of His death, but the surviving remnant will have peace for several generations. Nephi sorrows over the coming destruction of his people. The record of the people will be preserved and come forth in the latter days. The Gentiles will stumble because of their false churches and foster secret combinations. The Lord invites all to come unto Him.

1–6 Nephi prophesies that the resurrected Christ will appear to his descendants. Signs of His birth and His death and resurrection will appear. Great disruptions will come at the time of His death, resulting in the destruction of the wicked who slay the prophets.

> *7 O the pain, and* ***the anguish of my soul*** *for the loss of the slain of my people! For I, Nephi, have seen it, and it well nigh consumeth me before the presence of the Lord; but I must cry unto my God: Thy ways are just.*

The anguish of my soul

With prophetic vision, Nephi sees the time when the Savior will visit the Nephites following His ministry in the Holy Land. The prelude to that visit is to be an unprecedented natural catastrophe that will leave much of the land in ruins and bring about the destruction of the wicked. Nephi is consumed with pain and grief over the loss of life. He has witnessed in vision the decline and destruction of his people. Those among us who observe the waywardness of loved ones can understand and grieve with Nephi.

Memories: The Broken Heart of Charity

Within the magnificent six-spired Washington D.C. Temple there is a wall-size mural depicting the Day of Judgment. The Savior stands majestically in the center, His joyful followers to His right and the lost hordes of the shame-filled and wayward to His left. The point of departure is the scripture in Matthew that reads: "And before him shall be gathered all nations: and he shall separate them one from another, as a shepherd divideth *his* sheep from the goats: And he shall set the sheep on his right hand, but the goats on the left. Then shall the King say unto them on his right hand, Come, ye blessed of my Father, inherit the kingdom prepared for you from the foundation of the world" (Matthew 25:32–34).

My wife and I were living in that area of the country during the construction of the temple and thus had the opportunity to participate in the dedicatory session on November 19, 1974, conducted under the direction of Spencer W. Kimball. During our subsequent visits to the temple, I would look intently at the mural of the "sheep and the goats" and ponder on the significance of the doctrine reflected in it. More often than not I would find myself instinctively associating with those happy souls to the Savior's right-hand side (after all, was I not in the House of the Lord?) and sensing relief at not finding fellowship with those on his left. But was that the appropriate sentiment?

When Nephi was granted a vision of the unfolding of his people's destiny leading up to the time of the resurrected Savior's visit in America, he perceived the judgment that took place at that time, including the widespread destruction of the wicked. Was *his* mindset one of relief at not having affinity with the wayward and prideful? Listen to his expression: "O the pain, and the anguish of my soul for the loss of the slain of my people! For I, Nephi, have seen it, and it well nigh consumeth me before the presence of the Lord; but I must cry unto my God: Thy ways are just" (2 Nephi 26:7). And further: "And when these things have passed away a speedy destruction cometh unto my people; for, not withstanding the pains of my soul, I have seen it; wherefore, I know that it shall come to pass. . . . For the Spirit of the Lord will not always strive with man. And when the Spirit ceaseth to strive with man then cometh speedy destruction, and this grieveth my soul" (2 Nephi 26:10–11).

Pain and anguish of soul over the wicked? Being consumed with grief over the sinful? That is the perspective of a prophet and a man of charity. Throughout the Book of Mormon we are presented with portraits of individuals who reflect either hearts that are soft and humble or hearts that are hard and rebellious. This is one of the grand themes of the book, summarized in the essential quality of having a "broken heart and a contrite spirit" (see 2 Nephi 2:7; 4:32; 3 Nephi 9:20; 12:19; Mormon 2:14; Ether 4:15; Moroni 6:2). We are prone to think of this phrase as pertaining to our inward humility and contrition of soul before our Father in Heaven—and so it does. But does the phrase not also refer to the quality of heart we bring to bear in our relationships with others—in our ability to suspend judgment and exercise service-minded forbearance when others seem to stray or fall short in some way? Does a broken heart not also mean broken over the loss of blessings that others seem to relinquish when they wander into forbidden pathway? Does a contrite spirit not also imply being consumed with grief over the suffering that others must go through based on their choices? Is this compassionate quality of soul not a quality of the discipleship of charity?

"And he spake this parable unto certain which trusted in themselves that they were righteous, and despised others: Two men went up into the temple to pray; the one a Pharisee, and the other a publican. The Pharisee stood and prayed thus with himself, God, I thank thee, that I am not as other men are, extortioners, unjust, adulterers, or even as this publican. I fast twice in the week, I give tithes of all that I possess. And the publican, standing afar off, would not lift up so much as his eyes unto heaven, but smote upon his breast, saying, God be merciful to me a sinner. I tell you, this man went down to his house justified rather than the other: for every one that exalteth himself shall be abased; and he that humbleth himself shall be exalted" (Luke 18:9–14).

Thus it seems that the broken heart of charity—as it reaches out to do all in its power to rescue the disenfranchised, to reclaim the transgressor, to give hope through the gospel to the lost—comes very close to resonating with the Savior's pattern of love because, while not robbing justice one whit, it extends gentle service to all, even those who may find themselves shifting toward His left-hand side. (Richard J. Allen)

> *8 But behold, the righteous that hearken unto the words of the prophets, and destroy them not, but look forward unto Christ with steadfastness for the signs which are given, notwithstanding all persecution—behold, they are they which shall not perish.*
> *9 But the Son of righteousness shall appear unto them; and* ***he shall heal them,*** *and* ***they shall have peace with him,*** *until three generations shall have passed away, and many of the fourth generation shall have passed away in righteousness.*

He shall heal them; they shall have peace with him

Nephi takes comfort in seeing that the obedient are to be spared to enjoy the experience of the coming of the resurrected Savior. The righteous will be blessed at the coming of the Savior, whose influence and love will establish a canopy of righteousness and peace over the people that will last for over three generations.

> *10 And when these things have passed away a speedy destruction cometh unto my people; for, notwithstanding the pains of my soul, I have seen it; wherefore, I know that it shall come to pass; and they sell themselves for naught; for, for the reward of their pride and their foolishness they shall reap destruction; for because they yield unto the devil and choose works of darkness rather than light, therefore they must go down to hell.*
> *11 For* ***the Spirit of the Lord will not always strive with man.*** *And when the Spirit ceaseth to strive with man then cometh speedy destruction, and this grieveth my soul.*

The Spirit of the Lord will not always strive with man

When we are prideful and yield ourselves to the enticements of the devil, we lose the Spirit. The expression concerning the Spirit of the Lord not always striving with man is encountered from the beginning of time: "And the LORD said, My spirit shall not always strive with man, for that he also *is* flesh: yet his days shall be an hundred and twenty years" (Genesis 6:3). Besides the reference from 2 Nephi 26:11, the Book of Mormon provides an additional passage of this kind (see Ether 2:15), and latter-day scriptures also reconfirm this doctrine (see D&C 1:33; Moses 8:17). The application of this warning in our lives will enable us to take every action that will ensure our being able to enjoy the Spirit throughout our mortal days.

12–15 Nephi predicts that the record of his people, though they be destroyed as a result of wickedness, will come forth in the latter days at a time when the Gentiles shall have smitten the remnant of his seed, "yet the words of the righteous shall be written, and the prayers of the faithful shall be heard, and all those who have dwindled in unbelief shall not be forgotten" (verse 15).

> *16 For those who shall be destroyed* ***shall speak unto them out of the ground,*** *and their speech shall be* ***low out of the dust,*** *and their voice shall be as one that hath a familiar spirit; for the Lord God will give unto him power, that he may whisper concerning them, even as it were out of the ground; and their speech* ***shall whisper out of the dust.***
> *17 For thus saith the Lord God: They shall write the things which shall be done among them, and they shall be written and* ***sealed up in a book,*** *and those who have dwindled in unbelief shall not have them, for they seek to destroy the things of God.*

Shall speak unto them out of the ground; low out of the dust; shall whisper out of the dust; sealed up in a book

Nephi envisions the time when his record and that of future record keepers in the land of promise will be restored and speak to the people in the latter days, as it were, from the dust. His language parallels that of Isaiah, who foresaw the same future restoration of the word of God: "And thou shalt be brought down, and shalt speak out of the ground, and thy speech shall be low out of the dust, and thy voice shall be, as of one that hath a familiar spirit, out of the ground, and thy speech shall whisper out of the dust" (Isaiah 29:4).

18–22 Nephi prophesies that the Gentiles of the latter days will stumble because of pride and secret combinations inspired of the devil.

> *23 For behold, my beloved brethren, I say unto you that the Lord God worketh not in darkness.*

24 He doeth not anything save it be for ***the benefit of the world;*** *for he loveth the world, even that he layeth down his own life that he may draw all men unto him. Wherefore, he commandeth none that they shall not partake of his salvation.*

The benefit of the world

Nephi is filled with the spirit of the Atonement and emphasizes the universal love of the Savior. Gratitude for our Savior's sacrifice should draw us to Him that we might partake of His salvation.

25 Behold, doth he cry unto any, saying: Depart from me? Behold, I say unto you, Nay; but he saith: ***Come unto me all ye ends of the earth,*** *buy milk and honey, without money and without price.*
26 Behold, hath he commanded any that they should depart out of the synagogues, or out of the houses of worship? Behold, I say unto you, Nay.
27 Hath he commanded any that they should not partake of his salvation? Behold I say unto you, Nay; but he hath given it free for all men; and he hath commanded his people that they should persuade all men to repentance.
28 Behold, hath the Lord commanded any that they should not partake of his goodness? Behold I say unto you, Nay; but ***all men are privileged the one like unto the other,*** *and none are forbidden.*

Come unto me all ye ends of the earth; all men are privileged the one like unto the other

All are invited to partake of salvation. All are equal in the sight of God. If the Lord extends His invitation to everyone, should we not also seek to do our part and encourage all people to repent and partake of the salvation of the Lord?

29–32 The Lord forbids priestcraft (preaching for money) and all violations against the Ten Commandments.

33 For none of these iniquities come of the Lord; for he doeth that which is good among the children of men; and he doeth nothing save it be plain unto the children of men; and he inviteth them all to come unto him and partake of his goodness; and he denieth none that come unto him, black and white, bond and free, male and female; and he remembereth the heathen; and ***all are alike unto God,*** *both Jew and Gentile.*

All are alike unto God

The Lord loves all mankind, His concern being evident throughout the scriptures. He seeks our welfare and happiness. He wants all mankind to come unto Him and be saved. His love is made evident through His infinite and vicarious Atonement for the sins of mankind and making possible the Resurrection. The plan of happiness is designed to bless Heavenly Father's children that they might gain immortality and eternal life. To bring this to pass, our Savior, along with His disciples, invites all to come unto Christ and be perfected in Him. This is our glory and joy. This is the purpose of the Church and kingdom of God here upon the earth. In this dispensation of the fulness of times, the Restoration brought forth the Book of Mormon, the priesthood, and The Church of Jesus Christ of Latter-day Saints—with all of the saving ordinances—so that all mankind might have the opportunity of coming unto Christ.

CHAPTER 27

OVERVIEW

Nephi quotes much of Isaiah chapter 29 (with variations and commentary)—the last of the Isaiah chapters that he enters into his record for the good of his people and coming generations.

1–35 In the last days the Lord will bring forth the light of the Book of Mormon to illuminate, in a world of wickedness, the secret combinations and false churches established by the Gentiles. Three witnesses shall testify of the authenticity of the sealed work. Through the inspiration of the Almighty, it will speak, as it were, from the dust—"a marvelous work and a wonder" (2 Nephi 27:26; compare Isaiah 29:14) given to restore the fulness of the gospel of Jesus Christ and bring joy and understanding to the faithful.

1–11 In the last days the nations of the Gentiles and the remnants of the house of Israel will be obsessed with wickedness. The Lord will visit them in great judgment. They will be as if in a deep sleep—oblivious to the truths of eternity. At that time the Lord will bring forth a sealed book that will reveal all truth from the beginning to the end of the world.

> *12 Wherefore, at that day when the **book** shall be delivered unto the man of whom I have spoken, the **book** shall be hid from the eyes of the world, that the eyes of none shall behold it save it be that **three witnesses** shall behold it, by the power of God,*

*besides him to whom the **book** shall be delivered; and they shall testify to the truth of*
*the **book** and the things therein.*
13 And there is none other which shall view it, save it be a few according to the will of
God, to bear testimony of his word unto the children of men; for the Lord God hath
said that the words of the faithful should speak as if it were from the dead.
*14 Wherefore, the Lord God will proceed to bring forth the words of the **book;** and in*
*the mouth of as **many witnesses** as seemeth him good will he establish his word; and*
wo be unto him that rejecteth the word of God!

BOOK; THREE WITNESSES; MANY WITNESSES

The Lord always works through the testimony of witnesses, that "in the mouth of two or three witnesses every word may be established" (Matthew 18:16; compare 2 Nephi 11:3; 2 Corinthians 13:1; D&C 128:3).

EVIDENCE: THREE WITNESSES—FORM OF IMPORTANT DOCUMENTS (1 Nephi 1:17; 19:1; 2 Nephi 27:12–14; 3 Nephi 5:18; Mormon 6:6; Words of Mormon 1:3, 6; Moroni 10:27)

According to recent archaeological discoveries, many ancient Israelites—including those in Lehi's day—used doubled, sealed, and witnessed documents. In the two-part documents, one section was left open for easy access, and the second was sealed for later reference by the persons involved or by a judge in a court of law. Interestingly, when written on papyrus or parchment, a legal document would be written twice on the same sheet—at the top and at the bottom. The document was then folded and sealed, making one part open for inspection but keeping the other part sealed. With records engraved on metal, two or more plates were used, with the second "copy" often made more hurriedly. In addition, witnesses were necessary to verify a document; for instance, the Babylonian Talmud stated that the law required three witnesses to a sale of property. At least three witnesses to the Book of Mormon were necessary, but the Lord provided many more than this; in fact, he established His word by "as many witnesses as seemeth him good" (2 Nephi 27:14). In light of the way the plates of Mormon were put together and the law of witnesses satisfied, this ancient method of document preservation makes sense. However, the ancient practice was not known until long after the publication of the Book of Mormon (see *Echoes,* 374–379).

In the case of the Book of Mormon, the three witness were Oliver Cowdery, David Whitmer, and Martin Harris (see their testimony at the beginning of the published edition). The eight witnesses included four Whitmers (Christian, Jacob, Peter Jr., and John), three Smiths (Joseph Sr., Hyrum, and Samuel H.), plus Hiram Page (see also their testimony at the beginning of the published edition).

*15 But behold, it shall come to pass that the Lord God shall say unto him to whom
he shall deliver the book: Take these words which are not sealed and deliver them to
another, that he may* ***show them unto the learned,*** *saying: Read this, I pray thee.
And the learned shall say: Bring hither the book, and I will read them.
16 And now, because of the glory of the world and to get gain will they say this, and
not for the glory of God.
17 And the man shall say:* ***I cannot bring the book, for it is sealed.***
18 Then shall the learned say: ***I cannot read it.***
*19 Wherefore it shall come to pass, that the Lord God will deliver again the book and
the words thereof to him that is not learned; and the man that is not learned shall say:*
I am not learned.
*20 Then shall the Lord God say unto him: The learned shall not read them, for they
have rejected them, and* ***I am able to do mine own work;*** *wherefore thou shalt read
the words which I shall give unto thee.*

Show them unto the learned; I cannot bring the book, for it is sealed; I cannot read it; I am not learned; I am able to do mine own work

This reference is to the Book of Mormon, which has come forth by the power of God to establish the truth of the Bible and the verity of the gospel of Jesus Christ.

As the Words of a Book That Is Sealed

In 2 Nephi chapter 27 the terms "words of a book" and the "words of them which have slumbered" found in verse 6 refer to the teachings and message of the full record of the Nephites. In the golden plates (referred to as "the book" in verse 7) there is a sealed portion that is not to be given to us at this time. Verse 9 refers to the Prophet Joseph and his bringing forth of the Book of Mormon (that portion of the record not held back by the Lord) and sending some of the words to Charles Anthon (see JS—H 1:64). These events are encompassed in Isaiah's prophecy concerning the coming forth of the Book of Mormon. Joseph Fielding McConkie and Robert L. Millet have explained Isaiah (Isaiah 29:11–12 and 2 Nephi 27:15–20) and the Anthon transcript as follows:

> Isaiah spoke in cryptic language words which have special meaning to the Latter-day Saints, a people who have lived in the days when the prophecies of Isaiah have come to pass (see 2 Nephi 25:8): "And the vision of all is become unto you as the words of a book that is sealed, which men deliver to one that is learned, saying, Read

this, I pray thee: and he saith, I cannot; for it is sealed; and the book is delivered to him that is not learned, saying, Read this, I pray thee: and he saith, I am not learned" (Isaiah 29:11–12). The latter-day fulfillment of this prophecy is recorded by Joseph Smith as follows: "In the midst of our afflictions we found a friend in a gentleman by the name of Martin Harris, who came to us and gave me fifty dollars to assist us on our journey [to Harmony, Pennsylvania]. Mr. Harris was a resident of Palmyra township, Wayne county, in the State of New York, and a farmer of respectability.

"By this timely aid was I enabled to reach the place of my destination in Pennsylvania; and immediately after my arrival there I commenced copying the characters off the plates. I copied a considerable number of them, and by means of the Urim and Thummim I translated some of them, which I did between the time I arrived at the house of my wife's father, in the month of December, and the February following.

"Sometime in this month of February [1828], the aforementioned Mr. Martin Harris came to our place, got the characters which I had drawn off the plates, and started with them to the city of New York. For what took place relative to him and the characters, I refer to his own account of the circumstances, as he related them to me after his return, which was as follows:

"'I went to the city of New York, and presented the characters which had been translated, with the translation thereof, to Professor Charles Anthon, a gentleman celebrated for his literary attainments. Professor Anthon stated that the translation was correct, more so than any he had before seen translated from the Egyptian. I then showed him those which were not yet translated, and he said that they were Egyptian, Chaldaic, Assyriac, and Arabic; and he said they were true characters. He gave me a certificate, certifying to the people of Palmyra that they were true characters, and that the translation of such of them as had been translated was also correct. I took the certificate and put it into my pocket, and was just leaving the house, when Mr. Anthon called me back, and asked me how the young man found out that there were gold plates in the place where he found them. I answered that an *angel* of God had revealed it unto him.

"'He then said to me, "Let me see that certificate." I accordingly took it out of my pocket and gave it to him, when he took it and tore it to pieces, saying that there was no such thing now as ministering of angels, and that if I would bring the plates to him he would translate them. I informed him that part of the plates were *sealed,* and that I was forbidden to bring them. He replied, "I cannot read a sealed book." I left him and went to Dr. Mitchell, who sanctioned what Professor Anthon had said respecting both the characters and the translation.'" (JS—H 1:61–65)

2 Nephi 27:15. **[Take these words . . . and deliver them to another]** Here is the prophetic word which attests that Martin Harris's trip to New York was based upon more than his own curiosity or desire for academic substantiation for the Book of Mormon translation. Joseph Smith was commanded of the Lord to send another, Martin Harris, to New York.

2 Nephi 27:15. **[Show them unto the learned]** Charles Anthon was indeed a learned man by the world's standards: he was a professor of classics—Greek and Latin—at Columbia University in New York.

2 Nephi 27:16. **[Because of the glory of the world and to get gain]** This phrase identifies Professor Anthon's motivation. Further, it seems apparent that Anthon, though certainly a noted scholar in his day, was stretching the truth to suggest that he could translate the golden plates. According to Martin Harris's account, the learned professor indicated that the translation of what Moroni called reformed Egyptian was the most correct translation he had seen. Yet the work of Champollion, the French genius who broke the Egyptian language code through the Rosetta Stone, had not yet made its way to the United States. Anthon could not have known how to translate Egyptian antiquities.

2 Nephi 27:18. **[The learned]** "The learned" are Charles Anthon, Samuel Mitchell, and any other academician in any age who trusts in his own wisdom and rejects revelation.

2 Nephi 27:19. **[Him that is not learned]** Joseph Smith, who the God of heaven and earth chose to immerse in the mysteries of the universe, was, by man's myopic standards, "unlearned."

2 Nephi 27:19. **[I am not learned]** The Palmyra Seer, like so many of his prophetic colleagues, felt unworthy and ill-prepared to accomplish so great a task (cf. Moses 6:31; Exodus 3:11; Exodus 4:10; Jeremiah 1:6). But it is through such persons—men and women ever sensitive to their limitations, who thus trust in him who is able to transform weaknesses into strengths—that mighty things are accomplished. "The weak things of the world shall come forth and break down

the mighty and strong ones, that man should not counsel his fellow man, neither trust in the arm of flesh—but that every man might speak in the name of God the Lord, even the Savior of the world; that faith also might increase in the earth; that mine everlasting covenant might be established; that the fulness of my gospel might be proclaimed by the weak and the simple unto the ends of the world, and before kings and rulers" (D&C 1:19–23).

2 Nephi 27:20. **[I am able to do mine own work]** It would be delightful if kings and presidents the world over were to announce in regal splendor that God had spoken anew in this final dispensation. It would be helpful to the missionary cause if preachers and evangelists of all persuasions were to bear witness of the Prophet Joseph Smith and the work he set in motion. And it would be glorious indeed if linguists and archaeologists and anthropologists and scientists without number were to establish empirically what the Latter-day Saints have been saying about the Book of Mormon for over a century and a half. Such occurrences, however, do not appear to be on the horizon of possibility, at least not until the Lord returns in glory. But such things are not necessary; at least they are not necessary for the Lord. His work will move forward in humility and with quiet dignity. The simple but profound testimonies of thousands of Mormon missionaries and faithful members of the Church will continue to be borne to all the world and to be received by honest truth-seekers. The Lord is able to do his own work in his own way, and his way is not man's way (see Isaiah 55:8–9). (*Doctrinal Commentary on the Book of Mormon,* 4 vols. [Salt Lake City: Bookcraft, 1987–1992], 1:321–323).

21 Touch not the things which are sealed, for I will bring them forth in mine own due time; for I will show unto the children of men that I am able to do mine own work.
22 Wherefore, when thou hast read the words which I have commanded thee, and obtained the witnesses which I have promised unto thee, then shalt thou seal up the book again, and hide it up unto me, that I may preserve the words which thou hast not read, until I shall see fit in mine own wisdom to reveal all things unto the children of men.
23 For behold, I am God; and I am a God of miracles; and I will show unto the world that I am the same yesterday, today, and forever; and ***I work not among the children of men save it be according to their faith.***

I am the same yesterday, today, and forever; I work not among the children of men save it be according to their faith

We must strengthen your faith that the Lord might use us as instruments in His hands to fulfill the promises of the Abrahamic covenant in bringing the saving and exalting truths of the gospel of Jesus Christ to all the world.

> *24 And again it shall come to pass that the Lord shall say unto him that shall read the*
> *words that shall be delivered him:*
> *25 Forasmuch as this people draw near unto me with their mouth, and with their lips*
> *do honor me, but have removed their hearts far from me, and their fear toward me is*
> *taught by the precepts of men—*
> *26 Therefore, I will proceed to do a marvelous work among this people, yea,* ***a marvel-***
> ***ous work and a wonder,*** *for the wisdom of their wise and learned shall perish, and*
> *the understanding of their prudent shall be hid.*

A marvelous work and a wonder

This reference is to the miracle of the restoration of the gospel in our time, including the coming forth of the Book of Mormon (compare Isaiah 29:13–14). The Lord will bring about a marvelous work among this people, but the wisdom of the learned and wise who work darkness shall perish. The Lord can work with His children only according to their faith. The application is clear: We are to further the cause of this "marvelous work and a wonder" in our own lives so that the light of the gospel can shine forth and invite all to come unto Christ.

EVIDENCE: Process of Translation

The translation process itself, wherein Joseph worked by the gift and power of God, fulfilled Isaiah's prophecy that the Lord would do "a marvelous work among this people, yea, a marvelous work and a wonder" (2 Nephi 27:26; compare Isaiah 29:14). Joseph endured persecutions and numerous attempts by evil men to steal the plates, making the translation itself even more wondrous (see *Echoes,* 3).

Power to Translate

While the Prophet Joseph Smith never disclosed the exact details of the translation process, the testimonies of others provide us with some insight. Both David Whitmer and Martin Harris explained that as the Prophet used the instrument provided by the Lord, the hieroglyphics would appear along with the translation in English. Then Joseph would read the text to the scribe. It appears from such statements that Joseph did not need to be an expert in hieroglyphics in order to discern the English translation. In fact, he did not necessarily even need to scrutinize the actual characters on the plates (see *Echoes,* 4).

Brief Translation Time

The actual translation of the book took approximately sixty-five working days, with Joseph translating up to ten pages in a single day. In comparison, over fifty scholars worked for seven years to produce the King James Version of the Bible—about one page per day. Translating the Book of Mormon in such a short amount of time is even more extraordinary considering that Joseph often had to discontinue translating for hours at a time to do chores and care for his family. (See *Echoes,* 5–7).

Testimony of Joseph's Scribe

An important witness to the divine origin of the Book of Mormon, Oliver Cowdery, was also deeply involved with the book's translation. He stated, "I wrote with my own pen the intire (sic) [B]ook of Mormon (save a few pages) as it fell from the Lips of the prophet." (Compare also Oliver's detailed statement included in the footnote at the end of Joseph Smith—History in the *Pearl of Great Price*.) Oliver never denied his testimony, and though he fell away from the Church for a time, he eventually came back. On his deathbed, Oliver raised up and told his family and friends to "live according to the teachings in the [B]ook of Mormon and they would meet him in Heaven." (See *Echoes,* 11).

27–28 Though many hide their counsel from the Lord, He will bless the righteous in the latter days and make them fruitful.

> *29 And in that day shall **the deaf hear** the words of the book, and the eyes of **the blind shall see** out of obscurity and out of darkness.*

The blind shall see; the deaf hear

The Lord has a design in preserving and bringing forth the Book of Mormon. He has a design in raising up chosen prophets to convey His word to the honest at heart. Nephi has learned from his father much detail concerning the latter's visions about the course of Israel's history and future destiny. Nephi himself, after much prayer and fasting, is privileged to partake of the heavenly vision firsthand (see 2 Nephi 12–14). Thus he is schooled of the Lord in the design of heaven and in the essence of the prophecies of Isaiah (who saw in vision the unfolding of the very same covenant plan) and can speak with authority about the nature and implications of Isaiah's words. In particular, Nephi clarifies Isaiah Chapter 29 concerning the mysterious sealed book—a reference that has seemed to the world to be fairly cryptic. Nephi makes clear that this sealed book is none other than the record that he himself has initiated at God's command. With prophetic eye he looks forward to a time when this very record, extended and completed by a series of inspired prophets and compilers over the ages, will be brought forth "by the power of God" (Mormon 8:16) to a latter-day world hungry for the fulness of the everlasting gospel of Jesus Christ.

It would appear that one of the principal reasons the Lord directs the recording of so many of Isaiah's words in the Book of Mormon is so that the inspired commentary of Nephi concerning these words can be placed in juxtaposition to the original text. This allows the inspired commentary to shed additional light and truth on important themes "according to my plainness; in the which I know that no man can err" (2 Nephi 25:7).

30–32 The meek and the poor shall be blessed and have joy in the Lord. The wicked shall be consumed.

> *33 Therefore, thus saith the Lord, who redeemed Abraham, concerning the house of Jacob: Jacob shall not now be ashamed, neither shall his face now wax pale.*
> *34 But* ***when he seeth his children,*** *the work of my hands, in the midst of him, they* ***shall sanctify my name,*** *and* ***sanctify the Holy One of Jacob,*** *and shall* ***fear the God of Israel.***
> *35 They also that erred in spirit shall* ***come to understanding,*** *and they that murmured shall* ***learn doctrine.***

When he seeth his children; shall sanctify my name; sanctify the Holy One of Jacob fear the God of Israel; come to understanding; learn doctrine

The grand promises of the Lord, as conveyed through the lips of Isaiah, kindle hope, restore confidence, lift the burdens of sin, and fill the soul with joy. The Lord's work is to "bring to pass the immortality and eternal life of man" (Moses 1:39). The work of the prophets is to teach the word of God and administer keys in the kingdom. Man's work is "to keep my commandments, yea, with all your might, mind and strength" (D&C 11:20). Nephi blends his witness to these truths with that of Isaiah. They both reflect the vision of the destiny and potential of the sons and daughters of God.

CHAPTER 28

OVERVIEW

Nephi exposes the false philosophies of churches in the last days and the stealthy strategies of Satan for leading the wicked to destruction. Wo be unto those who fall prey to these practices. We are to learn line upon line and precept upon precept the things of God and avoid the precepts of men.

1–3 Nephi foresees the great value that will be added through the power of the Book of Mormon when it comes forth in a day of wickedness.

> *4 And they shall contend one with another; and their priests shall contend one with another, and they shall teach with their learning, and* ***deny the Holy Ghost,*** *which giveth utterance.*
> *5 And they deny the power of God, the Holy One of Israel; and they say unto the people: Hearken unto us, and hear ye our precept; for behold there is no God today, for the Lord and* ***the Redeemer hath done his work,*** *and* ***he hath given his power unto men;***
> *6 Behold, hearken ye unto my precept; if they shall say there is a miracle wrought by the hand of the Lord, believe it not; for this day* ***he is not a God of miracles; he hath done his work.***
> *7 Yea, and there shall be many which shall say:* ***Eat, drink, and be merry, for tomorrow we die;*** *and it shall be well with us.*
> *8 And there shall also be many which shall say: Eat, drink, and be merry; nevertheless, fear God—he will justify in committing a little sin; yea, lie a little, take the advantage of one because of his words, dig a pit for thy neighbor; there is no harm in this; and do all these things, for tomorrow we die; and if it so be that we are guilty,* ***God will beat us with a few stripes, and at last we shall be saved*** *in the kingdom of God.*
> *9 Yea, and there shall be many which shall teach after this manner, false and vain and foolish doctrines, and shall be puffed up in their hearts, and shall seek deep to hide their counsels from the Lord; and their works shall be in the dark.*
> *10 And the blood of the saints shall cry from the ground against them.*
> *11 Yea, they have all gone out of the way; they have become corrupted.*
> *12 Because of* ***pride,*** *and because of* ***false teachers,*** *and* ***false doctrine,*** *their churches have become corrupted, and their churches are lifted up; because of pride they are puffed up.*

DENY THE HOLY GHOST; THE REDEEMER HATH DONE HIS WORK; HE HATH GIVEN HIS POWER UNTO MEN; HE IS NOT A GOD OF MIRACLES; EAT, DRINK, AND BE MERRY, FOR TOMORROW WE DIE; GOD WILL BEAT US WITH A FEW STRIPES, AND AT LAST WE SHALL BE SAVED; PRIDE; FALSE TEACHERS; FALSE DOCTRINE

Nephi is looking forward into the future some 2,400 years and sees the present day. He is viewing with the spiritual eye, with the vision of the Lord, who declares unto Moses: "There is no God beside me, and all things are present with me, for I know them all" (Moses 1:6). What Nephi sees is an array of misguided churches in the latter days whose constitutions and policies are aptly described by the bolded key words from the scriptural passages just cited. With amazing accuracy, these words characterize the ecclesiastical world in which the young Joseph Smith found nothing but confusion, as confirmed for him by the voice of the Father: "I was answered that I must join none of them, for they were all wrong; and the Personage who addressed me said that all their creeds were an abomination in his sight; that those professors were all corrupt; that: 'they draw near to me with their lips, but their hearts are far from me, they teach for doctrines the commandments of men, having a form of godliness, but they deny the power thereof.'" (JS—H 1:19).

13–19 The churches rob the poor, teach the precepts of men, pervert the ways of the Lord, denigrate the worth of that which is good, and—save they repent—will be destroyed.

> *20 For behold, **at that day shall he rage** in the hearts of the children of men, and stir them up to anger against that which is good.*
> *21 And **others will he pacify,** and lull them away into carnal security, that they will say: All is well in Zion; yea, Zion prospereth, all is well—and thus the devil cheateth their souls, and leadeth them away carefully down to hell.*
> *22 And behold, others he flattereth away, and telleth them there is no hell; and he saith unto them: **I am no devil, for there is none**—and thus he whispereth in their ears, until he grasps them with his awful chains, from whence there is no deliverance.*
> *23 Yea, **they are grasped with death, and hell;** and death, and hell, and the devil, and all that have been seized therewith must stand before the throne of God, and be judged according to their works, from whence they must go into the place prepared for them, even a lake of fire and brimstone, which is endless torment.*

At that day shall he rage; others will he pacify; I am no devil, for there is none; they are grasped with death, and hell

Satan shall rage in the hearts of men with increasing vehemence in the last days. He seeks to destroy the souls of men with false doctrines and pride, and by lulling them away into false security. He stirs them to anger against that which is good. He flatters them into thinking there is no devil and no hell, while stealthily leading them directly there. If, like Nephi, we could witness in visionary revelation the enormous destructive turbulence and dislocation caused by Satan when he is to "rage in the hearts of the children of men" in the latter days (see 2 Nephi 28:20), would we not want to warn our posterity by revealing the secrets of his diabolical strategies? That is precisely what Nephi does. This portion of his record is the playbook of Lucifer exposed in plainness for all too see. Nephi's strategy makes eerie sense to us today as our nation's leadership expends enormous amounts of time and resources to learn the playbook and plans of the terrorist groups who constantly plot the destruction of our way of life. To know and understand the enemy is to be forewarned; to have insight into the enemy's tactics is the first step in overthrowing the enemy's design and in creating security for one's family. The Lord wants us to be on full alert against the incursions of evil, and Nephi is the Lord's voice on the battlefield of daily life where our chief defense is "the truth of God," which is "the rock" upon which we can establish our stand and achieve our victory (see 2 Nephi 28:28).

24 Therefore, ***wo be unto him that is at ease in Zion!***
25 Wo be unto him that crieth: ***All is well!***
26 Yea, wo be unto him that ***hearkeneth unto the precepts of men,*** *and* ***denieth the***
power of God, *and the gift of the Holy Ghost!*
27 Yea, wo be unto him that saith: We have received, and ***we need no more!***
28 And in fine, wo unto all ***those who tremble,*** *and are angry because of the truth of*
God! For behold, he that is built upon the rock receiveth it with gladness; and he that
is built upon a sandy foundation trembleth lest he shall fall.
29 Wo be unto him that shall say: We have received the word of God, and ***we need no***
more of the word of God, *for we have enough!*

Wo be unto him that is at ease in Zion; all is well! hearkeneth unto the precepts of men; denieth the power of God; those who tremble; we need no more of the word of God

Nephi identifies the leading objections that people bring up against the restored gospel and the Book of Mormon. The opposite constitutes the agenda of the disciples of the Lord: to be constantly engaged in a good cause (never at ease with mediocrity), to hearken to the precepts of God, to uphold the power of God, to look forward to greater light and understanding from on high, and to rejoice in the revelations from the Almighty.

> *30 For behold, thus saith the Lord God: I will give unto the children of men* ***line upon line, precept upon precept, here a little and there a little;*** *and blessed are those who hearken unto my precepts, and lend an ear unto my counsel, for they shall learn wisdom; for unto him that receiveth I will give more; and from them that shall say, We have enough, from them shall be taken away even that which they have.*

Line upon line, precept upon precept, here a little and there a little

God is the master teacher. He endows us with truth in accordance with our capacity to receive: "For precept must be upon precept, precept upon precept; line upon line, line upon line; here a little, and there a little (Isaiah 28:10, see also Isaiah 28:13; D&C 98:12; 128:21; Alma 12:9–11). We grow line upon line and precept upon precept—it is a process. As we hearken to the Lord's precepts (listen to them and do them), we gain wisdom and then qualify to receive more. Let us be patient and diligent in the things of the Lord, and He will endow us with an increasing measure of truth and light. "And if your eye be single to my glory, your whole bodies shall be filled with light, and there shall be no darkness in you; and that body which is filled with light comprehendeth all things" (D&C 88:67).

> *31 Cursed is he that putteth his trust in man, or maketh flesh his arm, or shall* ***hearken unto the precepts of men,*** *save their precepts shall be given by the power of the Holy Ghost.*

Hearken unto the precepts of men

The precepts of men are not of God. Decisions that matter most need to be made by following the Spirit (see 1 Nephi 4:6; 2 Nephi 32:5). We should trust in the Lord in all things (see 2 Nephi 4:34). Here is a question of conscience: Do we put our trust in man, his precepts, and the arm of flesh—or in God?

32 If the Gentiles repent, God will bless them.

CHAPTER 29

OVERVIEW

The Lord assures Nephi that his writings will be part of the great latter-day Restoration of truth. He is the same yesterday, today, and forever, and will continue to speak and reveal His word to each nation. Out of that which is written the nations will be judged. In the latter days He will gather His people and His word into one.

1–6 The Lord speaks to Nephi and assures him that his words will come forth in support of the divine plan to gather the scattered of Israel in the latter days and provide the world with another testament of Jesus Christ. Many in that day will reject the new witness—the Book of Mormon—saying they already have a Bible. But the Lord condemns such narrow-mindedness in those who have scant gratitude for the travail of the Jews who brought forth the Bible.

> *7 Know ye not that there are* ***more nations than one?*** *Know ye not that I, the Lord your God, have created all men, and that I remember those who are upon the isles of the sea; and that I rule in the heavens above and in the earth beneath; and I bring forth my word unto the children of men, yea, even upon all the nations of the earth?*
> *8 Wherefore murmur ye, because that ye shall receive more of my word? Know ye not that the testimony of two nations is a witness unto you that I am God, that I remember one nation like unto another? Wherefore, I speak the same words unto one nation like unto another. And when the two nations shall run together the* ***testimony of the two nations shall run together*** *also.*
> *9 And I do this that I may prove unto many that* ***I am the same yesterday, today, and forever;*** *and that I speak forth my words according to mine own pleasure. And because that I have spoken one word ye need not suppose that I cannot speak another; for* ***my work is not yet finished;*** *neither shall it be until the end of man, neither from that time henceforth and forever.*

More nations than one; testimony of the two nations shall run together; I am the same yesterday, today, and forever; my work is not yet finished

From these statements by the Lord, we understand better the importance and power of the Book of Mormon. Through the Book of Mormon we learn how to build a closer relationship with our Father in Heaven. The Prophet Joseph said, "I told the brethren that the Book of Mormon was the most correct of any book on earth, and the keystone of our religion, and a man would get nearer to God by abiding by its precepts, than by any other book" (*HC* 4:461).

Nephi knows through prophetic insight that the record he is initiating will be brought forth in the fulness of times as a light shining out of the darkness, illuminating the pathway for mankind. He also knows that the record will be received with disbelief because of the sectarian philosophy that the canon of scripture is closed. It must thrill Nephi to engrave upon his plates the Lord's own response to such narrow-mindedness: "Know ye not that there are more nations than one? Know ye not that I, the Lord your God, have created all men, and that I remember those who are upon the isles of the sea; and that I rule in the heavens above and in the earth beneath; and I bring forth my word unto the children of men, yea, even upon all the nations of the earth?" (2 Nephi 29:7).

Ezra Taft Benson points out the key place this new scripture occupies in the process of the Restoration:

> A powerful testimony to the importance of the Book of Mormon is to note where the Lord placed its coming forth in the timetable of the unfolding Restoration. The only thing that preceded it was the First Vision. In that marvelous manifestation, the Prophet Joseph Smith learned the true nature of God and that God had a work for him to do. The coming forth of the Book of Mormon was the next thing to follow.
>
> Think of that in terms of what it implies. The coming forth of the Book of Mormon preceded the restoration of the priesthood. It was published just a few days before the Church was organized. The Saints were given the Book of Mormon to read before they were given the revelations outlining such great doctrines as the three degrees of glory, celestial marriage, or work for the dead. It came before priesthood quorums and Church organization. Doesn't this tell us something about how the Lord views this sacred work? (*The Teachings of Ezra Taft Benson* [Salt Lake City: Bookcraft, 1988], 49)

10 Wherefore, because that ye have a Bible ye need not suppose that it contains all my words; neither need ye suppose that I have not caused more to be written.
11 For I command all men, both in the east and in the west, and in the north, and in the south, and in the islands of the sea, that they shall write the words which I speak unto them; for ***out of the books which shall be written I will judge the world,*** *every man according to their works, according to that which is written.*

> *12 For behold, I shall speak unto the Jews and they shall write it; and I shall also speak unto the Nephites and they shall write it; and I shall also speak unto the other tribes of the house of Israel, which I have led away, and they shall write it; and* ***I shall also speak unto all nations*** *of the earth and they shall write it.*

Out of the books which shall be written I will judge the world; I shall also speak unto all nations

We are judged by our works according to the standard of the written word of God given to us through mercy and love. We are blessed when we consistently and devotedly base our values and standards for living upon the word of God as given in the scriptures and through His living prophets.

> *13 And it shall come to pass that the Jews shall have the words of the Nephites, and the Nephites shall have the words of the Jews; and the Nephites and the Jews shall have the words of the lost tribes of Israel; and the lost tribes of Israel shall have the words of the Nephites and the Jews.*
>
> *14 And it shall come to pass that* ***my people, which are of the house of Israel, shall be gathered home*** *unto the lands of their possessions; and* ***my word also shall be gathered in one.*** *And I will show unto them that fight against my word and against my people, who are of the house of Israel, that I am God, and that I covenanted with Abraham that I would remember his seed forever.*

My people, which are of the house of Israel, shall be gathered home; my word also shall be gathered in one

According to the Lord's divine plan, the righteous are to be gathered together in the last days, and the words given unto them are also to be gathered in—that all might be brought together in unity. Thus the word of the Lord, dispensed as seeds of truth to each nation of the world as the Lord deems appropriate, will sprout and unfold, becoming a tree of everlasting life.

Sprouting Seeds

The Book of Mormon is the textbook of conversion. Later in its pages, one of its principal figures and teachers, Alma the Younger, a descendant of Lehi and Nephi, compares faith to a seed and inspires his listeners to undertake a practical strategy in spiritual horticulture: "But behold, if ye will awake and arouse your faculties, even to an experiment upon my words, and exercise a particle of faith, yea, even if ye can no more than desire to believe, let this desire work in you, even until ye believe in a manner that ye can give place for a portion of my words" (Alma 32:27). He then unfolds his memorable counsel for understanding the principle of how the Lord cultivates within us the power to rise to our divine potential based on faith.

From the earliest days of the Restoration, the Book of Mormon has served as a magnet, drawing truth-seekers into the fold. Take the story of Joseph Smith's younger brother, Samuel Harrison Smith. As a twenty-two-year-old returned from his mission, he was somewhat discouraged with the results. But look what came of his labors: On Saturday, April 14, 1832, Brigham Young, "the Lion of the Lord" (*HC* 7:435), was baptized after two years of intensive study and prayer centered on the Book of Mormon, a copy of which his brother Phineas had given him. Phineas had purchased the copy from the Prophet's younger brother, Samuel Harrison, in April 1830, during the latter's early missionary labors. Samuel also provided a copy to Reverend John P. Greene, husband of Phineas' sister, Rhoda. Both were subsequently converted. Brigham Young had given his copy of the Book of Mormon to his sister, Fanny Young Murray, the mother-in-law of Heber C. Kimball, who, along with his family, also became converted because of it. These families were thus brought into the Church through the Book of Mormon. And the Book of Mormon became accessible to them as a result of the devoted missionary labors of the twenty-two-year-old Samuel Harrison Smith. Young Samuel had returned home discouraged from this early mission to upstate New York—unaware at the time that his labors would eventually yield such extraordinary fruit. (See *Church History in the Fulness of Times*, 74–75).

The sprouting seeds that come from a sincere study of the Book of Mormon lead to the growth and maturation of a tree of faith from which "by and by ye shall pluck the fruit thereof, which is most precious, which is sweet above all that is sweet, and which is white above all that is white, yea, and pure above all that is pure; and ye shall feast upon this fruit even until ye are filled, that ye hunger not, neither shall ye thirst" (Alma 32:42).

Is it any wonder that the Lord has commanded us to share the Book of Mormon with our friends and colleagues so that they, too, can feast upon the fruit—learn divine truth through spiritual confirmation (see Moroni 10:4)? (Richard J. Allen)

CHAPTER 30

OVERVIEW

In the last days, the Lord will gather together His people under the banner of restored truth. The Gentiles who embrace the gospel will be numbered among the covenant flock. The remnants of the house of Israel who believe in the Savior will rejoice and become a pure and delightsome people. The wicked will be destroyed and the millennial period of peace will commence. Satan will be bound for a time.

> *1 AND now behold, my beloved brethren, I would speak unto you; for I, Nephi, would not suffer that ye should suppose that ye are more righteous than the Gentiles shall be. For behold,* ***except ye shall keep the commandments of God ye shall all likewise perish;*** *and because of the words which have been spoken ye need not suppose that the Gentiles are utterly destroyed.*
>
> *2 For behold, I say unto you that* ***as many of the Gentiles as will repent are the covenant people of the Lord;*** *and as many of the Jews as will not repent shall be cast off; for the* ***Lord covenanteth with none save it be with them that repent and believe in his Son,*** *who is the Holy One of Israel.*

Except ye shall keep the commandments of God ye shall all likewise perish; as many of the Gentiles as will repent are the covenant people of the Lord; Lord covenanteth with none save it be with them that repent and believe in his Son

Nephi gives his people a view of their descendants and the Gentiles in the latter days. He warns his people that they will be punished like the wayward Gentiles unless they repent and honor their covenants. Who are the covenant peoples of the Lord? All who come unto Christ in faith and repentance, thus becoming the seed of Abraham: "And I will bless them through thy name; for as many as receive this Gospel shall be called after thy name, and shall be accounted thy seed, and shall rise up and bless thee, as their father" (Abraham 2:10).

The Lord favors Nephi with a vision of His dealings with mankind from the beginning of time unto the end when He will institute His millennial reign. Nephi is able to experience vicariously the agony and anguish of those who relinquish their covenant blessing through apostasy and rebellion; he is able to savor the unspeakable joy of those who purify themselves and participate in the blessings of covenant obedience. Everyone can have a place among the covenant people of the Lord through faith in Christ, repentance, baptism, and receiving the gift of the Holy Ghost.

How can we liken this doctrine unto ourselves? When we choose to repent and follow the steps of spiritual rebirth, we make a covenant with the Lord. He will honor this covenant. Through obedience, we can have the blessings of eternal life by enduring to the end.

3 And now, I would prophesy somewhat more concerning ***the Jews and the Gentiles.*** *For after the book of which I have spoken shall come forth, and be written unto the* ***Gentiles,*** *and sealed up again unto the Lord, there shall be many which shall believe the words which are written; and they shall carry them forth unto the* ***remnant of our seed.***
4 And then shall the ***remnant of our seed*** *know concerning us, how that we came out from Jerusalem, and that they are* ***descendants of the Jews.***

The Jews and the Gentiles; remnant of our seed; descendants of the Jews

The Book of Mormon is to have a unifying influence on the righteous in the latter days. Many Gentiles will come into the fold and spread the word of truth to the remnant of Israel. How are the Book of Mormon peoples descendants of the Jews? Even though Lehi is a descendant of Manasseh, son of Joseph (see Alma 10:3), and Ishmael a descendant of Ephraim, son of Joseph (see *Journal of Discourses*, 23:184–185), these families originate in Jerusalem and spring from the Jewish national culture. Mulek, founder of the Mulekites, a people that later coalesces into the Nephite culture, is of the tribe of Judah (see Omni 1:12–16; Mosiah 25:2; Helaman 8:21). When the Lord speaks to Martin Harris concerning the Book of Mormon in our day, He declares: "And again, I command thee that thou shalt not covet thine own property, but impart it freely to the printing of the Book of Mormon, which contains the truth and the word of God—Which is my word to the Gentile, that soon it may go to the Jew, of whom the Lamanites are a remnant, that they may believe the gospel, and look not for a Messiah to come who has already come" (D&C 19:26–27). Thus the Lamanites are identified as a remnant of the Jews, based on their cultural origins in the Holy Land. Nevertheless, all are part of the house of Israel, including those Gentiles who are adopted into the fold through a covenant relationship.

5 And the gospel of Jesus Christ shall be declared among them; wherefore, they shall be ***restored unto the knowledge of their fathers,*** *and also to the* ***knowledge of Jesus Christ,*** *which was had among their fathers.*
6 And ***then shall they rejoice;*** *for they shall know that it is a blessing unto them from the hand of God; and their scales of darkness shall begin to fall from their eyes; and many generations shall not pass away among them, save they shall be* ***a pure and a delightsome people.***
7 And it shall come to pass that the Jews which are scattered also shall begin to believe in Christ; and they shall begin to gather in upon the face of the land; and as many as shall believe in Christ shall also become a ***delightsome*** *people.*

RESTORED UNTO THE KNOWLEDGE OF THEIR FATHERS; KNOWLEDGE OF JESUS CHRIST; THEN SHALL THEY REJOICE; A PURE AND DELIGHTSOME PEOPLE
As Nephi comes to the close of his portion of the sacred chronicle, he focuses on the good news—on the fruits of the Restoration in the latter days and on the effects of a revived spirituality among the gathering remnants of Israel and the responsive Gentile nations. Through the blessings of the gospel of Jesus Christ, new light is introduced into the lives of the faithful as they return to the fold. Their eyes see spiritual things and their hearts perceive spiritual truth. The "scales of darkness" fall away from their eyes and they become pure and delightsome.

8–18 Nephi presents a summary of the times of Restoration and cleansing, leading up to the millennial advent and the subsequent blessings of peace that will prevail among all creatures as foretold also by Isaiah (compare Isaiah 11:6–9; 2 Nephi 21:6–9). All shall be revealed in that day and Satan shall be bound for a time.

CONCLUDING THOUGHTS

Through the prophet Nephi's inspired vision we can look forward to the Second Coming of the Savior. We can deepen our understanding of the Lord's design in bringing forth the Book of Mormon in our day. We can become more skillful in anticipating and neutralizing the strategies of Satan. We can appreciate with greater insight the importance and power of the Book of Mormon. We can live more righteously as a covenant people, preparing ourselves and our posterity for the millennial reign.

CHAPTER 31

OVERVIEW

Nephi explains the doctrine of Christ. Though perfect, Christ was baptized to "fulfil all righteousness" (verse 5) and demonstrate His willingness to enter into a covenant of obedience with the Lord in all humility. One enters the strait and narrow way through faith, repentance, baptism, and receiving the gift of the Holy Ghost. By enduring to the end through obedience and devotion, one receives eternal life.

> *1 AND now I, Nephi, make an end of my prophesying unto you, my beloved brethren. And I cannot write but a few things, which I know must surely come to pass; neither can I write but a few of the words of my brother Jacob.*

2 Nephi 31:2–3

> 2 *Wherefore, the things which I have written sufficeth me, save it be a few words which I must speak concerning* ***the doctrine of Christ;*** *wherefore,* ***I shall speak unto you plainly,*** *according to the plainness of my prophesying.*
> 3 *For my soul delighteth in* ***plainness;*** *for after this manner doth the Lord God work among the children of men. For the Lord God giveth light unto the understanding; for he speaketh unto men according to their language, unto their understanding.*

THE DOCTRINE OF CHRIST; I SHALL SPEAK UNTO YOU PLAINLY; PLAINNESS

Nephi gives an inspired formulation of the doctrine of Christ—embracing the first four principles and ordinances of the gospel: faith in the Lord Jesus Christ, repentance, baptism by immersion, and the reception of the Holy Ghost through the laying on of hands (see 1 Nephi 10:17; 2 Nephi 31:12; 3 Nephi 19:20). Thereafter, one must press forward with a steadfastness in Christ, having hope and the love of God and of all men. We are to feast upon the word of God and endure to the end to receive eternal life (see 2 Nephi 31:20)

Elder Jeffrey R. Holland points out that the essence of the gospel of Jesus Christ has to do with these first principles and ordinances:

> In a marvelous final testimony to his people, as well as to the unborn and unseen of the last dispensation yet to come, Nephi made "an end" of his prophesying (including prophesying about the coming forth of the Book of Mormon) and concluded his writing—and his lifetime of teaching—with "a few words . . . concerning the doctrine of Christ." [2 Nephi 31:1–2.]
>
> Although a phrase like "the doctrine of Christ" could appropriately be used to describe any or all of the Master's teachings, nevertheless those magnificently broad and beautiful expressions spread throughout the Book of Mormon, New Testament, and latter-day scriptures might more properly be called "the *doctrines* of Christ." Note that the phrase Nephi used is distinctly singular. In Nephi's concluding testimony, and later in the Savior's own declaration to the Nephites at his appearance to them, the emphasis is on a precise, focused, singular sense of Christ's doctrine, specifically that which the Prophet Joseph Smith declared to be "the first principles and ordinances of the Gospel." [Articles of Faith 1:4.]
>
> The "doctrine of Christ" as taught by Nephi in his grand, summational discourse focuses on faith in the Lord Jesus Christ, repentance, baptism by immersion, receiving the gift of the Holy Ghost, and enduring to the end. It does not, in

this declaration, attempt to cover the entire plan of salvation, all the virtues of a Christian life, or the rewards that await us in differing degrees of heavenly glory. It does not, in this declaration, deal with the offices of the priesthood, the ordinances of the temple, or many other true doctrines. All these are important, but as used in the Book of Mormon, "the doctrine of Christ" is simple and direct. It focuses on the first principles of the gospel exclusively, including an expression of encouragement to endure, to persist, to press on. Indeed, it is in the clarity and simplicity of "the doctrine of Christ" that its impact is found. Nephi knew it would be so. He wrote, "I shall speak unto you plainly, according to the plainness of my prophesying." [2 Nephi 31:2.] (*Christ and the New Covenant: The Messianic Message of the Book of Mormon* [Salt Lake City: Deseret Book, 1997], 49–50)

4 Wherefore, I would that ye should remember that I have spoken unto you concerning that prophet which the Lord showed unto me, that should baptize the Lamb of God, which should take away the sins of the world.
5 And now, if the Lamb of God, he being holy, should have need to be baptized by water, ***to fulfil all righteousness,*** *O then, how much more need have we, being unholy, to be baptized, yea, even by water!*
6 And now, I would ask of you, my beloved brethren, wherein the Lamb of God did ***fulfil all righteousness*** *in being baptized by water?*
7 Know ye not that he was holy? But notwithstanding he being holy, he showeth unto the children of men that, according to the flesh ***he humbleth himself*** *before the Father, and* ***witnesseth unto the Father*** *that he would be obedient unto him in keeping his commandments.*
8 Wherefore, after he was baptized with water the Holy Ghost descended upon him in the form of a dove.

To fulfil all righteousness; he humbleth himself; witnesseth unto the Father
The Savior, though a perfect Being without spot or blemish, nevertheless suffers Himself to be baptized to "fulfil all righteousness," demonstrating His willingness to be humble and enter into a covenant of obedience, just as He requires of us all.

EVIDENCE: The Prophetic Perfect (1 Nephi 5:5, 2 Nephi 31:8, Jarom 1:11, Mosiah 16:6)
Nephi's statement speaks about the baptism of Christ as if it had already occurred. This kind of

grammatical construction is not unusual. Prophets in the Old Testament often used past tense, present perfect tense, or past perfect tense when they prophesied about future events. This phenomenon is referred to as the "prophetic perfect." For instance, in Isaiah 53, the prophet uses the prophetic perfect as he describes the future sufferings of the Savior, "He *hath borne* our griefs and *carried* our sorrows; yet we *did* esteem him stricken, smitten of God, and afflicted. But he *was wounded* for our transgressions, he *was bruised* for our iniquities: the chastisement of our peace *was* upon him." In the Book of Mormon, many prophets, including Lehi, Nephi, Abinadi, and King Benjamin, use the prophetic perfect when they prophesy. (See *Echoes,* 164–166).

9–12 Christ sets the example for entering in upon the strait and narrow pathway. He says, "**follow me,** and do the things which ye have seen me do" (verse 12).

Follow me

Having come to the moment in his ministry where he must bring his sacred account on the small plates to a close, Nephi shares his innermost thoughts. He has been favored of the Lord to behold many grand and extraordinary things pertaining to the design of heaven for mankind. He has viewed the generations of time, witnessed the coming and going of nations, perceived the flow of history from the beginning even until the end, and watched in anguish the inevitable decline of the rebellious and with joy the spiritual prosperity of the covenant faithful.

After all these grand episodes and revelations what does Nephi, in his final remarks, choose to emphasize in his closing witness for future readers? It is the simple and pure doctrine of Christ. It is a solemn reminder of the efficacy of the principles of faith, repentance, baptism, and the gift of the Holy Ghost. It is an earnest plea to his readers to take upon themselves the name of Christ and endure to the end. Nephi places his seal of confirmation upon these final words of counsel central to the gospel of Jesus Christ.

> *13 Wherefore, my beloved brethren, I know that if ye shall follow the Son, with full purpose of heart, acting no hypocrisy and no deception before God, but with real intent, repenting of your sins, witnessing unto the Father that ye are willing to take upon you the name of Christ, by baptism—yea, by following your Lord and your Savior down into the water, according to his word, behold, then shall ye receive the Holy Ghost; yea, then cometh the baptism of fire and of the Holy Ghost; and then can ye* ***speak with the tongue of angels,*** *and shout praises unto the Holy One of Israel.*

Speak with the tongue of angels

When we cross the threshold of conversion and comply with the requirements of covenant ordinances, having purified ourselves to the extent that the Holy Ghost becomes our constant companion, we can speak with the tongue of angels (see also 2 Nephi 32:2; Alma 29:1–9; 32:23). Angels speak the words of Christ. The words of Christ embrace and convey the essence of salvation and exaltation. We can speak this language when we follow the promptings of the Spirit and follow the footsteps of the Redeemer.

The question of conscience is this: Can we truly speak this new language, as if with the tongue of angels? When we follow Christ, we do our best to emulate His life and keep His commandments. This is not always an easy task—and it was not intended to be easy. It takes effort and diligence. Like Nephi (see the "Psalm of Nephi," 2 Nephi 4:17–35), we often struggle, but having acknowledged our weaknesses before the Lord, we will indeed be strengthened by Him (see Ether 12:27). The questions in our heart and soul are these: Are we doing our very best? Do we follow the Savior Jesus Christ with full purpose of heart? Are we speaking His words—both with our mouths and with our actions? If we prayerfully seek His guidance and support, we will be filled with the Spirit and speak the language of the gospel in all we do.

Memories: With the Tongue of Angels

Many years ago I became acquainted with a noble and sincere gentleman who had an Evangelical Christian background. He had studied the Book of Mormon and became convinced of its truth. Having attended our church meetings on several occasions, he mentioned to me one day that our worship pattern is fairly restrained, with little of the enthusiastic and spontaneous "Praise the Lord" occurrences from the audience that he had become accustomed to in his own religious upbringing. In response, I opened the Book of Mormon and read with him a passage from 2 Nephi 31 concerning the promise of the Lord that the converted would be able to speak a new kind of language: "then shall ye receive the Holy Ghost; yea, then cometh the baptism of fire and of the Holy Ghost; and then can ye speak with the tongue of angels, and shout praises unto the Holy One of Israel" (2 Nephi 31:13; compare 2 Nephi 32:2; Alma 29:1–9; 32:23).

My friend was intrigued with this passage. I explained to him that this new language is made manifest in several ways: through the speeches and lessons we may be invited to give from time to time; through the bearing of testimonies on fast Sunday and on other occasions where our feelings of praise and gratitude for the Lord come forth naturally and with heartfelt sincerity; through our hymns of praise and thanksgiving; and, most especially, through our patterns of behavior. It is how we *live* that reflects our understanding of the words of Christ. Our actions speak louder than our words. The Lord commanded: "And the members shall manifest before the church, and also before the elders, by a godly walk and conversation, that they are worthy of it, that there may be works and faith agreeable to the holy scriptures—walking in holiness before the Lord" (D&C 20:69).

My friend seemed satisfied with our discussion. Since then, I have thought about his question often, remembering also what Alma said on one occasion: "O THAT I were an angel, and could have the wish of mine heart, that I might go forth and speak with the trump of God, with a voice to shake the earth, and cry repentance unto every people!" (Alma 29:1). But when he thought about that wish, and about his circumstances, he restrained himself with the consolation: "I know that which the Lord hath commanded me, and I glory in it. I do not glory of myself, but I glory in that which the Lord hath commanded me; yea, and this is my glory, that perhaps I may be an instrument in the hands of God to bring some soul to repentance; and this is my joy" (Alma 29:9). We can indeed be instruments in the hands of the Lord in carrying His gospel message to the ends of the earth—doing so in meekness and gratitude by using the words of salvation and inspiration. The Lord has stated: "He that speaketh, whose spirit is contrite, whose language is meek and *edifieth* the same is of God if he obey mine ordinances" (D&C 52: 16). It is in this manner, as we are moved upon by the Holy Ghost, that we can speak with the tongues of angels. (Richard J. Allen)

14–18 After one has sincerely repented and witnessed to the Father a willingness to keep the commandments through the baptism of water and fire, that person is on the strait and narrow path leading to salvation—but that is not yet enough.

> *19 And now, my beloved brethren, after ye have gotten into this strait and narrow path, I would ask if all is done? Behold, I say unto you, Nay; for ye have not come thus far save it were by the word of Christ with unshaken faith in him, relying wholly upon the merits of him who is mighty to save.*
> *20 Wherefore, ye must* ***press forward with a steadfastness in Christ,*** *having a perfect brightness of hope, and a love of God and of all men. Wherefore, if ye shall press forward, feasting upon the word of Christ, and endure to the end, behold, thus saith the Father:* ***Ye shall have eternal life.***

PRESS FORWARD WITH A STEADFASTNESS IN CHRIST; YE SHALL HAVE ETERNAL LIFE

This statement by Nephi is among the most often quoted passages from the Book of Mormon. To press forward with steadfastness, with a firm and constant devotion to the Savior, and to endure to the end with unrelenting and fixed determination—these are the crowning attributes of discipleship. Nephi was the Lord's witness of the fact that entering into a covenant relationship with God, though indispensable for salvation and exaltation, is, in and of itself, not enough. One has to extend the covenant fidelity without limit. One has to endure to the end with an unyielding steadfastness in Christ—just as Nephi exemplified through his ministry, and just as the prophets of the Lord have demonstrated in all dispensations of time.

Elder Joseph B. Wirthlin draws our attention to enduring to the end in the marathon of life: "An obvious parallel between life and a marathon is the necessity to run diligently and endure to the end. Among Nephi's final words to his people were these: 'And now, . . . after ye have gotten into this strait and narrow path, I would ask if all is done? Behold, I say unto you, Nay; . . . Ye must press forward with a steadfastness in Christ . . . and endure to the end' (2 Nephi 31:19–20). I think of this promise of the Lord: 'They that wait upon the Lord shall renew their strength; they shall mount up with wings as eagles; they shall run, and not be weary; and they shall walk, and not faint.' (Isaiah 40:31.) We have that promise." (*Finding Peace in Our Lives* [Salt Lake City: Deseret Book, 1995], 153).

> *21 And now, behold, my beloved brethren, this is the way; and there is none other way nor name given under heaven whereby man can be saved in the kingdom of God. And now, behold, this is the doctrine of Christ, and* ***the only and true doctrine of the Father, and of the Son, and of the Holy Ghost, which is one God,*** *without end. Amen.*

The only and true doctrine of the Father, and of the Son, and of the Holy Ghost, which is one God

The doctrine of Christ is, in effect, the doctrine of the Father, the Son, and the Holy Ghost. We recognize that the Godhead consists of three distinct beings as noted in the scriptures (see Matthew 3:17; 3 Nephi 11:7; D&C 130:22; JS—H 1:17; Articles of Faith 1:1). Nevertheless, they are "one God." Oneness has many definitions, but when used in the scriptures by the Lord in reference to the oneness of the Godhead, it refers to unity of mission, being of one accord and purpose—just as the Lord prayed for His disciples to be one as He and His Father are one (see John 17:20–21). Another example is the occasion when the Apostle Paul speaks of husband and wife being one flesh (see Ephesians 5:31). The multitude is described as being of one heart and one soul (see Acts 4:32). We are one in the Lord (see Galatians 3:28). We are told to be one with the Lord as He is one with the Father (see D&C 35:2). We are commanded to be one, else we are not considered to be the

Lord's (see D&C 38:27). The Lord states that we are one in unity with Him and our Heavenly Father (see D&C 50:43). The doctrine of unity and oneness is the opposite of division and contention—which is fostered by the father of contention (see 3 Nephi 11:29).

CHAPTER 32

OVERVIEW

Nephi gives his parting instructions: Feast on the words of Christ and follow the guidance of the Holy Ghost, and you will know how to endure to the end and be saved. Remember to pray always to the Father in the name of Jesus Christ.

> *1 AND now, behold, my beloved brethren, I suppose that ye ponder somewhat in your hearts concerning that which ye should do after ye have entered in by the way. But, behold,* ***why do ye ponder these things in your hearts?***
> *2 Do ye not remember that I said unto you that after ye had received the Holy Ghost ye could speak with the tongue of angels? And now, how could ye speak with the tongue of angels save it were by the Holy Ghost?*
> *3 Angels speak by the power of the Holy Ghost; wherefore, they speak the words of Christ. Wherefore, I said unto you,* ***feast upon the words of Christ;*** *for behold, the words of Christ will tell you all things what ye should do.*

Why do ye ponder these things in your hearts? Feast upon the words of Christ

We have been encouraged by all the prophets and the holy scriptures to live by the word of God. The only way to know the word is by diligent study of the word. The Lord condemns the people for treating lightly the Book of Mormon and the commandments (see D&C 84:57). The regular study of the scriptures literally brings Christ into our lives, for He is indeed the Word of God (see John 1; Revelation 19:13). Do we feast upon the word of God by searching the scriptures daily? The word will tell us how to proceed on the strait and narrow course and back home again.

Memories: Feasting on the Word Will Inspire Us to Action

I was traveling to the Salt Lake City airport with my friend Robert Matthews on our way to a "Know Your Religion" lecture. He was in the midst of working on the topical guide, footnotes, and cross references for the new edition of the scriptures. I inquired as to the progress. He mentioned that things were going well and then said, "Last week I had an interesting experience. I was reading all the scriptures concerning prayer. It took several days and at the end of the project I had an overwhelming desire to pray."

I have thought about that experience over the years. Surely when we truly feast upon the words of Christ by searching the scriptures and listening to our living prophets—I mean truly feast—we will be inspired to action. The word becomes our Liahona (see Alma 37:37–44); tells us all things to do. It is the food for our spirit. Our spirits direct our bodies. If we are not diligent in keeping the commandments, our spiritual strength will wane. We need strength. We need to increase our faith. Faith comes by hearing the word of God (see Romans 10:17). Through faith, we, like Father Lehi, will be blessed with the Holy Spirit (see 1 Nephi 10:17). We can claim these blessings of the Lord by obedience, which begins with feasting upon the word. (Ed J. Pinegar)

> *4 Wherefore, now after I have spoken these words, if ye cannot understand them it will be* ***because ye ask not,*** *neither do ye knock; wherefore, ye are not brought into the light, but must perish in the dark.*

Because ye ask not

We are to actively seek to understand the word of God. We must ask in faith that we might understand rather than fall into a condition of disbelief because of neglected prayers and study.

> *5 For behold, again I say unto you that if ye will enter in by the way, and* ***receive the Holy Ghost,*** *it will show unto you all things what ye should do.*

Receive the Holy Ghost

The Holy Ghost will show you all things. Seek the Holy Ghost through faith, love, and obedience—that you might be guided in all things.

6–8 Nephi closes his comments on the doctrine of Christ. He is grieved because men do not follow the word of God, even when it is given to them in plainness, "even as plain as word can be" (verse 7).

> *9 But behold, I say unto you that ye must* ***pray always,*** *and not faint; that ye must not perform any thing unto the Lord save in the first place ye shall* ***pray unto the Father in the name of Christ,*** *that he will consecrate thy performance unto thee, that thy performance may be for the welfare of thy soul.*

Pray always; pray unto the Father in the name of Christ

Nephi, being both a visionary servant of the Lord and a practical guide for his people, leaves a legacy of inspired advice. Follow divine counsel. Follow the Spirit. Pray always in the name of the Christ "that thy performances may be for the welfare of thy soul" (2 Nephi 32:9).

CHAPTER 33

OVERVIEW

Nephi bears his witness that the words he has written are true, for they are the words of Christ spoken by the power of the Holy Ghost. Nephi glories in truth and plainness. He glories in the Savior. He acts out of charity for Jew and Gentile, encouraging his readers to hearken to the word of Christ and to be faithful. He bids them farewell until he should meet them before the judgment bar of God.

> *1 AND now I, Nephi, cannot write all the things which were taught among my people; neither am I mighty in writing, like unto speaking; for* ***when a man speaketh by the power of the Holy Ghost*** *the power of the Holy Ghost carrieth it unto the hearts of the children of men.*

When a man speaketh by the power of the Holy Ghost

We must be worthy of the Spirit. When we speak by the Spirit, the Spirit will carry our message into the hearts of those whom we teach. Every missionary knows of this commandment and promise of the Lord:

> Therefore, verily I say unto you, lift up your voices unto this people; speak the thoughts that I shall put into your hearts, and you shall not be confounded before men;
>
> For it shall be given you in the very hour, yea, in the very moment, what ye shall say.
>
> But a commandment I give unto you, that ye shall declare whatsoever thing ye declare in my name, in solemnity of heart, in the spirit of meekness, in all things.
>
> And I give unto you this promise, that inasmuch as ye do this the Holy Ghost shall be shed forth in bearing record unto all things whatsoever ye shall say. (D&C 100:5–8; compare Romans 5:5.)

2 But behold, there are ***many that harden their hearts*** *against the Holy Spirit, that it hath no place in them; wherefore, they cast many things away which are written and esteem them as things of naught.*

Many that harden their hearts

The Holy Spirit carries the word of God "unto" our hearts—not "into" our hearts (see 2 Nephi 33:1). We are to do our part in allowing the word to penetrate "into" our hearts. That means have a heart softened and prepared to yield to the Spirit and to God. We really are an expression of the condition of our hearts. We think and act according to our hearts (see Proverbs 23:7). As we become even as He is, we find that it is our heart that is changing. That is why Alma asked the question, "Have ye experienced this mighty change in your hearts?" (Alma 5:14) How soft are our hearts? Are we easily entreated? (See Alma 7:23.) Do we yield our hearts to the enticings of the Holy Spirit (see Mosiah 3:19) and to God (see Helaman 3:35)—and thus receive the blessings of doing so?

3 But I, Nephi, have written what I have written, and I esteem it as of great worth, and especially unto my people. For I pray continually for them by day, and mine eyes water my pillow by night, because of them; and I cry unto my God in faith, and I know that he will hear my cry.
4 And I know that the Lord God will consecrate my prayers for the gain of my people. And the words which I have written in weakness will be made strong unto them; for ***it persuadeth them to do good;*** *it maketh known unto them of their fathers; and it speaketh of Jesus, and* ***persuadeth them to believe in him,*** *and to* ***endure to the end, which is life eternal.***
5 And it speaketh harshly against sin, according to the ***plainness of the truth;*** *wherefore, no man will be angry at the words which I have written save he shall be of the spirit of the devil.*

Persuadeth them to do good; persuadeth them to believe in him; endure to the end, which is life eternal; plainness of the truth

Nephi bears his testimony about the truth of his words and the integrity of his motivation on behalf of his people. The purpose of the word of God is to persuade us to do good, to believe in Christ, and endure to the end. Nephi is conscious of his weakness in writing. But the Lord compensates for that weakness just as He can compensate for our weaknesses. When we pray for strength and support, He can make up the difference as an act of grace. In this regard, the Lord said to Moroni: "And if men come unto me I will show unto them their weakness. I give unto men weakness that they may be humble; and my grace is sufficient for all men that humble themselves before me; for if they humble themselves before me, and have faith in me, then will I make weak things become strong unto them" (Ether 12:27).

EVIDENCE: Endure to the end, which is life eternal—Merismus

A "merismus" is an ancient rhetorical device wherein a topic or statement is divided into parts, the division allowing the entire topic or statement to be brought to mind by listing only one or more of the parts. The Savior taught six major points of doctrine: faith, repentance, baptism, the gift of the Holy Ghost, enduring to the end, and eternal life. We could label these six points A, B, C, D, E, and F, establishing a pattern. In a merismus, naming at least two of these points of doctrine—for instance, faith and enduring to the end—would bring to mind the entire list. Similarly, the expression cited above ("Endure to the end, which is life eternal") would have the same effect. The Hebrew Bible frequently uses the merismus, and in the Book of Mormon, there are at least 130 meristic statements regarding Christ's doctrine. (See *Echoes,* 141–143).

> *6 **I glory in plainness; I glory in truth; I glory in my Jesus,** for he hath redeemed my soul from hell.*
> *7 **I have charity for my people,** and great faith in Christ that I shall meet many souls spotless at his judgment-seat.*
> *8 **I have charity for the Jew**—I say Jew, because I mean them from whence I came.*
> *9 **I also have charity for the Gentiles.** But behold, for none of these can I hope except they shall be reconciled unto Christ, and enter into the narrow gate, and **walk in the strait path** which leads to life, and continue in the path until the end of the day of probation.*

I glory in plainness; I glory in truth; I glory in my Jesus; I have charity for my people; I have charity for the Jew; I also have charity for the Gentiles

Nephi bears witness of the enduring values of his heart. He loves the truth and acts out of charity. His closing comments are remarkably personal. We can relate to the humanness of Nephi. Though a grand prophet of the Lord, he is also a friend to the readers of the Book of Mormon.

EVIDENCE: Different Cultural Settings (1 Nephi 1:2; 2 Nephi 33:8; Jacob 7:26; Mormon 9:32; Alma 49:11)

Compared to so-called similar books of its day, including *The Book of Pukei, Manuscript Found,* and *View of the Hebrews,* the Book of Mormon's cultural setting is markedly different. Where the former three works are set in a world heavily influenced by Roman culture, the Book of Mormon's setting is dominated by ancient Near Eastern and Mesoamerican cultures. After Lehi's group arrived in the New World, they started to assimilate the environment of their promised land. If Joseph Smith had read a book such as *View of the Hebrews* and used it in "writing" the Book of Mormon, as some critics mistakenly supposed he did, the cultures portrayed in the two books would not be so noticeably different. (See *Echoes,* 313–314).

Walk in the strait path. More Desert Imagery (2 Nephi 33:9)

Desert imagery is a vital and colorful facet of ancient Jewish writings, and related imagery is found throughout Nephi's accounts in the Book of Mormon. Hugh Nibley explains that in Western civilization, we consider the widest roads to be the most reliable and safe, whereas in the desert these roads are considered the most dangerous. Nephi's admonition to walk in the strait path and continue in it until the end of one's earthly life is strikingly similar to apocryphal excerpts. For example, in late Egyptian antiquity (1000 to 300 B.C.) it was popularly taught that a man should be righteous and always remain on the "right road." According to Nibley, this idea "had actually become a literary convention in Lehi's day; and in his culture, it is very closely connected with the Israelite use of it." The image of a "strait road" in the desert is but one instance of the desert imagery that appears abundantly in Nephi's writings. (See *Echoes,* 482–483).

> *10 And now, my beloved brethren, and also Jew, and all ye ends of the earth,* ***hearken unto these words and believe in Christ;*** *and if ye believe not in these words believe in Christ. And if ye shall believe in Christ ye will believe in these words, for they are the words of Christ, and he hath given them unto me; and they teach all men that they should do good.*

Hearken unto these words and believe in Christ

As we hearken to the Lord, we not only listen but act accordingly. Hearken means to listen *and* obey. The word hearken occurs hundreds of times in the scriptures. Many of those references refer to us and our willingness to listen to and obey the word of the Lord (see 1 Nephi 7:9). Do we hearken to the words of Christ (see D&C 84:43–46)? What do the words of Christ teach us (see 2 Nephi 32:3)?

Nephi reminds us that the words of Christ "teach all men that they should do good" (2 Nephi 33:10).

2 Nephi 33:11–15

11–15 Nephi ends his account with a prophecy that he will one day meet his readers before the judgment seat of God. He makes an impassioned plea that all who receive his words believe in them. To those of the house of Israel and mankind in general he says, "Farewell until that great day shall come" (verse 13), and to those who refuse to show respect for the word of God—whether from his own record (i.e., Nephi's), or from the record of the Jews (i.e., the Bible)—he says: "I bid you an everlasting farewell, for these words shall condemn you at the last day" (verse 14).

CONCLUDING THOUGHTS

There is power in the doctrine of Christ, because Christ is a Being of infinite power and majesty. His doctrine and His words can bring life eternal to those who chose to accept and follow His teachings. We come to know our Heavenly Father and our Savior through the word of God—whether we receive it in printed format, through the words of living prophets, or by personal revelation. Our hearts receive the word and our lives are changed. We truly cannot live without the spiritual nourishment that the word of God gives us. We should make goals and plans to feast upon the word every day of our lives and to follow the promptings of the Spirit in all we do.

THE BOOK OF
JACOB
THE BROTHER OF NEPHI

The words of his preaching unto his brethren. He confoundeth a man who seeketh to overthrow the doctrine of Christ. A few words concerning the history of the people of Nephi. [Note: This preamble was included in the original edition of the Book of Mormon published in 1830.]

BOOK OVERVIEW

Jacob is commissioned by the aging Nephi to keep the sacred records. Nephi passes away and Jacob assumes the spiritual mantle for guiding the people in righteousness. He condemns pride and immorality and enjoins the people to build upon the sure foundation of Christ and not look "beyond the mark" (Jacob 4:14). He presents and interprets the allegory of Zenos as a representation of the cultivation and gathering of the house of Israel and its interactions with the Gentiles in the latter days. He confounds the anti-Christ Sherem and restores peace to the land, urging the people to follow the words of Christ. Jacob turns the sacred records over to his son Enos.

CHAPTER 1

OVERVIEW

Jacob is commissioned by Nephi to keep the sacred records. He labors diligently to guide the people to believe in the Savior and to relinquish their prideful ways. Nephi passes away and is honored by the people. Having been consecrated by Nephi as priests and teachers, Jacob and Joseph strive with all their heart and soul to preach repentance and magnify their callings.

> *1 FOR behold, it came to pass that fifty and five years had passed away from the time that Lehi left Jerusalem; wherefore, Nephi gave me,* ***Jacob,*** *a commandment concerning the small plates, upon which these things are engraven.*

> *2 And he gave me,* ***Jacob,*** *a commandment* ***that I should write upon these plates a few of the things which I considered to be most precious;*** *that I should not touch, save it were lightly, concerning the history of this people which are called the people of Nephi.*

Jacob, Prophet of the Gathering

Jacob, soon to become the successor to Nephi as the leader of the people, is among the greatest of the doctrinal analysts and preachers in the Book of Mormon. Jacob is the consummate observer and articulator of the scattering and gathering the Lord's people. Having been born, like his younger brother Joseph, during Lehi's transit through the wilderness (see 1 Nephi 18:7), Jacob has no personal acquaintance with a life rooted in a permanent home, but instead is a wanderer and stranger. At the end of his days, Jacob takes a somewhat melancholy look back: "The time passed away with us, and also our lives passed away like as it were unto us a dream, we being a lonesome and a solemn people, wanderers, cast out from Jerusalem, born in tribulation, in a wilderness, and hated of our brethren, which caused wars and contentions; wherefore, we did mourn out our days" (Jacob 7:26).

Nevertheless, Jacob is able, through the strength of the Lord, to overcome the effects of the travail of the scattering and experience the joy of the gathering. Upon this solid gospel foundation, Jacob builds his life-long ministry. His father knew of his innate goodness: "And thou hast beheld in thy youth his [the Redeemer's] glory; wherefore, thou art blessed even as they unto whom he shall minister in the flesh; for the Spirit is the same, yesterday, today, and forever. And the way is prepared from the fall of man, and salvation is free" (2 Nephi 2:4). Even after the death of Lehi, when he follows Nephi and the other faithful descendants of Lehi away from the wicked sphere of Laman and Lemuel to start life anew, Jacob finds reason to rejoice: "And it came to pass that we lived after the manner of happiness" (2 Nephi 5:27). In his discourses and writings, Jacob eloquently relates mankind's journey from the foundation of time to the ultimate Judgment and bestowal of heavenly rewards.

EVIDENCE: That I should write upon these plates a few of the things which I considered to be most precious—Colophons (Similar examples in 1 Nephi 1:1–3; Jacob 7:27; Jarom 1:1–2; Omni 1:1, 3–4; Words of Mormon 1:9; Helaman 16:25)

As mentioned previously, major sections of the Book of Mormon are introduced and concluded with constructions known as "colophons," which inform the reader of the author and source of the material. In the words of Hugh Nibley, "This complacent advertising of one's own virtues, in particular one's reliability, is a correct and indeed a required fixture of any properly composed

Egyptian autobiography of Nephi's time." (See *Echoes,* 474; compare the information given earlier after 1 Nephi 1:3.)

*3 For he said that the **history of his people** should be engraven upon **his other plates,** and that I should preserve **these plates** and hand them down unto my seed, from generation to generation.*
*4 And if there were preaching which was sacred, or revelation which was great, or prophesying, that I should engraven the heads of them upon **these plates,** and touch upon them as much as it were possible, for Christ's sake, and for the sake of our people.*

HISTORY OF HIS PEOPLE; HIS OTHER PLATES; THESE PLATES

Jacob continues, after the pattern of Nephi, to record the actions and experiences of his people—both in the historical sense (large plates) as well as in the spiritual sense (small plates). Each of us likewise develops a history of his or her own life, including desires, plans, actions, challenges, and accomplishments. Each of us has eternal roles, Church callings, and personal responsibilities. In all things we are to progress and grow. We seek to improve and magnify our callings—this is our mission. We are responsible and accountable for our actions. Our actions are a result of our thoughts, which, when dwelt upon, become the desires that eventually result in action. Surely the scripture is true, "For as he thinketh in his heart, so is he . . ." (Proverbs 23:7). When we think in misguided patterns, we act with misguided deeds.

5 For because of faith and great anxiety, it truly had been made manifest unto us concerning our people, what things should happen unto them.
*6 And we also had **many revelations,** and the spirit of **much prophecy;** wherefore, we knew of Christ and his kingdom, which should come.*
*7 Wherefore **we labored diligently among our people,** that we might **persuade them** to come unto Christ, and partake of the goodness of God, that they might enter into his rest, lest by any means he should swear in his wrath they should not enter in, as in the **provocation** in the days of temptation while the children of Israel were in the wilderness.*
*8 Wherefore, we would to God that we could **persuade all men** not to rebel against God, to provoke him to anger, but that all men would believe in Christ, and view his death, and suffer his cross and bear the shame of the world; wherefore, I, Jacob, take it upon me to fulfil the commandment of my brother Nephi.*

Many revelations; much prophecy; we labored diligently among our people; persuade them; persuade all men

In just a few words, Jacob lays out the full agenda of his ministry: He knows the things of God by revelation; therefore, he labors to persuade his people to believe in Christ and come unto Him and partake of His goodness.

Provocation

The word "provocation" (verse 7) has reference to the mindset and behavior of the ancient Israelites following their liberation from Egyptian bondage. The Lord commanded that they should prepare themselves to meet Him, but they were fearful and demurred, preferring to stand behind Moses: "And all the people saw the thunderings, and the lightnings, and the noise of the trumpet, and the mountain smoking: and when the people saw it, they removed, and stood afar off. And they said unto Moses, Speak thou with us, and we will hear: but let not God speak with us, lest we die. And Moses said unto the people, Fear not: for God is come to prove you, and that his fear may be before your faces, that ye sin not. And the people stood afar off, and Moses drew near unto the thick darkness where God was" (Exodus 20:18–21). But the people would not fully turn to the Lord in righteousness, for their hearts were hardened. Therefore, His anger was provoked, and He withdrew the higher priesthood blessings from Israel and instituted a lesser program of rites and ceremonies to shape their devotion toward the Savior. Paul refers to this event in calling his associates to repentance: "Harden not your hearts, as in the provocation, in the day of temptation in the wilderness" (Hebrews 3:8; compare Hebrews 3:15; compare also Numbers 13:11; Psalm 95:8; Alma 12:36). Jacob, too, invokes the lessons of history in guiding his people to a better way of life in keeping with the principles of the gospel of Jesus Christ.

> *9 Now Nephi began to be old, and he saw that he must soon die; wherefore, he anointed a man to be a king and a ruler over his people now, according to the reigns of the kings.*
> *10 The people having loved Nephi exceedingly, he having been* ***a great protector*** *for them, having* ***wielded the sword of Laban in their defence,*** *and having* ***labored in all his days for their welfare—***
> *11 Wherefore, the people were desirous to* ***retain in remembrance his name.*** *And whoso should reign in his stead were called by the people, second Nephi, third Nephi, and so forth, according to the reigns of the kings; and thus they were called by the people, let them be of whatever name they would.*
> *12 And it came to pass that Nephi died.*

A great protector; wielded the sword of Laban in their defence; labored in all his days for their welfare; retain in remembrance his name

From Jacob's words, we gain a clear understanding of what draws individuals toward a leader and kindles the desire to honor the memory of that leader forever: *protection, defense, service*. If that leader, like Nephi, displays an enduring commitment toward the protection and defense of his associates and a life-long dedication of service on behalf of their welfare, then he becomes, as it were, unforgettable to them. We can liken our own situation to Nephi by strengthening our commitment of protection, defense, and service to our families and all others for whom we have responsibility.

13–17 Jacob organizes the various constituencies of people into two key designations—Nephites and Lamanites. He observes with sadness that the Nephites under Nephi's successor on the throne begin to grow more wicked and prideful. By virtue of his office, he calls them to repentance.

> *18 For I, Jacob, and my brother Joseph had been consecrated* ***priests and teachers*** *of this people, by the hand of Nephi.*
> *19 And we did* ***magnify*** *our office unto the Lord, taking upon us the responsibility, answering the sins of the people upon our own heads if we did not teach them the word of God with all diligence; wherefore, by laboring with our might their blood might not come upon our garments; otherwise their blood would come upon our garments, and we would not be found spotless at the last day.*

Priests and teachers; magnify

Great blessings flow when we receive our callings with gratitude and accept the responsibility to perform to our utmost ability—with faithful accountability and steadfastness of purpose—while we are on the errand of the Lord.

Both Jacob and Joseph are consecrated by Nephi to be priests and teachers of the people. Upon the passing of Nephi (see Jacob 1:12), Jacob succeeds his older brother, a giant of spirituality, and assumes the prophetic guidance of the people. His words at this point provide a lesson in how to receive a calling from the Lord in humility and all diligence. It is this context that allows us to learn the true definition of "magnifying a calling" with accountability and devotion (see verse 19).

Jacob is responsible and accountable for his stewardship. He will take the sins of the people upon his own head if he fails to teach them the word of God with all diligence. Therefore, he magnifies his calling. We, too, are responsible and accountable to the Lord to perform our duties with love and devotion. How we magnify our callings affects the lives of those around us. Let us resolve to make a list of priorities of things we are responsible and accountable for and then ensure that we do these things with all faith, diligence, and patience. President Gordon B. Hinckley gives us further insight into this responsibility:

Pres. Hinkley on magnifying our callings.

> To every officer, to every teacher in this Church who acts in a priesthood office, there comes the sacred responsibility of magnifying that priesthood calling. Each of us is responsible for the welfare and the growth and development of others. We do not live only unto ourselves. If we are to magnify our callings, we cannot live only unto ourselves. As we serve with diligence, as we teach with faith and testimony, as we lift and strengthen and build convictions of righteousness in those whose lives we touch, we magnify our priesthood. To live only unto ourselves, on the other hand, to serve grudgingly, to give less than our best effort to our duty, diminishes our priesthood just as looking through the wrong lenses of binoculars reduces the image and makes more distant the object. . . .
>
> We magnify our priesthood and enlarge our calling when we serve with diligence and enthusiasm in those responsibilities to which we are called by proper authority. I emphasize the words, "diligence and enthusiasm." This work has not reached its present stature through indifference on the part of those who have labored in its behalf. The Lord needs men, both young and old, who will carry the banners of His kingdom with positive strength and determined purpose. . . .
>
> We magnify our calling, we enlarge the potential of our priesthood when we reach out to those in distress and give strength to those who falter. ("Magnify Your Calling," *Ensign,* May 1989, 47–49)

An Illustration of How Wilford Woodruff Magnified His Calling

> I was still holding the office of a Teacher, and knowing for myself that the fulness of the gospel of Christ, which God had revealed to Joseph Smith, was true, I had a great desire to preach it to the inhabitants of the earth, but as a Teacher I had no authority to preach the gospel to the world. I went into the forest near Lyman Wight's [in Daviess County, Missouri . . .] one Sunday morning, aside

from the abodes of men, and made my desire known unto the Lord. I prayed that the Lord would open my way and give me the privilege of preaching the gospel. I did not make my request expecting any honor from man, for I knew that the preaching of the gospel was attended with hard labor and persecution. While I was praying, the Spirit of the Lord rested upon me, and testified to me that my prayer was heard, and that my request would be granted. I arose to my feet and walked some three hundred yards into a broad road, rejoicing. As I came into the road I saw Judge Elias Higbee standing before me. As I walked up to him he said, "Wilford, the Lord has revealed to me that it is your duty to go into the vineyard of the Lord and preach the gospel." I told him if that was the will of the Lord I was ready to go. I did not tell him that I had been praying for that privilege. I had been boarding at Lyman Wight's with Judge Higbee for months, and it was the first time he had ever named such a thing to me. (B. H. Roberts, *New Witnesses for God* [Salt Lake City: The Deseret News, 1951], 238–39)

CHAPTER 2

OVERVIEW

Jacob condemns pride and immorality. Charity and chastity should be the governing principles in life. God delights in the chastity of women.

1–4 Jacob speaks to the people in the temple following the death of Nephi and shares with them his anguish over their lapse into the ways of wickedness.

5 But behold, hearken ye unto me, and know that by the help of the all-powerful Creator of heaven and earth I can tell you concerning your ***thoughts,*** *how that ye are beginning to labor in sin, which sin appeareth very abominable unto me, yea, and abominable unto God.*
6 Yea, it grieveth my soul and causeth me to shrink with shame before the presence of my Maker, that I must testify unto you concerning the ***wickedness of your hearts.***

THOUGHTS; WICKEDNESS OF YOUR HEARTS

By the power of discernment, Jacob perceives the hidden agenda of his people as they begin to slide into sin. Our thoughts and feelings are the gateway to our actions. Great blessings attend pure devotion to the Lord; great sorrow stems from pride, greed, and unrighteousness. The gift of discernment is often reflected in the events of the Book of Mormon. Amulek perceives the thoughts of his detractors (see Alma 10:17). Alma reads the thoughts of Zeezrom (see Alma 12:7). Ammon is able to discern the thoughts of King Lamoni (see Alma 18:18). The Lord reads the thoughts of the three disciples (see 3 Nephi 28:6). The gift of discernment enables leaders to detect inward patterns of thinking and thus be of service to others in guiding them onto the pathway of righteousness.

7–10 Jacob is grieved that he has to speak boldly of dark and unpleasant things before an audience that includes women and children who have come to hear instead "the pleasing word of God" (verses 8, 9). But he is constrained by God to speak candidly.

> *11 Wherefore, I must tell you the truth according to the* ***plainness of the word of God.*** *For behold, as I inquired of the Lord, thus came the word unto me, saying: Jacob, get thou up into the temple on the morrow, and* ***declare the word which I shall give thee*** *unto this people.*

PLAINNESS OF THE WORD OF GOD; DECLARE THE WORD WHICH I SHALL GIVE THEE

Having assumed the role of spiritual leader of the people and curator of the sacred records following the ministry of Nephi, Jacob is mindful of the responsibility to cultivate and foster among the people an uncompromisingly obedient walk in life. Some fifty-five years have passed since Lehi and his family have left Jerusalem (see Jacob 1:1), and the little colony in the New World is now beginning to grow larger and more susceptible to the creeping malignancies of pride, materialism, and immorality. Blessed with the spirit of prophecy and revelation, Jacob perceives with utter clarity what lies ahead for his people, based on the consequences of their choices in life: "For because of faith and great anxiety, it truly had been made manifest unto us concerning our people, what things should happen unto them" (Jacob 1:5). He fears that the great "provocation" (Jacob 1:7) committed by the Israelites at the time of Moses and the giving of the Ten Commandments is about to be replayed in his day, and thus he prays unto the Lord for guidance and is commanded to assemble the people at the temple and call them to repentance (see Jacob 2:11). This he does with unfiltered frankness, exposing the sins of pride and immorality that are threatening to tear families apart and, as he later observes, causing the "fair daughters of this people" (Jacob 2:32) to cry unto the Lord in anguish. Jacob's sermon on overcoming wickedness is one of the masterpieces of the scriptures.

12–15 Jacob candidly exposes the pride and worldliness of the people.

> *16 O that he would rid you from this iniquity and abomination. And, O that ye would listen unto the word of his commands, and* ***let not this pride of your hearts destroy your souls!***

Let not this pride of your hearts destroy your souls!

Pride is a dominant theme of the Book of Mormon. It is a central issue in the warnings of the Lord to the people of the latter days: "And if ye seek the riches which it is the will of the Father to give unto you, ye shall be the richest of all people, for ye shall have the riches of eternity; and it must needs be that the riches of the earth are mine to give; but beware of pride, lest ye become as the Nephites of old" (D&C 38:39). Elder Dallin H. Oaks speaks about the danger of the pride of comparison:

> When the Lord showed him the thoughts of the people, the prophet Jacob told them that he "must testify unto [them] concerning the wickedness of [their] hearts" (Jacob 2:6). After reminding them how they had been blessed to obtain riches, Jacob condemned the effect of their riches on their thoughts and their behavior:
>
> "And because some of you have obtained more abundantly than that of your brethren ye are lifted up in the pride of your hearts, and wear stiff necks and high heads because of the costliness of your apparel, and persecute your brethren because ye suppose that ye are better than they" (Jacob 2:13).
>
> In this passage Jacob defined the elements of the pride of comparison: (1) a person obtains something more abundantly than others; (2) he is lifted up in pride because of this possession; and (3) he persecutes others because he supposes he is better than they. Jacob underlined the seriousness of this kind of pride when he pleaded, "Let not this pride of your hearts destroy your souls!" (Jacob 2:16).
>
> In the Book of Mormon accounts, the pride of comparison resulted most frequently from the acquisition and use of riches, such as by wearing fine

apparel. Thus, Alma the Younger gave this description of the Nephites in the land of Zarahemla, who "began to wax proud" because of their possessions, including their flocks, their gold, and their fine apparel: "The people of the church began to be lifted up in the pride of their eyes, and to set their hearts upon riches and upon the vain things of the world, that they began to be scornful, one toward another" (Alma 4:8). (*Pure in Heart* [Salt Lake City: Bookcraft, 1988], 97)

Pride, the universal sin, is at the crux of almost every other sin. Pride is expressed in arrogance, haughtiness, self-love, vanity, and egotism. Because pride involves man setting his will against God's, it creates enmity between God and man. The sin of pride is directly opposed to the Christlike quality of humility. President Ezra Taft Benson pointed out where pride carries us afoul at the crossroads of life: "Pride is characterized by 'What do I want out of life?' rather than by 'What would God have me do with my life?' It is self-will as opposed to God's will. It is the fear of man over the fear of God" ("Cleansing the Inner Vessel," *Ensign,* May 1986, 6–7). In the Book of Mormon, pride is the downfall of the Jaredite and Nephite peoples, and pride can be our downfall as well if we are not careful. Prideful thoughts are so powerful that they can lead to sinful thoughts and behavior, such as selfishness, greed, lust, jealousy, power-seeking, envy, and a whole host of related sins. This is why the Lord continually counsels us against pride (see Proverbs 16:18; James 4:6; Alma 1:32; Moroni 8:27; D&C 23:1). Pride can destroy our very souls.

17 Think of your brethren like unto yourselves, and be familiar with all and free with your substance, that they may be rich like unto you.
18 But before ye seek for riches, ***seek ye for the kingdom of God.***
19 And after ye have obtained a hope in Christ ***ye shall obtain riches, if ye seek them;*** *and ye will seek them* ***for the intent to do good****—to clothe the naked, and to feed the hungry, and to liberate the captive, and administer relief to the sick and the afflicted.*

Seek ye for the kingdom of God; ye shall obtain riches, if ye seek them for the intent to do good

Jacob does not condemn wealth, per se, but only greed and selfishness. Wealth can be a blessed opportunity for exhibiting charity toward those with less substance. The wealthy who withhold their gifts from the poor will suffer remorse, as latter-day scriptures confirm: "Wo unto you rich men, that will not give your substance to the poor, for your riches will canker your souls; and this shall be your lamentation in the day of visitation, and of judgment, and of indignation: The harvest is past, the summer is ended, and my soul is not saved!" (D&C 56:16). At the same time, the poor who likewise suffer a deficiency of spiritual contrition will also pay a price: "Wo unto you poor men, whose hearts are not broken, whose spirits are not contrite, and whose bellies are not satisfied, and whose hands are not stayed from laying hold upon other men's goods, whose eyes are full of greediness, and who will not labor with your own hands!" (D&C 56:17). The abundance of the earth is reserved for those with the right quality of heart: "But blessed are the poor who are pure in heart, whose hearts are broken, and whose spirits are contrite, for they shall see the kingdom of God coming in power and great glory unto their deliverance; for the fatness of the earth shall be theirs" (D&C 56:18). The governing question of conscience in such matters is this: What is the actual quality of our hearts?

20–26 Jacob turns from the subject of pride to an urgent call to cease from the "grosser crimes" (verse 23) of immorality.

> *27 Wherefore, my brethren, hear me, and hearken to the word of the Lord: For there shall not any man among you have save it be* ***one wife;*** *and concubines he shall have none;*
> *28 For I, the Lord God, delight in the* ***chastity of women.*** *And whoredoms are an abomination before me; thus saith the Lord of Hosts.*
> *29 Wherefore, this people shall keep my commandments, saith the Lord of Hosts, or cursed be the land for their sakes.*
> *30 For if I will, saith the Lord of Hosts,* ***raise up seed unto me,*** *I will command my people; otherwise they shall hearken unto these things.*
> *31 For behold, I, the Lord, have seen the sorrow, and heard the* ***mourning of the daughters*** *of my people in the land of Jerusalem, yea, and in all the lands of my people, because of the wickedness and abominations of their husbands.*
> *32 And I will not suffer, saith the Lord of Hosts, that the* ***cries of the fair daughters*** *of this people, which I have led out of the land of Jerusalem, shall come up unto me against the men of my people, saith the Lord of Hosts.*

ONE WIFE; CHASTITY OF WOMEN; RAISE UP SEED UNTO ME; MOURNING OF THE DAUGHTERS; CRIES OF THE FAIR DAUGHTERS

Jacob implores his fellow colleagues to purge their lives of all immorality and to protect and foster the happiness of their chaste women. Plural marriage is not sanctioned; such a practice can only come at the command of God if He chooses to "raise up seed" unto Himself (verse 30). The concubines and whoredoms of the ancient world, specifically the acts of David and Solomon in this regard, are an abomination in the sight of the Lord.

33–34 Jacob accentuates the pain and anguish suffered by the tender daughters of the people because of the cruelty and thoughtless immorality of men.

> *35 Behold, ye have done greater iniquities than the Lamanites, our brethren. Ye have* ***broken the hearts*** *of your tender wives, and* ***lost the confidence of your children,*** *because of your bad examples before them; and the* ***sobbings of their hearts ascend up to God*** *against you. And because of the strictness of the word of God, which cometh down against you, many hearts died, pierced with deep wounds.*

BROKEN THE HEARTS; LOST THE CONFIDENCE OF YOUR CHILDREN; SOBBINGS OF THEIR HEARTS ASCEND UP TO GOD

Jacob appeals to the perpetrators of immorality, pleading on behalf of the women who are made to suffer needlessly through unchaste deeds. Immorality exacts an immeasurable toll from its innocent victims—typically women.

Example is the great teacher. We have all learned from good and bad examples. We all serve as leaders and examples to someone in some capacity. Our example becomes the ever-present teacher every moment of every day. What is our example teaching those around us?

CHAPTER 3

OVERVIEW

Jacob continues his discourse to the people assembled at the temple. The pure in heart who receive the pleasing word of God will enjoy His love forever. The Lamanites are more righteous than the Nephites, for they remember to keep the moral law within their families. Jacob warns his listeners to repent lest they lose the land of their inheritance.

1 BUT behold, I, Jacob, would speak unto you that are ***pure in heart. Look unto God with firmness of mind,*** *and pray unto him with exceeding faith, and he will console you in your afflictions, and he will plead your cause, and send down justice upon those who seek your destruction.*
2 O all ye that are ***pure in heart,*** *lift up your heads and receive the pleasing word of God, and feast upon his love; for ye may, if your minds are firm, forever.*

Look unto God with firmness of mind

Having warned the people boldly concerning the insidious effects of their emerging pride and immorality, Jacob now brings forward the glorious case for embracing with full devotion the Lord's plan of salvation, with all of its attendant blessings of hope and joy. Thus he labors diligently to record on his plates the Lord's antidote to the darkness of sin, i.e., to accept the word of prophecy and revelation that we might know of Christ and His atoning sacrifice and align ourselves with the principles of happiness and redemption.

Pure in heart

Jacob extols the pure in heart (in general referring to the chaste and fair women and innocent children in his audience—see Jacob 2:10) and promises them grand blessings from the Lord. If they will receive His "pleasing" word, they may feast upon His love forever. The expression "pure in heart" is used frequently in the scriptures. In the Sermon on the Mount, the Savior says, "Blessed are the pure in heart: for they shall see God" (Matthew 5:8; compare the similar statement in 3 Nephi 12:8). In addition, the "pure in heart" are promised deliverance and abundant blessings at the Second Coming (D&C 56:18), the privilege of seeing God in His holy temple (see D&C 97:15–16), the blessings of returning to their inheritance with joy as part of the latter-day gathering (see D&C 101:17–18), counsel and authority at the hands of the Prophet Joseph Smith (see D&C 122:1–2), the bestowal of saving and exalting truths of the gospel (see D&C 123:11–12), and the opportunity to be part of Zion, "for this is Zion—THE PURE IN HEART" (D&C 97:21).

The Lord has promised those that are pure in heart that they shall see God (see 3 Nephi 12:8). The purpose of our lives is to become worthy to return to the presence of our Heavenly Father. This is His work and glory. He seeks for us to love Him with all our hearts (see Mark 12:30). Are we pure in heart?

3 But, wo, wo, unto you that are ***not pure in heart,*** *that are filthy this day before God; for except ye repent the land is cursed for your sakes; and the Lamanites, which*

> *are not filthy like unto you, nevertheless they are cursed with a sore cursing, shall scourge you even unto destruction.*
> *4 And the time speedily cometh, that except ye repent they shall possess* ***the land of your inheritance,*** *and the Lord God will lead away the righteous out from among you.*

NOT PURE IN HEART; THE LAND OF YOUR INHERITANCE

The consequence of being found "not pure in heart" is daunting—to have the land cursed and to be the target of Lamanite scourges that may result in the loss of the land of inheritance. This latter aspect of the covenant with God is emphasized in modern revelation, where it is made clear that the "pure in heart" will assuredly receive their inheritance in Zion:

> Therefore, let your hearts be comforted concerning Zion; for all flesh is in mine hands; be still and know that I am God.
>
> Zion shall not be moved out of her place, notwithstanding her children are scattered.
>
> They that remain, and are pure in heart, shall return, and come to their inheritances, they and their children, with songs of everlasting joy, to build up the waste places of Zion—(D&C 101:16–18).

EVIDENCE: LAND OF INHERITANCE (1 Nephi 2:4; Jacob 3:4; Alma 22:28; 54:12–13; Ether 7:16; Mormon 2:27–28; 3:17)

According to scholar Eduard Meyer, Israel's power and authority referred back to the first allotments of land made by the leaders when they settled in their land of promise. Only one who possessed "the land of his inheritance" could be a part of the aristocracy. This tradition is apparent in the Book of Mormon, where we learn that when Lehi leaves the land of Jerusalem, he is leaving "the land of his inheritance." Furthermore, when a group of people in the Book of Mormon moves to a different geographical location, the first land they obtain is always referred to as "the land of their inheritance" or "the land of their first inheritance." The ancient idea of a permanent inheritance of land was largely unknown until modern times, and Joseph Smith certainly would not have been familiar it. (See *Echoes* 466–467).

5–6 Jacob reminds his Nephite listeners that the Lamanites are more righteous than they are, for they remember and abide by the moral code and therefore will merit the mercy of God and become one day "a blessed people" (verse 6).

7 Behold, their husbands ***love*** *their wives, and their wives* ***love*** *their husbands; and their husbands and their wives* ***love*** *their children; and their unbelief and their hatred toward you is because of the* ***iniquity of their fathers;*** *wherefore, how much better are you than they, in the sight of your great Creator?*

Love; iniquity of their fathers

The Lamanites cultivate love in their families. They are burdened with unbelief and hatred toward the Nephites primarily because of the traditions of their Lamanite fathers.

Nothing is needed more than to give and receive love—the ultimate concern that brings about righteous service. Everything our Heavenly Father and our Savior do is motivated by love (see John 3:16; 2 Nephi 26:24). If we are selfless and think of our companions and families first, we will be happy. There is no worse feeling than that of being unloved. It is important to express love in word and deed. We must strive to have love, and expressions of love must become the watchwords of our homes. Is love nurtured in our marriages and families?

8–12 Jacob admonishes his brethren to cease reviling against the Lamanites and instead look to their own weaknesses and root out the immorality in their own lives for the sake of their grieving children: "Remember that ye may, because of your filthiness, bring your children unto destruction, and their sins be heaped upon your heads at the last day" (verse 10; compare Jacob 1:19; Mosiah 21:30; D&C 68:25–28). President David O. McKay reminds us that this counsel has relevance to modern moral laxity: "Infidelity and sexual immorality are two principal evils that threaten to weaken and to wreck present-day civilization. Unfortunately, the trends of modern life are tending to disintegrate the very foundation of the Christian home. Sexual laxity among young people, birth control, and intemperance are its insidious and vicious enemies. When family life disintegrates, the foundation and bulwark of human society is undermined" (CR, October 1947, 119; *Gospel Ideals: Selections from the Discourses of David O. McKay* [Salt Lake City: Improvement Era, 1953], 487)

If Only I Had Known

This story, as told by my friend Jaynann Payne to a BYU assembly, portrays the sorrow of sexual transgression:

> We will never forget that sweet young girl of sixteen who came to live with us one summer for the remaining months of her unwed pregnancy. My husband is an

> attorney and was handling the adoption of her baby. She hadn't wanted to marry the boy who was the father of her unborn child. She had been beguiled and had partaken of the bitter fruit.
>
> In September she gave birth to a beautiful little boy, and the day she was to leave the hospital, Dean and I had to go to Salt Lake City. We stopped at the hospital long enough to meet the couple who were adopting the baby. Under hospital rules, this young mother, sixteen years old, had to take her beautiful nine-pound boy from the arms of the nurse and hand him over to my husband, who then stepped outside the room and gave the baby to the adopting parents. It tore me apart to watch her and to see that young couple leave with her baby.
>
> She said to me, "Sister Payne, he lied to me when he said nobody would get hurt, and that because we loved each other, anything we did was all right. He didn't really love me. That is why I didn't marry him, because he wasn't worthy to be the father of my little boy. It's all a great big lie, and I don't want to live a lie!
>
> "Oh, if only I had known five minutes before I was immoral how I would feel five minutes after I gave my baby away!"
>
> For this girl not to have thought ahead about the consequences of her actions and not to have realized that lust is the mere image of love is indeed heart-breaking. It is so important to keep in tune, keep in touch, to receive the Spirit each and every day. We never know what is going to happen; and if we make the commitment in our private rooms, by the side of our beds, to our Father in heaven, of what we want to be in life—what we will do and what we won't do-and then ask for his help in keeping our commitments, he will help us in public and private. (Jaynann Payne, *BYU Speeches,* 10 February 1970.) (Ed J. Pinegar)

Great story on the evils of Immorality

13–14 Not even a hundredth part of the history of the people, "which now began to be numerous" (verse 13), can be written on the plates.

CHAPTER 4

OVERVIEW

Jacob rejoices that his words will be preserved as a blessing unto his posterity. All the holy prophets have spoken of the Savior and His atoning mission. By searching their words we gain a hope for the future and our faith becomes unshakable. The Lord will strengthen us beyond our weaknesses through His grace. We are to seek the counsel of the Lord and be reconciled to Him through the Atonement. We are to build upon the sure foundation of Christ and not "look beyond the mark."

1–2 Jacob confirms that only a small part of his discourses can be preserved because of the difficulty of engraving the words on the plates. At least this form of archiving will be permanent, whereas other forms will perish and be lost.

> *3 Now in this thing we do* ***rejoice;*** *and we labor diligently to engraven these words upon plates, hoping that our beloved brethren and our children will receive them with* ***thankful hearts,*** *and look upon them that they may* ***learn with joy*** *and not with sorrow, neither with contempt, concerning their first parents.*
>
> *4 For, for this intent have we written these things, that they may know that* ***we knew of Christ,*** *and we had a hope of his glory many hundred years before his coming; and not only we ourselves had a hope of his glory, but also* ***all the holy prophets*** *which were before us.*

Rejoice; thankful hearts; learn with joy; we knew of Christ; all the holy prophets

Jacob expresses the central force behind his motivation—the hope that his readers will receive the message of the gospel with thanksgiving and rejoice over the knowledge that their progenitors and all previous prophets knew about the coming mission of Jesus Christ and believed in Him. The question of conscience for us today is this: Do we receive the Book of Mormon with thankful hearts and rejoice in the universal knowledge concerning the Savior and His atoning sacrifice on our behalf?

EVIDENCE: Plates vs. Parchment (1 Nephi 1:2; Jacob 4:1–3; Mormon 1:4; Mormon 9:32–33)

In his 1825 work titled *View of the Hebrews,* Ethan Smith wrote that Americans Indians did not have books and letters. Furthermore, Reverend Solomon Spaulding, whose novel *Manuscript Story* paralleled the recently published Book of Mormon, declared that an ancient American manuscript would be written in an elegant hand—with Roman letters and Latin language—on rolls of parchment. Joseph Smith's claim that the Book of Mormon was engraved on metal plates in reformed Egyptian was a direct contradiction to these ideas. If Joseph had created the Book of Mormon narrative from his own knowledge, he surely would have conformed to the opinions of the religious scholars of his day. (See *Echoes,* 317–318).

> *5 Behold, they believed in Christ and worshiped the Father in his name, and also we worship the Father in his name. And for this intent* ***we keep the law of Moses,*** *it pointing our souls to him; and for this cause* ***it is sanctified unto us for righteousness,*** *even as it was accounted unto Abraham in the wilderness to be obedient unto the commands of God in offering up his son Isaac, which is a similitude of God and his Only Begotten Son.*
>
> *6 Wherefore,* ***we search the prophets,*** *and we have many revelations and the spirit of prophecy; and having all these witnesses* ***we obtain a hope,*** *and* ***our faith becometh unshaken,*** *insomuch that we truly can command in the name of Jesus and the very trees obey us, or the mountains, or the waves of the sea.*

We keep the law of Moses; it is sanctified unto us for righteousness; we search the prophets; we obtain a hope; our faith becometh unshaken

Jacob, with his characteristic economy of words, expresses in just a few lines the righteous lifestyle that he and his associates are leading and commends to others of their contemporaries that they should live the law of Moses for the right reason, i.e., because it points their souls to Christ. Moreover, all should search the prophets and receive ongoing revelation willingly, thereby being strengthened in their hope and faith and thus enabled to act with power in the name of Jesus.

> *7 Nevertheless, the Lord God showeth us* ***our weakness*** *that we may know that it is by his* ***grace,*** *and his great* ***condescensions*** *unto the children of men, that we have power to do these things.*

Our weakness; grace

Jacob was doubtless familiar with the great lesson taught by Nephi on this subject:

- "Nevertheless, I do not write anything upon plates save it be that I think it be sacred. And now, if I do err, even did they err of old; not that I would excuse myself because of other men, but because of the weakness which is in me, according to the flesh, I would excuse myself" (1 Nephi 19:6).

- "And I know that the Lord God will consecrate my prayers for the gain of my people. And the words which I have written in weakness will be made strong unto them; for it persuadeth them to do good; it maketh known unto them of their fathers; and it speaketh of Jesus, and persuadeth them to believe in him, and to endure to the end, which is life eternal" (2 Nephi 33:4).

The principle of weak things becoming strong through the blessings and grace of the Lord is a pervasive theme in the Book of Mormon and other holy scriptures. The Lord comforts Moroni in regard to his perceived weakness in translating the writings of Ether: "And if men come unto me I will show unto them their weakness. I give unto men weakness that they may be humble; and my grace is sufficient for all men that humble themselves before me; for if they humble themselves before me, and have faith in me, then will I make weak things become strong unto them" (Ether 12:27). See similar references in modern-day revelation (D&C 1:24; 35:17; 38:14; 62:1; 135:5; JS—H 1:28–29).

If we feel inadequate in our roles and callings, if we feel weak in relation to the duties and obligations placed upon us, if we feel humble and dependent upon our God for strength and vitality—then it is well, for the Lord will make up the difference through His benevolence and grace, and we will come off the victor in contributing in full measure to the welfare and prosperity of Zion. As Nephi stated: "For we labor diligently to write, to persuade our children, and also our brethren, to believe in Christ, and to be reconciled to God; for we know that it is by grace that we are saved, after all we can do" (2 Nephi 25:23).

Condescensions

Jacob is likewise aware of what Nephi had learned about the condescension of the Lord when he received his great vision concerning the dealings of God with mankind (see 1 Nephi 11:16, 26). Nephi later declared: "then, if I have seen so great things, if the Lord in his condescension unto the children of men hath visited men in so much mercy, why should my heart weep and my soul linger in the valley of sorrow, and my flesh waste away, and my strength slacken, because of mine afflictions?" (2 Nephi 4:26). Through the condescension of the Lord we can be lifted up to achieve the divine potential within us.

> *8 Behold, great and **marvelous are the works of the Lord.** How unsearchable are the depths of the mysteries of him; and it is impossible that man should find out all his ways. And no man knoweth of his ways save it be revealed unto him; wherefore, brethren, **despise not the revelations** of God.*

9 For behold, by the power of his word man came upon the face of the earth, which earth was created by the power of his word. Wherefore, if God being able to speak and the world was, and to speak and man was created, O then, why not able to command the earth, or the workmanship of his hands upon the face of it, according to his will and pleasure?
10 Wherefore, brethren, ***seek not to counsel the Lord, but to take counsel from his hand.*** *For behold, ye yourselves know that he counseleth in wisdom, and in justice, and in great mercy, over all his works.*
11 Wherefore, beloved brethren, ***be reconciled unto him through the atonement of Christ,*** *his Only Begotten Son, and ye may obtain a resurrection, according to the power of the resurrection which is in Christ, and be presented as the first-fruits of Christ unto God, having faith, and obtained a good hope of glory in him before he manifesteth himself in the flesh.*

Marvelous Are the Works of the Lord; Despise Not the Revelations; Seek Not to Counsel the Lord, but to Take Counsel from His Hand; Be Reconciled unto Him through the Atonement of Christ

These poetic words of Jacob resonate within the soul of the earnest seeker of truth. Just as Jacob engraves these words on the plates of gold, we, too, can engrave them in our hearts. As we search the scriptures and the words of the living prophets, we receive inspiration and revelation through which we obtain hope. Our faith becomes firm in that we can do many things in our weakness through the grace of God—and all His works are done through faith by the power of His word (see also Mormon 9:17; Moses 1:32).

Be Reconciled unto Him through the Atonement of Christ

We become reconciled to God through the Atonement of the Savior, who mediates, intercedes, and reunites. Through His redeeming love and grace we receive the free gift of the resurrection and the hope of immortality and eternal life "after all we can do" (2 Nephi 25:23). Let us never forget our debt to our Savior, recognizing our plight without the Atonement. To remember Him always instills within us a sense of enduring gratitude. We are inspired to change ourselves for the better and seek to become like Christ.

What Is the Will of the Lord in Our Lives?

Jacob preached the word and recorded the word according to the will of God. The Prophet Joseph Smith did the same, as the following account confirms:

> The word is the gospel of Jesus Christ. To preach the word is to bear testimony of Christ, of his atoning sacrifice and all that flows therefrom. It is, therefore, to teach the gospel by the power of the Holy Ghost, testifying of the Father and the Son, of Joseph Smith and the Restoration, of the Book of Mormon and the revelations that have come in this dispensation, and of the apostolic and prophetic ministry of those ordained in this day. To preach the word is to bear testimony that The Church of Jesus Christ of Latter-day Saints is the kingdom of God on earth and that it holds the keys, ordinances, powers, and truths of salvation.
>
> One of the great evidences that people have the spirit of the gospel is that they desire to share with others what they have. Father Smith, even before the Lord began to give revelations commanding men to share the gospel, felt the spirit of what was to come and desired to share what he knew with others. The Prophet Joseph Smith, of course, was the first missionary in this dispensation. The moment he returned from the grove and told his mother (or was it his parents?) that he had learned for himself "that Presbyterianism is not true"—and presumably he would soon relate to her and other family members the experience of his vision—at that moment he was involved in missionary service, first to his family and then to others. Father and Mother Smith were but a step behind him, and our records show that they were soon out speaking of their son's experiences to their neighbors. This was the pattern that characterized their entire lives: the Prophet Joseph called the cadence, and his humble parents nobly marched the distance. (Mark L. McConkie, *The Father of the Prophet: Stories and Insights from the Life of Joseph Smith Sr.* [Salt Lake City: Bookcraft, 1993], 108)

Each of us should testify of Christ and His atoning sacrifice in all that we do. Our lives should reflect our willingness to take counsel from the Lord. What is the will of the Lord in our lives? We can search our patriarchal blessing and seek to fulfill it. We can search the scriptures and apply them to our lives. We should always remember the counsel: "Wherefore, seek not the things of this world but seek ye first to build up the kingdom of God, and to establish his righteousness, and all these things shall be added unto you" (JST Matthew 6:38). (Ed J. Pinegar)

12 And now, beloved, marvel not that I tell you these things; for why not speak of the atonement of Christ, and attain to a perfect knowledge of him, as to attain to the knowledge of a resurrection and the world to come?
13 Behold, my brethren, he that prophesieth, let him prophesy to the understanding of men; for the Spirit speaketh the truth and lieth not. Wherefore, it speaketh of ***things as they really are, and of things as they really will be;*** *wherefore, these things are* ***manifested unto us plainly,*** *for the salvation of our souls. But behold, we are not witnesses alone in these things; for God also spake them unto prophets of old.*
14 But behold, the Jews were a stiffnecked people; and they despised the words of plainness, and killed the prophets, and sought for things that they could not understand. Wherefore, because of their blindness, which blindness came by ***looking beyond the mark,*** *they must needs fall; for God hath taken away his plainness from them, and delivered unto them many things which they cannot understand, because they desired it. And because they desired it God hath done it, that they may stumble.*

Things as they really are, and of things as they really will be; manifested unto us plainly; looking beyond the mark

The Lord speaks plainly. The gospel is elegant in its simplicity and easy for the humble and contrite to understand: "And truth is knowledge of things as they are, and as they were, and as they are to come" (D&C 93:24). But men have a way of imposing a laminate upon the gospel truth to make it more sophisticated and complex, and to make themselves the intended interpreters upon whom others must depend for the key to the mysteries. This is an act of pride that is described by Jacob as "looking beyond the mark." What does this image call to mind? Consider the following:

EVIDENCE: Looking Beyond the Mark (Jacob 4:14)

A unique expression in the Book of Mormon is "looking beyond the mark," i.e., the boundary set between good judgment and mere tradition, the frontier separating practice that depends on the promptings of the Spirit and practice devised of men. If one looks beyond this mark, then he or she ventures into unknown and dangerous territory. The ecclesiastical leaders in Judah to whom Jacob refers preferred complexity and superficial patterning over essence and purity of content. Thus they overlooked the vital truths concerning the Atonement of the Messiah. Hugh Nibley states that in the Zadokite Fragment of the Dead Sea Scrolls, "the false teachers of the Jews are charged with having 'removed the mark which the forefathers had set up in their inheritance,'

"looking beyond the mark"

and there is a solemn warning to 'all those of the members of the covenant who have broken out of the boundary of the Law,' or stepped beyond the designated mark." Nibley says that the early Christian gospel declared that Israel erred in looking "for that which is beyond the mark." (See *Echoes,* 477).

15 And now I, Jacob, am led on by the Spirit unto prophesying; for I perceive by the
workings of the Spirit which is in me, that by the stumbling of the Jews they will reject
the stone** upon which they might build and have **safe foundation.
*16 But behold, according to the scriptures, this **stone** shall become the great, and **the***
***last, and the only sure foundation,** upon which the Jews can build.*
*17 And now, my beloved, how is it possible that these, after having rejected **the sure***
foundation,** can ever build upon it, that it may become **the head of their corner?
18 Behold, my beloved brethren, I will unfold this mystery unto you; if I do not, by
any means, get shaken from my firmness in the Spirit, and stumble because of my over
anxiety for you.

The Stone; Safe Foundation; The Last, and the Only Sure Foundation; The Sure Foundation; The Head of Their Corner

Jacob uses a metaphor for Christ that is found throughout the scriptures. The Psalmist prophetically declared, "The stone which the builders refused is become the head stone of the corner" (Psalms 118:22). During His mortal ministry, Jesus called attention to this same theme: "Jesus saith unto them, Did ye never read in the scriptures, The stone which the builders rejected, the same is become the head of the corner: this is the Lord's doing, and it is marvellous in our eyes?" (Matthew 21:42; compare Luke 20:17). Peter announced: "This is the stone which was set at nought of you builders, which is become the head of the corner. Neither is there salvation in any other: for there is none other name under heaven given among men, whereby we must be saved" (Acts 4:11–12; compare 1 Peter 2:6–7). Paul declared: "And are built upon the foundation of the apostles and prophets, Jesus Christ himself being the chief corner stone" (Ephesians 2:20). In modern-day revelation, the Lord stated: "Wherefore, I am in your midst, and I am the good shepherd, and the stone of Israel. He that buildeth upon this rock shall never fall" (D&C 50:44). Thus Jacob is in very good company to speak about the "stone" and "the head of their corner" some five and a half centuries before the coming of Jesus Christ.

CONCLUDING THOUGHTS

Jacob magnifies his calling to preach the word and to engrave upon the plates the sacred things as pertaining to the revelations of God. His example is a beacon of light that shines down through the ages. He preaches and testifies of Christ and His atoning sacrifice. He condemns sin and exhorts the people to seek the kingdom of God and not the things of the world. He implores his people to avoid pride and, above all, to be pure and clean. He pleads with his brethren to be true to their covenants of marriage. Jacob's words are written for our day that we might learn from those who have gone before by being reconciled to God through the Atonement of Christ. We should take counsel from Jacob and repent of those things that are keeping us from the blessings of the gospel.

CHAPTER 5

"Allegory of Zenos" scattering & gathering of house of Israel.

ancient Hebrew prophet; martyr of the truth

OVERVIEW

Jacob cites the allegory of Zenos for the edification of his people and future readership. The development of the house of Israel and its future relationship with the Gentile nations in the latter days is explained by comparison with the cultivation of tame and wild olive trees. The scattering and gathering of Israel, together with the adoption of believing Gentiles into the fold, is portrayed. The Lord of the vineyard and his servants lay up fruit against the season, until the end comes and the vineyard is to be burned.

> 1 *BEHOLD, my brethren, do ye not remember to have read* ***the words of the prophet Zenos,*** *which he spake unto the house of Israel, saying:*
>
> 2 *Hearken, O ye house of Israel, and hear the words of me,* ***a prophet*** *of the Lord.*

The words of the prophet Zenos

Zenos is a Hebrew prophet of the lineage of Joseph whose writings are included in the brass plates and are thus available to the Book of Mormon prophets (see 1 Nephi 19:21; 3 Nephi 10:15–17). As cited by Nephi, Zenos prophesies that the Redeemer will be buried in a sepulchre after His crucifixion, with three days of attending darkness experienced by those "who should inhabit the isles of the sea, more especially given unto those who are of the house of Israel" (1 Nephi 19:10). Zenos also prophesies of the widespread natural calamities that will occur at the time, with the result that "many of the kings of the isles of the sea shall be wrought upon by the Spirit of God, to exclaim: The God of nature suffers" (1 Nephi 19:12)—while those in Jerusalem will be scourged and scattered for rejecting the Holy One of Israel. Nevertheless, when the House of Israel turns their hearts again to the Savior, He will remember the covenants He has made with their fathers and "all the earth shall see the salvation of the Lord, saith the prophet; every nation, kindred, tongue and people shall be blessed" (1 Nephi 19:17).

Jacob includes Zenos' allegory of the tame and wild olive trees as a symbol of the divine scattering and gathering of Israel over the generations of time. Additionally, Alma quotes Zenos at length in teaching the Zoramites about the doctrine and practice of prayer (see Alma 33:3–11). Amulek reinforces Alma's witness that Zenos taught "that redemption cometh through the Son of God" (Alma 34:7). Moreover, Nephi, son of Helaman, references Zenos in bearing witness before his recalcitrant countrymen about the mission of the Savior: "And now I would that ye should know, that even since the days of Abraham there have been many prophets that have testified these things; yea, behold, the prophet Zenos did testify boldly; for the which he was slain" (Helaman 8:19). Samuel the Lamanite, as well, cites Zenos in prophesying to the people that the Lamanites will one day be restored to a knowledge of the truths of the gospel (see Helaman 15:11).

Next to Isaiah, the prophet Zenos is quoted in the Book of Mormon more extensively than any other of the ancient Hebrew prophets.

> *3 For behold, thus saith the Lord,* ***I will liken thee, O house of Israel, like unto a tame olive-tree,*** *which a man took and nourished in his vineyard; and it grew, and waxed old, and began to decay.*

I will liken thee, O house of Israel, like unto a tame olive-tree

The allegory of the olive tree, which Jacob preserves on the plates of gold, is about us—and how we can participate in the glorious unfolding of the Lord's plan for the redemption of Israel and all those of the Gentiles who, through faith and obedience, confess His hand and are adopted into the fold. This allegory is a symbolic history of the Lord's dealings with His sons and daughters of the second estate—the mortal probationary phase of existence that gives us the opportunity to prosper spiritually and magnify our place in the covenant circle.

Among Jacob's inventory of gospel resources is the record of his family's experiences, including the prophecies of Lehi and Nephi, and the brass plates of Laban, containing the sacred writings from the beginning of prophetic history. It is among the latter records that he finds the words of Zenos, a prophet of ancient times about whom we know very little—except that he is a martyr for the truth (see Helaman 8:19)—and whose elegant and powerful witness has been lost from our current Old Testament compilation. Like his predecessors, Jacob is consumed by a desire to see that his posterity and future readers have a clear understanding of their place in the Lord's plan of covenant redemption. Thus he turns to Zenos to convey the meticulous design of the Lord in guiding His people through mortality. Zenos' allegory and Jacob's commentary confirm that the mighty promises made by the Lord to Abraham and the seed of Israel will be fulfilled on behalf of the whole world concerning the establishment of His gospel and kingdom here upon the earth.

President Joseph Fielding Smith provides a wonderful framework in which to view and interpret the allegory, or parable, as he calls it:

> The parable of Zenos, recorded by Jacob in chapter five of his book, is one of the greatest parables ever recorded. This parable in and of itself stamps the Book of Mormon with convincing truth. No mortal man, without the inspiration of the Lord, could have written such a parable. It is a pity that too many of those who read the Book of Mormon pass over and slight the truths which it conveys in relation to the history, scattering, and final gathering of Israel. Such members of the Church unto whom attention has been called to the great significance of this parable have said they fail to comprehend it. It is simple and very clear to the minds of those who earnestly seek to know the truth. No man without divine inspiration could have written such a parable as this.
>
> In brief, it records the history of Israel down through the ages, the scattering of the tribes to all parts of the earth; their mingling with, or being grafted in, the wild olive trees, or in other words the mixing of the blood of Israel among the Gentiles by which the great blessings and promises of the Lord to Abraham are fulfilled. After Abraham had been proved even to the extent of being willing to offer Isaac as a sacrifice, the Lord blessed him with the greatest of blessings, and said to him:
>
> . . . By myself have I sworn, saith the Lord, for because thou hast done this thing, and hast not withheld thy son, thine only *son*:
>
> That in blessing I will bless thee, and in multiplying I will multiply thy seed as the stars of the heaven, and as the sand which *is* upon the sea shore; and thy seed shall possess the gate of his enemies;

And in thy seed shall all the nations of the earth be blessed; because thou hast obeyed my voice (Genesis 22:16–18).

This remarkable parable portrays how, as branches of the olive tree (Israelites) were carried to all parts of the earth (the Lord's vineyard) and grafted into the wild olive trees (the Gentile nations). Thus they are fulfilling the promise that the Lord had made.

Today Latter-day Saints are going to all parts of the world as servants in the vineyard to gather this fruit and lay it in store for the time of the coming of the Master. This parable is one of the most enlightening and interesting in the Book of Mormon. How can any person read it without feeling the inspiration of this ancient prophet? (*Answers to Gospel Questions,* 5 vols. [Salt Lake City: Deseret Book, 1957–1966], 4:141–142)

EVIDENCE: I WILL LIKEN THEE, O HOUSE OF ISRAEL, LIKE UNTO A TAME OLIVE-TREE—OLIVE CULTURE

The allegory of Zenos derives its symbolic meaning from the well-established olive horticulture tradition of the Middle East. Carefully managed and nourished olive trees bear fruit for centuries, and the root system of such trees can retain vitality for millennia. The analogy with the enduring blessings of the gospel and the abiding sanctity of God's covenant relationship with His children is appropriate. The olive branch itself is a long-standing symbol for peace. The dove returning to Noah's ark bore an olive leaf in its beak—a powerful image for the restoration of peace to the earth (see Genesis 8:11). Peace comes through the gospel of Jesus Christ. The Savior said, "I AM the true vine, and my Father is the husbandman" (John 15:1). Nephi was fully oriented to the power of such imagery through his grand vision of the unfolding of Israel's destiny (see 1 Nephi 11–14). He explained to his hard-hearted older brothers the essence of the simile:

> And now, the thing which our father meaneth concerning the grafting in of the natural branches through the fulness of the Gentiles, is, that in the latter days, when our seed shall have dwindled in unbelief, yea, for the space of many years, and many generations after the Messiah shall be manifested in body unto the children of men, then shall the fulness of the gospel of the Messiah come unto the Gentiles, and from the Gentiles unto the remnant of our seed—
>
> And at that day shall the remnant of our seed know that they are of the house of Israel, and that they are the covenant people of the Lord; and then shall

Allegory: Development => Progress => Blessings

they know and come to the knowledge of their forefathers, and also to the knowledge of the gospel of their Redeemer, which was ministered unto their fathers by him; wherefore, they shall come to the knowledge of their Redeemer and the very points of his doctrine, that they may know how to come unto him and be saved.

And then at that day will they not rejoice and give praise unto their everlasting God, their rock and their salvation? Yea, at that day, will they not receive the strength and nourishment from the true vine? Yea, will they not come unto the true fold of God?

Behold, I say unto you, Yea; they shall be remembered again among the house of Israel; they shall be grafted in, being a natural branch of the olive-tree, into the true olive-tree. (1 Nephi 15:13–16).

Joseph Smith would never have known or understood the complexity of the allegory or the cultivating that goes on with the Mediterranean olive trees — he was an instrument in God's hands!

* What did Joseph Smith know of the traditions of the olive culture that figures so prominently in the allegory of Zenos? The young Joseph Smith, instrument in the hands of the Lord and inspired translator of the Book of Mormon, residing as he did in the forested American Northeast, could not have been familiar with the details of olive culture of the Mediterranean. In Jacob 5, the extended allegory of the olive tree—with its complex and realistic unfolding of the process of production and harvesting of fruit—is strikingly consistent with what we learn from ancient treatises on olive cultivation. (See *Echoes,* 198.)

Memories: The Drama of the Lord of the Vineyard

Over the years I have enjoyed discussing the allegory of Zenos (Jacob Chapter 5) with various priesthood, gospel doctrine, and institute classes. There are many layers of meaning in this masterful allegory—which seems to incorporate endless variations on the theme of development, progress, and the blessings of the harvest. I have found that it has often proven helpful, with such a long discourse—the longest chapter in the Book of Mormon—to view the events of the allegory as a grand drama reflecting the principles and milestones of spiritual progression, including conflict, early harvest, tragedy and faith, and final labors and harvest. The acts and scenes of the drama can be outlined as follows:

Verses 2–3: **Preamble**—The Lord's introduction to the allegory.

Act I. The Conflict

Verses 4–6: Scene 1—The initial strategy of the Lord: nurturing.

Verses 7–14: Scene 2—Subsequent strategies: grafting, transplanting, burning.

Act II. Early Harvest

Verses 15–18: Scene 1—The natural tree bears fruit.

Verses 19–28: Scene 2—The transplanted branches bear fruit.

Act III. Tragedy and Faith

Verses 29–37: Scene 1—The roots are overrun.

Verses 38–60: Scene 2—Loftiness brings about destruction.

Act IV. Final Labors and Harvest

Verses 61–72: Scene 1—The master strategy: restoration and balance.

Verses 73–75: Scene 2—Resolution: all is accomplished.

Verses 76–77: **Postlude—**Looking to the future and the end.

By experiencing the allegory of Zenos as an epic play, one can often more readily relate to the principal players, including the servant advocate ("Spare it a little longer"—verse 50) and Lord of the vineyard himself ("What could I have done more for my vineyard?"—verse 41; "For it grieveth me that I should lose the trees of my vineyard"—verse 66).

By likening scriptures such as these unto ourselves, as Nephi counseled (see 1 Nephi 19:23–24), we can gain perspective on how to magnify our offices and callings in the vineyard of the Lord, trimming away the nonproductive growth from our lives, and cultivating vitality of spirit and fruitfulness of service.

The vineyard of the Lord is the venue of miracles. The transformation that comes from living the gospel as part of the vineyard service is a miracle. (Richard J. Allen)

4–77 The Lord of the vineyard and his servant administer the strategies of cultivating and nurturing the trees of the vineyard—including grafting, transplanting, pruning, digging, burning the discarded branches, and harvesting the fruit—all in preparation for the end of the season.

> *7 And it came to pass that the master of the vineyard saw it, and he said unto his servant:* ***It grieveth me that I should lose this tree;*** *wherefore, go and pluck the branches from a wild olive-tree, and bring them hither unto me; and we will pluck off those main branches which are beginning to wither away, and we will cast them into the fire that they may be burned.*

It grieveth me that I should lose this tree

The care and succor that are characteristic of the Lord of the vineyard toward his trees is manifested throughout the allegory (see also verses 11, 13, 32, 46, 47, 51, 66). In his grand vision of the unfolding of human history, Enoch observes the heavens weep over the wickedness of the inhabitants of the earth. He asks the Lord: "How is it that thou canst weep, seeing thou art holy, and from all eternity to all eternity?" (Moses 7:29). The Lord responds with words to explain His grieving: "Behold these thy brethren; they are the workmanship of mine own hands, and I gave unto them their knowledge, in the day I created them; and in the Garden of Eden, gave I unto man his agency; And unto thy brethren have I said, and also given commandment, that they should love one another, and that they should choose me, their Father; but behold, they are without affection, and they hate their own blood" (Moses 7:32–33). In a similar manner, the Lord of the vineyard in the allegory of Zenos continually expresses grief when the progress of his trees is diminished or faltering. The Lord Almighty is concerned about the welfare of His children. He weeps over our failures and He rejoices over our victories.

12 Wherefore, go thy way; ***watch the tree, and nourish it,*** *according to my words.*

Watch the tree, and nourish it

Work to be done to fulfill Heavenly Fathers plan.

The allegory is filled with expressions of action—digging, pruning, nourishing, plucking, grafting, tasting, planting, dunging, laying up fruit. The work of the building up the kingdom of God and carrying out the duties inherent in the Abrahamic covenant is likewise demanding of our industry, effort, and commitment. "Verily I say, men should be anxiously engaged in a good cause, and do many things of their own free will, and bring to pass much righteousness; For the power is in them, wherein they are agents unto themselves. And inasmuch as men do good they shall in nowise lose their reward" (D&C 58:27–28). We observe in the allegory of the tame olive tree the endless labor of love (see 1 Thessalonians 1:3 and Hebrews 6:10 for this expression in the writings of Paul) in which the Lord of the vineyard and His servants are engaged on behalf of the harvest—the sons and daughters of God. We are engaged in the mighty work of the gathering and the perfecting of the Saints—both living and deceased. The allegory is a compelling view of the ongoing work leading to salvation and exaltation.

41 And it came to pass that the Lord of the vineyard wept, and said unto the servant:
What could I have done more for my vineyard?

What could I have done more for my vineyard?

The anguish of the Lord of the vineyard as He beholds, from time to time, the decline of his trees and the lack of good fruit is reflected in the question just cited (repeated also in verses 47 and 49). The same theme is sounded in a parable from Isaiah: "What could have been done more to my vineyard, that I have not done in it? wherefore, when I looked that it should bring forth grapes, brought it forth wild grapes?" (Isaiah 5:4; see 2 Nephi 15:4). The doctrine behind the allegory is the certainty of God's unremitting service on behalf of His children, whose immortality and eternal life constitute His mission and His glory (see Moses 1:39). God will never give up the fight. The forward motion of the plan is inexorable, despite disappointments and reversals along the way. Elder Neal A. Maxwell confirms this truth: "Prophets have a special appreciation, too, for Jacob's allegory of the olive trees. They can identify with the feelings of the Lord of the vineyard who, after all His labors, saw much evil fruit come forth. The twice-given lamentation of the Lord of the vineyard was: 'What could I have done more for my vineyard?' (Jacob 5:41, 47.)" (*If Thou Endure It Well* [Salt Lake City: Bookcraft, 1996], 72.)

We, too, sometimes might feel that our labors are not fully productive when children stray from the path or when our missionary outreach is not welcomed by those whom we try to teach. In such cases, the allegory of Zenos lends comfort and hope to our efforts, since, in the broad contours of God's plan for His children there will be the ultimate harvest of joy and triumph. From our modest position as servants of the Lord, we realize that our efforts will bear fruit if we endure to the end and place our faith in the "Lord of the harvest" (Alma 26:7).

Our work here on earth as it pertains to preaching the gospel may never be rendered "useless".

> *61 Wherefore, go to, and call servants, that we may labor diligently with our might in the vineyard,* ***that we may prepare the way,*** *that I may bring forth again the natural fruit, which natural fruit is good and the most precious above all other fruit.*

That we may prepare the way

The dispensation of the fulness of times has the divine mandate to prepare the world for the Second Coming. A central part of that role is to gather the dispersed of Zion and the willing and honest among the Gentiles unto Christ, to receive the saving principles and ordinances of the gospel. The Prophet and preparer of this, the final dispensation, was Joseph Smith:

> Joseph Smith was a messenger sent before the face of the Lord to prepare a people on earth for that day which will be both great and dreadful (Malachi 3:1; 3 Nephi 24:1; JS—H 1:36). For that matter, the gospel plan restored through him—the new

> and everlasting covenant—was dispensed to earth to serve a preparatory function. "I have sent mine everlasting covenant into the world," the Savior declared, "to be a light to the world, and to be a standard for my people, and for the Gentiles to seek to it, and *to be a messenger before my face to prepare the way before me*" (D&C 45:9; italics added). (Joseph Fielding McConkie and Robert L. Millet, *Doctrinal Commentary on the Book of Mormon,* 4 vols. [Salt Lake City: Bookcraft, 1987–1992], 2:71)

62 Wherefore, let us go to and labor with our might this last time, for behold the end draweth nigh, and this is for ***the last time that I shall prune my vineyard.***

The last time that I shall prune my vineyard

This verse reflects the work of the Restoration in the latter days:

> The Lord gave instructions to Joseph Smith to call others to assist him in gathering Israel in the final dispensation. "*Thou art called to prune my vineyard with a mighty pruning,*" the Savior said in July 1830, "yea, *even for the last time*; yea, and also all those whom thou hast ordained" (D&C 24:19; italics added). "Ye are called to lift up your voices as with the sound of a trump," the Lord explained in a later revelation, "to declare my gospel unto a crooked and perverse generation. For behold, the field is white already to harvest; and *it is the eleventh hour*, and *the last time that I shall call laborers into my vineyard.* And my vineyard has become corrupted every whit; and there is none which doeth good save it be a few." (D&C 33:2–4; italics added. Cf. D&C 39:17.) (Joseph Fielding McConkie and Robert L. Millet, *Doctrinal Commentary on the Book of Mormon,* 4 vols. [Salt Lake City: Bookcraft, 1987–1992], 2:70)

63 Graft in the branches; begin at the last that they may be first, and that the first may be last, and dig about the trees, both old and young, ***the first and the last; and the last and the first,*** *that all may be nourished once again for the last time.*

The first and the last; and the last and the first

During His earthly ministry, the Lord Jesus Christ conveyed the gospel first to the Jewish people, from which lineage He descended. He then directed that His Apostles and servants take the gospel to the Gentiles in surrounding lands. In the dispensation of the fulness of times, the order was reversed, the restored gospel going first to the Gentiles, among whom were mingled those of Israelite heritage, and then to the remnant of the house of Israel, including the descendants of the Lamanites and, eventually, to the Jewish people themselves. President Joseph Fielding Smith summarized this principle succinctly:

> FIRST TO BE LAST AND LAST TO BE FIRST. In the former dispensation, the gospel was first preached to the Jews and then, after they had rejected it, it was taken to the Gentiles. In the dispensation in which we live, the gospel was first taken to the Gentile nations, and scattered Israel other than the Jews were gathered out; and after being preached among the Gentile nations, it shall go to the Jews, the first being last and the last being first, as the Savior promised. [Compare Matthew 19:30; 20:16.] (*Doctrines of Salvation,* 3 vols., ed. Bruce R. McConkie [Salt Lake City: Bookcraft, 1954–1956], 3:259)

The Gospel will ultimately taken (preached) to the Jews.

Jacob is familiar with this principle from his studies of the brass plates and from statements by his brother Nephi. According to the message conveyed to Nephi by an angel of God we learn: "And the time cometh that he shall manifest himself unto all nations, both unto the Jews and also unto the Gentiles; and after he has manifested himself unto the Jews and also unto the Gentiles, then he shall manifest himself unto the Gentiles and also unto the Jews, and the last shall be first, and the first shall be last" (1 Nephi 13:42; compare Ether 13:12; D&C 29:30; 88:59).

> *68 And the branches of the natural tree will I graft into the natural branches of the tree; and thus will I bring them together again, that they shall bring forth the natural fruit, and* ***they shall be one.***

THEY SHALL BE ONE

The design of the Lord is to bring together in one all things of righteousness in the last days (see 2 Nephi 29:14). The word of the Lord in the Bible will blend with the word of the Lord in the Book of Mormon to establish the fulness of the gospel on behalf of the faithful and to serve as the basis for judging the deeds of those who have been given the opportunity to access to the word.

> *69 And* ***the bad shall be cast away,*** *yea, even out of all the land of my vineyard; for behold, only this once will I prune my vineyard.*

The bad shall be cast away

The allegory of Zenos is structured about elements of urgency—the Lord of the vineyard being anxious to gather up the harvest before the end of the season, or "against the season" (Jacob 5:13, 18, 19, 20, 23, 27, 29, 31, 46, 76), for "the end is nigh at hand, and the season speedily cometh; and if ye labor with your might with me ye shall have joy in the fruit which I shall lay up unto myself against the time which will soon come" (verse 71).

> The "end of the world" is the destruction of the wicked (Joseph Smith Matthew 1:4), the destruction of those who are not either terrestrial or celestial at the time of Christ's coming in glory. "The righteous need not fear," Nephi taught, "for they are those who shall not be confounded. But it is the kingdom of the devil, which shall be built up among the children of men, which kingdom is established among them which are in the flesh—for the time speedily shall come that all churches which are built up to get gain, and all those who are built up to get power over the flesh, and those who are built up to become popular in the eyes of the world; and those who seek the lusts of the flesh and the things of the world, and to do all manner of iniquity; yea, in fine, all those who belong to the kingdom of the devil are they who need fear, and tremble, and quake; they are those who must be brought low in the dust; they are those who must be consumed as stubble" (1 Nephi 22:22–23). In short, "the time speedily cometh that the Lord God shall cause a great division among the people [cf. D&C 63:54], and the wicked will he destroy; and he will spare his people, yea, even if it so be that he must destroy the wicked by fire" (2 Nephi 30:10). (Joseph Fielding McConkie and Robert L. Millet, *Doctrinal Commentary on the Book of Mormon,* 4 vols. [Salt Lake City: Bookcraft, 1987–1992], 2:71)

> *70 And it came to pass that the Lord of the vineyard sent his servant; and the servant went and did as the Lord had commanded him, and brought other servants; and* ***they were few.***

They were few

The Savior told His disciples, "The harvest truly is plenteous, but the labourers are few" (Matthew 9:37; compare Luke 10:2). In his great vision of the coming events associated with the Restoration, Nephi observes, "And it came to pass that I beheld the church of the Lamb of God, and its numbers were few, because of the wickedness and abominations of the whore who sat upon many waters; nevertheless, I beheld that the church of the Lamb, who were the saints of God, were also upon all the face of the earth; and their dominions upon the face of the earth were small, because of the wickedness of the great whore whom I saw" (1 Nephi 14:12). We are the other servants depicted in the allegory of Zenos. We are few in number but in the strength of the Lord we surely can go and do as He has commanded by bringing His truth to the nations of the earth.

> *76 For behold, for a long time will I lay up of the fruit of my vineyard unto mine own self against the season, which speedily cometh; and* ***for the last time*** *have I nourished my vineyard, and pruned it, and dug about it, and dunged it; wherefore I will lay up unto mine own self of the fruit, for a long time, according to that which I have spoken.*
>
> *77 And when the time cometh that evil fruit shall again come into my vineyard, then will I cause the good and the bad to be gathered; and the good will I preserve unto myself, and the bad will I cast away into its own place. And* ***then cometh the season and the end;*** *and my vineyard will I cause to be burned with fire.*

For the Last Time; Then Cometh the Season and the End

How do we apply the allegory of Zenos to our own lives? The servant (prophet) brings other servants (us) to go into the vineyard (the earth) for the last time (dispensation of the fulness of times) to labor (do missionary work) that we might have joy in our fruit (bringing souls unto Christ—convert baptisms) until finally the season ends and the earth is burned. It is our duty to preach the gospel to every creature (see Mormon 9:22). The Prophet Joseph Smith declared, "After all that has been said, [our] greatest and most important duty is to preach the Gospel" (*Teachings of the Prophet Joseph Smith,* sel. by Joseph Fielding Smith [Salt Lake City: Deseret Book Company, 1938], 112). Remember that we are the missionaries who will prune the vineyard for the last time by sharing the gospel. We can have joy in bringing souls to Christ.

Time Considerations in the Allegory of the Olive Tree

The allegory of the olive tree relates to the dealings of the Lord, the Master of the vineyard, with the House of Israel. In general, the following chronology may be helpful for understanding the allegory:

- First period—Jacob 5:4–14: 1800 B.C. (Jacob/Israel) to 400 B.C. (Malachi)
- Long time passes—Jacob 5:15: 400 B.C. (Malachi) to A.D. 30 (The Lord Jesus Christ)

Jacob 5:77

- Second period—Jacob 5:16–28: A.D. 30 to A.D. 100 (The Lord Jesus Christ and His Apostles) Note: The death of Peter and Paul in approximately A.D. 65 would indicate the end of the quorums; however, the writings of John were near the end of the first century.
- Long time passes—Jacob 5:29: A.D. 100 to A.D. 1820 (Apostasy to the Restoration)
- Third period—Jacob 5:30–60: A.D. 1820 to present day (Restoration and Gathering)
- Fourth period—Jacob 5:61–75: Present day—gathering of Israel and preparing for the Second Coming of the Lord
- Long time passes—Jacob 5:76: The Millennial reign
- End of the Millennium—Jacob 5:77: End of the world and then the earth shall be renewed

Summary of Interpretations:

- Tame olive tree—the House of Israel
- Vineyard—the world
- Master of the vineyard—the Lord Jesus Christ
- Servant—the prophets
- Wild olive tree—Gentiles or non-Israelites
- Branches—different groups of the House of Israel
- Roots—blood of Israel or the seed of Abraham or the gospel covenants
- Fruit—good works and converted Saints
- Digging, pruning, and dunging—nourishing and persuading the children of God with the word of God to come unto Christ and do good works
- Grafting—coming to Christ and becoming part of the House of Israel
- Transplanting the branches—sending groups through out the world
- Decaying branches—wickedness and apostasy
- Casting branches into the fire—judgment of God (Ed J. Pinegar)

Memories: Leadership Principles for the Gathering

The gathering is a central part of the Lord's design to establish His kingdom once more upon the earth, never again to be diminished or removed. The gathering is accomplished according to leadership principles defined and confirmed from before the foundation of the earth.

Even though the purpose of Zenos' narrative may not have been to teach leadership principles per se, we can see from the masterful leadership of the Lord of the vineyard specific ways whereby we can improve and advance in our own roles as stewards of the gathering—whether in the family, in the branches, wards, and stakes of the Church, or in missionary endeavors. Each of the questions in the following checklist reflects a leadership principle embodied in the narrative of the allegory. You might wish to score yourself and then go back through Jacob 5 to determine how the Lord acted in order to maximize the harvest. What better leadership model is there than the Lord Himself?

A. General Principles

Leadership qualities of Christ.

1. Do I have an overarching, governing sense of purpose and mission in what I do? (see verses 9, 49, 54, 61)
2. Do I maintain focus without ever losing sight of the objective? (see verses 13, 35, 61)
3. Do I understand and remain aligned with the "root" values of my enterprise? (see verse 59)
4. Am I firm in your commitment to action? (see verses 14, 75; compare Abraham 3:17; 2 Nephi 24:24)
5. Is my engagement total and "impassioned"? (see entire allegory; compare Mark 12:30, 2 Nephi 25:29; D&C 4:2)
6. Do I maintain an attitude of faith and hope? (see verses 53–54, 60, 77)

B. Leadership Structure and Style

7. Do I plan before taking action? (see entire allegory)
8. Do I follow through with the steps of my plan? (see verses 37, 61–62, 71–72, 74–75)
9. Do I understand the time framework within which I operate? (see verses 29, 47, 71)
10. Am I a team builder? (see verses 15, 19, 61, 70)
11. Do I delegate effectively? (see verses 12, 72, 75)
12. Do I understand how to apply rewards effectively? (see verses 53–54, 60, 71, 75)
13. Am I a participative leader who works alongside team members? (see verse 72)
14. Am I an effective listener? (see verses 27, 33, 47–48, 50)
15. Do I take responsibility for my decisions? (see verses 27, 29, 45)
16. Do I discipline effectively? (see verse 22)

C. Leadership Strategies

17. Am I adaptable and resilient? (see verses 22, 48)
18. Do I operate from a contingency perspective, always with a careful fallback position? (see verse 13)
19. Do I constantly evaluate and monitor results? (see verse 31)
20. Am I able to deal resourcefully with crises? (see verses 34, 36)
21. Do I understand the techniques and science of vitality and growth? (see verses 61, 64)
22. Is my approach balanced and fine-tuned? (see verses 48, 65, 74)
23. Do I harvest as I go—"against the season"? (throughout allegory)
24. Am I able to "close the circle"—to restore, to complete, to resolve, to bring things to a successful conclusion? (see verses 63, 68, 75)

Every servant and steward in the Lord's vineyard is admonished to "learn his duty, and to act in the office in which he is appointed, in all diligence" (D&C 107:99). (Richard J. Allen)

CHAPTER 6

OVERVIEW

Jacob confirms the truth of the allegory and offers his own interpretive summary. The Lord will gather the faithful in the latter days. He will consign the wicked to endless torment. Jacob entreats his listeners solemnly to repent and be counted among the chosen and elect of God.

1 AND now, behold, my brethren, as I said unto you that I would prophesy, behold, this is my ***prophecy—****that the things which this prophet Zenos spake, concerning the house of Israel, in the which he likened them unto a tame olive-tree,* ***must surely come to pass.***

2 And the day that he shall set his hand again ***the second time*** *to recover his people, is the day, yea, even the last time, that the servants of the Lord shall go forth in his power, to nourish and prune his vineyard; and after that the end soon cometh.*

3 And ***how blessed*** *are they who have labored diligently in his vineyard; and* ***how cursed*** *are they who shall be cast out into their own place! And the world shall be burned with fire.*

> *4 And* ***how merciful*** *is our God unto us, for* ***he remembereth the house of Israel,***
> *both roots and branches; and he stretches forth his hands unto them all the day long;*
> *and they are a stiffnecked and a gainsaying people; but as many as will not harden*
> *their hearts shall be saved in the kingdom of God.*

Prophecy; must surely come to pass; the second time; how blessed; how cursed; how merciful; he remembereth the house of Israel

Jacob recaptures the essence of the allegory of the tame and wild olive trees in just four verses. He speaks by way of prophecy to confirm the certainty of Zenos' words and to present a plain and simple view of the latter-day Restoration in which the Lord's faithful are gathered to Zion. The Lord is a God of mercy and compassion, saving as many as will respond to His universal invitation to come unto Him. Those who reject Him will be separated and isolated in their own place.

5–10 Jacob calls upon his listeners to repent and enjoy the blessings of Christ rather than persist in wickedness and be consigned to endless torment.

> *11 O then, my beloved brethren, repent ye, and enter in at the strait gate, and continue*
> *in the way which is narrow, until ye shall* ***obtain eternal life.***
> *12* ***O be wise;*** *what can I say more?*

Obtain eternal life; O be wise

The message of Jacob is to be wise in honoring our covenant vows. Jacob has already experienced a major social division when the Nephites separate themselves from the murderous circle of Laman and Lemuel. Now he looks out over the growing branch of Israel under his stewardship and senses forces that threaten, once again, to polarize the population into two camps—the chaste and obedient on the one hand, and the prideful and corrupt on the other. Thus his fervent appeal to his people to repent or be "hewn down and cast into the fire" (Jacob 6:7). He warns his listeners to be wise and repent at once.

We can apply Jacob's counsel to ourselves as we seek to participate in the ongoing unfolding of the restoration of the gospel in its fulness. Those who come unto Christ experience the opening of windows of eternal blessings upon themselves and their families. Those who eschew righteousness and refuse to repent are consigned to damnation, Jacob reminds us that now is the time for us to repent and align ourselves with the word of God. We cannot set our repentance aside, because we will stand accountable for everything we have done.

* Jacob had experienced a divide with his brothers. No wonder he was so observant to the fact that the Nephites were splitting into 2 separate groups under his leadership. Pride vs. chaste & obedient.

13 Finally, I bid you farewell, until I shall ***meet you before the pleasing bar of God,*** *which bar striketh the wicked with awful dread and fear. Amen.*

Meet you before the pleasing bar of God

What a daunting assemblage of chosen servants we will encounter on the Day of Judgment! Jacob will be there, according to his testimony. Nephi will be there, too: "You and I shall stand face to face before his bar; and ye shall know that I have been commanded of him to write these things, notwithstanding my weakness" (2 Nephi 33:11). The final words of the Book of Mormon attest that Moroni will also be present, "to meet you before the pleasing bar of the great Jehovah, the Eternal Judge of both quick and dead. Amen" (Moroni 10:34). And many other servants of the Lord will doubtless be present as witnesses to confirm the words of truth that they were commanded to give unto the children of God—words by which we will be judged on that great day of accountability.

CHAPTER 7

OVERVIEW

Jacob confounds the anti-Christ Sherem and restores peace to the land. He enjoins the people to follow the words of Christ. The Nephites fail in an attempt to bring the truth to the Lamanites. They arm themselves against Lamanite attacks. Jacob waxes nostalgic that his people are wanderers in a strange land. He turns the sacred records over to his son Enos.

1 AND now it came to pass after some years had passed away, there came a man among the people of Nephi, whose name was ***Sherem.***

Sherem, Anti-Christ

Sherem is the first of several anti-Christ figures included in the Book of Mormon. He is known for his skillful and proud orating during the tenure of the prophet Jacob. "And he [Sherem] was learned, that he had a perfect knowledge of the language of the people; wherefore, he could use much flattery, and much power of speech, according to the power of the devil" (Jacob 7:4). His message is an explicit denial of the being and mission of Christ—"for no man knoweth of such things; for he cannot tell of things to come . . ." (Jacob 7:7). Having drawn away many of the people of God into his perverted pathway, Sherem is called before Jacob, where he attempts to justify his untenable position. "But behold, the Lord God poured in his Spirit into my soul," declares Jacob, "insomuch that I did confound him in all his words" (Jacob 7:8).

Sherem insists on a sign to substantiate the gospel position. By the intercession of the power of the Lord, he is rendered incapacitated for many days. He then arranges for the people to congregate to hear his confession of guilt and his witness about the verity of Christ and the power of the Holy Ghost—after which he dies in dire fear of having committed the unpardonable sin (see Jacob 7:20). Jacob feels relief at the conclusion of this ordeal: "And it came to pass that peace and the love of God was restored again among the people; and they searched the scriptures, and hearkened no more to the words of this wicked man" (Jacob 7:23).

2–4 Sherem attempts to lead the people of Nephi away from the pathway of Christ through his deceiving flattery and gift of oratory.

> 5 *And he had hope to shake me from the faith, notwithstanding the many revelations and the many things which I had seen concerning these things; for I truly had seen angels, and they had ministered unto me. And also, I had heard the voice of the Lord speaking unto me in very word, from time to time; wherefore,* ***I could not be shaken.***

I could not be shaken

It is inconceivable how an individual could hope to dislodge a prophet of God from his station of certainty in the faith. But Sherem brazenly makes the attempt. How might we apply this encounter to our own situation? Are we unshakable in our faith? Is the foundation upon which we stand as sure as the foundation upon which the prophets of the Lord stand? Through faith, devotion, continually studying and pondering the word of God, constant prayer, and the cultivation of a service-minded love for our fellowmen, we can also become unshakable so that no anti-Christ or evil influence can dislodge us from our spiritual moorings. The Lord said to Oliver Cowdery: "Wherefore, if you shall build up my church, upon the foundation of my gospel and my rock, the gates of hell shall not prevail against you" (D&C 18:5). Yet Oliver failed to secure himself upon the rock of the Savior and fell away from his high office. We can learn a lesson from that and do better. We can follow the counsel of the Lord's prophets.

(Oliver Cowdry Shaken)

6–7 Sherem contends against Jacob, saying that no one can know of the coming of a being such as Christ.

*8 But behold, the Lord God poured in his Spirit into my soul, insomuch that I did **confound him** in all his words.*

Confound him

Sherem is a prototype for endless varieties of disgruntled and misguided enemies of the truth who emerge in all generations of time only to be confounded by the chosen representatives of the Lord. In the strength of God the righteous can prevail against those who scheme to overthrow the doctrines of Christ. Elder Neal A. Maxwell considers the pitiful plight of all such self-appointed torch bearers:

> Just how crucial access is to time-transcending truth may be pondered in the setting in which Sherem, an agnostic, berated a prophet for preaching a Christ to come "many hundred years hence." Sherem declared that "there should be no Christ." Indeed, he said, it was even blasphemous for prophets to teach of things to come, for "no man knoweth of such things; for he cannot tell of things to come" (Jacob 7:1–7). The anti-Christ was a "here and now" person who, ironically, put himself forward as if he were the judge of what constituted orthodoxy. So, alas, today—like Sherem, who ostensibly wished to uphold the law of Moses—some denounce modern prophets for telling of plain and precious things yet to come. Provincialism wears many blinders, and each is designed to deflect those fundamental truths which transcend time. How relentlessly the adversary seeks to grind mortals down to a single plane, knowing, as he does, that if mortals can be confined to now, then it is so easy to declare present appetite, instead of Jesus, as king. (*Plain and Precious Things* [Salt Lake City: Deseret Book, 1983], 58–59)

9 And I said unto him: Deniest thou the Christ who shall come? And he said: If there should be a Christ, I would not deny him; but I know that there is no Christ, neither has been, nor ever will be.
*10 And I said unto him: **Believest thou the scriptures?** And he said, Yea.*
*11 And I said unto him: **Then ye do not understand them;** for **they truly testify of Christ.** Behold, I say unto you that none of the prophets have written, nor prophesied, save they have spoken concerning this Christ.*
*12 And this is not all—it has been made manifest unto me, for I have heard and seen; and it also has been made manifest unto me by the **power of the Holy Ghost;** wherefore, I know if there should be no atonement made all mankind must be lost.*

Believest thou the scriptures? They truly testify of Christ; power of the Holy Ghost

The armor of God in confounding such false contenders as Sherem is the word of God, which testifies plainly of Christ, and the power of the Spirit. Those who fail to comprehend true doctrine either do not read the scriptures or do not understand them through the promptings of the Holy Ghost. They are left to their own capacity, which, on its own, will always fall short of penetrating to the heart of the mysteries of God.

12–16 Sherem demands a sign and is consequently rendered powerless and immobile by an act of God. He calls the people together and confesses his wrongs.

> *17 And it came to pass that on the morrow the multitude were gathered together; and he spake plainly unto them and denied the things which he had taught them, and* ***confessed the Christ,*** *and the power of the Holy Ghost, and the ministering of angels.*
> *18 And he spake plainly unto them, that he had been* ***deceived by the power of the devil.*** *And he spake of hell, and of eternity, and of eternal punishment.*

Confessed the Christ; deceived by the power of the devil

Sherem, who is deceived by the devil, soon comes to retract his false teachings. Why are people deceived by the devil? Because they are enticed by the things that are pleasing to the carnal mind (see Alma 30:53). We are counseled to do all in our power to be spiritually minded (see 2 Nephi 9:39). The carnal mind has been described as follows: "Unconverted men are so called (1 Cor. 3:3). They are represented as of a 'carnal mind, which is enmity against God' (Rom. 8:6, 7). Enjoyments that minister to the wants and desires of man's animal nature are so called (Rom. 15:27; 1 Cor. 9:11)." (*Illustrated Bible Dictionary,* M. G. Easton.)

19–22 Sherem completes his confession and expires—all in answer to Jacob's prayer for the protection of his people.

I Cried unto the Lord for Strength and Wisdom

Anti-Christs are always deceived by the devil (see Jacob 7:18–19; compare the case of Korihor in Alma 30:52–53). In our day the devil seeks to deceive people in a variety of ways. Some are captured strategically and chained by the devil in subtle and delicate ways. Some instances are more dramatic, as described by Newel Knight in the following account:

> After the close of the meeting Brother Hyrum [Smith] and myself intended going to spend the night with one of the brethren who lived a short distance from my uncle's, but as we were ready to start, the Spirit whispered to me that I should tarry there at my uncle's all night. I did so, and retired to bed, where I rested till midnight when my uncle came to my room and desired me to get up, saying he feared his wife [Electa Peck] was about to die. This surprised me, as she was quite well when I went to bed.
>
> I dressed myself, and having asked my Heavenly Father to give me wisdom and power to rebuke the destroyer from the habitation, I went to the room where my aunt lay. She was in a most fearful condition; her eyes were closed, and she appeared to be in the last agonies of death. Presently she opened her eyes, and bade her husband and children farewell, telling them she must die for the redemption of this generation, as Jesus Christ had died for the generation in His day. Her whole frame shook, and she appeared to be racked with the most exquisite pain and torment; her hands and feet were cold, and the blood settled in her fingers; while her husband and children stood weeping around her bed.
>
> This was a scene new to me, and I felt she was suffering under the power of Satan—that was the same spirit that had bound and overpowered me at the time Joseph cast him out. I now cried unto the Lord for strength and wisdom that we might prevail over this wicked and delusive power. Just at this time my uncle cried aloud to me saying: "O, Brother Newel, cannot something be done?"
>
> I felt the Holy Spirit of the Lord rest upon me as he said this, and I immediately stepped forward, took her by the hand, and commanded Satan, in the name of the Lord Jesus Christ, to depart. I told my aunt she would not die, but that she should live to see her children grown up; that Satan had deceived her, and put a lying spirit in her mouth; that Christ had made the only and last atonement for all who would believe on His name; and that there should be no more shedding of blood for sin. She believed and stretched forth her hand, and cried unto me, and Satan departed from her. (*Scraps of Biography,* 66–67; Jack M. Lyon, Jay A. Parry, and Linda R. Gundry, eds., *Best-Loved Stories of the LDS People, vol. 2* [Salt Lake City: Deseret Book, 1999], 155–156.) (Ed J. Pinegar)

23–25 With the demise of Sherem, peace is again restored to the land and the people return to searching the word of God. A campaign to restore the Lamanites to the truth fails, and the Nephites fortify themselves against their continual assaults.

26 And it came to pass that I, Jacob, began to be old; and the record of this people being kept on the other plates of Nephi, wherefore, ***I conclude this record,*** *declaring that I have written according to the best of my knowledge, by saying that the time passed away with us, and also our lives passed away like as it were unto us a dream, we being* ***a lonesome and a solemn people, wanderers,*** *cast out from Jerusalem, born in tribulation, in a wilderness, and hated of our brethren, which caused wars and contentions; wherefore, we did* ***mourn out our days.***

I CONCLUDE THIS RECORD; A LONESOME AND A SOLEMN PEOPLE; WANDERERS; MOURN OUT OUR DAYS

Having lost their ageless inheritance in the Old World, the Nephites hold firmly to the hope of a heavenly inheritance in the realms to come. Through the Atonement of Christ, they have the assurance of happiness and hope for a better world. But for the time being, they retain their spot of ground in the land of promise through ceaseless defensive measures against their enemies—not knowing from moment to moment what the next assault will bring. Are we not in a similar circumstance? We are beset on all sides by endless attacks from the forces of evil. We are wanderers in a telestial world where the only enduring light is the light of the gospel of Jesus Christ, and sometimes we mourn out our days, yearning for the security of our heavenly home.

27 Jacob commissions his son Enos to take over the sacred duty to keep and add to the plates.

CONCLUDING THOUGHTS

The Lord has a great work for us to do in this the dispensation of the fulness of times. We are the servants in the Lord's vineyard who have the charge to help cultivate, nurture, and harvest the covenant crop. We are to take the gospel to every kindred, tongue, and people. This is the last time He will set His hand to recover and gather His people leading up the Second Coming that will usher in the millennial reign. Let us watch and be ready and prepare ourselves against the power of Satan, for he seeks to bring us down to hell. Let us not be deceived by the sophistries of men, the lusts of the flesh, or any influence that takes us away from the gospel of Jesus Christ. The gospel message resounds with clarion purpose: Hold to the iron rod, pray with faith, listen to the Spirit, and follow the living prophets.

In fulfilling his office with dignity, Jacob sets a glorious example for us. He becomes an eyewitness of angels (see Jacob 7:5) and beholds the Redeemer Himself (see 2 Nephi 10:3). He is continually nourished by the Spirit (see Jacob 7:12). He is faithful in keeping and augmenting the sacred account on the plates of Nephi. He teaches humility and morality to his fellow Saints (see Jacob 2:1–35). He is a witness of the reality of Christ and the verity of the Atonement. Toward the end of his ministry, he confounds the anti-Christ Sherem with a powerful testimony of the Savior and thus restores unity to his people. In the life of Jacob we have proof of the harvest of joy that flows into the life of all who are gathered home to the Good Shepherd. By following the example of Jacob, as a type and shadow of the eternal example of the Messiah, we, too, can live "after the manner of happiness" (2 Nephi 5:27).

THE BOOK OF
ENOS

The Transitional Record Keepers

Between the time of Jacob, brother of Nephi, and the reign of King Benjamin (around 130 B.C.), a sequence of seven record keepers preserved and augmented the sacred history of the people. These transitional curators were:

- Enos, son of Jacob
- Jarom, son of Enos
- Omni, son of Jarom
- Amaron, son of Omni
- Chemish, brother of Amaron
- Abinadom, son of Chemish
- Amaleki, son of Abinadom, who passed the records on to Benjamin

BOOK OVERVIEW

Enos remembers the inspiring words of his father, Jacob, and prays mightily to the Lord for the welfare of his own soul. The voice of the Lord confirms that he is forgiven because of his faith. Enos then prays for the welfare of the Nephites and Lamanites. The Lord covenants with Enos that the sacred records will go forth in the Lord's due time as a blessing to future generations. Enos spends the remainder of his life preaching and guiding the people. He looks forward with rejoicing to his coming reunion with the Lord.

> *1 BEHOLD, it came to pass that I,* ***Enos,*** *knowing my father that he was a just man—for he taught me in his language, and also in the nurture and admonition of the Lord—and blessed be the name of my God for it—*
> *2 And I will tell you of the* ***wrestle*** *which I had before God, before I received a* ***remission of my sins.***

Enos, the One Who Prayed with Faith

The Savior taught: "Therefore, ye must always pray unto the Father in my name; And whatsoever ye shall ask the Father in my name, which is right, believing that ye shall receive, behold it shall be given unto you" (3 Nephi 18:19–20). Enos desires a remission of his sins. He hungers to be spiritually liberated and enjoy "eternal life, and the joy of the saints" (verse 3)—blessings that his father, Jacob, has unveiled to him as part of "the nurture and admonition of the Lord" (verse 1). What Enos does in the pursuit of this worthy goal, while alone in the out-of-doors, is something that resonates in the hearts and minds of all who search the scriptures in quest of enlightenment and encouragement: "And my soul hungered;" Enos says, "and I kneeled down before my Maker, and I cried unto him in mighty prayer and supplication for mine own soul; and all the day long did I cry unto him; yea, and when the night came I did still raise my voice high that it reached the heavens" (verse 4). The Lord hears his supplication and speaks to him the words he hungers after: "Enos, thy sins are forgiven thee, and thou shalt be blessed" (verse 5). When he asks the Lord how such a thing is done, the answer comes: "Because of thy faith in Christ . . . " (verse 8).

It is faith that brings forgiveness to Enos through the power of the Atonement; and it is forgiveness that brings an overpowering surge of charity into his soul—as evidenced by his longing for the blessings of the Lord to be extended to his brethren, the Nephites, and then, in turn, to the Lamanites. Thus he prays fervently that the Lord will preserve the records of His dealings with the people and cause that these records will be made available to his brethren as an instrumentality of salvation. As a result, the Lord covenants with Enos that this will be fulfilled "in his own due time" (verse 16).

Enos is the son of Jacob, brother of Nephi. His celebrated prayer experience takes place sometime in the period 544 B.C. to 421 B.C. Following his spiritual rejuvenation, Enos serves his people in righteousness all the remaining days of his life. He learns that the most effective strategy for keeping his people on the pathway of obedience is "exceedingly great plainness of speech" (verse 23). Thus his message to us about prayer, forgiveness, and charity is short, austere, and directly to the point.

Wrestle; remission of my sins

The story of Enos is one about the power of fervent prayer. Prayer is the gateway to the "mighty change" (Mosiah 5:2) that will sweep away the guilt from our lives and align us with the patterns of divine truth. Enos continues in the righteous pathways commended to him by his father, Jacob. However, at the outset of his ministry, he feels driven to seek a spiritual confirmation of his spiritual worthiness—what he calls "the wrestle which I had before God" (verse 2)—and the means whereby his guilt can be "swept away" (verse 6). The contribution of Enos to the ongoing sacred record of the people is limited, mostly, to this single experience with prayer and its impact on his compassionate but futile mission to restore the Lamanites to a place among the covenant people. Nevertheless, righteous prayer is an indispensable element in the process of forgiveness and the dispensing of divine blessings.

*3 Behold, I went to hunt beasts in the forests; and the **words which I had often heard my father speak** concerning eternal life, and the joy of the saints, sunk deep into my heart.*
*4 And my soul hungered; and I kneeled down before my Maker, and I cried unto him in **mighty prayer** and supplication for mine own soul; and all the day long did I cry unto him; yea, and when the night came I did still raise my voice high that it reached the heavens.*

Words which I had often heard my father speak; mighty prayer

Enos remembers the counsel of his father concerning the gospel—and he is thus moved to pray for his own soul all the day and into the night. Which words of our own parents do we remember with thanksgiving and appreciation? Which of our own words will our children and grandchildren, our students and our wards, remember at a time when their souls hunger and they are seeking answers? Let us take care to bring forth words of counsel that our own families will long remember. Let us speak of joy and the blessings of the gospel, of hope, and of the precious gift of the Atonement, of comfort and the promptings of the Holy Ghost in our lives—that the coming generation may hold to the iron rod and live "after the manner of happiness" (2 Nephi 5:27).

*5 And there came a voice unto me, saying: Enos, **thy sins are forgiven** thee, and thou shalt be blessed.*
*6 And I, Enos, knew that God could not lie; wherefore, **my guilt was swept away.***
7 And I said: Lord, how is it done?
*8 And he said unto me: **Because of thy faith in Christ,** whom thou hast never before heard nor seen. And many years pass away before he shall manifest himself in the flesh; wherefore, go to, thy faith hath made thee whole.*

Thy sins are forgiven; my guilt was swept away; because of thy faith in Christ

"How is it done?" is a question natural and appropriate for all who have experienced blessed relief from the crushing burden of sin. The voice of the Savior provides the simple answer: "Because of thy faith in Christ." Of this event, President Ezra Taft Benson has said, "Enos was spiritually healed. Through his mighty supplications to God, he experienced what the faithful of any dispensation can experience, do experience, and must experience if they are to see God and be filled with His Spirit. We should become acquainted with Enos and the entire Book of Mormon, the greatest book in the world—a new witness for Christ" (*Come unto Christ* [Salt Lake City: Deseret Book, 1983], 93).

President Spencer W. Kimball had similar thoughts on the subject of prayer:

> If you have not, I sincerely hope that the time will soon come when, as others before you have, you will struggle in the spirit and cry mightily and covenant sincerely, so that the voice of the Lord God will come into your mind, as it did to Enos, saying:
>
> . . . thy sins are forgiven thee, and thou shalt be blessed.
>
> Because of thy faith in Christ . . .
>
> I will grant unto thee according to thy desires. . . . (Enos 5, 8, 12.)
>
> For this is the ultimate object of all prayer, to bring men closer to God, to give them a new birth, to make them heirs of his kingdom. (*Faith Precedes the Miracle* [Salt Lake City: Deseret Book, 1972], 211)

Enos, concerned for the welfare of his own soul, prays mightily for forgiveness. His guilt is swept away through faith in Jesus Christ. From this we see that a gateway can be opened for each of us: The Lord has provided a way for us to repent. We are to come forward with a broken heart and contrite spirit, confessing and forsaking our sins (see Alma 34:15–17).

> *9 Now, it came to pass that when I had heard these words* ***I began to feel a desire for the welfare of my brethren, the Nephites;*** *wherefore,* ***I did pour out my whole soul*** *unto God for them.*
>
> *10 And while I was thus struggling in the spirit, behold, the voice of the Lord came into my mind again, saying: I will visit thy brethren according to their diligence in keeping my commandments. I have given unto them this land, and it is a holy land; and I curse it not save it be for the cause of iniquity; wherefore, I will visit thy brethren according as I have said; and their transgressions will I bring down with sorrow upon their own heads.*
>
> *11 And after I, Enos, had heard these words, my faith began to be unshaken in the Lord; and I prayed unto him with many long strugglings* ***for my brethren, the Lamanites.***
>
> *12 And it came to pass that after I had prayed and labored with all diligence, the Lord said unto me: I will grant unto thee according to thy desires, because of thy faith.*

after forgiveness, anguish is replaced with charity (love of Christ)

I began to feel a desire for the welfare of my brethren, the Nephites; I did pour out my whole soul for my brethren, the Lamanites

Why is it that repentance and forgiveness result in the desire to bless the lives of others? Why is charity the first tenant in a house purged of sin? Because the love of God fills the vacuum left in a heart when its anguish over personal weakness and shortcomings has been eliminated: "And hope maketh not ashamed; because the love of God is shed abroad in our hearts by the Holy Ghost which is given unto us" (Romans 5:5). The presence of the love of God within us extends to a love of our fellowmen and a desire for them to have the same feelings of joy we have experienced. Missionaries who have prepared themselves with care to labor in the mission field will, in most cases, sense within themselves a deep love for the people they teach—even if they do not know any of these people ahead of time. It is a gift of the Spirit, a miracle of the gospel. Enos had this same experience. Are we truly converted? The depth of our conversion is manifested in our caring for our fellowmen.

Memories: Something Happened Inside

I taught Book of Mormon classes at BYU for eighteen years, and I was always astounded when I would talk about something in class and a student would observe, "Oh, I read that once."

"Oh, you read it once?" I would reply. "Well, I teach this book every year and find things I've never even seen before. And you've read it once?"

So, we had an assignment. I gave extra credit to students who read 2 Nephi 9 or Enos for thirty days in a row before going to bed. A student once asked me: "Why? Why do we need to read it every day? I mean, I'll get it after just a night or two."

"You just read it and see," is all I answered.

Well, one day I was walking to class, and all of a sudden this young man was waiting for me by the door. He literally leapt upon me, gave me a hug, and said, "Oh, Brother Ed, Brother Ed, it's true, it's true!"

I said, "I know it's true, Elder."

"I understand what you mean now," he said. "I read Enos, and on the twenty-first day something happened inside. I wanted everybody to be converted. Brother Ed, I'm thinking of checking out of school and going on my mission today."

"Can't you just wait two more weeks until the semester ends?" I asked.

This young man fell in love with the Book of Mormon because he did what the prophet said, again and again and again, and then he applied it in his life. Until we apply it to our lives, we will not delight in it. We will not enjoy this feeling. We will not be enthusiastic about it. We'll say, "Yeah, I read the book this morning." But when we love it, we'll live it because we apply it.

Nephi understood this principle: "For my soul delighteth in the scriptures, and my heart pondereth them" (2 Nephi 2:15). President Benson also understood: "Now, my beloved brethren and sisters, let us read the Book of Mormon and be convinced that Jesus is the Christ. Let us continually reread the Book of Mormon so that we might more fully come to Christ, be committed to Him, centered in Him, and consumed in Him" ("'Come unto Christ,'" *Ensign,* Nov. 1987, 83). (Ed J. Pinegar)

13–14 Enos supplicated the Lord to preserve the sacred records that they might serve at some future date as an instrument in convincing the Lamanites of the truthfulness of the gospel.

> *15 Wherefore, I knowing that the Lord God was able to preserve our records, I cried unto him continually, for he had said unto me: Whatsoever thing ye shall* ***ask in faith,*** *believing that ye shall receive in the name of Christ,* ***ye shall receive it.***
> *16 And I had faith, and I did cry unto God that he would preserve the records; and he covenanted with me that he would bring them forth unto the Lamanites* ***in his own due time.***

Ask in faith; ye shall receive it in his own due time

One of the eternal principles of the gospel is the efficacy of prayer. Whatever righteous things we ask for in faith will be granted—in the due time of the Lord. That appendage—in the due time of the Lord—is sometimes overlooked by the devout petitioner. All prayers are answered according to the timetable of the Lord, as the following illustration confirms.

Memories: In the Due Time of the Lord

The scriptures make frequent reference to the phrase "in the own due time of the Lord" (see, for example, 1 Nephi 10:3; 2 Nephi 14:26; Enos 1:16)—especially when it comes to such milestone events as the coming forth of the word of the Lord, the gathering of Israel, the redemption of Zion, and the inauguration of the millennial reign.

How long is the "due time of the Lord"? We mortals often yearn to know the Lord's timetable when it comes to our individual circumstances. In some cases, the timing is explicit: "Yea, I would that ye would come forth and harden not your hearts any longer; for behold, now is the time and the day of your salvation; and therefore, if ye will repent and harden not your hearts, *immediately* shall the great plan of redemption be brought about unto you" (Alma 34:31, italics added). At other times, for our own blessing and instruction, the Lord wisely leaves the timing open-ended: "Humble yourselves therefore under the mighty hand of God, that he may exalt you in due time" (1 Peter 5:6).

In our prayers do we not sometimes couch our words in the context of personal urgency and express our desire for the prompt flow of blessings in fulfillment of our needs? I recall as a young boy my first lesson in the efficacy of prayer:

A dense fog descended upon the countryside as our family was en route to a neighboring city one evening for a night at the movies. We crept along the deserted highway scarcely able to see more than a few feet ahead of the car. The headlights made an eerie glow in the impenetrable fog. Suddenly two figures loomed up into view directly before us, standing in the middle of the road. My father slammed on the brakes—but too late. A sickening thud signaled the tragic collision. In shock, we stumbled out of the car to view the two bodies lying by the side of the road. The fog covered everything like a blanket of death. There was panic. The two men who had been hit were still alive but seriously injured.

What to do? I signaled my friend to follow me up the road embankment. We were perhaps eleven years old at the time. Faintly visible were two other vehicles a few yards away, apparently having collided with each other earlier. Moments later several other vehicles plummeted along the highway and crashed into the abandoned cars. Then all was silent. It was a scene of mass confusion. People were wandering around. I suddenly had the urge to pray. So with my friend, I knelt on the embankment and offered a prayer to our Heavenly Father to watch over the injured and protect the rest from further harm. We prayed that all would be well. We prayed for help. Seconds later, the lights of some vehicles came into view on the highway. The vehicles stopped, including one police car. Help had arrived. Things were quickly brought under control. Flares were deployed. An ambulance retrieved the injured and delivered them to the hospital. We later learned they would be all right. It was a night never to be forgotten, and two young boys learned firsthand the power of prayer.

In this case, "the own due time of the Lord" was, miraculously, a matter of only several minutes. In other cases, we are instead left to cultivate patience, strengthen faith, practice long-suffering, and wait upon the Lord until, in His infinite wisdom, the time is right—which, in earthly terms, may seem very long. The Psalmist counseled: "Wait on the LORD: be of good courage, and he shall strengthen thine heart: wait, I say, on the LORD" (Psalms 27:14).

When Enos had his "wrestle" before God concerning forgiveness of his sins, the "due time of the Lord" was a full day: "and all the day long did I cry unto him; yea, and when the night came I did still raise my voice high that it reached the heavens" (verse 4). It was then that the answer to his prayer came, and the "due time of the Lord" was fulfilled rather quickly. For the Prophet Joseph Smith, the trials and tribulations, the prayers and supplications, extended across endless seasons before his mission was completed.

How much patience is reflected in our prayers? How much faith do we bring to bear when it comes to pleading with the Lord on behalf of our families and our own personal lives? When it comes to the "due time of the Lord," do we have the courage to imbue our prayers, in all humility, with the essence of these words from the dedicatory prayer of the Kirtland Temple: "Thy will be done, O Lord, and not ours" (D&C 109:44)? (Richard J. Allen)

17–26 Enos receives a confirmation that his prayers on behalf of the Lamanites will be fulfilled. He testifies to the Nephites of the marvelous things he has experienced. The Lamanites reject the message of the gospel. He uses "exceedingly great plainness of speech" (verse 23) to keep his people, in their prosperity, on the pathway of righteousness. Many wars take place. Enos grows old and brings his ministry to an end around 421 B.C.

> *27 And I soon go to the place of my rest, which is with my Redeemer; for I know that* ***in him I shall rest.*** *And* ***I rejoice*** *in the day when my mortal shall put on immortality, and shall stand before him;* ***then shall I see his face with pleasure,*** *and he will say unto me: Come unto me, ye blessed, there is a place prepared for you in the mansions of my Father. Amen.*

IN HIM I SHALL REST; I REJOICE; THEN SHALL I SEE HIS FACE WITH PLEASURE

Enos' Testimony

Enos ends his account by bearing his testimony about the coming rest of the Lord that awaits him. His last words recorded on the plates raise a question of conscience for us all: Do we look forward with rejoicing to the time when we will be brought into the presence of the Lord? Do we have the certainty that our mortal probation will have been completed with full devotion and acceptable valor? Just prior to his benedictory statement, Enos gives the key to the matter: "And I saw that I must soon go down to my grave, having been wrought upon by the power of God that I must preach and prophesy unto this people, and declare the word according to the truth which is in Christ. And I have declared it in all my days, and have rejoiced in it above that of the world" (verse 26). Enos is about to depart with rejoicing because he has honored his covenant service all his days and rejoiced in the word of God above the things of the world. May we do the same.

THE BOOK OF JAROM

OVERVIEW

Jarom labors diligently to preach the word of God among the people to help them overcome pride and hardness of heart. Their leaders ("mighty men in the faith"—verse 7) help the people defend themselves against the continual attacks of the Lamanites. The prophets, priests, and teachers exhort the people to repent and look forward to the Messiah. The people prosper and spread across the land. At the end of his ministry, around 361 B.C., Jarom commissions his son, Omni, to keep the sacred records.

> *1 NOW behold, I, **Jarom,** write a few words according to the commandment of my father, Enos, that our genealogy may be kept.*

JAROM, SON OF ENOS

Jarom, son of Enos, continues the process of record keeping on the small places of Nephi from around 420 to 361 B.C. His contribution is fairly brief, comprising only fifteen verses, the shortest book in the Book of Mormon. But his words include precious insights concerning the work of the Lord during his time.

> *2 And as these plates are small, and as these things are written for the intent of the benefit of our brethren the Lamanites, wherefore, it must needs be that I write a little; but I shall not write the things of my prophesying, nor of my revelations. For what could I write more than my fathers have written? For have not they revealed the plan of salvation? I say unto you, Yea; and **this sufficeth me.***
> *3 Behold, it is expedient that much should be done among this people, because of the **hardness of their hearts,** and the deafness of their ears, and the blindness of their minds, and the stiffness of their necks; nevertheless, God is exceedingly **merciful** unto them, and has not as yet swept them off from the face of the land.*

THIS SUFFICETH ME; HARDNESS OF THEIR HEARTS; MERCIFUL

Jarom follows in the footsteps of his predecessors by keeping the sacred records of the covenant to preserve the chronicles of the Lord's dealings with His people. We know that Jarom is a spiritual person, for he refers to his own "prophesying" and "revelations" (verse 2). However, he is also humble and self-effacing in that he declines to provide much detail of his own ministry, preferring instead to confirm the witness of those who have gone before him concerning the plan of salvation. However, he provides a compelling portrait of the prevailing tendency among many of his countrymen to fall short of spiritual progress because of their hardness, deafness, blindness, and stiffness. Nevertheless, God is merciful to them.

4–7 Jarom proceeds to give a summary of the ministry of his day: many receive revelations and commune with God in faith. The kings and leaders of his day, being "mighty men in the faith of the Lord" (verse 7), are effective in defending the people against the incursions of the Lamanites. In all of this we see the interplay of a dual pattern among the people: on the one hand, adherence to righteous gospel principles according to the teachings of the prophets, and on the other, the manifestation of "the hardness of their hearts, and the deafness of their ears, and the blindness of their minds, and the stiffness of their necks" (verse 3). For the time being, the Lord allows this dichotomy to prevail. He blesses the people to increase in numbers and prosperity through industry and craftsmanship.

> *8 And **we multiplied exceedingly,** and spread upon the face of the land, and became exceedingly rich in gold, and in silver, and in precious things, and in fine workmanship of wood, in buildings, and in machinery, and also in iron and copper, and brass and steel, making all manner of tools of every kind to till the ground, and weapons of war—yea, the sharp pointed arrow, and the quiver, and the dart, and the javelin, and all preparations for war.*

We multiplied exceedingly

Through the eyes of Jarom we see that the people expand and spread across the land, building mighty cities and a prosperous culture (in the case of the Nephites), or following a warlike and wild existence (in the case of the more numerous Lamanites).

9–10 The Lamanites fail to overcome the Nephites, who are continually being exhorted by the prophets to keep the commandments so that the Lord will preserve them in the land.

> *11 Wherefore, the prophets, and the priests, and the teachers, did labor diligently, **exhorting** with all long-suffering the people to diligence; **teaching** the law of Moses, and the intent for which it was given; **persuading** them to look forward unto the Messiah, and believe in him to come as though he already was. And after this manner did they teach them.*

,

2050233 - CLEVELAND ES(EME

2050233

CLEVELAND ES(EME
New Student

12 And it came to pass that by so doing they kept them from being destroyed upon the face of the land; for ***they did prick their hearts with the word,*** *continually stirring them up unto repentance.*

Exhorting; teaching; persuading; they did prick their hearts with the word

Jarom and his colleagues understand the intent of the law of Moses—to help people look forward to the Messiah, even the Lord Jesus Christ, and believe in Him as if He had already come. The prophet leaders of the Nephites continually teach the people the ways of the Lord—to repent and keep the commandments. Their priesthood agenda is much like it is today: "to preach, teach, expound, exhort, and baptize, and administer the sacrament" (D&C 20:46). The tendency of the people to harden their hearts can be kept in check only by the valiant, proactive ministry of the prophets, priests, and teachers: "for they did prick their hearts with the word, continually stirring them up unto repentance" (verse 12). Thus Jarom confirms that the promptings of the Spirit can prevail above the allure of worldly pride and materialism, if the people will only give heed and obey.

The word of God has power to encourage us to do what is right and to move us to repentance. If we hearken to the word of God, we will be inspired to repent. Let us encourage our families to abide by gospel principles and honor our covenants with the Lord. Let us do better in keeping the commandments and avoiding the sin of pride. Let us bring ourselves to a higher level of obedience and devotion. Our duty to God is too sacred to neglect, our destiny too glorious to ignore.

Walking in the Ways of the Lord

Since Old Testament times, our prophets have admonished us to walk in the ways of the Lord. Jarom recorded, along with the other Book of Mormon prophets, that the leaders taught the people the ways of the Lord. Our prophets today continue to exhort us to righteousness by teaching us the ways of the Lord. Our beloved prophet President Gordon B. Hinckley has recently given us the magnificent talk about the "B's":

Be grateful. There are two little words in the English language that perhaps mean more than all others. They are "thank you." Comparable words are found in every other language. . . .

Be smart. You are moving into the most competitive age the world has ever known. All around you is competition. You need all the education you can get. . . .

Be clean. We live in a world that is filled with filth and sleaze, a world that reeks of evil. It is all around us. It is on the television screen. It is at the movies. It is in the popular literature. It is on the

Internet. You can't afford to watch it, my dear friends. You cannot afford to let that filthy poison touch you. Stay away from it. Avoid it. You can't rent videos and watch them as they portray degrading things. You young men who hold the priesthood of God cannot mix this filth with the holy priesthood. . . .

Be true. Said Shakespeare, "To thine own self be true; and it must follow, as the night the day, thou canst not then be false to any man" (*Hamlet,* I, iii, 78–81). You have a tremendous inheritance. You have a great background of noble ancestry. Many of you are descendants of the pioneers, who died by the hundreds and thousands in testimony of the truth of this work. If they were to look down upon you, they would plead with you: "Be true. Be loyal. Be 'true to the faith that our parents have cherished, true to the truth for which martyrs have perished.'" They would say, "Faith of our fathers, holy faith, we will be true to thee till death . . ." (*Hymns,* 254, 84).

Be humble. There is no place for arrogance in our lives. There is no place for conceit. There is no place for egotism. . . . The Lord has said, "Be thou humble; and the Lord thy God shall lead thee by the hand, and give thee answer to thy prayers . . ." (D&C 112:10).

Be prayerful. You cannot do it alone. I look at this vast congregation, and I know that you are young people who pray, who get on your knees and speak with the Lord. You know that He is the source of all wisdom.

> You need His help, and you know that you need His help. You cannot do it alone. You will come to realize that and recognize that more and more as the years pass. So live that in good conscience you can speak with the Lord. Get on your knees and thank Him for His goodness to you and express to Him the righteous desires of your hearts. The miracle of it all is that He hears. He responds. He answers—not always as we might wish He would answer, but there is no question in my mind that He answers. ("A Prophet's Counsel and Prayer for Youth," *Ensign,* Jan. 2001, 2–10)

Oh how grateful we should be for living prophets whose sole desire is to help us keep on the strait and narrow path. (Ed J. Pinegar)

13–15 Around the year 361 B.C., Jarom delivers the plates into the hands of his son, Omni, and counsels his readers that they can go to the larger plates of Nephi, kept by the kings, if they want additional details concerning the broader history of the people, their wars, etc.

THE BOOK OF
OMNI

OVERVIEW

The words of Omni, Amaron, Chemish, Abinadom, and Amaleki—five of the seven transitional record keepers in the time frame between Jacob and King Benjamin—are included in the Book of Omni. Their overarching message is that the Lord blesses and prospers those who keep His commandments and brings judgment upon those who fail to do so. We are to come unto Christ and be saved. Amaleki reports that Mosiah is led by the Lord to discover the people of Zarahemla, descendants of the Mulekites who fled Jerusalem shortly after the exodus of Lehi and his group. The two groups are united under the leadership of King Mosiah, who brings with him the records of the Jews. The people of Zarahemla had earlier encountered the last of the remaining Jaredites, Coriantumr. Thus all three major population groups in the Book of Mormon—Nephites, Mulekites, and Jaredites—cross paths in the account included in the Book of Omni. King Benjamin succeeds his father, Mosiah, as king.

> *1 BEHOLD, it came to pass that I,* ***Omni,*** *being commanded by my father, Jarom, that I should write somewhat upon these plates, to preserve our genealogy—*

2–3 Omni gives a brief statement of his service as a defender of the people during a long period of alternating war and peace to around 317 B.C.

Omni, Son of Jarom

Omni receives the sacred records from his father, Jarom, around 361 B.C., with the commission that they "be kept according to the commandments of my fathers" (Jarom 1:15). Omni complies with the task to "write somewhat upon these plates, to preserve our genealogy" (verse 1)—yet he does so with a unique confession: "But behold, I of myself am a wicked man, and I have not kept the statutes and the commandments of the Lord as I ought to have done" (verse 2). Wicked or not, Omni is a defender of his people—"Wherefore, in my days, I would that ye should know that I fought much with the sword to preserve my people, the Nephites, from falling into the hands of their enemies, the Lamanites" (verse 2)—and he faithfully guards and preserves the records for some forty-four years during a time of considerable turmoil and warfare. Around 317 B.C. he delegates the task of maintaining the records to his son Amaron.

*4 And now I, **Amaron,** write the things whatsoever I write, which are few, in the book of my father [Omni].*

5–8 In his brief statement, Amaron confirms the covenant principle of the Lord that the people in the promised land will prosper if they keep His commandments and decline if they do not. The greater part of the wicked Nephites have been destroyed by their enemies.

Amaron, Record Keeper

By the command of God, the records of the people have been compiled and passed down from generation to generation—from the exodus of Lehi around 600 B.C. until the time of Mormon and, finally, to his son Moroni, who buries the plates around A.D. 421. Between the time of Jacob (son of Lehi and brother of Nephi) and the reign of King Benjamin (around 130 B.C.), a sequence of seven transitional curators of the sacred records preserves the word of God in abbreviated format. One of these is Amaron, who makes his short entry around 279 B.C., on the day he delivers the plates to his brother, Chemish (see Omni 1:9). Amaron's message makes clear that "the more wicked part of the Nephites were destroyed" in his day (verse 5), while "he [the Lord] did spare the righteous that they should not perish" (verse 7). The essence of Amaron's warning concerning the wicked is preserved in one verse: "For the Lord would not suffer, after he had led them out of the land of Jerusalem and kept and preserved them from falling into the hands of their enemies, yea, he would not suffer that the words should not be verified, which he spake unto our fathers, saying that: Inasmuch as ye will not keep my commandments ye shall not prosper in the land" (verse 6).

*8 And it came to pass that I [Amaron] did deliver the plates unto my brother **Chemish.***
*9 Now I, **Chemish,** write what few things I write, in the same book with my brother; for behold, I saw the last which he wrote, that he wrote it with his own hand; and he wrote it in the day that he delivered them unto me. And after this manner we keep the records, for it is according to the commandments of our fathers. And I make an end.*

Chemish, Scribe of Few Words

All seven of the record keepers following Jacob and continuing down to the time of King Benjamin, are fairly economical with words. Surely the most taciturn is Chemish, who simply states that he has observed his brother writing in the records: "according to the commandments of our fathers. And I make an end" (verse 9). Of all the Book of Mormon scribes, Chemish contributes the fewest words to the spiritual record. It is possible that he and his colleagues contribute more material to the historical account of their times preserved on the larger plates.

We can perhaps extract from Chemish a lesson about our own personal journal-writing: Should we not strive to pass on to our posterity a more abundant account of our spiritual dealings "according to the commandments of our fathers"?

> *10 Behold, I,* ***Abinadom,*** *am the son of Chemish. Behold, it came to pass that I saw much war and contention between my people, the Nephites, and the Lamanites; and I, with my own sword, have taken the lives of many of the Lamanites in the defence of my brethren.*
> *11 And behold, the record of this people is engraven upon plates which is had by the kings, according to the generations; and I know of no revelation save that which has been written, neither prophecy; wherefore, that which is sufficient is written. And I make an end.*

Abinadom, Son of Chemish

Abinadom is the next in line among the seven transitional record keepers between the time of Jacob and the reign of King Benjamin (around 130 B.C.). Abinadom's contribution to the record consists of just two verses, which inform us of the wars and contentions of his day (he being an active defender of the people) and of the fact that he is aware of no revelation or prophecy beyond that which is already written.

> *12 Behold, I am* ***Amaleki,*** *the son of Abinadom. Behold, I will speak unto you somewhat concerning* ***Mosiah,*** *who was made king over the land of Zarahemla; for behold, he being warned of the Lord that he should flee out of the land of Nephi, and as many as would hearken unto the voice of the Lord should also depart out of the land with him, into the wilderness—*

Amaleki, Last Record Keeper before Benjamin

Amaleki, the son of Abinadom, is the last in the sequence of seven transitional curators of the sacred records extending from the time of Jacob to the time of King Benjamin (about 130 B.C.). Amaleki (pronounced A-mal-ak-eye) preserves for us what little information we have concerning the first Mosiah, a Nephite who was commanded by the Lord to leave the land of Nephi with his followers and travel through the wilderness, eventually uniting with the people of Zarahemla (the

Mulekites). Mosiah brought with him the plates of brass "which contained the record of the Jews" (verse 14). Presumably, Amaleki travels with Mosiah and brings with him the small plates of Nephi on which he records his brief account, comprising only nineteen verses of the Book of Mormon (see Omni 1:12–30).

Mosiah I, Unifier of Nations

Mosiah, father of King Benjamin and grandfather of the second Mosiah (the last of the Nephite kings), is a descendant of Lehi. He lives in the southern area of the country where Lehi and his group from Jerusalem first settle in the promised land. In those early days, Nephi and his righteous followers, having been warned of the Lord, separate themselves from Laman and Lemuel for reasons of safety (see 2 Nephi 5:5–7). The animosity of the Lamanite branch of the family against the Nephites continues for many generations so that Mosiah is likewise warned of the Lord to flee into the wilderness to preserve his life from the enemies. Mosiah's willingness to heed the counsel of the Lord is evidence of the quality of his character. The Book of Mormon provides scant detail concerning Mosiah's life—there are only a dozen verses of scripture about him from the hand of his contemporary, Amaleki, one of the curators of the sacred text (see Omni 1:12–23). We can conclude that Mosiah is active in the period between around 279 B.C. to 130 B.C.

> *13 And it came to pass that he [Mosiah] did according as the Lord had commanded him. And they departed out of the land into the wilderness, as many as would hearken unto the voice of the Lord; and they were led by many preachings and prophesyings. And they were admonished continually by the word of God; and they were led by the power of his arm, through the wilderness until they came down into the land which is called the land of* ***Zarahemla.***
>
> *14 And they discovered a people, who were called the people of Zarahemla. Now, there was great* ***rejoicing*** *among the people of Zarahemla; and also Zarahemla did rejoice exceedingly, because the Lord had sent the people of Mosiah with the* ***plates of brass*** *which contained the record of the Jews.*

Zarahemla; rejoicing; plates of brass

The information contained in these and the succeeding verses, though very brief, is exceptionally important, for it confirms the coming together of two of the three major populations (Nephites and Mulekites) covered by the record of the Book of Mormon—plus information about an earlier contact between the last of the Jaredites (the third main group of emigrants) and the Mulekite people. Mosiah soon discovers that the people of Zarahemla have origins closely paralleling his ancestral source—Lehi and his family—with one important exception: the Mulekites have brought with them none of the records concerning their genealogy or their scriptural foundations. The appearance of Mosiah and his group, therefore, engenders considerable excitement among the people. In his wisdom, Mosiah has appropriated the sacred records before fleeing the land of Nephi and has carried them forth to preserve the written language of his forebears and the record of God's dealings with His people. We can only imagine how much we ourselves would rejoice if, believing in the traditions of prophetic discourse and having been deprived for generations of the scriptures, we suddenly found ourselves in possession of the priceless treasure of God's word to His children.

Zarahemla, Leader of the Mulekites

Readers of the Book of Mormon are disposed to think of Zarahemla as a place—the capital city of the Nephite nation. Logically so, since the name Zarahemla is used some 150 times in this volume of scripture, overwhelmingly in regard to a geographical location. However, there is also a man named Zarahemla—a descendant of Mulek, the lone surviving son of king Zedekiah of Judah (see Mosiah 25:2). The Mulekites have been led out of Jerusalem concurrent with the Babylonian conquest of 587 B.C., just over a decade after Lehi's exodus. When Mosiah I is commanded of the Lord to leave the land of Nephi—the area where Lehi originally settle—he and his group are guided northward to a city populated by the descendants of Mulek and governed by one called Zarahemla—which is also the name of the city (see Omni 1:14–16). We know little about the personality of Zarahemla, except that he places great value in the scriptural records of the Lord and apparently accedes humbly to the leadership of Mosiah, who is appointed king over the united peoples (see Omni 1:19).

> *15 Behold, it came to pass that Mosiah discovered that the people of Zarahemla came out from Jerusalem at the time that **Zedekiah,** king of Judah, was carried away captive into Babylon.*
>
> *16 And they journeyed in the wilderness, and were brought by the hand of the Lord across the great waters, into the land where Mosiah discovered them; and they had dwelt there from that time forth.*

Zedekiah, Last King of Judah

Zedekiah was the last king of Judah. He was "one and twenty years old when he began to reign, and reigned eleven years in Jerusalem" (2 Chronicles 36:11). Nephi informs us that it was during the first year of Zedekiah's rule that Lehi was called to warn the people of Jerusalem about the impending judgments of God about to befall them (see 2 Nephi 1:4). Zedekiah's tenure ends with the Babylonian conquest of Jerusalem in 587 B.C. Jeremiah reports: "And the king of Babylon slew the sons of Zedekiah before his eyes: he slew also all the princes of Judah in Riblah. Then he put out the eyes of Zedekiah; and the king of Babylon bound him in chains, and carried him to Babylon, and put him in prison till the day of his death" (Jeremiah 52:10–11; compare 2 Kings 25:7). The implication is that all the sons of Zedekiah perish in this way; however, the Book of Mormon makes clear that Zedekiah's youngest son, Mulek, survives the ordeal and is guided by the Lord to the promised land, where he establishes a colony and founds a new nation (see Helaman 8:21). Mormon gives the geographical orientation as follows: "Now the land south was called Lehi, and the land north was called Mulek, which was after the son of Zedekiah; for the Lord did bring Mulek into the land north, and Lehi into the land south" (Helaman 6:10). When the Nephite leader Mosiah I is commanded of the Lord to flee from the land south (the land of Lehi, also called the land of Nephi) sometime in the period 279 B.C. to 130 B.C., he and his loyal followers are guided northward to Zarahemla, where the Mulekites eventually settle (see Omni 1:12–16). Thereafter the Mulekites and the Nephites are united as one nation.

Mulekites & Nephites become one nation.

17 And at the time that Mosiah discovered them, they had become exceedingly numerous. Nevertheless, they had had many wars and serious contentions, and had fallen by the sword from time to time; and ***their language had become corrupted;*** *and they had brought* ***no records*** *with them; and they denied the being of their Creator; and Mosiah, nor the people of Mosiah, could understand them.*
18 But it came to pass that Mosiah caused that they should be taught in his language. And it came to pass that after they were taught in the ***language of Mosiah,*** *Zarahemla gave a genealogy of his fathers, according to his memory; and they are written, but not in these plates.*

Their language had become corrupted; no records; language of Mosiah

From the record we learn that the people of Zarahemla "denied the being of their Creator" (Omni 1:17) and have to be instructed in the written and spoken language of the Nephites, their language having become "corrupted" (verse 17). Once the people are able to communicate with Mosiah and his followers, he is able to orient them concerning the history and lineage of the Nephites. Thereafter, the Mulekites of Zarahemla are absorbed into the Nephite flow of events.

The cultural/linguistic information provided by this historic account is most interesting. Over a period of several hundred years, the Mulekites, having no written record, experience a corruption and decline of their language. Doubtless it has transformed itself into quite a different dialect than the original mother tongue. Mosiah turns out to be a divinely appointed language teacher. He instructs the people in his language so that all can understand one another. No doubt he also instructs the people in the principles of the gospel in order to correct their lapse of testimony, for, prior to his coming, they are in a state of mind where "they denied the being of their Creator" (verse 17).

> *19 And it came to pass that the people of Zarahemla, and of* ***Mosiah,*** *did unite together;*
> *and Mosiah was* ***appointed to be their king.***

MOSIAH; APPOINTED TO BE THEIR KING

So much does Mosiah endear himself to the hearts and minds of the people of Zarahemla that he is appointed king over the united population. As the righteous unifier of nations, he is responsible for blending together the two streams of peoples—Nephites and Mulekites—into one people under God. Mosiah's son and successor, Benjamin, carries on his father's righteous leadership and becomes one of the greatest prophet-rulers in the Book of Mormon.

> *20 And it came to pass in the days of Mosiah, there was a* ***large stone*** *brought unto him*
> *with engravings on it; and he did interpret the engravings by the gift and power of God.*
> *21 And they gave an account of one* ***Coriantumr,*** *and the slain of his people. And*
> *Coriantumr was discovered by the people of Zarahemla; and he dwelt with them for*
> *the space of nine moons.*
> *22 It also spake a few words concerning his fathers. And his first parents came out from*
> *the* ***tower,*** *at the time the Lord confounded the language of the people; and the severity*
> *of the Lord fell upon them according to his judgments, which are just; and their bones*
> *lay scattered in the land northward.*

LARGE STONE; CORIANTUMR; TOWER

During his reign as king, the people bring Mosiah an archaeological artifact—a "large stone"—displaying engravings, which Mosiah is able to interpret "by the gift and power of God" (verse 20). The stone tells of the last days of Coriantumr, the final Jaredite ruler, who has been discovered by the people of Zarahemla and dwells among them for the better part of a year (see Omni 1:21)—

perhaps in the time frame around 500 B.C. Thus the story of Mosiah also blends with the history of the Jaredites, who have been led by the Lord to the northern part of the land of promise at the time of the Tower of Babel—approximately 2000 B.C. It is within the lifetime and tenure of Mosiah, therefore, that we find the footprints of all three major migrant peoples of the Book of Mormon—Jaredites to the north, Mulekites in the central area, and Nephites to the south—crossing in the sands of time. It is Mosiah's grandson, also named Mosiah, who will translate the twenty-four gold plates later discovered by Limhi's group, giving the history of the Jaredites written by the prophet Ether (Ether 4:1; 13:14; 15:33; Mosiah 21:26–28) and incorporated into Moroni's abridgment called the Book of Ether (see Ether 1:2). Thanks to Mosiah and his successor archivists, the origins and histories of these peoples have been preserved for our edification and learning.

> *23 Behold, I, Amaleki, was born in the days of Mosiah; and I have lived to see his*
> *death; and* ***Benjamin,*** *his son, reigneth in his stead.*
> *24 And behold, I have seen, in the days of king* ***Benjamin,*** *a serious war and much*
> *bloodshed between the Nephites and the Lamanites. But behold, the Nephites did*
> *obtain much advantage over them; yea, insomuch that king* ***Benjamin*** *did drive them*
> *out of the land of Zarahemla.*
> *25 And it came to pass that I began to be old; and, having no seed, and* ***knowing king***
> ***Benjamin to be a just man before the Lord,*** *wherefore, I shall deliver up these*
> *plates unto him, exhorting all men to come unto God, the Holy One of Israel, and*
> *believe in prophesying, and in revelations, and in the ministering of angels, and in*
> *the gift of speaking with tongues, and in the gift of interpreting languages, and in all*
> *things which are good; for there is nothing which is good save it comes from the Lord;*
> *and that which is evil cometh from the devil.*

Amaleki (records) ↓ King Benjamin

BENJAMIN, A JUST MAN BEFORE THE LORD

Here we have an introduction to King Benjamin, one of the most beloved personalities in the Book of Mormon. Amaleki closes the transitional period by giving the sacred records to Benjamin as he bears his final testimony about the Savior, about the ministering of angels, and about the gifts of the Spirit.

> *26 And now, my beloved brethren, I would that ye should* ***come unto Christ,*** *who is*
> *the Holy One of Israel, and partake of his salvation, and the power of his redemption.*
> *Yea, come unto him, and offer your whole souls as an offering unto him, and continue*
> *in fasting and praying, and* ***endure to the end;*** *and as the Lord liveth ye will be saved.*

Come unto Christ; endure to the end

Across the centuries of time comes to us this brief, final exhortation of Amaleki. His counsel is the same as that of all prophets in every dispensation, including our own: Come unto Christ, give unto Him an offering of your whole soul, and endure to the end. We know little about Amaleki the person, but we know that he speaks the word of God, and we can apply his counsel with the certain knowledge that it is true, and that great blessings will come to us if we do so.

A Missionary Example

Missionary work, family work, Church work, and life's work are about inviting all to come unto Christ. This is the purpose of the Church and kingdom of God. This is what the prophets do. This is the main thrust of the Book of Mormon. Moroni ends with the plea, "come unto Christ, and be perfected in Him . . . " (Moroni 10:32).

How do you come unto Christ? Faith in Jesus Christ, taking upon us the name of Jesus Christ, repentance and baptism through Jesus Christ, and the gift of the Holy Ghost from God—these are the principles of the gospel that allow us to come unto Christ. We apply the Atonement to our lives and to the lives of our investigators as we teach them. This is the most incredible thing you will ever see in conversion. When the power of God is placed in an anointed servant of God, and that servant gives it by the power and authority of God to someone who is honest in heart, you can watch that person change before your very eyes. All of a sudden, their eyes will start to light up. They'll say, "Oh yes, I see, tell me more!" And in this process of enlightenment, guess what they receive? The Spirit.

They know who they are. They recognize where they came from—"I am a child of God and I now understand his plan for me, and I need it in my life. I want to be baptized." (Ed J. Pinegar, Adapted from *Especially for Missionaries,* 4 vols. [American Fork, UT: Covenant Communications, 1997], 3.) (Ed J. Pinegar)

27–29 Amaleki ends his record by telling of a group of individuals who leave Zarahemla in his day to go up to the land of their origin where Lehi originally settled. Because of contention in the party, many are slain and the remainder return to Zarahemla. The party is then reconstituted and sets out once again.

> *30 And I, Amaleki, had a* ***brother,*** *who also went with them; and I have not since known concerning them. And I am about to lie down in my grave; and these plates are full. And I make an end of my speaking.*

Omni 1:30

BROTHER

Though his account is short, Amaleki is a faithful and devoted servant of the Lord who plays a vital part in the process of ensuring continuity of the word of God down through time. In this context, Amaleki also alludes to the fact that his brother (unnamed) has participated in the exploratory group of men desiring to return to the land of Nephi, the land of their origin. It is a man named Zeniff who leads the group back to the land of Nephi, his grandson Limhi being responsible for discovering the records of the Jaredites contained on the twenty-four gold plates of Ether (see Mosiah 8:9; 21:27). Thus Amaleki's final words anticipate a future event that will lead to the addition of valuable scriptural treasures to be preserved and made available for modern-day readers.

CONCLUDING THOUGHTS

The transitional record keepers bridging the time frame between Jacob and King Benjamin cover a great many years in very few pages. Jarom, son of Enos and great-grandson of Lehi, conveys the engraved records to his son, Omni, around 361 B.C. The period of time subsequently covered by the ministry of Omni, Omni's son Amaron, Amaron's brother Chemish, Abinadom the son of Chemish, and Abinadom's son Amaleki, is evidently somewhat over two centuries long (to around 130 B.C.). The entire transitional period from Enos to Amaleki is covered in around seven pages of modern text, of which the last major part is written by Amaleki. Amaleki is a personal witness to the events surrounding the life of the first Mosiah and his faithful group, who are led to safety by the Lord and discover the parallel civilization founded by immigrants who fled Jerusalem through divine intervention at the time of the Babylonian conquest. Amaleki's testimony reflects the joy of the enlightened citizens of the newly discovered city and their leader Zarahemla when they once again have access to the brass plates and a record of their forefathers (see Omni 1:14). We learn that the last vestige of a third civilization, the people of Ether (the Jaredites), including examples of their records, have come to the attention of the people of Zarahemla some time before Mosiah comes onto the scene. Thus we see the Lord's design in bringing together His word for the blessing of mankind. Though short, Amaleki's account contains a priceless witness concerning "Christ, who is the Holy One of Israel" (verse 26) and a memorable exhortation to his readers to honor the covenant principles "and endure to the end; and as the Lord liveth ye will be saved" (verse 26). Thereafter, Amaleki turns the sacred chronicle over to King Benjamin, the son of Mosiah. Thus the continuity of testimony pointing to Christ is preserved uninterrupted.

THE
WORDS OF MORMON

OVERVIEW

Mormon makes an abridgment of the history of the people from the time of Lehi to the time of King Benjamin. He inserts the small plates of Nephi into his abridgment "for a wise purpose" known to God, and then continues to finish his work preparatory to turning the records over to his son Moroni. King Benjamin defends his people from the Lamanites, puts down false preachers, and establishes peace in the land once again.

1–4 The time flashes forward to around A.D. 385. Most of the Nephite civilization has been destroyed. Mormon reports that he is about to convey the sacred records to his son Moroni. He (Mormon) has abridged the plates of Nephi concerning the events from Lehi down to King Benjamin when he discovers the smaller plates of Nephi containing the prophecies of the coming of Christ and other inspiring words of the prophets. Mormon includes the smaller plates of Nephi in his archive and adds his own account to them.

> *6 But behold, I shall take these plates, which contain these* ***prophesyings and revelations,*** *and put them with the remainder of my record, for they are* ***choice*** *unto me; and I know they will be* ***choice*** *unto my brethren.*
> *7 And I do this* ***for a wise purpose;*** *for thus it whispereth me, according to the* ***workings of the Spirit*** *of the Lord which is in me. And now, I do not know all things; but the Lord knoweth all things which are to come; wherefore, he worketh in me to do according to his will.*

Prophesyings and revelations; choice; for a wise purpose; workings of the Spirit

It is an attribute of Christ-centered living to follow the promptings of the Spirit with full faith in the Lord's divine will and wisdom, just as Mormon does in compiling his record. When Mormon, the principal compiler and abridger of the sacred records, discovers the smaller plates of Nephi among the engraved annals of his people, he feels inspired to include these remarkable spiritual testimonies with his abridgment "for a wise purpose" (Words of Mormon 1:7). He is pleased with the character of the added records—which cover the same time period as the larger plates of Nephi—"because of the prophecies of the coming of Christ" (verse 4) contained therein. Mormon's successor, his son Moroni, carries this same theme into his summary overview of the purposes of the completed work: "And also to the convincing of the Jew and Gentile that Jesus is the Christ, the Eternal God, manifesting himself unto all nations" (from the Title Page to the Book of Mormon).

Elder Jeffrey R. Holland argues convincingly that the "wise purpose" behind the inspired action of preserving and including the smaller plates of Nephi in the final compilation of the Book of Mormon—beyond resolving the problem of the lost 116 pages of the initial translation—was to memorialize and emphasize the testimony of three key witnesses to the truth of the gospel: Nephi, Jacob, and Isaiah.

> In keeping with this same covenantal principle, it is interesting to note that there were three earlier witnesses—special witnesses—not only of the divine origins of the Book of Mormon but also of Divinity himself. These early witnesses were Nephi, Jacob, and Isaiah, and it is not by coincidence that their testimonies appear so conspicuously at the beginning of this ancient record.
>
> Their opening testimonies come in the Book of Mormon from what we know as the small plates of Nephi. At least six times in the Book of Mormon, the phrase *for a wise purpose* is used in reference to the making, writing, and preserving of the small plates. One such wise purpose—the most obvious one—was to compensate for the future loss of 116 pages of manuscript translated by the Prophet Joseph Smith from the first part of Mormon's abridgment of the large plates of Nephi.
>
> But there is another "wise purpose" for the inclusion of these smaller plates in the highly edited material that would constitute the Book of Mormon. In Doctrine and Covenants 10:45 the Lord declared to Joseph Smith, "Behold, there are many things engraven upon the [small] plates of Nephi which do throw *greater views* upon my gospel."
>
> All the details and information contained in those first 116 pages of manuscript are not yet known. What *is* known is that most of the "greater views" of the gospel found in the teachings of the small plates of Nephi come from the personal declarations of these three great prophetic witnesses of the premortal Jesus Christ—Nephi, Jacob, and Isaiah. These three doctrinal and visionary voices make clear at the very outset of the Book of Mormon why it is "another testament of Jesus Christ."
>
> In declaring the special preparation these three had for receiving and teaching such "greater views" of the gospel, Nephi revealed the most persuasive qualification of all: They had seen the premortal Jesus Christ . . . [2 Nephi 11:2–4.].

> One could argue convincingly that the primary purpose for recording, preserving, and then translating the small plates of Nephi was to bring forth to the dispensation of the fulness of times the testimony of these three witnesses. Their writings constitute a full 135 of the 145 pages from the small plates. By the time one has read Nephi, Jacob, and Isaiah in these first pages, a strong foundation has been laid for what Nephi called "the doctrine of Christ." [2 Nephi 31:21.] It is a foundation conforming perfectly to the title page of the Book of Mormon. After reading these three witnesses from the small plates of Nephi, the reader knows two things in bold relief: that Jesus is the Christ, the Son of the Living God, and that God will keep his covenants and promises with the remnants of the house of Israel. Those two themes constitute the two principal purposes of the Book of Mormon, and they are precisely the introductory themes addressed by Nephi, Jacob, and Isaiah.
>
> Obviously it would be exciting if someone were one day to find the lost 116 pages of the original manuscript of the Book of Mormon. But whatever those pages contain, it could not be more important or more fundamental to the purpose of the Book of Mormon than the teachings of these three prophets recorded on the small plates. Standing like sentinels at the gate of the book, Nephi, Jacob, and Isaiah admit us into the scriptural presence of the Lord. (*Christ and the New Covenant: The Messianic Message of the Book of Mormon* [Salt Lake City: Deseret Book, 1997], 34–36)

The Lord knows all things. Mormon follows the Lord's promptings obediently (see Words of Mormon 1:7). When we trust in the Lord in faith and obey His counsel, we—and everyone we serve—will be blessed.

For a wise purpose

Mormon includes the small plates of Nephi in his record "for a wise purpose" as inspired by the Spirit. He does not know why but seeks to do the will of the Lord. Little does he know of the future tragic loss of the first 116 pages translated from the larger plates of Nephi—and the need to provide an alternative record of a more spiritual character concerning the same time period in the Book of Mormon account.

The Story of the 116 Lost Pages

> Martin Harris, having written some one hundred and sixteen pages for Joseph, asked permission of my son to carry the manuscript home with him, in order

to let his wife read it, as he hoped it might have a salutary effect upon her feelings.

Joseph was willing to gratify his friend as far as he could consistently, and he inquired of the Lord to know if he might do as Martin Harris had requested, but was refused. With this, Mr. Harris was not altogether satisfied, and, at his urgent request, Joseph inquired again, but received a second refusal. Still, Martin Harris persisted as before, and Joseph applied again, but the last answer was not like the two former ones. In this, the Lord permitted Martin Harris to take the manuscript home with him, on condition that he would exhibit it to none, save five individuals whom he had mentioned, and who belonged to his own family.

Mr. Harris was delighted with this, and bound himself in a written covenant of the most solemn nature, that he would strictly comply with the injunctions which he had received. Which being done, he took the manuscript and went home.

Joseph did not suspect but that his friend would keep his faith, consequently, he gave himself no uneasiness with regard to the matter. . . .

[After several weeks with no news from Martin Harris, Joseph travels a great distance to meet with him and check on the manuscript.]

"Martin, have you lost that manuscript? Have you broken your oath, and brought down condemnation upon my head as well as your own?"

"Yes; it is gone," replied Martin, "and I know not where."

"Oh, my God!" said Joseph, clinching his hands. "All is lost! all is lost! What shall I do? I have sinned—it is I who tempted the wrath of God. I should have been satisfied with the first answer which I received from the Lord; for he told me that it was not safe to let the writing go out of my possession." He wept and groaned, and walked the floor continually.

At length he told Martin to go back and search again.

"No," said Martin, "it is all in vain; for I have ripped open beds and pillows; and I know it is not there."

"Then must I," said Joseph, "return with such a tale as this? I dare not do it. And how shall I appear before the Lord? Of what rebuke am I not worthy from the angel of the Most High?"

I besought him not to mourn so, for perhaps the Lord would forgive him, after a short season of humiliation and repentance. But what could I do to comfort

> him, when he saw all the family in the same situation of mind as himself; for sobs and groans, and the most bitter lamentations filled the house. However, Joseph was more distressed than the rest, as he better understood the consequences of disobedience. And he continued pacing back and forth, meantime weeping and grieving, until about sunset, when, by persuasion, he took a little nourishment.
>
> The next morning, he set out for home. We parted with heavy hearts, for it now appeared that all which we had so fondly anticipated, and which had been the source of so much secret gratification, had in a moment fled, and fled forever. (Lucy Mack Smith, *History of Joseph Smith by His Mother* [Salt Lake City: Stevens & Wallis, Inc., 1945], 124–129)

8–16 Mormon continues to finish his record, taken from the plates of Nephi. Amaleki conveys his record to King Benjamin, who puts it with the other records of historical interest. Mormon prays that the records will be preserved, "for there are great things written upon them, out of which my people and their brethren shall be judged at the great and last day, according to the word of God which is written" (verse 11). King Benjamin defends his people from the Lamanites and, with the help of prophets, defeats the work of false preachers.

> *17 For behold, king **Benjamin was a holy man,** and he did reign over his people in righteousness; and there were many holy men in the land, and they did speak the **word of God** with power and with authority; and they did use much sharpness because of the stiffneckedness of the people—*
>
> *18 Wherefore, with the help of these, king Benjamin, by laboring with all the might of his body and the faculty of his whole soul, and also the prophets, did once more establish **peace in the land.***

Benjamin was a holy man; word of God; peace in the land

The fruit of the Spirit is peace. The harvest of gospel living is peace. Like Melchizedek, King Benjamin is a king of peace—both of these monarchs having taken their pattern of leadership from the Prince of Peace Himself, the Lord Jesus Christ. The peace of the gospel comes through the power of fervent prayer administered for the understanding of the word of God.

THE BOOK OF
MOSIAH

BOOK OVERVIEW

The reign of King Mosiah, beloved prophet-leader, is unfolded. His benedictory sermon is given. The people experience a mighty change and covenant to take upon themselves the name of Jesus Christ. King Benjamin's son, Mosiah, succeeds his father around 124 B.C. and rules in righteousness. Mosiah sends an expeditionary force under the leadership of Ammon to discover the state of affairs of the people of Zeniff, who left around 200 B.C. to settle in the land of the Lamanites. Ammon discovers Limhi, grandson of Zeniff, who is currently the king over the Nephite colony. An account of the experiences of Zeniff and his successors is given. They constantly struggle to preserve themselves from Lamanite attacks and oppression. Noah succeeds his father and rules in wickedness with his priests. The prophet Abinadi is sent by the Lord to call the people to repentance and warn them of impending destruction. Abinadi is martyred by fire. Alma believes the words of Abinadi and establishes the Church at the Waters of Mormon. The Lamanites attack and the colony is dispersed. Noah is burned to death by his own people in fulfillment of Abinadi's prophecy.

Limhi becomes king and establishes an uneasy peace with the Lamanites, who increase their oppression of the people. Ammon arrives and helps Limhi and his people to escape, and they return to Zarahemla around 121 B.C. Alma and his people suffer painful burdens at the hands of the Lamanites, now in league with the renegade priests of Noah. Alma and his people escape through the help of the Lord and return to Zarahemla around 120 B.C. Mosiah authorizes Alma to establish the Church throughout the land. Mosiah translates the twenty-four plates of gold written by Ether and discovered by Limhi's people. Alma the Younger and the sons of Mosiah rebel against the Church. An angel of God intervenes and turns them from their destructive course. The sons of Mosiah depart on a mission among the Lamanites. Mosiah establishes a system of elected judges among the people. Alma the Younger is appointed the first chief judge of the land around 91 B.C. Peace is preserved. Alma the Elder and Mosiah both pass away.

CHAPTER 1

OVERVIEW

King Benjamin instructs his three sons in the language and prophecies of their forefathers and exhorts them to hold to the word of God in all diligence. The sacred records kept over the generations have preserved their spiritual heritage. Benjamin confers the kingship upon his son Mosiah, who is to convene the people on the morrow so that they might hear the royal proclamation and also receive a new name to distinguish them from all other peoples brought by the Lord from the land of Jerusalem. Mosiah receives the sacred records.

> *1 AND now there was no more contention in all the land of Zarahemla, among all the people who belonged to king Benjamin, so that king Benjamin had continual peace all the remainder of his days.*

King Benjamin, Monarch of the Mighty Change

King Benjamin is one of the most beloved and oft-quoted personalities in the Book of Mormon. His valedictory discourse to his people, given about 124 B.C. to articulate the essential Christ-centered life of service and spiritual integrity (see Mosiah 2:9 to 4:30), is among the most celebrated gospel sermons ever recorded. Benjamin is the son of the first Mosiah, who is commanded of the Lord to depart from the land of Nephi with as many as will hearken unto the voice of the Lord, to preserve their lives and the records of their ancestors. Guided by the Lord through the wilderness, they find their way northward to safety in Zarahemla, where they join with the descendants of Mulek—"for the Lord did bring Mulek [surviving son of King Zedekiah of Judah] into the land north, and Lehi into the land south" (Helaman 6:10). Mosiah is named king over the union of the two peoples and serves in righteousness and devotion all his days, conferring the kingdom in his old age upon his son.

King Benjamin receives custody of the sacred records from Amaleki, and, like his father, serves the people with distinction, having established peace in the land of Zarahemla through outstanding leadership and military prowess: "And he did fight with the strength of his own arm, with the sword of Laban" (Words of Mormon 1:13). He teaches his three sons—Mosiah, Helorum, and Helaman—the supreme importance of the scriptures (see Mosiah 1:5–6). Toward the end of his life, Benjamin appoints his son Mosiah to be king of the land. In Benjamin's farewell address to his assembled people—much of it imparted to him previously by a heavenly messenger in the night—he fulfills his promise to give them a new name, i.e., the name of Christ. So powerful are the words of King Benjamin that his people experience a complete spiritual transformation—"a mighty change" (Mosiah 5:2).

EVIDENCE: King Benjamin had continual peace—"Wordprint": Internal Proof of the Book of Mormon

The small plates were written by two primary authors, Nephi and Jacob, with large quotes from

Isaiah. When we begin Mosiah the book speaks in the third person, for this is now Mormon's abridgement. Authors have different styles of writing. This is called wordprint or stylometry—a concept unknown to the Prophet Joseph Smith. Note the following:

> John L. Hilton [leader of a group of scientists in Berkeley, California] approaches texts quite differently, letting his computer do the analysis by counting and comparing selected words in defined relationships. It has been demonstrated elsewhere that individual authors leave a unique stamp or wordprint on their writings that can usually be detected through this kind of analysis. On the basis of this finding, Hilton asserts that neither Joseph Smith nor any of the other candidates for authorship of the book set forward by critics could have written the Book of Mormon. Their wordprints are closer to each other than to any part of the book. Furthermore, the parts of the book that claim to be authored by different prophets do in fact have distinguishable wordprints. Statistical analysis of the text confirms Joseph Smith's explanation of the book's origins. (Noel B. Reynolds, ed., *Book of Mormon Authorship Revisited: The Evidence for Ancient Origins* [Provo: Foundation for Ancient Research and Mormon Studies, 1997]; compare *Echoes,* 132–135)

> *2 And it came to pass that he had three sons; and he called their names Mosiah, and Helorum, and Helaman. And he caused that they should be taught in all the* ***language of his fathers,*** *that thereby they might become* ***men of understanding;*** *and that they might know concerning the* ***prophecies*** *which had been spoken by the mouths of their fathers, which were delivered them by the hand of the Lord.*
> *3 And he also taught them concerning the records which were engraven on the plates of brass, saying: My sons, I would that ye should remember that were it not for these plates, which contain these records and these* ***commandments,*** *we must have suffered in ignorance, even at this present time, not knowing the* ***mysteries of God.***

Language of his fathers; men of understanding; prophecies; commandments; mysteries of God

There is no more valuable legacy for parents to leave to their children than to teach them to value, search, understand, and heed the word of the God as embodied in the holy scriptures and in the spoken word of God's chosen servants. King Benjamin, being both a great spiritual leader and political leader, cultivates an environment where his people can enjoy "continual peace" (Mosiah 1:1) throughout his tenure. As he reaches the end of his mortal sojourn, he calls his three sons to his side and instructs them in many important matters, the majority of which "are not written in this book" (Mosiah 1:8). What Mormon singles out from among King Benjamin's instructions to his sons is his impressive benedictory statement concerning the central place of the word of God in the plan of salvation. Thus King Benjamin causes his sons to be taught in the language of their forefathers, that they might become men of a sound understanding and come to know of the prophecies of their fathers and the indispensable value of the records (see Mosiah 1:2).

Mysteries of God

What is meant by the "mysteries of God"? Essentially, the mysteries of God constitute the principles and ordinances of salvation and exaltation—the essence of the gospel of Jesus Christ. Elder Bruce R. McConkie gives the following explanation:

> A mystery is something which cannot be explained, either because it is beyond human comprehension in general, or because some particular man has not learned enough to understand it. Accordingly, some matters of doctrine, philosophy, or science may be a mystery to one person and not to another. When a thing is understood it is no longer a mystery. In the eternal sense there are no mysteries; all things are known to and understood by Deity; and there will be no mysteries among exalted beings, for they too shall know all things.
>
> A knowledge of the mysteries of God comes by obedience to gospel law. "It is given unto many to know the mysteries of God," Amulek taught. "He that will harden his heart, the same receiveth the lesser portion of the word; and he that will not harden his heart, to him is given the greater portion of the word, until it is given unto him to know the mysteries of God until he know them in full" (Alma 12:9–11) [Compare also D&C 42:61–65; 6:7, 11; 8:11; 11:7; 76:5–10]. (*Mormon Doctrine,* 2d ed. [Salt Lake City: Bookcraft, 1966], 523)

4 For it were not possible that our father, Lehi, could have remembered all these things, to have taught them to his children, except it were for ***the help of these plates;*** *for he having been taught in the language of the Egyptians therefore he could read these engravings, and teach them to his children, that thereby they could teach them to their children, and so fulfilling the commandments of God, even down to this present time.*

Mosiah 1:5

> *5 I say unto you, my sons,* ***were it not for these things,*** *which have been kept and preserved by the hand of God, that we might read and understand of his mysteries, and have his commandments always before our eyes, that* ***even our fathers would have dwindled in unbelief,*** *and we should have been like unto our brethren, the Lamanites, who know nothing concerning these things, or even do not believe them when they are taught them, because of the traditions of their fathers, which are not correct.*

THE HELP OF THESE PLATES; WERE IT NOT FOR THESE THINGS EVEN OUR FATHERS WOULD HAVE DWINDLED IN UNBELIEF

To the modern reader with ready access to the scriptures of God, it is difficult to fathom the enormous value that these ancient prophets placed on having access to the word of God and making that priceless word available to the people so that they might attain joy and eternal blessings. Without the word of God, the ancient Mulekites, whose descendants Mosiah I discovered at Zarahemla, had "denied the being of their Creator" (Omni 1:17). Without the word of God, the Lamanites had lost their spiritual anchor and pursued a lifestyle of limited perspective and self-serving aggression. Josiah, king of Judah from 640 B.C. to 610 B.C., and therefore an older contemporary of Lehi, is overjoyed when, during the renovation of the temple, the high priest Hilkiah discovers a book of the law, originating from the time of Moses (see 2 Kings 22:8f; 2 Chronicles 34:15f). Says Josiah: "Go ye, enquire of the LORD for me, and for the people, and for all Judah, concerning the words of this book that is found: for great is the wrath of the LORD that is kindled against us, because our fathers have not hearkened unto the words of this book, to do according unto all that which is written concerning us" (2 Kings 22:13). The king reads the long-lost book before the people and causes them to covenant to live by its teachings (see 2 Kings 23:3). President Spencer W. Kimball has declared: "I feel strongly that we must all of us return to the scriptures just as King Josiah did and let them work mightily within us, impelling us to an unwavering determination to serve the Lord. Josiah had the law of Moses only. In our scriptures we have the gospel of Jesus Christ in its fulness; and if a taste is sweet, in fulness there is joy" ("How Rare a Possession—the Scriptures!" *Ensign*, Sept. 1976, 2).

INFLUENCE OF DARKNESS AGAINST THE LORD'S SERVANT, JOSEPH SMITH

The coming forth of the Book of Mormon was countered with insidious hatred by enemies of the word of God. Satan and his minions spared no effort in attempting to thwart the emergence of this witness of Jesus Christ, as the following narrative from Lucy Mack Smith, mother of the prophet, attests:

The plates were secreted about three miles from home, in the following manner: Finding an old birch log much decayed, excepting the bark, which was in a measure sound, [Joseph] took his pocket knife and cut the bark with some care, then turned it back and made a hole of sufficient size to receive the plates, and, laying them in the cavity thus formed, he replaced the bark; after which he laid across the log, in several places, some old stuff that happened to lay near, in order to conceal as much as possible the place in which they were deposited.

Joseph, on coming to them, took them from their secret place, and, wrapping them in his linen frock, placed them under his arm and started for home.

After proceeding a short distance, he thought it would be more safe to leave the road and go through the woods. Traveling some distance after he left the road, he came to a large windfall, and as he was jumping over a log, a man sprang up from behind it and gave him a heavy blow with a gun. Joseph turned around and knocked him down, then ran at the top of his speed. About half a mile farther he was attacked again in the same manner as before; he knocked this man down in like manner as the former and ran on again; and before he reached home he was assaulted the third time. In striking the last one, he dislocated his thumb, which, however, he did not notice until he came within sight of the house, when he threw himself down in the corner of the fence in order to recover his breath. As soon as he was able, he arose and came to the house. He was still altogether speechless from fright and the fatigue of running.

After resting a few moments, he desired me to send Carlos for my husband, Mr. Knight, and his friend Stoal, and have them go immediately and see if they could find the men who had been pursuing him. And after Carlos had done this, he wished to have him sent to Hyrum's, to tell him to bring the chest.

I did as I was requested, and when Carlos arrived at Hyrum's, he found him at tea with two of his wife's sisters. Just as Hyrum was raising a cup to his mouth, Carlos touched his shoulder. Without waiting to hear one word from the child, he dropped the cup, sprang from the table, caught the chest, turned it upside down, and emptying its contents on the floor, left the house instantly with the chest on his shoulder.

The young ladies were greatly astonished at his singular behavior and declared to his wife—who was then confined to her bed, her eldest daughter, Lovina, being but four days old—that he was certainly crazy.

His wife laughed heartily and replied, "Oh, not in the least; he has just thought of something which he has neglected; and it is just like him to fly off on a tangent when he thinks of anything in that way."

When the chest came, Joseph locked up the Record, then threw himself upon the bed and after resting a little, so that he could converse freely, he arose and went into the kitchen, where he related his recent adventure to his father, Mr. Knight, and Mr. Stoal, besides many others who had by this time collected, with the view of hearing something in regard to the strange circumstance which had taken place. He showed them his thumb, saying, "I must stop talking, father, and get you to put my thumb in place, for it is very painful."

I will here mention that my husband, Mr. Knight, and Mr. Stoal went in pursuit of those villains who had attempted Joseph's life, but were not able to find them (*History of Joseph Smith,* ed. Preston Nibley [Salt Lake City: Bookcraft, 1958], 107–9).

6 O my sons, I would that ye should ***remember*** *that these sayings are true, and also that these records are true. And behold, also the plates of Nephi, which contain the records and the sayings of our fathers from the time they left Jerusalem until now, and they are true; and we can know of their surety because we have them before our eyes.*
7 And now, my sons, I would that ye should ***remember*** *to search them diligently, that ye may profit thereby; and I would that ye should keep the commandments of God, that ye may prosper in the land according to the promises which the Lord made unto our fathers.*

Remember

King Benjamin teaches his sons concerning the value of the scriptures, without which they would dwindle in unbelief. He testifies of the truthfulness of the word of God and encourages them to diligently search the sacred records. Let us come to realize why the prophets continually exhort us to search, hearken, and live by the word of God: The word of God is given to nourish us that we might know the commandments and understand the mysteries of God.

Without the word of God, the iron rod, we would have no knowledge of the plan of salvation, the goodness and mercy of God, and all the commandments we should obey. We would live in ignorance. The only sure way to overcome temptation and return to the presence of God is to feast upon the word of God, holding to the iron rod so we can live by the word of God. Do we have a scripture study plan in place in our homes—a time, a place, and a way to search the scriptures together?

Memories: The Precious Student

A blessed event some years ago was the birth of a precious and beautiful granddaughter. I thought it not inappropriate to select a verse of scripture to share with her parents during the initial visit to the hospital by the doting grandparents to celebrate the new arrival. Quite by coincidence I was pondering at the time one of my favorite passages concerning the transition of God's children from the First Estate to the mortal world: "Even before they were born, they, with many others, received their first lessons in the world of spirits and were prepared to come forth in the due time of the Lord to labor in his vineyard for the salvation of the souls of men" (D&C 138:56). Looking down upon the newborn babe, only a few hours old, I wondered at the wisdom already invested in her heart and mind by virtue of the preparation and instruction she had received in the premortal realm. What she would later find arrayed in the scriptures, and what her parents would soon be teaching her about the gospel of Jesus Christ, would be a harmonizing echo of distant lessons already learned, a wondrous review of divine instruction gleaned firsthand from the Creator Himself.

It is the nature of scripture study to be an adventure in remembering. Those who read and ponder the word of God through the Spirit will experience that remarkable sensation of seeming to recover, line upon line, what was known long ago before the veil of forgetfulness was placed upon them at birth. Thus the messengers of the holy scriptures will speak to us, "and their voice shall be as one that hath a familiar spirit" (2 Nephi 26:16; compare Isaiah 29:4). According to this perspective, our learning is essentially an "unforgetting"—as the ancient Greeks expressed it, not knowing how close upon the heels of the truth they really were. This is what awaited our newest grandchild—to be able to relearn in life, by a process of unforgetting through the blessings of the Spirit, what the Father and the Son had already taught her in her previous home on high. (Richard J. Allen)

> *8 And **many more things** did king Benjamin teach his sons, which are not written in this book.*

Many more things—A Preview

King Benjamin's teachings to his sons and his magnificent sermon comprise the first five chapters of the book of Mosiah. Much of his sermon consists of the divine message imparted to him by an angel of the Lord. His teachings embrace a variety of key gospel themes: the value of the scriptures in our lives, obedience to the commandments, cultivating universal love of God and all mankind, the goodness of God and His blessings to His children, the infinite indebtedness of mankind to God (i.e., that we are all unprofitable servants), the importance of continually praising and thanking God for all things, avoiding contention, the dire consequences of transgression (loss of the Spirit), rebellion as the essence of enmity toward God, the happy state of those who keep the commandments, the coming of Christ and His atoning sacrifice, the role and function of prophets in declaring the word of the Lord, the name of Jesus Christ as the only source of salvation, the natural man being an enemy to God, the indispensable need to yield to the enticings of the Holy Spirit, and many other important doctrines. King Benjamin teaches only the things that the Lord commands him to teach. He gives great emphasis to the principle that we will be judged according to our works.

9–18 Benjamin arranges for his son Mosiah to call the people together on the morrow at the temple to proclaim Mosiah the new king and to give the people a new name to distinguish them as a highly favored people among all others brought forth from the land of Jerusalem. Benjamin commissions Mosiah to keep the sacred records and also gives him the artifacts of their lineage: the Liahona and the sword of Laban.

CHAPTER 2

OVERVIEW

The people are assembled in large numbers, their tent doors facing the temple, to hear King Benjamin's address. He revisits his many years of concerned service on their behalf and exhorts them to serve God and their fellowmen, remembering always to keep the commandments with full devotion. They are dependent upon God for all blessings—even life from one day to the next. The faithful will have "never-ending happiness" (verse 41).

1–3 The people gather in large numbers to listen to King Benjamin. They offer sacrifices according to the law of Moses.

> *4 And also that they might give **thanks** to the Lord their God, who had brought them out of the land of Jerusalem, and who had **delivered them** out of the hands of their enemies, and had appointed **just men to be their teachers,** and also **a just man to***

be their king, *who had established* ***peace*** *in the land of Zarahemla, and who had* ***taught them*** *to keep the commandments of God, that they might* ***rejoice*** *and be* ***filled with love*** *toward God and all men.*

Thanks; delivered them; just men to be their teachers; a just man to be their king peace; taught them; rejoice; filled with love

The account of the people of Zarahemla gathering for a meeting—a general conference—raises an interesting question of conscience. As we gather to our appointed Church meetings, what is the attitude we have in our hearts? Do we thank the Lord for having given us deliverance from our burdens—or at least the strength to overcome? Are we grateful for devoted teachers and leaders? Do we feel joy in the gospel and love for our fellowmen? When we bring our families together for family home evenings and family councils, do family members come with thanksgiving in their hearts? If so, then such Church and family meetings will be open to the guidance of the Lord.

5 And it came to pass that when they came up to the temple, they ***pitched their tents***
round about, every man according to his family, consisting of his wife, and his sons,
and his daughters, and their sons, and their daughters, from the eldest down to the
youngest, every family being separate one from another.
6 And they pitched their tents round about the temple, every man having his tent ***with***
the door thereof toward the temple, *that thereby they might remain in their tents*
and hear the words which king Benjamin should speak unto them;

Pitched their tents with the door thereof toward the temple

Many testimonies in the Book of Mormon take the form of benedictory statements from revered leaders—Lehi's remarkable discourse on the Atonement and on the destiny of Israel, Nephi's final discourse on the doctrine of Christ, Jacob's allegory of the olive trees, and King Benjamin's masterful sermon before the people of Zarahemla. The king's son and heir apparent, Mosiah, sends a proclamation for the people to gather at the temple to hear the speech. Significantly, the congregation is united by positioning their tent doorways toward the temple. One can imagine row upon row of concentric family semicircles radiating outward from the temple grounds as far as the eye can see, all hearts tuned to receive the sacred instruction "that they might rejoice and be filled with love toward God and all men" (Mosiah 2:4). In a similar way, we can unitedly open our hearts toward the source of all truth and salvation, even the Lord Almighty, from whom all blessings flow.

Mosiah 2:7–17

> *7 For the multitude being so great that king Benjamin could not teach them all within the walls of the temple, therefore he caused a* ***tower*** *to be erected, that thereby his people might hear the words which he should speak unto them.*
> *8 And it came to pass that he began to speak to his people from the tower; and they could not all hear his words because of the greatness of the multitude; therefore he caused that the words which he spake should be* ***written and sent forth*** *among those that were not under the sound of his voice, that they might also receive his words.*

Tower; written and sent forth

The king takes steps to ensure that his words are accessible to all assembled. When the tower is not adequate to the task, he causes his words to be written and disseminated—the first ensign in the New World! It is instructive that Ammon, the leader of the exploratory group from Zarahemla that is soon to discover the people of Limhi, has with him a copy of Benjamin's speech, which he reads to the colonists (see Mosiah 8:3). Thus the Book of Mormon peoples are favored to have excerpts from the words of the prophets in written format from time to time, even though they have no published editions of the scriptures as we do today.

9–16 Benjamin commences his speech. The people are to give earnest heed to his words: "**Hearken unto me,** and open your ears that ye may hear, and your hearts that ye may understand, and your minds that the mysteries of God may be unfolded to your view" (verse 9). His tenure has been one of service on their behalf, he having been called of the Lord and "kept and preserved by his matchless power, to serve you with all the might, mind and strength which the Lord hath granted unto me" (verse 11). He comes before them for the last time with a clear conscience, having labored alongside them and spared them heavy taxes.

Hearken unto me

We are to sustain and follow our prophets. They will teach and lead us in truth and righteousness.

> *17 And behold, I tell you these things that ye may learn* ***wisdom;*** *that ye may learn that when ye are in the* ***service of your fellow beings*** *ye are only in the* ***service of your God.***

Wisdom; service of your fellow beings; service of your God

This is one of the most famous maxims in the Book of Mormon. It declares the equivalency of service to man and service to God. In its parallelism, it is reminiscent of the Savior's statement about the great commandment in the law: "Jesus said unto him [an inquiring lawyer among the Pharisees who tempted Him], Thou shalt love the Lord thy God with all thy heart, and with all thy soul, and with all thy mind. This is the first and great commandment. And the second is like unto it, Thou shalt love thy neighbour as thyself" (Matthew 22:37–39).

Service of your fellow beings (Mosiah 2:17)

As we serve others we serve our Heavenly Father. There is an important question of conscience prompted by this verse. To be easily entreated and submissive to the commandments of God requires one to be humble. When we recognize the tender mercies of God in our lives, we love God and are filled with gratitude. We want to do good. We want to keep the commandments to show our love (see John 14:15). Let's consider our responsibilities: What does it take to stir us up to do our duty? (Read Jacob 1:19; 2:2; Alma 7:22; Moroni 9:6; and D&C 107:99–100 for counsel from the Lord on this question.)

How Do We Show Our Love?

Though we may not necessarily forfeit our lives in service to our God, we can certainly demonstrate our love for Him by how well we serve Him. He who hears our silent prayers, He who observes our unheralded acts will reward us openly when the need comes. President Thomas S. Monson relates this story:

> [An] example is a family in the mission over which I presided, a family by the name of Agnew. They were difficult people to convert. William Agnew, particularly, would not listen to the missionaries, but finally he consented to attend our Sunday School with his wife, three children, and the two missionaries. However, when the missionaries came on Sunday morning to escort the family to the chapel, there had been a little disagreement in their home. Brother Agnew had insisted, "I will not go to the Mormon Sunday School."
>
> His wife replied, "But you promised, Bill. You promised these young men that you would go."
>
> "I'm not going, and that's that!" he said. He became rather angry, but somewhat reluctantly he permitted his wife and children to go to Sunday School. He later told me of the events of that morning. He said, "When my wife and children shut the door and left me alone in the living room, I had nothing good to say about the Mormon faith. I was about as angry a man as one could imagine. I picked up the morning newspaper to see if I could read about the problems of

the world and get my mind off religion, but it was to no avail. I kept thinking, my wife and my children have gone to meet with the Mormons. I then went into my daughter Isabel's bedroom. I thought that perhaps I could turn on the news and hear something different. As I turned on the little radio on her nightstand, what do you think I heard? The Mormon Tabernacle Choir! What message do you think I heard? Richard L. Evans spoke on the subject 'Let Not the Sun Go Down on Thy Wrath.' I felt as though the Lord were talking to me personally. I got down upon my knees and promised my Heavenly Father that I would no longer rail against Him—that I would do what these young missionaries had taught me to do."

When his wife and children returned from Sunday School, they found a new husband and a new father. They couldn't understand why he was in such a pleasant mood. Finally they asked him what had happened to change his attitude.

He said: "I'll tell you. I was so upset when you left that I read the paper in an attempt to get my mind off all of you. No success. Then I went to Isabel's bedroom and turned on the radio to hear the news, and of all things, I heard the Mormon Tabernacle Choir. This man, Richard L. Evans, spoke to me and said, 'Don't let the sun go down on thy wrath.' I felt closer to God at that moment than I have ever felt in my life. I am ready to go with you to the meetings. I am ready to pursue a diligent study with the missionaries."

Isabel said, "Dad, that's a wonderful story—if only it were true."

Her father said, "Isabel, it's true."

She said, "No, Dad. Did you say that you turned on the radio on my nightstand?"

He replied, "That's the one—the little white one."

"Dad," she said, "that radio hasn't worked for several weeks. I think the tubes are burned out."

"Isabel," he said, "that radio works. Come with me." He led his family into Isabel's bedroom, walked over to the nightstand next to her bed, and turned on the radio as he had done just one hour earlier, but no sound came forth. That radio did not work! But when our Heavenly Father needed to communicate a message to an honest seeker after truth, that radio not only worked, but it tuned him into the very program and to the very message he needed to bring him to a recognition of the truth. Little wonder that he later became the bishop of that ward. Little wonder that all three of his children are active in the Church and continue to fill positions of responsibility.

When we serve our God, when we love Him, He knows it, and He will take us by the hand and give us answers to our prayers.

"Thou shalt love thy neighbour as thyself." ("How Do We Show Our Love?" *Ensign*, Jan. 1998, 2)

18 Behold, ye have called me your king; and if I, whom ye call your king, do labor to serve you, then ought not ye to labor to ***serve one another?***
19 And behold also, if I, whom ye call your king, who has spent his days in your service, and yet has been in the service of God, do merit any thanks from you, O how you ought to ***thank your heavenly King!***
20 I say unto you, my brethren, that if you should render all the thanks and praise which your whole soul has power to possess, to that God who has created you, and has kept and preserved you, and has caused that ye should rejoice, and has granted that ye should live in peace one with another—
21 I say unto you that if ye should serve him who has created you from the beginning, and is preserving you from day to day, by ***lending you breath,*** *that ye may live and move and do according to your own will, and even supporting you from one moment to another—I say,* ***if ye should serve him with all your whole souls yet ye would be unprofitable servants.***

SERVE ONE ANOTHER; THANK YOUR HEAVENLY KING; LENDING YOU BREATH; IF YE SHOULD SERVE HIM WITH ALL YOUR WHOLE SOULS YET YE WOULD BE UNPROFITABLE SERVANTS

King Benjamin continually teaches of the goodness of God. It is a central tenet of the Christian faith that we come to this understanding of our dependence on Him, for, in view of the infinite Atonement, we are indeed all unprofitable servants—no matter how devoted our worship and service. We are perpetually indebted to God. This truth is explained by President Joseph F. Smith:

> I am inclined to acknowledge the hand of God in all things. If I see a man inspired with intelligence, with extraordinary ability and wisdom, I say to myself he is indebted to God for that wisdom and ability; and that, without the providence or interposition of the Almighty, he would not have been what he is. He is indebted to the Lord

Almighty for his intelligence, and for all that he has; for the earth is the Lord's and the fulness thereof. God originated and designed all things, and all are his children. We are born into the world as his offspring; endowed with the same attributes. The children of men have sprung from the Almighty, whether the world is willing to acknowledge it or not. He is the Father of our spirits. He is the originator of our earthly tabernacles. We live and move and have our being in God our Heavenly Father. And having sprung from him with our talents, our ability, our wisdom, we should at least be willing to acknowledge his hand in all the prosperity that may attend us in life, and give to him the honor and glory of all we accomplish in the flesh. We are particularly dependent upon the Almighty for everything we possess of a worldly character. There is not a man on the earth possessed of the wisdom or power of himself to cause even a spear of grass to grow, or to produce a kernel of wheat or of corn, or any fruit, vegetable, or any material whatever which is essential for the sustenance, the happiness and the well-being of a human creature in the world. It is true we can go to the earth, we find it prepared to a certain extent, and we cultivate, plow and plant, and we reap the harvest; but God has ordained that the fruits of our labor shall be in subjection and in obedience to certain laws which he himself controls, and which he has kept out of the power of man. Man may boast of having a great deal of wisdom; of having accomplished a great deal in this nineteenth century; but, if he did but know it, he derives the ability by which he accomplishes these things from God his Father, who is in heaven. He does not possess the power in and of himself. (*Gospel Doctrine: Selections from the Sermons and Writings of Joseph F. Smith,* comp. John A. Widtsoe (Salt Lake City: Deseret Book, 1939), 62)

Elder Neal A. Maxwell adds these thoughts on the subject of our dependence upon the Lord:

While the egoistic urge of the natural man is to invite others, "Look at me," instead we should increasingly say, "Look to God and live" (Alma 37:47). When our natural instinct is to claim credit, increasingly we should ponder what they have done for us—a rescuing which we mortals were absolutely powerless to effect for ourselves. No wonder we are comparatively "unprofitable servants" (Mosiah 2:21). . . .

Both premortally and after the astonishing atonement, Jesus said "Glory be to the Father" (see Moses 4:2; D&C 19:19). What a contrast to those of us unprofitable servants who, after doing a few good deeds, insist on keeping score!

We worry over whether or not our little deed is noticed. We notice the size of the letters on the mortal marquees over the tiny little theaters where our "own little plot is always being played."

We continue to be overly concerned with getting mortal credit and over-establishing our worth. As God's children we do have great value and genuine intrinsic, individual worth. Must that intrinsic worth ever be at the mercy of our moods or of extrinsic, ephemeral measuring rods? (*Men and Women of Christ* [Salt Lake City: Bookcraft, 1991], 31, 128)

The Principle of Indebtedness According to C. S. Lewis

Our sense of gratitude for the Lord's mercies ought to create a ready acknowledgment of our utter ineptitude without him. "Every faculty you have," Lewis taught, "your power of thinking or of moving your limbs from moment to moment, is given you by God. If you devoted every moment of your whole life exclusively to His service you would not give Him anything that was not in a sense His own already. So that when we talk of a man doing anything for God or giving anything to God, I will tell you what it is really like. It is like a small child going to its father and saying, 'Daddy, give me sixpence to buy you a birthday present.' Of course, the father does, and he is pleased with the child's present. It is all very nice and proper, but only an idiot would think that the father is sixpence to the good on the transaction."

Does that sound a bit like Benjamin in the Book of Mormon? "I say unto you," the righteous prophet-king declared, "that if ye should serve him who has created you from the beginning, and is preserving you from day to day, by lending you breath, that ye may live and move and do according to your own will, and even supporting you from one moment to another—I say, if ye should serve him with all your whole souls yet ye would be unprofitable servants" (Mosiah 2:21). (Andrew C. Skinner and Robert L. Millet, *C. S. Lewis, the Man and His Message: An LDS Perspective* [Salt Lake City: Deseret Book, 1999], 145–146)

22 And behold, all that he requires of you is to ***keep his commandments;*** *and he has promised you that if ye would keep his commandments ye should prosper in the land; and he never doth vary from that which he hath said; therefore, if ye do* ***keep his commandments*** *he doth bless you and prosper you.*
23 And now, in the first place, he hath created you, and ***granted unto you your lives,*** *for which ye are indebted unto him.*
24 And secondly, he doth require that ye should do as he hath commanded you; for which if ye do, ***he doth immediately bless you;*** *and therefore he hath paid you. And*

ye are ***still indebted unto him,*** *and are, and will be, forever and ever; therefore, of what have ye to boast?*

KEEP HIS COMMANDMENTS; GRANTED UNTO YOU YOUR LIVES; HE DOTH IMMEDIATELY BLESS YOU; STILL INDEBTED UNTO HIM

King Benjamin teaches us concerning the blessings of God that flow to us every day of our lives and how He preserves us hour by hour, even lending us our very breath—and all He requires of us is to keep His commandments. When we do, then He immediately blesses us. Let us take the opportunity to see, feel, and appreciate all the blessings of God in our lives every day. When we realize the goodness of God, we will be filled with gratitude, knowing full well that we can never repay Him for our abundant blessings. This gratitude will motivate us to keep the commandments.

25 And now I ask, can ye say aught of yourselves? I answer you, Nay. Ye cannot say that ye are even as much as the dust of the earth; yet ye were created of the dust of the earth; but behold, it belongeth to him who created you.
26 ***And I, even I,*** *whom ye call your king, am no better than ye yourselves are; for I am also of the dust. And ye behold that I am old, and am about to yield up this mortal frame to its mother earth.*

EVIDENCE: AND I, EVEN I—EMPHATIC PRONOUN

To emphasize a subject or object, the Hebrew language of the Bible often repeats a personal pronoun that is the subject of a sentence or phrase. For instance, we read in Genesis 6:17, "Behold, *I*, even *I*, do bring a flood of waters upon the earth" (emphasis added). This also occurs on many occasions when the pronoun is the object, as in Esau's injunction to Jacob: "bless *me*, even *me* also, O my father" (Genesis 27:38, emphasis added). The emphatic pronoun is used in the Book of Mormon as well. For example, we read in Mosiah 2:26, "And *I*, even *I*, whom ye call your king, am no better than ye yourselves are" (emphasis added). Thus ancient patterns of expression occur in the Book of Mormon, reminding us again of its authenticity. (See *Echoes,* 180).

27–29 King Benjamin announces that he can no longer teach them or serve as their king.

30 For even at this time, ***my whole frame doth tremble*** *exceedingly while attempting to speak unto you; but* ***the Lord God doth support me,*** *and hath suffered me that I* *should speak unto you, and hath commanded me that I should declare unto you this day, that my son Mosiah is a king and a ruler over you.*

My whole frame doth tremble; the Lord God doth support me

There is nobility inherent in the final words of this and other aging leaders. We tend to invest greater attention to such pronouncements, knowing that the wisdom of a lifetime is encapsulated in the expression of last words.

Memories: Last Words

"The tongues of dying men enforce attention like deep harmony." Thus spake William Shakespeare in Richard II (II.1.5–6). We are attuned to the benedictory pronouncements of those we admire and respect.

In a special way, we accord lasting significance to the final recorded pronouncements of the great prophets such as Jacob (Israel) in the Old Testament, and Lehi, Nephi, Jacob, King Benjamin, Abinadi, Samuel, Mormon, Moroni, and others from the Book of Mormon. King Benjamin, in his last days, at a time when he declared "my whole frame doth tremble exceedingly" (Mosiah 2:30), exhorted his people in a final, masterful sermon, to obey the commandments of God: "And again, believe that ye must repent of your sins and forsake them, and humble yourselves before God; and ask in sincerity of heart that he would forgive you; and now, if you believe all these things see that ye do them" (Mosiah 4:10).

I can recall the last words my father said to me. In his senior years, he had become increasingly feeble, so, to assist him in his personal care, I had given him a new electric razor. He looked at it, smiled gratefully, and then, much to my surprise, returned it to me, saying in a weak voice, "Do this for me," since he was at the time too weak to do it on his own. I bent over and carefully shaved away his whiskers—a kind of father-son celebration of a long and productive life. He passed away not long thereafter. "Do this for me." The symbolic meaning of that phrase echoes still in my mind. To me it implies the exhortation to do those things of righteousness and follow those principles of obedience that he had exemplified throughout his life. What better way for children to honor the name of their parents than to follow their example and emulate the "godly walk and conversation" (D&C 20:69) cultivated as a legacy of faith and courage. (Richard J. Allen)

31–40 King Benjamin exhorts his people to keep the commandments of the Lord and avoid the enticements of the evil one—"For behold, there is **a wo pronounced upon him** who listeth to obey that spirit" (verse 33). If we persist in evil, then the Spirit of the Lord "**may have no place in [us]** to guide us in wisdom's paths" (verse 36), and we become "**an enemy to God**" (verse 38).

Three Applications Arising from These Scriptures

A wo pronounced upon him. We must beware, lest we succumb to the devil's temptations and worldliness. The consequence of listening to the devil is that we receive the wages of sin.

May have no place in us. When we go contrary to what we have been taught or know to be true, we lose the Spirit and have no direction in our lives.

An enemy to God. If we do not repent, we become an enemy to God. We shrink in His presence and live with the burden of guilt.

> *41 And moreover, I would desire that ye should consider on the* ***blessed and happy state*** *of those that keep the commandments of God. For behold, they are blessed in all things, both temporal and spiritual; and if they hold out faithful to the end they are received into heaven, that thereby they may dwell with God in a state of never-ending happiness.* ***O remember, remember that these things are true; for the Lord God hath spoken it.***

Blessed and happy state; O remember, remember that these things are true; for the Lord God hath spoken it

King Benjamin concludes this segment of his speech by bearing his testimony that his words are true. They are not his words. They are the words of the Lord. When one speaks according to the Spirit, one speaks scripture, as the Lord confirmed in modern-day revelation:

> And this is the ensample unto them, that they shall speak as they are moved upon by the Holy Ghost.
>
> And whatsoever they shall speak when moved upon by the Holy Ghost shall be scripture, shall be the will of the Lord, shall be the mind of the Lord, shall be the word of the Lord, shall be the voice of the Lord, and the power of God unto salvation.
>
> Behold, this is the promise of the Lord unto you, O ye my servants (D&C 68:3–4).

EVIDENCE: NEW YEAR RITES (Mosiah 1–2)

Hugh Nibley states that King Benjamin's farewell address, Mosiah's coronation, and the accompanying events are exemplary of a typical year-rite or great assembly. While the rituals in Mosiah chapters 1 and 2 are on a much higher spiritual level than those written about in Old World texts, Nibley reveals that "not a single element of the primordial rites is missing, and nothing is added, in the Book of Mormon version." (See *Echoes,* 472).

CHAPTER 3

OVERVIEW

The Savior is to come among men and bring about the Atonement. The only name given whereby salvation can come is the name of Christ, the Lord Omnipotent. We are to put off the natural man and respond to the enticings of the Holy Spirit, becoming as a little child, submissive in all things. The gospel will be spread throughout the world as a standard for judging the people. Those who fail to accept it will be consigned to endless torment.

> *1 AND again my brethren, I would call your attention, for I have somewhat more to speak unto you; for behold, I have things to tell you concerning* ***that which is to come.***
> *2 And the things which I shall tell you are made known unto me by* ***an angel from God.*** *And he said unto me:* ***Awake;*** *and I awoke, and behold he stood before me.*
> *3 And he said unto me:* ***Awake,*** *and hear the words which I shall tell thee; for behold, I am come to declare unto you the* ***glad tidings of great joy.***
> *4 For the Lord hath heard thy prayers, and hath judged of thy righteousness, and hath sent me to declare unto thee that thou mayest rejoice; and that thou mayest* ***declare unto thy people,*** *that they may also be filled with joy.*

THAT WHICH IS TO COME; AN ANGEL FROM GOD; AWAKE; GLAD TIDINGS OF GREAT JOY; DECLARE UNTO THY PEOPLE

King Benjamin continues his discourse by speaking the words of an angel who appears to him during the night. Thus the king, who has been judged of the Lord as righteous, can literally "speak with the tongue of angels, and shout praises unto the Holy One of Israel," as Nephi proclaimed on behalf of all the faithful (see 2 Nephi 31:13). The process of divine communication in this case is clear: one is called to serve, one lives a life worthy of the Lord's favor, one remains receptive to the word, the word is given, then the word is delivered to the people—that they likewise can experience the joy and edification of heavenly guidance. Elder Bruce R. McConkie explains the significance of the words King Benjamin is about to speak:

> An angel from heaven recited to King Benjamin what well may be the greatest sermon ever delivered on the atonement of Christ the Lord. (Mosiah 3) Abinadi made it clear that God himself would redeem his people (Mosiah 13:32–33), that were it not for this redemption all mankind must have perished, and that the Lord redeemeth none of those who rebel against him and die in their sins (Mosiah 15). (*The Promised Messiah: The First Coming of Christ* [Salt Lake City: Deseret Book, 1978], 232)

5 For behold, ***the time cometh,*** *and is not far distant, that with power, the Lord Omnipotent who reigneth, who was, and is from all eternity to all eternity, shall come down from heaven among the children of men, and shall dwell in a tabernacle of clay, and shall go forth amongst men, working mighty miracles, such as healing the sick, raising the dead, causing the lame to walk, the blind to receive their sight, and the deaf to hear, and curing all manner of diseases.*
6 And he shall cast out devils, or the evil spirits which dwell in the hearts of the children of men.
7 And lo, ***he shall suffer*** *temptations, and pain of body, hunger, thirst, and fatigue, even more than man can suffer, except it be unto death; for behold,* ***blood cometh from every pore,*** *so great shall be his anguish for the wickedness and the abominations of his people.*
8 And he shall be called ***Jesus Christ,*** *the Son of God, the Father of heaven and earth, the Creator of all things from the beginning; and his mother shall be called* ***Mary.***

The time cometh; he shall suffer; blood cometh from every pore; Jesus Christ; Mary

These words are spoken 124 years prior to the birth of the Savior. Without exception, the prophets of God have focused their message on the mission and Atonement of the Savior. Jesus Christ is the central theme of all prophetic discourse.

9 And lo, he cometh unto his own, ***that salvation might come unto the children of men even through faith on his name;*** *and even after all this they shall consider him*

a man, and say that he hath a devil, and shall scourge him, and shall crucify him.
10 And he shall rise the third day from the dead; and behold, he standeth to judge the world; and behold, all these things are done that a righteous judgment might come upon the children of men.

THAT SALVATION MIGHT COME UNTO THE CHILDREN OF MEN EVEN THROUGH FAITH ON HIS NAME

Christ offers salvation to all—and will judge all mankind.

11–16 According to the words of the angel, Christ's sacrifice atones for the Fall of Adam, covers those who are ignorant of the law—including innocent little children—and extends mercy to those who repent in faith and follow the words of the prophets whom God sends "**to declare these things to every kindred, nation, and tongue**" (verse 13) so that they might be redeemed and have great joy.

TO DECLARE THESE THINGS TO EVERY KINDRED, NATION, AND TONGUE

The calling of the Lord's prophets is to preach repentance and faith on the Lord Jesus Christ. Let us therefore repent and exercise faith in the Savior to receive a remission of our sins. Let us obey and rejoice rather than rebel and be filled with sorrow and anguish.

17 And moreover, I say unto you, that there shall be ***no other name given*** *nor any other way nor means whereby salvation can come unto the children of men, only in and through the name of Christ, the Lord Omnipotent.*
18 For behold he judgeth, and his judgment is just; and the infant perisheth not that dieth in his infancy; but men drink damnation to their own souls except they ***humble themselves*** *and become as little children, and believe that* ***salvation was, and is, and is to come, in and through the atoning blood of Christ,*** *the Lord Omnipotent.*

NO OTHER NAME GIVEN; HUMBLE THEMSELVES; SALVATION WAS, AND IS, AND IS TO COME, IN AND THROUGH THE ATONING BLOOD OF CHRIST

King Benjamin, like all the prophets before him, prophesies and preaches concerning the coming of the Savior and His Atonement. The crowning testimony of King Benjamin's final discourse to his people is a report given him by an angel of God about the mission of the Redeemer. King Benjamin conveys to his listeners (and by extension to his modern-day readers) a compelling witness of what the angel has instructed him to say about the need to repent, overcome the natural man, and become as a saint through the Atonement of Christ. There is no other name given for salvation other than the name of Jesus Christ—no philosophy of man, no scientific process, no sectarian creed, no political platform—just the name of Jesus Christ. We are to become like little children and come unto the Lord, the only source of salvation.

> *19 For **the natural man is an enemy to God,** and has been from the fall of Adam, and will be, forever and ever, **unless he yields to the enticings of the Holy Spirit,** and putteth off the natural man **and becometh a saint through the atonement of Christ** the Lord, and becometh as a child, submissive, meek, humble, patient, full of love, willing to submit to all things which the Lord seeth fit to inflict upon him, even as a child doth submit to his father.*

The natural man is an enemy to God unless he yields to the enticings of the Holy Spirit and becometh a saint through the atonement of Christ

This celebrated and oft-cited passage is not a statement from King Benjamin, but a quotation from the angel of God—a messenger speaking the words of the Messiah. It is a formula for the miraculous unfolding of our spiritual potential through the Atonement. The natural man does not receive the things of God (see 1 Corinthians 2:14). The natural man chooses to love Satan more than God, thus becoming carnal, sensual, and devilish (see Moses 5:13). The natural man does not repent. The natural man does not yield to the enticings of the Holy Spirit. The natural man is not a saint. Man is a dual being—with a mortal body and a spirit endowed with divine potential and with the capacity to choose what kind of person he will become. We are in a fallen state, thus needing the help of an all-merciful God to return to His presence. Mortality does not equate with being a natural man, for the natural man is such by choice. We choose to become a saint through the Atonement of Christ. Elder Neal A. Maxwell described the significance of this doctrine:

> Of the great invitation we have received to "come home," the Prophet Joseph Smith declared, "If you wish to go where God is, you must be like God, or possess the principles which God possesses." King Benjamin was specific in saying that if one wishes to become a saint, he must become "as a child, submissive, meek, humble, patient, full of love, willing to submit to all things which the Lord seeth fit to inflict upon him, even as a child doth submit to his father" (Mosiah 3:19).

> The more one sees of life, the more one understands why there is such a scriptural stress on submissiveness and meekness. The dangers flowing from an excess of ego are real and constant. Would that we first placed an ego-filtering screen over all our thoughts, words, and actions before they hurt others or embarrassed us. If we are steadily becoming more and more the man or woman of Christ, the filtering mesh in that ego screen will become finer; fewer things will slip through to harm.
>
> Some questions may help us to "audit" how much operative faith we have in the Father's plan of salvation.
>
> - How perceptibly are we developing the Christlike qualities enumerated by King Benjamin?
> - What will our sons, daughters, grandsons, and granddaughters learn from us about gospel doctrines? Or will we depend entirely upon Church classrooms to teach our children?
> - Does our understanding of the plan of salvation help us to handle disappointments in life? Can we partake of our tiny, bitter cups without becoming bitter?
> - How often do we render quiet, Christian service? A lack of sufficient love for others constitutes a major failure for which no other successes can ever fully compensate.
>
> (*Lord, Increase Our Faith* [Salt Lake City: Bookcraft, 1994], 48–49)

King Benjamin teaches us that the natural man—i.e., one who is unrepentant (see Mosiah 2:38)—is an enemy to God. The natural man will continue in his downward course unless he yields to the enticings of the Holy Spirit, becoming a saint through the Atonement of our Savior Jesus Christ, becoming as a child—willing to submit to all things according to the will of the Lord. The application of this scripture to our lives has an exalting power. It is the pathway to salvation and exaltation.

The Price of Spirituality

To become a Saint we must yield to the enticings of the Holy Spirit. There is a price to pay if we are to be worthy of these blessings. Elder Marion G. Romney recommended four things for obtaining and keeping the guidance of the Spirit:

Mighty Prayer—Pray and fast for the blessing of the Holy Ghost (see 3 Nephi 19:9).

Search the Scriptures (see 2 Nephi 32:3)—Faith comes by hearing the word (see Romans 10:17). The Holy Ghost is a blessing that comes through faith (see 1 Nephi 10:17). We live by the word of God (see D&C 84:44–46) and the word is given by the power of the Holy Ghost (see D&C 68:4).

Live Righteously—When we keep the commandments, we are blessed always to have the Spirit (see D&C 20:77, 79). Through purity and by showing love we are blessed by the Spirit (see D&C 76:116). The fruits of the Spirit are in goodness, righteousness, and truth (see Ephesians 5:9).

Church Service—We can teach only by the Spirit (see D&C 42:14). Our meetings must be directed by the Spirit (see Moroni 6:9). In all of our Church service we rely on the Spirit in every facet of the work, whether it is to testify (see 3 Nephi 28:11) or do the work of the ministry (see Acts 13:2–4; 16:6). As disciples we have the joy of the Spirit (see Acts 13:52). (Adapted from Marion G. Romney, "Guidance of the Holy Spirit," *Ensign,* Jan. 1980, 5.) (Ed J. Pinegar)

20–27 King Benjamin concludes this aspect of his discourse. The gospel will be spread throughout the world as a standard for judging the people. Those who fail to heed and comply will find that justice overrides mercy and consign them to endless torment.

CHAPTER 4

OVERVIEW

King Benjamin continues with his discourse. Forgiveness and peace come alone through the Atonement of Christ. We are to remember our nothingness in comparison with the majesty and greatness of God. Repent and believe in God in order to retain a remission of sins. "If you believe all these things see that ye do them" (verse 10). We must teach our children to love one another and serve one another. We must succor the poor and give of our substance to the beggar, for we are all beggars before the Lord. We must act in wisdom and order. "And now, O man, remember, and perish not" (verse 30).

> *1 AND now, it came to pass that when king Benjamin had made an end of speaking the words which had been delivered unto him by the angel of the Lord, that he cast his eyes round about on the multitude, and behold they had fallen to the earth, for* ***the fear of the Lord*** *had come upon them.*
> *2 And they had viewed themselves in their own carnal state, even less than the dust of the earth. And they all cried aloud with one voice, saying: O have mercy, and apply*

the atoning blood of Christ that we may receive ***forgiveness*** *of our sins, and our hearts may be purified; for* ***we believe in Jesus Christ,*** *the Son of God, who created heaven and earth, and all things; who shall come down among the children of men.*
3 And it came to pass that after they had spoken these words the ***Spirit of the Lord*** *came upon them, and they were* ***filled with joy,*** *having received a* ***remission of their sins,*** *and having* ***peace of conscience,*** *because of the* ***exceeding faith*** *which they had in Jesus Christ who should come, according to the words which king Benjamin had spoken unto them.*

The fear of the Lord; forgiveness; we believe in Jesus Christ; Spirit of the Lord; filled with joy; remission of their sins; peace of conscience; exceeding faith

The event now reported in the abridgment of Moroni is miraculous. The words of the angel, straight from the Lord, have a rejuvenating impact on the people, who experience an immediate transformation through the power of the Atonement. As King Benjamin finishes delivering the message to his people, he witnesses a singularly remarkable event—the members of his audience fall to the earth, having been given a startling new insight as to their need for the mercy of the Lord. Thus he sees that the Spirit has enabled them to view themselves from a higher perspective where mortal weaknesses are placed in sharp contrast with saintly patterns of living. Consequently, the process of repentance can proceed unimpeded even to the remission of sins and the ushering in of illuminating joy—"because of the exceeding faith which they had in Jesus Christ" (Mosiah 4:3).

4 And king Benjamin again opened his mouth and began to speak unto them, saying: My friends and my brethren, my kindred and my people, I would again call your attention, that ye may ***hear and understand*** *the remainder of my words which I shall speak unto you.*

Hear and understand

King Benjamin continues and completes his sermon before the people of Zarahemla. He integrates into his discourse many of the central themes of the gospel: salvation through Christ, the goodness of God, our own nothingness and fallen state, trust in the Lord, the need to repent and humble ourselves before the Lord, the need to remember our dependence on God, standing steadfast in the faith, and much more. His message conveys the promise that if we follow covenant principles we will be filled with the love of God and retain a remission of our sins. He admonishes us to teach our children to honor the laws of God by walking in truth and soberness. Above all, we are to help those in need.

5 For behold, if the knowledge of ***the goodness of God*** *at this time has awakened you*
to a sense of ***your nothingness,*** *and* ***your worthless and fallen state—***
6 I say unto you, if ye have come to a knowledge of the goodness of God, and his matchless
power, and his wisdom, and his patience, and his long-suffering toward the children
of men; and also, the atonement which has been prepared from the foundation of the
world, that thereby salvation might come to him that should put his trust in the Lord,
and should be diligent in keeping his commandments, and continue in the faith even
unto the end of his life, I mean the life of the mortal body—
7 I say, that this is the man who receiveth salvation, through ***the atonement*** *which*
was prepared from the foundation of the world for all mankind, which ever were since
the fall of Adam, or who are, or who ever shall be, even unto the end of the world.

The goodness of God; your nothingness; your worthless and fallen state; the atonement

There is a moment in the life of every true follower of the Lord when he or she gains insight concerning the grandeur and perfection of God in contrast with the infancy and imperfection of man. This overwhelming contrast of divine versus human of necessity renders the station of man as one of nothingness and worthlessness. But through the Savior's love, manifested by the Atonement, the faithful and obedient can be elevated to a higher station of perfectibility. Thus, nothingness becomes supreme potential. (through Atonement)

8 And this is ***the means whereby salvation cometh.*** *And there is* ***none other sal-***
vation *save this which hath been spoken of; neither are there any conditions whereby*
man can be saved except the conditions which I have told you.

The means whereby salvation cometh; none other salvation

President Ezra Taft Benson summarizes this central doctrine: "The Book of Mormon tells us of the Messiah's great atoning sacrifice. It describes how Jesus willingly suffered the pains of all men and specifies the conditions by which His atonement may bring us to a remission of our sins, a peace of conscience, and great joy" (Ezra Taft Benson, *The Teachings of Ezra Taft Benson* [Salt Lake City: Bookcraft, 1988], 55). James E. Talmage expressed this truth as follows: "Thus no man can consistently hope for salvation in the kingdom of God except through the Atonement of Jesus Christ; and the Atonement is made operative for the remission of sins through individual compliance with the conditions explicitly set forth by "the author of eternal salvation unto all them that obey him." (Heb. 5:9). Christ's method of saving souls is that of providing definite means, which any one may accept or reject to his own eternal gain or loss" (*The Vitality of Mormonism* [Boston: Gorham Press, 1919], 64).

> *9* ***Believe in God;*** *believe that he is, and that he created all things, both in heaven and in earth; believe that he has all wisdom, and all power, both in heaven and in earth; believe that man doth not comprehend all the things which the Lord can comprehend.*
>
> *10 And again,* ***believe that ye must repent*** *of your sins and forsake them, and humble yourselves before God; and ask in sincerity of heart that he would forgive you; and now,* ***if you believe all these things see that ye do them.***

Believe in God; believe that ye must repent; if you believe all these things see that ye do them

These two simple verses (Mosiah 4:9–10) contain an appropriate credo for all to follow. They define the character and quality of faith; they identify the steps that lead to forgiveness and peace. Above all, they transform concept and principle into action: "if you believe all these things see that ye do them" (verse 10). What could be a more suitable covenant motto to use in speeches, lessons, and family home evenings than the formula presented by King Benjamin on the temple grounds in Zarahemla that day: *believe and do*.

> *11 And again I say unto you as I have said before, that as ye have come to the knowledge of the glory of God, or if ye have known of his goodness and have tasted of his love, and have received a remission of your sins, which causeth such exceedingly great joy in your souls, even so I would that ye should remember, and* ***always retain in remembrance, the greatness of God, and your own nothingness,*** *and his goodness and long-suffering toward you, unworthy creatures, and humble yourselves even in the depths of humility, calling on the name of the Lord daily, and standing steadfastly in the faith of that which is to come, which was spoken by the mouth of the angel.*
>
> *12 And behold, I say unto you that if ye do this ye shall always rejoice, and* ***be filled with the love of God,*** *and always* ***retain a remission of your sins;*** *and ye shall grow in the knowledge of the glory of him that created you, or in the knowledge of that which is just and true.*

Always retain in remembrance, the greatness of God, and your own nothingness; be filled with the love of God; retain a remission of your sins

Remembrance brings blessings. King Benjamin reminds us, as part of our gratitude for having received a remission of our sins, to always ponder the goodness of God and retain in remembrance the following: God's greatness, our nothingness (without the help of the Lord), His long-suffering toward us, the need for humility and daily prayer, and the need to stand steadfastly in the faith. By doing these, we will be filled with His love, retain a remission of our sins, and grow in the knowledge of His glory.

Think of what has just transpired in Zarahemla: King Benjamin has just brought his people to the point where they have repented in full faith, being "filled with joy, having received a remission of their sins, and peace of conscience" (Mosiah 4:3). He then guides the people toward a firm understanding of how they, having tasted the love of God, might assure the continuation of this divine blessing in their lives, and "always retain a remission of your sins" (Mosiah 4:12). We can go through precisely this same process as a continual experience in renewal and rejuvenation through the power of the Atonement of Jesus Christ.

> *13 And ye will not have a mind to injure one another, but to* ***live peaceably,*** *and to render to every man according to that which is his due.*
> *14 And ye will not suffer your children that they go hungry, or naked; neither will ye suffer that they transgress the laws of God, and fight and quarrel one with another, and serve the devil, who is the master of sin, or who is the evil spirit which hath been spoken of by our fathers, he being an enemy to all righteousness.*
> *15 But ye will* ***teach them to walk in the ways of truth and soberness;*** *ye will teach them to* ***love one another,*** *and to* ***serve one another.***

Live peaceably; teach them [your children] to walk in the ways of truth and soberness; love one another; serve one another

King Benjamin reminds us that when we remember and apply the principles of the gospel we will have a desire to live a Christlike life. We will live peaceably with one another. We will bless our children so that they will not go hungry or transgress the laws of God or quarrel one with another. We will teach our children to walk in truth and soberness (i.e., being serious minded as to the things of the Lord) and to serve and love one another. The following questions of conscience for us arise from this: Do we impart to our children, our grandchildren, our students, or anyone for whom we have responsibility, clear instructions about maintaining the standards of Zion and serving one another? Do we use our leadership to supplant contention with peace, enmity with love, evil with goodness?

16 And also, ye yourselves will ***succor those that stand in need of your succor;*** *ye will administer of your substance unto him that standeth in need; and ye will not suffer that the beggar putteth up his petition to you in vain, and turn him out to perish.*
17 Perhaps thou shalt say: The man has brought upon himself his misery; therefore I will stay my hand, and will not give unto him of my food, nor impart unto him of my substance that he may not suffer, for his punishments are just—
18 But I say unto you, O man, whosoever doeth this the same hath great cause to repent; and except he repenteth of that which he hath done he perisheth forever, and hath no interest in the kingdom of God.
19 For behold, ***are we not all beggars?*** *Do we not all depend upon the same Being, even God, for all the substance which we have, for both food and raiment, and for gold, and for silver, and for all the riches which we have of every kind?*
20 And behold, even at this time, ye have been calling on his name, and begging for a remission of your sins. And has he suffered that ye have begged in vain? Nay; ***he has poured out his Spirit upon you,*** *and has caused that your hearts should be filled with joy, and has caused that your mouths should be stopped that ye could not find utterance, so exceedingly* ***great was your joy.***
21 And now, if God, who has created you, on whom you are dependent for your lives and for all that ye have and are, doth grant unto you whatsoever ye ask that is right, in faith, believing that ye shall receive, O then, how ye ought to ***impart of the substance that ye have*** *one to another.*

Succor those that stand in need of your succor; are we not all beggars? He has poured out his Spirit upon you; great was your joy; impart of the substance that ye have

Living a Christlike life requires that we begin to take upon ourselves His divine nature (see 2 Peter 1:3–10; D&C 4:6). The Lord is the supreme benefactor of the needy, the bestower of mercy upon the helpless. His invites all to come unto Him, turning away none. Beneath the canopy of His goodness, we are all beggars. How then can we choose not to succor the beggars in our midst when we indeed are among them?

What are the fruits of possessing the love of God? When the love of God is within us, we have an overwhelming desire to do good to all. When we are fully aware of our utter dependence upon God for all things, then we are disposed to give freely to others who are in need.

Mosiah 4:21

Memories: A New Way of Looking at Things

One beautiful spring day several colleagues and I were participating in a business retreat. Two of us were walking along the streets of the city preparing to rejoin our wives and other family members when, all at once, we came upon a teenaged boy who seemed to be disoriented and in distress. As we passed by, he looked at us with fear and longing in his eyes. His arms reached out in a beckoning way to the pedestrians around him. He seemed to be challenged in multiple ways. Without stopping, we walked around the spot where he was standing and continued silently on our way. Then our pace slackened. Suddenly, my friend stopped and turned around. He walked back toward the young man and began to speak with him. "What can we do to help?" was the question. The young man seemed to be somewhat relieved but was uncommunicative. My friend attempted for some time to explore various options for being of assistance but could not seem to find any resolution. Finally, we concluded that nothing could be done at that time. We waved good-bye and continued down the street.

What was the outcome? Perhaps nothing more than an attempt to be of service. But there was more than that, for the effects of the action have continued to this day, and I have often thought with admiration about the charity of my friend. Why was this simple event so memorable for me? Because my friend has a son who is similarly challenged—and so do I. Any family who is blessed to care for a challenged child will never again look upon an individual in that situation with the same eyes. There will always be more compassion than before. There will always be a greater level of understanding, because life will have imparted a new kind of perspective, a new way of looking at things.

In a miraculous way, the gospel of Jesus Christ also provides a new way of looking at things, one that has enduring consequences. King Benjamin warned us not to withhold our assistance and compassion under any circumstances. "For behold, are we not all beggars? Do we not all depend upon the same Being, even God, for all the substance which we have?" (Mosiah 4:19). So powerful was the king's masterful discourse that his listeners collapsed under the burden of their own nothingness, perceiving themselves as "even less than the dust of the earth" (Mosiah 4:2; compare Helaman 12:7–23). It was only in this state of perception—this new way of looking at things—that they could admit utter dependence upon the Lord, through whose redeeming merits and mercy alone can the joy of redemption come into one's life.

The gospel of Jesus Christ has a way of making people look at things differently.

And that is the surprising vista that the gospel gives, for once we perceive our nothingness ("which thing I had never supposed" was the way Moses characterizes this traumatic insight; see Moses 1:10), the Spirit can lift our sight to a crystal clear vision of the pathway of salvation.

When we see a beggar, a challenged person, we see ourselves, and in this perspective, we also see our pathway home. And that is the pathway of service, obedience, charity, faith, hope, diligence, compassion, humility, even a broken heart and a contrite spirit—the "mighty change" (Mosiah 5:2) to which King Benjamin gave us the master key. (Richard J. Allen)

> 22 *And* ***if ye judge the man who putteth up his petition to you*** *for your substance that he perish not, and condemn him, how much more just will be your condemnation for withholding your substance, which doth not belong to you but to God, to whom also your life belongeth; and yet ye put up no petition, nor repent of the thing which thou hast done.*
> 23 *I say unto you, wo be unto that man, for his substance shall perish with him; and now, I say these things unto those who are rich as pertaining to the things of this world.*

If ye judge the man who putteth up his petition to you

There is spiritual peril in judging those who petition for our help. Our substance does not belong to us, but to God. We must beware of judging others and their situations—giving freely to all. We must never deny a generous thought.

22–26 King Benjamin finishes his point: to withhold from the poor will bring the condemnation of God. The poor who have naught to give but whose attitude is nonetheless charitable—"If I had I would give" (verse 24)—will be blessed. Retaining a remission of sins requires unconditional charity to all.

> 27 *And see that all these things are* ***done in wisdom and order;*** *for it is not requisite that a man should run faster than he has strength. And again, it is expedient that he should* ***be diligent,*** *that thereby he might win the prize; therefore, all things must be done in order.*

Done in wisdom and order; be diligent

Charity is wise, acting according to principles of order and available resources. Nevertheless, charity is diligent—not giving up until the destination is reached. The same counsel is given to Joseph Smith in 1828 regarding the work of bringing forth the Book of Mormon: "Do not run faster or labor more than you have strength and means provided to enable you to translate; but be diligent unto the end" (D&C 10:4). We must plan well, organize every needful thing, count the cost in time and effort, and be charitable—then we will succeed.

28 Return that which you have borrowed and avoid sin for both borrower and giver.

29 And finally, I cannot tell you all the things whereby ye may commit sin; for there are divers ways and means, even so many that I cannot number them.
30 But this much I can tell you, that if ye do not ***watch yourselves,*** *and your* ***thoughts,*** *and your* ***words,*** *and your* ***deeds,*** *and* ***observe the commandments of God,*** *and* ***continue in the faith*** *of what ye have heard concerning the coming of our Lord, even unto the end of your lives, ye must perish. And now, O man,* ***remember, and perish not.***

WATCH YOURSELVES; THOUGHTS; WORDS; DEEDS; OBSERVE THE COMMANDMENTS OF GOD; CONTINUE IN THE FAITH; REMEMBER, AND PERISH NOT

King Benjamin's parting statement is "remember, and perish not." President Spencer W. Kimball stated, "When you look in the dictionary for the most important word, do you know what it is? . . . 'Remember' is the word." ("Circles of Exaltation," [Address to religious educators, BYU, 28 June 1968], 8). President Harold B. Lee provides a three-step program for remembering our covenants and moving forward on the pathway prescribed by the Savior:

> What must I do to be saved? As I pondered these words, I thought of three essentials that are necessary to inspire one to live a Christlike life—or, speaking more accurately in the language of the scriptures, to live more perfectly as the Master lived. The first essential I would name in order to qualify is: There must be awakened in the individual who would be taught or who would live perfectly an awareness of his needs. . . . The second essential for perfection that I would name is found in the conversation the Master had with Nicodemus . . . A man must be "born again" if he would reach perfection, in order to see or enter into the kingdom of God. . . . And then finally the third essential: to help the learner to know the gospel by living the gospel. Spiritual certainty that is necessary to salvation must be preceded by a maximum of individual effort. Grace, or the free gift of the Lord's atoning power, must be preceded by personal striving. Repeating again what Nephi said, "By grace . . . we are saved, after all we can do." (*Stand Ye in Holy Places* [Salt Lake City: Deseret Book, 1974], 208–213)

MEMORIES: THE YELLOW PANSIES

Some people seem to be blessed with a "green thumb." My wife is like that, always cultivating and preserving a touch of natural color in the flower beds around our home. I fondly recall how she managed to coax persistent growth from a small bed of yellow pansies around the base of a tree in the front yard throughout the entire winter. Where the neighboring yards had been dutifully purged of all floral expression, here was this radiant bed of yellow pansies.

Gospel flower beds are like that. We plant and cultivate the seeds of repentance and faith in our lives, and we receive joy in verdant beginnings and early blossoms. But it takes commitment and valor to maintain the lasting bloom of the fruits of righteousness. When the winters of life come, and the winds of adversity and temptation whistle through our mortal landscape, it is only through our enduring faith, anchored in the "merits, and mercy, and grace of the Holy Messiah" (2 Nephi 2:8), that we can hope to keep our spiritual garden alive and prospering. (Richard J. Allen)

CHAPTER 5

OVERVIEW

King Benjamin desires to know the disposition of the people concerning his final discourse. They report unanimously having experienced a "mighty change" (verse 2)—with no more desire to do evil. By making a covenant to obey God forever, they "have become his sons and his daughters" (verse 7). They receive His name, even the name of Jesus Christ, which can never be blotted out except through transgression. King Benjamin exhorts them to be "steadfast and immovable, always abounding in good works, that Christ, the Lord God Omnipotent, may seal you his" (verse 15).

> *1 AND now, it came to pass that when king Benjamin had thus spoken to his people, he sent among them, desiring to know of his people if they believed the words which he had spoken unto them.*
> *2 And they all cried with one voice, saying: Yea, **we believe all the words** which thou hast spoken unto us; and also, we know of their surety and truth, because of **the Spirit** of the Lord Omnipotent, which **has wrought a mighty change in us,** or in our hearts, that we have no more disposition to do evil, but to do good continually.*

WE BELIEVE ALL THE WORDS; THE SPIRIT HAS WROUGHT A MIGHTY CHANGE IN US

The mighty change of heart referenced here comes as a result of covenant commitment. The Spirit of the Lord can, if we are submissive and easily entreated, bring about a mighty change in our hearts. If we seek the Spirit, we will change and lose the desire to do evil. The people of King Benjamin believe his words as the Holy Spirit manifests the truth unto them, causing a mighty change to take place in their hearts. Let us likewise seek to know the truth by the power of the Holy Spirit. It will show us all things to do (see 2 Nephi 32:5) and testify of the truth of all things (see Moroni 10:5)—thus we will be blessed to receive and maintain the mighty change of heart. President Ezra Taft Benson spoke of this change as follows:

> When we have undergone this mighty change, which is brought about only through faith in Jesus Christ and through the operation of the Spirit upon us, it is as though we have become a new person. Thus the change is likened to a new birth. Thousands of you within the sound of my voice have experienced this change. You have forsaken lives of sin, sometimes deep and offensive sin, and through applying the blood of Christ in your lives, have become clean. You have no more disposition to return to your old ways. You are in reality a new person. This is what is meant by a change of heart. (*The Teachings of Ezra Taft Benson* [Salt Lake City: Bookcraft, 1988], 470)

The Mighty Change

Stephen Robinson illustrates the ongoing process and challenges entailed in the mighty change:

> From the moment of their conversion (or reconversion), the people of Benjamin changed their orientation and wanted righteousness rather than wickedness. It became their one goal. But that does *not* mean they achieved their goal instantaneously! It does *not* mean they never had another carnal thought or that they never subsequently lost any struggle against their carnal natures. At that moment, filled with the Spirit and clearly seeing the two paths before them, the people of Benjamin lost all desire to follow the path of evil. I feel the same way when I feel the Spirit, but I do not always feel the Spirit. And as with Moses, when the epiphany (divine appearance) is over, Satan sometimes takes his best shot (Moses 1:9–12). Therefore we must recharge our spiritual batteries regularly.
>
> Great spiritual damage can be done by teaching the Saints that "the mighty change" means once truly converted we are never again tempted to sin. For if the Saints believe that the *truly* converted are never subsequently tempted, then when they are tempted—and they will be—they will conclude they are not really converted. However, being truly converted does not end the tests of mortality, for we will continue to be tested and tempted as long as we are in the flesh. Even as

> covenant members of the church of Jesus Christ, we will continue to be subject to the carnal impulses and other weaknesses that are a consequence of the Fall.
>
> Since my own conversion, if at any time an angel had somehow presented me with two options and said, "Push button A and you will never sin again; push button B and you will," I'd have pushed button A—without hesitation and hard enough to break my thumb! Imperfect as I am, since my conversion I in fact "have no more disposition to do evil but to do good continually," and most of us feel that way. It's just that we have difficulty overcoming our carnal natures and the effects of the Fall at all times in order to act according to our predisposition. That our disposition is *good* is proven by the fact that when we occasionally act otherwise, we feel bad about it, repent, and return to our previous heading toward righteousness. Like a compass needle that may swing this way or that but always comes again to point north, so are the believers who may make this or that temporary misstep but always correct their course and return to their original heading. That is a clear disposition to do good. "The mighty change" is a change of heart, a change of desires, and a change of disposition concerning our goals. It is not a complete victory over the Fall or over our carnal natures all at once. (*Following Christ: The Parable of the Divers and More Good News* [Salt Lake City: Deseret Book, 1995], 41–42)

> *3 And we, ourselves, also, through the infinite goodness of God, and the manifestations of his Spirit, have* ***great views of that which is to come;*** *and were it expedient,* ***we could prophesy of all things.***
>
> *4 And it is the* ***faith*** *which we have had on the things which our king has spoken unto us that has brought us to this great knowledge, whereby we do rejoice with such exceedingly* ***great joy.***

Faith

We can gain sure knowledge and joy as we exercise our faith.

Great views of that which is to come; we could prophesy of all things; faith; great joy

The scriptures are imbued with the spirit of prophecy—"great views"—concerning the mission and Atonement of the Savior. The Lord uses a similar phrase when He commands Joseph Smith to translate from the small plates of Nephi after the loss of the initial 116 pages of the Book of Mormon: "Behold, there are many things engraven upon the plates of Nephi which do throw greater views upon my gospel; therefore, it is wisdom in me that you should translate this first part of the engravings of Nephi, and send forth in this work. And, behold, all the remainder of this work does contain all those parts of my gospel which my holy prophets, yea, and also my disciples, desired in their prayers should come forth unto this people" (D&C 10:45–46).

Great views of the future in hope and faith—this is a central theme that resonates in King Benjamin's speech. He has loved and served his people, and they are willing to listen to their prophet-king. He teaches them great truths that they understand and appreciate—truths that bring about a "mighty change" in their hearts (see Mosiah 5:2–4). If we choose to hearken to the words of the gospel from the scriptures and our living prophets, we too can have this mighty change of heart and receive "great views of that which is to come." The gospel of Jesus Christ is the gospel of joy—in infinitely greater measure than is possible from any other source.

*5 And we are willing to enter into a **covenant** with our God to do his will, and to be obedient to his commandments in all things that he shall command us, all the remainder of our days, that we may not bring upon ourselves a never-ending torment, as has been spoken by the angel, that we may not drink out of the cup of the wrath of God.*
*6 And now, these are the words which king Benjamin desired of them; and therefore he said unto them: Ye have spoken the words that I desired; and the **covenant** which ye have made is a righteous **covenant.***
*7 And now, because of the **covenant** which ye have made ye shall be called the children of Christ, his sons, and his daughters; for behold, **this day he hath spiritually begotten you;** for ye say that your hearts are changed through faith on his name; therefore, ye are born of him and **have become his sons and his daughters.***
*8 And under this head ye are made free, and there is no other head whereby ye can be made free. There is **no other name given** whereby salvation cometh; therefore, I would that ye should take upon you the name of Christ, all you that have entered into the **covenant** with God that ye should be obedient unto the end of your lives.*
*9 And it shall come to pass that whosoever doeth this shall be found at the right hand of God, for he shall know the name by which he is called; for he shall be **called by the name of Christ.***

Covenant; this day he hath spiritually begotten you; have become his sons and his daughters; no other name given; called by the name of Christ

When King Benjamin gives his son Mosiah instructions to gather the people of Zarahemla together to hear his final counsel, he makes this promise and commitment: "And moreover, I shall give this people a name, that thereby they may be distinguished above all the people which the Lord God hath brought out of the land of Jerusalem; and this I do because they have been a diligent people in keeping the commandments of the Lord. And I give unto them a name that never shall be blotted out, except it be through transgression" (Mosiah 1:11–12). True to his promise, the king declares to his people at the conclusion of his discourse the new name by which they will become known in all eternity: "And under this head ye are made free, and there is no other head whereby ye can be made free. There is no other name given whereby salvation cometh; therefore, I would that ye should take upon you the name of Christ, all you that have entered into the covenant with God that ye should be obedient unto the end of your lives" (Mosiah 5:8).

By what process is the name of Christ imparted to us? The miracle of the mighty change is more than a spiritual transformation—it is a covenant process. Faith and repentance are followed by requisite ordinances at the hands of authorized priesthood holders commissioned to baptize and impart the gift of the Holy Ghost. It is through this process that we come to be known under the name of Christ.

His sons and His daughters

When we make covenants with Christ through baptism we become His sons and daughters. We are changed through faith on His name. We are born of Christ. We can be free from sin as we repent and take upon ourselves the name of Jesus Christ and obediently endure to the end.

The Power and Joy of Conversion

The Prophet Joseph describes as follows the joyous occasion when he and Oliver Cowdery were baptized for the remission of sins:

> On the 5th day of April, 1829, Oliver Cowdery came to my house, until which time I had never seen him. He stated to me that having been teaching school in the neighborhood where my father resided, and my father being one of those who sent to the school, he went to board for a season at his house, and while there the family related to him the circumstances of my having received the plates, and accordingly he had come to make inquiries of me.

Joseph Smith's & Oliver Cowdery's baptism

Two days after the arrival of Mr. Cowdery (being the 7th of April) I commenced to translate the Book of Mormon, and he began to write for me.

We still continued the work of translation, when, in the ensuing month (May, 1829), we on a certain day went into the woods to pray and inquire of the Lord respecting baptism for the remission of sins, that we found mentioned in the translation of the plates. While we were thus employed, praying and calling upon the Lord, a messenger from heaven descended in a cloud of light, and having laid his hands upon us, he ordained us, saying:

Upon you my fellow servants, in the name of Messiah, I confer the priesthood of Aaron, which holds the keys of the ministering of angels, and of the gospel of repentance, and of baptism by immersion for the remission of sins; and this shall never be taken again from the earth until the sons of Levi do offer again an offering unto the Lord in righteousness.

He said this Aaronic Priesthood had not the power of laying on hands for the gift of the Holy Ghost, but that this should be conferred on us hereafter; and he commanded us to go and be baptized, and gave us directions that I should baptize Oliver Cowdery, and that afterwards he should baptize me.

Accordingly we went and were baptized. I baptized him first, and afterwards he baptized me—after which I laid my hands upon his head and ordained him to the Aaronic Priesthood, and afterwards he laid his hands on me and ordained me to the same Priesthood—for so we were commanded.

The messenger who visited us on this occasion and conferred this Priesthood upon us, said that his name was John, the same that is called John the Baptist in the New Testament, and that he acted under the direction of Peter, James and John, who held the keys of the priesthood of Melchizedek, which Priesthood, he said, would in due time be conferred on us, and that I should be called the first Elder of the Church, and he (Oliver Cowdery) the second. It was on the fifteenth day of May, 1829, that we were ordained under the hand of this messenger, and baptized.

Immediately on our coming up out of the water after we had been baptized, we experienced great and glorious blessings from our Heavenly Father. No sooner had I baptized Oliver Cowdery, than the Holy Ghost fell upon him, and he stood up and prophesied many things which should shortly come to pass. And again, so soon as I had been baptized by him, I also had the spirit of prophecy, when,

> standing up, I prophesied concerning the rise of this Church, and many other things connected with the Church, and this generation of the children of men. We were filled with the Holy Ghost, and rejoiced in the God of our salvation. (JS—H 1:66–73)

10–14 King Benjamin reinforces the doctrines discussed in his discourse: The mighty change results in the granting of a new name to be written in our hearts—even the name of Jesus Christ—which will never be blotted out except through transgression. We are to remember this new name always and act in keeping with the principles of righteousness.

> *15 Therefore, I would that ye should be steadfast and immovable,* ***always abounding in good works,*** *that Christ, the Lord God Omnipotent, may seal you his, that you may be brought to heaven,* ***that ye may have everlasting salvation and eternal life,*** *through the wisdom, and power, and justice, and mercy of him who created all things, in heaven and in earth, who is God above all. Amen.*

Always abounding in good works; that ye may have everlasting salvation and eternal life

This section of the Book of Mormon is a refreshing lesson for those who desire to receive a remission of their sins by living a Christlike life—resulting in a mighty change of heart that alone can serve as a sure and immovable foundation for honoring covenant commitments. An authentic change of heart brings a transformation in our attitudes and behavior. Our affections are directed toward our God in love, and because of our love we obey. Our decisions will be according to the commandments and the will of God, because it is not our own will or the enticements of the world but the will of God we seek to obey. The doctrines, principles, and covenants that King Benjamin teaches, when understood and appreciated, will fill our hearts with gratitude, and we too will make the mighty change and keep our covenants, faithfully enduring to the end.

Here is a question of conscience: King Benjamin's magnificent sermon is a demonstration of the power of the word (see Alma 31:5) and of the Holy Spirit (see 2 Nephi 33:1)—plus the goodness of the people to come and willingly hear the word of God (see Mosiah 2:1). The people offer sacrifices to demonstrate their thanks to the Lord for their blessings. They rejoice in being filled with love toward God and toward all men (see Mosiah 2:3–6). Will we make King Benjamin's sermon a part of our lives, that we might say as those who were there: "we believe all the words which thou hast spoken unto us; and also, we know of their surety and truth, because of the Spirit of the Lord Omnipotent, which has wrought a mighty change in us, or in our hearts, that we have no more disposition to do evil, but to do good continually (Mosiah 5:2)"?

EVIDENCE: Classic Farewell Address (Mosiah 2–5)

Recently, scholars studying the farewell speeches of ancient leaders, both military and political, found many similarities. Several specific themes stand out in the speeches, making it seem as if most of the speakers followed a traditional pattern. These same themes are present in the farewell speeches in the Book of Mormon, including in King Benjamin's final address to his people. It would have been nearly impossible for Joseph Smith to know the themes of a classic farewell address, as no significant information about these patterns had been published at the time. (See *Echoes,* 338–340).

CHAPTER 6

OVERVIEW

King Benjamin determines that all of his listeners, save little children only, have entered into a covenant to serve the Lord. King Benjamin consecrates his son to be ruler and king and appoints priests to teach the people. Mosiah commences his reign and Benjamin passes away. Mosiah reigns in righteousness and peace among the people.

> *1 AND now, king Benjamin thought it was expedient, after having finished speaking to the people, that he should take* ***the names of all those who had entered into a covenant*** *with God to keep his commandments.*
> *2 And it came to pass that there was not one soul, except it were little children, but who had entered into the covenant and had taken upon them the name of Christ.*

The names of all those who had entered into a covenant

Among the thousands assembled at the temple in Zarahemla there is not one (save little children) who does not enter into the covenant of obedience in the wake of the mighty change experienced that day. Universal repentance—what a glorious outcome for the assembly. It reminds us of the triumph of the high priest Melchizedek in Jerusalem at a time when the people had all gone astray. Alma includes the example of Melchizedek in his discourse on the priesthood before the hard-hearted leadership in the city of Ammonihah:

> Now this Melchizedek was a king over the land of Salem; and his people had waxed strong in iniquity and abomination; yea, they had all gone astray; they were full of all manner of wickedness;
>
> But Melchizedek having exercised mighty faith, and received the office of the high priesthood according to the holy order of God, did preach repentance unto his people. And behold, they did repent; and Melchizedek did establish peace in the land in his days; therefore he was called the prince of peace, for he was the king of Salem; and he did reign under his father.
>
> Now, there were many before him, and also there were many afterwards, but none were greater; therefore, of him they have more particularly made mention (Alma 13:17–19).

For Melchizedek they all repented. For Benjamin likewise. How extraordinary to achieve such a blessed outcome through the power of the Atonement and the Spirit—in both cases before the actual atoning sacrifice has been made. Elder Jeffrey R. Holland comments on the miraculous results of King Benjamin's inspired appeal:

2 great leaders who had faith & preached repentance to their people insomuch that all took upon them the name of Christ.

> King Benjamin was delighted with this response from the congregation and informed them that in this covenant-making process, they had become "children of Christ, his sons, and his daughters." "For behold," he told them, "this day he hath spiritually begotten you; for ye say that your hearts are changed through faith on his name; therefore, ye are born of him and have become his sons and his daughters . . ." (Mosiah 5:7).
>
> This is one way in which that title [Father] is appropriately applied to him who is customarily referred to as "Son." He is the Father of redeemed, restored, spiritual life—in short, eternal life. The faithful are born again—of Christ and by Christ and through Christ—when this mighty change wrought by him comes into their hearts. As is appropriate at the time of a new birth, a name is given, and the name the redeemed take upon themselves is "the name of Christ," evidence that all such have entered into a covenant with God that they would be obedient to the gospel to the end of their lives. . . .
>
> That this sermon carried a spiritual power beyond the clarity of the written word is undeniable, for following the close of the discourse and wishing to take "the names of all those who had entered into a covenant," this mighty servant

> of God realized "there was not one soul, except it were little children, but who had entered into the covenant and had taken upon them the name of Christ." (Mosiah 6:1–2.) Oh that we might have more such sermons, and, even more important, that all who hear them might make such honest and binding covenants as a result. (*Christ and the New Covenant: The Messianic Message of the Book of Mormon* [Salt Lake City: Deseret Book, 1997], 102–103)

By keeping our covenants, we receive the blessings of exaltation. Every commandment and covenant honored has a blessing (see D&C 130:20–21), just as every one that is broken has a consequence and punishment (see 2 Nephi 2:26; Amos 2:4; D&C 58:29). Do we keep the covenants we make with the Lord? (See also Mosiah 5:5.)

Mosiah was 30 yrs old when he took over as king.

3–7 King Benjamin consecrates his son to be king and appoints priests to teach the people. Mosiah commences his reign in the thirtieth year of his life (about 124 B.C.), it being 476 years from the time Lehi left Jerusalem. Benjamin lives three more years and passes away. Mosiah reigns in righteousness and peace among the people.

EVIDENCE: Treaty/Covenant Pattern (Mosiah 1–6)

King Benjamin's farewell address and related events reflect a literary pattern used by ancient Israelites. In 1954, biblical scholar George Mendenhall detailed this connection between Hittite treaties and Israelite covenant making, giving six specific elements of the pattern. In summary, the king/prophet (1) introduces God as the one making the covenant, or introduces himself as the spokesman for God; (2) briefly reviews the Lord's past dealings with Israel; (3) lists the terms of the covenant, including the commandments God expects Israel to obey; (4) acknowledges the people's formal acceptance of the covenant; (5) notes the blessings for obeying (and cursings for disobeying) the covenant; and (6) arranges for the safekeeping of a copy of the covenant and for reading it to the people in the future. King Benjamin's address and the events that follow it conform to these six elements of the treaty/covenant pattern, and other connections exist as well. It is important to note that this pattern was completely unknown when the Book of Mormon was published in 1830, and was probably not studied until the 1930s. (See *Echoes,* 389–394).

EVIDENCE: Mosiah's Coronation Ceremony (Mosiah 1–6)

The first six chapters of Mosiah describe the coronation of King Benjamin's son, Mosiah. The account of the coronation conforms to three important elements of ancient Israelite coronations, including (1) the coronation is held at the sanctuary—a society's most sacred spot (in this case, the temple); (2) insignia are conferred upon the king (in this case Mosiah received the brass plates, Laban's sword, and the Liahona); and (3) the king is anointed with oil. A fourth element of an ancient Israelite coronation involved the king receiving a throne name—a new name—when he was crowned. While it is not specified that Mosiah receives his throne name as part of the coronation rite, in light of other Book of Mormon patterns, it is highly likely. (See *Echoes,* 394–395).

CHAPTER 7

OVERVIEW

Mosiah sends an expeditionary force, led by Ammon, to discover the group that has left Zarahemla many years previous to return to the land of Lehi-Nephi. Ammon discovers Limhi and his colony in bondage among the Lamanites. Limhi is overjoyed that deliverance is nigh. He recounts the history of the colony, noting with sorrow that bondage has come because of the wickedness of the people, who have slain a prophet of God [Abinadi] and rejected the message of the gospel. Limhi proclaims before the people that hope for deliverance is now a possibility if they will "turn to the Lord with full purpose of heart" (verse 33).

1–3 After three years of peace in the land, Mosiah authorizes an expeditionary force, led by **Ammon,** to go southward to the land of Lehi-Nephi in search of Limhi's people.

Ammon, Explorer

Ammon is "a strong and mighty man" and a descendant of Zarahemla of Mulekite lineage (Mosiah 7:3). He is the leader of a group sent out around 121 B.C. by Mosiah, son of Benjamin and grandson of Mosiah I, to determine the whereabouts and circumstances of a group of colonists that left Zarahemla about 200 B.C., bound for the land of Nephi (see Omni 1:27–30). As a preview to what will follow below, we note that Ammon is to be successful in his mission. He discovers Limhi and his followers, who are in bondage to the Lamanites. Limhi is the son of Noah, who was the son of Zeniff, the original colonizer. Limhi and his people are enlightened by Ammon concerning the affairs of the people in Zarahemla since the departure of Zeniff, including the last words of King Benjamin (see Mosiah 8:3), delivered around 124 B.C. With the help of Ammon, the colonists eventually escape from Lamanite bondage and return to Zarahemla to join the remainder of the Nephites.

The Principle of Scattering and Gathering

From the higher perspective of the Lord's dealings with His people over the generations, a consistent pattern emerges: He moves and scatters both the righteous and the wicked according to His far-reaching plan to maximize the blessings of redemption for the greatest number of souls. Thus we have seen the influence of His merciful hand in removing Lehi and his family from the dangers of impending bondage in Jerusalem (where the wicked were to be scattered by the Babylonians) to the security of the promised land. And yet, only a generation later, Nephi and his faithful few are again removed from the peril of unrighteous fraternity to the safety of a refuge where they could live in peace "after the manner of happiness" (2 Nephi 5:27). Not many generations hence we see the first Mosiah and his people again warned of the Lord to flee the wrath of their enemies (see Omni 1:12). Thus he and his righteous group are led from the land of Nephi northward to Zarahemla, where they come upon yet another group (the Mulekites) who have likewise been guided by the hand of the Lord to a place of safety. In turn, this new group has come upon the last survivor of yet an earlier nation (the Jaredites) who had followed the Lord's counsel in removing themselves from the scattering associated with the Tower of Babel (see Omni 1:20–22).

The principle of scattering is part of the Lord's agenda for His people, just as the principle of gathering is an instrument of strategic restoration for building, strengthening, and enlarging the tent of Zion. Thus it should not surprise us to see this divine process of diaspora (dispersion) and recovery played out multiple times as evidence of the Lord's infinite love and concern for His sons and daughters. It is only three years into the reign of the second Mosiah (son of King Benjamin) that the persistent "teasings" of the people (see Mosiah 7:1) induce him to yield to their request to organize an expeditionary force to locate the missing group of explorers who had traveled southward to investigate the land of their inheritance (Nephi-Lehi) from whence the first Mosiah has emigrated. As a result, Ammon and his group wander some forty days in the wilderness before coming upon the residue of the earlier expeditionary group, now led by Limhi.

Limhi and his people, as it turns out, are in bondage to the Lamanites because of the iniquity that has crept in among them through the materialistic pride and lascivious living of the previous King Noah and his so-called priests. We are shown the joy of Limhi and his people upon the arrival of Ammon, in whom they see the answer to their prayers for deliverance. It is a chronic pattern described once again by the ancient prophet-historians for the benefit of modern readers: sin and depravity lead to bondage; repentance and righteous obedience lead to liberty.

4–18 Ammon and his group wander forty days in the wilderness before coming upon Limhi's colony in the land occupied by the Lamanites. At first suspicious, the king is soon overjoyed to learn that the party has been sent from Zarahemla to locate them. He explains the dire circumstances the colonists face in being heavily taxed by the increasingly belligerent Lamanites. He calls an assembly to declare unto his people that deliverance is nigh.

> *19 Therefore, lift up your heads, and* ***rejoice,*** *and* ***put your trust in God,*** *in that God who was the God of Abraham, and Isaac, and Jacob; and also, that God who brought the children of Israel out of the land of Egypt, and caused that they should walk through the Red Sea on dry ground, and fed them with manna that they might not perish in the wilderness; and many more things did he do for them.*
> *20 And again, that same God has brought our fathers out of the land of Jerusalem, and has kept and preserved his people even until now; and behold,* ***it is because of our iniquities and abominations that he has brought us into bondage.***

Rejoice; put your trust in God; it is because of our iniquities and abominations that he has brought us into bondage

Limhi rises to declare true principles to the people concerning a way out of their dilemma. As both political and spiritual leader, he exercises authority on behalf of the people. Will they choose to follow his counsel? Consider the statements of latter-day prophets on this important subject. President George Albert Smith declared:

> The path of safety is to follow Church leaders. We are living not only in the day in which [Heavenly Father] has spoken, but we are offered the opportunity to listen to the voices of men who receive his inspiration when they teach us. If therefore we fall into and by forbidden paths we will not be able to blame anybody but ourselves, because if we are teachable, if we are humble, if we are willing to do what the Lord would have us do, we have the information at hand, not only in the records that have been handed down to us by those who have given their lives that we might have the truth, but we also have the privilege of listening to the voices of living oracles who are as unselfish and faithful as those that we revere because of the records that they have left behind. (*The Teachings of George Albert Smith,* ed. Robert McIntosh and Susan McIntosh [Salt Lake City: Bookcraft, 1996], 68)

President Howard W. Hunter confirmed this truth as well: "If we follow the counsel of Church leaders we will not be led astray. If we follow the advice, counsel, and teachings of the leaders of the Church in their instruction to us, we will not go amiss in that which is important for our own personal salvation and exaltation" (*The Teachings of Howard W. Hunter*, ed. Clyde J. Williams [Salt Lake City: Bookcraft, 1997], 223).

21–27 King Limhi rehearses before the people the history of their colony, beginning with Zeniff, the first king who has entered into a treaty with the king of the Lamanites to occupy part of the land. The king of the Lamanites has agreed in order to support his hidden agenda of eventually taxing the Nephites to the extent of half of all their increase. The people fall into wickedness and cause bloodshed among themselves. They slay a prophet of God [Abinadi] who comes among them to teach true principles of the gospel of Jesus Christ. Having rejected the counsel of a living prophet, they are exposed to the judgment of the Almighty God.

> *28 And now, because he [Abinadi] said this, they did put him to death; and many more things did they do which brought down the wrath of God upon them. Therefore,* ***who wondereth that they are in bondage,*** *and that they are smitten with sore afflictions?*

WHO WONDERETH THAT THEY ARE IN BONDAGE?
The people of the Nephite colony fail to heed the counsel of a prophet of God and therefore continue their accelerated decline into bondage and oppression at the hands of their enemies. It is no surprise when the decrees of a just God come to pass.

29–32 King Limhi confirms that the suffering of his people stems directly from their disobedience to the commandments of God. However, he holds out hope for deliverance, based on a change in their desires and actions.

> *33 But if ye will* ***turn to the Lord with full purpose of heart,*** *and put your trust in him, and serve him with all diligence of mind, if ye do this,* ***he will, according to his own will and pleasure, deliver you out of bondage.***

TURN TO THE LORD WITH FULL PURPOSE OF HEART; HE WILL, ACCORDING TO HIS OWN WILL AND PLEASURE, DELIVER YOU OUT OF BONDAGE
There is always the light of hope in the gloom of bondage. The lessons of history resound with these truths: sin leads to bondage; hope and faith lead to deliverance.

CHAPTER 8

OVERVIEW

At King Limhi's request, Ammon reports to the people concerning events in Zarahemla from the time Zeniff first departs for the land of Lehi-Nephi and the time Ammon himself follows in his footsteps. Ammon learns of the twenty-four gold plates discovered by Limhi's search party and reports to Limhi that the king at Zarahemla (Mosiah) has a gift from God that enables him to translate the plates. Ammon explains to King Limhi the nature of the office of a seer, who is both a revelator and a prophet. Limhi rejoices in the greatness of God as contrasted with the blindness of men.

1–12 King Limhi arranges for Ammon to share with the people all that has transpired in Zarahemla from the time that Zeniff has departed on his exploratory excursion (around 200 B.C.) until the time that Ammon sets out on his journey (around 121 B.C.). Ammon rehearses for them the final discourse of King Benjamin before they are dismissed to return to their homes. Limhi shares with Ammon the record of the colonists from the time of Zeniff to the current day and also the story of the discovery of twenty-four plates of gold brought back by a search party sent out from the colony to find Zarahemla (verse 9). Limhi inquires whether Ammon knows of anyone who can translate the plates and reveal how the source nation has been destroyed.

> *13 Now Ammon said unto him: I can assuredly tell thee, O king, of a man that can translate the records; for he has wherewith that he can look, and translate all records that are of ancient date; and it is* ***a gift from God.*** *And the things are called interpreters, and no man can look in them except he be commanded, lest he should look for that he ought not and he should perish. And whosoever is commanded to look in them,* ***the same is called seer.***

A GIFT FROM GOD; THE SAME IS CALLED SEER

The vision of a seer is the Lord's blessing for mankind. The Lord has not left us to wander blindly upon the mortal landscape, but has illuminated the pathway with light imparted through his chosen servants—prophets, seers, and revelators.

> *14 And behold, the king of the people who are in the land of Zarahemla is the man that is commanded to do these things, and who has this* ***high gift from God.***
> *15 And the king said that* ***a seer is greater than a prophet.***

16 And Ammon said that ***a seer is a revelator and a prophet also;*** *and a gift which is greater can no man have, except he should possess the power of God, which no man can; yet a man may have great power given him from God.*
17 But ***a seer can know of things which are past, and also of things which are to come,*** *and by them shall all things be revealed, or, rather, shall secret things be made manifest, and hidden things shall come to light, and things which are not known shall be made known by them, and also things shall be made known by them which otherwise could not be known.*
18 Thus God has provided a means that man, through faith, might work ***mighty miracles;*** *therefore he becometh a great benefit to his fellow beings.*

High gift from God; a seer is greater than a prophet; a seer is a revelator and a prophet also; a seer can know of things which are past, and also of things which are to come; mighty miracles

Limhi is overjoyed to learn from Ammon concerning Mosiah's remarkable ability to interpret ancient languages such as that found on the twenty-four plates. In this context, we have from Ammon the essential explanation of the role of seer in the priesthood of God.

19 And now, when Ammon had made an end of speaking these words ***the king rejoiced*** *exceedingly,* ***and gave thanks to God,*** *saying: Doubtless a great mystery is contained within these plates, and these interpreters were doubtless prepared for the purpose of unfolding all such mysteries to the children of men.*
20 O ***how marvelous are the works of the Lord,*** *and how long doth he suffer with his people; yea, and how blind and impenetrable are the understandings of the children of men; for they will not seek wisdom, neither do they desire that she should rule over them!*
21 Yea, they are ***as a wild flock*** *which fleeth from the shepherd, and scattereth, and are driven, and are devoured by the beasts of the forest.*

The king rejoiced and gave thanks to God; how marvelous are the works of the Lord; as a wild flock

The response of the king is to rejoice and express thanksgiving for the divine solution at hand for interpreting the mysterious gold plates containing the record made by the hand of Ether, the last of the Jaredite prophets, which will be abridged in due time by Moroni (see Ether 1:2). Then the king utters an impressive poetic expression concerning the contrast between the wonders of the

Lord and the blindness and hard-heartedness of men who eschew wisdom and wander without aim as a wild flock.

THE RECORD OF ZENIFF

An account of his people, from the time they left the land of Zarahemla until the time that they were delivered out of the hands of the Lamanites. [Note: This preamble was included in the original edition of the Book of Mormon published in 1830.]

OVERVIEW OF SECTION

The history of the people of Zeniff, beginning with their departure from Zarahemla around 200 B.C. until the time they are delivered from Lamanite bondage through the hand of the Lord and thereafter returned to Zarahemla to unite with the people of Mosiah around 121 B.C. (Chapters 9 through 22.)

CHAPTER 9

OVERVIEW

During the original excursion from Zarahemla to the land of Lehi-Nephi (around 200 B.C.), Zeniff discerns merit in the Lamanite people and counters the orders, albeit in vain, of the commander to slay them. Zeniff survives the resulting battle and returns to Zarahemla to organize a second excursion. The Lamanites permit the Nephites to settle in part of the land—but only for the purpose of enslaving them. Zeniff and his people defend themselves over a period of many years "in the strength of the Lord" (verse 17).

*1 I, **ZENIFF,** having been taught in all the language of the Nephites, and having had a knowledge of the land of Nephi, or of the land of our fathers' first inheritance, and having been sent as a spy among the Lamanites that I might spy out their forces, that our army might come upon them and destroy them—but when I saw that which was good among them I was desirous that they should not be destroyed.*

Zeniff: Zealous Colonizer

It is a natural inclination in the hearts of most people to retain an attachment to the place of their origin after they have moved away. So it is with Zeniff. Zeniff is a decent and principled individual, "having been taught in all the language of the Nephites, and having had a knowledge of the land of Nephi, or of the land of our fathers' first inheritance" (Mosiah 9:1). We gain insight into Zeniff's honorable character when we learn that he refuses to participate in the destruction of the Lamanites according to the orders of his army leader, saying "When I saw that which was good among them I was desirous that they should not be destroyed" (verse 1).

2–8 The leader of Zeniff's party, "being an austere and a blood-thirsty man" (verse 2), orders Zeniff's execution, thus causing the eruption of an intense battle in which all but fifty of the contingent perish. Having survived, Zeniff returns to Zarahemla for a time; however, "being over-zealous to inherit the land of our fathers" (verse 3), he reorganizes the party and sets out again to obtain the land of Nephi, then controlled by the Lamanites. He makes a treaty with Laman, the king of the Lamanites, to occupy a part of the land where the Nephites can begin to settle and sustain themselves.

> *9 And we began to till the ground, yea, even with all manner of seeds, with seeds of corn, and of wheat, and of barley, and with neas, and with* ***sheum,*** *and with seeds of all manner of fruits; and we did begin to multiply and prosper in the land.*

EVIDENCE: Sheum. Akkadian "She'um"

When Zeniff, the Nephite ruler, lists the crops his people cultivate, he names corn, wheat, barley, and *sheum,* a term with which most English-speaking people are unfamiliar. In the last forty years, *she'um* has been identified as the most important grain among the Akkadians (or Babylonians) of Mesopotamia. Interestingly, in Akkadian the word *she'um* means barley, while in Old Assyrian it signifies *wheat.* Since these two specific grains are already listed in Mosiah 9:9, it is probable that the Jaredites or Nephites gave another cultivable plant the name *she'um.* (See *Echoes,* 288).

10–19 Zeniff eventually learns that the accommodation made by the Lamanites has the hidden purpose of enslaving the Nephites, "that they might glut themselves with the labors of our hands; yea, that they might feast themselves upon the flocks of our fields" (verse 12). Over a period of several decades, Zeniff and his people labor to preserve and sustain their families through diligence and hard work, while at the same time defending themselves "in the strength of the Lord" (verse 17; compare Mosiah 10:10) against periodic incursions from the Lamanite forces.

CHAPTER 10

OVERVIEW

Zeniff and his people prosper in the land for some twenty-two years. They are industrious and productive. They defend themselves against the brutality of the Lamanites, who foster the false tradition that they have been wronged by the Nephites for generations. Zeniff and his people are victorious in a battle against the successor son of King Laman. The aging Zeniff confers the kingdom upon his son Noah.

1–10 Zeniff and his people flourish in the land of their fathers, toiling and laboring to sustain themselves and to defend themselves against the Lamanites. "In the strength of the Lord" (verse 10) they battle against the successor to King Laman.

> *11 Now,* ***the Lamanites knew nothing concerning the Lord,*** *nor the strength of the Lord, therefore they depended upon their own strength. Yet they were a strong people, as to the strength of men.*
> *12 They were* ***a wild, and ferocious, and a blood-thirsty people,*** *believing in the tradition of their fathers, which is this—Believing that they were driven out of the land of Jerusalem because of the iniquities of their fathers, and that they were* ***wronged*** *in the wilderness by their brethren, and they were also* ***wronged*** *while crossing the sea;*
> *13 And again, that they were* ***wronged*** *while in the land of their first inheritance, after they had crossed the sea, and all this because that Nephi was more faithful in keeping the commandments of the Lord—therefore he was favored of the Lord, for the Lord heard his prayers and answered them, and he took the lead of their journey in the wilderness.*
> *14 And his brethren were wroth with him because they understood not the dealings of the Lord; they were also wroth with him upon the waters because they hardened their hearts against the Lord.*
> *15 And again, they were wroth with him when they had arrived in the promised land, because they said that he had taken the ruling of the people out of their hands; and they sought to kill him.*
> *16 And again, they were wroth with him because he departed into the wilderness as the Lord had commanded him, and took the records which were engraven on the plates of brass, for they said that he* ***robbed*** *them.*

17 And thus they have ***taught their children*** *that they should hate them, and that they should murder them, and that they should rob and plunder them, and do all they could to destroy them; therefore they have an eternal hatred toward the children of Nephi.*

The Lamanites knew nothing concerning the Lord; a wild, and ferocious, and a blood-thirsty people; wronged; robbed; taught their children

From the words of Zeniff we have the most comprehensive statement in the Book of Mormon concerning the traditional Lamanite perspective vis-à-vis the Nephites and why the Lamanites cultivate an insatiable desire to kill them. Three factors are at work in their belief system; they believe (1) that they have been wrongly deprived of their inheritance in Jerusalem; (2) that they ha been wronged in transit to the New World and during the initial settlement period when Nephi wrested from them their right to leadership; and (3) that they have been robbed of the plates of brass. To this, Zeniff counters with the observation that "Nephi was more faithful in keeping the commandments of the Lord—therefore he was favored of the Lord, for the Lord heard his prayers and answered them, and he took the lead of their journey in the wilderness" (verse 13) because his brethren "understood not the dealings of the Lord" (verse 14).

The Lamanites depend upon their own strength. Their vengeful anger toward the Nephites is anchored in the false traditions of their fathers. They are full of hatred because they know not the dealings of the Lord. Thus they teach their children to hate the Nephites and to snub the Lord. What application for our own lives can we draw from this unfortunate situation? We learn that when people separate themselves from the Lord they are left to themselves. They know not the dealings of the Lord, and thus they often feel hurt, become angry, and then rebel. As we ponder these events, we can learn from them and realize that when we find ourselves inclined to complain about something in the Church or find fault with our leaders, we are in need of repentance.

A Story to Help Us Remember the Lord Always

When hatred fills the human heart, it obscures and filters out the beauty that is constantly around us. Elder Elray L. Christiansen confirms this sad truth in the following illustration:

> Some time ago I read a story that had a profound influence upon me. . . . It was about a young man who had committed a serious crime and was languishing in jail, awaiting execution in payment for the crime (if that will pay it). During his last night on earth, of course, he did not sleep. Dawn found him standing at the

window of his cell, holding the bars, looking out. He could see over the prison walls and behold the countryside around about and the sky.

As the sky brightened with the dawning of the day, a changed seemed to come over him—a change of values, a change of appreciation for what he had hitherto considered commonplace, unworthy of his notice. He observed the rich, brown earth, and the leaves of the trees and the bright green fields and the sky. He gripped the bars of his cell and stared intently at the scene which lay before him, but which had been unnoticed through his lifetime. Tears came to his eyes, and he realized for the first time the glory and the magnificence of the world about him. As the muffled footsteps of the jailors could be heard on their way to the cell, he still stood at his window, transfixed by the unspeakable beauty of the dawning of the day and the rising of the sun.

Of course, the beauty and the wonder of it had been there all during his twenty-three years. He had simply let *time* run out on him until now it was too late to fully enjoy it. I doubt if he is the only one who has failed to make the most of his opportunities and appreciate while there is still time to do so.

"Time is so fleeting," said Hans Christian Andersen, "that if we do not remember God and learn of him in our youth, age may find us incapable of thinking of him." ("The Endowment Time," *BYU Speeches of the Year,* March 14, 1962, 3–4)

18–22 Zeniff teaches his people the cause of the chronic hatred felt by the Lamanites for the Nephites. The people respond by contending with the Lamanites face-to-face, doing so by "putting their trust in the Lord" (verse 19). The people of Zeniff triumph and return to their homes in peace. The aging Zeniff confers his kingdom upon one of his sons (Noah) around 160 B.C. The last words we have from Zeniff are these: "And may the Lord bless my people" (Mosiah 10:22).

CONCLUDING THOUGHTS

Under a covenant banner of truth, Zeniff, as king of the Nephite colony, is able to lead the people to victory over the Lamanites and preserve at least a semblance of stability and peace for a period of time. This delicate balance between Nephite and Lamanite interests ends to the disadvantage of the colonists soon after Zeniff confers the kingdom upon his son Noah, who becomes a wicked ruler. Nevertheless, during his days of service, Zeniff remembers the Lord and attempts to guide his people in righteous paths. That his prayer is answered is later confirmed by King Mosiah in Zarahemla, who rejoices in the deliverance of the Zeniff/Limhi colony from bondage (Mosiah 25:5–8). And Zeniff's prayer continues to be answered on behalf of all sincere readers of the Book of Mormon who acquire through their study the yearning to return once again to their homelands—even the home of Deity in the celestial realm.

CHAPTER 11

OVERVIEW

King Noah and his priests revel in immorality and squander tax revenues on lavish structures. They defeat the Lamanites for a time and boast in their own strength. Abinadi comes among the people to call them to repentance. Noah seeks to take his life.

> *1 AND now it came to pass that Zeniff conferred the kingdom upon* ***Noah,*** *one of his sons; therefore Noah began to reign in his stead; and he did not walk in the ways of his father.*

NOAH, WICKED KING

Noah is the second of the Nephite kings in the colony established by Zeniff among the Lamanites in the land of Nephi (south of the land of Zarahemla) beginning around 200 B.C. The aging Zeniff confers the kingdom upon his son, Noah, around 160 B.C. But Noah's greed and lasciviousness propel the people into a state of godlessness, leading to bondage and oppression at the hands of their Lamanite hosts. The Lord sends the prophet Abinadi to call Noah and his complicit priests to repentance (see Mosiah 11:20–29; chapters 12–17). Noah is struck with fear at the compelling message of the impending judgments of God, but his priests stir him to anger anew against Abinadi, who is then delivered to a fiery death. Before his demise, the prophet declares to Noah: "Behold, even as ye have done unto me, so shall it come to pass that thy seed shall cause that many shall suffer the pains that I do suffer, even the pains of death by fire; and this because they believe in the salvation of the Lord their God" (Mosiah 17:15).

2–14 Noah sets his heart on wealth and riotous living. He replaces all of Zeniff's priests with minions of his own and cultivates a pattern of worldliness, oppression of the people, and promiscuity, building lavish palaces and towers with revenues derived from excessive taxation.

15 And it came to pass that he planted vineyards round about in the land; and he built wine-presses, and made ***wine*** *in abundance; and therefore he became a wine-bibber, and also his people.*

EVIDENCE: WINE

Some scholars have asserted that wine produced from grapes was not made or used in ancient America, so they discount the reference to wine in Mosiah 11:15. But the scripture does not mention grapes, and many other types of drinks are often referred to as wine. The Spaniards who came to Mesoamerica hundreds of years ago wrote of several varieties of native "wines," including an intoxicating beverage made with water, a specific type of tree bark, and honey. Other groups fermented juices from bananas, pineapples, hearts of palm, or the agave plant, and the Europeans applied the term *wine* to all of these beverages. Furthermore, it is possible that Nephite wine was actually made from grapes, as the grape plant was recently identified near ancient ruins in the Mexican state of Chiapas. (See *Echoes,* 288–289).

16–19 The Lamanites begin to come against the colony with some success, since Noah has failed to set up sufficient defenses on the perimeter. Noah unleashes his army against the intruders and drives them back for a time—causing the Nephites to boast "in their own strength" (verse 19) and rejoice in the victory and bloodshed.

20 And it came to pass that there was a man among them whose name was ***Abinadi;*** *and he went forth among them, and began to prophesy, saying: Behold, thus saith the Lord, and thus hath he commanded me, saying, Go forth, and say unto this people, thus saith the Lord—Wo be unto this people, for I have seen their abominations, and their wickedness, and their whoredoms; and except they repent I will visit them in mine anger.*

ABINADI, TRIUMPH OF VALOR

Abinadi is an enduring symbol of the triumph of divine standards over sinful pride. When the Lord sends Abinadi to preach repentance and warn the people against the inevitable destructive outcomes of their behavior, the prophet's compelling words are rejected. Before the court of wicked King Noah, Abinadi fulfills with boldness the commission of crying repentance to the debauched and profligate leadership of the Nephite colony. Abinadi is forced to flee. Two years later, however, he returns in disguise to convey the dire pronouncement of the Lord: "And it shall come to pass that except they repent I will utterly destroy them from off the face of the earth" (Mosiah 12:8). Abinadi delivers his message with courage and inspiration, then seals his testimony as a martyr in the flames of retribution. By his actions, Abinadi is a type and shadow of the Redeemer. Like Christ, he shrinks not from the charge to stand firm against evil and to carry out the will of the Father in giving his life for the cause of spiritual liberty.

> *21 And **except they repent** and turn to the Lord their God, behold, I will deliver them into the hands of their enemies; yea, and they shall be into **bondage;** and they shall be afflicted by the hand of their enemies.*
> *22 And it shall come to pass that they shall know that I am the Lord their God, and am a jealous God, visiting the iniquities of my people.*
> *23 And it shall come to pass that **except this people repent** and turn unto the Lord their God, they shall be brought into **bondage;** and none shall deliver them, except it be the Lord the Almighty God.*

Except they repent; bondage

Abinadi exhorts the people to repent or the Lord will deliver them into the hands of their enemies. Let us learn that being accepted of the Lord requires repentance. He will have his people be humbled in order that they might repent (see Helaman11:4–11). Our choice in life is to repent in all sincerity or receive the condemnation of the Lord.

Hope in the Lord Jesus Christ

Of all the doctrines found in the scriptures and preached from the pulpit, without doubt the most repeated principle taught is repentance. That is the message of Abinadi and all the Lord's prophets. M. G. Easton describes the elements well:

> (1) A true sense of one's own guilt and sinfulness; (2) an apprehension of God's mercy in Christ; (3) an actual hatred of sin (Ps. 119:128; Job 42:5, 6; 2 Cor. 7:10) and turning from it to God; and (4) a persistent endeavour after a holy life in a walking with God in the way of his commandments. The true penitent is conscious of guilt (Ps. 51:4, 9), of pollution (51:5, 7, 10), and of helplessness (51:11; 109:21, 22). Thus he apprehends himself to be just what God has always seen him to be and declares him to be. But repentance comprehends not only such a sense of sin, but also an apprehension of mercy, without which

there can be no true repentance (Ps. 51:1; 130:4). (M. G. Easton, *Illustrated Bible Dictionary*).

The Book of Mormon teaches us that we should preach nothing save it be faith and repentance (see Mosiah 18:20; Mosiah 25:15; Alma 37:33; Helaman 6:4). As missionaries, we teach discussions about the plan of redemption, the gospel of Jesus Christ, the principles of a Christlike life, and the doctrines of the kingdom of God as promulgated by the Lamb of God. An integral part of each discussion is to have faith to accept the teaching and courage to repent and live it. In every lesson taught, with every principle or doctrine expounded upon, and in every situation when the word of God is preached, we are to embrace the principles of faith and repentance. Thus we see that faith is the foundation of all righteousness and that through repentance we can become righteous—even clean and pure. How do we become perfect? Repent perfectly.

I will never forget Cecil B. DeMille's talk at BYU in the 1950s. The *Ten Commandments* had been released and everyone was seeing this epic film. He talked about the commandments of God and how they could not be broken. As I sat there wondering what he meant, he then said, "You can't break the Ten Commandments—they are God's commandments. You can only break yourself against them." It was a profound truth taught by a master teacher. When we break the commandments, we are the ones who lose. We separate ourselves from God. We lose His Spirit. There is only one hope in this life and that is in the Lord Jesus Christ. We must strive to obey His commandments, and repent when we have broken ourselves against them. He has redeemed our souls if we will but repent. Yes, repenting of our sins is the greatest thing we will do for our lives. (Ed J. Pinegar)

24 Yea, and it shall come to pass that when they shall cry unto me ***I will be slow to hear their cries;*** *yea, and I will suffer them that they be smitten by their enemies.*
25 And except they repent in sackcloth and ashes, and cry mightily to the Lord their God, I will ***not hear their prayers,*** *neither will I deliver them out of their afflictions; and thus saith the Lord, and thus hath he commanded me.*

I WILL BE SLOW TO HEAR THEIR CRIES; NOT HEAR THEIR PRAYERS

King Noah, the paragon of evil, greed, and promiscuity, is diametrically opposite of the nobility and valor of his namesake from the Old Testament. When a branch of the House of Israel descends to the depths of depravity displayed by King Noah's generation in what the Lord has decreed will be a land of promise for the faithful, there is always an inexorable and predictable response from heaven: prophetic intervention. In this case, King Noah encounters Abinadi. It is an encounter that begins with a majestic call to repentance (Mosiah 11:20–25) and continues with the predictable rejection of that call, bringing a second encounter of greater forcefulness. This, in turn, leads to the martyrdom of the Lord's anointed and, eventually, the demise of the forces of evil. This is a case study in the condition of the heart, for Noah and his people display hearts so hardened that they are impenetrable. From them we can extract a lesson for our day, i.e., the Lord commands that we bring before Him the acceptable offering of a broken heart and a contrite spirit (see Psalm 51:17; 2 Nephi 2:7; 3 Nephi 9:20; Mormon 2:14; Moroni 6:2; D&C 59:8).

26–28 In their anger the people seek to slay Abinadi. King Noah condemns him to die.

> *29 Now the eyes of the people were blinded; therefore* ***they hardened their hearts*** *against the words of Abinadi, and they sought from that time forward to take him. And* ***King Noah hardened his heart*** *against the word of the Lord, and he did not repent of his evil doings.*

THEY HARDENED THEIR HEARTS; KING NOAH HARDENED HIS HEART

Upon the prideful and impenitent the word of God falls as the sword of justice, but upon the humble and obedient it distills as comforting dews from heaven. When people reject the word of God, dire consequences inevitably follow. Elder Mark E. Petersen confirms this truth:

> Abinadi came as a prophet of the Lord to call the people to repentance. He went among them and began to prophesy, saying: "Behold, thus saith the Lord, and thus hath he commanded me, saying, Go forth, and say unto this people, thus saith the Lord—Wo be unto this people, for I have seen their abominations, and their wickedness, and their whoredoms; and except they repent I will visit them in mine anger." (Mosiah 11:20.)
>
> Note that Abinadi received a revelation from the Lord calling him to confront the king, and giving him instructions as to what he should say. His words were forceful: "Thus saith the Lord," he cried out, "and thus hath he commanded me," and then he quotes the language of the Lord.
>
> God always directs his prophets. There was revelation in those days even as now. And so the Lord commanded Abinadi to give his warning, "Thus saith the Lord, Wo be unto this people."

This was revelation, and it was God's message to those people. Abinadi was but the instrument of communication. The language is in the first person, as the Lord himself addressed them. . . .

Abinadi's visit left the people more than ever entrenched in their sins. Their "hearts were hardened" against the words of the prophet as they searched for him that they might kill him.

"And King Noah hardened his heart against the word of the Lord, and he did not repent of his evil doings" (Mosiah 11:21–29.). (*Alma and Abinadi* [Salt Lake City: Deseret Book, 1983], 8–9)

CONCLUDING THOUGHTS

From these episodes in the Book of Mormon we are renewed in our conviction that the gospel of Jesus Christ brings us the light of hope in the darkness of bondage—whether that bondage be discouragement, uncorrected sinfulness, or rebelliousness and pride. Through modern-day scriptures, we receive confirmation that the Lord has again restored to the earth the blessings of the vision of prophets, seers, and revelators, just as in ages past. When we ponder the written word of God and listen to the inspired pronouncements of His chosen servants, we show our love for God and His servants. We then find ourselves on the strait and narrow path where rich blessings wait in store, the greatest being eternal life.

CHAPTER 12

OVERVIEW

Abinadi returns after two years to continue warning the people to repent. He is imprisoned by the king and subjected to a cross-examination intended to silence him. Instead, his words expose the hypocrisy and wickedness of his accusers in their failing to live and teach the Ten Commandments given unto Moses.

1 AND it came to pass that ***after the space of two years that Abinadi came among them*** *in disguise, that they knew him not, and began to prophesy among them, saying: Thus has the Lord commanded me, saying—Abinadi,* ***go and prophesy unto this my people,*** *for they have hardened their hearts against my words; they have repented not of their evil doings; therefore,* ***I will visit them in my anger,*** *yea, in my fierce anger will I visit them in their iniquities and abominations.*

Mosiah 12:1–8

After the space of two years Abinadi came among them; go and prophesy unto this my people; I will visit them in my anger

Two years after Abinadi delivers his initial call to repentance before the people of King Noah, he returns in disguise to deliver his final and ultimate declaration that God's judgments will be poured out upon this impenitent and rebellious generation. In the Spirit of the Lord, Abinadi tries, convicts, and sentences his detractors in the court of God's justice, rendering them incapable of countering his irrefutable evidence of their wickedness in wantonly violating the Ten Commandments.

> 2 *Yea,* ***wo be unto this generation!*** *And the Lord said unto me: Stretch forth thy hand and prophesy, saying: Thus saith the Lord, it shall come to pass that this generation, because of their iniquities, shall be brought into bondage, and shall be smitten on the cheek; yea, and shall be driven by men, and shall be slain; and the vultures of the air, and the dogs, yea, and the wild beasts, shall devour their flesh.*
>
> 3 *And it shall come to pass that* ***the life of King Noah shall be valued even as a garment in a hot furnace;*** *for he shall know that I am the Lord.*

EVIDENCE: Wo be unto this generation; the life of King Noah shall be valued even as a garment in a hot furnace—Simile Curses (Mosiah 12:3, Mosiah 12:11, Alma 46:22)

Simile curses are found in many ancient Near Eastern writings, including treaties, prophecies, and religious texts dealing with covenants. In a simile curse, an invocation for harm to come upon the recipient is given in the form of a comparison between two objects, often using *like* or *as.* Since simile curses appear only a handful of times in the Old Testament, Joseph Smith was probably unaware of the concept. Therefore, the presence of numerous simile curses in the Book of Mormon attests its Near Eastern background. (See *Echoes,* 156–159).

4–7 Abinadi quotes the Lord in projecting inevitable consequences of destruction upon the people (famine, pestilence, burdens, hail, wind storms, insects)—unless they repent.

> 8 *And it shall come to pass that* ***except they repent I will utterly destroy them*** *from off the face of the earth; yet they shall* ***leave a record behind them,*** *and I will preserve them for other nations which shall possess the land; yea, even this will I do that*

I may discover the abominations of this people to other nations. And many things did Abinadi prophesy against this people.

EXCEPT THEY REPENT I WILL UTTERLY DESTROY THEM; LEAVE A RECORD BEHIND THEM
The universal message of the prophets to a wayward people is repent or be destroyed. Salvation comes solely through the redemptive mission of Jesus Christ. The message of the Savior, through His prophets, is that the faithful and obedient may come and freely partake of the eternal joys of the gospel, while the rebellious and impenitent will suffer the consequences of damnation. The record concerning the wickedness of the people is the record that readers of the Book of Mormon hold in their hands. The words of Abinadi concerning the evil of King Noah and his people resound to the four quarters of the earth as a warning of the consequences of unrepentant disobedience. The imminent destruction of Noah and his circle of wicked followers corroborates of the truth that the word of the Lord will always be fulfilled.

9–18 The people bring Abinadi before the king and falsely accuse the prophet of condemning them and prophesying evil concerning the king. As evidence of Abinadi's error, they pridefully ascribe to themselves invincible strength. Noah imprisons Abinadi and holds a council concerning his fate.

19 And they began to question him, that they might cross him, that thereby they might have wherewith to accuse him; but he answered them boldly, and withstood all their questions, yea, to their astonishment; for ***he did withstand them in all their questions,*** *and did confound them in all their words.*
20 And it came to pass that one of them said unto him: What meaneth the words which are written, and which have been taught by our fathers, saying:
21 ***How beautiful upon the mountains are the feet of him that bringeth good tidings;*** *that publisheth peace; that bringeth good tidings of good; that publisheth salvation; that saith unto Zion, Thy God reigneth;*
22 Thy watchmen shall lift up the voice; with the voice together shall they ***sing;*** *for they shall see eye to eye when the Lord shall bring again Zion;*
23 Break forth into ***joy;*** *sing together ye waste places of Jerusalem; for the Lord hath* ***comforted*** *his people, he hath* ***redeemed*** *Jerusalem;*
24 The Lord hath made bare his holy arm in the eyes of all the nations, and all the ends of the earth shall see the ***salvation*** *of our God?*

He did withstand them in all their questions; How beautiful upon the mountains are the feet of him that bringeth good tidings; sing; joy; comforted; redeemed; salvation

Before the court of the king, Abinadi is subjected to a cross-examination intended to expose his fraudulent claims. One of the priests asks him about the meaning of the scripture from Isaiah which reads, "How beautiful upon the mountains are the feet of him that bringeth good tidings; that publisheth peace; that bringeth good tidings of good; that publisheth salvation; that saith unto Zion, Thy God reigneth" (Mosiah 12:21; compare Isaiah 52:7). The priest seems to imply with this reference that the gospel should be all about peace and good tidings, comfort and joy rather than inveighing against the good name of the king and his court. In this misguided effort to contrast the biblical prophecy about peace and good news with Abinadi's divinely commissioned invective against sin, the priest reveals his ignorance of scripture and his serious misjudgment about the power behind Abinadi's mission as a servant of the Almighty.

25–37 Abinadi accuses his audience of hypocrisy in teaching what they fail to understand. "Ye have not applied your hearts to understanding; therefore, ye have not been wise. Therefore, what teach ye this people?" (verse 27). When they respond that they teach the law of Moses, Abinadi points out their obvious failure to live the Ten Commandments and to teach the people to abide by the word of the Lord.

CHAPTER 13

OVERVIEW

Abinadi is protected from his angry assailants by the power of God. He completes his discourse on the Ten Commandments and declares the people guilty of violating these commandments. He teaches that the law of Moses points to the coming Atonement of the Messiah, without which all would be lost.

> *1 AND now when the king had heard these words, he said unto his priests: Away with this fellow, and* ***slay him;*** *for what have we to do with him, for he is mad.*
> *2 And they stood forth and attempted to lay their hands on him; but he withstood them, and said unto them:*

3 ***Touch me not,*** *for God shall smite you if ye lay your hands upon me, for* ***I have***
not delivered the message *which the Lord sent me to deliver; neither have I told you*
that which ye requested that I should tell; therefore, God will not suffer that I shall be
destroyed at this time.
4 But ***I must fulfil the commandments*** *wherewith God has commanded me; and*
because I have told you the truth ye are angry with me. And again, because I have
spoken the word of God ye have judged me that I am mad.
5 Now it came to pass after Abinadi had spoken these words that the people of King
Noah durst not lay their hands on him, for ***the Spirit of the Lord was upon him;***
and his face shone with exceeding luster, even as Moses' did while in the mount of
Sinai, while speaking with the Lord.

SLAY HIM; TOUCH ME NOT; I HAVE NOT DELIVERED THE MESSAGE; I MUST FULFIL THE COMMANDMENTS; THE SPIRIT OF THE LORD WAS UPON HIM

Abinadi is protected from his assailants because his divine mission is as yet incomplete. Abinadi overpowers his audience with prophetic utterances anchored in the word of God and conveyed by the power of the Spirit to the extent that his enemies dare not lay their hands on him.

6 And he spake ***with power and authority from God;*** *and he continued his words,*
saying:
7 Ye see that ye have not power to slay me, therefore I finish my message. Yea, and I perceive
that it cuts you to your hearts because I tell you the truth concerning your iniquities.
8 Yea, and my words fill you with wonder and amazement, and with anger.
9 But I finish my message; and then it matters not whither I go, if it so be that I am
saved.
10 But this much I tell you, ***what you do with me, after this, shall be as a type and***
a shadow of things which are to come.

WITH POWER AND AUTHORITY FROM GOD; WHAT YOU DO WITH ME, AFTER THIS, SHALL BE AS A TYPE AND A SHADOW OF THINGS WHICH ARE TO COME

Abinadi speaks with the power of God and prophesies that his treatment hereafter will prefigure future outcomes—in particular for his detractors. Abinadi continues his delivery, repudiating the court for its failure to teach and exemplify the Ten Commandments and uphold the law of Moses, and he emphatically declares the coming Atonement of Christ as the ordained fulfillment of the law.

Mosiah 13:11–35

11–26 Abinadi teaches the Ten Commandments and holds the people accountable for not keeping them.

> *27 And now ye have said that salvation cometh by the law of Moses. I say unto you that it is expedient that ye should* ***keep the law of Moses as yet;*** *but I say unto you, that the time shall come when it shall no more be expedient to keep the law of Moses.*
> *28 And moreover, I say unto you, that* ***salvation doth not come by the law alone;*** *and were it not for* ***the atonement,*** *which God himself shall make for the sins and iniquities of his people, that they must unavoidably perish, notwithstanding the law of Moses.*

KEEP THE LAW OF MOSES AS YET; SALVATION DOTH NOT COME BY THE LAW ALONE; THE ATONEMENT

Law of Moses & Atonement

Law of Moses

Abinadi sets forth the relationship between the law of Moses and the Atonement. The former is a provisional pathway to a higher manifestation of saving doctrine; the latter is essential for salvation, for without the Atonement, all are lost.

29–31 The law of Moses is a program of "performances and ordinances" (verse 30) given to the children of Israel to remind them of their duty to God. But they fail to understand that the law points to something more important to come.

> *32 And now, did they understand the law? I say unto you, Nay, they did not all understand the law; and this because of the hardness of their hearts; for they understood not that there could not any man be saved* ***except it were through the redemption of God.***
> *33 For behold, did not Moses prophesy unto them concerning the coming of* ***the Messiah,*** *and that God should redeem his people? Yea, and even* ***all the prophets*** *who have prophesied ever since the world began—have they not spoken more or less concerning these things?*
> *34 Have they not said that God himself should come down among the children of men, and take upon him the form of man, and go* ***forth in mighty power*** *upon the face of the earth?*
> *35 Yea, and have they not said also that he should bring to pass the resurrection of the dead, and that he, himself, should be oppressed and afflicted?*

EXCEPT IT WERE THROUGH THE REDEMPTION OF GOD; THE MESSIAH; ALL THE PROPHETS; GO FORTH IN MIGHTY POWER

Abinadi is assailed by his interrogators because his message does not conform with the tenor of Isaiah's pronouncements about "good tidings of good" (verse 21) and the comforts that accompany the salvation of Zion. What they fail to perceive is that "there could not any man be saved except it were through the redemption of God" (verse 32) and that, as Abinadi later testifies, the Redeemer, for all His compassion and mercy, "cannot deny justice when it has its claim" (Mosiah 15:27). Thus King Noah and his priests (except for Alma) stand ready to condemn Abinadi to death for telling the truth "with power and authority from God" (Mosiah 13:6).

CHAPTER 14

OVERVIEW

Abinadi quotes Isaiah chapter 53 for his audience.

1–12 Isaiah prophesies that the Messiah will undertake His mortal mission with the appearance of being just an ordinary person—but one who will be despised and rejected, one who will give his life to heal men of their iniquities. With a life foreshortened, who would be His seed? Those who accept His Atonement and make His soul an offering for sin will be His seed, for it pleased the Lord to offer His Son that life could be preserved and an intercession accomplished for the transgressor.

The entire 53rd chapter of Isaiah is of inestimable worth in the canon of Messianic scripture. Here is just one reference that Abinadi returns to later:

> *8 He was taken from prison and from judgment; and* ***who shall declare his generation?*** *For he was cut off out of the land of the living; for the transgressions of my people was he stricken.*
> *9 And he made his grave with the wicked, and with the rich in his death; because he had done no evil, neither was any deceit in his mouth.*
> *10 Yet it pleased the Lord to bruise him; he hath put him to grief;* ***when thou shalt make his soul an offering for sin he shall see his seed,*** *he shall prolong his days, and the pleasure of the Lord shall prosper in his hand.*

WHO SHALL DECLARE HIS GENERATION; WHEN THOU SHALT MAKE HIS SOUL AN OFFERING FOR SIN HE SHALL SEE HIS SEED

The question of conscience raised by this passage is profound: Do we consider ourselves to be of the seed of Christ? Do we accept His offering and demonstrate that acceptance by responding with obedience and valor? If so, then He shall declare us to be of His generation, to be His seed—His sons and daughters as joint-heirs with Him in the courts of the Father. Abinadi confirms this hope in a later passage (see Mosiah 15:11, 14).

CHAPTER 15

OVERVIEW

Abinadi explains how Christ is both the Father and the Son. The seed of Christ includes all who accept His Atonement on their behalf and who live in accordance with the commandments. Little children have eternal life. "And O how beautiful upon the mountains were their feet!" (verse 15) applies to all of Christ's seed (the obedient), to all of the prophets from the beginning, and to Christ Himself. The Atonement brings to pass the resurrection of all mankind and makes eternal life possible for those who keep the commandments.

> *1 AND now Abinadi said unto them: I would that ye should understand that God himself shall come down among the children of men, and shall redeem his people.*
> *2 And because he dwelleth in flesh he shall be called the Son of God, and having subjected the flesh to the will of the Father,* ***being the Father and the Son—***
> *3 The Father, because he was conceived by the power of God; and the Son, because of the flesh; thus becoming the Father and Son—*
> *4 And they are one God, yea, the very Eternal Father of heaven and of earth.*
> *5 And thus the flesh becoming subject to the Spirit, or the Son to the Father, being one God, suffereth temptation, and yieldeth not to the temptation, but suffereth himself to be mocked, and scourged, and cast out, and disowned by his people.*

BEING THE FATHER AND THE SON

Elder Bruce R. McConkie helps us understand how Christ fulfills both roles:

Although Christ—the Firstborn in the spirit and the Only Begotten in the flesh—is the Son of God the Father, and as such is a separate and distinct personage from the Father, yet there are three senses in which Christ is called the Father. These are clearly set forth in a document entitled, "The Father and the Son: A Doctrinal Exposition by the First Presidency and the Twelve." ([James E. Talmage,] *Articles of Faith,* 465–473.)

1. Christ is the Father in the sense that he is the Creator, the Maker, the Organizer of the heavens and of the earth, and all things that in them are. (Isa. 9:6; 2 Nephi 19:6; Mosiah 15:4; 16:15; Alma 11:38–39; Ether 4:7.)
2. He is the Father of all those who are born again (Mosiah 27:24–29), who "are begotten sons and daughters unto God" through his atoning Sacrifice (D&C 76:24), who are "spiritually begotten" through faith, thus becoming "his sons and his daughters." (Mosiah 5:7.)
3. He is the Father by what has aptly been termed divine investiture of authority. That is since he is one with the Father in all of the attributes of perfection, and since he exercises the power and authority of the Father, it follows that everything he says or does is and would be exactly and precisely what the Father would say and do under the same circumstances.

Accordingly, the Father puts his own name on the Son and authorizes him to speak in the first person as though he were the Father. This is similar to the situation in which Christ puts his name on an angel so that the designated heavenly ministrant can speak in the first person as though he were Christ himself. (Rev. 1:1; 19:9–10; 22:8–14.) Thus it is that our Lord can begin a revelation by saying, "Listen to the voice of Jesus Christ," and shortly thereafter speak of "mine only Begotten" (D&C 29:1, 41–46), such latter expression being made by Christ, but under that divine investiture of authority which permits him to speak as though he were the Father. (D&C 93:3–5; Mosiah 15:1–5.) (*Mormon Doctrine,* 2d ed. [Salt Lake City: Bookcraft, 1966], 130)

6–9 Abinadi offers commentary on Isaiah chapter 53, which he has just cited: The Savior willingly gives Himself over to be crucified, "the will of the Son being swallowed up in the will of the Father" (verse 7), and thus effects the grand Atonement by means of which victory over death is assured and the demands of justice are satisfied through eternal mercy extended to the penitent.

> *10 And now I say unto you,* ***who shall declare his generation?*** *Behold, I say unto you, that when his soul has been made an offering for sin he shall see his seed. And now what say ye? And who shall be his seed?*
> *11 Behold I say unto you, that whosoever has heard the words of the prophets, yea, all the holy prophets who have prophesied concerning the coming of the Lord—I say unto you, that all those who have hearkened unto their words, and believed that the Lord would redeem his people, and have looked forward to that day for a remission of their sins, I say unto you, that* ***these are his seed, or they are the heirs of the kingdom of God.***

Who shall declare his generation? these are his seed, or they are the heirs of the kingdom of God

Abinadi masterfully explains the nature and relationship of the Father and the Son in connection with the divine mission of the Atonement (Mosiah 15:1–11) and provides the correct interpretation of the Isaiah scripture invoked earlier by the wicked priest. Who become the heirs of the kingdom of God and the seed of Christ? Who publishes peace upon the mountains? Those who hearken to the words of the prophets, look forward in faith for the remission of sins, and spread the gospel of salvation to others.

Memories: The Royal Adoption

Elder Theodore M. Burton served as mission president in the West German Mission during my time there as a young missionary. The last part of my service was spent in the mission home in Frankfurt where it was my great honor to get to know President Burton and his wife well. One of the choice blessings that came with that opportunity was to spend the first part of each morning in gospel study with the mission home staff, learning from President Burton, an eminent student of the scriptures. I shall never forget the day he offered his insightful commentary on Abinadi, in particular on those passages that dealt with Isaiah's compelling question concerning the Savior: "and who shall declare his generation?" (Mosiah 14:8). President and Sister Burton had an adopted son who accompanied them on their mission. Because they were familiar with the complex legal process by means of which an adoption is consummated, it was natural for President Burton to relate his personal experiences to the doctrine of adoption into the kingdom of God whereby we can become part of the family of Christ, as King Benjamin explained: "And now, because of the covenant which ye have made ye shall be called the children of Christ, his sons, and his daughters; for behold, this day he hath spiritually begotten you; for ye say that your hearts are changed through faith on his name; therefore, ye are born of him and have become his sons and his daughters" (Mosiah 5:7).

During our scripture study sessions and in a celebrated speech delivered to various congregations in our mission, President Burton amplified this doctrine by explaining the exceptional transition through which adults go in adopting a child. They must appear before the court and answer the sobering question (in effect): "Are you willing to take upon yourself all responsibility for the welfare and well-being of this child, to nurture and care for the child under all circumstances just as if the child were your natural-born child?" To answer yes to this question, and to complete the legally binding covenants relative to the adoption, brings about an extraordinary change in the status of the adopting adults: the man becomes a father, the woman a mother. Later, as a General Authority, Elder Burton expressed it this way: "When we are baptized, we actually make a new covenant with God the Eternal Father to take upon us the name of his Only Begotten Son. Jesus Christ thus becomes by adoption our covenant Father. Thus, though he was, and is, our Elder *Brother,* he is also *now* our covenant *Father,* and we have become his covenant sons and daughters. We desire to be respectful and show our gratitude to him for the opportunity we have to become members of his royal family" ("To Be Born Again," *Ensign,* Sept. 1985, 66ff; taken from a devotional address delivered at Brigham Young University, 26 October 1982).

It was in reference to this exalted process of the Savior's transformation to covenant Fatherhood that Abinadi, citing Isaiah, raised the question: "and who shall declare his generation?" (Mosiah 14:8; compare Isaiah 53:8). Expressed in another way, the question might read: Who shall be able to identify Christ's children, His seed, since He was "cut off out of the land of the living" (Mosiah 14:8)? The answer to that question is given succinctly by Isaiah, as quoted by Abinadi: "when thou shalt make his soul an offering for sin [i.e., when we accept the Atonement and keep the covenant commandments], he shall see his seed, he shall prolong his days, and the pleasure of the LORD shall prosper in his hand" (Isaiah 53:10).

Abinadi, as President Burton reminded us, expanded on this doctrine before the incorrigibly hard-hearted priests of Noah, driving home the acute need for their repentance. "And now what say ye? And who shall be his seed? Behold I say unto you, that whosoever has heard the words of the prophets, yea, all the holy prophets who have prophesied concerning the coming of the Lord—I say unto you, that all those who have hearkened unto their words, and believed that the Lord would redeem his people, and have looked forward to that day for a remission of their sins, I say unto you, that these are his seed, or they are the heirs of the kingdom of God" (Mosiah 15:10–11).

Similarly, all of God's holy prophets since the world began are Christ's seed: "And these are they who have published peace, who have brought good tidings of good, who have published salvation; and said unto Zion: Thy God reigneth!" (Mosiah 15:14).

Prophets

In a powerfully ironic echo of the very words of Noah's wicked priests, who had earlier condemned Abinadi for failing to prophecy of such "good tidings" and how the Lord was to comfort his people (Mosiah 12:21–22), Abinadi gives this magnificent portrait of the righteous harbingers of true peace and comfort: "And O how beautiful upon the mountains were their feet! And again, how beautiful upon the mountains are the feet of those that are still publishing peace! And again, how beautiful upon the mountains are the feet of those who shall hereafter publish peace, yea, from this time henceforth and forever! And behold, I say unto you, this is not all. For O how beautiful upon the mountains are the feet of him that bringeth good tidings, that is the founder of peace, yea, even the Lord, who has redeemed his people; yea, him who has granted salvation unto his people" (Mosiah 15:15–18).

Because Christ is the founder of peace, and because "he became the author to eternal salvation unto all them that obey him" (Hebrews 5:9), He brought to completion His role as the most exalted adopting figure of all existence and became, in that sense, the Father of the faithful. Before the supernal court of justice, Christ became the adopting covenant Father: "Having ascended into heaven, having the bowels of mercy; being filled with compassion toward the children of men; standing betwixt them and justice; having broken the bands of death, taken upon himself their iniquity and their transgressions, having redeemed them, and satisfied the demands of justice" (Mosiah 15:9). In effect, the Savior took upon Himself the responsibility to be our eternal Caregiver and to assure that we, as His sons and daughters, enjoy everlasting vitality and nurture, being born again through a royal adoption into the family of Christ.

Thus Abinadi exhorts his recalcitrant audience to teach the truth about the doctrine of eternal adoption that applies to all of the faithful and obedient: "Teach them that redemption cometh through Christ the Lord, who is the very Eternal Father. Amen" (Mosiah 16:15). Shortly thereafter Abinadi completes his prophetic mission through the process of martyrdom whereby he seals his testimony with his life, having left a legacy of truth concerning the dual role of the Savior, "being the Father and the Son" (Mosiah 15:2), and having explained with unmistakable clarity the essence of what Paul would later refer to as "the Spirit of adoption, whereby we cry, Abba, Father" (Romans 8:15). (Richard J. Allen)

1–18 Abinadi concludes his line of reasoning concerning the seed of Christ who publish peace. These are they whom He redeems from their transgressions. These are all the holy prophets from the beginning of time "who have published peace" (verse 14)—the good news of the gospel. These are those who in the future will carry the gospel message to the world. These merit the characterization "O how beautiful upon the mountains were their feet!" (verse 15)—just as it applies to the Savior Himself, "the founder of peace, yea, even the Lord, who has redeemed his people; yea, him who has granted salvation unto his people" (verse 18).

Who have published peace

Every member a missionary—that is the motto that celebrates the opportunity we have to share the gospel. It is the responsibility of the seed of Abraham to take the gospel message to every nation, kindred, tongue, and people (see Mosiah 15:28; Mormon 9:22). How beautiful are those that publish peace—the peace that only the Lord can give to those who come unto Him through repentance.

EVIDENCE: Abinadi on Isaiah 52–53 (Mosiah 15:13–15, 18)

While Abinadi refers to and quotes portions of Isaiah 52–53, the Book of Mormon prophet's *explanations* of Isaiah's prophecies are not taken from the Bible. These interpretations appeared to be Abinadi's and his alone, until the twentieth-century discoveries of other ancient Christian documents including the Dead Sea scrolls. For example, after quoting Isaiah's prophecy that begins "How beautiful upon the mountains are the feet of him that bringeth good tidings" (Isaiah 52:7), Abinadi explains that the scripture refers to all the holy prophets, as well as to the founder of peace, the Lord Himself. Interestingly, this explanation is similar to that in 11QMelchizedek of the Dead Sea Scrolls. After referencing the Isaiah passage, the narrative indicates that "the mountains are the pro[phets] . . . And the messenger is [the ano]inted of the spirit about whom Dan[iel] spoke" (Col. II, lines 15–17). The Hebrew term translated as "anointed" is *masiah,* or Messiah. Unlike Abinadi's treatise, this Jewish text compares the prophets with the mountains, while another—*Midrash Tanhuma*—implies that the mountain cited in Zechariah 4:7 is the Messiah. (See *Echoes,* 240–241).

19–31 Abinadi concludes his exposition on the Atonement: the bands of death are broken through the Resurrection; little children have eternal life; those who have known the commandments and fail to keep them will not take part in the first resurrection and will not have eternal life; the gospel will be preached in all the world "and all the ends of the earth shall see **the salvation of our God**" (verse 31).

The salvation of our God

The essence of Abinadi's message to this point—and in subsequent passages—is expertly captured by Elder Jeffrey R. Holland:

> Abinadi, that prophetic prefiguration of Christ whose sermon will be addressed in detail later, underscored the fact that in his ministry he was doing only what his predecessors and contemporaries had done:
>
> "For behold, did not Moses prophesy unto them concerning the coming of the Messiah, and that God should redeem his people? Yea, and even *all the prophets who have prophesied ever since the world began*—have they not spoken more or less concerning these things?
>
> "Have they not said that God himself should come down among the children of men, and take upon him the form of man, and go forth in mighty power upon the face of the earth?
>
> "Yea, and have they not said also that he should bring to pass the resurrection of the dead, and that he, himself, should be oppressed and afflicted?" (Mosiah 13:33–35)
>
> In another of those consummate sermons on the Savior laced throughout the Book of Mormon, Abinadi made these declarations about the Son of God:
>
> - "God himself" would atone for the sins and iniquities of his people. (Mosiah 13:28; see also Mosiah 13:34; 15:1; 17:8; Alma 42:15)
> - Christ would play mortal roles as Father and as Son. (see Mosiah 15:2–7)
> - The law of Moses was to be a type and shadow, a prefiguration of Christ who would come. (see Mosiah 13:31; 16:14)
> - Christ would dwell in the flesh and suffer temptation but not yield to it. (see Mosiah 15:5)
> - The Savior would suffer himself to be mocked, scourged, cast out, and disowned by his own people. (see Mosiah 15:5)
> - He would work "many mighty miracles" only to be led without resistance to the crucifixion. (see Mosiah 15:6–7)
> - His "intercession for the children of men" reflecting his mercy and compassion would allow him to stand "betwixt" these people and the demands of justice. (see Mosiah 15:8–9)

- In this atoning process he would break the bands of death, take upon himself the transgressions of all, satisfy the demands of justice, and redeem his people. (see Mosiah 15:9)
- Christ's "seed" (the "children of Christ" spoken of by King Benjamin) would be those who have believed the prophets and looked forward to Christ for a redemption of their sins. These are they whose sins Christ would bear and for whom his death would be wholly efficacious. (see Mosiah 15:11–12)
- Were it not for this redemption and resurrection, all mankind would perish. (see Mosiah 15:19)
- Christ would bring a "first resurrection" that would include the faithful who lived and died before Christ's death, including little children and those in their maturity who died without any saving knowledge of the gospel. (see Mosiah 15:21–25)
- There would be no resurrection of the willfully rebellious at the time of Christ's (or "the first") resurrection. (see Mosiah 15:26)

These truths, he testified, have constituted "the words of the prophets, *yea, all the holy prophets who have prophesied concerning the coming of the Lord.*" (see Mosiah 15:11) Abinadi then concluded his masterful sermon with this declaration: "If Christ had not come into the world, *speaking of things to come as though they had already come,* there could have been no redemption.

"And if Christ had not risen from the dead, or have broken the bands of death that the grave should have no victory, and that death should have no sting, there could have been no resurrection.

"But there is a resurrection, therefore the grave hath no victory, and the sting of death is swallowed up in Christ.

"He is the light and the life of the world; yea, a light that is endless, that can never be darkened; yea, and also a life which is endless, that there can be no more death. . . .

"Teach . . . that redemption cometh through Christ the Lord." (Mosiah 16:6–9,15) (*Christ and the New Covenant: The Messianic Message of the Book of Mormon* [Salt Lake City: Deseret Book, 1997], 103–105)

CONCLUDING THOUGHTS

Abinadi's extraordinary pronouncements about the Atonement and the redeeming mission of the Savior constitute one of the most compelling witnesses of Christ's divinity in all scripture. Like Nephi and Jacob before him, he offers up a commentary on Isaiah that renders many of the cited passages transparently clear and vibrantly instructive. Without fear of his life, Abinadi brings King Noah and his priests face to face with the unassailable truth that Christ is the author of their salvation.

In our day and age the prophets of God continue to deliver the word of God concerning repentance and acceptance of the gospel plan. For example, President Harold B. Lee stated:

> The only thing the Savior expects from us in return for his suffering is that we repent of our sins and keep his commandments. Although his sufferings were so intense that he the Son of God was caused "to tremble because of pain and to bleed at every pore, and to suffer both body and spirit, and would that (he) might not drink the bitter cup, and shrink," (Doc. and Cov. 19:18.) yet he, as would a true mother, counts it all worthwhile if, at the end of the earth, mankind, for whom he died, might gain eternal life and become his sons and daughters eternally through the acceptance of his gospel, which is God's plan for man's salvation. (*Decisions for Successful Living* [Salt Lake City: Deseret Book, 1973], 115)

CHAPTER 16

OVERVIEW

All shall "see the salvation of the Lord" (verse 1)—for all shall stand as resurrected beings before the judgment bar and be consigned our reward according to our obedience and faithfulness: the wicked will be cast out as though no redemption had been made, and the righteous who accept Christ as "the light and the life of the world" (verse 9) will receive "endless light and happiness" (verse 11).

> *1 AND now, it came to pass that after Abinadi had spoken these words he stretched*
> *forth his hand and said: The time shall come when* ***all shall see the salvation of the***

***Lord;** when every nation, kindred, tongue, and people shall see eye to eye and shall confess before God that his judgments are just.*

All shall see the salvation of the Lord

This expression derives from the prophetic writings of Isaiah concerning the last days and the Second Coming: "Break forth into joy, sing together, ye waste places of Jerusalem: for the LORD hath comforted his people, he hath redeemed Jerusalem. The LORD hath made bare his holy arm in the eyes of all the nations; and all the ends of the earth shall see the salvation of our God" (Isaiah 52:9–10; compare Isaiah 40:5).

Just prior to the parting of the Red Sea, Moses had spoken a portion of this phrase when the Israelites feared the oncoming assault of Pharaoh's army: "And Moses said unto the people, Fear ye not, stand still, and see the salvation of the LORD, which he will shew to you to day: for the Egyptians whom ye have seen to day, ye shall see them again no more for ever. The LORD shall fight for you, and ye shall hold your peace" (Exodus 14:13–14).

Nephi echoed a variation of the expression generations before the time of Abinadi: "Yea, and all the earth shall see the salvation of the Lord, saith the prophet; every nation, kindred, tongue and people shall be blessed" (see 1 Nephi 19:17). The wicked priests of King Noah unwisely raise this same expression in an attempt to cross Abinadi (see Mosiah 12:24). Abinadi turns the expression back upon their heads twice during his fervent call to repentance (see Mosiah 15:31; 16:1). The Savior Himself brings forth this exact expression to assure His listeners at Bountiful that the word of the Lord given through Isaiah will be fulfilled in the last days (see 3 Nephi 16:17–20).

"All shall see the salvation of the Lord" has a bipolar consequence: joy for the faithful and righteous, fear and anguish for the wicked. It reflects redemption and exaltation as well as condemnation and damnation—depending upon the level of obedience and acceptance of gospel principles demonstrated in the life of each individual.

The Justice of God

Under certain conditions God commands men to take up arms and defend themselves (see Alma 43:47), while at other times he tells His people that He will fight their battles for them (see D&C 98:37; 105:14). It is the latter situation that pertains to this day, Thursday, June 19, 1834, when members of Zion's Camp are protected by divine power in the form of a severe thunder storm at Fishing River in Clay County, Missouri. A mob of nearly 400 men who have vowed "to kill Joe Smith and his army" (*HC,* 2:104) are converging upon the Saint's location. Five scouts from the mob visit the Camp of Zion and threaten that the Mormons "will see hell before morning" (2:103).

Some of the brethren desire to load their weapons and fight, but Joseph tells them, "Stand still and see the salvation of God" (*Church History in the Fulness of Times*, 148; compare Moses' words in Exodus 14:13).

Elder Wilford Woodruff records what appeared in the hitherto cloudless heavens moments after the scouts' departure: "a small cloud like a black spot appeared in the north west, and it began to unroll itself like a scroll, and in a few minutes the whole heavens were covered with a pall as black as ink" (*HC* 2:104). An ensuing storm of unprecedented violence entirely frustrates the schemes of the scattering mob. Joseph declares: "God is in this storm" (ibid.). The surviving mobocrats decide that "when Jehovah fights they would rather be absent" (ibid.). The same will be said by the wicked at the time of the Second Coming when the Lord will make "bare his holy arm in the eyes of all the nations; and all the ends of the earth shall see the salvation of our God" (Isaiah 52:10). The wicked will howl in anguish while the righteous will rejoice and welcome their Lord and Savior. Meanwhile, the Saints can endure in faith and echo the words of Moses: "The Lord shall fight for you, and ye shall hold your peace" (Exodus 14:14). (Richard J. Allen)

2–4 The wicked will be cast out, having forfeited redemption.

> *5 But remember that he that persists in his own carnal nature, and goes on in the ways of sin and rebellion against God, remaineth in his fallen state and the devil hath all power over him. Therefore, he is* ***as though there was no redemption made,*** *being an enemy to God; and also is the devil an enemy to God.*

As though there was no redemption made

The expression "carnal nature" or "carnal mind" describes those who love Satan more than God (see Moses 5:13). These are they who wilfully rebel against God. People become carnal, sensual, and devilish as they yield to the temptations of the devil (see Moses 6:49). "Carnal mind" sometimes refers to the mortal or temporal mind (see Alma 36:4). Alma describes people "that are in a state of nature" or "in a carnal state" as being "in the bonds of iniquity; they are without God in the world, and they have gone contrary to the nature of God; therefore, they are in a state contrary to the nature of happiness" (Alma 41:11) and thus become "carnal, sensual, and devilish, by nature" (Alma 42:10). Mortality does not make man inherently evil or wicked, for even without a body in the premortal life, some of God's children chose evil rather than good. Thus we see that we are free to choose eternal life or captivity and the devil (see 2 Nephi 2:27). We are to realize that we can emerge from our lost and fallen state as we rely upon our Savior, repent, and come unto Him (see 1 Nephi 10:6; 2 Nephi 25:17). We remain in our fallen state if we continue in our wickedness (Mosiah 16:2), or "carnal nature," by sinning and rebelling against God (see Mosiah 16:2–5).

Abinadi teaches the people that the wicked who will not repent are not redeemed of the Lord. They are carnal-minded and are subject to the devil—and they remain in a fallen state as an enemy to God. Let us be confirmed in our belief that redemption is in and through the Lord Jesus Christ. To take full advantage of His atoning sacrifice requires that we repent and follow His commandments. There is no other way.

6–8 Redemption can come only through Christ, who alone brings about the Resurrection.

> *9 He is* ***the light and the life of the world;*** *yea, a light that is endless, that can never be darkened; yea, and also a life which is endless, that there can be no more death.*

The light and the life of the world

The resurrected Savior would identify Himself by these same words to the ancient American Saints: "I am the light and the life of the world. I am Alpha and Omega, the beginning and the end" (3 Nephi 9:18; Ether 4:12; D&C 10:70; 93:9).

10–14 In the resurrected state, all of God's children will stand before the bar of judgment to receive either "endless life and happiness" (verse 11) if they were good, or "endless damnation" (verse 11) if they were evil. How important it is therefore that all repent and "remember that only in and through Christ ye can be saved" (verse 13).

> *15 Teach them that* ***redemption cometh through Christ*** *the Lord, who is the very Eternal Father. Amen.*

Redemption cometh through Christ

The final words of Abinadi's discourse on the Atonement give the essence of all the grand principles he is commanded to declare. Christ is the key to salvation, eternal life, and exaltation. It is Christ that we are to teach. It is Christ we are to follow. To know whether we are on the divine pathway we need only inquire of ourselves—do we teach Christ to our families and exemplify His matchless love in our lives?

CHAPTER 17

OVERVIEW

Alma attempts to intercede on behalf of Abinadi but is forced to flee for his life. He records Abinadi's words. Abinadi is sentenced to death unless he agrees to recant. He refuses and is burned to death while prophesying that a similar fate will befall future righteous descendants of Noah, and that the judgments of God will fall upon the wicked, including Noah himself.

> *1 AND now it came to pass that when Abinadi had finished these sayings, that the*
> *king commanded that the priests should take him and cause that he should be put*
> *to death.*
> *2 But there was one among them whose name was* ***Alma,*** *he also being a descendant*
> *of Nephi. And he was a young man, and he believed the words which Abinadi had*
> *spoken, for he knew concerning the iniquity which Abinadi had testified against them;*
> *therefore he began to plead with the king that he would not be angry with Abinadi,*
> *but suffer that he might depart in peace.*

Alma the Elder, Founder of the Church

Alma the Elder is the inspiring example of a repentant soul and a courageous leader who guides the honest-in-heart into the fold of the Lord. As a member of the court of wicked King Noah, Alma is, by his own words, "caught in a snare, and did many things which were abominable in the sight of the Lord" (Mosiah 23:9). However, when the Lord sends Abinadi around 150 B.C.—and again two years later—to warn the people of impending destruction because of their wickedness, Alma "believed the words which Abinadi had spoken" (Mosiah 17:2) and experiences a mighty change of heart. When Alma pleads for the prophet's release, the king orders Alma's execution. He flees for his life and secretly gathers together at the Waters of Mormon all those who want to begin a new existence defined by obedience to the principles of the gospel. Having founded the Church among the faithful, Alma leads his followers through the wilderness to escape Lamanite persecution. Because of his valor, he receives a remarkable promise from the Lord: "Thou art my servant; and I covenant with thee that thou shalt have eternal life; and thou shalt serve me and go forth in my name, and shalt gather together my sheep" (Mosiah 26:20). Eventually Alma and his group find their way to Zarahemla where he continues his inspired ministry among the Saints until his death at age eighty-two (Mosiah 29:45).

EVIDENCE: The Name "Alma"

If Joseph Smith had known the name *Alma* from his life experiences in upstate New York, it probably would have been as a woman's name, not a man's, as it occurs in the Book of Mormon. In recently discovered documents from the Near East, Alma also appears as a Semitic masculine personal name. (See *Echoes,* 210–211).

3 But the king was more wroth, and caused that ***Alma should be cast out*** *from*
among them, and sent his servants after him that they might slay him.
4 But he fled from before them and hid himself that they found him not. And he being
concealed for many days ***did write all the words which Abinadi had spoken.***

Alma should be cast out; did write all the words which Abinadi had spoken

Alma flees under threat of his life. As an eyewitness to the proceedings, he makes a written record of Abinadi's words. Although the Book of Mormon, as such, is not available to the world before the Restoration, parts are in circulation among the ancient American Saints. The words of Benjamin are recorded and circulated to later generations (see the example of Ammon reading them to the people of Limhi—Mosiah 8:3). Now Abinadi's words are preserved in the same manner.

5–8 Abinadi is condemned and sentenced to die unless he disclaims the words he has spoken.

9 Now Abinadi said unto him: I say unto you, ***I will not recall the words*** *which I*
have spoken unto you concerning this people, for they are true; and that ye may know
of their surety I have suffered myself that I have fallen into your hands.
10 Yea, and ***I will suffer even until death,*** *and* ***I will not recall my words, and***
they shall stand as a testimony against you. *And if ye slay me ye will shed innocent*
blood, and this shall also stand as a testimony against you at the last day.

I will not recall the words; I will suffer even until death; they shall stand as a testimony against you

Abinadi's demeanor and courage are a type and shadow of the Lord's willingness to suffer the will of the Father and complete His mission of atoning grace on behalf of all mankind. If we are to liken Abinadi's words and example unto our own lives, then we will prayerfully muster the courage to stand up for the principles of righteousness—no matter the consequences.

11–14 King Noah is struck with fear at Abinadi's words and is about to release him. However, his priests rekindle Noah's anger against the prophet. Abinadi is subjected to the horrible pain of flaming faggots (bundles of wood and branches used for that purpose) pressed relentlessly against his body, and is brought within moments of death, at which point he raises his voice in prophetic pronouncements.

> *15 Behold, even as ye have done unto me, so shall it come to pass that thy seed shall cause that* ***many shall suffer the pains that I do suffer,*** *even the pains of death by fire; and this because they believe in the salvation of the Lord their God.*
> *16 And it will come to pass that* ***ye shall be afflicted*** *with all manner of diseases because of your iniquities.*
> *17 Yea, and ye shall be* ***smitten*** *on every hand, and shall be* ***driven*** *and* ***scattered*** *to and fro, even as a wild flock is driven by wild and ferocious beasts.*
> *18 And in that day ye shall be* ***hunted,*** *and ye shall be taken by the hand of your enemies, and* ***then ye shall suffer, as I suffer, the pains of death by fire.***
> *19 Thus God executeth vengeance upon those that destroy his people. O God, receive my soul.*

Many shall suffer the pains that I do suffer; ye shall be afflicted, smitten, driven, scattered, hunted; then ye shall suffer, as I suffer, the pains of death by fire

Under inspiration, Abinadi perceives that others of a righteous character will suffer as he suffers (see ahead to Alma 25:5–11), and that the wicked will succumb to a similar fate, even death by fire (see Mosiah 19:20, recounting the death of Noah by fire).

> *20 And now, when Abinadi had said these words, he fell, having suffered death by fire; yea, having been put to death because he would not deny the commandments of God, having* ***sealed the truth of his words by his death.***

Sealed the truth of his words by his death

These words anticipate the words of Brigham Young on January 14, 1847, concerning the martyrdom of the Prophet Joseph Smith: "Many have marveled because of his death; but it was needful that he should seal his testimony with his blood, that he might be honored and the wicked might be condemned" (D&C 136:39). The sacrifice of life in the cause of eternal salvation and exaltation—if requisite in the designs of God—is a principle of faith and devotion. The Lord proclaimed through the voice of the Prophet Joseph on August 2, 1833 in the midst of severe persecution and suffering by the Saints in Missouri: "Verily I say unto you, all among them who know their hearts are honest, and are broken, and their spirits contrite, and are willing to observe their covenants by sacrifice—yea, every sacrifice which I, the Lord, shall command—they are accepted of me" (D&C 97:8). Sacrifice was, is, and always will be a central dimension of the gospel of Jesus Christ. In comparison with the transcendent atoning sacrifice of the Savior, there is nothing that man can do to come close. Thus the sacrifice of all things in devotion to the cause of immortality and eternal life is never too high a price to pay, for even the sacrifice of all things leaves man a debtor before God (see Mosiah 2:21).

After refuting the evil position of King Noah and his priests through the exquisite word of God, Abinadi dies as a martyr, "having sealed the truth of his words by his death" (Mosiah 17:20). He has had but one purpose—to do the will of the Father.

Here is an application for our times: Abinadi would not recall his words, for they would stand as a testimony against his unrighteous detractors. He suffered death by fire because he would not deny the commandments of God—thus sealing his testimony of truth by his death. We may not be asked to die for them, but we have certainly been asked to live for our beliefs. Let us realize that standing for, living by, and testifying of the truth is our duty (see Mosiah 18:8–9). To abdicate this sacred responsibility, either through a sin of omission, or worse, through a sin of commission in willfully teaching that which is false, carries severe consequences. President Joseph Fielding Smith stresses this point:

> We who are called and ordained to the ministry or to teach in The Church of Jesus Christ of Latter-day Saints carry a very grave responsibility. Every man that teaches holds a great responsibility. And he that teaches error and leads men from the path of truth is committing one of the greatest crimes that it is possible for man to commit. If he, through his teachings, is presenting false doctrine, and leading men astray from that which is eternal truth, away from the kingdom of God, he is taking upon himself a grave responsibility for which he will have to answer at the judgment seat of God.
>
> The Lord said in one of the early revelations before the organization of the Church that the worth of souls is great in the sight of God. Then he said if a man should labor all his days and convert but one soul, he should have great joy in the kingdom of our Father, and if he should convert many souls, then much greater would be that joy (see D&C 18:10–16). Reversing the picture, he who

> blinds one soul, he who spreads error, he who destroys, through his teachings, divine truth, truth that would lead a man to the kingdom of God and to its fulness, how great shall be his condemnation and his punishment in eternity. For the destruction of a soul is the destruction of the greatest thing that has ever been created. (*Take Heed to Yourselves* [Salt Lake City: Deseret Book, 1966], 190)

Only One Convert

> Another example of far-reaching effects of an inspired testimony is that of the prophet Abinadi. The testimony he bore as he called an apostate king, Noah, and his priests to repentance is one of the most significant doctrinal discourses in the Book of Mormon. The king and his priests, except one, rejected Abinadi's teachings and had him put to death. That one was Alma.
>
> Abinadi may have felt that he failed as a missionary because he had only one convert, so far as the record shows. However, that one convert, Alma, and his descendants were spiritual leaders among the Nephites and Lamanites for about three hundred years. His son Alma became the first chief judge of the Nephite people and the high priest over the Church. Alma's other descendants who became prominent religious leaders include his grandson Helaman; his great-grandson Nephi; and his great-great-great-grandson Nephi, who was the chief disciple of the resurrected Jesus Christ. All of this resulted from Abinadi's lone convert. (Joseph B. Wirthlin, *Finding Peace in Our Lives* [Salt Lake City: Deseret Book, 1995], 220)

CONCLUDING THOUGHTS

In Abinadi's teaching and exhortations we come to know the goodness of God and His masterful plan of redemption that comes only through His beloved Son Jesus Christ. To take full advantage of His atoning sacrifice, we must repent and come unto Him. The plea of Abinadi, like that of all the holy prophets, past and present, resonates through generations of time: Repent and come unto Christ. Through sincere repentance and faithfully honoring our gospel covenants, we can become the sons of daughters of God and thus, through spiritual adoption into the family of Christ, come to understand that "redemption cometh through Christ the Lord, who is the very Eternal Father" (Mosiah 16:15).

CHAPTER 18

OVERVIEW

Alma repents and organizes a clandestine church at the Waters of Mormon near the borders of the land. He teaches the doctrine of baptism—including obedience to the commandments and committed service one to another—baptizes his gatherers (some 204 in number), and ordains priests to carry on the work of the ministry. He teaches them to have "their hearts knit together in unity and in love one toward another" (verse 21). When King Noah discovers their activities, Alma and his followers (numbering now around 450) flee farther into the wilderness.

> *1 AND now, it came to pass that* ***Alma,*** *who had fled from the servants of King Noah,*
> ***repented of his sins*** *and iniquities, and went about privately among the people, and*
> ***began to teach*** *the words of Abinadi—*
> *2 Yea, concerning that which was to come, and also concerning the resurrection of the dead, and the redemption of the people, which was to be brought to pass through the power, and sufferings, and death of* ***Christ,*** *and his resurrection and ascension into heaven.*

Alma repented of his sins; began to teach [of] Christ

Alma has been a member of the court of King Noah, presumably caught up in the sinful practices of that group. Inspired and changed by the words of Abinadi, Alma repents and does that which the honestly penitent do—reach out to serve others.

3–8 Alma gathers the believers to an isolated place called Mormon, located on the borders of the land and featuring "a fountain of pure water" (verse 5) near a grove of trees that affords seclusion and privacy from the king's guard. There he teaches them "repentance, and redemption, and faith on the Lord" (verse 8).

> *8 And it came to pass that he said unto them: Behold, here are the waters of Mormon (for thus were they called) and now, as ye are desirous to come into the fold of God, and to be called his people, and are* ***willing to bear one another's burdens,*** *that they may be light;*
> *9 Yea, and are* ***willing to mourn with those that mourn;*** *yea, and comfort those that stand in need of comfort, and to* ***stand as witnesses of God*** *at all times and*

in all things, and in all places that ye may be in, even until death, that ye may be redeemed of God, and be numbered with those of the first resurrection, ***that ye may have eternal life—***

Willing to bear one another's burdens; willing to mourn with those that mourn; stand as witnesses of God; that ye may have eternal life

In the time frame of approximately 147 B.C., Alma gathers the faithful around him in seclusion to teach faith, repentance, and redemption through the Lord Jesus Christ. He explains to the eager congregants the commitments required as part of the baptismal covenant—to genuinely love and care for our brothers and sisters as we bear one another's burdens, to mourn with those that mourn, to comfort those who stand in need of comfort, and to seek their welfare by standing as a willing witness of the truth in all places and circumstances (see also Mosiah 28:3; Alma 36:24). The people believe and desire to be baptized.

We should also be willing and eager to stand as a witness of God and to testify of the truths of the gospel. We are to open our mouths with courage (see D&C 33:8–11) and share the gospel with everyone we meet (see D&C 88:81; Mormon 9:22). We covenant with the Lord to serve Him and keep His commandments (see D&C 20:37, 68–70, 77, 79; Moroni 6:1–4).

The application of these passages to our own lives is this: When we accept and follow Christ through baptism we should remember our duties and obligations with full commitment. To do so is an indication that we are qualified through the Spirit to be Saints in the kingdom of God.

10 Now I say unto you, if this be the ***desire of your hearts,*** *what have you against* ***being baptized*** *in the name of the Lord, as a* ***witness*** *before him that ye have entered into a covenant with him, that ye will* ***serve him*** *and* ***keep his commandments,*** *that he may pour out his* ***Spirit*** *more abundantly upon you?*
11 And now when the people had heard these words, they clapped their hands for ***joy,*** *and exclaimed: This is the desire of our hearts.*

Being baptized; witness; serve him; keep his commandments; Spirit; joy

The ordinance of baptism is the sacred ceremonial declaration that one is willing to take upon himself or herself the name of Christ and live by solemn covenant in accordance with His laws. Such an ordinance, being of the nature of renewal, rebirth, cleansing, liberation, and spiritual adoption into the family of Christ, is a thing of transcendent beauty and all-encompassing joy. Concerning the sacred nature of the baptismal covenant, President Joseph Fielding Smith has stated:

Every person baptized into this Church has made a covenant with the Lord to keep his commandments. We are to serve the Lord with all the heart, and all the mind, and all the strength that we have, and that too in the name of Jesus Christ. Everything that we do should be done in the name of Jesus Christ.

In the waters of baptism, we covenanted that we would keep these commandments; that we would serve the Lord; that we would keep this first and greatest of all commandments, and love the Lord our God; that we would keep the next great commandment, we would love our neighbor as ourselves; and with all the might that we have, with all the strength, with all our hearts, we would prove to him that we would "live by every word that proceedeth forth from the mouth of God"; that we would be obedient and humble, diligent in his service, willing to obey, to hearken to the counsels of those who preside over us and do all things with an eye single to the glory of God.

We should not forget these things, for this commandment is binding upon us as members of the Church. (*Doctrines of Salvation,* 3 vols., ed. Bruce R. McConkie [Salt Lake City: Bookcraft, 1954–1956], 2:328)

12 And now it came to pass that Alma took Helam, he being one of the first, and went and stood forth in the water, and cried, saying: O Lord, pour out thy Spirit upon thy servant, that he may do this work with holiness of heart.
13 And when he had said these words, the Spirit of the Lord was upon him, and he said: Helam, ***I baptize thee, having authority from the Almighty God,*** *as a testimony that ye have entered into a covenant to serve him until you are dead as to the mortal body; and may the Spirit of the Lord be poured out upon you; and may he grant unto you eternal life, through the redemption of Christ, whom he has prepared from the foundation of the world.*
14 And after Alma had said these words, both Alma and Helam were buried in the water; and they arose and came forth out of the water rejoicing, being filled with the Spirit.

I baptize thee, having authority from the Almighty God

Alma prays for the Spirit of the Lord to accomplish his duty "with holiness of heart" (verse 12) as he prepares to baptize Helaman. The wording used in the performance of the baptismal ordinance at the Waters of Mormon is similar to our wording today—which states (calling the person by name): "Having been commissioned of Jesus Christ, I baptize you in the name of the Father, and of the Son, and of the Holy Ghost. Amen" (D&C 20:73; compare 3 Nephi 11:25)—except that Alma also includes an expression of the attendant blessings of eternal life through the redemption of Christ.

15–17 After this manner, Alma baptizes every one of the assemblage at the Waters of Mormon, in all about 204 souls. They are "filled with the grace of God" (verse 16) and are called "the church of God, or the church of Christ, from that time forward" (verse 17). Others are added to the Church as they are baptized.

Yellow Canaries with Gray on Their Wings

President Monson illustrates in this story that everyone, in even the smallest ways, can help ease the burdens of their fellowmen:

> When I was a young man serving as the bishop of a large ward in Salt Lake City, one evening, at a late hour, my telephone rang. I heard a voice say, "Bishop Monson, this is the hospital calling. Kathleen McKee, a member of your congregation, has just passed away. Our records reveal that she had no next of kin, but your name is listed as the one to be notified in the event of her death. Could you come to the hospital right away?"
>
> Upon arriving there, I was presented with a sealed envelope that contained a key to the modest apartment in which Kathleen McKee had lived. A childless widow seventy-three years of age, she had enjoyed but few of life's luxuries and possessed scarcely sufficient of its necessities. In the twilight of her life, she had become a member of The Church of Jesus Christ of Latter-day Saints. Being a quiet and overly reserved person, little was known about her.
>
> That same night I entered her tidy basement apartment, turned on the light switch, and in a moment discovered a letter written ever so meticulously in Kathleen McKee's own hand. It rested face up on a small table and read:
>
> *Bishop Monson,*
>
> *I think I shall not return from the hospital. In the dresser drawer is a small insurance policy that will cover funeral expenses. The furniture may be given to my neighbors.*

In the kitchen are my three precious canaries. Two of them are beautiful, yellow-gold in color, and are perfectly marked. On their cages I have noted the names of friends to whom they are to be given. In the third cage is "Billie." He is my favorite. Billie looks a bit scrubby, and his yellow hue is marred by gray on his wings. Will you and your family make a home for him? He isn't the prettiest, but his song is the best.

She had also left two Alka-Seltzer bottles filled with quarters, and this message: "Bishop, here is my fast offering. I am square with the Lord." A spirit of peace filled that apartment. A silent sermon had been delivered.

In the days that followed, I learned much more about Kathleen McKee. She had befriended many neighbors in need. She had given cheer and comfort almost daily to a physically handicapped person who lived down the street. Indeed, she had brightened each life she touched.

Kathleen McKee was much like "Billie," her prized yellow canary with gray on its wings. She was not blessed with beauty, gifted with poise, or honored by posterity. Yet her song helped others to more willingly bear their burdens and more ably shoulder their tasks. (*Inspiring Experiences That Build Faith: From the Life and Ministry of Thomas S. Monson* [Salt Lake City: Deseret Book, 1994], 221–223)

18 And it came to pass that Alma, having authority from God, ***ordained priests;*** *even*
one priest to every fifty of their number did he ordain to preach unto them, and to
teach them concerning the things pertaining to the kingdom of God.
19 And he commanded them that they should teach nothing save it were the things
which he had taught, and which had been spoken by the mouth of the holy prophets.
20 Yea, even he commanded them that ***they should preach nothing save it were***
repentance and faith on the Lord, *who had redeemed his people.*
21 And he commanded them that there should be no contention one with another, but
that they should look forward with one eye, having one faith and one baptism, ***having***
their hearts knit together in unity and in love *one toward another.*

They Should Preach Nothing Save It Were Repentance and Faith on the Lord

The responsibility of a teacher in the kingdom of God is to teach faith and repentance.

Alma organizes the Church in smaller units of fifty, each with its own priest. Only the fundamentals of the gospel as spoken by the prophets of God are to be taught (compare Alma 37:33).

Their hearts were to be "knit together in unity and love." The question of conscience that applies to our time would be this: Do we focus our teaching at home and at Church on the fundamentals of the gospel and avoid getting into themes and topics of a marginal and speculative nature?

22–29 They are to observe the Sabbath day, pray always, maintain a lay priesthood, teach with the Spirit, and gather together weekly to worship. Each member is to give to the poor, **"according to that which he [the giver] had"** (Mosiah 18:27). All are to sustain one another.

According to that which he [the giver] had

We are to give to the poor and needy according to our capacity to give. If we have more, we give more. The counsel is clear: Give readily and of your own free will (see Jacob 2:17; Mosiah 4:26; Alma 1:27; 4:13) and not to be seen of men (see 3 Nephi 13:1–4). Your prayers are vain if you fail to care for the needy, the sick, and afflicted (see Alma 34:27–29). You are to serve and help others both temporally and spiritually according to their needs. Ministering to others by sharing the word of God will bring about the greatest blessings of change in their lives (see Jacob 4:1; Alma 31:5).

> *30 And now it came to pass that all this was done in Mormon, yea, by the waters of Mormon, in the forest that was near the waters of Mormon; yea, the place of Mormon, the waters of Mormon, the forest of Mormon,* ***how beautiful*** *are they to the eyes of them who there* ***came to the knowledge of their Redeemer;*** *yea, and how blessed are they, for they shall* ***sing to his praise forever.***

How beautiful; came to the knowledge of their Redeemer; sing to his praise forever

We can remind ourselves that Alma, having been touched by the Spirit as he feasted upon the words of truth delivered by the prophet Abinadi, has importuned King Noah to spare the life of this holy man. In so doing, Alma places himself in mortal peril and has to flee for his life and take refuge in the wilderness. The account of his secret convocations at the Waters of Mormon with a small group of enthusiastic and receptive followers is one of the most powerful accounts of conversion and baptism in all scripture. Isaiah intones the famous words: "How beautiful upon the mountains are the feet of him that bringeth good tidings, that publisheth peace; that bringeth good tidings of good, that publisheth salvation; that saith unto Zion, Thy God reigneth!" (Isaiah 52:7). Alma embodies the spirit of these same words, but with the variation, "how beautiful at the

Waters of Mormon . . . !" The redemptive process (in whatever venue) is indeed a thing of beauty, involving as it does the radiance, glory, and light of the gospel of Jesus Christ.

Memories: Sacred Precincts

For every person whose life has been touched by the gospel there is at least one place on the mortal landscape to which a fond spiritual memory is attached. For some that might be the scene where the Holy Ghost first whispered the comforting truth of redemption. For others that might be a room within one of the Holy temples of God, or a place where communion with loved ones has rendered sacred the walls of a home or dwelling place.

I can still recall as if it were yesterday the pleasant surroundings of a certain secluded grove on a beautiful summer day many years ago where I had retired, following an extended fast, to pour out my heart in prayer for confirmation of the decision I had made to propose to a certain noble and fair daughter of Zion. It was there that the Spirit proffered a blessing of truth and comfort in unmistakable terms, and I cannot drive past that spot without thinking of the words "Did I not speak peace to your mind concerning the matter? What greater witness can you have than from God?" (D&C 6:23.) That scene, together with the sealing room in one of the holy temples where she and I soon thereafter consummated our wedding vows, remains fixed in my mind as an unforgettable, sacred precinct to which fond memories will forever be associated.

In the account of Alma's ministry at the secluded Waters of Mormon, we read of an event that would become unforgettable for a small group of enthusiastic converts—and by extension for the countless readers of the Book of Mormon who have since vicariously experienced this same event with much edification: "And now it came to pass that all this was done in Mormon, yea, by the waters of Mormon, in the forest that was near the waters of Mormon; yea, the place of Mormon, the waters of Mormon, the forest of Mormon, how beautiful are they to the eyes of them who there came to the knowledge of their Redeemer; yea, and how blessed are they, for they shall sing to his praise forever" (Mosiah 18:30).

It is through such experiences that we come to understand that there are many traces of the infinite scattered through the finite mortal landscape. Indeed, revisiting such places of spiritual resort (either in reality or within our active memory), and reliving the ennobling events that transpired there, can become for many a source of strength and vitality, and an inducement to remember with gratitude the Lord's compassion in walking with us, as it were, along the pathway of life. (Richard J. Allen)

31 The king discovers Alma's clandestine church and sends his army to destroy them. Alma is alerted to the advance and flees farther into the wilderness with his group, now numbering some 450 souls.

CHAPTER 19

OVERVIEW

A division occurs within the Nephite colony. Gideon attempts to slay King Noah. The king is spared when the Lamanites invade the land, forcing all to flee into the wilderness. The king tries to force the men to abandon their wives and children. Those who refuse and stay behind are spared for the sake of their fair daughters. The Lamanites grant the captured people a protectorate in Lamanite territory in exchange for a tribute of half their goods annually. The escaping Noah refuses to allow other men in his group to return to their wives and children. In anger, they execute him by fire. Limhi, son of Noah, is appointed king by the people.

1–3 Noah's army returns, not having discovered Alma and the people of the Lord. A division arises among the people, with a lesser part rising up in contention against the king.

> *4 And now there was a man among them whose name was* ***Gideon,*** *and he being a strong man and an enemy to the king, therefore he drew his sword, and swore in his wrath that he would slay the king.*

Gideon, Defender of the Truth

Gideon is a physically strong man in the army of King Noah. Until his death, Gideon stands firm against those who would act contrary to the laws of God and violate the inalienable rights of God's children. From the scriptural account, we learn of three separate occasions where he rises boldly to take action against tyranny or evil: once in opposition to the abuses of wicked King Noah around 145 B.C., subsequently in devising a successful plan to liberate the people of Limhi from Lamanite bondage, and finally in defying the false preaching of Nehor in Zarahemla during the first year of the reign of Alma as chief judge of the land. It is in this last episode that Gideon gives his life in defending the truth, for he is unable—"being stricken with many years" (Alma 1:9)—to withstand the lethal blows inflicted upon him by Nehor. Gideon serves as an example of "a righteous man" (Alma 1:13), one with the courage to rise fearlessly in supporting the cause of freedom and in upholding the principles of the gospel.

5–18 Gideon battles Noah one on one, forcing the king to escape to the tower near the temple. Gideon pursues him and is about to slay him when the king spies the approaching Lamanites on the horizon. Gideon spares the king's life. The king and those who follow him flee into the wilderness. When they are about to be captured, the king orders the men to abandon their wives and children. Those who refuse to do so remain behind and plead with the Lamanites to spare their lives. The Lamanites, enchanted by the fair daughters of the Nephites, spare the people and give them a protectorate in Lamanite territory on condition that they pay a tribute of half their goods annually and capture Noah and turn him over to them. Among those taken by the Lamanites is Limhi, one of the sons of King Noah. From the record we learn that Limhi "was desirous that his father should not be destroyed; nevertheless, Limhi was not ignorant of the iniquities of his father, he himself being a just man" (Mosiah 19:17). Meanwhile, Gideon sends men to find Noah and his priests. Instead they come upon some of the men who have abandoned their wives and children.

> *19 Now they had sworn in their hearts that they would return to the land of Nephi, and if their wives and their children were slain, and also those that had tarried with them, that they would seek revenge, and also perish with them.*
> *20 And the king commanded them that they should not return; and* ***they were angry with the king,*** *and caused that he should suffer, even unto* ***death by fire.***
> *21 And they were about to take the priests also and put them to death, and they fled before them.*

THEY WERE ANGRY WITH THE KING; DEATH BY FIRE

Abinadi has warned the rebellious and prideful King Noah and his courtiers that the same fate they have chosen to inflict upon him will, in turn, be inflicted upon them and their followers. Abinadi's last words amidst his fiery grave, are: "Thus God executeth vengeance upon those that destroy his people. O God, receive my soul" (Mosiah 17:19). It is not long thereafter that the Lamanites invade the colony, causing Noah and his priests to flee for their lives. When a search party comes after Noah and his group to deliver him to the Lamanites, Noah refuses to let his companions return, and they pronounce summary judgment upon him "and caused that he should suffer, even unto death by fire" (Mosiah 19:20). Thus we see that the Lord's word, delivered through the voice of His servant, is inviolate.

The justice of God is immovable. Just as God will fulfill His promised blessings to the righteous without fail, He will also execute judgment upon those who reject His word and turn back His servants. President Spencer W. Kimball emphasized this point with stark clarity: "Remember, God is in his heavens. He knew what he was doing when he organized the earth. He knows what he is doing now. Those of us who break his commandments will regret and suffer in remorse and pain. God will not be mocked. Man has his free agency, it is sure, but remember, GOD WILL NOT BE

MOCKED. (See D&C 63:58.) Our counsel then to you is to live strictly the laws of your Heavenly Father" ("God Will Not Be Mocked," *Ensign,* Nov. 1974, 4ff).

King Noah suffers death by fire as Abinadi has prophesied (see Mosiah 17:18). Let us realize that when the prophets speak, it is the same as if the Lord were speaking. The words of our prophets will be fulfilled. When we come to understand and appreciate this eternal truth, we will be more obedient to prophets both living and dead. We shall see in later scriptures that the wicked priests of Noah and their successors, in league with the Lamanites, cause much pain and suffering among the people over the next generation or two before they are subjected to the judgments of God (see Alma 25:4–13). Thus we will see how much destruction one wicked king can cause, just as Mosiah later reminds us: "Yea, remember King Noah, his wickedness and his abominations, and also the wickedness and abominations of his people. Behold what great destruction did come upon them; and also because of their iniquities they were brought into bondage" (Mosiah 29:18). But there is to be a favorable and comforting side to the story as well, for the faithful Nephites who put their trust in the Lord will be liberated by a merciful Lord (see Mosiah 29:19–20).

22–24 The people who execute King Noah encounter the men of Gideon and learn that their wives and children have been spared and taken to Lamanite lands. They report the death of Noah and the flight of the priests into the wilderness. All return rejoicing to Zarahemla.

> *25 And it came to pass that the king of the Lamanites made an oath unto them, that his people should not slay them.*
> *26 And also **Limhi,** being the son of the king, having the kingdom conferred upon him by the people, made oath unto the king of the Lamanites that his people should pay tribute unto him, even one half of all they possessed.*

Limhi, a Just King

We have already encountered Limhi in the context of his coming role as successor to Noah. Limhi is discovered by Ammon, who has been sent from Zarahemla to locate the Nephite colonists in Lamanite lands (see Mosiah 7–8). The current scriptural account is a flashback leading up to the discovery by Ammon. Here is the situation with regard to Limhi: He is the last of the Nephite kings in the colony established by Zeniff among the Lamanites in the land of Nephi beginning around 200 B.C. We have seen that the aging Zeniff confers the kingdom upon his son, Noah, around 160 B.C. But Noah's profligacy and wickedness propel the people into a state of bondage and oppression at the hands of their Lamanite hosts. With the demise of Noah, the people confer the kingdom on his son, Limhi, around 145 B.C. (see Mosiah 19:26).

Limhi's leadership is defined by a threefold agenda: (1) to remind the people continually that wickedness leads to enslavement, both physical and spiritual—"and behold, it is because of our iniquities and abominations that he [the Lord] has brought us into bondage" (Mosiah 7:20); (2) to preserve peace, order, and a prevailing attitude of trust in God and hope for deliverance—"Therefore, lift up your heads, and rejoice, and put your trust in God, in that God who was the God of Abraham, and Isaac, and Jacob; and also, that God who brought the children of Israel out of the land of Egypt" (Mosiah 7:19); and (3) to seek an effective means for escape and eventual return to the homeland of Zarahemla.

27–29 Limhi establishes peace in their territory for the space of two years, even while their community is being contained by Lamanite guards who are supported out of the tribute the Nephites have to pay.

CHAPTER 20

OVERVIEW

The fugitive priests of King Noah abduct twenty-four Lamanite maidens from their place of recreation. In revenge, the Lamanites attack Limhi and his people as the perceived perpetrators, but are repulsed. When it comes to light through Gideon who the real culprits are, the Lamanites, along with their wounded king, are pacified and return to their territory in peace.

1–5 The priests of King Noah, fearful of returning to their city, abduct twenty-four daughters of the Lamanites from a place where these maidens are singing and dancing.

EVIDENCE: Courtship and Romance (1 Nephi 7:1–5; 1 Nephi 16:7; Mosiah 20:4–5; Ether 8:9–10)

Many works popular around the time of the Book of Mormon's publication were romances. In fact, *Manuscript Story* by Reverend Solomon Spaulding—a book some dissenters erroneously thought to be the original source of the Book of Mormon—devotes more than one-fourth of its pages to romance, courtship, and marriage. Furthermore, Jane Austen's novels—icons of traditional romance—appeared in the same time period as the Book of Mormon. While courtship and marriage do show up in the Book of Mormon—an example being the abduction of the Lamanite maidens by the wicked priests of King Noah—the details are related matter-of-factly, and neither the patterns nor the treatment of the subjects remotely resembles nineteenth-century notions of romantic love. (See *Echoes,* 311–312).

6–26 The Lamanites, incensed at the abduction of their daughters, assume that the people of Limhi are the perpetrators. Consequently they attack the Nephites but are repelled. The wounded king of the Lamanites is captured and taken before Limhi. During the ensuing dialogue, Limhi pleads ignorance of the deed and Gideon, captain of Limhi's army, comes forward to attribute the abduction to the priests of King Noah. Gideon advocates a strategy of pacification, "for it is better that we should be in bondage than that we should lose our lives; therefore, let us put a stop to the shedding of so much blood" (verse 22). The king of the Lamanites concurs. He recommends that the Nephites go before his army unarmed and, with his help, appeal for peace in light of the new disclosure. The Lamanites return in peace to their own land with their king.

CHAPTER 21

OVERVIEW

Peace prevails for a time in the city of Nephi before Lamanite oppression increases, causing the people to murmur against the king. He allows them to go against the enemy, but they are defeated three times with much loss of life. The people mourn. They descend into the depths of humility and pray for deliverance. The Lord softens the hearts of their oppressors and the burdens are lightened, but deliverance must wait as the people pay the price for their iniquities. Ammon and his party arrive. There is rejoicing over the hope of deliverance and over the plates of metal discovered by a search party looking for the route to Zarahemla. There is mourning over the loss of life and the evils caused by King Noah and his priests. Limhi and his people covenant to serve the Lord and desire to be baptized at the first opportunity.

1–3 Limhi and his people dwell in peace until the Lamanite guards begin to plague them and increase the level of oppression brought to bear against them—always coming just short of slaying them in order to honor the oath of protection the Lamanite king has made.

> *4 Yea, all this was done that the **word of the Lord** might be fulfilled.*

Word of the Lord

As part of his call to repentance before the people, Abinadi declares: "Yea, wo be unto this generation! And the Lord said unto me: Stretch forth thy hand and prophesy, saying: Thus saith the Lord, it shall come to pass that this generation, because of their iniquities, shall be brought into bondage, and shall be smitten on the cheek; yea, and shall be driven by men, and shall be slain; and the vultures of the air, and the dogs, yea, and the wild beasts, shall devour their flesh" (Mosiah 12:2).

5–12 The afflictions of the Nephites become so great that they begin to murmur against the king and insist on waging war against the Lamanites. Finally the king acquiesces to their demands and gives them leave to do as they wish. Three times they come against the Lamanites to battle, and three times they suffer terrible defeat. Mourning and lamentation fill the air.

> *13 And* ***they did humble themselves*** *even to the dust, subjecting themselves to the yoke of bondage, submitting themselves to be smitten, and to be driven to and fro, and burdened, according to the desires of their enemies.*
> *14 And* ***they did humble themselves even in the depths of humility;*** *and they did cry mightily to God; yea, even* ***all the day long did they cry unto their God*** *that he would deliver them out of their afflictions.*

They did humble themselves even in the depths of humility; all the day long did they cry unto their God

It is according to the mercy and benevolence of the Lord that the chastened and humbled are to be delivered. There is a principle in the heavens according to which blessings are predicated upon obedience to divine law (see D&C 130:20–21). The scriptures provide ample evidence that the degree of liberty enjoyed by the Saints of God is a function of their humility, valor, and willingness to be entreated and instructed of the Spirit. Limhi's people are in bondage to the Lamanites, which fulfills Abinadi's prophetic warning. Thus Limhi's people are chastened of the Lord that they might learn obedience and humility. They finally humble themselves to the point that the seeds of deliverance are sown whereby they are ultimately delivered by the Lord out of the hands of their enemies (see Mosiah 7:33; 20:21; 21:4; 22:13). What are those seeds? Even before they are buried in the depths of humility and petition their Lord for deliverance, Ammon and his group are already en route, seeking to discover them. Thus the principle enunciated by Isaiah long before is again substantiated: "And it shall come to pass, that before they call, I will answer; and while they are yet speaking, I will hear" (Isaiah 65:24).

Mosiah 21:15–23

> *15 And now* ***the Lord was slow to hear their cry*** *because of their iniquities; nevertheless* ***the Lord did hear their cries,*** *and began to* ***soften the hearts of the Lamanites*** *that they began to ease their burdens; yet the Lord did not see fit to deliver them out of bondage.*

The Lord was slow to hear their cry

How can we be delivered out of our afflictions? In life we sometimes are casual in our relationship with God and in our prayers of thanksgiving. We do as we wish until the afflictions and need are so severe that we feel overwhelmed—and then we call upon the Lord for help. Because of our iniquity and lack of faith, the Lord is slow to hear our cries. It is vital to remember that blessings are given according to our faith, diligence, and patience as we receive the word and give heed to it (see 1 Nephi 16:28; Alma 7:26; 37:44; 49:30; 3 Nephi 12:1). It is important to do all we can to succeed rather than just ask the Lord and expect that He will deliver us and do all the work. Oliver Cowdery learned why he was unable to translate—he had to do his part in order to succeed (see D&C 9:3–9). Limhi's people finally counsel together and, under the inspired plan of Gideon, are delivered out of bondage (see Mosiah 22:1–13)

The Lord did hear their cries; soften the hearts of the Lamanites

The Lord would deliver them from oppression in His own due time—but for now they pay the price of their iniquities. Their burdens become lighter because the Lord softens the hearts of their enemies. Ultimate deliverance, however, is still in the future. We can apply this to our own circumstances. Let us learn to exercise our faith, even though we are not perfect, in order to receive answers to our prayers (see Mosiah 27:14). We sometimes take no thought save to ask (see D&C 9:7) and wonder why our prayers are not answered. Our prayers are answered according to our faith and our commitment to do right and honor our covenants (see Mormon 9:37).

16–23 Gradually, conditions for the Nephites improve. Their crops and herds become more abundant as a solution to hunger. The widows and their children are supported. The people remain unified and vigilant against their enemy. The king does not venture outside the city walls without his guard. They keep an eye out to capture the fugitive priests of Noah who have caused them so much suffering. It is at that point that Ammon and his contingent are discovered outside the city walls and mistaken for the priests of Noah.

24 But when he [Limhi] found that they were not, but that they were his brethren, and had come from the land of Zarahemla, he was filled with ***exceedingly great joy.***

Exceedingly great joy

At this point, the narrative picks up once again where the events around the arrival of Ammon and his brethren are placed on hold to accommodate the interposition of the account of Zeniff and his successors (see Mosiah 8).

25–30 A brief account is given concerning the party sent out earlier by Limhi to discover the route to Zarahemla. Instead, the party discovers the remains of an extinct nation (the Jaredites) and returns a few days prior to Ammon's arrival with a record engraved on plates of ore (the record of Ether on twenty-four plates of gold; see Ether 1:2) (see verse 27). Ammon and his brethren sorrow over many things: the loss of life among the colonists, the wicked influence of Noah and his priests over the people, the death of Abinadi, and the departure of Alma and his group.

31 Yea, they did mourn for their departure, for they knew not whither they had fled. Now they would have gladly joined with them, for ***they themselves had entered into a covenant with God*** *to serve him and keep his commandments.*
32 And now since the coming of Ammon, king ***Limhi had also entered into a covenant with God,*** *and also many of his people, to serve him and keep his commandments.*

They themselves had entered into a covenant with God; Limhi had also entered into a covenant with God

By guiding the people into the depths of humility and dependence upon the will of the Lord, Limhi is at last able to bring about a change in their disposition: "And they did humble themselves even in the depths of humility; and they did cry mightily to God; yea, even all the day long did they cry unto their God that he would deliver them out of their afflictions" (Mosiah 21:14). Signifying their commitment to righteousness, Limhi and many of his people enter into a covenant with God "to serve him and keep his commandments" (Mosiah 21:31).

33 And it came to pass that king Limhi and many of his people were ***desirous to be baptized;*** *but there was none in the land that had authority from God. And* ***Ammon declined doing this thing,*** *considering himself an unworthy servant.*

34 Therefore they did not at that time form themselves into a church, ***waiting upon***
the Spirit of the Lord. *Now they were desirous to become even as Alma and his*
brethren, who had fled into the wilderness.
35 They were ***desirous to be baptized as a witness and a testimony*** *that they*
were willing to serve God with all their hearts; nevertheless they did prolong the
time; and an account of their baptism shall be given hereafter.
36 And now all the study of Ammon and his people, and king Limhi and his
people, was to deliver themselves out of the hands of the Lamanites and from
bondage.

DESIROUS TO BE BAPTIZED; AMMON DECLINED DOING THIS THING; WAITING UPON THE SPIRIT OF THE LORD; DESIROUS TO BE BAPTIZED AS A WITNESS AND A TESTIMONY

Alma has organized the Church at the Waters of Mormon, and then is forced by the Lamanites to flee into the wilderness. Limhi is aware of Alma's actions and wishes to follow in his footsteps. Lacking authority, however, Limhi patiently looks forward to the time when this blessing can be granted.

CHAPTER 22

OVERVIEW

The Nephites escape bondage by making their Lamanite captors drunk. The people return safely to Zarahemla with their records and join with the people of Mosiah.

1–13 Ammon and Lehi consider strategies for liberating the people from Lamanite bondage. Gideon conceives a plan to make the enemy guards drunk. Limhi provides tribute wine in abundance, and the people escape into the wilderness with all of their valuables. They make their way to Zarahemla where they join with the people of Mosiah. The period of bondage comes to an end.

Ammon arrives from Zarahemla with a rescue party around 121 B.C. and aids in the escape. Limhi and his party reach the safety of Zarahemla around 121 B.C. (see Mosiah 22:13). As it turns out, Alma and his party follow shortly thereafter, arriving in Zarahemla around 120 B.C. (see Mosiah 24:25).

What Delivers a People from Bondage?

Having examined the different types of bondage and the steps that lead people into bondage, we need to examine the process that leads people out of bondage. On the subject of deliverance from bondage, the stories of Limhi and his people and that of Alma the Elder and his people present some unique insights. . . .

The first step outlined in the Book of Mormon for removing the chains of bondage is to be humble before the Lord. Because of heartache and the heavy yoke of bondage, Limhi and his people humbled themselves before the Lord (Mosiah 21:13), "turn[ing] to the Lord with full purpose of heart" as Limhi had instructed (7:33). Notice that the command to turn to the Lord is not to be half-hearted, but rather requires one's "*full* purpose of heart." This process of being humbled requires a changing or "turning" that must occur in individual lives if they are to be spared or delivered from bondage. President N. Eldon Tanner declared: "A person who is guilty of a serious transgression cannot progress, and he is not happy while the guilt is upon him. Until he has confessed and repented he is in bondage" (78). Limhi's people acknowledged their guilt and turned to the Lord for his help.

The second step that leads away from bondage is for people to engage in mighty prayer. Prayer should automatically accompany being humbled before the Lord. In Mosiah 21 we read that the people of Limhi "did humble themselves even in the depths of humility; and they did cry mightily to God; yea, even all the day long did they cry unto their God that he would deliver them out of their afflictions" (v 14). These Nephites learned to put their trust in the Lord as Limhi had encouraged them to do (Mosiah 7:33). Even though they sincerely and humbly relied on the Lord, "the Lord was slow to hear their cry" (Mosiah 21:15) because they had been slow to hear and respond to his word.

The third step of Limhi's people toward deliverance from bondage was their willingness to covenant with the Lord to keep his commandments (Mosiah 21:32). Their obedience not only moved them toward freedom from physical bondage, it also enabled them to begin to enjoy a release from spiritual bondage before they had actually escaped from the hands of the Lamanites. In the words of President Marion G. Romney:

"Freedom thus obtained—that is, by obedience to the law of Christ—is freedom of the soul, the highest form of liberty. And the most glorious thing about it is that it is within the reach of every one of us, regardless of what people about us, or even nations, do. All we have to do is learn the law of Christ and obey it. To learn it and obey it is the primary purpose of every soul's mortal life." (Marion G. Romney, "The Perfect Law of Liberty." *Ensign,* Nov. 1981, 45)

The fourth and final step in escaping bondage is to serve the Lord with all diligence (see Mosiah 7:33; 21:32). To both the Nephites and the Jaredites the Lord declared that freedom from bondage would continue for those who inhabit this choice land as long as they "serve the God of the land, who is Jesus Christ" (Ether 2:12; compare 2 Nephi 1:7). Once Limhi and his people had covenanted with God to serve him and keep his commandments, they were able to devise a plan of escape from their Lamanite captors (Mosiah 22). That Limhi and his people began to witness the hand of the Lord helping them in their time of bondage confirms the promise of the Lord "that he [would] pour out his Spirit more abundantly" upon those who would serve him and keep his commandments (Mosiah 18:10)." (Monte S. Nyman and Charles D. Tate Jr., eds., *Mosiah: Salvation Only through Christ* [Provo: Religious Studies Center, 1991], 269–270)

14 And it came to pass that ***Mosiah received them with joy;*** *and* ***he also received their records,*** *and also the* ***records*** *which had been found by the people of Limhi.*

Mosiah received them with joy; he also received their records

When Ammon and his expeditionary group from Zarahemla discover Limhi's people around 121 B.C., hope for relief is rekindled. Limhi is overjoyed to learn from Ammon that King Mosiah is a seer—"a revelator and a prophet also" (Mosiah 8:16)—who can interpret the twenty-four plates of gold discovered and retrieved by Limhi's search party venturing inadvertently into former Jaredite territory while on a quest to find Zarahemla (see Mosiah 8:9; 21:27). At that time, Limhi, being a Nephite wanderer himself, separated from the place of his origins at Zarahemla, is moved to articulate his feelings about the challenges of mortality in light of the fate of the extinct nation of the Jaredites. "O how marvelous are the works of the Lord, and how long doth he suffer with his people; yea, and how blind and impenetrable are the understandings of the children of men; for they will not seek wisdom, neither do they desire that she should rule over them! Yea, they are as a wild flock which fleeth from the shepherd, and scattereth, and are driven, and are devoured by the beasts of the forest" (Mosiah 8:20–21).

Like the Jaredites, the people of the Nephite colonies, through their pride and lack of faith, have been scattered and driven from time to time by their captors, coming face to face finally with the prospect of utter destruction. But unlike the Jaredites, the people of Limhi spiritually turn themselves about and are blessed, with the help of the Lord, to return safely to Zarahemla and bring with them all of their records (Mosiah 22:13–14). In this manner, invaluable treasures of truth are preserved for our day by the hand of the Lord.

The leadership of Mosiah is a model for all to follow. As leaders, do we consider our ways in order to be sure we are blessing the lives of those we serve?

15–16 The Lamanites discover that the Nephites have escaped and pursue them for two days until they can no longer follow the tracks.

> *An account of Alma and the people of the Lord, who were driven into the wilderness by the people of King Noah.* [Note: This preamble was included in the original edition of the Book of Mormon published in 1830.] (Chapters 23 and 24.)

CHAPTER 23

OVERVIEW

The people of Alma flee to a secluded area called Helam where they can settle in safety. Alma refuses to become their king. He reminds them of the evil that a wicked king such as Noah can cause. The people are to choose only righteous leaders to preside over them. The Lord tests the faith of the people by sending the Lamanites as oppressors. Alma exhibits calm leadership. The Lamanites under Amulon, one of the priests of Noah now subject to the Lamanite king, surround and confine the colony.

1–7 Alma is warned of the Lord to flee from the armies of King Noah. He gathers his people together and they flee for eight days into the wilderness. They discover a fertile area where they can settle in safety. The people ask Alma to be their king, but he refuses, saying that they should "not esteem one flesh above another" (verse 7).

8 Nevertheless, if it were possible that ye could always have just men to be your kings it would be well for you to have a king.
9 But ***remember the iniquity of King Noah*** *and his priests; and* ***I myself was caught in a snare,*** *and did many things which were abominable in the sight of the Lord, which caused me sore repentance;*
10 Nevertheless, after much tribulation, the Lord did hear my cries, and did answer my prayers, and has made me ***an instrument in his hands*** *in bringing so many of you to a knowledge of his truth.*
11 Nevertheless, in this I do not glory, for I am unworthy to glory of myself.

Remember the iniquity of King Noah; I myself was caught in a snare; an instrument in his hands

The lesson of this section of the Book of Mormon is that evil men can readily extend their evil influence to others who all too easily succumb to misguided practices, as did Alma. His repentance enables the Lord to make him an instrument of service in gathering the people to the Lord.

12 And now I say unto you, ye have been oppressed by King Noah, and have been in bondage to him and his priests, and have been brought into iniquity by them; therefore ***ye were bound with the bands of iniquity.***
13 And now as ye have been delivered by the power of God out of these bonds; yea, even out of the hands of King Noah and his people, and also from the bonds of iniquity, even so I desire that ye should ***stand fast in this liberty wherewith ye have been made free,*** *and that ye trust no man to be a king over you.*
14 And also trust no one to be your teacher nor your minister, ***except he be a man of God,*** *walking in his ways and keeping his commandments.*

Ye were bound with the bands of iniquity; stand fast in this liberty wherewith ye have been made free; except he be a man of God

The people of Alma understandably accept him as their benevolent and charitable leader. They want him to be their king, for they love him and know of his goodness. However, Alma sees beyond the present moment and perceives the potential danger of an unrighteous king. He therefore declines the invitation to serve as king and uses the opportunity to teach an important lesson about the need to be cautious in facilitating the rise of people to leadership. After all, the people have just experienced the lethal dangers of being under the influence of King Noah. In a sense, they have allowed this to happen because they did not stand up for truth and righteousness. Alma therefore teaches the people that they should trust no one to be a teacher or minister unto them save he be a man of God, walking in His ways and keeping His commandments.

The application to our own situation today is this: Let us always stand for truth and righteousness. Let us expect integrity and honesty from our government leaders and from those whom we choose to heed. It is our duty to follow our living prophets—not the voice anti-Christs like Sherem, Nehor, or Korihor. The erroneous philosophies of men and misguided secular teachings of men can lead us away from our Savior. By following the Spirit, we can discern such falsehoods and avoid them.

> *15 Thus did Alma teach his people, that* ***every man should love his neighbor as himself,*** *that there should be no contention among them.*
> *16 And now, Alma was their high priest, he being the founder of their church.*
> *17 And it came to pass that none received authority to preach or to teach except it were by him from God. Therefore he consecrated all their priests and all their teachers; and* ***none were consecrated except they were just men.***
> *18 Therefore* ***they did watch over their people, and did nourish them*** *with things pertaining to righteousness.*
> *19 And it came to pass that* ***they began to prosper exceedingly*** *in the land; and they called the land Helam.*

EVERY MAN SHOULD LOVE HIS NEIGHBOR AS HIMSELF; NONE WERE CONSECRATED EXCEPT THEY WERE JUST MEN; THEY DID WATCH OVER THEIR PEOPLE, AND DID NOURISH THEM; THEY BEGAN TO PROSPER EXCEEDINGLY

The contrast between the culture of Helam and that of King Noah is striking. Within a very short time the people are redirected into paths of prosperity and unity. The previous conditions of depravity and oppression are transformed into a state of unity and integrity—all because Alma has taught the people to follow principles of righteousness, sustain authorized priesthood service, and practice charity among themselves. If we apply divine principles in our lives, joy will result just as surely as day follows night. It is so today just as it was in Alma's day, for God is "the same God yesterday, today, and forever" (D&C 20:12).

> *20 And it came to pass that they did multiply and prosper exceedingly in the land of Helam; and they built a city, which they called the city of Helam.*
> *21 Nevertheless the* ***Lord seeth fit to chasten his people;*** *yea, he trieth their patience and their faith.*

*22 Nevertheless—**whosoever putteth his trust in him the same shall be lifted up at the last day.** Yea, and thus it was with this people.*
*23 For behold, I will show unto you that they were brought into bondage, and **none could deliver them but the Lord their God,** yea, even the God of Abraham and Isaac and of Jacob.*

LORD SEETH FIT TO CHASTEN HIS PEOPLE; WHOSOEVER PUTTETH HIS TRUST IN HIM THE SAME SHALL BE LIFTED UP AT THE LAST DAY; NONE COULD DELIVER THEM BUT THE LORD THEIR GOD

Mormon inserts this commentary as a preamble to the events that follow. At the very time the people are beginning to prosper and multiply, the Lord deems it appropriate to test their faith and bless them with the insight that He will liberate those who trust in Him. In a sense He reminds them that life is a test, that faith and patience are tried through chastening, that we are here on earth to prove ourselves worthy (see Abraham 3:25). But because He is a loving Father, He also reinforces the doctrine that by exercising faith and trusting in the strength of the Lord, we will be lifted up and blessed (see 2 Nephi 26:13; 2 Nephi 4:34; Moroni 7:33; Alma 26:12; Alma 61:13; Ether 12:27).

24–26 The Lamanites begin to attack. The people are gripped with fear.

*27 But Alma went forth and stood among them, and exhorted them that **they should not be frightened,** but that **they should remember the Lord their God** and he would deliver them.*
28 Therefore they hushed their fears, and began to cry unto the Lord that he would soften the hearts of the Lamanites, that they would spare them, and their wives, and their children.
*29 And it came to pass that **the Lord did soften the hearts of the Lamanites.** And Alma and his brethren went forth and delivered themselves up into their hands; and the Lamanites took possession of the land of Helam.*

THEY SHOULD NOT BE FRIGHTENED; THEY SHOULD REMEMBER THE LORD THEIR GOD; THE LORD DID SOFTEN THE HEARTS OF THE LAMANITES

Alma exhibits steady and comforting leadership at a time of crisis.

Calm Leadership

If life were devoid of sudden reversals, unexpected challenges, and the unpredictable onslaught of stealthy intruders, then it would not be the mortality we are all used to. Such events, though taxing, present opportunities for the manifestation of leadership that is circumspect and calm.

The crisis in Helam occasioned by the attack of the Lamanites is an example of how calm leadership can carry the day. Alma is approached by frantic citizens upon the invasion by the enemy. The citizens have rushed from their farms to seek guidance from Alma, their high priest. Note what transpires: He invokes the principle of trusting in the Lord. Therefore they hush their fears and begin to cry unto the Lord that He will soften the hearts of the Lamanites, that they might spare them, and their wives, and their children. "And it came to pass that the Lord did soften the hearts of the Lamanites" (Mosiah 23:29). As a result of this prudent and steady leadership, the community is spared bloodshed. They are eventually led by the Lord out of bondage and are able to join the main body of the Nephites in the capital Zarahemla.

This incident reminds me of the deportment of the Prophet Joseph when he had been unjustly accused of the attempted murder of Missouri's ex-governor, Lilburn W. Boggs. In May 1842, a would-be assassin wounded Boggs in Missouri, and local authorities and apostate John C. Bennett accused Joseph Smith of complicity in the crime. As a result, a second attempt was made to extradite the Prophet to Missouri for a sham trial, causing Joseph to flee into hiding on a Mississippi River island to elude his enemies and protect his life. Rumors began to multiply in Nauvoo regarding possible attacks from the militia, mob violence, writs, etc., so that when some of the brethren (including his brother Hyrum) hastened to the Prophet on Monday, August 15, 1842, to warn him of all sorts of real or imagined dangers, they had worked themselves into somewhat of a frenzy. Joseph calmly evaluated the situation, recalling: "I discovered a degree of excitement and agitation manifested in those who brought the report, and I took occasion to gently reprove all present for letting report excite them, and advised them not to suffer themselves to be wrought upon by any report, but to maintain an even, undaunted mind. Each one began to gather courage, and all fears were soon subsided, and the greatest union and good feeling prevailed amongst all present. Various subjects were then conversed upon, and counsel given which was felt to be most seasonable and salutary" (*HC* 5:97–98).

By this we see the wisdom of cultivating composure under stress, of carefully separating fact from fiction when making judgments, and, above all, of continually maintaining faith in the guidance of the Lord. (Richard J. Allen)

30–39 Which contingent of the Lamanites has come upon Helam? The background is given by Mormon: The armies of the Lamanites who have been pursuing Limhi and his people instead come upon the fugitive priests of King Noah and their leader Amulon. Amulon and the abducted Lamanite maidens now part of the Nephite group plead with the Lamanites for mercy. The Lamanites spare them and allow them to join with them as they set out to find their way back to the city of Nephi (the former headquarters of the Nephite colony). En route they stumble upon the settlement at Helam. They agree to spare the people and grant unto them their liberty if Alma will show them the way to Nephi. Alma does so, but the Lamanites fail to keep their promise. Instead, they surround Helam with guards under the charge of Amulon, the Nephite turncoat now subject to the Lamanite king. The shackles of bondage are once again placed upon the people of the Lord.

CHAPTER 24

OVERVIEW

The people of Alma are persecuted bitterly by Amulon and the Lamanite guards. Amulon threatens to kill anyone caught praying. The people of the Lord privately pour out their hearts before God. The Lord gives them the strength to bear their burdens. He delivers them from bondage, and they return to Zarahemla and join with the people of Mosiah.

1–2 Amulon, former chief priest of Noah, gains favor with the king of the Lamanites. The king assigns him and his fellow priests to be teachers in the cities over which the Lamanites have gained possession.

> *3 And now the name of the king of the Lamanites was Laman, being called after the name of his father; and therefore he was called king Laman. And he was king over a numerous people.*

4–10 Amulon and his priests teach the language of the Nephites to their Lamanite colleagues and encourage them to keep written records and correspond with one another. However, they do not teach things of righteousness. The Lamanites flourish in the ways of the world. Amulon is angry with Alma for believing the words of Abinadi. Amulon places heavy burdens upon Alma and his people so that they suffer greatly.

11 And Amulon commanded them that they should stop their cries; and he put guards over them to watch them, that ***whosoever should be found calling upon God should be put to death.***
12 And ***Alma and his people did not raise their voices to the Lord their God, but did pour out their hearts to him;*** *and he did know the thoughts of their hearts.*
13 And it came to pass that the voice of the Lord came to them in their afflictions, saying: ***Lift up your heads and be of good comfort,*** *for I know of the covenant which ye have made unto me; and I will covenant with my people and deliver them out of bondage.*

Whosoever should be found calling upon God should be put to death; Alma and his people did pour out their hearts to him; lift up your heads and be of good comfort

The Lord will gather the faithful out of bondage. The Lord answers the prayers of the humble and faithful by granting them strength to meet the challenges of life, courage to face adversity, and resilience to endure the burdens of mortality. The citizens of Helam are placed under grievous burdens by the vengeful Amulon, and it is only through their humble prayers and faithful dependence on the Lord that they are ultimately freed from bondage and find their way to the central locus of Nephite leadership at Zarahemla.

14 And ***I will also ease the burdens*** *which are put upon your shoulders, that even you cannot feel them upon your backs, even while you are in bondage; and this will I do that ye may* ***stand as witnesses for me hereafter,*** *and that ye may know of a surety that I, the Lord God, do visit my people in their afflictions.*
15 And now it came to pass that the burdens which were laid upon Alma and his brethren were made light; yea, ***the Lord did strengthen them*** *that they could bear up their burdens with ease, and they did submit cheerfully and with patience to all the will of the Lord.*

I will also ease the burdens; stand as witnesses for me hereafter; the Lord did strengthen them

Like Moses, Alma liberates his people from both physical and spiritual bondage. Alma's statement concerning the theme of preserving personal and community liberty—"Stand fast in this liberty wherewith ye have been made free" (Mosiah 23:13)—depicts the operation of eternal principles in our lives. Alma also teaches the universal truth that seeking and obtaining the strength of God is what transcends mortal suffering and hardship.

> *16 And it came to pass that so great was their faith and their patience that the voice of the Lord came unto them again, saying: Be of good comfort, for on the morrow* ***I will deliver you out of bondage.***

I will deliver you out of bondage

We must pray with faith and be patient. The Lord will provide. In the Lord's own time, sooner or later things will be better.

17–25 Alma directs his people to prepare to flee during the night. The Lord brings a deep sleep upon the Lamanite guards so that the people can escape. The people pour out their hearts in thanksgiving. The Lord warns them to hasten their escape, for the enemy has awakened. After a flight of twelve days they arrive safely in Zarahemla, to the great joy of king Mosiah. This occurs approximately 120 B.C.

A Scholarly Note on Bondage

> Because Alma and his people had been humbled by the word of God rather than being compelled to be humble by their bondage as Limhi's group had been, the Lord made the bondage of Alma and his people much easier to endure. The message for us is that it is better to repent sooner than later. The slower we are to hearken to the Lord, the slower he must be in responding to our needs. How reassuring it must have been to Alma's people to experience the miracle of not feeling the burdens which were placed upon their backs. They could have no question in their minds about whose power it was that delivered them and led them back to the land of Zarahemla.
>
> The question may be asked why Alma's group was put into bondage since they had repented, had made covenants, and had served the Lord for some time. The answer seems to go back to Abinadi's prophecy. When he first came to the Nephites in the land of Nephi, he warned that they would be brought into bondage if they did not repent (see Mosiah 11:21). This warning went unheeded until Abinadi returned two years later. His warning then

proclaimed that they *would* be brought into bondage, and if they still refused to repent they would be destroyed (see Mosiah 12:2, 8). It was at this time that Alma was converted and began to teach the words of Abinadi secretly to those Nephites who would listen. Thus, even though Alma and his people had repented, it was still necessary that Abinadi's first prophecy be fulfilled.

A great principle we can learn from this portion of the book of Mosiah (chapters 19–24) is that the longer we wait to repent and forsake our sins, the more serious the consequences will be. Elder Melvin J. Ballard reiterated this principle: "Every man and woman who is putting off until the next life the task of correcting and overcoming the weakness of the flesh are sentencing themselves to years of bondage, for no man or woman will come forth in the Resurrection until he has completed his work, until he has overcome, until he has done as much as he can do" (242).

Sadly, for many this bondage has already begun in this life. As with Limhi and his people, if we are slow to hearken to the counsel of the Lord, we only make our transformation to freedom more difficult and increase the degree of our bondage. (Monte S. Nyman and Charles D. Tate Jr., eds., *Mosiah: Salvation Only through Christ* [Provo: Religious Studies Center, 1991], 272)

Counsel from the Prophet Joseph Smith

From the *Lectures on Faith* we have a statement confirming the faith of leaders such as Alma, who prepared the people for deliverance by planting in their hearts a sure conviction of the greatness and goodness of God:

> It is also of equal importance that men should have the idea of the existence of the attribute judgment in God, in order that they may exercise faith in him for life and salvation; for without the idea of the existence of this attribute in the Deity, it would be impossible for men to exercise faith in him for life and salvation, seeing that it is through the exercise of this attribute that the faithful in Christ Jesus are delivered out of the hands of those who seek their destruction; for if God were not to come out in swift judgment against the workers of iniquity and the powers of darkness, his saints could not be saved; for it is by judgment that the Lord delivers his saints out of the hands of all their enemies, and those who reject the gospel of our Lord Jesus Christ. But no sooner is the

> idea of the existence of this attribute planted in the minds of men, than it gives power to the mind for the exercise of faith and confidence in God, and they are enabled by faith to lay hold on the promises which are set before them, and wade through all the tribulations and afflictions to which they are subjected by reason of the persecution from those who know not God, and obey not the gospel of our Lord Jesus Christ, believing that in due time the Lord will come out in swift judgment against their enemies, and they shall be cut off from before him, and that in his own due time he will bear them off conquerors, and more than conquerors, in all things. (*Lectures on Faith* [Salt Lake City: Deseret Book, 1985], 4:14)

CONCLUDING THOUGHTS

In just a few chapters we discover a treasure of spiritual wisdom: the sacred baptismal covenant, the inexorable justice of God, the means whereby the chastened can look forward to deliverance, and the compassion of the Lord in gathering the faithful out of bondage. There are many great lessons that can be learned from these passages and just as many questions of conscience we might ask ourselves.

Do we remember our baptismal covenants and the obligation of renewing them weekly? Review them carefully in Mosiah 18:8–9, Moroni 6:1–4, and Doctrine and Covenants 20:37, as well as the many scriptures concerning discipleship, i.e., 3 Nephi 5:13; John 13:34–35; Matthew 25:40; and Doctrine and Covenants 88:81, to name a few. What does it mean to stand as a witness? (see Mosiah 18:9). How do we put ourselves in bondage? (compare the stories of Limhi and Alma and the instrumentality of ultimate deliverance.) As leaders, are we worthy of people's trust? (see Mosiah 23:14).

CHAPTER 25

OVERVIEW

Mosiah brings the people of Zarahemla together into two groups—Nephites and Mulekites, or descendants of Mulek—and reads to them the records of Zeniff and of Alma. The people are amazed and overjoyed over the blessings of deliverance granted by the Lord to His people, but also saddened at the loss of so many lives and the grievous condition of the Lamanites. Alma speaks to the people and reminds them that the Lord is the source of their deliverance. He then baptizes Limhi and his followers. Mosiah authorizes Alma to organize seven churches (congregations) throughout the land and to ordain priests and teachers to serve the needs of the people. Only faith and repentance are taught.

1–4 King Mosiah assembles the people of **Zarahemla** into two great bodies: the Nephites, and the more numerous descendants of Mulek.

EVIDENCE: ZARAHEMLA—LOCATION FOR ZARAHEMLA (Mosiah 25:4)

Next to the Grijalva River in the Mexican state of Chiapas lies an archaeological site that meets all the geographical requirements for the Nephite city of Zarahemla. Though the ruin, known half a century ago as Santa Rosa, now sits under water, earlier excavations point to a great deal of building activity around the first century B.C. Large earthen mounds were formed, and a huge platform was built in the center of the city. Details surrounding this platform suggest the division of the community into two social groups. This recalls the situation of the city of Zarahemla at the time of King Mosiah when his subjects—who spoke two different languages—gathered to hear him in two separate bodies. (See *Echoes,* 296–298).

5–8 Mosiah reads the records of Zeniff and Alma. The people are amazed as they behold in their midst the people who have escaped bondage, and "they were filled with exceedingly **great joy**" (verse 8).

GREAT JOY

The last words we have from Zeniff are these: "And may the Lord bless my people" (Mosiah 10:22). That this prayer is answered is confirmed by the event just described, for the people have indeed been blessed through deliverance from their oppressors and reunion with their fellow saints in Zarahemla.

9–13 Emotions at this time are somewhat mixed: sorrow for those who have been slain by the Lamanites, thanksgiving for the goodness of God in liberating His people, anguish for the welfare of the misguided Lamanites, and (on the part of the children of Amulon and the other priests of Noah) disappointment with the conduct of their fathers—to the extent that these children abandon their family name and take on the name of the Nephites. In fact, all the people are numbered among the Nephites, who provide the governing leadership.

14 And now it came to pass that when Mosiah had made an end of speaking and reading
to the people, he desired that Alma should also speak to the people.
15 And ***Alma did speak unto them,*** *when they were assembled together in large bod-*
ies, and he went from one body to another, preaching unto the people repentance and
faith on the Lord.
16 And he did exhort the people of Limhi and his brethren, all those that had been
delivered out of bondage, that ***they should remember that it was the Lord that***
did deliver them.

Alma did speak unto them; they should remember that it was the Lord that did deliver them

The colonists have now been repatriated to Zarahemla, from whence Zeniff first ventured forth to regain the land of their first inheritance. They are now secure. No attacks threaten them, they have adequate food and shelter, they have networks of support and encouragement under peaceful conditions, and they have regained their strength. Alma reminds them that they should be thinking about the Lord and His mercy and kindness toward them. He teaches them "that they should remember that it was the Lord that did deliver them" (verse 16).

It reminds us of the miracle performed by Jesus in healing the ten lepers: "And one of them, when he saw that he was healed, turned back, and with a loud voice glorified God, And fell down on his face at his feet, giving him thanks: and he was a Samaritan. And Jesus answering said, Were there not ten cleansed? but where *are* the nine? There are not found that returned to give glory to God, save this stranger. And he said unto him, Arise, go thy way: thy faith hath made thee whole" (Luke 17:15–19).

Through the service and leadership of Alma, we might suppose, indeed we hope, that all of the people—not just one out of ten—remembered to offer sincere thanks to the Lord for His blessings of mercy and deliverance.

17 And it came to pass that after Alma had taught the people many things, and had
made an end of speaking to them, that king ***Limhi was desirous that he might be***
baptized; *and all his people were desirous that they might be baptized also.*
18 Therefore, ***Alma did go forth into the water and did baptize them;*** *yea, he did*
baptize them after the manner he did his brethren in the waters of Mormon; yea, and
as many as he did baptize did belong to the church of God; and this because of their
belief on the words of Alma.

Limhi was desirous that he might be baptized; Alma did go forth into the water and did baptize them

The first action on the part of the repatriates after arriving in Zarahemla is to request baptism. They are baptized by Alma who, in like manner, has also escaped from Lamanite bondage. It is instructive that Limhi and his followers request to be baptized prior to their return, "but there was none in the land that had authority from God. And Ammon declined doing this thing, considering himself an unworthy servant" (Mosiah 21:33). It is also of interest that Ammon's namesake, the son of Mosiah, would later become, with his brothers, the instrument in the hands of God to return to the Lamanite region and bring thousands of the people into the fold of God.

19–23 With authorization from Mosiah, Alma establishes seven churches (or congregations) throughout the land and ordains priests and teachers over each church. The churches are unified in the faith, "for there was nothing preached in all the churches except it were **repentance and faith** in God" (verse 22). Those who desire to take upon themselves the name of God join the churches.

Repentance and faith

We read that there was nothing preached in the newly organized churches (congregations) in Zarahemla "except it were repentance and faith in God" (verse 22). To live the gospel, enjoy the blessings of the Spirit, and endure to the end, we are entreated to exercise our faith in Jesus Christ and become perfected in Him by applying the Atonement to our lives through repentance (see 3 Nephi 27:20).

> *24 And they were called* ***the people of God.*** *And* ***the Lord did pour out his Spirit upon them,*** *and they were blessed, and prospered in the land.*

The people of God; the Lord did pour out his Spirit upon them

In those days in Zarahemla, the process of building the kingdom of God moves forward upon the same principles that will later apply during the Restoration in our day. Brigham Young identifies the master key for governing the people of Zion:

> One of the simplest things in the world is to control a people. Is there any particular art in making this people obedient? There is just one. If you, Elders of Israel, can get the art of preaching the Holy Ghost into the hearts of the people, you will

> have an obedient people. This is the only art required. Teach the people truth, teach them correct principles; show them what is for their greatest good and don't you think they will follow in that path? They will, just as far as it is consistent with their weaknesses and the power of darkness that is over the inhabitants of the earth—with us as with others. (*Discourses of Brigham Young,* comp. John A. Widtsoe [Salt Lake City: Deseret Book, 1954], 225)

Building the Kingdom of God in Our Day

The teachings of King Mosiah and particularly Alma help establish the Church in Zarahemla. Every day throughout the world, missionaries are teaching the gospel, inviting people to come unto Christ, and establishing the Church and kingdom of God upon the earth. This is the great purpose of this last dispensation—to take the gospel of Jesus Christ to every nation, kindred, tongue, and people. Here are a few examples of establishing the Church in our day:

The Church in the Philippines

Joseph Fielding Smith, an apostle, dedicated the Philippines for the preaching of the gospel on August 21, 1955, and the first four missionaries arrived from Hong Kong in June 1961. Establishing the Church in the Philippines progressed more smoothly than in any other part of Asia because over 90 percent of the population were Christian, almost 50 percent used English to some degree, and Americans who were teaching a religion with American origins were generally popular. By 1967, the Philippines was made a separate mission with Paul Rose as president, and by 1973, over 13,000 Filipinos had been baptized. On May 20, 1973, Ezra Taft Benson, an Apostle, organized the Manila Philippines Stake with Agusto A. Lim as president. Four years later the Manila stake was divided into three stakes. The developing of experienced leadership and building of adequate meetinghouses have been a challenge, but members have had the full program of the Church, including seminaries and institutes since 1972. Selections from the Book of Mormon were published in Tagalog (1987); a missionary training center was established in Manila (1986); and on September 25–27, 1984, President Gordon B. Hinckley dedicated the Manila Philippines Temple. In 1988 the First Presidency made Manila the headquarters for the Philippines/Micronesia area of the Church and assigned an area president to live there. Church growth in the Philippines has been the most rapid of all Asian countries, and over 80 percent of the missionaries in 1990 were local Filipinos. (*Encyclopedia of Mormonism,* 1–4 vols., ed. Daniel H. Ludlow (New York: Macmillan, 1992), 79.)

The Church in Chile

After Parley P. Pratt's unsuccessful attempt to establish a Church foothold in Chile in 1851–1852, the Church did not officially come to Chile until Brother William Fotheringham moved to Santiago, Chile, in 1952, and requested that the Church send missionaries there. The first regular missionaries arrived in Santiago just two weeks before Elder Henry D. Moyle, then of the Quorum of the Twelve Apostles, called Brother Fotheringham as the president of the first Chilean branch on July 5, 1956. It was made up primarily of expatriate members, the first local Chilean convert being baptized that same year.

The first mission in Chile was organized on October 8, 1961, with A. Delbert Palmer presiding. That single mission has grown to become six missions, with more than 50 percent of the missionaries called from the local members, many of whom have been prepared in large measure by their seminary and institute training. They are generally called to attend the Missionary Training Center in Santiago, the second such center in South America. The Church has grown rapidly in Chile, with almost 298,000 members on March 31, 1990. On January 1991, Carlos Cifuentes, one of those local converts, became the first native Chilean branch president and stake president. On September 15, 1983, the Santiago Chile Temple was dedicated. Eugene F. and Rae Stephens Jones Olsen were the president and matron. On March 31, 1990, Elder Eduardo Ayala, a former mission president in Uruguay, became the first native Chilean called to be a Seventy. (*Encyclopedia of Mormonism,* 1–4 vols., ed. Daniel H. Ludlow (New York: Macmillan, 1992), 1399.)

The Church in Russia

During the 1988 commemoration of 1000 years of Christianity in Russia, it became apparent large numbers of Russians had preserved a heritage of faith despite more than seven decades of official Soviet atheism. Many of these Russians turned for spiritual nourishment to the centuries-old Russian Orthodox Church. Others sought renewal from Christian faiths brought to Russia in the 19th century.

In the late 1980s and early 1990s, some Russians began to direct their spiritual quests toward a study of religious faiths just entering the country, including The Church of Jesus Christ of Latter-day Saints.

In October 1989 Dennis B. Neuenschwander (now of the Seventy), president of the Austria Vienna East Mission; and Steven R. Mecham, president of the Finland Helsinki Mission, were authorized to take the gospel into the Soviet Union. Within months, Elder Russell M. Nelson of the Quorum of the Twelve Apostles formally dedicated Estonia for the preaching of the restored gospel and offered a prayer of gratitude in a spirit of rededication in Leningrad, invoking the blessings of heaven upon the Estonian and Russian peoples. (Elder Francis M. Lyman of the Quorum of the Twelve Apostles had dedicated Russia in July 1903.) In 1990 the Church was officially recognized in Estonia and Russia.

In December 1989 President Mecham and the first full-time missionaries visited Leningrad (now St. Petersburg) and the Estonian capital, Tallinn, to support members and teach investigators. By July 1990 the Church numbered 156 Soviet members: 80 in Leningrad, 43 in Tallinn, 26 in Vyborg, and 7 in Moscow.

Early Russian investigators and new members encountered daunting obstacles to embracing the restored gospel. Paramount was the common perception that joining another church implied a betrayal of Russian Christianity, which was embodied in distinctive images of the Russian Orthodox Church: cathedrals with gilded cupolas and icons, beautiful liturgical music and priestly vestments, and elaborate worship services. (Gary Browning, "Pioneering in Russia," *Ensign,* June 1997, 25.)

CHAPTER 26

OVERVIEW

Many of the rising generation become rebellious and hard-hearted, and lead many souls away from the Church. Alma seeks help from the Lord, who responds that the faithful and penitent are to be received into the Church and forgiven as often as they repent, while those who refuse to repent are not to be numbered among the Church membership. Alma and those he has called to leadership positions regulate the Church in all diligence, despite much persecution. Many are baptized.

> *1 NOW it came to pass that there were many of* ***the rising generation*** *that could not understand the words of king Benjamin, being little children at the time he spake unto his people; and* ***they did not believe the tradition of their fathers.***
> *2 They did not believe what had been said concerning the resurrection of the dead, neither did they believe concerning the coming of Christ.*
> *3 And now because of their unbelief* ***they could not understand the word of God;*** *and* ***their hearts were hardened.***
> *4 And* ***they would not be baptized; neither would they join the church.*** *And they were a separate people as to their faith, and remained so ever after, even in their carnal and sinful state; for* ***they would not call upon the Lord*** *their God.*

THE RISING GENERATION DID NOT BELIEVE THE TRADITION OF THEIR FATHERS COULD NOT UNDERSTAND THE WORD OF GOD; THEIR HEARTS WERE HARDENED; THEY WOULD NOT BE BAPTIZED; NEITHER WOULD THEY JOIN THE CHURCH; THEY WOULD NOT CALL UPON THE LORD

Because of unbelief, the rising generation does not understand the things of God and thus their hearts are hardened. The antidote to this condition is to exercise faith and be believing (see D&C 90:24). Exercising faith to believe and then seeking understanding is pleasing to God (see Hebrews 11:6). Unbelief precipitates apathy, which is the antithesis of love—hence, obedience wanes, the heart is hardened, the Spirit is lost, and sin is the result. In our own lives, let us therefore seek and pray for understanding, that we may act with faith. When we act with faith, we remain easily entreated and prevent our hearts from becoming hardened to the things of the Lord.

5–6 The dissenters, still a minority, grow in number. They flatter many in the Church into the byways of sin. Such are "**admonished by the church**" (verse 6).

ADMONISHED BY THE CHURCH

What is the nature of our influence in home, church, and community? We need to ensure that our influence serves as a lighthouse rather than a shadow. The Book of Mormon often teaches by using contrasts, just as Lehi observed: "For it must needs be, that there is an opposition in all things" (2 Nephi 2:11). We observe the exemplary position of Alma and the people of the Lord, on the one hand, and the contrasting position of the rebellious and self-centered youth who were too young to understand or remember the words of King Benjamin. Thus we see in the lives of the rising generation in Zarahemla, including Alma the Younger and the sons of Mosiah, the seeds of dissent germinating and sprouting. Such minds seek followership. In our own lives let us remember that our influence is felt far beyond the confines of our own personal space and time.

7–13 The rebels are brought before Alma. Witnesses attest to their misdeeds. Troubled, Alma seeks to have Mosiah judge the accused, but Mosiah demurs, leaving the ecclesiastical administration in the hands of Alma. Alma goes before the Lord to inquire what He would have him do.

> *14 And it came to pass that after he had poured out his whole soul to God, the voice of the Lord came to him, saying:*

15 ***Blessed art thou,*** *Alma, and* ***blessed are they who were baptized*** *in the waters of Mormon.* ***Thou art blessed*** *because of thy exceeding faith in the words alone of my servant Abinadi.*
16 And ***blessed are they because of their exceeding faith*** *in the words alone which thou hast spoken unto them.*
17 And ***blessed art thou because thou hast established a church*** *among this people; and they shall be established, and they shall be my people.*
18 Yea, ***blessed is this people who are willing to bear my name;*** *for in my name shall they be called; and they are mine.*
19 ***And because thou hast inquired*** *of me concerning the transgressor,* ***thou art blessed.***
20 Thou art my servant; and ***I covenant with thee that thou shalt have eternal life;*** *and thou shalt* ***serve me*** *and go forth in my name, and shalt* ***gather together my sheep.***

Blessed are thou; blessed are they; I covenant with thee that thou shalt have eternal life

In seven verses the Lord expresses His blessing seven times! What an inspiring response from the Savior of the world! He covenants with Alma that he shall have eternal life by serving Him and gathering His sheep. That is the context for Church service in the kingdom of God. Within that context, problems can be solved, including the one that Alma brings before the Lord.

21–32 The Lord sets forth the process for dealing with those who fall by the wayside. He will be the ultimate judge in the day of accountability. By virtue of the Atonement, the righteous who believe "shall have a place eternally at my right hand" (verse 24), while those who fail to come unto Christ will not be redeemed but "depart into everlasting fire prepared for the devil and his angels" (verse 27). Meanwhile, in the kingdom of God on the earth, those who hear the voice of the Lord are received into the Church and are forgiven of their trespasses as often as they repent, while he who "will not repent of his sins the same shall not be numbered among my people; and this shall be observed from this time forward" (verse 32). In any case, members of the Church are to forgive one another always. "And ye shall also **forgive one another** your trespasses; for verily I say unto you, he that forgiveth not his neighbor's trespasses when he says that he repents, the same hath brought himself under condemnation" (verse 31). The Lord's message to Alma is similar to His message today: "I, the Lord, will forgive whom I will forgive, but of you it is required to forgive all men" (D&C 64:10). Nevertheless, those called to administer the affairs of the Church are to take the action of excluding those who refuse to repent from being numbered among the membership of the Church.

Forgive one another

Forgiveness of others is the key to complete repentance and forgiveness of our own sins. Taking offense is caused by the inability to understand or forgive another. Taking offense is a choice we make. To contend is a choice we make. To be unforgiving is a choice we make. There will be people who, through ignorance or weakness of the flesh, will do things that are unseemly and unkind. If an offense is dropped—don't pick it up. Our test is to act as the Savior would act, do the things He would do. This is easy to say—but it *is* doable. Are we easily offended? Are we forgiving? Do we hold grudges?

Perspectives on the Doctrine of Forgiveness

The capacity to forgive is one of the most divine attributes we can possess. It is a commandment of God to forgive others (see 3 Nephi 13:15). Forgiveness brings peace to the forgiver as well as those forgiven. Without a doubt, true forgiveness is one of the most difficult aspects of human behavior to perfect. Forgiveness is tied to our righteousness to such an extent that we are condemned of the Lord and we have the greater sin if we fail to forgive others. We may wonder how this can be so when we are sometimes victims. However, the Lord was the greatest victim of all and yet He uttered, "Father, forgive them; for they know not what they do" (Luke 23:34). Christ was forgiving by nature: though the soldiers crucified Him, He forgave them. We are commanded to be like Him (see 3 Nephi 27:27), so we ought to be forgiving like He is. Forgiveness is an expression of godliness. Remember, as we confess and forsake our sins, the Lord remembers them no more (see D&C 58:42–43). (Ed J. Pinegar)

> *33 And it came to pass when Alma had heard these words* ***he wrote them down*** *that he might have them, and* ***that he might judge the people*** *of that church* ***according to the commandments of God.***

He wrote them down; that he might judge the people according to the commandments of God

Alma's record serves as a handbook of instructions for Church leadership.

34–36 Alma carries out the command of the Lord, retaining the penitent and faithful among the ranks of the Church and blotting out the names of the incorrigible and impenitent.

> *37 And it came to pass that Alma did* ***regulate all the affairs of the church;*** *and they began again to have* ***peace*** *and to prosper exceedingly in the affairs of the church, walking circumspectly before God, receiving many, and* ***baptizing many.***

Regulate all the affairs of the church; peace; baptizing many
Through communion with the Lord, Alma learned how to govern the Church according to the principles of moral agency. It is so today. The kingdom of God is governed according to the operation of priesthood keys and through revelation and the blessings of the Spirit of the Lord.

38–39 Alma and his associates continue their ministry in all diligence. Though they suffer much persecution by those outside the Church, they admonish all to walk by the word of God, pray continually, and "give thanks in all things" (verse 39).

CONCLUDING THOUGHTS

Through the Book of Mormon record we relive the formal organization of the Church among the branch of Israel gathered in Zarahemla. We see the commitment of these early members. We will soon see the patience and love of a father—himself reformed—for his bright but misdirected son, Alma the Younger, who later (along with his colleagues of the rising generation) cultivates a single-minded devotion to missionary work and the service to God. All of this is part of the epic saga of building up the kingdom of God on earth.

The Book of Mormon confirms that where there is covenant leadership on earth, with authorized representatives of the Lord's priesthood power, the Church will emerge in its divinely appointed structure to administer the ordinances and blessings of the gospel to the sons and daughters of God.

CHAPTER 27

OVERVIEW

Persecution against the Church intensifies. Mosiah sends out a proclamation forbidding persecution and upholding universal equality. Alma the Younger and his colleagues, the four sons of Mosiah, commit destructive acts against the Church and lead people astray. An angel of the Lord intervenes and commands them to desist. Alma is rendered helpless and dumb. His father prays for him. He revives and bears witness to his miraculous conversion. Alma and the four sons of Mosiah commence their ministry to repair the harm they have done, and they preach the gospel throughout the land.

1–7 The persecutions against Church members in the land become so acute that Alma appeals to Mosiah for help. Mosiah makes a proclamation prohibiting such persecution. He declares that "there should be an equality among all men" (verse 3). Peace is restored, a lay priesthood is maintained, and the people begin to multiply and build large cities throughout the land.

> *8 Now* ***the sons of Mosiah were numbered among the unbelievers;*** *and also* ***one of the sons of Alma was numbered among them, he being called Alma,*** *after his father; nevertheless, he became a very wicked and an idolatrous man. And he was a man of many words, and did speak much flattery to the people; therefore he led many of the people to do after the manner of his iniquities.*
> *9 And he became a great hinderment to the prosperity of the church of God; stealing away the hearts of the people; causing much dissension among the people; giving a chance for the enemy of God to exercise his power over them.*

The sons of Mosiah were numbered among the unbelievers; one of the sons of Alma was numbered among them, he being called Alma

Here is a great tragedy—the offspring of noble and righteous men turn against the principles espoused of their fathers and go their own rebellious and destructive way. Alma the Elder, a former member of King Noah's notorious court, has a personal understanding of the transition from a state of ungodliness to a state of penitent spirituality. He has freely confessed his shadowy background to the congregants who have gathered in self-imposed exile in the wilderness: "But remember the iniquity of King Noah and his priests; and I myself was caught in a snare, and did many things which were abominable in the sight of the Lord, which caused me sore repentance" (Mosiah 23:9). In a remarkable foreshadowing of the life of his future son, Alma, he adds: "Nevertheless, after much tribulation, the Lord did hear my cries, and did answer my prayers, and has made me an instrument in his hands in bringing so many of you to a knowledge of his truth" (Mosiah 23:10).

Alma the Younger is a member of the rising, free-spirited generation at Zarahemla who have not personally witnesses the extraordinary teachings of King Benjamin and thus are not aligned with the spiritual traditions of the prophet-kings (Mosiah 26:1–4). He and his colleagues, the sons of Mosiah, are renegades. Their injurious behavior draws many from the fountain of truth (see Mosiah 27:8–9). Years later, the reformed and valiant Alma characterizes his earlier behavior in strong terms before his son Helaman: "Yea, and I had murdered many of [God's] children, or rather led them away unto destruction; yea, and in fine so great had been my iniquities, that the very thought of coming into the presence of my God did rack my soul with inexpressible horror" (Alma 36:14).

In two of the most compelling spiritual "come back" stories in the scriptures, the two Almas provide persuasive testimony that an influence of darkness can be transformed into an influence of overwhelming light through repentance and faith grounded in "the merits, and mercy, and grace of the Holy Messiah" (2 Nephi 2:8).

The Power of Example

> I would like to tell you a story about a friend of mine whom I shall call Bill, for the sake of anonymity. During Bill's last year at school, he met a lovely young woman named Helen. They became very good friends, and it wasn't very long until they began to talk about the possibility of their getting married.
>
> During that same last year of school Bill fell in with a group of fellows who were known as the most popular group on the campus. They taught Bill some bad habits.
>
> When Helen first saw Bill with a cigarette in his mouth, it nearly broke her heart. She talked with him and pleaded with him, but he felt that smoking cigarettes was one of the things that went with the popularity of this group on the campus. So her pleadings brought no results. Helen began to wonder if she should stay with Bill or not, whether she should allow their courtship to end in marriage. She wanted to be married in the temple, and she knew that if Bill continued to smoke cigarettes they would not get to the temple.
>
> When graduation time came, Bill offered a formal proposal to Helen and asked her to set the date of their wedding. She thought it over long and seriously. She loved Bill a very great deal and did not like the idea of losing him. But neither did she like the idea of marrying a smoking man, one who could not take her into the temple where she had wanted to go.

After some days' consideration, Helen finally came to the conclusion that when school was out, Bill would be separated from this group of boys and that possibly, if she married him, under her influence he might leave off the bad habits which he had acquired and get back into activity in the Church. And then, probably within a year or so, they could go to the temple together; so she consented, and they were married by her bishop in her living room at home.

A year or so went by, and a lovely baby boy was born to them. They called him John. In due time another boy was born to them. They called him James, but he was soon known as Jim.

Bill loved his two boys, and every night after he came home from work, he would play with them and have just a grand time. He would hold them way above his head and laugh at them and talk to them, and they would laugh back. Then he would bring them down and hug them to him.

This show of affection made Helen very happy, but Bill played with them while he had a cigarette in his mouth, and when Helen saw those little baby hands reach out for that smoldering white thing between Bill's lips, her heart sank, and she began to wonder what that example might mean in the future lives of those boys.

Years went by. John became twenty years of age and was called on a mission. He was thrilled with the call and so was his mother. Bill—well, on the night of the farewell testimonial, Bill sat on the stand with his wife and son and he was just about as proud as any father could be, because John was really a remarkably fine young man.

About three weeks after John's departure for his mission, Bill was sitting one evening in front of the big, open fireplace in the living room reading the evening paper and smoking a cigarette. While he was doing so, in came Jim, a young man by this time. Jim said, "Hi Dad."

Without looking up from his paper, Bill said, "Hello, Son. How are you?"

"I'm fine, Dad. I want to ask you a question."

"All right, Son, what is it?"

"What's the best brand of cigarettes?"

Bill stiffened in his chair. For a moment it seemed as if he were frozen there. Then his hands relaxed, and the paper slipped from his fingers and fell to the floor. He flipped his cigarette over into the open fire and then stood up and faced his son.

He said, "Jim, you cannot start to smoke."

"But I have started already, and I want to know what is the best brand of cigarettes?"

"Son, I am telling you," Bill said, "you cannot start to smoke."

"Well, why not, Dad? You've smoked as long as I can remember, and it hasn't hurt you any. I've watched you."

Those last words Jim spoke cut into Bill's heart. "I've watched you. I've watched you." Then Helen was right, Bill thought to himself. All these years Helen had told him that his cigarette habit—the example he was holding before his sons—would result like this, and he had never believed her. Now Helen was right. Here was Jim saying, "I've watched you. I've watched you."

Then Bill felt a consciousness of guilt, a note of self-accusation, and there were words going through his mind saying, "I taught him, I taught him, I taught him."

Bill shook himself and walked over to his son and took hold of both shoulders and looked him square in the eye and said, "Son, you say these cigarettes didn't ever hurt me. And you say you've watched me. I want you to know that these cigarettes have done me more harm than anything else in my life. Nothing has hurt me, nothing has handicapped me so much as these cigarettes. Why, I'd give anything that I own if I had never started to use them, and I don't want to see the same handicaps come to you. Why, Jim, these cigarettes have raised a barrier between me and happiness right here in my own home, and they have caused your mother many hours of weeping. I know that, and I don't want you to undertake a habit of this kind."

He talked so earnestly and so unusually that Jim at first thought that his Dad was putting on an act and told him so. Again Bill began to talk and plead with his son never to smoke again, to get rid of this habit that he had just begun.

Then Jim, realizing that his dad was really serious, said, "Well, Dad, if this cigarette habit is so bad, why haven't you quit?"

Bill said, "I've tried to quit. I've tried many times, but I have never been able to—the habit is too strong. I'm just like a slave to the cigarette, and I don't want you to become a slave. Now, Son, cut it out."

Jim said, "Well, Dad, you see all the fellows I go with—they all smoke. They'll think I'm a sissy. I couldn't face those fellows and tell them I wasn't going to smoke any more. They are the most popular crowd I know."

Bill said, "Popular or not, stop this habit and if necessary get a new crowd. Find new friends who don't smoke, but let cigarettes alone."

Jim said, "Well, I don't know whether I can do that or not. I'll have to think this over."

Then his dad said, "Jim, I'll make a bargain with you. If you'll quit smoking, I'll quit."

Jim, quick as a flash said, "Well, Dad, you just told me you couldn't quit. Are you trying to lead me along?"

Bill's answer to that was that he walked over to the fire-place, put his hand in his pocket, pulled out the package of cigarettes and the folder of matches, and threw them into the open fireplace. Then he turned around and faced his son and said, "Son, I've quit. I'm all through. Now, will you do the same thing?"

"Well I don't know, Dad; I've got to think this over," Jim said, "I'll tell you in the morning."

That night Bill couldn't sleep. He rolled and tossed in bed as long as he could stand it and then got up and went into the living room and closed the door. He didn't turn on the lights. He just walked the floor there in the dark. Jim's words kept going through his head, "I've watched you. I've watched you," followed by his own sense of self-accusation, "I taught him. I taught him."

It had been a long time since Bill had said a prayer. He had left that pretty much with Helen. But this night he wanted more than anything else to have Jim quit smoking; so there in the darkness and the stillness of his home he slipped down on his knees and began to pray. He poured out his soul to the Lord and told him all of his faults and shortcomings, confessed all of his sins to the Lord—the first time he'd ever done that. Then he told the Lord about Jim and their conversation of the evening.

He didn't pray with much faith. The cigarettes had pretty well weakened what faith he had, but he did pray from a sense of fear—fear for the future of that boy—and from a sense of love—love for a son for whom he would give his own life, if necessary. But it seemed like asking a great deal of the Lord to erase in one night an example which he had held before his son ever since that son was a tiny baby.

At last morning came. Bill slowly climbed the stairs up to Jim's room and went in and sat down on the edge of the bed. He put one hand on Jim's shoulder. Jim turned over, and Bill said, "Son, what's your answer?"

Jim looked up into his dad's tired face and sleepless eyes and said, "Dad, I surely don't want to hurt your feelings, but the fellows—I couldn't face them. I guess I won't quit. I'll wait awhile."

Deeply disappointed, but without saying another word, Bill got up and walked slowly out of the room. He felt like he had been whipped. But he was more than ever determined to keep his own resolution. He would never go back to his cigarettes.

The next Sunday he went to church, the first time in years. He went again the next Sunday and the next, and he continued to go and enjoyed it.

About a year afterwards the bishop came to him one day and said, "Bill, how would you like to be ordained an elder?"

A lump came into Bill's throat, and his eyes filled with tears as he took hold of the bishop's hand and said, "Bishop, do you mean that at last I can take Helen to the temple?"

The bishop squeezed his hand and said, "Yes, Bill, at last you can take Helen to the temple."

Another year went by, and John came home from his mission. One day when John and his father were alone together, John went over and put his arm around his dad and said, "Dad, I want you to know how deeply grateful I am to you for the wonderful thing you have done. You know, as a boy I always used to think that my dad was just about perfect, and I guess every boy thinks that his dad is the greatest man in the world. But every time you took a cigarette, it hurt me deep inside. I knew you had a weakness you couldn't control. But now, Dad, all that is over, and I want you to know how grateful I am to you."

But what about Jim? Well, Jim is married now and has a little boy of his own, and he comes home at night and plays with his boy just as Bill used to play with Jim. And when Jim gets his own little son up in his arms, that little baby, just as his father did, reaches out for that smoldering white thing between his dad's lips.

The other day I rode home on the bus with Bill, and he was telling me how happy he is in his new life. And then he told me about Jim, and said that if nearly twenty years of bad example would put Jim where he now is, possibly another twenty years of a good example might bring him back to where he ought to be. And I thought, "God bless you, Bill."

And God bless all other men like him in the wonderful struggle they are making for the right.

And God bless Jim and all other boys like him that they may recognize tobacco for what it is—a narcotic which enslaves human beings and helps to destroy their faith in God. This is my prayer, in Jesus' name. Amen. (Mark E. Peterson, CR, September 1950, 38–42)

10 And now it came to pass that while he [Alma] was going about to destroy the church of God, for he did go about secretly with the sons of Mosiah seeking to destroy the church, and to lead astray the people of the Lord, contrary to the commandments of God, or even the king—
11 And as I said unto you, as they were going about rebelling against God, behold, ***the angel of the Lord appeared unto them;*** *and he descended as it were in a cloud; and he spake as it were with a voice of thunder, which caused the earth to shake upon which they stood;*
12 And so great was their astonishment, that they fell to the earth, and understood not the words which he spake unto them.
13 Nevertheless he cried again, saying: Alma, arise and stand forth, for ***why persecutest thou the church of God?*** *For the Lord hath said: This is my church, and I will establish it; and nothing shall overthrow it, save it is the transgression of my people.*
14 And again, the angel said: Behold, the ***Lord hath heard the prayers of his people, and also the prayers of his servant, Alma, who is thy father;*** *for he has prayed with much faith concerning thee that thou mightest be brought to the knowledge of the truth; therefore, for this purpose have I come to convince thee of the power and authority of God, that the prayers of his servants might be answered according to their faith.*

The angel of the Lord appeared unto them; why persecutest thou the church of God? Lord hath heard the prayers of his people, and also the prayers of his servant, Alma, who is thy father

Alma importunes the Lord to bless his wayward son. An angel of the Lord intervenes to set the young man on a sounder course—because the Lord has a mission for young Alma, just as He had a mission for Saul of Tarsus. Alma is to repent, just as his father has earlier. Young Alma takes up and continues the work of the ministry in the pathway established by his father, "the founder of their church" (Mosiah 29:47).

Among other things, the Book of Mormon offers modern readers an inventory of the Lord's means of communicating with mortals. Nephi reminded his older brothers of their chronic insensitivity to the Lord's attempts to signal them the truth: "Ye are swift to do iniquity but slow to remember the Lord your God. Ye have seen an angel, and he spake unto you; yea, ye have heard his voice from time to time; and he hath spoken unto you in a still small voice, but ye were past feeling, that ye could not feel his words; wherefore, he has spoken unto you like unto the voice of thunder, which did cause the earth to shake as if it were to divide asunder" (1 Nephi 17:45). Similarly, in our day, there is wisdom in staying tuned to the Lord's communications extended to us through His Spirit, through the voices of the prophets, and through the scriptures, so that He is not constrained, as with Alma the Younger, to resort to more dramatic means:

> O, ye nations of the earth, how often would I have gathered you together as a hen gathereth her chickens under her wings, but ye would not!
>
> How oft have I called upon you by the mouth of my servants, and by the ministering of angels, and by mine own voice, and by the voice of thunderings, and by the voice of lightnings, and by the voice of tempests, and by the voice of earthquakes, and great hailstorms, and by the voice of famines and pestilences of every kind, and by the great sound of a trump, and by the voice of judgment, and by the voice of mercy all the day long, and by the voice of glory and honor and the riches of eternal life, and would have saved you with an everlasting salvation, but ye would not!" (D&C 43:24–25).

In the case of Alma the Younger and his royal colleagues, the word of the Lord comes through an angel of God who commands them to cease their evil ways and repent of their errors. It is on the basis of this angelic intervention, resulting from the sincere and fervent prayer of the fathers, that these young men are redirected into righteous channels and converted to the Church.

Alma the Younger suffers great pains of remorse and shame but is forgiven. The conversion of these young men to the Savior and His gospel is deep and complete. They have an overwhelming desire to redress the evils they have perpetrated and to preach the gospel—especially to the Lamanites. Alma and King Mosiah grant permission and receive the assurance of the Lord that these stalwart missionaries will be preserved through their faith.

15 And now behold, can ye dispute the power of God? For behold, doth not my voice shake the earth? And can ye not also behold me before you? And ***I am sent from God.***
16 Now I say unto thee: Go, and ***remember the captivity of thy fathers*** *in the land of Helam, and in the land of Nephi; and* ***remember how great things he has done for them;*** *for they were in bondage, and he has delivered them. And now I say unto thee, Alma, go thy way, and* ***seek to destroy the church no more,*** *that their prayers may be answered, and this even if thou wilt of thyself be cast off.*

I am sent from God; remember the captivity of thy fathers; remember how great things he has done for them; seek to destroy the church no more

The Lord answers the prayers of the people according to their faith. Therefore an angel is sent to convince Alma of the power and authority of God. We can have the blessings of God in our lives as we exercise our faith through prayer. Alma changes after this experience. Laman and Lemuel do not change after their angelic visitations. Agency is supreme—everyone can choose to obey or disobey. Let us realize that angels (messengers of God) can be in the form of mortals (see D&C 42:6) as well as from beyond the veil. President Thomas S. Monson has taught us that in our eternal roles and duties within the Church we can be inspired to be an answer to someone's prayer. He said, "As we love the Lord, as we love our neighbor, we discover that our Heavenly Father will answer the prayers of others through our ministry" (*Live the Good Life* [Salt Lake City: Deseret Book, 1988], 114).

17–23 Alma and his four colleagues collapse in shock over the heavenly manifestation. Alma is taken, mute and helpless, before his father, who rejoices that God has displayed His power in this manner. The father and his associates of the priesthood fast and pray for the younger Alma. After two days and nights the young man regains his strength and bids them be of good comfort.

24 For, said he, ***I have repented of my sins, and have been redeemed*** *of the Lord; behold I am born of the Spirit.*

Mosiah 27:25–27

> *25 And the Lord said unto me: Marvel not that all mankind, yea, men and women, all nations, kindreds, tongues and people, must be* ***born again;*** *yea, born of God, changed from their carnal and fallen state, to a state of righteousness, being redeemed of God, becoming his sons and daughters;*
> *26 And thus they become new creatures; and unless they do this, they can in nowise inherit the kingdom of God.*
> *27 I say unto you, unless this be the case, they must be cast off; and this I know, because* ***I was like to be cast off.***

I HAVE REPENTED OF MY SINS, AND HAVE BEEN REDEEMED; BORN AGAIN

Born of God or "born again" refers to the personal spiritual experience in which repentant individuals receive a forgiveness of sins and a witness from God that if they continue to live the commandments and endure to the end, they will inherit eternal life. The scriptures teach that just as each individual is "born into the world by water, and blood, and the spirit," so must one be "born again" of water and the Spirit and be cleansed by the blood of Christ (John 3:5; Moses 6:59). To be born of God implies a sanctifying process by which the old or natural man is supplanted by the new spiritual man who enjoys the companionship of the Holy Ghost and hence is no longer disposed to commit sin (see Colossians 3:9–10; Mosiah 3:19; *TPJS*, 51). When individuals are born again they are spiritually begotten sons and daughters of God and more specifically of Jesus Christ (see Mosiah 5:7; 27:25). The Book of Mormon prophet Alma calls this inner transformation a "mighty change in your hearts" (Alma 5:14). Enos relates that after "mighty prayer and supplication" the Lord declared that his sins had been forgiven (Enos 1:1–8). After King Benjamin's discourse, the people said that the Spirit had "wrought a mighty change in us, or in our hearts," and that they had "no more disposition to do evil, but to do good continually" (Mosiah 5:2).

Of his conversion experience, Alma the Younger says, "Nevertheless, after wading through much tribulation, repenting nigh unto death, the Lord in mercy hath seen fit to snatch me out of an everlasting burning, and I am born of God" (Mosiah 27:28). Persons who have experienced this mighty change manifest attitudinal and behavioral changes. Feeling their hearts riveted to the Lord, their obedience extends beyond performance of duty. President Harold B. Lee taught, "Conversion must mean more than just being a 'card-carrying' member of the Church with a tithing receipt, a membership card, a temple recommend, etc. It means to overcome the tendencies to criticize and to strive continually to improve inward weaknesses and not merely the outward appearances" ("The Iron Rod," *Ensign*, June 1971, 8). (Ed J. Pinegar, *Encyclopedia of Mormonism,* 1–4 vols. ed. Daniel H. Ludlow [New York: Macmillan, 1992], 218–219)

Memories: I was like to be cast off

All of us, from time to time, become subject to feelings of separation and disconnection from our roots and our home. In many respects, life is an experience in finding our way repeatedly back home to the familiar shores of our sustaining connections. This is particularly true when our detours and separations occur because of wayward behavior and sin. The Savior's parable of the prodigal son (Luke 15:11–32) recounts the anxiety that besets a family when a loved one chooses to depart from the strait pathways. The parable also celebrates the joy that attends a homecoming after unfortunate choices have led not only to separation but also to anguish. Alma's reprieve of the agony of his repentance is captured in this verse: "I say unto you, unless this be the case, they must be cast off; and this I know, because I was like to be cast off" (Mosiah 27:27).

This theme about the peril of being "cast off" occurs again and again in the Book of Mormon. In fact, the expression "cast off" occurs fourteen times in the narrative text and once in the title page. It is in this last instance that the recurring theme of being "cast off" is used in the context of the fourfold purpose of the Book of Mormon: "Which is to show unto the remnant of the House of Israel what great things the Lord hath done for their fathers; and that they may know the covenants of the Lord, that they are not cast off forever—And also to the convincing of the Jew and Gentile that Jesus is the Christ, the Eternal God, manifesting himself unto all nations."

It becomes clear that "not cast off" is the equivalent of having *hope* for spiritual deliverance and thus eventual everlasting reunion with the Lord and the hosts of heaven. With this understanding, we could restate the elements in the purpose of the Book of Mormon. In essence, Moroni entreats us to learn these four things: what great things the Lord has done for our forefathers, how the covenant promises apply to us personally today, and how we can have hope for the future (i.e., not be "cast off")—all because of the merits, mercy, and grace of the atoning Redeemer, even Jesus Christ.

It is inspiring to discover how these four interrelated elements recur throughout the Book of Mormon. Thus in Alma's experience of transforming change and repentance, the angel reminds him to "remember the captivity of thy fathers . . . and how great things he has done for them; for they were in bondage, and he has delivered them" (Mosiah 27:16). He is thus reminded of what his father, the elder Alma, had doubtless rehearsed to him many times before, having himself learned this truth from the Lord firsthand: "Thou art my servant; and I covenant with thee that thou shalt have eternal life; and thou shalt serve me and go forth in my name, and shalt gather together my sheep" (Mosiah 26:20). It is through the intervention of the angel and the agony of remorse that Alma the Younger discovers a buoyant spiritual hope. And, finally, he anchors all of his newly discovered truths on the sure foundation of his testimony of Jesus Christ because of what he experienced even while he was still being "racked with torment" and "harrowed up by the memory" of his many sins. He later recounted this event to his son Helaman: "Behold, I remembered also to have heard my father prophesy unto the people concerning the coming of one Jesus Christ, a son of God, to atone for the sins of the world. Now, as my mind caught hold upon this thought, I cried within my heart: O Jesus, thou son of God, have mercy on me, who am in the gall of bitterness, and am encircled about by the everlasting chains of death. And now, behold when I thought this, I could remember my pains no more" (Alma 36:17–19).

Having been launched into his ministry by this remarkable conversion, Alma thereafter spends all his days preaching of the Savior, reminding the people of the goodness of God to their fathers, guiding them to honor their covenants, and inspiring them with the hope of eternal life. (Richard J. Allen)

> *28 Nevertheless, after wading through much tribulation, repenting nigh unto death, the Lord in mercy hath seen fit to snatch me out of an everlasting burning, and I am* ***born of God.***
> *29 My soul hath been redeemed from the gall of bitterness and bonds of iniquity.* ***I was in the darkest abyss;*** *but now I behold the marvelous light of God. My soul was racked with eternal torment; but I am snatched, and my soul is pained no more.*

Born of God

All must repent and come unto Christ through the waters of baptism. When we keep the commandments, we become the children of Christ.

EVIDENCE: I was in the darkest abyss—Apocalyptic Imagery (Mosiah 27:29; 1 Nephi 14:3; 22:14)

If the Book of Mormon had been written by Joseph Smith, Hugh Nibley explains, it would have been full of imagery of the apocalyptic destruction, as this doctrine was popular in Joseph's day. But apocalyptic imagery is noticeably absent in the Book of Mormon. According to Nibley, "The fire and smoke of hell, and other apocalyptic images, are clearly stated to be types, rather than realities, as is the monster death and hell. This practice agrees with the old apocrypha." Alma's utterance, "I was in the darkest abyss; but now I behold the marvelous light of God" (Mosiah 27:29) is noticeably similar to Barnabas' declaration, "He has freed us from the darkness to prepare himself a holy people" (*Epistola Catholica*). Numerous Book of Mormon passages mirror those found in the apocrypha, which of course Joseph Smith had no access to as they were not discovered until long after his death. (See *Echoes,* 484).

30 I rejected my Redeemer, and denied that which had been spoken of by our fathers;
but now that they may foresee that he will come, and that he remembereth every creature
of his creating, he will make himself manifest unto all.
31 Yea, ***every knee shall bow, and every tongue confess before him.*** *Yea, even*
at the last day, when all men shall stand to be judged of him, then shall they confess
that he is God; then shall they confess, who live without God in the world, that the
judgment of an everlasting punishment is just upon them; and they shall quake, and
tremble, and shrink beneath the glance of his all-searching eye.
32 And now it came to pass that ***Alma began from this time forward to teach the***
people, *and those who were with Alma at the time the angel appeared unto them,*
traveling round about through all the land, publishing to all the people the things
which they had heard and seen, and preaching the word of God in much tribula-
tion, being greatly persecuted by those who were unbelievers, being smitten by many
of them.

Every knee shall bow, and every tongue confess before him; Alma began from this time forward to teach the people

By this may one know that conversion is complete: if the convert is spiritually moved by an overwhelming desire to share the good news with others, even as Alma and the sons of Mosiah are motivated to do missionary work. Enos has the same experience following his redemption (see Enos 1:9, 11). All who taste of the fruit of the tree of life desire that others should join them (see Lehi's dream as reported in 1 Nephi 8). The operation of the Holy Spirit imparts a singular devotion to the cause of service and missionary labor. That is one of the miracles of gospel living.

33 But notwithstanding all this, ***they did impart much consolation to the church,***
confirming their faith, and exhorting them with long-suffering and much travail to
keep the commandments of God.
34 And four of them were the sons of Mosiah; and their names were Ammon, and
Aaron, and Omner, and Himni; these were the names of the sons of Mosiah.
35 And they traveled throughout all the land of Zarahemla, and among all the people
who were under the reign of king Mosiah, ***zealously striving to repair all the injuries***
which they had done to the church, confessing all their sins, and ***publishing all the***
things which they had seen, *and* ***explaining the prophecies and the scriptures*** *to*
all who desired to hear them.

*36 And thus they were **instruments in the hands of God** in bringing many to the knowledge of the truth, yea, to the knowledge of their Redeemer.*
*37 And how blessed are they! For **they did publish peace;** they did publish good tidings of good; and they did declare unto the people that **the Lord reigneth.***

THEY DID IMPART MUCH CONSOLATION TO THE CHURCH ZEALOUSLY STRIVING TO REPAIR ALL THE INJURIES; PUBLISHING ALL THE THINGS WHICH THEY HAD SEEN, EXPLAINING THE PROPHECIES AND THE SCRIPTURES; INSTRUMENTS IN THE HANDS OF GOD; THEY DID PUBLISH PEACE; THE LORD REIGNETH

Repentance yields a harvest of charitable service. Charity is a natural outgrowth of repentance. Why? Because when the burden of sin is removed, the Spirit of the Lord cultivates in its place a love for all and the desire to bless others (see Romans 5:5). Alma and the sons of Mosiah are overcome with the desire to bless lives. Their example gives us hope that we, too, can displace iniquity within our beings and be transformed into "instruments in the hands of God" (verse 36) to lift others and invite them to come unto Christ with a firm knowledge "that the Lord reigneth" (verse 37).

CHAPTER 28

OVERVIEW

The sons of Mosiah have a fervent desire to go among the Lamanites to preach the gospel. Mosiah inquires of the Lord and receives the assurance that they will be protected and have great success. Mosiah translates the plates of gold discovered by the people of Limhi concerning the origin and destruction of the Jaredites. Mosiah turns the sacred records over to Alma the Younger.

*1 NOW it came to pass that after the sons of Mosiah had done all these things, they took a small number with them and returned to their father, the king, and desired of him that he would grant unto them **that they might,** with these whom they had selected, **go up to the land of Nephi** that they might preach the things which they had heard, **and that they might impart the word of God to their brethren, the Lamanites—***
2 That perhaps they might bring them to the knowledge of the Lord their God, and convince them of the iniquity of their fathers; and that perhaps they might cure them of their hatred toward the Nephites, that they might also be brought to rejoice in the Lord

their God, that they might become friendly to one another, and that there should be no more contentions in all the land which the Lord their God had given them.
3 Now they were desirous that salvation should be declared to every creature, ***for they could not bear that any human soul should perish;*** *yea, even the very thoughts that any soul should endure endless torment did cause them to quake and tremble.*

That they might go up to the land of Nephi; and that they might impart the word of God to their brethren, the Lamanites—for they could not bear that any human soul should perish

The words of the sons of Mosiah concerning their deep concern to save souls is a classic missionary scripture. Like their colleague Alma, the sons of Mosiah, following their conversion, have a great desire to share the gospel with all people—especially the Lamanites. As a result, they dedicate their lives to preaching the gospel, and continue, even today, by their example, to radiate an influence for good in the ongoing process of building up the kingdom of God. President Ezra Taft Benson shares the following words concerning a member's responsibility to share the gospel:

> Early in this dispensation the Savior placed on the Church the responsibility to share the gospel. On November 1, 1831, He said: "The voice of warning shall be unto all people, by the mouths of my disciples, whom I have chosen in these last days. And they shall go forth and none shall stay them, for I the Lord have commanded them." (Doctrine and Covenants 1:4–5.)
>
> Again, on December 27, 1832, He commanded: "Behold, I sent you out to testify and warn the people, and it becometh every man who hath been warned to warn his neighbor. Therefore, they are left without excuse, and their sins are upon their own heads." (Doctrine and Covenants 88:81–82.)
>
> When the Saints came West, President Brigham Young declared: "We wish the brethren to understand the facts just as they are; that is, there is neither man or woman in this Church who is not on a mission. That mission will last as long as they live, and it is to do good, to promote righteousness, to teach the principles of truth, and to prevail upon themselves and everybody around them to live those principles that they may obtain eternal life. This is the mission of every Latter-day Saint" (*Journal of Discourses* 12:19). (*Come unto Christ* [Salt Lake City: Deseret Book, 1983], 89)

Mosiah 28:3

In our day President David O. McKay pronounced a mandate that has become our watchword concerning missionary work:

> Every member is a missionary. He or she has the responsibility of bringing somebody: a mother, a father, a neighbor, a fellow worker, an associate, somebody in touch with the messengers of the gospel. If every member will carry that responsibility, and if the arrangement to have that mother, or that father, or somebody meet the authorized representatives of the Church, no power on earth can stop this Church from growing. And personal contact is what will influence those investigators. That personal contact, the nature of it, its effect depends upon you. And that's one thing which I wish to emphasize. There's one responsibility which no man can evade, and that's the responsibility of personal influence. What you are thunders so loud in my ears, I cannot hear what you say. And what you are is the result of a silent, subtle radiation of your personality. The effect of your words and acts is tremendous in this world. Every moment of life you are changing, to a degree, the life of the whole world. (Address to the North British Mission, 1961).

More recently, we received this counsel from President Spencer W. Kimball:

> We are still just scratching the surface of the needs of our Father's other children who dwell upon the earth. Many still hunger and thirst after truth and are kept from it only "because they know not where to find it." (Doctrine and Covenants 123:12.) There are still more places to go than there are full-time missionaries and organized missions to serve them. There are still millions more being born, living, and dying, than are hearing testimonies borne to them by the servants of the Lord.
>
> All of this means, quite frankly, brethren, that we cannot share the gospel with every nation, kindred, tongue, and people with [our present number of] missionaries (as wonderful as they are), but we must have several million more to help them. We must, therefore, involve the members of the Church more effectively in missionary work. Member-missionary work is the key to the future growth of the Church, and it is one of the great keys to the individual growth of our members.
>
> Leaders and members alike need in their lives the special renewal and enthusiasm which comes from regular personal involvement in missionary work.

> If personal missionary work is something someone has always been *meaning* to do, but has never gotten around to, then something very important and rewarding is missing in that person's life.
>
> Good neighbors are best suited to bringing to others the good news of the gospel, just as righteous members, living the gospel by example, as well as by precept, are the Church's best advertisement. (Regional Representatives Seminar, October 3, 1980; italics added).

These statements summarize the responsibility the Lord has laid upon us to share the gospel with all of our Father's children. We cannot avoid it. Let no man or woman think that because of where we live or because of our place in society or because of our occupation or status, we are exempt from this responsibility.

> Membership in the Lord's church is a gift and a blessing that the Lord has given us in mortality, and He expects us to share that blessing with those who do not have it.
>
> We need to live the gospel. When we live the gospel, there is a spirit that emanates from us, and good people will be attracted by that spirit. Though nothing may be said about the Church, there will be an affinity between those who have the truth and those who love truth. That is the principle of attraction to which President McKay was referring. I know it is true. (Ezra Taft Benson, *Come unto Christ* [Salt Lake City: Deseret Book, 1983], 89–91)

For they could not bear that any human soul should perish

The sons of Mosiah are truly converted to the Lord. They are filled with charity. They cannot bear that any human soul should perish and endure endless torment. This thought causes them to quake and tremble. When we are truly converted, we feel like the sons of Mosiah. We have an overwhelming concern for the welfare of others. We seek to serve and bless lives (see Mosiah 18:8–9; D&C 108:7; Matthew 25:40).

Sharing the Gospel Is for Everyone

> I had an experience some time ago in Idaho when I attended a stake conference there. The stake president mentioned he had a surprise for me and asked, "Will

you trust me?" I responded, "Well, we trust all of our stake presidents; I trust you if you are right." He said, "Well, I think you will enjoy what is going to happen tomorrow in the general session of the conference."

Here is what happened. In the Sunday morning session, he called upon a little girl who was about ten years of age to come up to the pulpit and bear her testimony about being a "Primary missionary." What had happened was that the stake president had authorized the high council adviser to the Primary to implement an idea that children can also be missionaries. This high councilor went to the ward Primaries to teach the little children that they were missionaries too. This sweet little girl, whom we shall call Katie, learned from the high councilor that she could be a missionary. She came home to her father, who was the bishop of one of the wards, and said, "Daddy, I'm a Primary missionary, and I want to share the gospel with somebody." The bishop said, "Well, sweetheart, that's a wonderful thing, but we have only one or two non-member families in our whole ward, so it might be a little difficult." But this little girl asked, "Who are they?" The bishop named the nonmember families, and his daughter promptly responded, "Let's you and me go visit them, and we'll invite them to come to our home for family home evening." Those of you who are fathers of little girls know how easily you succumb when a sweet daughter looks at you imploringly out of innocent, trusting eyes. And that's what happened to the bishop. So he and Katie went and knocked on the door of one nonmember family. When the mother of the family answered the door, little Katie said, "I am a Primary missionary, and we want you to come to our house for family home evening." This wonderful mother, I guess, had the same problem with those big, innocent eyes, and she agreed to bring her family to home evening. They came; they had a nice evening; they were not converted.

About two weeks later, Katie came home just as her mother was taking some banana bread out of the oven. Katie asked, "Can I have a loaf of that bread?" Her mother said, "Yes sweetheart, but what do you want it for?"

"I want to take it to Mrs. Johnson," she replied.

When Mrs. Johnson came to the door, Katie said, "I have something for you that I would like to give you, but I can only give it to you on one condition." When Mrs. Johnson asked what the condition was, Katie responded, "That you let the missionaries teach you the gospel." Mrs. Johnson smiled and said, "If that's the only condition for us to have the banana bread, then I'll agree that we will let the missionaries teach us the gospel."

The missionaries taught the gospel to the Johnsons, and they were baptized.

After Katie finished her testimony at the conference, Sister Johnson was the next to speak. I shall never forget what I felt when she thanked a little ten-year-old Primary missionary who had had the courage to invite her family to learn about the gospel.

When it was my turn to speak, I invited the bishop and his family, including Katie, to come up and stand by me, and then I invited the Johnson family to come up—mother, father, and three children. I said to them, "You have had a wonderful experience together. Bishop, you and Katie have shared with your neighbor the most precious thing in life, the gospel of Jesus Christ. But I want to tell you that if you think your heart is filled with joy today, wait till that day one year from now when the Johnson family kneels at the altar in the Idaho Falls Temple to be sealed for time and all eternity. That will be a moment in mortality that you will never, ever forget."

One year later, I performed their sealing. When I walked into the temple, there in the waiting room was Katie, now age eleven, the Primary missionary. She was not able to go to the sealing room because she wasn't old enough, but she was there waiting for her convert family to be sealed. The sealing room was filled with members of the ward. When the three Johnson children knelt around that altar and I sealed them to their parents, it was a bit of heaven on earth—all made possible because a little girl took seriously an assignment from an inspired and motivated high councilor who had the idea that children could be missionaries too and who taught little Katie that she could share the gospel with others. (M. Russell Ballard, *Counseling with Our Councils: Learning to Minister Together in the Church and in the Family* [Salt Lake City: Deseret Book, 1997], 86–88)

4–6 The sons of Mosiah suffer much anguish of soul because of their previous iniquities, but the Spirit of the Lord continues to work through them and they persist in their petition before their father, the king, to go among the Lamanites as missionaries. Mosiah inquires of the Lord and receives an answer.

7 And the Lord said unto Mosiah: ***Let them go up,*** *for* ***many shall believe*** *on their*
words, and they shall have eternal life; and ***I will deliver thy sons out of the hands***
of the Lamanites.
8 And it came to pass that Mosiah granted that they might go and do according to
their request.
9 And they took their journey into the wilderness to go up to preach the word among
the Lamanites; and I shall give an account of their proceedings hereafter.

Let them go up; many shall believe; I will deliver thy sons out of the hands of the Lamanites

As with all missionary callings, this one is sanctioned by the Lord. He promises Mosiah that his sons will be preserved and have much success in their endeavors. We are privileged to have the actual wording of this missionary call preserved for our edification and instruction.

10–20 Using the Urim and Thummim, Mosiah translates the plates of gold found by Limhi's search party. It is the record of the Jaredite people from the time of the great tower and the confounding of the language down to the time of their destruction because of wickedness (see the book of Ether). Thereafter, Mosiah appoints Alma the Younger to be the curator of the sacred things and keeper of the sacred records.

CONCLUDING THOUGHTS

Fervent convictions can be cultivated as we study these stirring Book of Mormon stories about building up the kingdom of God. Through the inspired teachings of Mosiah and Alma the Elder, many were brought into the fold. The power of the word and the Spirit was manifested in their preaching. The conversion of young Alma and the sons of Mosiah gives hope to all and verifies the principle of repentance, for they experienced a "mighty change."

CHAPTER 29

OVERVIEW

The aging Mosiah inquires of the people who they desire to be his successor. They choose Aaron, his son. However, neither Aaron nor any of the king's other sons are willing to serve as king; they having departed on their missions to the Lamanites. Therefore, Mosiah sends an epistle among the people calling for a system of governance based on elected judges. He renounces the preservation of the monarchy because of the dangers of wicked kings such as Noah. He counsels: "Do your business by the voice of the people" (verse 26), because the voice of the people commonly chooses that which is righteous and good. The people accept Mosiah's wisdom and elect judges. Alma the Younger is chosen as the first chief judge. He acts according to principles of righteousness. Both Alma the Elder and Mosiah pass away.

1–15 When none of Mosiah's sons want to succeed their father as king, Mosiah institutes a system of government by the people. If just men such as King Benjamin could serve as kings, it would be expedient to have kings—but such is not always the case.

> *16 Now I say unto you, that because **all men are not just** it is not expedient that ye should have a king or kings to rule over you.*
> *17 For behold, **how much iniquity doth one wicked king cause** to be committed, yea, and what great destruction!*

EVIDENCE: ALL MEN ARE NOT JUST; HOW MUCH INIQUITY DOTH ONE WICKED KING CAUSE—DISTINCTIVE POLITICS (Mosiah 29:17)

In most cases, Book of Mormon politics are vastly different from the American politics of Joseph Smith's day. Joseph would have been exposed to the idea that the American Revolution involved "heroic resistance," with the colonists fighting for freedom from monarchial tyranny. But the Book of Mormon account of the Revolution speaks more of divine intervention than of bravery in battle. In fact, as Noel B. Reynolds points out, "Book of Mormon peoples never overthrow an established government, no matter how tyrannical." Nephite peoples frequently desire to live under a monarchy, whereas their leaders—even some of the kings themselves—warn of the precarious situation the people face when an evil king takes the throne. This is a significant difference from widespread American ideas at the time that Joseph translated the Book of Mormon, when the people viewed monarchs as oppressive. (See *Echoes,* 146–148.)

18–24 Mosiah reminds the people of the abominations of King Noah and his people. It was only through the "interposition of their all-wise Creator" (verse 19) that the people were able to escape bondage. It takes much bloodshed and contention to dethrone a wicked king, because he is surrounded by his iniquitous friends and guards and "enacteth laws, and sendeth them forth among his people, yea, laws after the manner of his own wickedness" (verse 23) and destroys all who rebel against him.

25 Therefore, ***choose you by the voice of this people,*** *judges, that ye may be judged*
according to the laws which have been given you by our fathers, which are correct, and
which were given them by the hand of the Lord.
26 Now ***it is not common that the voice of the people desireth anything contrary to that which is right;*** *but it is common for the lesser part of the people to desire*
that which is not right; therefore this shall ye observe and make it your law—to ***do your business by the voice of the people.***

Choose you by the voice of this people; it is not common that the voice of the people desireth anything contrary to that which is right; do your business by the voice of the people

What government structure is the best? - one based on eternal principles.

This passage of scripture resonates well with the modern-day reader who lives in an age when democratic principles upholding the inalienable rights of the people are constantly under barrage from those who would subvert agency and the right to choose. Righteous government is based on eternal principles (compare D&C 134). There is wisdom in elevating wise and righteous people to positions of leadership according to the voice of the people, for the majority of the people commonly desires that which is right; therefore, it is prudent "to do your business by the voice of the people" (Mosiah 29:26).

27 And if the time comes that the voice of the people doth choose iniquity, then is the
time that ***the judgments of God will come upon you;*** *yea, then is the time he will*
visit you with great destruction even as he has hitherto visited this land.

The judgments of God will come upon you

One sign of the times is the perilous moment when the voice of the people chooses iniquity. The Book of Mormon includes multiple cases where that turns out to be the case—resulting in the destruction of entire nations. On a massive scale, the fates of the Jaredites and the Nephites are the most compelling cases in point. As members of any society, we are duty bound to become involved in the process of encouraging and enacting laws and government policies that will be for the good of all and that will sustain the momentum of the majority electing righteous patterns of behavior and governance.

28–31 Mosiah sets forth a system of checks and balances for ensuring justice and equality: judges who fail to judge according to the law can be referred to a higher judge; higher judges who judge unrighteously can be adjudicated by panels of lower judges; do things "in the fear of the Lord" (verse 30).

> 32 *And now I desire that this inequality should be no more in this land, especially among this my people; but I desire that this land be* ***a land of liberty,*** *and every man may enjoy his* ***rights and privileges*** *alike, so long as the Lord sees fit that we may live and inherit the land, yea, even as long as any of our posterity remains upon the face of the land.*

A land of liberty; rights and privileges

These words echo with a familiar sound in the post-Constitutional era. "Therefore, it is not right that any man should be in bondage one to another. And for this purpose have I established the Constitution of this land, by the hands of wise men whom I raised up unto this very purpose, and redeemed the land by the shedding of blood" (D&C 101:79–80). The Restoration of the gospel in our day was made possible because the Lord established a framework in which agency played a central role and equality enabled the promulgation of eternal principles. Brigham Young said, "I am for the kingdom of God. I like a good government, and then I like to have it wisely and justly administered. The government of heaven, if wickedly administered, would become one of the worst governments upon the face of the earth. No matter how good a government is, unless it is administered by righteous men, an evil government will be made of it" (*Discourses of Brigham Young,* comp. John A. Widtsoe [Salt Lake City: Deseret Book, 1954], 147).

Joseph Fielding Smith makes the case for learning from the past. He stated: "As were the ancient inhabitants, so we are under commandment to make our government conform to the righteous principles of the government of God" (*The Progress of Man* [Salt Lake City: Deseret Book, 1964], 261).

President Smith also cites the testimony of Calvin Coolidge that good government has spiritual principles at its core:

> I have here something that is just as good as scripture, written by President Calvin Coolidge; I am going to read it to you: "Our government rests upon religion. It is from that source that we derive our reverence for truth and justice, for equality and liberality, and for the rights of mankind. Unless the people believe in these principles they cannot believe in our government. There are only two main theories of government in the world. One rests on righteousness and the other on force. One

appeals to reason, and the other appeals to the sword. One is exemplified in the republic, the other is represented by a despotism.

"The government of a country never gets ahead of the religion of a country. There is no way by which we can substitute the authority of law for the virtue of man. Of course we endeavor to restrain the vicious, and furnish a fair degree of security and protection by legislation and police control, but the real reform which society in these days is seeking will come as a result of our religious convictions, or they will not come at all. Peace, justice, humanity, charity—these cannot be legislated into being. They are the result of divine grace."

Well, words like that, I believe, are spoken by inspiration. This is a warning to the people of this nation, coming from a former president of the United States. It is in full harmony with the word of the Lord in the Book of Ether in the Book of Mormon, in regard to this land. We cannot get away from the God of this land, without dire consequences following. (*Doctrines of Salvation,* 3 vols., ed. Bruce R. McConkie [Salt Lake City: Bookcraft, 1954–1956], 3:317)

33–39 Mosiah continues to offer evidence of the dangers of having a wicked king at the helm. He convinces the people of this fact. Therefore, rejoicing in their liberty, they cast their voices to elect righteous judges.

40 And they did wax strong in love toward Mosiah; yea, they did esteem him more than any other man; for they did not look upon him as a tyrant who was seeking for gain, yea, for that lucre which doth corrupt the soul; for he had not exacted riches of them, neither had he delighted in the shedding of blood; but he had established peace in the land, and he had granted unto his people that they should be delivered from all manner of bondage; therefore they did esteem him, yea, exceedingly, beyond measure.

41–47 Alma is appointed to be the first chief judge in the land. He also serves as high priest, having been appointed to that office by his father. Alma judges righteously. He preserves peace in the land. Thus the reign of the judges commences in approximately 91 B.C. During this time frame, Alma's father passes away at age eighty-two. Mosiah also passes away, but at the younger age of sixty-three, having reigned thirty-three years. The time frame at the end of the era of Nephite kings is therefore 509 years since the departure of Lehi from Jerusalem. Thus ends the Book of Mosiah.

THE BOOK OF
ALMA
THE SON OF ALMA

The account of Alma, who was the son of Alma, the first and chief judge over the people of Nephi, and also the high priest over the Church. An account of the reign of the judges, and the wars and contentions among the people. And also an account of a war between the Nephites and the Lamanites, according to the record of Alma, the first and chief judge. [Note: This preamble, which has been slightly modified in the intervening years, was included in the original edition of the Book of Mormon published in 1830.]

CHAPTER 1

OVERVIEW

Alma commences his tenure around 91 B.C. as the first chief judge in the land and high priest of the Church. Nehor introduces priestcraft and establishes a church of his own, drawing many away from the gospel. An aging Gideon rises to counter these false practices, but Nehor slays him. Alma sentences Nehor to death. Nehor recants but is executed. The people of the Lord experience much persecution. Those who endure in patience prosper greatly. They maintain a lay priesthood and practice equality in caring for the poor and needy. Those outside the Church continue their prideful and wicked practices but are restrained by the law. There is peace in the land.

1 NOW it came to pass that in the first year of the reign of the judges over the people of Nephi, from this time forward, King Mosiah having gone the way of all the earth, having warred a good warfare, walking uprightly before God, leaving none to reign in his stead; nevertheless he had established laws, and they were acknowledged by the people; therefore they were obliged to abide by the laws which he had made.
2 And it came to pass that in the first year of the reign of ***Alma*** *in the* ***judgment-seat,*** *there was* ***a man brought before him to be judged,*** *a man who was large, and was noted for his much strength.*

Alma the Younger, Tireless Champion of Faith

Alma was the son of Alma the Elder, who had been at the court of wicked King Noah when the prophet Abinadi preached his ultimate sermon there on repentance before being burned at the stake. The elder Alma fled with his righteous followers via the Waters of Mormon and eventually reached Zarahemla. Like the sons of King Mosiah, young Alma is initially "numbered among the unbelievers" (Mosiah 27:8) and "the very vilest of sinners" (Mosiah 28:4). But the Lord has an important calling for him and his young colleagues. When a heavenly messenger intervenes and brings about their spiritual transformation (sometime between 100 B.C. and 92 B.C.—see Mosiah 27:11–18), they redirect their lives toward service and honor. Young Alma is appointed chief judge of the land (around 91 B.C.) and commences his service by overcoming the forces of incipient priestcraft in the land. Then, as we shall see, he defeats the conspirator Amlici, who has designed the overthrow of the government. A few years later, Alma is consecrated high priest of the Church by his father (see Alma 4:4; 5:3) and subsequently delegates his judgment office to another, that he "might go forth among his people, or among the people of Nephi, that he might preach the word of God unto them, to stir them up in remembrance of their duty, and that he might pull down, by the word of God, all the pride and craftiness and all the contentions which were among his people" (Alma 4:19).

Alma reforms the Church in Zarahemla and then travels to other cities in the region, preaching the gospel of Jesus Christ and bringing order and harmony into the fold. In the city of Ammonihah around 82 B.C., however, Alma is rejected outright and forced to abandon his mission. An angel of the Lord intervenes and commands him to return to the city. He returns "speedily" (Alma 8:18) and is met by Amulek, whom the angel had commissioned to receive and house the traveling prophet. Alma delivers his timeless speech on faith (Alma 32). From that point he and Amulek continue to preach repentance and the Atonement to the hard-hearted citizens and warn them of the impending destruction of the city, but they are again rejected by the local leadership (including the lawyer Zeezrom). Alma and Amulek are cast into prison to suffer for days until they are liberated through the power of God. Zeezrom is converted and returns with them to Zarahemla.

Alma's ministry thereafter consists of a long sequence of valiant achievements, including making arrangements for the safety and settlement of the righteous Lamanites (the people of Anti-Nephi-Lehi, or the people of Ammon, who were converted by the sons of Mosiah), confounding of the sign-seeking anti-Christ Korihor, preaching in the regions round about, and providing remarkable counsel and blessings for his sons, Helaman, Shiblon, and Corianton around 73 B.C. Shortly thereafter, Alma sets off for the land Melek but is never heard of again, presumably being translated after the manner of Moses (see Alma 45:18–19).

EVIDENCE: JUDGMENT SEAT

In the time of king Zedekiah of Judah, the council of elders—a centuries-old institution—was overthrown. Proud and aspiring men assumed the powerful judgment seats, then systematically abused their power, oppressed the nation of Israel, and suppressed criticism of their own unrighteous actions. The idea of ruling judges was not new, according to Hugh Nibley, who explains that in 1085 B.C., one called Korihor, Ammon's chief priest, had seized the Egyptian throne, and the priests of Ammon ran the country as judges. Lehi and his descendants would have been familiar with the concepts of judges and judgment seats, so the smooth transition from kings to judges in the Book of Mormon is perfectly comprehendible. (See *Echoes,* 467–468.)

A MAN BROUGHT BEFORE HIM TO BE JUDGED

The reference is to Nehor, a rebel preacher, first named in Alma 1:15. This man, large of stature and "noted for his much strength" (Alma 1:2), is brought before Alma during his first year as chief judge around 91 B.C. Nehor's agenda among the people is to persuade them that the ministry should be supported out of the public coffers. His philosophy is designed to appeal to the masses: "And he also testified unto the people that all mankind should be saved at the last day, and that they need not fear nor tremble, but that they might lift up their heads and rejoice; for the Lord had created all men, and had also redeemed all men; and, in the end, all men should have eternal life" (Alma 1:4).

Intoxicated with success and inflated in his pride, Nehor begins to build up a church of his own consisting of the followers he is able to lure away from the people of God. In this he is met with resistance from the faithful, including the aging Gideon who has been instrumental in assisting the colony of Limhi to escape Lamanite bondage and return to Zarahemla (see Mosiah 22:3–9).

His devious philosophy, however, is not even expunged from the undercurrent of society with his death, "for there were many who loved the vain things of the world, and they went forth preaching false doctrines; and this they did for the sake of riches and honor" (Alma 1:16). Not many years later, Amlici, another disciple of Nehor, arises to cause difficulty among the people. Alma contends with Amlici "face to face" (Alma 2:29), putting down the insurrection he has caused. Thereafter the Nehoristic philosophy rears its ugly head from time to time among the people in the form of factions desirous to undermine liberty and righteousness (see Alma 14:16–18; 15:15; 16:11; 21:4; 24:28–29). Nehor is one example among many in the Book of Mormon concerning "the great wickedness one very wicked man can cause to take place among the children of men" (Alma 46:9).

3–6 Nehor advances his agenda of deception, calling for a paid ministry, claiming that all mankind will be redeemed and have eternal life, and promoting a church featuring costly trappings.

George Q. Cannon points out the contrast between the authority of the priesthood of God and the soulless, counterfeit initiatives of Satan:

> The full recognition of God's authority as bestowed by Him and man's equality with his fellow man constitute the vitality of the kingdom of God. But Satan prompts man to establish creeds of man worship, in which priestcraft, as opposed to priesthood, prevails. He appeals to the avarice and ambition of men and divides society into classes, making worldly learning, the possession of wealth, and the "accident of birth," the distinctions which command respect and honor" (*The Life of Joseph Smith, the Prophet* [Salt Lake City: Deseret Book, 1986], 80).

Nehor serves as a good example of someone laboring under the banner of "irreligion," as Elder Neal A. Maxwell aptly expressed it:

> Even in the seemingly miscellaneous gospel gems there is plainness and preciousness. If, for instance, we assume there is only ancient relevance concerning the practice and purposes of priestcraft, we need to be braced by how germane that definition is for our time. "He commandeth that there shall be no priestcrafts; for, behold, priestcrafts are that men preach and set themselves up for a light unto the world, that they may get gain and praise of the world; but they seek not the welfare of Zion." (2 Nephi 26:29.) Do we not see such people working today (minus the label, of course) among the children of men? Alas, such match the criteria set forth not only as some lead out in the realm of religion but in the realm of irreligion. (*Plain and Precious Things* [Salt Lake City: Deseret Book, 1983], 86–87)

7 And it came to pass as he was going, to preach to those who believed on his word, he met a man who belonged to the church of God, yea, even one of their teachers; and he began to contend with him sharply, that he might lead away the people of the church; but the man withstood him, ***admonishing him with the words of God.***

Admonishing him with the words of God

The man who stands up to Nehor is none other than Gideon, the same strong, righteous defender of truth who rose up in opposition to the abuses of wicked King Noah around 145 B.C. and subsequently devised a successful plan to liberate the people of Limhi from Lamanite bondage. Now he again rises in courage to defy the assaults of Nehor. In this capacity, Gideon gives his life in defending the truth, for he is unable—"being stricken with many years" (Alma 1:9)—to withstand the blows inflicted upon him by Nehor.

8–15 Nehor slays Gideon. He is then taken in his pride and haughtiness before Alma to be judged. Alma condemns him for his priestcraft—"this is the first time that priestcraft has been introduced among this people . . . and were priestcraft to be enforced among this people it would prove their entire destruction" (verse 12)—and sentences him to death for shedding the blood of Gideon—"a righteous man, yea, a man who has done much good among this people" (verse 13). Nehor subsequently acknowledges "between the heavens and the earth, that what he had taught to the people was contrary to the word of God" (verse 15) and is then executed at the top of a hill called Manti.

EVIDENCE: Death of Nehor (Alma 1:11–15)

A forceful and articulate man, Nehor preached false doctrine and introduced priestcraft among the Nephites, even establishing his own church. When he attempted to enforce his priestcraft with the sword, Nehor received the penalty of death. His execution, as well as that of the later traitor, Zemnarihah (see 3 Nephi 4:28–33), hearkens back to an ancient practice. According to Hugh Nibley, tradition holds that fallen angels named Harut and Marut "first corrupted the word of God and as a result hang to this day between heaven and earth confessing their sin. Their counterpart in Jewish tradition is the angel Shamhozai, who 'repented, and by way of penance hung himself up between heaven and earth'" (*Echoes,* 476).

16–19 Despite the death of Nehor, undercurrents of priestcraft continue to fester across the land. Sympathizers who subscribe to such false movements remain in the shadows out of fear of the law but still "**persecute those that did belong to the church** of God, and [have] taken upon them the name of Christ" (verse 19). The seeds of priestcraft are sown, and Amlici, a Nehorian disciple, soon launches a revolution to challenge not only the Church but the very institutions of civil liberty established by Mosiah.

Persecute those that did belong to the church

It is the duty of the servants of God to be vigilant against any incursion by interlopers with an agenda to undermine spiritual institutions by offering their own false imitation of the gospel for commercial gain and power. "Beware of false prophets, which come to you in sheep's clothing, but inwardly they are ravening wolves," is how the Savior expresses it (Matthew 7:15). We should be willing, despite the threat of force or the pain of persecution, to rise up in defense of the Church and kingdom of God—just as Gideon and Alma.

Priestcraft

Definition:

> Priestcraft is the sin committed by the combination of a good act—such as preaching or teaching the gospel—and a bad motive. The act may be good and visible, but the sin is in the motive. On earth, the wrong motive may be known only to the actor, but in heaven it is always known to God. . . . The sin of priestcraft is a grievous one. Time after time the Lord has condemned those who appear to men to be his servants, but who, though they draw near to him with their lips, have removed their hearts far from him. This description of those who have no true motive to serve the Lord appears in Isaiah (29:13), in Matthew (15:8), in 2 Nephi (27:25), and in Joseph Smith's History (JS—H 1:19). In modern as in ancient times, those who appear to be servants of the Lord and present themselves to labor in his vineyard are subject to the prophetic principle: "The laborer in Zion shall labor for Zion; for if they labor for money they shall perish" (2 Nephi 26:31).
>
> The prototype of those who appear to serve God but actually have other motives is King Amaziah, who "did that which was right in the sight of the Lord, but not with a perfect heart" (2 Chronicles 25:2).
>
> During my lifetime, I have seen more than a few persons in positions of responsibility in various churches whose activities in the "work of the Lord" seemed to be motivated predominantly by personal interest. The commandment to avoid priestcraft is a vital challenge to religious persons in every age of time. (Dallin H. Oaks, *Pure in Heart* [Salt Lake City: Bookcraft, 1988], 16–17)

Purity of Motivation Is Essential

> The Book of Mormon says, "Priestcrafts are that men preach and set themselves up for a light unto the world, that they may get gain and praise of the world; but they seek not the Welfare of Zion. . . . But the laborer in Zion shall labor for Zion;

for if they labor for money they shall perish" (2 Nephi 26:29, 31). Inherent in this definition is the concern that Church leaders must labor to build Zion into the hearts of the people, and not for their personal aggrandizement or reward. When leaders "make merchandise" of men's souls (2 Peter 2:3), they turn religion into a business, and pride, materialism, and unrighteous dominion follow.

Both in scripture and in literature priestcraft is condemned. Peter cursed Simon the sorcerer, who wanted to purchase the priesthood for money (Acts 8:14–24). Dante's Peter castigates several popes and priests for not serving freely and for making a sewer of the sepulchre of Peter by selling priesthood appointment (*Paradiso* 27:22–57). Chaucer observed that greed for personal gain and glory often replaced genuine priesthood service ("General Prologue" and "Introduction to the Pardoner's Tale," *Canterbury Tales*). Milton's lines from *Lycidas* condemning a clergy who "for their bellies' sake, / Creep and intrude, and climb into the fold" (ll. 114–15) sum up the evil of priestcraft: "The hungry sheep look up, and are not fed, / But swoln with wind and the rank mist they draw, / Rot inwardly, and foul contagion spread" (ll. 125–27). (Charles D. Tate Jr., *Encyclopedia of Mormonism,* 1–4 vols., ed. Daniel H. Ludlow [New York: Macmillan, 1992], 1133)

20–25 Persecution against the Church continues. Despite the law forbidding persecution in any sector of society, some members of the Church pridefully begin to counter their tormentors with force, persecuting those who do not belong to the Church. This action results in the excommunication of many, much to the sadness of those who are standing fast in the faith with diligence and patience.

26 And when the priests left their labor to impart the word of God unto the people, the people also left their labors to hear the word of God. And when the priest had imparted unto them the word of God they all returned again diligently unto their labors; and the priest, not esteeming himself above his hearers, for the preacher was no better than the hearer, neither was the teacher any better than the learner; and thus ***they were all equal,*** *and they did all labor, every man according to his strength.*

They were all equal

All are considered important in the community of the Lord. Each person is responsible for seeking the Spirit in the learning process, where both teacher and learner are edified in the experience—

one is not above the other. We grow together. Each labors faithfully according to his or her role. Teachers are to speak by the Spirit, while learners are to use their ears, minds, and hearts in humility, being "easy to be entreated" (Alma 7:23), so that they might understand and feel the Spirit and thereby know that what is being said is true. Thus both are edified, for it is done in the Spirit of truth (see D&C 50:17–22).

> *27 And they did impart of their substance, every man according to that which he had, to the poor, and the needy, and the sick, and the afflicted; and* ***they did not wear costly apparel, yet they were neat and comely.***
> *28 And thus they did establish the affairs of the church; and thus they began to have continual peace again, notwithstanding all their persecutions.*

They did not wear costly apparel, yet they were neat and comely

Do we maintain a good balance in our lives—being "neat and comely" without going to prideful excess in our appearance? The word *comely* comes from an Old English word meaning lovely or delicate—hence the modern implication is to be wholesomely pleasing and attractive in appearance. The word comely is used in the scriptures to describe that which is suitable and appropriate, for example, "In that day shall the branch of the LORD be beautiful and glorious, and the fruit of the earth shall be excellent and comely for them that are escaped of Israel" (Isaiah 4:2). "I have likened the daughter of Zion to a comely and delicate woman" (Jeremiah 6:2).

29–32 The people of the Lord prosper over the next few years, but they remember to be charitable to the poor and needy without discrimination, being "liberal to all, both old and young, both bond and free, both male and female, whether out of the church or in the church, having no respect to persons as to those who stood in need" (verse 30). Those outside the Church continue to cultivate worldly and unrighteous pursuits, though the law holds them in check and forces them to conceal their activities.

> *33 And it came to pass that by thus exercising the law upon them, every man suffering according to that which he had done, they became more still, and* ***durst not commit any wickedness*** *if it were known; therefore,* ***there was much peace*** *among the people of Nephi until the fifth year of the reign of the judges.*

Durst not commit any wickedness; there was much peace

A society based on the rule of law benefits from the tangible blessings of order and peace. Discipleship brings blessings. Let us seek to uphold the laws of the land and of God—at home, school, work, and in the community—that we might enjoy peace.

CHAPTER 2

OVERVIEW

Amlici, a rebel after the order of Nehor, aspires to become king. The voice of the people rejects him. Nevertheless, his followers make him their king. The Amlicites come against Alma's army and are defeated. They repeat their assault, this time in confederacy with the invading Lamanites. Alma slays Amlici and leads his army against the enemy in the strength of the Lord. The righteous prevail.

> *1 AND it came to pass in the commencement of the fifth year of their reign there began to be a contention among the people; for a certain man, being called* ***Amlici,*** *he being a very cunning man, yea, a wise man as to the wisdom of the world, he being after the order of the man that slew Gideon by the sword, who was executed according to the law—*

Amlici, Enemy of Freedom

Amlici (pronounced AM-li-sigh), a Nephite trouble maker, has a short-lived career during the early tenure of Alma the Younger. Before the rise of Amlici, Alma has already taken steps to purge from the social fabric of the people an insidious movement known as "priestcraft" (Alma 1:12), whereby cunning individuals with keen oratorical skills cultivate their own power-hungry group of followers for purposes of greed. Nephi had warned against this trend, saying that the Lord "commandeth that there shall be no priestcrafts; for, behold, priestcrafts are that men preach and set themselves up for a light unto the world, that they may get gain and praise of the world; but they seek not the welfare of Zion" (2 Nephi 26:29). Nehor, the first such practicer of priestcraft during the ministry of Alma, has been put to death for his mockery of truth and for murder (see Alma 1:15). But this does not stop the undercurrent of selfishness among the people. Amlici is the next in line to emerge as a champion of this evil scourge. He is a person after the order of Nehor, "being a very cunning man, yea, a wise man as to the wisdom of the world" (Alma 2:1).

Alma 2:1–7

Amlici attracts a large and powerful following that endeavors to make him king over all the people around 87 B.C. But the voice of the people rejects this initiative, and Amlici, being enthroned by his followers and energized by his greed and lust for power, rises up in arms against the remainder of the people.

> 2 *Now this Amlici had, by his cunning, drawn away much people after him; even so much that they began to be very powerful; and they began to endeavor to establish Amlici to be a king over the people.*
> 3 *Now this was alarming to the people of the church, and also to all those who had not been drawn away after the persuasions of Amlici; for they knew that according to their law that such things* ***must be established by the voice of the people.***
> 4 *Therefore, if it were possible that Amlici should gain the voice of the people, he, being a wicked man, would deprive them of their* ***rights and privileges*** *of the church; for it was his intent to destroy the church of God.*

MUST BE ESTABLISHED BY THE VOICE OF THE PEOPLE; RIGHTS AND PRIVILEGES

The designs of Amlici to become a self-elevated king over the people fly in the face of the principle of preserving a framework of liberty and freedom of conscience. The kingdom of God can best flourish in an environment where the inviolable agency of mankind is upheld through laws and institutions of liberty. It is incumbent upon every free people to take every needful action to preserve and maintain freedom of conscience, including the freedom to worship Almighty God in peace.

5–7 The people assemble to vote concerning the Amlici issue and decide against him, "that he was **not made king**" (verse 7).

NOT MADE KING

Elder Mark Peterson summarized the principles involved in this:

> The scripture says that every man could speak according to his own mind, "whether it were for or against Amlici . . . having much dispute and wonderful contentions one with another. And thus they did assemble themselves together to cast in their voices concerning the matter," [Alma 2:5] and their arguments were laid before the judges of the land.

> Those who were against Amlici, being in the majority, were grateful that the voice of the people could be expressed and that the decisions would be made through the system of judges.
>
> But this did not please Amlici. He refused to abide by the free choice of the people. His followers grouped together and consecrated Amlici to be king over the land. He armed his followers and immediately ordered them to begin a war against the rest of the people. (*Alma and Abinadi* [Salt Lake City: Deseret Book, 1983], 59)

8–17 The followers of Amlici, known as Amlicites, rise up in arms against the Nephites. However, the Nephites, under the personal leadership of Alma, are prepared to courageously defend their freedoms.

> *18 Nevertheless* ***the Lord did strengthen the hand of the Nephites,*** *that they slew the Amlicites with great slaughter, that they began to flee before them.*

The Lord did strengthen the hand of the Nephites

In the colossal battle that ensues, the people of God, under command of Alma, prevail for two principal reasons: because of their careful preparations, and because the Lord strengthens their hand. They are on the side of right. They fight to defend their lives and freedoms in accordance with correct principles.

19–27 The Nephites pursue the Amlicites all day long, slaying thousands but also suffering many casualties. Alma sends spies during the night to observe the enemy. They return the following day, astonished, and report that the Amlicites have aligned themselves with the Lamanites and that their joint armies are now advancing and causing great destruction. As they hasten to return to Zarahemla to protect their possessions and families, Alma's forces are attacked by the enemy, who are "as numerous almost, as it were, as the sands of the sea" (verse 27).

> *28 Nevertheless, the Nephites being* ***strengthened by the hand of the Lord,*** *having prayed mightily to him that he would deliver them out of the hands of their enemies, therefore the Lord did hear their cries, and did strengthen them, and the Lamanites and the Amlicites did fall before them.*

Strengthened by the Hand of the Lord

What hope is there in the face of an enemy as numerous as the sands of the sea? The only hope is in the Lord—and that is where the Nephites place their faith and trust. The people of God pray earnestly for the help of God, and He hears their prayers and strengthens them so that they can prevail. Who are our enemies today? What are the forces against which we must contend? We can apply the example of Alma and his followers by appealing to the Lord in humility for strength to overcome and preserve the right.

29 And it came to pass that ***Alma fought with Amlici*** *with the sword, face to face; and they did contend mightily, one with another.*
30 And it came to pass that Alma, being a man of God, being exercised with much faith, cried, saying: ***O Lord, have mercy and spare my life,*** *that I may be an instrument in thy hands to save and preserve this people.*
31 Now when Alma had said these words he contended again with Amlici; and ***he was strengthened,*** *insomuch that he slew Amlici with the sword.*

Alma fought with Amlici; O Lord, have mercy and spare my life; he was strengthened

It is a dramatic moment. Alma himself comes up against Amlici, "face to face," in mortal combat. It is a moment for importuning divine help. The Lord hears Alma's solemn prayer and strengthens him so that he can send Amlici to his just reward. The Lord then helps the Nephites repel the Lamanite hordes and their confederates—at least for the time being. This example of Alma encourages us to seek the strength and wisdom sufficient to be worthy instruments in the Lord's hands for blessing and protecting our families and liberties.

32–36 Alma and his forces succeed in driving the Lamanites and their Amlicite confederates into the wilderness.

37 Yea, they were met on every hand, and slain and driven, until they were scattered on the west, and on the north, until they had reached the wilderness, which was called ***Hermounts;*** *and it was that part of the wilderness which was infested by wild and ravenous beasts.*
38 And it came to pass that many died in the wilderness of their wounds, and were devoured by those beasts and also the vultures of the air; and their bones have been found, and have been heaped up on the earth.

EVIDENCE: HERMOUNTS

Of all the names in the Book of Mormon account, many scholars have found the name *Hermounts* the most peculiar, because it is neither classical nor oriental. *Hermounts* is "that part of the wilderness which was infested by wild and ravenous beasts" (verse 37); in other words, it is the wild country or hunting grounds. Nibley declares that the "equivalent of such a district in Egypt is *Hermonthis,* the land of Month, the Egyptian Pan—the god of wild places and things. *Hermounts* and *Hermonthis* are close enough to satisfy the most exacting philologist." (See *Echoes,* 474–475.)

NAME PECULIARITIES

In the Old Testament, not a single surname is given; each person is simply known by one name. When translated into English, no biblical name includes the letters *q, x,* or *w,* and none begins with *F.* Similarly, of the hundreds of characters named in the Book of Mormon, no surnames are mentioned, and no names use the letters *q, x,* or *w,* or begin with *F.* If Joseph Smith had fabricated the manuscript of the Book of Mormon, it is likely that he would have inadvertently given at least one character a surname, since this was a long-held tradition in his day. Furthermore, it is improbable that the Prophet would have noticed the lack of the letters *q, x,* and *w* in Biblical names. (See *Echoes,* 159–160).

CHAPTER 3

OVERVIEW

The violent confrontations with the Amlicites exact an enormous toll on human life. The Amlicites mark their foreheads with red, thus unknowingly fulfilling a prophecy that those who rebel against the work of God will be cursed, just as the Lamanites were cursed and separated from the people of the Lord. By the misuse of agency, men bring a curse upon themselves. The Nephites repel another Lamanite invasion.

1–7 The toll of dead from the battle is enormous on both sides and includes men, women, and children. The Amlicites mark themselves, as did the Lamanites. In addition, the Lamanites shear their heads, and their bodies are naked except for loin cloths and armor.

> *8 And this was done that their seed might be distinguished from the seed of their brethren, that thereby* ***the Lord God might preserve his people,*** *that they might not mix and believe in incorrect traditions which would prove their destruction.*

THE LORD GOD MIGHT PRESERVE HIS PEOPLE

In His wisdom, the Lord brings about the scattering, gathering, and separation of His children from time to time for the purpose of blessing them according to their faith and to enact judgment upon them according to their transgressions. In the case of the Lamanites, the Lord's design was to separate them from the Nephites so that the latter would be protected from the false traditions of the former. The darkness becomes a sign of warning. At the same time, the Lord gives the promise that when false traditions are overcome and the people return to the pathway of the gospel, the sign will be removed and they will become a "pure and delightsome people" (see 2 Nephi 30:6–7).

9–18 Unknowingly, the Amlicites fulfill a prophecy that those who mingle with the Lamanites will bring upon themselves the mark of separation (see 2 Nephi 30:4–7). From this time forth, those who do not believe in the traditions of the Lamanites but instead believe in the word of God are known as Nephites, or the people of Nephi (verse 11).

> *19 Now I would that ye should see that* ***they brought upon themselves the curse;*** *and even so doth every man that is cursed bring upon himself his own condemnation.*

THEY BROUGHT UPON THEMSELVES THE CURSE

Mormon interposes an editorial statement confirming that the judgments of God—"the curse"—come as a result of man's misusing his God-given agency. Indeed, we bring upon ourselves such a judgment when we violate the commandments of God.

20–26 Several months after the monumental battle with the Amlicites, the Nephites are again attacked by the Lamanites, who are then driven out of the land so that peace once more prevails. In these confrontations, many thousands are sent to their reward "according to their works, whether they were good or whether they were bad, to reap eternal happiness or eternal misery, according to the spirit which they listed to obey, whether it be a good spirit or a bad one" (verse 26).

> *27 For every man receiveth wages* ***of him whom he listeth to obey,*** *and this according to the words of the spirit of prophecy; therefore let it be according to the truth. And thus endeth the fifth year of the reign of the judges.*

Of him whom he listeth to obey

The Lord stands ready to reward us according to our faith, works, and the desires of our hearts (see Alma 41:3; compare Mosiah 2:33, 37). The devil, on the other hand, will never support those who follow him but will speedily bring them down to hell (see Alma 30:60). Let us come unto the Lord and "enjoy the words of eternal life in this world, and eternal life in the world to come, even immortal glory" (Moses 6:59).

CHAPTER 4

OVERVIEW

Peace returns to the land and Alma baptizes thousands of converts. But pride and wickedness again creep into the hearts of the people. Alma transfers the chief judgeship to Nephihah and devotes his full time to preaching repentance to the people.

1–2 Peace prevails in the land, but the people mourn because of their losses.

> *3 And so great were their afflictions that every soul had cause to mourn; and they believed that it was the judgments of God sent upon them because of their wickedness and their abominations; therefore they were awakened to* ***a remembrance of their duty.***

A remembrance of their duty

In good times and bad, let us always remember the goodness of God in all things. Not so surprisingly, we tend to remember Him more when we are in greatest need. Therefore, let us make it our practice to remember Him at all times, for we truly need His blessings continually.

4–6 Thousands of people are baptized into the Church; however, prosperity rekindles the flames of pride and worldliness in the hearts of the people, "because of their exceeding riches, and their **fine silks,** and their **fine-twined linen**" (verse 6).

EVIDENCE: Fine silks, fine-twined linen—Native American Fabrics (Alma 4:6; Ether 10:24)

Critics of the Book of Mormon cite references to the Nephites' and Jaredites' "silks" and "fine-twined linen" as proof that the book is flawed. It is true that cultural records for pre-Columbian

America mention neither silk nor linen, and that European conquerors apparently did not find silkworms or flax when they arrived in the Americas. However, several fabrics have recently been identified in ancient Mesoamerica that could reasonably be termed "silk" and "linen."

Various Mesoamerican fabrics were considered silk (or its equivalent) by the Spanish invaders; one of these fabrics was spun from cocoons gathered from wild trees. Likewise, the word "linen" often applies to types of cloth not made from flax but having similar characteristics. It is now known that in pre-Spanish America, native people made at least two kinds of cloth using a process similar to the one used to make linen, using the leaves of the ixtle, maguey, or agave plant. (See *Echoes,* 289–292.)

7–9 The upsurge in pride and wickedness is of great concern to Alma and the other priesthood leaders.

> *10 And thus ended the eighth year of the reign of the judges; and the wickedness of the church was a* ***great stumbling-block*** *to those who did not belong to the church; and thus the church began to fail in its progress.*
> *11 And it came to pass in the commencement of the ninth year, Alma saw the wickedness of the church, and he saw also that the* ***example of the church*** *began to lead those who were unbelievers on from one piece of iniquity to another, thus bringing on the destruction of the people.*

Great stumbling-block; example of the church

There is great power in example. Example can bless or curse. Remember, we are always leading someone somewhere.

12–14 Alma grieves over the inequality among the people. Many are neglecting the poor and needy, while others remember to display great charity according to the principles of the gospel of Jesus Christ.

> *15 And now it came to pass that Alma, having seen the afflictions of the humble followers of God, and the persecutions which were heaped upon them by the remainder of his people, and seeing all their inequality, began to be very sorrowful; nevertheless the Spirit of the Lord did not fail him.*
> *16 And he selected a wise man who was among the elders of the church, and gave him power according to the voice of the people, that he might have power to enact laws*

according to the laws which had been given, and to put them in force according to the
wickedness and the crimes of the people.
17 Now this man's name was ***Nephihah,*** *and he was appointed chief judge; and he sat*
in the judgment-seat to judge and to govern the people.
18 Now Alma did not grant unto him the office of being high priest over the church,
but he retained the office of high priest unto himself; but he delivered the judgment-
seat unto Nephihah.

Nephihah

Nephihah is the second chief judge in Zarahemla, succeeding Alma the Younger around 83 B.C. Alma is increasingly concerned about the declining spirituality of the people and feels moved by the Spirit to shift his emphasis away from political involvements toward the ministry. Nephihah serves in his public leadership capacity until his death, around 67 B.C., "having filled the judgment-seat with perfect uprightness before God" (Alma 50:37). Among the noteworthy events during his tenure are the destruction of the city of Ammonihah by Lamanite invaders, the establishment of the protectorate at Jershon for the Lamanite converts (from the missionary labors of the sons of Mosiah), the dissention of the Zoramites, and the insurrection of Amalickiah and his involvement in Lamanite invasions. Nephihah's years of service also include considerable commercial progress and increased prosperity for the people. He declines Alma's invitation to take over the management of the sacred records of the people; thus Alma commissions his son Helaman to this stewardship (see Alma 50:38). Pahoran, son of Nephihah, succeeds his father as chief judge and governor of the land.

+ Nephihah

Helaman takes over sacred records.

19 And this he did that he himself might go forth among his people, or among the
people of Nephi, that he might preach the word of God unto them, to ***stir them up in***
remembrance of their duty, *and that he might* ***pull down, by the word of God,***
all the pride and craftiness *and all the contentions which were among his people,*
seeing no way that he might reclaim them save it were in ***bearing down in pure***
testimony *against them.*
20 And thus in the commencement of the ninth year of the reign of the judges over
the people of Nephi, Alma delivered up the judgment-seat to Nephihah, and confined
himself wholly to the high priesthood of the holy order of God, to the testimony of the
word, according to the spirit of revelation and prophecy.

Stir them up in remembrance of their duty; pull down, by the word of God, all the pride and craftiness; bearing down in pure testimony

The ministry of Alma helps us gain perspective on the cycle of prosperity and pride manifested so persistently in the history of the Book of Mormon. So often individuals, communities, and entire nations allow abundance and prosperity to cloud spiritual vision and make pride the prime motivator in life. It is of utmost urgency that we follow prophetic counsel in avoiding pride and hard-heartedness, which inevitably lead to the collapse of moral values and the destruction of the spiritual framework of life. There is no lesson from the Book of Mormon that is more pervasive than the admonition to avoid pride.

Following the defeat of Amlici and his revolutionary initiatives, many members of the Church become prosperous, forget God, and acquire the spiritually-suffocating characteristic of pride. Many become unkind and uncharitable, and their behavior negatively affects the growth of the Church. To counter this pernicious influence, Alma relinquishes the judgeship seat to preach the "word of God unto them, to stir them up in remembrance of their duty" (verse 19). This campaign of "**bearing down in pure testimony** against them" (verse 19) is the only action that seems to Alma capable of defeating pride.

Bearing down in pure testimony

The power of the word of God is without limit or boundaries. As we speak, let us never doubt the power of the word. When spoken by the Spirit, it has power to change souls. We should seek to bless others who are struggling by touching their hearts with the Spirit through the word of God.

Beware of Pride

> One of Satan's greatest tools is pride: to cause a man or a woman to center so much attention on self that he or she becomes insensitive to his Creator or fellow beings. It is a cause for discontent, divorce, teenage rebellion, family indebtedness, and most other problems we face. . . .
>
> In the scriptures there is no such thing as righteous pride. It is always considered as a sin. We are not speaking of a wholesome view of self-worth, which is best established by a close relationship with God. But we are speaking of pride as the universal sin, as someone has described it. Mormon writes that "the pride of this nation, or the people of the Nephites, hath proven their

destruction" (Moroni 8:27). The Lord says in the Doctrine and Covenants, "Beware of pride, lest ye become as the Nephites of old" (D&C 38:39). Essentially, pride is a "my will" rather than "thy will" approach to life. The opposite of pride is humbleness, meekness, submissiveness, or teachableness (see Alma 13:28). . . .

Pride does not look up to God and care about what is right. It looks sideways to man and argues who is right. Pride is manifest in the spirit of contention. Was it not through pride that the devil became the devil? Christ wanted to serve. The devil wanted to rule. Christ wanted to bring men to where He was. The devil wanted to be above men. Christ removed self as the force in His perfect life. It was not my will, but thine be done (see Mark 14:36; Luke 22:42).

Pride is characterized by "What do I want out of life?" rather than by "What would God have me do with my life?" It is self-will as opposed to God's will. It is the fear of man over the fear of God. . . .

Humility responds to God's will—to the fear of His judgments and to the needs of those around us. To the proud, the applause of the world rings in their ears; to the humble, the applause of heaven warms their hearts. Someone has said, "Pride gets no pleasure out of having something, only out of having more of it than the next man." Of one brother, the Lord said, "I, the Lord, am not well pleased with him, for he seeketh to excel, and he is not sufficiently meek before me" (D&C 58:41). . . .

As we cleanse the inner vessel, there will have to be changes made in our own personal lives, in our families, and in the Church. The proud do not change to improve, but defend their position by rationalizing. Repentance means change, and it takes a humble person to change. But we can do it. (Ezra Taft Benson, *The Teachings of Ezra Taft Benson* [Salt Lake City: Bookcraft, 1988], 435–436)

Pride, the Great Sin

C. S. Lewis's recognition of the legitimacy of a "self" that is grounded in Christ also comes with a warning: "The moment you have a self at all, there is a possibility of putting yourself first—wanting to be the centre—wanting to be God, in fact. That was the sin of Satan: and that was the sin he taught the human race."

Perhaps the most meaningful counsel given in all of his writings is contained in Lewis's warnings about pride: "The essential vice, the utmost evil, is Pride. Unchastity, anger, greed, drunkenness, and all that, are mere fleabites in comparison: it was through Pride that the devil became the devil: Pride leads to every other vice: it is the complete anti-God state of mind."

On 30 January 1930 Lewis wrote to his friend Arthur Greeves and told him that though he felt he was being supported in overcoming anger and immorality, he was alarmed concerning his own pride. Lewis wrote:

"I have found out ludicrous and terrible things about my own character. Sitting by, watching the rising thoughts to break their necks as they pop up, one learns to know the sort of thoughts that do come. And, will you believe it, one out of every three is a thought of self-admiration: when everything else fails, having had its neck broken, up comes the thought, 'what an admirable fellow I am to have broken their necks!' I catch myself posturing before the mirror, so to speak, all day long. I pretend I am carefully thinking out what to say to the next pupil (for *his* good, of course) and then suddenly realize I am really thinking how frightfully clever I'm going to be and how he will admire me . . . when you force yourself to stop it, you admire yourself for doing *that*. It's like fighting the hydra. . . . There seems to be no end to it. Depth under depth of self-love and self-admiration. . . . *Pride* . . . is the mother of *all sins*, and the original sin of Lucifer."

Latter-day Saints will remember President Ezra Taft Benson's landmark address entitled, "Beware of Pride," wherein our dear prophet quoted C. S. Lewis in warning the membership of the Church concerning "the sin of pride." Though President Benson and Professor Lewis both described the manifestation of pride where we look "down on things and people," President Benson articulated another: "Pride is a sin that can readily be seen in others but is rarely admitted in ourselves. Most of us consider pride to be a sin of those on the top, such as the rich and the learned, looking down at the rest of us (see 2 Nephi 9:42). There is, however, a far more common ailment among us—and that is *pride from the bottom looking up*."

Lewis alluded to the bidirectional nature of pride when he taught that Satan always delivers heresy in pairs: "He always sends errors into the world in pairs—pairs of opposites. And he always encourages us to spend a lot of time thinking which is the worse. You see why, of course? He relies on your extra dislike of the one error to draw you gradually into the opposite one."

Elder Dallin H. Oaks shares this challenging insight on "pride from the bottom looking up" in his life:

"A few months after my calling to the Council of the Twelve, I expressed my feelings of inadequacy to one of the senior members of my quorum. He responded with this mild reproof and challenging insight: 'I suppose your feelings are understandable. But you should work for a condition where you will not be pre-occupied with yourself and your own feelings and can give your entire concern to others, to the work of the Lord in all the world.'

"Whenever we focus on ourselves, even in our service to others, we fall short of the example of our Savior, who gave himself as a total and unqualified sacrifice for all mankind. Those who seek to follow his example must lose themselves in their service to others."

Pride from the bottom looking up and the top looking down. Lewis taught that if we think ourselves not guilty of pride "it means [we] are very conceited indeed." Lewis further taught: "The real test of being in the presence of God is that you either forget about yourself altogether or see yourself as a small, dirty object. It is better to forget about yourself altogether." (Daniel K. Judd, in Andrew C. Skinner and Robert L. Millet, eds., *C. S. Lewis, the Man and His Message: An LDS Perspective* [Salt Lake City: Deseret Book, 1999], 65–67)

Memories: The Milk of Kindness

My father was a generous man. I can recall with utter clarity the scene I saw through the front porch windows of my childhood home one blistering-hot summer day. There was a gruff-looking stranger out there cutting down the weeds along the edge of the street. He would pause to mop his brow from time to time. My father was also watching. Suddenly my father went to the kitchen and retrieved a new, unopened quart bottle of milk and, much to my amazement, he walked passed me (I was perhaps five or six years old at the time) and went directly outside to speak with the stranger. I watched with fascinating as they exchanged a few words. Then my father handed the milk bottle to the man, who gratefully accepted it, opened it, and drank down the contents in nearly one draught.

There were two aspects to this memory for me. The one was seeing a total stranger drink down a quart of milk right from the jar—quite a feat in itself. The other was the grateful look on his face, which was matched only by the glow on my father's. Despite its simplicity, this example from my father has been a lasting legacy concerning the milk of human kindness and a vivid reminder to be generous and charitable to others in their need.

Alma 4:20

In the eighth year of his tenure as chief judge and high priest among the people at Zarahemla, Alma the Younger perceived a destructive rift in the social fabric of his nation. A large segment of the population became dominated by self-consuming pride because of their abundant wealth and prosperity: "Yea, he saw great inequality among the people, some lifting themselves up with their pride, despising others, turning their backs upon the needy and the naked and those who were hungry, and those who were athirst, and those who were sick and afflicted" (Alma 4:12). He also saw others who remained compassionate and caring, "abasing themselves, succoring those who stood in need of their succor, such as imparting their substance to the poor and the needy, feeding the hungry, and suffering all manner of afflictions, for Christ's sake, who should come according to the spirit of prophecy" (Alma 4:13). Because of this dangerous rift, Alma conveyed his chief judgeship to a worthy colleague and took upon himself the responsibility to go forth and preach the word of God to the people, "to stir them up in remembrance of their duty, and that he might pull down, by the word of God, all the pride and craftiness and all the contentions which were among his people, seeing no way that he might reclaim them save it were in bearing down in pure testimony against them" (Alma 4:19).

In effect, he was extending to them the promise that Isaiah, before him, had extended to the people: "Ho, every one that thirsteth, come ye to the waters, and he that hath no money; come ye, buy, and eat; yea, come, buy wine and milk without money and without price" (Isaiah 55:1; compare 2 Nephi 9:50; 26:25). In his extraordinary discourse to the people, Alma was to ask them this compelling question: "Have ye experienced this mighty change in your hearts" (Alma 5:14)—this change that would cause them to keep all of the Lord's commandments, including repenting of the prideful denial of the petitions of the destitute and "turning your backs upon the poor and the needy, and in withholding your substance from them" (Alma 5:55). Charity to one's fellows is a reflection of the matchless charity of the Savior who imparted the bread of life and the water of salvation freely to all of God's children. Charity, rather than pride, is what we must each develop to become like our Great Exemplar, Jesus Christ. (Richard J. Allen)

CONCLUDING THOUGHTS

The initial chapters of the book of Alma remind us of deep and cherished values that the Lord commands us to maintain and cultivate, including the principles of righteous government within a framework of liberty and freedom of conscience, honoring our priesthood covenants in the face of incursions by those operating with priestcraft motivation, and avoiding pride, selfishness, and hard-heartedness at all times, especially when the Lord has blessed us with prosperity. There is only one way to happiness and peace—the Lord's way. When we go against the word of God or seek to follow our own prideful will instead of the Lord's will, we separate ourselves from the Lord and the Spirit. Pride surely is the destroyer of happiness. Let us sincerely seek to overcome pride with humility and charity as exemplified by our willingness to follow the Lord and His designated leaders and our selflessness in serving our fellowmen.

> *The words which Alma, the High Priest according to the holy order of God, delivered to the people in their cities and villages throughout the land.* [Note: This preamble was included in the original edition of the Book of Mormon published in 1830.]

CHAPTER 5

OVERVIEW

Alma provides a series of compelling questions and wise answers to enable the people to bring their lives into alignment with the standards and principles of the gospel. We can enjoy the blessings of the Atonement if we repent of our pride and iniquity and come unto Christ. Alma bears his witness of the truth of the word of Christ and commands all to repent. "For the names of the righteous shall be written in the book of life" (verse 58).

> *1 NOW it came to pass that* ***Alma began to deliver the word of God*** *unto the people, first in the land of Zarahemla, and from thence throughout all the land.*

Alma began to deliver the word of God

Alma seeks to awaken the minds and hearts of the citizens of Zarahemla to a higher level of spirituality through a series of searching questions designed to prick their consciences and inspire them to righteousness. Question after question is boldly asked that the listeners might be touched. As a result of Alma's ministry, many repent though some retain their pride. The order of the Church is established. Being full of charity, the members of the Church pray for all those who do not know of God and His ways. Alma will later go to Gideon (chapter 6) to continue testifying of the truth and encouraging the people to follow Him. Studying these events can help us evaluate our lives and bring us closer to our Savior.

Consider what has transpired in the years leading up to this significant discourse by the prophet Alma. The Church has survived the onslaught of two highly articulate deceivers, Nehor and Amlici. Amlici, having failed to gain the voice of the people to make him king, has organized a revolutionary movement to seize power and undermine all civil liberties, even entering into an alliance with the invading Lamanites. Thousands on both sides of this conflict lose their lives, and it is only through their faith and diligence that the Nephites, led by Alma, come out victorious, but not without great cause to mourn. The Church, brought to a state of humility, experiences a great expansion. Peace returns to the land. The people once again prosper. But with that prosperity comes the chronic malaise of pride. So great is the rift between the proud and the humble in the land that Alma steps down from his judgeship and initiates great reform empowered by the word of God. His speech stands as a stark warning to our own generation to repent and experience the mighty change of heart that alone can lead to spiritual rebirth.

2–5 The words of Alma to his people are presented, "according to his own record" (verse 2). He reviews the history of the founding of the Church through his father, Alma the Elder, at the Waters of Mormon.

> *6 And now behold, I say unto you, my brethren, you that belong to this church, have you sufficiently* ***retained in remembrance*** *the captivity of your fathers? Yea, and have you sufficiently* ***retained in remembrance*** *his mercy and long-suffering toward them? And moreover, have ye sufficiently* ***retained in remembrance*** *that he has delivered their souls from hell?*

Retained in remembrance

This preamble to Alma's speech is a reminder to remain ever conscious of the blessings of the Lord to our progenitors. We are defined by our actions in the context of our heritage as part of God's family. The application is clear: We are to do whatever is requisite to remember the goodness and mercy and loving-kindness of God. If we forget, we will be disposed to go the ways of the world.

> *7 Behold, he changed their hearts; yea, he awakened them out of a deep sleep, and they awoke unto God. Behold, they were in the midst of darkness; nevertheless, their souls were illuminated by* ***the light of the everlasting word;*** *yea, they were encircled about by the bands of death, and the chains of hell, and an everlasting destruction did await them.*

The light of the everlasting word

There is power in the word of God. The word of God originates with the Word, even Jesus Christ. He is all-powerful in bringing to pass the immortality and eternal life of man (see Moses 1:39). It is this Word who empowers the gospel plan in our lives.

8–11 Alma reminds his listeners that his father's group was liberated from their physical and spiritual bands because they heeded the word of God as spoken through the prophet Abinadi.

> *12 And according to his faith there was* ***a mighty change*** *wrought in his heart. Behold I say unto you that this is all true.*
> *13 And behold, he preached the word unto your fathers, and* ***a mighty change*** *was also wrought in their hearts, and they humbled themselves and put their trust in the true and living God. And behold, they were faithful until the end; therefore they were saved.*

A Mighty Change

When we allow the word to take root in our hearts, we experience a mighty change. We are humble, trust in God, and are faithful in keeping the commandments.

> *14 And now behold, I ask of you, my brethren of the church, have ye spiritually been born of God? Have ye received his image in your countenances? Have ye experienced* ***this mighty change*** *in your hearts?*

This mighty change

Alma raises a question that should penetrate to the very center of our beings. Have we experienced the mighty change that Alma the Elder and his followers were blessed to receive through belief on the word of God and obedience to covenant requirements? Every individual who has a hope to one day inherit celestial glory and immortality must of necessity go through a mighty change of heart occasioned by faith, repentance, humility, and the transforming renewal of the Spirit. Only by strict obedience to all of the commandments of God can this mighty change of heart become a permanent part of one's life. The questions are these: Have we been born of God? Have we received His image in our countenance? Have we experienced this mighty change of heart? Elder Neal A. Maxwell states, "'In process of time' the patina of pride is burnished off. Hearts that were so set on the things of the world, if sufficiently meek, will either go through 'a mighty change' or be broken, so 'a new heart' can be given (see D&C 121:35; Alma 5:14; Ezekiel 18:31; 36:26). The righteous and covenant-keeping individuals who endure it well will inherit 'all that my Father hath' (D&C 84:38)" (*If Thou Endure It Well* [Salt Lake City: Bookcraft, 1996], 9).

A doctrinal understanding of the mighty change, i.e. being born again or born of God, is important for us to achieve, as this is our goal as children of God here upon the earth. The following treatment outlines the essential aspects of this process:

> Born of God or "born again" refers to the personal spiritual experience in which repentant individuals receive a forgiveness of sins and a witness from God that if they continue to live the commandments and endure to the end, they will inherit eternal life. The scriptures teach that just as each individual is "born into the world by water, and blood, and the spirit," so must one be "born again" of water and the Spirit and be cleansed by the blood of Christ (John 3:5; Moses 6:59). To be born of God implies a sanctifying process by which the old or natural man is supplanted by the new spiritual man who enjoys the companionship of the Holy Ghost and hence is no longer disposed to commit sin (Col. 3:9–10; Mosiah 3:19; *TPJS*, 51). When individuals are born again they are spiritually begotten sons and daughters of God and more specifically of Jesus Christ (Mosiah 5:7; 27:25). The Book of Mormon prophet Alma 1 calls this inner transformation a "mighty change in your hearts" (Alma 5:14).
>
> LDS scripture and literature contain numerous examples of individuals who have undergone this process of spiritual rebirth. Enos relates that after "mighty prayer and supplication" the Lord declared that his sins had been forgiven (Enos 1:1–8). After King Benjamin's discourse, the people said that the Spirit had "wrought a mighty change in us, or in our hearts," and that they had "no more disposition to do evil, but to do good continually" (Mosiah 5:2). Of his conversion experience, Alma 2 says, "Nevertheless, after wading through much tribulation, repenting nigh unto death, the Lord in mercy hath seen fit to snatch me out of an everlasting burning, and I am born of God" (Mosiah 27:28). Similar experiences are recounted about King Lamoni and his father (Alma 19, 22). In an account written in 1832, the Prophet Joseph Smith describes his first vision as being significant not only for opening a new dispensation of the gospel, but also for his personal conversion. He writes, "The Lord opened the heavens upon

me and I saw the Lord and he spake unto me saying Joseph my son thy sins are forgiven thee. [A]nd my soul was filled with love and for many days I could rejoice with great joy and the Lord was with me" (TPJS 1:6–7).

Mormon explains the "mighty change" that must occur if one is to be born of God. The first fruit of repentance is the baptism of water and fire, which baptism "cometh by faith unto the fulfilling of the commandments." Then comes a remission of sins that brings a meekness and lowliness of heart. Such a transformation results in one's becoming worthy of the companionship of the Holy Ghost, who "filleth with hope and perfect love, which love endureth by diligence unto prayer" (Moro. 8:25–26).

LDS scriptures teach that spiritual rebirth comes by the grace of God to those who adhere to the principles and ordinances of the gospel of Jesus Christ, namely, faith, repentance, baptism, and reception of the gift of the Holy Ghost. For the process to be genuine, however, one must be diligently engaged in good works, for as James says, "faith without works is dead; . . . by works [is] faith made perfect" (James 2:20, 22). A mere confession of change, or receiving baptism or another ordinance, does not necessarily mean that one has been born of God.

Other Christian faiths also emphasize the importance of being "born again." Unlike many of these, Latter-day Saints do not believe this experience alone is sufficient for salvation. Instead, the process of spiritual rebirth signals to Latter-day Saints the beginning of a new life abounding with faith, grace, and good works. Only by enduring to the end may the individual return to the presence of God. Those who receive the ordinance of baptism and are faithful in keeping the commandments may enjoy the constant presence of the Holy Ghost who, like fire, will act as a sanctifier, and will witness to the hearts of the righteous that their sins are forgiven, imparting hope for eternal life.

Persons who have experienced this mighty change manifest attitudinal and behavioral changes. Feeling their hearts riveted to the Lord, their obedience extends beyond performance of duty. President Harold B. Lee taught, "Conversion must mean more than just being a 'card-carrying' member of the Church with a tithing receipt, a membership card, a temple recommend, etc. It means to overcome the tendencies to criticize and to strive continually to improve inward weaknesses and not merely the outward appearances" (*Ensign*, June 1971, 8). Latter-day Saints believe that individuals who are truly born of God gladly give a life of service to their fellow beings—they share the gospel message, sacrifice their own time, energy, and resources for the benefit of others, and in general hold high the Light of Christ, being faithful to all the commandments." (Ed J. Pinegar, *Encyclopedia of Mormonism,* 1–4 vols., ed. Daniel H. Ludlow [New York: Macmillan, 1992], 218–219)

*15 Do ye exercise **faith in the redemption** of him who created you? Do you look forward with an eye of faith, and view this mortal body raised in immortality, and this corruption raised in incorruption, to **stand before God to be judged** according to the deeds which have been done in the mortal body?*
*16 I say unto you, can you imagine to yourselves that ye hear the voice of the Lord, saying unto you, in that day: **Come unto me ye blessed,** for behold, your works have been the works of righteousness upon the face of the earth?*

Faith in the redemption; stand before God to be judged; Come unto me ye blessed

There will be a Judgment Day. There will be a time of accounting for our deeds in mortality. Let us carefully consider our eventual position before the judgment bar of God and regulate our lives according to eternal principles. Marion G. Romney comments on this doctrine:

> Alma implies here that the "exercise of faith in the redemption" of Christ [verse 15] sufficient to bring about the mighty change in one's heart is prerequisite to obtaining a pure heart and clean hands. He also implies that if on the great judgment day one can look up to God with a pure heart and clean hands, he will hear the voice of the Lord saying unto him, "Come unto me ye blessed" [verse 16]; if he cannot do so, his soul will be filled with guilt and remorse. (*Learning for the Eternities* [Salt Lake City: Deseret Book, 1977], 127)

*17 Or do ye imagine to yourselves that ye can **lie unto the Lord** in that day, and say—Lord, our works have been righteous works upon the face of the earth—and that he will save you?*
*18 Or otherwise, can ye imagine yourselves brought before the tribunal of God with your souls filled with guilt and remorse, having **a remembrance** of all your guilt, yea,*

> ***a perfect remembrance*** *of all your wickedness, yea,* ***a remembrance*** *that ye have set at defiance the commandments of God?*
> *19 I say unto you, can ye look up to God at that day with a pure heart and clean hands? I say unto you, can you look up,* ***having the image of God*** *engraven upon your countenances?*

LIE UNTO THE LORD; A REMEMBRANCE, A PERFECT REMEMBRANCE; HAVING THE IMAGE OF GOD

The impenitent are promised the ability, at the time of the Great Judgment, to have a perfect remembrance of their sins and misdeeds—and consequently will be filled with guilt and remorse. The opposite of this condition is having the image of God engraved upon our countenances. The divine image confirms that the process of repentance and purification is complete.

> *20 I say unto you, can ye think of being saved when you have yielded yourselves to become subjects to the devil?*
> *21 I say unto you, ye will know at that day that ye cannot be saved; for there can no man be saved except his* ***garments are washed white;*** *yea, his garments must be purified until they are cleansed from all stain, through the blood of him of whom it has been spoken by our fathers, who should come to redeem his people from their sins.*

EVIDENCE: GARMENTS ARE WASHED WHITE (Alma 5:21; see also 2 Nephi 9:14; Alma 13:11–12; Alma 7:25)

Many passages in the Book of Mormon refer to white garments, and Alma declares that a man's garments must be washed white or he cannot be saved. Modern scholars such as Erwin Goodenough have identified the white garment as being of particular importance to the Jews. Paraphrasing Goodenough, Hugh Nibley states that "God himself may be represented in the earliest Jewish art as one of three men clothed in white. . . . This image [from the Dura Europos synagogue] wasn't even known to exist until 1958 . . . there are three men in white, or a single figure, the prophet in white. The symbol of the chosen prophet, an emissary from God, is always the white robe, which is reserved for heavenly beings." This coincides perfectly with Nephi's statement that the righteous will be "clothed with purity, yea, even with the robe of righteousness" (2 Nephi 9:14). (See *Echoes,* 485.)

Alma 5:22–33

22–25 Alma emphasizes the point that we cannot lie ourselves into a state of salvation.

> *26 And now behold, I say unto you, my brethren, if ye have experienced a change of heart, and if ye have felt to sing the song of redeeming love, I would ask,* ***can ye feel so now?***

Can ye feel so now?

This is a riveting question. The mighty change of heart is more than an event at one point in our lives: it is an ongoing process. The transforming change we feel through the Spirit needs to be preserved and prolonged across time as we seek to come unto God and honor our covenant obligations. Therefore, Alma asks "Can ye feel so now?" The answer is an indication of how faithfully we have been in keeping our commitment to endure to the end.

> *27 Have ye walked,* ***keeping yourselves blameless*** *before God? Could ye say, if ye were called to die at this time, within yourselves, that ye have been sufficiently humble? That your garments have been cleansed and made white through the blood of Christ, who will come to redeem his people from their sins?*
> *28 Behold, are ye stripped of pride? I say unto you, if ye are not ye are not prepared to meet God. Behold ye must* ***prepare quickly;*** *for the kingdom of heaven is soon at hand, and such an one hath not eternal life.*

Keeping yourselves blameless; prepare quickly

Evaluate your life. This is the time to prepare to meet God. We will receive our blessings or consequences.

29–32 Those who cultivate envy, mock others, and work iniquity have need to repent.

> *33 Behold, he sendeth an invitation unto all men, for* ***the arms of mercy are extended toward them,*** *and he saith: Repent, and I will receive you.*

EVIDENCE: The arms of mercy are extended toward them—Temple Imagery

(Alma 5:33)

Some critics have claimed that the Book of Mormon does not comprise the "fulness of the gospel" because it does not include temple ordinances. However, Hugh Nibley states that the Book of Mormon is full of temple imagery—particularly in the many discourses on the Atonement—and that the temple ordinances are "everywhere in the book if we know where to look for them." For example, Nibley explains that the literal meaning of *kaphar* and *kippurim* is a warm embrace, and that this embrace occurred anciently at the *kapporeth,* the front flap of the tabernacle or tent that housed first the Ark and later the Holy of Holies. The implication of phrases such as "the arms of mercy are extended toward them" (verse 33) is analogous to this "warm embrace" associated with the ancient temple rites. Moreover, Nephi's description of his redemption by the Lord, in particular his being "encircled about eternally in the arms of [the Lord's] love" [2 Nephi 1:15], is certainly reflective of this ancient temple rites. (See *Echoes,* 481–482.)

> *34 Yea, he saith: Come unto me and ye shall partake of* ***the fruit of the tree of life;*** *yea, ye shall eat and drink of the bread and the waters of life freely;*

The Fruit of the Tree of Life

Receive the love of God by coming unto Christ and He shall bless you.

35–37 Bring forth good works and heed the voice of the Good Shepherd.

> *38 Behold, I say unto you, that the good shepherd doth call you; yea, and* ***in his own name he doth call you,*** *which is the name of Christ; and if ye will not hearken unto the voice of the good shepherd, to the name by which ye are called, behold, ye are not the sheep of the good shepherd.*

In his own name he doth call you

Christ calls after us. Let us hearken unto His voice (i.e., listen and do)—and thus become part of His fold.

39–42 If you are not part of the Savior's fold, you belong to the fold of the devil and receive the wages of death.

> *43 And now, my brethren, I would that ye should hear me, for I speak in the energy of my soul; for behold,* ***I have spoken unto you plainly*** *that ye cannot err, or have spoken according to the commandments of God.*
> *44 For I am called to speak after this manner, according to the holy order of God, which is in Christ Jesus; yea,* ***I am commanded to stand and testify*** *unto this*

people the things which have been spoken by our fathers concerning the things which are to come.

45 And this is not all. Do ye not suppose that I know of these things myself? Behold, I testify unto you that I do know that these things whereof I have spoken are true. And how do ye suppose that I know of their surety?

46 Behold, I say unto you they are ***made known unto me by the Holy Spirit of God.*** *Behold, I have fasted and prayed many days that I might know these things of myself. And now I do know of myself that they are true; for the Lord God hath made them manifest unto me by his Holy Spirit; and this is the spirit of revelation which is in me.*

I have spoken unto you plainly; I am commanded to stand and testify; made known unto me by the Holy Spirit of God

Alma provides a succinct job description of a prophet: to speak plainly by command of God those things revealed by the Spirit. If we are to engage in this kind of communion, then we, too, should fast and pray to know the truth by the power of the Holy Ghost. In that way we can have the gift of prophecy to guide our own lives and bless the lives of our family members.

47–55 Alma confirms his witness of the truth of the words he has been commanded to speak. He asks "can ye withstand these sayings" (verse 53) and warns the people to respond and to repent of their pride and iniquity.

56 And finally, all ye that will persist in your wickedness, I say unto you that these are they who shall be hewn down and ***cast into the fire*** *except they speedily repent.*

Cast into the fire

What are the results of not hearkening to the word of God? The consignation to a state of damnation. Therefore, it is urgent that we ponder the fate of the wicked—which will be our fate if we don't repent—and then repent speedily so that the Lord will turn away the consequences of sin through the operation of the Atonement.

57 And now I say unto you, all you that are desirous to follow the voice of the good shepherd, come ye out from the wicked, and be ye separate, and touch not their unclean things; and behold, ***their names shall be blotted out,*** *that the names of the wicked*

shall not be numbered among the names of the righteous, that the word of God may be fulfilled, which saith: The names of the wicked shall not be mingled with the names of my people;
58 For the ***names of the righteous shall be written in the book of life,*** *and unto them will I grant an inheritance at my right hand. And now, my brethren, what have ye to say against this? I say unto you, if ye speak against it, it matters not, for* ***the word of God must be fulfilled.***

Their names shall be blotted out; names of the righteous shall be written in the book of life; the word of God must be fulfilled

According to the economy of heaven, the wicked are not numbered among the fold of Christ. Only the righteous are written in the "book of life" (verse 58) and receive an inheritance at the right hand of the Lord. The attitudes and opinions of men concerning this verity do not matter, for "the word of God must be fulfilled' (verse 58). Let us remember that we will be judged by one standard alone: the word of God.

59 For what shepherd is there among you having many sheep doth not watch over them, that the wolves enter not and devour his flock? And behold, if a wolf enter his flock doth he not drive him out? Yea, and at the last, if he can, he will destroy him.
60 And now I say unto you that ***the good shepherd doth call after you;*** *and if you will hearken unto his voice he will bring you into his fold, and ye are his sheep; and he commandeth you that ye suffer no ravenous wolf to enter among you, that ye may not be destroyed.*

The good shepherd doth call after you

Let us never forget that Christ continually calls after us to bless and strengthen us, to protect and guide us, to lift and purify us.

61 And now I, Alma, do ***command*** *you in the language of him who hath commanded me, that ye observe to do the words which I have spoken unto you.*
62 ***I speak by way of command*** *unto you that belong to the church; and unto those who do not belong to the church* ***I speak by way of invitation,*** *saying: Come and be baptized unto repentance, that ye also may be partakers of the fruit of the tree of life.*

Command; I speak by way of command; I speak by way of invitation

Alma provides many questions—plus plain and precious answers—to induce his listeners to evaluate their lives and rise to their divine potential. He now does that which all prophets do: he *commands* the people of the Church to obey so that they can be "partakers of the fruit of the tree of life" (verse 62). And Alma *invites* those not of the faith to come unto Christ and be baptized unto repentance.

A Review of Questions of Conscience

Alma 5 can be considered the great evaluation chapter in the Book of Mormon. Alma used questions of conscience to arouse the people to righteousness. By way of review, consider some of the following questions that Alma asks the people in Zarahemla:

v. 14 And now behold, I ask of you, my brethren of the church, have ye spiritually been born of God? Have ye received his image in your countenances? Have ye experienced this mighty change in your hearts?

v. 15 Do ye exercise faith in the redemption of him who created you? Do you look forward with an eye of faith, and view this mortal body raised in immortality, and this corruption raised in incorruption, to stand before God to be judged according to the deeds which have been done in the mortal body?

v. 16 I say unto you, can you imagine to yourselves that ye hear the voice of the Lord, saying unto you, in that day: Come unto me ye blessed, for behold, your works have been the works of righteousness upon the face of the earth?

v. 17 Or do ye imagine to yourselves that ye can lie unto the Lord in that day, and say—Lord, our works have been righteous works upon the face of the earth—and that he will save you?

v. 18 Or otherwise, can ye imagine yourselves brought before the tribunal of God with your souls filled with guilt and remorse, having a remembrance of all your guilt, yea, a perfect remembrance of all your wickedness, yea, a remembrance that ye have set at defiance the commandments of God?

v. 19 I say unto you, can ye look up to God at that day with a pure heart and clean hands? I say unto you, can you look up, having the image of God engraven upon your countenances?

v. 27 Have ye walked, keeping yourselves blameless before God? Could ye say, if ye were called to die at this time, within yourselves, that ye have been sufficiently humble? That your garments have been cleansed and made white through the blood of Christ, who will come to redeem his people from their sins?

v. 28 Behold, are ye stripped of pride? I say unto you, if ye are not ye are not prepared to meet God. Behold ye must prepare quickly; for the kingdom of heaven is soon at hand, and such an one hath not eternal life.

v. 29 Behold, I say, is there one among you who is not stripped of envy? I say unto you that such an one is not prepared; and I would that he should prepare quickly, for the hour is close at hand, and he knoweth not when the time shall come; for such an one is not found guiltless.

v. 53 And now my beloved brethren, I say unto you, can ye withstand these sayings; yea, can ye lay aside these things, and trample the Holy One under your feet; yea, can ye be puffed up in the pride of your hearts; yea, will ye still persist in the wearing of costly apparel and setting your hearts upon the vain things of the world, upon your riches?

Alma concludes by exhorting the people to observe the words he has spoken, even as he has observed to follow the commandments of the Lord (see Alma 5:61). That is what prophets do. It is their divine role to seek to persuade and influence people to be good and keep the commandments. Alma's questions are not designed to engender guilt as much as to inspire and motivate us to righteousness, to help us experience a change of heart, and ultimately to become like the Christ. When we give our hearts to the Lord we become as He is—His will is our will, His joy is our joy, and His work is our work. What could be more wonderful?

CHAPTER 6

OVERVIEW

Alma sets in order the Church in Zarahemla. To serve the needs of the people, priests and elders are ordained by the laying on of hands. Alma goes to the city of Gideon to preach to the people.

1–4 Alma ordains priests and elders "by laying on his hands **according to the order of God**" (verse 1) to watch over the Church in Zarahemla. The penitent are received into the Church. The names of wicked are not numbered among the righteous.

According to the Order of God

The Church is a house of order governed by the spirit of prophecy and revelation. God has ordained that prophets shall regulate the affairs of His Church and kingdom according to eternal principles. Following Alma's extraordinary discourse to the people of Zarahemla, the people begin again to have a clear vision of the covenant duties incumbent upon them, and the order of the Church is established in Zarahemla. President John Taylor explains the concept of the order of the Church: "The order of the church is for us to fulfil and magnify the calling to which we are called, and do it with an eye single to the glory of God, each man fulfilling the various duties and responsibilities of his office" (John Taylor, *The Gospel Kingdom: Selections from the Writings and Discourses of John Taylor,* comp. G. Homer Durham [Salt Lake City: Improvement Era, 1941], 150–151).

President David O. McKay added the following:

> Establishing the order of the Church refers to the method of regular arrangements, procedures, rules, regulations and operations so that everything is in its proper place and working well . . . being directed by the priesthood.
>
> "The Church of Jesus Christ was organized in accordance with the order of the Church as recorded in the New Testament," said Joseph Smith. The practical and beneficent workings of this organization prove its divine authenticity. (*Gospel Ideals: Selections from the Discourses of David O. McKay* [Salt Lake City: Improvement Era, 1953], 85)

> *5 Now I would that ye should understand that the word of God was* ***liberal unto all,*** *that none were deprived of the privilege of assembling themselves together to hear the word of God.*

Liberal unto all

The word of God is sent without restriction to all of mankind. All are invited to come unto Christ and partake of the living waters and the bread of life.

> *6 Nevertheless the children of God were commanded that they should gather themselves together oft, and join in fasting and mighty prayer* ***in behalf of the welfare of the souls of those who knew not God.***

In behalf of the welfare of the souls of those who knew not God

We should fast and pray for all people—especially for those who know not God, "For there are many yet on the earth among all sects, parties, and denominations, who are blinded by the subtle craftiness of men, whereby they lie in wait to deceive, and who are only kept from the truth because they know not where to find it—" (D&C 123:12).

In the Church in Zarahemla the people are commanded to meet together often. They are to fast and pray for those who know not God. Sometimes in our fasting we merely go without food. We fast without purpose. We forget to pray mightily to our Heavenly Father. If we are truly concerned for the well-being of Heavenly Father's children, we should pray for them to know God and come unto Christ. We should pray for world leaders to make choices that will bless lives—not destroy them. We should pray for the wicked to repent. In our personal lives, we should pray to increase our faith, to show more charity to our fellowmen, and to be more obedient to the commandments of God.

Order of the Church

> Everything of God is done in order. Orderliness in the Church surely sets the tone for the Spirit, reverence, and worship. As leaders who serve in the kingdom, we surely need to make sure that we do things according to the established order of the Church. We should administer the kingdom in an orderly fashion. This is essential so that the Spirit can be present. When we fail to administer wisely and carefully, according to the established order of the Church, we do not enjoy the Spirit. How many times have you witnessed the moment when someone is late, ill prepared, or does something contrary to the normally accepted practice? Sadly, the Spirit of the meeting or event is sometimes lost. We can all think of when this has happened in our lives. Let us remember what the prophet Joseph F. Smith said in regard to order:
>
> The house of God is a house of order, and not a house of confusion; and it could not be thus, if there were not those who had authority to preside, to direct, to counsel, to lead in the affairs of the Church. No house would be a house of order if it were not properly organized, as the Church of Jesus Christ of Latter-day Saints is organized. Take away the organization of the Church and its power would cease. Every part of its organization is necessary and essential to its perfect existence. Disregard, ignore, or omit any part, and you start imperfection in the Church; and if we should continue in that way we would find ourselves like those of old, being led by error, superstition, ignorance, and by the cunning and craftiness of men. We would soon leave out here a little and there a little,

> here a line and there a precept, until we would become like the rest of the world, divided, disorganized, confused and without knowledge; without revelation or inspiration, and without Divine authority or power. (*Gospel Doctrine: Selections from the Sermons and Writings of Joseph F. Smith,* comp. John A. Widtsoe [Salt Lake City: Deseret Book, 1939], 149)

7–8 After completing the regulations of the Church in Zarahemla, Alma goes to the city of Gideon to declare the word of God to the people there according to the spirit of prophecy and revelation.

> *The words of Alma which he delivered to the people in Gideon, according to his own record.* [Note: This preamble was included in the original edition of the Book of Mormon published in 1830.]

CHAPTER 7

OVERVIEW

Alma speaks with the people of Gideon. He prophecies of the coming of the Messiah to bring about the Atonement. He will be born of Mary in the land of Jerusalem. His suffering and affliction will enable Him to succor us in our infirmities. Our duty to God is to walk blameless before Him so that we can receive the gift of eternal life. Alma leaves a prophet's blessing of peace upon the faithful people of Gideon.

1–6 Alma addresses the saints in Gideon, reporting that he has given up the judgment seat to another in order to work toward the much needed regulation of the Church in Zarahemla. He expresses hope that the saints in Gideon are not afflicted with pride, worldliness, and unbelief, as were the Saints in Zarahemla prior to their spiritual rebirth. He trusts that those in Gideon do "worship the true and the living God, and that ye look forward for the remission of your sins, with an everlasting faith, which is to come" (verse 6).

> *7 For behold, I say unto you there be many things to come; and behold, there is* ***one thing which is of more importance than they all****—for behold, the time is not far distant that* ***the Redeemer liveth and cometh*** *among his people.*

8 Behold, I do not say that he will come among us at the time of his dwelling in his mortal tabernacle; for behold, the Spirit hath not said unto me that this should be the case. Now as to this thing I do not know; but this much I do know, that the Lord God hath power to do all things which are according to his word.
9 But behold, the Spirit hath said this much unto me, saying: Cry unto this people, saying—Repent ye, and prepare the way of the Lord, and walk in his paths, which are straight; for behold, the kingdom of heaven is at hand, and the Son of God cometh upon the face of the earth.
*10 And behold, **he shall be born of Mary,** at Jerusalem which is the land of our forefathers, she being a virgin, a precious and chosen vessel, who shall be overshadowed and conceive by the power of the Holy Ghost, and bring forth a son, yea, even the Son of God.*

One thing which is of more importance than they all; the Redeemer liveth and cometh

The knowledge of the Redeemer and His atoning mission is of transcendent value in the grand scheme of things—nothing surpasses this in importance. The Savior taught: "And this is life eternal, that they might know thee the only true God, and Jesus Christ, whom thou hast sent" (John 17:3).

EVIDENCE: He shall be born of Mary

According to the report of Alma, the Savior would be born of Mary "at Jerusalem which is the land of our forefathers" (verse 10). Alma's prophecy that Jesus would be born "at Jerusalem" has drawn significant criticism since the Book of Mormon's first publication in 1830. As all Christians know, Jesus was born in the town of Bethlehem. However, with the discovery of ancient documents such as the Dead Sea Scrolls, it has become apparent that Bethlehem was anciently considered part of the "land of Jerusalem." (See *Echoes,* 211.)

*11 And he shall go forth, **suffering pains and afflictions** and temptations of every kind; and this that the word might be fulfilled which saith he will take upon him the pains and the sicknesses of his people.*
*12 And he will take upon him death, that he may loose the bands of death which bind his people; and he will take upon him their infirmities, that his bowels may be **filled with mercy,** according to the flesh, that he may know according to the flesh **how to succor his people** according to their infirmities.*

SUFFERING PAINS AND AFFLICTIONS; FILLED WITH MERCY; HOW TO SUCCOR HIS PEOPLE
What Alma describes is the nurturing power of Christ, who suffered, sacrificed, and loosed the bands of death that He would better be able to bless us in our weakness and infirmities. The Savior makes possible the liberation from sin (see 2 Nephi 2:7). He opens the gates of resurrection through His infinite and eternal Atonement and frees us from the shackles of the devil (see 2 Nephi 9:6–12). He gives us strength to do all things (see Alma 26:11–12). He provides a way to overcome temptation through His word and the power of prayer (see 1 Nephi 15:24–25; 3 Nephi 18:18). When we are scattered, struggling, wayward, and endangered, He seeks to gather and nurture us even as a hen gathers her chicks (see 3 Nephi 10:4–6). He will consecrate our afflictions for our gain (see 2 Nephi 2:2). He will console us (see Jacob 3:1), give us success (see Alma 26:27), support us (see Alma 36:3), and nourish and strengthen us (see 1 Nephi 17:3; Jacob 5:3–5, 11–12, 20–24). We see that the work of the Lord is solely to help us to come unto Him that we might be perfected in Him (see Moroni 10:32).

How do we apply these insights to our own lives on a daily basis? We should come to understand the goodness of our Savior and His overwhelming concern for our well-being in all aspects of our lives. He not only suffered in Gethsemane, died on the cross at Calvary, opened the gates through the power of the Resurrection, and provided all things for us to gain eternal life, but He has a continual concern for each of us individually. He lends us breath (see Mosiah 2:21). He goes before our face to guide us (see D&C 84:85–88). He lends us strength (see Alma 26:12). And He succors us according to our infirmities. Now, are we not filled with gratitude? In humility and thanksgiving we ought to show our love and appreciation by keeping His commandments and serving our fellowmen.

> *13 Now the Spirit knoweth all things; nevertheless* ***the Son of God suffereth according to the flesh*** *that he might take upon him the sins of his people, that he might blot out their transgressions according to the power of his deliverance; and now behold, this is the testimony which is in me.*

THE SON OF GOD SUFFERETH ACCORDING TO THE FLESH
Christ suffered all things in the flesh in order to know how to relate to our circumstances with infinite charity and benevolence. Our hearts should be full of gratitude for our Savior. We can trust in Him. He will heal us.

> *14 Now I say unto you that ye must* ***repent, and be born again;*** *for the Spirit saith if ye are not born again ye cannot inherit the kingdom of heaven; therefore come and*

be baptized unto repentance, that ye may be washed from your sins, that ye may have faith on the Lamb of God, who taketh away the sins of the world, who is mighty to save and to cleanse from all unrighteousness.

Repent, and be born again

Christ is mighty to save. He commands us to repent and be born again in order to inherit the kingdom of heaven. Our testimony of the Savior gives us strength to obey. Joy centers in our testimony of Jesus Christ and in the confirmation that others who are in our care are likewise motivated by the testimony of the Savior. Elder Neal A. Maxwell eloquently confirms this truth:

> At the gate to heaven, Christ, the King of kings, waits for us with open arms. He awaits not only to certify us, but also to bestow a Shepherd's divine affection upon His sheep as we come Home. The reality that, if we are worthy, we should one day be so warmly received by the Lord of lords and King of kings is marvelous beyond comprehension!
>
> Yet He cannot fully receive us until we fully follow Him. His love for us is unconditional and perfect, but ours for Him is clearly not. Being just, He cannot deviate from His standards by giving us blessings without our obedience to the laws upon which such blessings are predicated. His devotion to truth is such that even in His mercy, He cannot lie, including to Himself, about our readiness. He knows our weaknesses, but, mercifully, He also knows how to succor us as we seek to cope with them. And whatever weaknesses remain in us, He will tutor us and train us to exculpate these, if we will but let Him.
>
> Let others, if they choose, advocate lesser lords or causes for mankind. Only Jesus, truly and fully, advocates the basic and central cause of mankind. Christ's advocacy is advocacy with perfect empathy and mercy. Being sinless Himself, the wounds and scars He bears are actually ours. After all, He was "wounded for our transgressions." He loved us so dearly that He voluntarily laid down His life for us. Furthermore, even though He gives us demanding commandments and stern tasks, He has mercifully promised to prepare a way for us to keep and to fulfill all of them.
>
> Oh, how glorious and wonderful is "this Jesus Christ"!
>
> If contemplating the doing of all these things—to become more and more like Him—makes us feel discouraged, intimidated, and overwhelmed, we

need to remember that He never said it all had to be done in a day. Rather, if we could not travel fast, we could at least be steadfast and press forward, doing things in wisdom and order and in a pattern of paced progress, first achieving correct direction and then added momentum. It is the labor of a lifetime and more. (*Even As I Am* [Salt Lake City: Deseret Book, 1982], 33–34)

Help All People Come unto Christ by Following Him and His teachings

Just as He organized His church in His day, conferring His authority upon His brethren, commanding them to pursue the salvation of mankind, so has He in these latter days restored His church, and revealed His priesthood, and commissioned those who receive the priesthood to warn, expound, exhort, teach, and invite all to come unto Christ. Then, as members do come into His Church, He also commissions His priesthood to visit the house of each member, exhorting them to pray vocally and in secret and to attend to all family duties. For this is the only way to keep His kingdom strong. His charge to us is to be with and strengthen our brethren.

To those who diligently pursue such a course, miracles come to pass, evidenced by testimonies that declare: "He was dead, and is alive again; he was lost, and is found."

So wrote one sister. She, having been born and raised in another church, states that she and her Mormon husband lived the first years of their marriage without any religious activity. One evening two pleasant fellows appeared at their door and introduced themselves as home teachers. With little encouragement, they kept coming, month after month. Then the husband began, for the first time, to read such Church books as he had.

The sister said that when they moved to another town she packed the books away where she hoped her husband would never find them again. Sure enough, the couple again forgot about religion until other home teachers arrived at their new home.

After the first visit of these new teachers, her husband searched for his books until he found them. The sister states that the one teacher was so friendly that they couldn't help liking him, and when he began inviting them to Church affairs, they accepted because he seemed to really want them there and they didn't want to disappoint him.

"Finally," said the sister, "after calling for many months, he asked if he could offer a prayer in our home, and we didn't know how to refuse. So the first prayer ever offered in our home was by this home teacher.

"About this time our teenage son began to complain at being sent to my church while neither his father nor I was attending church ourselves. So we compromised by attending the Mormon Church and my church on alternate Sundays.

"Our home teachers had been calling on us for about two years when they asked if the missionaries might call. (We had had them in our former town, but I had refused to listen to them.) This time I agreed to hear the missionaries, but failed to make any effort to listen or understand, and refused to read any of the material that was given to me. After the fourth call, the missionaries handed me more pamphlets and suggested that I read fifty more pages in the Book of Mormon (I had read none of the book yet); then one of them said good-naturedly, 'Now you can get further behind.'

"Suddenly I was ashamed of my attitude and determined to read the entire Book of Mormon before his next visit. I carried out this promise, and when the missionaries returned I told them I wanted to be baptized. As a result of these efforts by the priesthood brethren, the family was unified and is now enjoying the true purpose of life in harmony with the principles and teachings of the gospel." (John H. Vandenberg, CR, October 1970, 11)

15–21 Alma encourages the people of Gideon to repent and covenant with the Lord through baptism to keep His commandments faithfully and receive eternal life. He then declares that he discerns through the manifestation of the Spirit of the Lord that they are righteous and have a strong faith.

22 And now my beloved brethren, I have said these things unto you that I might awaken you to a sense of ***your duty to God,*** *that ye may* ***walk blameless before him,*** *that ye may walk after the holy order of God, after which ye have been received.*

Your duty to God; walk blameless before him

This scripture defines the essence of the "duty to God" achievement program for the Aaronic Priesthood. The underlying doctrine applies to us all—men, women, and children. We are to listen to the prophets and follow their counsel.

23 And now I would that ye should be humble, and be submissive and gentle; ***easy to be entreated;*** *full of patience and long-suffering; being temperate in all things; being diligent in keeping the commandments of God at all times; asking for whatsoever things ye stand in need, both spiritual and temporal; always returning thanks unto God for whatsoever things ye do receive.*
24 And see that ye ***have faith, hope, and charity,*** *and then ye will always abound in good works.*

Easy to be entreated; have faith, hope, and charity

This scripture outlines the qualities of righteousness that we should all aspire to cultivate. As we apply this scripture to our lives, we will abound in good works. Alma issues to the people of Gideon a divine pattern for attaining happiness. The entire seventh chapter is an inspired invitation to come unto Christ, recognize His goodness, and acknowledge His desire to bless us (verses 11–12). As Alma closes his discourse, he admonishes both the people of Gideon and us to righteousness and good works.

25–26 Alma rejoices in leaving a prophet's blessing with the people, invoking the influence of the Lord upon them to keep them clean that they might ultimately "be brought to sit down with Abraham, Isaac, and Jacob, and the holy prophets who have been ever since the world began" (verse 25).

27 And now, may the ***peace of God*** *rest upon you, and upon your houses and lands, and upon your flocks and herds, and all that you possess, your women and your children, according to your faith and good works, from this time forth and forever. And thus I have spoken. Amen.*

Peace of God

Let us understand that our prophets care about our well-being. As Alma states, we can have peace "according to [our] faith and good works."

CHAPTER 8

OVERVIEW

Alma journeys to the land of Melek to regulate the affairs of the Church. The people respond obediently to his message. He goes to Ammonihah where the people revile him and reject his message. As he departs in sorrow, an angel commands him to return to deliver this divine ultimatum: repent or be destroyed. He encounters Amulek, who has been instructed in a vision to receive the prophet of God. Together, the two witnesses of the Lord preach repentance unto the people.

1–5 Alma returns to rest at his home in Zarahemla after having established the order of the Church in Gideon. Soon thereafter, at the beginning of the tenth year of the reign of the judges, Alma travels to the land of Melek, where the people are baptized throughout all the land.

> *6 So that when he had finished his work at Melek he departed thence, and traveled three days' journey on the north of the land of Melek; and he came to a city which was called* ***Ammonihah.***

Ammonihah

In the ministry of Alma and Amulek among the wicked inhabitants of Ammonihah we see demonstrated the valor, courage, and indomitable will of holy men who are sustained and supported by the power of God. Like missionary companionships today, these two prophetic messengers of the Lord embody the law of multiple witnesses according to which our Heavenly Father always establishes His truth among men. The central theme of the message imparted by Alma and Amulek is the same as that issued by missionaries in all dispensations, for they preach faith unto repentance and call the people to practice righteousness.

7–9 Alma begins to preach the word of God among the inhabitants of Ammonihah, but Satan has captured their hearts to such an extent that "**they would not hearken** unto the words of Alma" (verse 9).

They would not hearken

The Lord's universal message to all mankind is to repent and come unto Christ. The clarion call of all prophets is repentance. After Alma enjoys remarkable success in his ministry in Gideon and Melek, he travels north to the city of Ammonihah where he finds himself among the hard-hearted who resolutely defy his entreaties. Just as in the parable of the sower (see Matthew 13:1–23), the word is received at various levels of acceptance and preparation. Concerning the prophetic office of issuing a call to repentance, President Joseph Fielding Smith explained:

> "I think it is high time," the Prophet [Joseph Smith] wrote, "for a Christian world to awake out of sleep, and cry mightily to that God, day and night, whose anger we have justly incurred." The condition of the world should be, he wrote, as a stimulant "to arouse the faculties, and call forth the energies of every man, woman or child that possesses feelings of sympathy for their fellows, or that is in any degree endeared to the budding cause of our glorious Lord." The Prophet was inspired to call upon the inhabitants to turn from their sins, and the Lord has called the weak to call upon the great to repent. This epistle [of the Prophet on January 4, 1833] was much like the calls to repentance by the prophets in ancient Israel, and without any questions was necessary to be given to the world shortly after the restoration of the Gospel and the priesthood. (*Church History and Modern Revelation,* 4 vols. [Salt Lake City: The Church of Jesus Christ of Latter-day Saints, 1946–1949], 2:139)

Memories: The Persistence of Alma

Missionaries sometimes encounter rejection and persecution as they seek to take the message of our Savior Jesus Christ to all the world. Every missionary can tell his or her story, "I'll never forget the time when . . ." Such was the case with Elder Simpson, a wonderful missionary I had the pleasure of serving with in the England London South Mission. He, like Alma, had not been successful in a certain area—but he had the persistence of Alma. He had reviewed the area control book (containing the vital information about the area, including the names of former investigators). He found a family that had been taught the discussions two or three times previously. As the Spirit worked upon him, he and his companion were inspired to return there. Sounds familiar, doesn't it? Yes, they had success. This time the family was ready to make the commitment to be baptized. I will never forget his phone call. He was full of excitement and joy when he said, "Remember that family in Southampton that had been taught several times? They are going to be baptized! Isn't that great, President?" I too was full of joy for the family and for Elder Simpson and his companion. As the elders were obedient in reviewing the area control book, the Lord inspired them to know what to do . . . just like Alma and Amulek. (Ed J. Pinegar)

> *10 Nevertheless Alma labored much in the spirit,* ***wrestling with God in mighty prayer,*** *that he would pour out his Spirit upon the people who were in the city; that he would also grant that he might baptize them unto repentance.*

Wrestling with God in mighty prayer

Missionaries pray continually for success in bringing souls to Christ. Orson Pratt set a goal of bringing two hundred souls into the Church in Scotland. It is not wrong to seek a goal of bringing so many people into the Church. Remember that the Lord wants baptisms (see 3 Nephi 11), for this is the symbol of people coming unto Christ and taking His name upon them. It is the Spirit that converts, so we pray constantly that the Spirit will be poured out upon the people (see Mosiah 18:10–12; Alma 16:16; 19:36; Helaman 6:36). How do we feel about the souls of our fellowmen? (see Mosiah 28:3; Alma 29:9–10).

11–14 Alma is rejected by the people in Ammonihah. In sorrow, he departs for the city of Aaron. But an angel appears unto him on the way.

> *15 Blessed art thou, Alma; therefore, lift up thy head and rejoice, for thou hast great cause to* ***rejoice;*** *for thou hast been faithful in keeping the commandments of God from the time which thou receivedst thy first message from him. Behold, I am he that delivered it unto you.*
> *16 And behold, I am sent to command thee that thou* ***return to the city of Ammonihah,*** *and preach again unto the people of the city; yea, preach unto them. Yea, say unto them, except they repent the Lord God will destroy them.*
> *17 For behold, they do study at this time that they may destroy the liberty of thy people, (for thus saith the Lord) which is contrary to the statutes, and judgments, and commandments which he has given unto his people.*
> *18 Now it came to pass that after Alma had received his message from the angel of the Lord* ***he returned speedily*** *to the land of Ammonihah. And he entered the city by another way, yea, by the way which is on the south of the city of Ammonihah.*

Rejoice; return to the city of Ammonihah; he returned speedily

There is a lesson in the experience of Alma. Even though the people fail to heed his word, he still has reason to rejoice, according to the angel, for he has been faithful in keeping the commandments of God. This is the same angel who has guided Alma himself from a state of impenetrable hard-heartedness to transformational repentance in the early years of his life (see verse 15). How long does it take Alma to obey and return to the city? He returns "speedily" (verse 18)—another lesson in the quality of obedience for us to remember and emulate. This time Alma's message is even more urgent and imperative than before: repent or be destroyed. His ultimatum to the people of Ammonihah is swift, sure, and powerful, for he is teaching with the Spirit of the Lord.

19 And as he entered the city he was an hungered, and he said to a man: Will ye give to an humble servant of God something to eat?
20 And the man said unto him: I am a Nephite, and I know that ***thou art a holy prophet of God,*** *for thou art the man whom an angel said in a vision: Thou shalt receive. Therefore, go with me into my house and I will impart unto thee of my food; and* ***I know that thou wilt be a blessing unto me and my house.***
21 And it came to pass that the man received him into his house; and the man was called ***Amulek;*** *and he brought forth bread and meat and set before Alma.*

AMULEK; THOU ART A HOLY PROPHET OF GOD; I KNOW THAT THOU WILT BE A BLESSING UNTO ME AND MY HOUSE

Amulek is prepared through a vision to receive Alma. He recognizes Alma as a prophet of God and serves alongside him as a second witness of the truth.

As the faithful missionary companion of Alma, Amulek shares in the tribulation often attending the errand of the Lord, but also harvests the blessings of joy that come with covenant obedience. When we think of Amulek, we remember the spiritual lessons he teaches with power and authority: that prayer is a potent force for good ("But it is by the prayers of the righteous that ye are spared"—Alma 10:23; compare Alma 34:17–28); that the Lord will not come to redeem the people "in their sins, but to redeem them from their sins" (Helaman 5:10; Alma 11:33–37); that we should follow the Spirit in all things ("For I shall say nothing which is contrary to the Spirit of the Lord"—Alma 11:22); that the Resurrection is a certainty ("And even there shall not so much as a hair of their heads be lost; but every thing shall be restored to its perfect frame"—Alma 11:44); and that the infinite Atonement is essential for the salvation of mankind: "And behold, this is the whole meaning of the law, every whit pointing to that great and last sacrifice; and that great and last sacrifice will be the Son of God, yea, infinite and eternal" (Alma 34:14).

In Amulek, as we shall see, we have an example of one who is willing to relinquish all of his worldly possessions "for the word of God" (Alma 15:16) and suffer rejection by his family when he takes up the ministry (Alma 15:16). Amulek continues to serve the Lord with complete loyalty and righteous commitment.

22–29 Alma unfolds his prophetic agenda to Amulek and tarries with him for days. The Lord commands Alma to commission Amulek to join in the ministry of preaching repentance to the people. Thus Amulek receives his official calling as Alma's companion, a calling that will shortly prove highly effective in establishing the truth of the Lord's word in the mouths of more than one witness.

The Law of Witnesses

Whenever the Lord has established a dispensation by revealing his gospel and by conferring priesthood and keys upon men, he has acted in accordance with the law of witnesses which he himself ordained. This law is: "In the mouth of two or three witnesses shall every word be established." (2 Cor. 13:1; Deut. 17:6; 19:15; Matt. 18:15–16; John 8:12–29.)

Never does one man stand alone in establishing a new dispensation of revealed truth, or in carrying the burden of such a message and warning to the world. In every dispensation from Adam to the present, two or more witnesses have always joined their testimonies, thus leaving their hearers without excuse in the day of judgment should the testimony be rejected.

Joseph Smith, for instance, conformed perfectly to the law of witnesses in that someone else was always with him when priesthood or keys were being conferred by heavenly messengers. Both he and Oliver Cowdery had the Aaronic Priesthood conferred upon them by John the Baptist (D&C 13); both were present when Peter, James, and John brought back the Melchizedek Priesthood (D&C 20:2–3; 27:12–13); both were present when Elias, Moses, and Elijah came with the keys of their dispensations (D&C 110:11–16); and so it was with reference to every key, power, and authority that the Lord restored anew in this final dispensation—someone was always with the Prophet so that two witnesses could leave a binding testimony to the world. (Bruce R. McConkie, *Mormon Doctrine,* 2d ed. [Salt Lake City: Bookcraft, 1966], 436.)

The Holy Ghost "witnesses of the Father and the Son" (2 Nephi 31:18); he "beareth record of the Father and the Son" (Moses 1:24); he, and he only, makes known those holy beings whom it is life eternal to know. Jesus said: "He shall testify of me" (John 15:26); and, he "beareth record of the Father and me" (3 Nephi 11:32). And Paul said: "No man can say [meaning know] that Jesus is the Lord, but by the Holy Ghost." (1 Corinthians 12:3.) Thus the Holy Ghost is the source of saving knowledge; his mission, assigned by the Father, is to bear witness to the truth of those things which enable men to gain eternal life. His witness is sure; it cannot be controverted; it will stand forever. (Bruce R. McConkie, *A New Witness for the Articles of Faith* [Salt Lake City: Deseret Book, 1985], 267)

Memories: My Sheep Hear My Voice

When Alvin R. Dyer arrived in Frankfurt, Germany, on January 28, 1960, to begin his tenure as European Mission President, he brought with him an inspiring and powerful testimony of missionary work. At the time, I was serving in the mission home in Frankfurt and thus was on hand to record in my journal these comments about Elder Dyer: "Our first impression was that he was a big rancher. He had long David O. McKay-type hair. . . . His powerful jaw gave him a certain force and one saw that he was a great personality. Like most general authorities, he could look right through you." The day after his arrival, Elder Dyer called the mission staff together to instruct them in the particulars of his strategy for missionary work. At the heart of his plan was the universal principle that one must teach by the Spirit (D&C 50) and never engage in debate: "Again I say, hearken ye elders of my church, whom I have appointed: Ye are not sent forth to be taught, but to teach the children of men the things which I have put into your hands by the power of my Spirit" (D&C 43:15). Like Alma and Amulek before the lawyers of Ammonihah, Elder Dyer shunned descending into nonproductive dialogue of worldly terms, and instead embraced the high road of bold testimony-bearing as guided by the Spirit of the Lord.

One of the most striking and memorable points he made about the power of bearing fervent testimony concerning the truth was the following: When he served as president of the Central States Mission, he conducted a mission-wide research poll among all the converts of the mission, asking them to declare when they first knew that the gospel was true. Several thousand participated in the project. Elder Dyer learned that 82 percent of the converts knew the gospel was true the *first time they heard the missionaries bear witness of it.* Thus in most cases the transforming witness came not after a period of experience with the Church but *immediately* upon hearing the message for the first time as the missionaries spoke with the power of the Spirit. Elder Dyer testified that this phenomenon was a substantiation of the Savior's statement: "My sheep hear my voice, and I know them, and they follow me" (John 10:27). What a lesson for all as we accept the Lord's errand to convey the good news of the gospel to the peoples of the world. (Richard J. Allen)

30 And Alma went forth, and also Amulek, among the people, to declare the words of God unto them; and they were ***filled with the Holy Ghost.***

31 And ***they had power given unto them,*** *insomuch that they could not be confined in dungeons; neither was it possible that any man could slay them; nevertheless they did not exercise their power until they were bound in bands and cast into prison. Now, this was done that the Lord might show forth his power in them.*

32 And it came to pass that ***they went forth and began to preach and to prophesy*** *unto the people, according to the spirit and power which the Lord had given them.*

FILLED WITH THE HOLY GHOST; THEY HAD POWER GIVEN UNTO THEM; THEY WENT FORTH AND BEGAN TO PREACH AND TO PROPHESY

Through the power of the Spirit, we can accomplish our duties with courage and confidence. King Lamoni later confirms this truth to his missionary messenger Ammon: "I know, in the strength of the Lord thou canst do all things" (Alma 20:4). The Savior declared: "With God all things are possible" (Matthew 19:26). Do we feel in our heart that we can accomplish all needful things with the help of the Lord?

THE WYOMING COWBOY

I am going to [tell you a] story, quickly, about a young man who was called into the mission field. He felt inadequate for the call—his grammar was poor, he did not know how to talk to people, and he felt that he could not carry out his mission. The reason he had this inferiority complex was because he had to quit school when he was 15 years of age because his father passed away. This boy became the family breadwinner—he had to take over the ranch in Wyoming. The bishop assured him, however, that his place was in the mission field now that he was nineteen.

So into the mission field he traveled, half-way around the world, and there on his very first day he was told that Sister Johnson was having the missionaries for dinner, which was the custom of that mission. On the first day they went to her home and tasted the food of that land and learned something of the customs. Sister Johnson's husband was not a member of the Church. He knew the scriptures very, very well—he knew everything that a Mormon missionary did *not* know on his first day in the mission field. After dinner he would get these missionaries in a corner. He would try to embarrass them, and he found great delight in doing so. More often than not the missionaries went home determined that was not going to happen to them again, so they set their alarm clocks up thirty minutes earlier in order that they might get some extra studying in.

But here comes our young cowboy from Wyoming, feeling inadequate in his calling. Mr. Johnson was in the corner with him after dinner, and the missionary was embarrassed til tears came to his eyes. The thought came into his heart, "I will go to my mission president in the morning and tell him that I must be released. I have come into the mission field unprepared." Just then something lifted him right out of his chair, and he stood up to his full six-foot-four-inches of Wyoming cowboy. He reached over and took Mr. Johnson by the shoulders, and he pulled him in real close. He said, "Now, Mr. Johnson, I do not know how to argue these things with you. I do not know how to debate with you. I have not had a lot of schooling, but I know *why* I had to come half-way around the world. If you will just stand here for four or five minutes, I am going to tell you about it." Mr. Johnson had no choice. The young elder from Wyoming then had a captive audience. Then, for the next five or six minutes, this young cowboy from Wyoming told the man the Joseph Smith story—the story that rang true in his heart. He had been taught the story at the knee of his mother. He used to read the story as he rode the range. He loved it and he *knew* that it was true, and so he told it to Mr. Johnson with all of the sincerity of his heart. After five or six minutes had gone by, there were tears in other eyes.

To make a long story short, there was a baptism about four or five weeks later. I think you know who was baptized and who did the baptizing. Mr. Johnson had heard the Joseph Smith story from every missionary who had ever been in his home—some who had been all of the way through college, some who had their gifts developed; but never had he heard it with *the gift of the Spirit of God* like he heard it from the unschooled lips of a cowboy from Wyoming on that wonderful day. He was listening to something beyond the words that were traveling from lip to ear. There was something from the heart of this young missionary into his heart—bearing witness to him, "This young man is telling me the truth. Poorly as he is telling it, poor as his grammar is, I know that it is true because God is revealing it to me." And he joined this great church. (Robert L. Simpson, "Gifts of the Spirit," in *Outstanding Stories by General Authorities,* comp. Leon R. Hartshorn [Salt Lake City: Deseret Book, 1970–73], 1:179–180)

The words of Alma, and also the words of Amulek, which were declared unto the people who were in the land of Ammonihah. And also they are cast into prison, and delivered by the miraculous power of God which was in them, according to the record of Alma. [Note: This preamble was included in the original edition of the Book of Mormon published in 1830.]

CHAPTER 9

OVERVIEW

Alma tells the people of Ammonihah the truth—that they have forgotten the goodness of God to their ancestors. He calls them to repentance. They are to remember to be righteous—"after having had so much light" (verse 19)—or they will be destroyed by the Lamanites. They reject his words in anger. He prophecies of the coming Savior, who will redeem those who obey and are baptized. They attempt to imprison Alma, but he is protected by the power of God.

1–8 Alma begins to preach unto the people. They reject his message, saying that he is but one witness and that God would not destroy the city in one day. He boldly calls them to repentance for having so easily forgotten the goodness of God.

> *9 Do ye not* ***remember*** *that our father, Lehi, was brought out of Jerusalem by the hand of God? Do ye not* ***remember*** *that they were all led by him through the wilderness?*
> *10 And have ye forgotten so soon how many times he delivered our fathers out of the hands of their enemies, and* ***preserved them from being destroyed,*** *even by the hands of their own brethren?*

Remember, remember; preserved them from being destroyed

Alma preaches of the goodness of God—which the people of Ammonihah have forgotten or choose to ignore. He reminds them how often the Lord has delivered their ancestors from harm and death. Alma's remarks remind us that we should never forget the goodness of the Lord and His tender care over his children.

> *11 Yea, and if it had not been for his matchless power, and his mercy, and his long-suffering toward us, we should unavoidably have been cut off from the face of the earth long before this period of time, and perhaps been consigned to a state of endless misery and woe.*
> *12 Behold, now I say unto you that he commandeth you to repent; and except ye repent, ye can in nowise inherit the kingdom of God. But behold, this is not all—he has commanded you to* ***repent, or he will utterly destroy you*** *from off*

the face of the earth; yea, he will visit you in his anger, and in his fierce anger he
will not turn away.
13 Behold, do ye not ***remember the words*** *which he spake unto Lehi, saying that:*
Inasmuch as ye shall keep my commandments, ye shall prosper in the land? And again
it is said that: Inasmuch as ye will not keep my commandments ye shall be cut off from
the presence of the Lord.
14 Now I would that ye should ***remember,*** *that inasmuch as the Lamanites have*
not kept the commandments of God, they have been cut off from the presence of
the Lord. Now we see that the word of the Lord has been verified in this thing,
and the Lamanites have been cut off from his presence, from the beginning of their
transgressions in the land.

Repent, or He Will Utterly Destroy You; Remember the Words; Remember

Alma teaches the people a lesson on forgetting and remembering. When we forget our God and Savior Jesus Christ, we are left to ourselves. We are led away by the devil (see Alma 46:8). When we are blessed and prospered, we tend to forget God due to the ease of the way (see Helaman 12:2). We are constantly admonished through the scriptures and by our living prophets to remember—remember the commandments, remember the goodness and mercy of God, remember to keep the covenants we have made.

The word *remember* or a form of that word occurs frequently throughout the scriptures—over 110 times in the Book of Mormon and Doctrine and Covenants alone. As we have made covenants with our Heavenly Father, it is clear that the power to do good and be good is tied to our ability to remember these covenants. The ability to keep sacred things in our minds is also a part of our covenants that we might remember the goodness of God and keep the commandments. To remember is more than just recollecting a thought periodically. It means always to have the principle, doctrine, and covenant in our mind continually. In remembering, we should think upon the things of the Lord and in particular our covenants. This is a key point in living the gospel: "For as he thinketh in his heart, so is he" (Proverb 23:7). President Kimball reminds us, "When you look in the dictionary for the most important word, do you know what it is? . . . 'Remember' is the word" ("Circles of Exaltation" [Address to religious educators, BYU, 28 June 1968], 8). In the sacred ordinance of partaking of the sacrament we are commanded to remember the Lord Jesus Christ and to keep His commandments, and He promises us the blessing of the Spirit in our lives. Remembering is a key to a righteous life.

15–17 Alma tells the people that the Lord will be merciful unto the Lamanites because they are ignorant of the Lord's principles, having been taught the false traditions of their fathers. But the people of Ammonihah know better than to persist in their iniquity.

> *18 But behold, I say unto you that if ye persist in your wickedness that your days shall not be prolonged in the land, for the Lamanites shall be sent upon you; and if ye repent not they shall come in a time when you know not, and ye shall be visited with* ***utter destruction;*** *and it shall be according to the fierce anger of the Lord.*
> *19 For he will not suffer you that ye shall live in your iniquities, to destroy his people. I say unto you, Nay; he would rather suffer that the Lamanites might destroy all his people who are called the people of Nephi, if it were possible that they could fall into sins and transgressions,* ***after having had so much light*** *and so much knowledge given unto them of the Lord their God;*

Utter destruction; after having had so much light

Alma speaks with the spirit of prophecy and revelation in disclosing to the people that if they fail to repent, "after having had so much light" (verse 19), the Lamanites will come upon them to destroy them. That is exactly what comes to pass (see Alma 16:3, 10). That is also what eventually comes to pass for the entire Nephite nation, of which Ammonihah is merely the microcosm that presages the fall of the entire civilization through pride and iniquity.

20–25 Alma enumerates the choice spiritual blessings that the Nephite people have received from the Lord, having been favored above all nations of the earth, having enjoyed miraculous spiritual gifts, having been repeatedly delivered from bondage by a merciful God. If such a people should transgress "contrary to the light and knowledge which they do have" (verse 23), then it will be more tolerable for the Lamanites than for them—for they will "utterly be destroyed from off the face of the earth" (verse 24).

> *26 And not many days hence the* ***Son of God*** *shall come in his glory; and his glory shall be the glory of the Only Begotten of the Father,* ***full of grace, equity, and truth, full of patience, mercy, and long-suffering,*** *quick to hear the cries of his people and to answer their prayers.*
> *27 And behold, he cometh to redeem those who will be baptized unto repentance, through faith on his name.*
> *28 Therefore,* ***prepare ye the way of the Lord,*** *for the time is at hand that all men shall reap a reward of their works, according to that which they have been—if they*

have been righteous they shall reap the salvation of their souls, according to the power
and deliverance of Jesus Christ; and if they have been evil they shall reap the damna-
tion of their souls, according to the power and captivation of the devil.
29 Now behold, this is the voice of the angel, crying unto the people.

Son of God; full of grace, equity, and truth, full of patience, mercy, and long-suffering; prepare ye the way of the Lord

The message of Alma is centered on the Son of God, Jesus Christ, the Great Judge. The most persuasive dimension of Alma's reasoning with the people is that the Savior will redeem all who believe in His name and obey His commandments. That is the message of angels and the message of prophets from the beginning of time.

30–33 Alma entreats the people to repent, emerge from their darkness as "a lost and a fallen people" (verse 30), and show forth works of righteousness. They are **"angry"** with him (verse 32) and attempt to imprison him, but he cannot be confined because of the power of the Lord.

Angry

The people are angry with Alma for telling them the truth. How do we respond when the prophets tell us the truth—is it uncomfortable? Alma chastens the people to bring forth works meet for repentance. Their hearts have been hardened against the word of God. They have become a lost and fallen people. Their response is anger, and they seek to cast him into prison. We should always know that our prophets seek our welfare. Everything they do is for our sake—and the greatest thing we can do for our personal welfare is to listen to them and repent. Chastening helps us repent and return to righteousness. Unfortunately, we often are hurt by such words, frequently become angry, and sometimes rebel. What we fail to recognize is that chastening is a form of God's love toward us (see D&C 95:1–2).

34 Alma and Amulek go forth to continue their preaching.

CHAPTER 10

OVERVIEW

Amulek teaches the people of Ammonihah. He states his lineage and background, being a descendant of Joseph through Manasseh and Lehi. He reveals the details of his angelic vision in which he has been commissioned to care for Alma and work with him in the ministry. Amulek perceives the sinister thoughts of his audience—"ye are laying traps and snares to catch the holy ones of God" (verse 17)—and calls the people to repentance. He declares that only the prayers of the righteous have spared the city from destruction. He denounces the unrighteousness of the judges and lawyers, among whom is a man named Zeezrom, "the foremost to accuse Amulek and Alma" (verse 31).

1–3 Amulek preaches to the people. He traces his lineage back to Aminadi, "who interpreted the writing which was upon the wall of the temple, which was written by the finger of God" (verse 2), and thence back to Nephi, son of Lehi, "who came out of the land of Jerusalem, who was a descendant of Manasseh, who was the son of Joseph who was sold into Egypt by the hands of his brethren" (verse 3).

> *4 And behold, I am also a man of* ***no small reputation*** *among all those who know me; yea, and behold, I have many kindreds and friends, and I have also acquired much riches by the hand of my industry.*
> *5 Nevertheless, after all this, I never have known much of the ways of the Lord, and his mysteries and marvelous power. I said I never had known much of these things; but behold, I mistake, for I have seen much of his mysteries and his marvelous power; yea, even in the preservation of the lives of this people.*
> *6 Nevertheless,* ***I did harden my heart, for I was called many times and I would not hear;*** *therefore I knew concerning these things, yet I would not know; therefore I went on rebelling against God, in the wickedness of my heart, even until the fourth day of this seventh month, which is in the tenth year of the reign of the judges.*

No small reputation; I did harden my heart; for I was called many times and I would not hear

Amulek's self-characterization is analogous to the pattern of life being practiced by his listeners, the leadership of the city. They too are people of repute; they too have been called upon many times to receive the word of God, and they too have hardened their hearts against it. Thus Amulek is relating to them on their own terms, but with one exception: he has obeyed and is now stepping forth with courage to tell them the truth in the words of an insider. Just as Alma the Elder rose in majesty to defend the prophet Abinadi from the wrath of King Noah and his priests, Amulek now speaks with authority to his fellow countrymen and confirms the words of another prophet, Alma the Younger.

7–11 Amulek recounts his experience in beholding the angel of God who commissioned him to feed and house the fasting prophet of God. Amulek testifies that Alma is indeed a holy man of God and that he (Amulek) and his family have been blessed for their service.

> *12 And now, when Amulek had spoken these words the people began to be astonished, seeing there was* ***more than one witness*** *who testified of the things whereof they were accused, and also of the things which were to come, according to the spirit of prophecy which was in them.*

More than one witness

The Lord has proclaimed that His doctrine shall be established through the testimony of multiple witnesses: "In the mouth of two or three witnesses shall every word be established" (2 Corinthians 13:1; compare Matthew 18:16; D&C 6:28; 128:3; 2 Nephi 11:1–3). There is power in testifying as a witness for the Lord and in blending our voices with others to confirm the truth of the gospel of Jesus Christ.

13–16 The lawyers among Amulek's audience aspire to contend with him through rhetorical subtleties, hoping to lead him into a corner where he will be forced to contradict himself.

> *17 Now they knew not that Amulek could know of their designs. But it came to pass as they began to question him,* ***he perceived their thoughts,*** *and he said unto them: O ye wicked and perverse generation, ye lawyers and hypocrites, for ye are laying the foundations of the devil; for* ***ye are laying traps and snares to catch the holy ones of God.***
>
> *18 Ye are laying plans to pervert the ways of the righteous, and to bring down the wrath of God upon your heads, even to the utter destruction of this people.*

He perceived their thoughts; ye are laying traps and snares to catch the holy ones of God

The enemies of God have no understanding of the gift of discernment (see 1 Corinthians 12:10; D&C 46:23). So often in the accounts of the prophets of God we read of their being able to read the thoughts of their interrogators and listeners—to the condemnation of the wicked (as in this case) or to the inspired guidance of those in whom the light of the gospel is beginning to dawn (see the experience of Ammon with King Lamoni—Alma 18:16, 20). Through the light of Christ, all individuals receive, to one degree or another, the gift of being able to discern between good and bad, right and wrong (see Moroni 7:12–19). Church leaders who are called upon to be judges in Israel (such as bishops and stake presidents) follow the Spirit in discerning the hearts of those for whom they are responsible so as to be able to guide them in righteous pathways. Missionaries learn through the Spirit to discern the attitudes and feelings of those whom they are teaching. In the case of the prophets of God, such as Amulek and Alma, even the thoughts of the listeners are revealed—thus enabling these teachers of the gospel to proceed according to the operation of the Spirit.

19–21 Amulek reminds the people that if the majority among them chooses evil, the people will be ripe for destruction, just as King Mosiah warned (see Mosiah 29:27).

> *22 Yea, and I say unto you that if it were not for the* ***prayers of the righteous,*** *who are now in the land, that ye would even now be visited with utter destruction; yet it would not be by flood, as were the people in the days of Noah, but it would be by famine, and by pestilence, and the sword.*
>
> *23 But* ***it is by the prayers of the righteous that ye are spared;*** *now therefore, if ye will cast out the righteous from among you then will not the Lord stay his hand; but in his fierce anger he will come out against you; then ye shall be smitten by famine, and by pestilence, and by the sword; and the time is soon at hand except ye repent.*

It is by the prayers of the righteous that ye are spared

Amulek reveals to the people something that they have not perceived: that they are actually already well past the hour of destruction, and that only the prayers of the few righteous among them have postponed the day of their utter annihilation. This is further evidence of the power of prayer. Let us pray in faith, and the Lord will hear and answer our prayers. We may even now be on our knees importuning the Lord of mercy to guide and influence those in our circle who've strayed off the beaten track. These souls may never know of our anguish and concern on their behalf—but the Lord knows, and He will save them in His own due time.

24–25 The people are angry with Amulek and condemn his actions as contrary to their laws. Amulek speaks out with greater intensity and asks how it is that they have allowed **Satan** to gain such a hold on their hearts.

Satan

How is it that Satan can acquire influence and power over us? Only when we allow him to. When we yield ourselves to the things of the world, we yield ourselves to the devil. We must set aside the things of the world and turn to the things of God. Then Satan will be powerless to stop our forward progress. It is a choice. Father Lehi put it this way: "Wherefore, men are free according to the flesh; and all things are given them which are expedient unto man. And they are free to choose liberty and eternal life, through the great Mediator of all men, or to choose captivity and death, according to the captivity and power of the devil; for he seeketh that all men might be miserable like unto himself (2 Nephi 2:27).

26–30 Amulek denies having testified against their law—"but I have spoken in favor of your law, to your condemnation" (verse 26). He condemns the unrighteousness of their lawyers and judges. The people reject his words and plot against him.

> *31 And there was one among them whose name was* ***Zeezrom.*** *Now he was the foremost to accuse Amulek and Alma, he being one of the most expert among them, having much business to do among the people.*
> *32 Now the object of these lawyers was to get gain; and they got gain according to their employ.*

Zeezrom

Zeezrom (pronounced Zee-EZ-rum) is an example of the process of spiritual transformation, of rebounding from a life of sin to a life of service. He is a lawyer in the city of Ammonihah during the time that Alma and Amulek are preaching repentance in that part of the land. Zeezrom is "the foremost to accuse Amulek and Alma, he being one of the most expert among them, having much business to do among the people" (Alma 10:31). The strategy used by the lawyers is to stir up the people in order to generate suits and increase employment opportunities. Thus Zeezrom, "who [is] expert in the devices of the devil, that he might destroy that which was good" (Alma 11:21), is determined to question both Amulek and Alma with an eye to catching them in contradictory statements that can be turned to their destruction. His favorite stratagem of trickery is to impute to Amulek the false claim that the Son of God "shall not save His people" (Alma 11:35)—whereas Amulek, in his teaching, is simply making clear that the Lord cannot save people "in their sins" because "he hath said that no unclean thing can enter the kingdom of heaven" (Alma 11:36–37).

Despite his devious methods, Zeezrom is no match for these prophets of God, who, acting under the power of the Spirit, discern his thoughts and render impotent his evil intentions.

The more Amulek and Alma expound the doctrines of Christ and His atoning mission, the more fearful Zeezrom becomes, trembling under the burden of his growing awareness that his position is altogether wrong. Then Alma plants a seed of hope in the conversation as conveyed by the words of the Lord: "Therefore, whosoever repenteth, and hardeneth not his heart, he shall have claim on mercy through mine Only Begotten Son, unto a remission of his sins; and these shall enter into my rest" (Alma 12:34). Zeezrom is illuminated with the light of the gospel and is moved to repentance, as are many others who witness the testimony of the servants of God (see Alma 14:6–7).

The story has a happy ending. The initial encounter between Zeezrom and Alma and Amulek takes place around 82 B.C. Zeezrom's subsequent healing and baptism occurs not long thereafter, and the new convert begins "from that time forth to preach unto the people" (Alma 15:12). Several years later, Alma calls Zeezrom to accompany him, along with Amulek and others, to preach to the Zoramites in the land of Antionum (see Alma 31:6–7, 32). Following this mission, Zeezrom presumably continues his service in the ministry back in Zarahemla.

CHAPTER 11

OVERVIEW

The money system of the Nephites is outlined. Amulek and Zeezrom engage in a dialogue about spiritual matters. Amulek speaks with the power of the Spirit concerning the Atonement. Through Christ all shall be resurrected, but people must repent in order to be saved in the kingdom of heaven and enjoy eternal life. Zeezrom begins to tremble under the consciousness of his guilt.

1–19 Those in the legal profession are remunerated according to the time they devote to their calling. Details of the Nephite **money system** are outlined.

EVIDENCE: Money System—Comparable Weight and Measures (Alma 11:3–19)

A collection of Babylonian inscriptions called the "Code of Eshnunna" includes a description of an elaborate system of weights and measures. Included among the initial provisions of this ancient law is the text, "One kor of barley is (priced) at 1 shekel of silver." This resembles the language of the weights and measures system described in the Book of Mormon, a portion of which reads: "A senum of silver was equal to a senine of gold" (Alma 11:7). Furthermore, in Babylon the primary conversion was between silver and barley—precious metal and grain values were convertible to each other. The law in Alma 11 has the same conversion factor; the basic measure for silver or gold was equal to "a measure of barley." These similarities reveal just one more way that the culture in the Book of Mormon relates surprisingly well to ancient cultures. (See *Echoes,* 348–350.)

> *20 Now, it was for the sole purpose to get gain, because they received their wages according to their employ, therefore,* ***they did stir up the people*** *to riotings, and all manner of disturbances and wickedness, that they might have more employ, that they might get money according to the suits which were brought before them; therefore they did stir up the people against Alma and Amulek.*
> *21 And this Zeezrom began to question Amulek, saying: Will ye answer me a few questions which I shall ask you? Now Zeezrom was a man who was* ***expert in the devices of the devil,*** *that he might destroy that which was good; therefore, he said unto Amulek: Will ye answer the questions which I shall put unto you?*

They did stir up the people; expert in the devices of the devil

Zeezrom has one ultimate objective in mind: to enhance his professional standing and income. Little does he know that his "few questions" will backfire. Zeezrom, a practiced orator with considerable intellect and subtle, highly developed entrapment skills, and a man of God filled with the Spirit of the Holy Ghost are unequally matched in a contest.

> *22 And Amulek said unto him: Yea, if it be* ***according to the Spirit*** *of the Lord, which is in me; for I shall say nothing which is contrary to the Spirit of the Lord. And Zeezrom said unto him: Behold, here are six onties of silver, and all these will I give thee if thou wilt deny the existence of a Supreme Being.*

According to the Spirit

Amulek boldly declares from the beginning the source of his power—it comes from the Spirit of the Lord. He will say nothing contrary to the Spirit. What an example! When we find ourselves at a crossroads in our mortal experience—where our standards are subjected to skeptical scrutiny by those who disclaim the validity and operation of spiritual values—how do we respond? We can say, with Amulek, that we will proceed according to the operation of the Spirit of God, saying and doing nothing contrary to the Spirit.

23 When Zeezrom tempts Amulek by offering him money if he will recant, Amulek responds according to priesthood principles: "Reproving betimes [i.e., right away] with sharpness, when moved upon by the Holy Ghost" (D&C 121:43). Later on, Amulek and Alma will show forth "an increase of love" (ibid.) toward a reformed Zeezrom. For the moment, Amulek characterizes him as a "child of hell" and begins his own interrogation into Zeezrom's spiritual understanding.

24 Believest thou that there is no God? I say unto you, Nay, ***thou knowest*** *that there is a God, but thou lovest that lucre more than him.*

Thou knowest

Amulek discerns Zeezrom's innermost, unspoken belief in a divine Being and the reason for his suppressing this conviction: money.

25–33 Amulek and Zeezrom engage in a dialogue about God and the Son of God. Zeezrom falsely believes he has discovered a chink in Amulek's armor.

34 And Zeezrom said again: Shall he save his people in their sins? And Amulek answered and said unto him: I say unto you he shall not, for it is impossible for him to deny his word.
35 Now Zeezrom said unto the people: See that ye remember these things; for he said there is but one God; yet he saith that the Son of God shall come, ***but he shall not save his people****—as though he had authority to command God.*
36 Now Amulek saith again unto him: Behold thou hast lied, for thou sayest that I spake as though I had authority to command God because I said he shall not save his people in their sins.
37 And I say unto you again that ***he cannot save them in their sins;*** *for I cannot deny his word, and he hath said that no unclean thing can inherit the kingdom of heaven; therefore, how can ye be saved, except ye inherit the kingdom of heaven? Therefore, ye cannot be saved in your sins.*

But he shall not save his people; he cannot save them in their sins

For a moment, Zeezrom believes he has caught Amulek in a contradiction, as if Amulek has imposed upon God an edict that He will not be able to save His people. In fact, Amulek speaks the truth, for God cannot save people *in* their sins. There is only one way to gain exaltation: through the grace of

God and obedience to the gospel principles and ordinances (see 2 Nephi 25:23). We must repent. Allowance is made for the sinner who repents but not for the sin (see D&C 1:31–33).

38–45 Amulek gives an impassioned and inspiring statement about the Atonement and the indispensable role of faith in bringing about a remission of sins leading to eternal life. All mankind will be redeemed from the bands of death and "**stand before God**" at the bar of justice (verse 43) as resurrected beings, where "the wicked remain as though there had been no redemption made" (verse 41).

Stand before God

We will remember our past sins that have not been remitted through repentance and the grace of the Atonement. It is best to repent rather than suffer with such guilt.

> *46 Now, when Amulek had finished these words the people began again to be astonished, and also* ***Zeezrom began to tremble.*** *And thus ended the words of Amulek, or this is all that I have written.*

Zeezrom began to tremble

The impact of the Spirit impresses itself upon the locked mind and hardened heart of the lawyer. Why does Zeezrom tremble? Because of the consciousness of his guilt and iniquity in denying what he knows is true—that the gospel of Jesus Christ is the only sure foundation for salvation and eternal life—not worldly power, not money, not professional mastery, not fellowship with secular associates. We need to embrace the gospel with all of our heart, might, mind, and strength (see D&C 4:2; 59:5)—lest we find ourselves trembling in fear and guilt as does Zeezrom.

CHAPTER 12

OVERVIEW

Alma confirms the testimony of Amulek. He discerns the devious mindset of Zeezrom and exposes his hypocrisy. The mysteries of God are accessible only to those with contrite hearts. We will be judged by our words, works, and thoughts. Life is a probationary state in which we can demonstrate our obedience to divine laws. Through the Atonement of Jesus Christ the gift of the Resurrection is made possible to all, and the gift of eternal life to the faithful and obedient who merit the mercy of God.

1–2 Alma validates the words of Amulek and carries the discourse further, based on the scriptures.

> *3 Now Zeezrom, seeing that thou hast been taken in thy lying and craftiness, for thou hast not lied unto men only but thou hast lied unto God; for behold, he knows all thy thoughts, and thou seest that* ***thy thoughts are made known unto us by his Spirit;***

Thy thoughts are made known unto us by his Spirit

The key for dealing with unbelievers is to follow the Spirit. All those who embark in the service of God will from time to time encounter contrary spirits who tend to vilify divine truth and disparage the good news of the gospel of Christ. The Lord has made clear that the most powerful strategy in such cases is to teach by the Spirit (see Alma 11:21–22). The lawyers of Ammonihah are skilled in cunning rhetoric and opportunism. Among these is Zeezrom, he "being one of the most expert among them, having much business to do among the people" (Alma 10:31). In the case of Alma and Amulek, he sees the opportunity to stir up a great deal of business for himself and his colleagues. But he has no idea what kind of power he is taking on. These men of God, whom he mentally dismisses as unworthy foes, can discern his thoughts through the Spirit of God (see Alma 12:3), and thus lay open to view his pernicious plans. What Zeezrom intends as an attack on Alma and Amulek actually is a turning point in his own spiritual life. He soon comes to realize that his opponents, these trouble-makers with a proclaimed divine agenda, in fact, speak the truth. Far from shaming them with his legal manipulations, he takes up their cause, so powerful and persuasive is their witness of the Savior and His plan of redemption.

Pen Pal Convert

The following story teaches the need for careful preparation in order to teach doctrine to unbelievers:

> Helen Patten was in the fifth grade when she began writing to a pen pal by the name of Charlotte Alvoet in Dundee, Scotland. Helen told her what she did in Primary, later Mutual, and sent pictures of the Church's temples and other buildings, and places of interest in Utah.
>
> Last year an elder from Helen's ward, Bruce Draper, was called on a mission to Scotland. Since Helen secretly wished that he might teach the gospel to Charlotte,

she wrote a letter to Elder Draper, telling him about Charlotte and giving her address in case he should be assigned to work in Dundee.

About a week later Charlotte wrote to Helen telling her of the visit of two "Yanks." It so happened that Charlotte had gone to a concert, so she was not home when they first called. The elders waited about two hours for her return but finally they had to leave. They left word with her grandmother that they wanted to call again the following Saturday. Charlotte returned home about fifteen minutes after they left. When she heard of the visit, she was so anxious to see these young men that she wrote to Helen that she could hardly wait for the next Saturday to come.

The next letter Helen received began, "Guess who was baptized yesterday! Guess who will be confirmed tomorrow! Guess who is the happiest girl in the world! ME ME ME!" She went on to write that both she and her mother had been converted in only two weeks.

Subsequent letters told of her interest in church activities, her new friends, and her part in the branch's roadshow.

On August 21, she wrote the following:

"I just had to write this to you. I absolutely had to. I guess if I did not I would burst. Oh, the marvelous happening all because of being a Mormon. I must tell you from the beginning or I'll get too mixed up.

"You see, in Scotland we have no LDS schools, so when I was baptized I stayed at the school I had been attending previously, the Harris Academy. This is a Presbyterian school, where pupils of all Protestant faiths attend (Methodists, Episcopalian, and all that). In school we have one period each week for instruction in religion, and this is in the Presbyterian faith. Well, when I was baptized, there was little change since all we did was read the Bible. But this year our teacher decided that our religion period should be informal and should be a period for debate, so he said he would ask us to write one question that he would try to answer and that the class would discuss.

"I didn't ask one question—I asked six! I knew all the answers, but I wanted to explain our teachings and doctrine to him.

"I asked: (1) the interpretation of Rev. 14:6; (2) the meaning of 1 Cor. 15:29 (baptism for the dead); (3) which is the true church of Jesus Christ; (4) the nature of the Godhead (if they were three in one or three separate beings); (5) the correct method of baptism; (6) the reason for baptism.

"None of my friends had questions, so mine were all copied. Well, a fortnight later (yesterday) the teacher decided that we would discuss the question concerning the personality of our Father in heaven. He blithered on for a wee while about heathens and atheists. Then we got down to business. I brought up the belief of some that our Father, Jesus Christ, and the Holy Ghost are three in one. Since we don't believe that, I told him so. He asked me for proof, and was he surprised when I rattled off a list of scriptures! You see, I had sat up the night before reading the books I was given when the elders were teaching me. I read scriptures concerning our Father being separate from Jesus Christ and the Holy Ghost. After I had proved my point that they were not three in one, my master went on to another subject, saying, 'Of course, we all know God is a spirit,' and I read more scriptures about our Father in heaven having a body, hair, eyes, and back parts. It was marvelous. One thing led to another, and soon I was deep in telling the class the Joseph Smith story. I was inspired, and I know I had the Holy Ghost and the Spirit of the Lord within me as I talked. At the end I took over the class and was answering questions. Now twenty-one people know about Joseph Smith and heard my testimony as I bore it to them. They also saw the Book of Mormon.

"May God bless you always,

Love,

Charlotte"

(*Improvement Era*, April 1962; Leon R. Hartshorn, comp., *Inspiring Stories for Young Latter-day Saints* [Salt Lake City: Deseret Book, 1975], 202–204)

4–6 Alma exposes the agenda of Zeezrom, his detractor.

7 Now when Alma had spoken these words, Zeezrom began to tremble more exceedingly, for he was convinced more and more of the power of God; and he was also convinced that Alma and Amulek had a knowledge of him, for he was convinced that ***they knew the thoughts and intents of his heart;*** *for power was given unto them that they might know of these things* ***according to the spirit of prophecy.***
8 And Zeezrom ***began to inquire of them diligently,*** *that he might know more concerning the kingdom of God. And he said unto Alma: What does this mean which Amulek hath spoken concerning the resurrection of the dead, that all shall rise from the*

dead, both the just and the unjust, and are brought to stand before God to be judged according to their works?

They knew the thoughts and intents of his heart; according to the spirit of prophecy; began to inquire of them diligently

The veneer of self-righteousness is penetrated by the Spirit. There can be no safe shell of hypocrisy in the presence of the prophets of God. Alma and Amulek can read the thoughts of Zeezrom—and he knows it. It causes him to tremble before the power of God, and his arrogant self-confidence begins to evaporate. His authentic interest in truth begins to blossom.

9 And now Alma began to expound these things unto him, saying: It is given unto many to know the ***mysteries of God;*** *nevertheless they are laid under a strict command that they shall not impart only according to the portion of his word which he doth grant unto the children of men, according to the heed and diligence which they give unto him.*

Mysteries of God

The learning objective for us as the children of God is to come to know in full His "mysteries"—meaning the fundamental truths of salvation (Alma 12:9). The degree to which we may know His truth is dependent upon how open our hearts are to receive such truth, and on the heed and diligence we give to it. Thus the quality of our heart—how receptive it is, or how rejecting it is—will determine how much of His word is "found in us" at the last day (Alma 12:13, see also Alma 12:36). And how much of His word is found in us will determine our ultimate celestial future. Those who teach by the Spirit of God will know how much of the word to impart unto learners based on their willingness to be entreated and respond with obedience.

10 And therefore, he that will ***harden his heart,*** *the same receiveth* ***the lesser portion*** *of the word; and he that will* ***not harden his heart,*** *to him is given* ***the greater portion*** *of the word, until it is given unto him to know the mysteries of God until he know them in full.*
11 And they that will harden their hearts, to them is given the lesser portion of the word until they know nothing concerning his mysteries; and then they are taken captive by the devil, and led by his will down to destruction. Now this is what is meant by the chains of hell.

Harden his heart, the lesser portion; not harden his heart, the greater portion

The heart is the decision-making center of the soul and the affection center of our very being. We are an expression of our heart—it is who you are. A hardened heart prevents us from hearkening to the word of God (see 1 Nephi 2:18). The devil through his temptations can blind our eyes and harden our hearts (see 1 Nephi 12:17). A hardened heart prevents us from seeking answers from the Lord (see 1 Nephi 15:3, 10–11). We become past feeling when our hearts are hardened (see 1 Nephi 17:45–46). Our softened and easily-entreated hearts—even a broken heart and contrite spirit—are the sacrifice that we are to offer (see 3 Nephi 9:20). As many as will not harden their hearts can be saved (see Jacob 6:4), while those who harden their hearts will not be able to enter into the Lord's rest (see Alma 12:35–37). When hearts are hardened, people receive a lesser portion of the word (see Alma 12:10–11). When our hearts are hardened, we will forget the Lord and trample Him under our feet (see Helaman 12:2). Remember that a softened heart is the key to belief (see 1 Nephi 2:16) and understanding (see 3 Nephi 19:33), and that those who have the Lord's law written in their hearts will hearken unto Him and know righteousness (see 2 Nephi 8:7). If our hearts are pure, we can see God (see 3 Nephi 12:8). We must remember to treasure the things of God, for where our treasures are, there will be our hearts also (see 3 Nephi 13:21).

12–13 Alma confirms the words of Amulek concerning the judgment of God.

> *14 For our **words** will condemn us, yea, all our **works** will condemn us; we shall not be found spotless; and our **thoughts will also condemn us;** and in this awful state we shall not dare to look up to our God; and we would fain be glad if we could command the rocks and the mountains to fall upon us to hide us from his presence.*

Words, works, thoughts will condemn us

Let us remember that we are blessed or condemned according to our total performance: our words, our works, and our thoughts.

15–19 The Atonement of Christ overcomes physical death—all will stand as resurrected beings before the judgment bar of God. But there is also a spiritual death for the person who persists in wickedness, for "he shall die as to things pertaining unto righteousness" (verse 16) and be consigned to "everlasting destruction" (verse 17) as "though there had been no redemption made" (verse 18).

*20 But there was one **Antionah,** who was a chief ruler among them, came forth and said unto him: What is this that thou hast said, that man should rise from the dead and be changed from this mortal to an immortal state that the soul can never die?*
*21 What does the scripture mean, which saith that God placed cherubim and a flaming sword on the east of the garden of Eden, lest our first parents should enter and partake of the fruit of the tree of life, and live forever? And thus we see that there was **no possible chance that they should live forever.***

ANTIONAH; NO POSSIBLE CHANCE THAT THEY SHOULD LIVE FOREVER

A man by the name of Antionah (pronounced an-tee-AH-nah) is "a chief ruler" among the people of Ammonihah at the time Alma is preaching there around 82 B.C. (see verse 20). He challenges Alma concerning the doctrine of immortality through the Resurrection, citing the reference in the scriptures that Adam and Eve were prevented from partaking of the fruit of the tree of life by the placement of cherubim to guard the way: "And thus we see that there was no possible chance that they should live forever" (verse 21). His point opens the way for Alma to explain that the blessing of eternal life is conditional on faith and obedience in mortality.

*22 Now Alma said unto him: This is the thing which I was about to explain. Now we see that **Adam did fall** by the partaking of the forbidden fruit, according to the word of God; and thus we see, that by his fall, all mankind became a lost and fallen people.*
23 And now behold, I say unto you that if it had been possible for Adam to have partaken of the fruit of the tree of life at that time, there would have been no death, and the word would have been void, making God a liar, for he said: If thou eat thou shalt surely die.
*24 And we see that death comes upon mankind, yea, the death which has been spoken of by Amulek, which is the temporal death; nevertheless there was a space granted unto man in which he might repent; therefore **this life became a probationary state;** a time to prepare to meet God; a time to prepare for that endless state which has been spoken of by us, which is after the resurrection of the dead.*

ADAM DID FALL; THIS LIFE BECAME A PROBATIONARY STATE

Mortality is a probationary state. It is a time to prepare to meet God. During this time we cultivate a covenant-anchored hope in a resurrection of glory and the transcendent blessing of eternal life—based on our faith, obedience, and persistence in enduring to the end.

25–29 The plan of redemption brings about the Resurrection. If Adam and Eve had partaken of the tree of life, they would have suffered eternal misery. Therefore, a preparatory state was provided, angels were sent to proclaim the gospel message, and mankind was given the chance to receive eternal life through the plan of redemption.

> *30 And they began from that time forth to call on his name; therefore **God conversed with men,** and made known unto them the plan of redemption, which had been prepared from the foundation of the world; and this he made known unto them according to their faith and repentance and their holy works.*

God conversed with men

Since it is "expedient that man should know" the principles upon which salvation is made possible (verse 28), the Lord publishes among men the good tidings about the plan of redemption. Thus saving and exalting truth is made known unto those who call upon Him through prayer, exercise faith, repent, and do good works.

31–33 God reveals His plan of salvation unto mankind and commands them to repent and receive divine mercy through the Atonement of the Son of God. The alternative is to suffer a "second death" (verse 32), since justice will have to prevail in the case of the impenitent.

> *34 Therefore, whosoever repenteth, and hardeneth not his heart, he shall have **claim on mercy** through mine Only Begotten Son, unto a remission of his sins; and these shall enter into my rest.*

Claim on mercy

Here is the seed of hope that Alma plants in his dialogue with Zeezrom, Antionah, and the other listeners in the city of Ammonihah. There is a way to receive mercy and to enter into the rest of the Lord—and that is to repent and demonstrate a softening of the heart toward the things of God.

35–37 Alma bears solemn witness concerning the plan of redemption and the fundamentals of faith and repentance. Those who provoke God by persisting in wickedness will not enter into the rest of the Lord. Alma calls upon the people to respond according to the principles of righteousness. Once Zeezrom has seen the error of his ways, he becomes open to the witness of Amulek and Alma as they present the Lord's plan of salvation by the power of the Holy Ghost. Alma testifies of and enlarges upon Amulek's teachings. He teaches the word of God, warns his listeners against being hard-hearted, and sets forth in clarity the consequences of persisting in the neglect of God's commandments. To persist in rejecting the invitation to come unto the Lord will provoke Him, just as the early Israelites discovered at Sinai ("the first **provocation**"—Alma 12:36) when they reject the invitation to enter His rest.

Provocation

Provoking the Lord through disobedience and rebellion will disqualify us from entering into His rest. We need to relinquish our unyielding hearts and turn resolutely toward God in order to enjoy His blessings. Elder Neal A. Maxwell reinforces this point: "Events may turn against us, but if we are turning ever more toward God, we are on course. This is the only turning that really matters. Though that turning may bring with it an attendant churning, better the spiritual churning of a broken heart than an unyielding, hard heart" (*Men and Women of Christ* [Salt Lake City: Bookcraft, 1991], 130).

CONCLUDING THOUGHTS

Among the important lessons reviewed in these passages of the Book of Mormon is that the Lord's universal message to all mankind is simply to repent and come unto Christ. This message, delivered with unmistakable clarity by the Lord's chosen servants is always confirmed through the power of a second witness or even multiple witnesses. Not all will receive these witnesses willingly. Antionah and his colleagues in the leadership of the city of Ammonihah—with the exception of Zeezrom—rejected the message of Alma and Amulek when they came to preach around 82 B.C. The following year, in 81 B.C., the Lamanites came upon the so-called invincible city and destroyed it "in one day" (Alma 16:10).

The Lord has ordained that the most effective strategy for dealing with unbelievers is to always follow the guidance of the Holy Spirit in teaching them the truth. The quality of the listeners' hearts will determine how much of the word of God they will accept: hardened hearts are not a fertile seedbed for truth; but hearts that are broken and spirits that are contrite will be open to the blessings of spiritual knowledge.

We are reminded in these sacred passages from the Book of Mormon that there is power in treasuring up the word in our minds so that we can teach by the Spirit and bear testimony of the truth—especially as an additional witness. The law of witnesses has majesty. It is another way the Lord has of bringing credibility to His work. It has the power to establish truth.

In our desire to follow our Savior, we should always remember to examine the "state of our heart." Is it broken, easily entreated, and yielding to the Lord? If it is, our becoming as He is will be the result of our having a willing and humble heart.

CHAPTER 13

OVERVIEW

Alma explains that the priesthood after the holy order of the Son is given unto men of exceeding faith and righteousness "according to the foreknowledge of God" (verse 3), whereas the wicked altogether relinquish this divine blessing. The faithful are sanctified and made pure, that they may teach the commandments of God. Alma calls on the people to humble themselves as the people did in the days of Melchizedek. He pleads with the people to repent and prepare themselves to enter into the rest of the Lord. Angels will soon announce that Christ has come to earth to fulfill his atoning mission.

1 AND again, my brethren, I would cite your minds forward to the time when the
Lord God gave these commandments unto his children; and I would that ye should
remember that the Lord God ordained priests, after his holy order, which was after the
order of his Son, to teach these things unto the people.
2 And those priests were ***ordained after the order of his Son,*** *in a manner that*
thereby the people might know in what manner to look forward to his Son for
redemption.
3 And this is the manner after which they were ordained—being called and prepared
from the foundation of the world ***according to the foreknowledge of God,*** *on*
account of their exceeding faith and good works; in the first place being left to choose
good or evil; therefore they having chosen good, and exercising exceedingly great faith,
are called with a holy calling, yea, with that holy calling which was prepared with,
and according to, a preparatory redemption for such.
4 And thus they have been called to this holy calling ***on account of their faith,*** *while*
others would reject the Spirit of God on account of the hardness of their hearts and
blindness of their minds, while, if it had not been for this they might have had as great
privilege as their brethren.

Ordained after the order of his Son according to the foreknowledge of God on account of their faith

Alma establishes a further dimension of the contrast between faith and hardened hearts. Those with enduring faith are called to the holy order of the priesthood of God, whereas those with hardened hearts renounce claim to this supreme opportunity and blessing. We are continually blessed according to our faith and good works, both in the premortal realm and in mortality. We were prepared for our callings here upon the earth long before our birth. In the premortal courts of heaven we received our "first lessons in the world of spirits and were prepared to come forth in the due time of the Lord to labor in his vineyard for the salvation of the souls of men" (D&C 138:56).

5–6 The faithful are called to teach the gospel of Jesus Christ to the children of men, "that they also might enter into his rest" (verse 6).

> *7 This* ***high priesthood*** *being* ***after the order of his Son,*** *which order was from the foundation of the world; or in other words, being without beginning of days or end of years, being prepared from eternity to all eternity, according to his* ***foreknowledge*** *of all things—*
> *8 Now they were ordained after this manner—being called with a holy calling, and ordained with a holy ordinance, and taking upon them the high priesthood of the holy order, which calling, and ordinance, and high priesthood, is without beginning or end—*
> *9 Thus they become* ***high priests forever,*** *after the order of the Son, the Only Begotten of the Father, who is without beginning of days or end of years, who is full of grace, equity, and truth. And thus it is. Amen.*

High priesthood after the order of his Son; foreknowledge; high priests forever

Alma continues to explain the principle of foreordination. Many children of God are foreordained (called and set apart) to future assignments prior to coming here to the earth (see also Jeremiah 1:5; D&C 138:53–57; Abraham 3:22–23). Those who are foreordained exhibited exceeding faith and good works. While it is true that we have all been sent to the earth to prove ourselves worthy through correct choices and righteous actions, foreordination does not override the agency of man—we are free to choose whether we will fulfill our mission in life or not.

President Spencer W. Kimball confirmed this truth:

> Remember, in the world before we came here, faithful women were given certain assignments while faithful men were foreordained to certain priesthood tasks. While we do not now remember the particulars, this does not alter the glorious reality of what we once agreed to. We are accountable for those things which long ago were expected of us just as are those whom we sustain as prophets and apostles. (*My Beloved Sisters* [Salt Lake City: Deseret Book, 1979], 37)

Moreover, concerning the principle of foreordination, Elder Bruce R. McConkie has stated:

> Since men are foreordained to gain exaltation, and since no man can be exalted without the priesthood, it is almost self-evident that worthy brethren were foreordained to receive the priesthood. And so we find Alma teaching that those who hold the Melchizedek Priesthood in this life were "called and prepared from the foundation of the world according to the foreknowledge of God." (Alma 13:1–12.) And Joseph Smith said, "Every man who has a calling to minister to the inhabitants of the world," and this includes all who hold the Melchizedek Priesthood, "was ordained to that very purpose in the Grand Council of heaven before this world was. I suppose that I was ordained to this very office in that Grand Council." (*Teachings,* 365.) (*Doctrinal New Testament Commentary* [Salt Lake City: Bookcraft, 1965–1973], 3:329)

The Doctrine of Foreordination

Foreordination is the premortal selection of individuals to come forth in mortality at specified times, under certain conditions, and to fulfill predesignated responsibilities. In LDS interpretation, "foreordained" does not mean predetermined (see Predestination). It is the outcome of voluntary choice, not the violation or abrogation of it. The idea of preexistence and premortal preparation for earth life is hinted at in biblical sources, and evidence of it appears in some early Jewish-Christian sources. But it has been less prominent in later thought.

Difference between Foreordination & Predestination outlined

Abraham was told that he was included among the valiant spirits and was therefore chosen or *foreordained* before his birth to be a leader in God's kingdom on earth (Abr. 3:22–23). The Lord likewise informed Jeremiah, "Before I formed thee in the belly I knew thee; and . . . I ordained thee a prophet unto the nations" (Jer. 1:5). Alma 2 taught that priests belonging to a "holy order" were foreordained "according to the foreknowledge of God, on account of their exceeding faith and good works" (Alma 13:1, 3). The Prophet Joseph Smith concluded that "every man who has a calling to minister to the inhabitants of the world was ordained to that very purpose in the Grand Council of heaven before this world was" (*TPJS,* 365). And in addition to these foreordinations to priesthood callings, many spirits may have been foreordained to specific nations and generations, which Paul characterized as the "bounds of habitation" (Acts 17:26), as well as to families and to varied assignments, work, or missions on earth.

While each of these selections is ultimately based on the omniscience and foreknowledge of God, several factors may influence one's earthly circumstances. Foreordination comes as a blessing or reward for premortal righteousness and valiant commitment to Jesus Christ. Birth into the house of Israel and heirship to all the blessings of Abraham, Isaac, and Jacob are often seen as the birthright of dedicated souls (see Eph. 1:4–5; Rom. 9:4). These rights and blessings may still be obtained by any and all who elect to receive them, whether in this life or the next. People sooner or later will manifest, as Elder B. H. Roberts, of the Seventy, taught, "the strength of that intelligence and nobility to which their spirits had attained in the heavenly kingdom before they took bodies upon earth" (T. Madsen, *Defender of the Faith* [Salt Lake City, 1980], 2). The Doctrine and Covenants teaches that men and women may come to God through righteousness and diligence and thus become numbered with those who are "sons [and daughters] of Moses and of Aaron and the seed of Abraham, and the church and kingdom, and the elect of God" (D&C 84:34).

Through faithfulness on earth, whatever one's premortal foreordination or prior covenants, one may, as Paul taught, become "adopted" into the favored lineage: "They are not all Israel, which are of Israel" (Rom. 9:6). Many, that is, may be foreordained to high missions in mortality, but may, through sin and rebellion, fail in their foreordinations and give up their blessings. Obedience to the covenants and ordinances of the gospel is a primary factor in determining ultimate election to the chosen lineage.

Latter-day Saints further believe that the times, places, and circumstances of birth into mortality may be the outcome of former covenants and decisions as well as that which would be best, in divine wisdom, to provide both opportunities and challenges for the individual's growth and development. Additionally, foreordination may also be based on God's own purposes and plans to bless all of his children. The specifics of these factors remain unclear. As a result, a person's premortal character can never be judged by his or her present station in life. Some of the most bitter and arduous circumstances may be, in the perspective of eternity, the most blessed, and perhaps even the situations that men and women elected and agreed to enter. Foreordination does not preclude the exercise of agency. Foreordination is a *conditional* preappointment to or bestowal of certain blessings and responsibilities.

Following Augustine and Calvin, some have interpreted the word "predestine" in Romans 8:29–30 and Ephesians 1:4–5 as meaning divine precausation. In this view, God is the ultimate causal agent, whereas man is always and only an effect. Latter-day Saints reject this interpretation. They believe that neither the Greek nor related scriptural sources lead to this view. Paul's usage of this term refers to being foreordained to divine sonship through Christ. Furthermore, since God knows "all things, for all things are present before [his] eyes" (D&C 38:1–2), he anticipates our choices. However, he does not make the choices for us. Knowing our potential, he foreordains those who will help to bring about his purposes. Latter-day Saints extend this concept to embrace foreordination to any divinely appointed ministry or function. (Brent L. Top in *Encyclopedia of Mormonism,* ed. Daniel H. Ludlow [New York: Macmillan, 1992], 521–522)

10 Now, as I said concerning the holy order, or this ***high priesthood,*** *there were many who were ordained and became high priests of God; and it was on account of their exceeding faith and repentance, and their righteousness before God, they choosing to repent and work righteousness rather than to perish;*
11 Therefore they were called after this holy order, and were ***sanctified,*** *and their garments were washed white through the blood of the Lamb.*
12 Now they, after being ***sanctified*** *by the Holy Ghost, having their garments made white, being pure and spotless before God, could not look upon sin save it were with abhorrence; and there were many, exceedingly great many, who were made pure and entered into the rest of the Lord their God.*

High priesthood; sanctified

What is meant by sanctification? Sanctification is a process of purification before God. We are sanctified when we are actually purified through the atoning blood of Christ and made innocent and holy. Through the grace of God, we can become sanctified in Christ, made clean and pure by the power of the Holy Ghost (see 3 Nephi 27:19–20; Alma 5:54; Moroni 10:32–33). This sanctification comes through the Atonement of Christ as we receive the principles and ordinances of His gospel and yield our hearts to God (Helaman 3:35). Sanctification is more than just doing: it is a "becoming" within our soul—a mighty change, a heart yielding to the enticings of the Spirit and to God (see Mosiah 3:19). Then we, being sanctified, are prepared, made holy, consecrated, and set apart for sacred service. Let us therefore seek to become clean and pure by the power of the Holy Ghost.

13 And now, my brethren, I would that ye should humble yourselves before God, and bring forth fruit meet for repentance, that ye may also enter into that rest.
14 Yea, humble yourselves even as the people in the days of ***Melchizedek,*** *who was also a high priest after this same order which I have spoken, who also took upon him the high priesthood forever.*
15 And it was this same ***Melchizedek*** *to whom Abraham paid tithes; yea, even our father Abraham paid tithes of one-tenth part of all he possessed.*
16 Now these ordinances were given after this manner, that thereby the people might look forward on the Son of God, it being a type of his order, or it being his order, and this that they might look forward to him for a remission of their sins, that they might enter into the rest of the Lord.
17 Now this ***Melchizedek*** *was a king over the land of Salem; and his people had waxed strong in iniquity and abomination; yea, they had all gone astray; they were full of all manner of wickedness;*
18 But ***Melchizedek*** *having exercised mighty faith, and received the office of the high priesthood according to the holy order of God, did preach repentance unto his people. And behold, they did repent; and* ***Melchizedek*** *did establish peace in the land in his days; therefore he was called the prince of peace, for he was the king of Salem; and he did reign under his father.*
19 Now, there were many before him, and also there were many afterwards, but none were greater; therefore, of him they have more particularly made mention.

Melchizedek, Ancient King of Righteousness

In his treatise on the priesthood before the hard-hearted leaders and citizens of Ammonihah around 82 B.C., Alma provides insights concerning the ancient king and priesthood leader to whom Abraham paid tithes (see Genesis 14:18–20; Hebrews 5:6; 7:1–3). Note the context for Alma's invoking the example of Melchizedek: Having explained to the people of Ammonihah that "it was expedient that man should know concerning the things whereof [the Lord] had appointed unto them" (Alma 12:28), Alma lays out the details of the plan of salvation as proclaimed by angels and confirmed and administered by those called and authorized "after the order of the Son, the Only Begotten of the Father" (Alma 13:9). In this remarkable discourse, Alma teaches the people that priesthood callings were initiated during the premortal existence where, in harmony with the principle of free agency, the faithful were foreordained "according to the foreknowledge of God, on account of their exceeding faith and good works" (Alma 13:3). Thus Alma impresses upon his listeners the startling truth about who they really are: sons and daughters of God with a marvelous opportunity and destiny to choose the right and honor their divine heritage.

Having established this eternal framework, Alma then reminds them of the example of their great forebear, King Melchizedek, who likewise had to issue the supreme call for repentance among his people before they could rise to the level of their potential and become a nation of peace. Here is evidence of the opportunity that lay before the people of Ammonihah. By honoring their relationship with God and fulfilling their covenant obligations through repentance and faith, they can participate in the glorious plan of redemption and look forward with hope to the imminent coming of the Son of God. This is Alma's impassioned and inspired appeal to the people—one that, with few exceptions, is rejected.

20–26 Alma consummates his discourse on the Atonement of Christ by reiterating the fact that angels are even now declaring the good news of salvation among all the Lord's people "in plain terms, that we may understand, that we cannot err" (verse 23). The prophecies of old will soon be confirmed by the angelic news that the Lord has come to earth to fulfill His mission of redemption and reconciliation.

> *27 And now, my brethren, I wish* ***from the inmost part of my heart,*** *yea, with great anxiety even unto pain, that ye would hearken unto my words, and cast off your sins, and not procrastinate the day of your repentance;*
> *28 But that ye would humble yourselves before the Lord, and call on his holy name, and watch and pray continually, that ye may not be tempted above that which ye*

> *can bear, and thus* ***be led by the Holy Spirit,*** *becoming humble, meek, submissive, patient, full of love and all long-suffering;*
> *29* ***Having faith on the Lord;*** *having a hope that ye shall receive eternal life; having the love of God always in your hearts, that ye may be lifted up at the last day and* ***enter into his rest.***
> *30 And may the Lord grant unto you repentance, that ye may not bring down his wrath upon you, that ye may not be bound down by the chains of hell, that ye may not suffer the second death.*

From the inmost part of my heart; be led by the Holy Spirit; having faith on the Lord; enter into his rest

What is the message of the prophets? That we accept the gospel, take upon ourselves the divine nature, and become worthy to enter into the rest of the Lord. This is Alma's final exhortation: to be repentant and faithful. His overwhelming concern for his fellowmen is demonstrated by his anxiety that they—and we—might hearken unto his words and take action by repenting and not procrastinating. The prophets and true Saints have these feelings for their fellowmen (see 2 Nephi 33:3; Enos 1:9,11; Mosiah 28:3; Alma 6:6; Alma 29:9–10; Alma 34:33–35). Alma exhorts us to be humble, watch always, and pray constantly. Faith in the Lord, hope for eternal life, and charity in our hearts will be the outcomes of our quest, and then we will be as He is (see Moroni 7:48).

> *31 And Alma spake many more words unto the people, which are not written in this book.*

EVIDENCE: Tenfold Repetitions (Mosiah 2–5; 2 Nephi 4:16–35; Alma 12–13; Alma 31:26–35; Alma 33:4–11)

Interestingly, the name of the Lord is mentioned ten times in King Benjamin's speech in the book of Mosiah—seven times as *Lord God* and three as *Lord Omnipotent.* In addition, the word *Lord* also appears ten times in the psalm of Nephi, and the words *Lord* and *Son* are each mentioned ten times in Alma's powerful speech found in Alma 12–13. Furthermore, the phrase *O Lord* is found ten times in Alma's prayer in Antionum, while the poem of Zenos quoted by Alma (see Alma 33) contains ten uses of the word *hear.* Though we do not know for certain, it would seem that these tenfold occurrences might relate to the Israelites' reverence for the Ten Commandments. It is doubtful that Joseph Smith noticed the tenfold repetitions in the Book of Mormon, and even more unlikely that *anyone* in 1829 would have sensed the important place of the number ten in ancient minds. (See *Echoes,* 332–333.)

CHAPTER 14

OVERVIEW

Many believe Alma's words and repent, but the majority revile against the two prophets. Zeezrom pleads their cause, but he is cast out and the believers are martyred in the fire. The Spirit constrains Alma to remain impassive for the sake of justice. Alma and Amulek are imprisoned and subjected to cruel abuse for many days. Alma prays for deliverance and the power of God is made manifest. The prison is destroyed by an earthquake. The wicked priests and lawyers perish. The people flee "even as a goat fleeth with her young from two lions" (verse 29).

1–7 Many who hear Alma believe his words and begin to repent and search the scriptures, but more revile against the two prophets and take them bound before the chief judge, accusing them of acting against the law of the land and promoting false doctrine. Zeezrom intervenes on behalf of Alma and Amulek, confessing his own guilt and proclaiming the two prophets to be "spotless before God" (verse 7). The people cast Zeezrom out and stone those who believe Alma and Amulek.

> *8 And they brought their wives and children together, and **whosoever believed** or had been taught to believe in the word of God **they caused that they should be cast into the fire;** and they also brought forth their records which contained the holy scriptures, and cast them into the fire also, that they might be burned and destroyed by fire.*
> *9 And it came to pass that they took Alma and Amulek, and carried them forth to the place of martyrdom, that they might witness the destruction of those who were consumed by fire.*
> *10 And when Amulek saw the pains of the women and children who were consuming in the fire, he also was pained; and he said unto Alma: How can we witness this awful scene? Therefore let us stretch forth our hands, and exercise the power of God which is in us, and save them from the flames.*
> *11 But Alma said unto him: **The Spirit constraineth me that I must not stretch forth mine hand;** for behold the Lord receiveth them up unto himself, in glory; and he doth suffer that they may do this thing, or that the people may do this thing unto them, according to the hardness of their hearts, that the judgments which he shall exercise upon them in his wrath may be just; and the blood of the innocent shall stand as a witness against them, yea, and cry mightily against them at the last day.*

Whosoever believed they caused that they should be cast into the fire; the Spirit constraineth me that I must not stretch forth mine hand

The righteous often suffer persecution for the sake of the gospel. The harvest of Alma and Amulek's season of preaching in the city of Ammonihah is only modest. The greater part of the people refuse to believe in the words they have heard, reviling instead against the men of God and condemning the circle of believers to a fiery martyrdom. The Spirit constrains Alma from intervening to stop this grievous persecution of the innocent. Why? Because the Lord has received the righteous victims "up unto himself" (verse 11)—and so that the impending judgments of God upon the wicked perpetrators "may be just" (ibid.).

Concerning the suffering of the innocent, Joseph Smith Jr., wrote these words from Liberty Jail on December 16, 1838: "Dear brethren, do not think that our hearts faint, as though some strange thing had happened unto us, for we have seen and been assured of all these things beforehand, and have an assurance of a better hope than that of our persecutors. Therefore God hath made broad our shoulders for the burden. We glory in our tribulation, because we know that God is with us, that He is our friend, and the He will save our souls. We do not care for them that can kill the body; they cannot harm our souls" (*HC* 3:227).

President Harold B. Lee formulated the following statement concerning universal persecution for the cause of righteousness:

> To be persecuted for righteousness sake in a great cause where truth and virtue and honor are at stake is god-like. Always there have been martyrs to every great cause. The great harm that may come from persecution is not from the persecution itself but from the possible effect it may have upon the persecuted who may thereby be deterred in their zeal for the righteousness of their cause. Much of that persecution comes from lack of understanding, for men are prone to oppose that which they do not comprehend. Some of it comes from men intent upon evil. But from whatever cause, persecution seems to be so universal against those engaged in a righteous cause. (*Decisions for Successful Living* [Salt Lake City: Deseret Book, 1973], 61–62)

12 Now Amulek said unto Alma: Behold, perhaps they will burn us also.
13 And Alma said: Be it according to the will of the Lord. But, behold, ***our work is not finished;*** *therefore they burn us not.*

Memories: Our Work Is Not Finished

During the throes of persecution and adversity, the Prophet Joseph Smith not infrequently consoled his companions with good cheer by saying that his mission was not yet complete and that the Lord would protect and preserve him until that day. When Alma and Amulek were forced to witness the fiery martyrdom of the faithful Saints in Ammonihah at the hands of the incorrigible priests of Nehor, a similar scene of concern and consolation transpired: "Now Amulek said unto Alma: Behold, perhaps they will burn us also. And Alma said: Be it according to the will of the Lord. But, behold, our work is not finished; therefore they burn us not" (Alma 14:12–13). And thus these two prophets of God were preserved miraculously to continue with their labors until their mission upon the earth was done.

That same kind of calm, dignified reassurance that God's work would move forward unimpeded was evidenced by the Prophet Joseph Smith while attending to some business in Montrose, Iowa, across the river from Nauvoo, on Saturday, August 6, 1842. On that occasion, he was engaging in relaxing conversation with some of his colleagues as they were drinking ice water in the shade of a school house. His tumbler in hand, the Prophet gave voice to visionary inspiration: "I prophesied that the Saints would continue to suffer much affliction and would be driven to the Rocky Mountains, many would apostatize, others would be put to death by our persecutors or lose their lives in consequence of exposure or disease, and some of you will live to go and assist in making settlements and build cities and see the Saints become a mighty people in the midst of the Rocky Mountains" (*HC* 5:85). A participant, Anson Call, recalled: "It is impossible to represent in words this scene which is still vivid in my mind, of the grandeur of Joseph's appearance, his beautiful description of this land, and his wonderful prophetic utterances as they emanated from the glorious inspirations that overshadowed him" (86). The Prophet gave voice to an inspired view of how God's people would continue the work of the Restoration and extend the blessings of the Abrahamic Covenant to the world—in spite of all persecution and reversal, all challenges and adversity. The Lord had already revealed to Joseph in reassuring words given in Liberty Jail that he would be preserved until the completion of his earthy mission. "Thy days are known, and thy years shall not be numbered less; therefore, fear not what man can do, for God shall be with you forever and ever" (D&C 122:9). Similarly, each one of us, through our prayers of faith and hope, can experience the calming peace of the Spirit in the assurance that our earthly sojourn will continue under the protection of the Almighty until our foreordained mission on earth is complete. (Richard J. Allen)

14–24 Alma and Amulek remain silent in the face of derision for their inaction to save the believers. They are confined to prison and deprived of the necessities of life for many days. Their detractors continue to threaten and cruelly torment them.

25 And it came to pass that they all went forth and smote them, saying the same words,
even until the last; and when the last had spoken unto them ***the power of God was***
upon Alma and Amulek, *and they rose and stood upon their feet.*
26 And Alma cried, saying: How long shall we suffer these great afflictions, O Lord?
O Lord, ***give us strength according to our faith which is in Christ,*** *even unto*
deliverance. And they broke the cords with which they were bound; and when the
people saw this, they began to flee, for the fear of destruction had come upon them.
27 And it came to pass that so great was their fear that they fell to the earth, and did
not obtain the outer door of the prison; and ***the earth shook mightily,*** *and the walls*
of the prison were rent in twain, so that they fell to the earth; and the chief judge, and
the lawyers, and priests, and teachers, who smote upon Alma and Amulek, were slain
by the fall thereof.

The power of God was upon Alma and Amulek; give us strength according to our faith which is in Christ; the earth shook mightily

Alma prays fervently for the power of God to be upon them in their dire circumstances. His example resonates with us today and raises an important question of conscience: When we face daunting challenges and adversity—particularly for the sake of the gospel cause—is our first thought to pray for strength to overcome and prevail?

28–29 After many days of silent suffering and abuse in prison, Alma and Amulek are empowered by the Spirit, **"according to their faith"** (verse 28), to invoke judgment upon the Nehorian priests of the city. The prison is destroyed by an earthquake, taking down the dynasty of wicked priests and allowing the two prophets of God to emerge unscathed. As the prophet-abridger Mormon aptly describes it, the people of the city flee in panic, "even as a goat fleeth with her young from two lions" (Alma 14:29).

According to their faith

There is a great principle demonstrated in how the Lord's anointed deal with the trials they encounter. Recall that when Nephi was bound by his brothers he prayed for strength to burst the bands (see 1 Nephi 7:17). So likewise did Alma pray for strength. Like Nephi, Alma and Amulek are freed according to their faith. This is the lesson: Pray for strength to overcome—not for the challenges and problems to go away. Remember, in the strength of the Lord we can do all things (see Alma 20:4; 26:11–12).

CHAPTER 15

OVERVIEW

Alma and Amulek are sent to Sidom, where they establish the Church among the refugees from Ammonihah and the faithful throughout the region. Alma heals Zeezrom, who is baptized and becomes a teacher among the people. Amulek, who has sacrificed all for the sake of Christ, goes with Alma to his home in Zarahemla.

1–4 Alma and Amulek are commanded by the Lord to leave the city of Ammonihah. They go to a neighboring area called Sidom, where the fleeing refugee families from Ammonihah have taken shelter, including the reformed persecutor, Zeezrom. The latter is languishing in the feverish agony of conscience, believing that his lifestyle of rebellion and wrongdoing is responsible for the deaths of the two prophets and many others. When he learns that Alma and Amulek have been preserved, he calls them to his sickbed.

> *5 And it came to pass that they went immediately, obeying the message which he had sent unto them; and they went in unto the house unto Zeezrom; and they found him upon his bed, sick, being very low with a burning fever; and his mind also was exceedingly sore because of his iniquities; and when he saw them he stretched forth his hand, and besought them that they would heal him.*
> *6 And it came to pass that Alma said unto him, taking him by the hand:* ***Believest thou in the power of Christ unto salvation?***
> *7 And he answered and said:* ***Yea, I believe*** *all the words that thou hast taught.*
> *8 And Alma said: If thou believest in the redemption of Christ thou canst be healed.*
> *9 And he said: Yea, I believe according to thy words.*
> *10 And then Alma cried unto the Lord, saying:* ***O Lord our God, have mercy on this man,*** *and heal him according to his faith which is in Christ.*
> *11 And when Alma had said these words, Zeezrom leaped upon his feet, and began to walk; and this was done to the great astonishment of all the people; and the knowledge of this went forth throughout all the land of Sidom.*
> *12 And* ***Alma baptized Zeezrom unto the Lord;*** *and he began from that time forth to preach unto the people.*

Believest thou in the power of Christ unto salvation? Yea, I believe; O Lord our God, have mercy on this man; Alma baptized Zeezrom unto the Lord

In the example of Zeezrom we see the agony of guilt and the ecstasy of deliverance. Through penitence and obedience, the Spirit can transform the guilt in an anguished soul into the joy of redemption. According to Zeezrom's faith, Alma is able to heal him through the Spirit. He is baptized and begins to preach the gospel. Do we have a Zeezrom element within us that needs to be reformed and converted into an element of strength in building the kingdom of God? We can learn from Zeezrom by placing our trust in the Lord and seeking to divest ourselves of worldly entanglements that detract from heavenly commitments, or worse, that enchain us to a life of sin. "O Lord our God," prayed the prophet, "have mercy on this man" (verse 10). In the same way we can ask our leaders and friends to pray for us, and we can pray for ourselves, that our lives may become kinder, gentler, and holier.

13–15 Alma, the chief high priest, establishes the Church in the land of Sidom. Many are baptized. The citizens of Ammonihah, however, persist in their evil ways.

> *16 And it came to pass that Alma and Amulek,* ***Amulek having forsaken all*** *his*
> *gold, and silver, and his precious things, which were in the land of Ammonihah,* ***for***
> ***the word of God,*** *he being rejected by those who were once his friends and also by his*
> *father and his kindred;*
> *17 Therefore, after Alma having established the church at Sidom, seeing a great*
> *check, yea, seeing that the people were checked as to the pride of their hearts, and*
> *began to humble themselves before God, and began to assemble themselves together*
> *at their sanctuaries to worship God before the altar, watching and praying con-*
> *tinually, that they might be delivered from Satan, and from death, and from*
> *destruction—*

Amulek having forsaken all for the word of God

Consider the price that Amulek pays for discipleship. He willingly sacrifices his wealth, his friends, and the companionship of his father and other relatives for the sake of the gospel. Even though Amulek would not hear the word of the Lord earlier, he truly repents and gives his all to the Lord. Let us ponder the price for our own discipleship. Are we willing to sacrifice all things for the building up of the kingdom of God? Said President Joseph F. Smith:

> True repentance is not only sorrow for sins, and humble penitence and contrition before God, but it involves the necessity of turning away from them, a discontinuance of all evil practices and deeds, a thorough reformation of life, a vital change from evil to good, from vice to virtue, from darkness to light. Not only so, but to make restitution, so far as it is possible, for all the wrongs we have done, to pay our debts, and restore to God and man their rights—that which is due to them from us. This is true repentance, and the exercise of the will and all the powers of body and mind is demanded, to complete this glorious work of repentance; then God will accept it. (*Gospel Doctrine: Selections from the Sermons and Writings of Joseph F. Smith,* comp. John A. Widtsoe [Salt Lake City: Deseret Book, 1939], 100)

She Laid Down Her Crutch

Alma and Amulek were the instruments of divine intercession on behalf of the ailing Zeezrom. Then, as now and at all times, blessings and healings through the priesthood are always accomplished through faith in Jesus Christ. The following story is related by President Wilford Woodruff:

> Mary Pitt . . . was something like the lame man who lay at the gate of the Temple called "Beautiful" at Jerusalem—she had not been able to walk a step for fourteen years, and confined to her bed nearly half that time. She had no strength in her feet and ankles and could only move about a little with a crutch or holding on to a chair. She wished to be baptized. Brother Pitt [Mary's brother] and myself took her in our arms, and carried her into the water and I baptized her. When she came out of the water I confirmed her. She said she wanted to be healed and she believed she had faith enough to be healed. I had had experience enough in this Church to know that it required a good deal of faith to heal a person who had not walked a step for fourteen years. I told her that according to her faith it should be unto her. It so happened that on the day after she was baptized, Brother Richards and President Brigham Young came down to see me. We met at Brother Kington's. Sister Mary Pitt was there also. I told President Young what Sister Pitt wished, and that she believed she had faith enough to be healed. We prayed for her and laid hands upon her. Brother Young was mouth, and commanded her to be made whole. She laid down her crutch and never used it after, and the next day she walked three miles. (*Journal of Discourses,* 26 vols. (London: Latter-day Saints' Book Depot, 1854–86), 15:344–345)

President Young Story about healing & faith.

18 Now as I said, Alma having seen all these things, therefore he took Amulek and came over to the land of Zarahemla, and took him to his own house, and did administer unto him in his tribulations, and ***strengthened him in the Lord.***
19 And thus ended the tenth year of the reign of the judges over the people of Nephi.

Strengthened him in the Lord

It was only a short time previous that Amulek had taken the fasting prophet Alma into his home and nurtured him. Now Alma returns the favor by taking Amulek into his home to administer unto him and strengthen him.

CHAPTER 16

OVERVIEW

Ammonihah is destroyed "in one day" (verse 10) by the invading Lamanites. Zoram, captain over the Nephite armies, is sent to recover those carried away into the wilderness. The Lamanites are repulsed and peace returns. Alma and Amulek establish the Church throughout all the Nephite territories. The people prepare themselves for the predicted appearance of the resurrected Lord among them.

1 AND it came to pass in the eleventh year of the reign of the judges over the people of Nephi, on the fifth day of the second month, there having been much peace in the land of Zarahemla, there having been no wars nor contentions for a certain number of years, even until the fifth day of the second month in the eleventh year, there was ***a cry of war*** *heard throughout the land.*
2 For behold, the armies of ***the Lamanites had come*** *in upon the wilderness side, into the borders of the land,* ***even into the city of Ammonihah,*** *and began to slay the people and destroy the city.*
3 And now it came to pass, before the Nephites could raise a sufficient army to drive them out of the land, ***they had destroyed the people*** *who were in the city of Ammonihah, and also some around the borders of Noah, and taken others captive into the wilderness.*

A cry of war; the Lamanites had come even into the city of Ammonihah; they had destroyed the people

Only a year after Alma and Amulek proclaim the Lord's ultimatum to the people of Ammonihah (spoken around 82 B.C.; see Alma 8:16; 9:24), the great city of wickedness is destroyed by the invading Lamanite hordes: "But behold, in one day it was left desolate; and the carcasses were mangled by dogs and wild bests of the wilderness" (Alma 16:10). So great is the stench of death in that vicinity that it is left desolate for many years, being referred to as "Desolation of Nehors; for they were of the profession of Nehor" (Alma 16:11). Alma and Amulek continue with their ministry, establishing the Church throughout the land, bringing many souls unto Christ, and preparing them for the prophesied coming of the Lord to their land following His resurrection.

Preparing for the Second Coming

Alma's prophecy of the destruction of the city of Ammonihah (see Alma 9:4–5,12,18) is fulfilled (Alma 16:2, 11). The prophets have declared throughout time: repent or perish. If not destroyed in mortality, then we will pay for our sins in the hereafter (see D&C 19:15–19). The question for today is where do we stand in regard to our own personal repentance? Where does the country we live in stand as to its reverence to God? Consider and ponder the following comment from noted scholars Joseph Fielding McConkie and Robert L. Millet:

> Ammonihah, a city pretending religion, a religion perfectly tolerant of any action save it be the preaching of the gospel of repentance! To preach repentance, to testify of Christ, to speak of the necessity of good works—these were sins too grievous to be borne. Their effect was to unite in wrath and bitterness the diversified factions within the congregations of this ever-tolerant religion. These missionaries of righteousness must be mocked, ridiculed, beaten, and imprisoned. Their adherents must be stoned, driven from the community, or burned at the stake. Such were the seeds they planted and such was the harvest they reaped in the desolation of Nehors. We are left to wonder to what extent Ammonihah is a prophetic foreshadowing of that which the scriptures denominate as the "desolation of abomination" (D&C 84:114, 117; D&C 88:85), events that will precede and attend the coming of our Lord and Master that will bring again that peace once known to the faithful of the Nephite nation. (*Doctrinal Commentary on the Book of Mormon* [Salt Lake City: Bookcraft, 1987–1992], 3:119)

4–8 The Nephites send **Zoram,** chief captain over the armies, to recover those who have been carried away by the Lamanites into the wilderness.

Zoram, Captain of Nephite Armies

Following the ministry of Alma and Amulek in the wicked city of Ammonihah, the Lamanites attack and destroy the city in the year 81 B.C. in fulfillment of prophecy. Some citizens are taken captive by the Lamanites and led into the wilderness. The chief captain over the Nephite armies at the time is a man named Zoram, who has two sons, Aha and Lehi. Zoram inquires of Alma where he should take his forces to recover the captives. Alma receives direction from the Lord, and Zoram takes his two sons and marches forth to engage the Lamanites. The Lamanites are scattered and driven into the wilderness and the Nephite prisoners are returned to their homes unharmed (see Alma 16:8).

Ammonihah becomes Desolation of Nehors

9–11 The city of Ammonihah—having been destroyed in one day" (verse 10), including "every living soul" (verse 9)—leaves behind the scent of decomposing bodies that lasts for many years. The area is known thereafter as the "Desolation of Nehors" (verse 11).

EVIDENCE: Following the Law of Apostate Cities (Alma 16:9–11)

The destruction of the corrupt city of Ammonihah by the Lamanites conforms to an ancient Israelite law described in Deuteronomy 13:12–16. As chief judge over the land of Zarahemla, Alma would have certainly known this law, which requires the utter annihilation of apostate cities by the sword. Many specifics of the destruction of Ammonihah fit the elements required in the ancient law. 1) For instance, before a city could be destroyed, a thorough investigation was required to determine if the inhabitants had indeed completely forsaken the Lord to worship false gods. 2) The law also demanded the testimony of at least two righteous witnesses as to the sinful state of the city, fulfilled in this case by Alma and Amulek. 3) When these two prophets preached repentance and proclaimed that Ammonihah would be destroyed if its people did not turn to their true God, another portion of the law was satisfied. Interestingly, the city was declared untouchable for approximately seven years, probably a ritual cleansing period in either the Nephite or Israelite world, or both. (Eight years and nine months pass between Alma 16:1 and Alma 49:1, when we learn that the city of Ammonihah had been rebuilt and fortified.) (See *Echoes,* 369–372.)

12–15 Peace returns for a period of time. Alma and Amulek establish the Church throughout all the territories of the Nephites, everyone being invited to come unto the Lord.

16 And there was ***no inequality*** *among them; the Lord did pour out his Spirit on all the face of the land to prepare the minds of the children of men, or to prepare their hearts to receive the word which should be taught among them at the time of his coming—*

No inequality

There are great blessings that flow from unity in a social environment where all are considered equal children of our Father in Heaven. When we are unified as one in all things, we are blessed with the Spirit of the Lord. Do we treat one another as equals before the Lord? Do we cultivate an environment where everyone is valued and considered worthy of respect as we labor cooperatively to fulfill our potential as sons and daughters of God?

17–21 The priests go forth in their ministry to help the people purge iniquity from their lives and prepare themselves for the coming of the Son of God. "They were taught that he would appear unto them after his resurrection; and this the people did hear with great joy and gladness" (verse 20). The word of God is preached "in its purity" (verse 21) throughout all the land.

CONCLUDING THOUGHTS

Our hearts swell with great confidence when we realize the knowledge and power of God. He knows the end from the beginning. He knows our hearts. He wants to bless us with His Holy Priesthood—and He does. We are always blessed according to our faithfulness. Many of us will be required to pay the price of enduring persecution in our lives, and for all of this we shall be blessed. Looking at the fate of Ammonihah should cause us to realize that our prophets speak for God. Today when our prophet asks us to obey the commandments and do certain things, we should realize that it is always for our own good. The blessings of heaven will be ours for obeying the commandment on which the blessing is predicated.

Let us consider that our mission upon the earth commenced in the premortal existence where we were called to service (as we were reminded in Alma chapter 13) based on the principle of foreordination as anchored in faith and valor. When we came here on our mortal journey we knew beforehand that the righteous would be persecuted for the sake of Christ. We were schooled in premortal classrooms to recognize both the agony of guilt and the ecstasy of deliverance—because we were taught there the first principles and ordinances of the gospel of Jesus Christ. We knew before the foundations of the earth were laid that God's word would always be fulfilled, then as now, and we rejoiced in the coming opportunity to complete our mortal probation with dignity, loyalty, and virtue—no matter what adversity might pour into our lives, no matter what sacrifice we might be called upon to make on behalf of the kingdom of God.

An account of the sons of Mosiah, who rejected their rights to the kingdom for the word of God, and went up to the land of Nephi to preach to the Lamanites; their sufferings and deliverance—according to the record of Alma. [Note: This preamble was included in the original edition of the Book of Mormon published in 1830.]

CHAPTER 17

OVERVIEW

En route to the land of Manti, Alma is overjoyed to encounter the four sons of Mosiah as they return home from their fourteen-year mission to the Lamanites. They have been blessed with the spirit of prophecy and revelation through diligent study, prayer, and fasting. The account of their mission is commenced. The Lord gives them comfort and promises that if they will show forth examples of patience and endurance they will be instruments in His hands "unto the salvation of many souls" (verse 11). Ammon goes to the land of Ishmael and becomes a servant to King Lamoni. By overpowering a group of attacking Lamanites through the power of God, Ammon rescues the king's flocks and herds and establishes his authority and legitimacy among the king's guard.

4 sons of Mosiah fulfilled a 14-year mission.

1 AND now it came to pass that as Alma was journeying from the land of Gideon southward, away to the land of Manti, behold, to his astonishment, he met with ***the sons of Mosiah*** *journeying toward the land of Zarahemla.*
2 Now these sons of Mosiah were with Alma at the time the angel first appeared unto him; therefore Alma did rejoice exceedingly to see his brethren; and what added more to his joy, they were still his brethren in the Lord; yea, and they had waxed strong in the knowledge of the truth; for they were men of a sound understanding and they had ***searched the scriptures*** *diligently, that they might know the word of God.*
3 But this is not all; they had given themselves to ***much prayer, and fasting;*** *therefore* ***they had the spirit of prophecy, and the spirit of revelation,*** *and when they taught,* ***they taught with power and authority of God.***
4 And they had been teaching the word of God for the space of fourteen years among the Lamanites, having had ***much success*** *in bringing many to the knowledge of the truth; yea, by the power of their words many were brought before the altar of God, to call on his name and confess their sins before him.*

THE SONS OF MOSIAH; SEARCHED THE SCRIPTURES; MUCH PRAYER, AND FASTING; SPIRIT OF PROPHECY, SPIRIT OF REVELATION; THEY TAUGHT WITH POWER AND AUTHORITY OF GOD; MUCH SUCCESS

These are among the most celebrated and instructive scriptures on missionary work. The formula for teaching with the power and authority of God is explained succinctly: search the word of God, pray, fast, and teach by the Spirit.

Consider what is taking place: As Alma is journeying toward the land of Manti one day, he is astonished to encounter his beloved colleagues, the sons of King Mosiah, who are now on their way back to Zarahemla after having labored some fourteen years in a highly successful missionary campaign to reclaim the Lamanites. The Book of Mormon record at this point turns to a recounting of the extraordinary experiences of the sons of Mosiah. We learn the secret of their success: from the beginning they practice the godly regimen of feasting upon the word of God, praying diligently in the attitude of fasting, and thus cultivating within themselves the spirit of missionary work, in effect, the spirit of prophecy and revelation. The gateway for gaining this marvelous gift is personal dedication, scripture study, fasting, and prayer—which enable us to teach with the power and authority of God. These principles are illustrated in great detail in the actual missionary report of the sons of Mosiah, beginning with the experiences of Ammon, "being the chief among them" (Alma 17:18), who is to win the heart of King Lamoni and his court through the influence of the Spirit.

President Gordon B. Hinckley discusses the kind of devotion needed in missionary preparation:

> [We must] cultivate in our homes a proper attitude toward missionary service. We enjoy the blessings we so greatly treasure because of those who have gone before us. Out of a sense of appreciation, out of simple gratitude, we should make an effort to extend these same blessings to others. Our young people have an obligation to prepare themselves for missionary service. . . .
>
> One of the great compliments paid the Savior was that he taught as one having authority. The missionary who knows scripture and can quote it speaks with the voice of authority. It is not essential to memorize five hundred citations, nor even three hundred. Fifty well chosen verses of scripture will become a remarkably effective tool in the hands of a missionary. May I suggest that in our family night gatherings we make it a project to memorize one scripture citation a week pertinent to this work. At the conclusion of a year our children will have on their lips a fund of scripture which will remain with them throughout their lives. . . .

> Live for the opportunity when you may go out as a servant of the Lord and an ambassador of eternal truth to the people of the world. "And this gospel of the kingdom shall be preached in all the world for a witness unto all nations; and then shall the end come." (Matt. 24:14.) This is our commission, and this is our obligation spoken anciently and reaffirmed in modern revelation. (*Teachings of Gordon B. Hinckley* [Salt Lake City: Deseret Book, 1997], 344–345)

Preparation to Teach and Preach

Alma 17:2–3 is the basic formula for preparing to teach and preach as a missionary.

Be "in the Lord"—by following our Savior and keeping His commandments.
1) Wax strong "in the knowledge of the truth."
2) Be of a "sound understanding."
3) Search the scriptures "diligently" to know the word of God.
4) Pray and fast.

The reward is to have the Spirit of prophecy and revelation so that we will teach with the power and authority of God. Missionaries who are prepared to serve and willing to work hard—being exactly, immediately, and courageously obedient—will always enjoy the Spirit on their missions and have greater success in working with the people (see Alma 19:35–36).

Pure motives help bring souls to repentance: "Therefore, this was the cause for which the sons of Mosiah had undertaken the work, that perhaps they might bring them unto repentance; that perhaps they might bring them to know of the plan of redemption" (Alma 17:16.). They truly cared about the people (see Mosiah 28:3).

5–8 Having declined the opportunity to serve on the throne, the sons of Mosiah depart from Zarahemla with their supplies. They are to face much affliction and suffering, "and also much labor in the spirit" (verse 5).

> *9 And it came to pass that they journeyed many days in the wilderness, and they fasted much and prayed much that the Lord would grant unto them a portion of his Spirit to go with them, and abide with them, that they might be* ***an instrument in the hands of God*** *to bring, if it were possible, their brethren, the Lamanites, to the knowledge of the truth, to the knowledge of the baseness of the traditions of their fathers, which were not correct.*

An instrument in the hands of God

The pure motivation of these young men is to follow the Spirit in order to be worthy instruments of the Lord in bringing people unto Him and blessing their lives. If our motivation is pure and righteous, a way will be opened for us to serve productively and effectively.

> *10 And it came to pass that the Lord did visit them with his Spirit, and said unto them:*
> ***Be comforted.*** *And they were comforted.*
> *11 And the Lord said unto them also: Go forth among the Lamanites, thy brethren, and*
> *establish my word; yet ye shall* ***be patient*** *in long-suffering and afflictions, that ye may* ***show forth good examples*** *unto them in me, and I will make an instrument of thee in my hands unto the salvation of many souls.*

Be comforted; be patient; show forth good examples

There is power in example. A central core of being a good example is to be patient in afflictions. We must set a good example so that the Lord can use us to build up the kingdom.

12–17 The sons of Mosiah take courage. They arrive in the borders of the land of the Lamanites and go their separate ways, "according to the word and power of God" (verse 17) given to each, with the objective of bringing this hard-hearted and murderous people unto Christ.

> *18 Now* ***Ammon*** *being the chief among them, or rather he did administer unto them, and he departed from them, after having blessed them according to their several stations, having imparted the word of God unto them, or administered unto them before his departure; and thus they took their several journeys throughout the land.*

Ammon, Man of God

Ammon, like his brother Aaron, is a missionary figure of the Book of Mormon. All four of the sons of King Mosiah—Ammon, Aaron, Omner, and Himni—were at first "numbered among the unbelievers" (Mosiah 27:8) and were "the very vilest of sinners" (Mosiah 28:4). But the Lord had an urgent, vital calling for these young men, and He sent an angel to intervene and bring about their spiritual transformation (see Mosiah 27:11–18). Afterwards, they went about preaching the gospel, confirming their testimony, and bringing about much good in their own land and later among the Lamanites with courage and enthusiasm.

Alma 17:18–25

Following their miraculous conversion, Ammon and his brethren desired more than anything else to declare the gospel of Jesus Christ to "every creature" (Mosiah 28:3). Thus they decided to embark on a missionary journey among the Lamanites that was to last fourteen years (approximately 90 B.C. to 77 B.C.; see Alma 17:4). Their preparation included much study, fasting, and prayer (see Alma 17:2–3). The Lord responded to their entreaties for a blessing by giving them comfort and assurance, promising He would make them instruments "unto the salvation of many souls" (Alma 17:11). For his part, Ammon was to journey to the land of Ishmael around 90 B.C., where he would win the respect of King Lamoni and his servants as a fearless defender of the royal flocks and herds—and then bring the gospel of Jesus Christ to the royal family and the entire nation (see Alma 17–18). Later, Ammon would provide a framework of strength and compassion to prepare the father of King Lamoni to respond to the missionary message of Aaron and come into the fold with much of his nation. Thus Ammon and his brethren would be instruments in establishing the gospel among the Lamanites.

19–21 Ammon goes to the land of Ishmael and is carried bound before King **Lamoni,** a descendant of Ishmael.

Lamoni, Royal Receptor of Light

Lamoni is the king over one region of the Lamanite territory known as the land of Ishmael, named after the descendants of the family that accompanied Lehi on his journey to the promised land. Lamoni is now about to cross paths with Ammon, one of the sons of Mosiah, and experience a mighty change of heart upon learning the message of the gospel. Through the Spirit of our Father in Heaven, Lamoni will be illuminated with the light of hope and transformed from his previous state of spiritual darkness to one of redemption and grace through the power of the Atonement. Lamoni responds with full heart and mind to the touch of the Master—even though it means relinquishing all the traditions and philosophies upheld by his fathers for five hundred years.

22–25 The king allows Ammon to dwell in the land and even offers him one of his daughters as a wife. But Ammon requests only one thing: "**I will be thy servant**" (verse 25).

I will be thy servant

How does one approach a king with any hope to influence his thinking and behavior? "Being wise, yet harmless" (Alma 18:22), Ammon first becomes a servant to the king and then seeks opportunities for awakening within him an awareness of the power of the Spirit of God. The formula is simple: first a servant, and then a teacher. Missionary work is a "labour of love" (Hebrews 6:10) that is anchored in an attitude of service toward those we teach. Let us become more effective teachers in family, Church, and community by ensuring that our motivation is centered in charity and service—and that we depend fully upon the Lord for guidance. President Ezra Taft Benson stated:

> It was while I was on my first mission that I discovered the constant need for dependence on the Lord. I learned through experience that I could not convince another soul to come unto Christ. I learned that one cannot convert another by just quoting scripture. Conversion comes when another is touched by the Spirit of the Lord and receives a witness, independent of the missionary, that what he or she is being taught is true.
>
> I learned that a missionary is only a vessel through whom the Lord can transmit His Spirit. To acquire that Spirit, a missionary must humble himself in prayer and ask our Heavenly Father to use him to touch the hearts of investigators.
>
> The first lesson of missionary work is to be dependent on the Lord for our success. (*Come unto Christ* [Salt Lake City: Deseret Book, 1983], 95)

Memories: How Much Do You Care?

Ammon sought to win the hearts of his Lamanite guards by showing forth the power of God in preserving the flocks of the king (see Alma 17:29–39). In missionary work, people must know we care before they will listen to our teachings. The old cliché is true: "I don't care about how much you know until I know how much you care." This was exemplified in the letters new converts would write me. I would ask them to tell me of their conversion. They would reply, "I felt the love of the missionaries so much I had to listen to what they were teaching. While listening I felt the Spirit and I knew the gospel was true and I wanted to be baptized." (Ed J. Pinegar)

26–28 Ammon becomes a servant to King Lamoni. He assists the king's guards in protecting the royal flocks and herds from the Lamanite interlopers who take pleasure in scattering the animals at the river Sebus. On the third day of Ammon's service, the royal flocks are again scattered, and the king's servants begin to weep.

> *29 Now they wept because of the fear of being slain. Now when Ammon saw this his heart was swollen within him with joy; for, said he,* ***I will show forth*** *my power unto these my fellow-servants, or* ***the power which is in me,*** *in restoring these flocks unto the king, that I may win the hearts of these my fellow-servants,* ***that I may lead them to believe in my words.***

I WILL SHOW FORTH THE POWER WHICH IS IN ME THAT I MAY LEAD THEM TO BELIEVE IN MY WORDS

Ammon rejoices in the opportunity to gain credibility with his colleagues through a demonstration of the power of God. As we live righteously, the power of God is made manifest in us. If we are willing, the Lord will provide the opportunity and give us the strength as well as the words to say to bless peoples' lives. Elder Neal A. Maxwell taught this principle: "God does not begin by asking us about our ability, but only about our availability, and if we then prove our dependability, he will increase our capability!" ("It's Service, Not Status, That Counts," *The Neal A. Maxwell Quote Book, ed.* Cory H. Maxwell [Salt Lake City: Bookcraft, 1997], xvii).

30–39 Ammon helps the king's guard to recover and to secure the scattered animals. He then contends with the attackers, who assume they can easily slay him, for "they [know] not that the Lord had promised Mosiah that he would deliver his sons out of their hands" (verse 35; see Mosiah 28:7). Before he is finished, Ammon slays many of the attackers and smites off the arms of a number who come against him. He then returns to the king with the evidence of his accomplishment.

EVIDENCE: LAMANITE GAMES AT THE WATERS OF SEBUS (Alma 17:25–39; 18:1–7)

Though it seems strange to modern readers, the "practice of plunder" (Alma 18:7) among the Lamanites at the Waters of Sebus was probably much like a game—a game that followed specific rules. Ammon's slaying of several men and smiting off the arms of others may appear harsh, but archaeological evidence shows that in many such ceremonial games the loser was killed. As examples of such deadly games, Hugh Nibley lists Aztec duels, chariot races of the princes, the ancient game of Nemi, "the Platanista, the Krypteia, the old Norse brain-ball, the hanging games of the Celts, and so on." The most dramatic example of this phenomenon may be the ball games played in ancient Mesoamerica, wherein members of the losing team were often beheaded. (See *Echoes,* 478–479.)

EVIDENCE: Smiting Off Arms (Alma 17)

Ammon's severing of the arms of King Lamoni's enemies leaves some readers wondering why such an honorable servant of God would perform such a gruesome feat. But Hugh Nibley points out that on ancient Egyptian monuments, depictions of battle scenes show piles of severed hands and arms delivered to the king as trophies. Recent research has revealed that in Mesoamerica, an arm was considered a war trophy, and was as valuable as fine jewelry taken from a dead opponent. In at least one firsthand account, Aztec warriors held up the severed arms of their sacrificed battle opponents to warn the Spanish and their allies against further aggression. According to scholars John Welch and John Lundquist, many ancient reliefs portray Assyrian troops cutting off the heads, hands, and feet of their conquered foes. It is highly improbable that Joseph Smith would have had access to this information; therefore, it is one more evidence of the Book of Mormon's authenticity. (See *Echoes,* 422–425.)

Postlude

The famous incident in which Ammon displays his amazing strength to protect the king's flocks serves as the tipping point for his missionary debut. Thereafter he will be able to gain the confidence of King Lamoni and guide him over the threshold of honest curiosity and into the realm of overwhelming spiritual enlightenment.

CHAPTER 18

OVERVIEW

Lamoni learns of Ammon's marvelous deeds and supposes that he is the Great Spirit. Ammon is summoned before the king and explains that his understanding and power come from the Holy Spirit. He teaches the king about God's dealings as preserved in the holy scriptures, including the plan of redemption. The king believes him, prays for mercy, and is rendered lifeless for two days and nights.

1–15 The king's guards report to Lamoni details concerning Ammon's power and invincibility. The king is persuaded that Ammon is the Great Spirit that his forefathers have spoken about. He fears that he has done wrong in slaying his servants for failing to protect his flocks from the plundering Lamanites. Ammon, who is preparing the king's horses and chariots for a trip to the land of Nephi, is summoned before the king.

> *16 And it came to pass that Ammon, being* ***filled with the Spirit of God,*** *therefore*
> *he* ***perceived the thoughts of the king.*** *And he said unto him: Is it because thou hast*

> *heard that I defended thy servants and thy flocks, and slew seven of their brethren with the sling and with the sword, and smote off the arms of others, in order to defend thy flocks and thy servants; behold, is it this that causeth thy marvelings?*
> *17 I say unto you, what is it, that thy marvelings are so great? Behold,* ***I am a man, and am thy servant;*** *therefore, whatsoever thou desirest which is right, that will I do.*

Filled with the Spirit of God; perceived the thoughts of the king; I am a man, and am thy servant

Ammon takes no honor unto himself, but nevertheless confirms that he can, indeed, discern the thoughts of the king, for he is inspired through the power of the Holy Ghost. It is the same power that will overcome Lamoni in due time when he, for the first time in his life, experiences a spiritual manifestation.

18–21 The king inquires how Ammon can discern his thoughts and how he has triumphed over the enemies of the crown.

> *22 Now Ammon* ***being wise, yet harmless,*** *he said unto Lamoni:* ***Wilt thou hearken unto my words,*** *if I tell thee by what power I do these things? And this is the thing that I desire of thee.*

Being wise, yet harmless; wilt thou hearken unto my words?

There are only two places in the scriptures where the words "wise" and "harmless" are used in counter-position to each other: Alma 18:22 (as above) and Matthew 10:16, where the Savior instructs the Twelve: "Behold, I send you forth as sheep in the midst of wolves: be ye therefore wise as serpents, and harmless as doves." Ammon was harmless, i.e., without guile, pure, with an eye single to the glory of God; and he was also wise, i.e., skillful in establishing a framework of operation where his listeners would be guided into a state of receptivity to the Spirit.

23–34 Ammon guides Lamoni into a dialogue where he can explain to the king in straight-forward terms the nature of God as creator, the nature of heaven, his (Ammon's) role as the messenger of truth, and his calling by the Holy Spirit.

> *35 And a portion of that Spirit dwelleth in me, which giveth me knowledge, and also* ***power according to my faith*** *and desires which are in God.*

POWER ACCORDING TO MY FAITH

Ammon explains the source of his power—it comes from the Spirit of God that dwells in him. Thus Ammon can know the king's thoughts and can perform with power to accomplish much good (in this case be an effective servant in protecting the king's estate). This miraculous process is sustained according to our faith. The lesson is that if we exercise our faith, the Spirit is given to us to bless others.

36–39 Beginning with the Creation, Ammon imparts to Lamoni an account of all God's dealings as contained in the holy scriptures, including the travels and sufferings of Lehi and his group, and the rebellion of Laman and Lemuel. He explains the plan of redemption and the Atonement.

> *40 And it came to pass that after he had said all these things, and expounded them to the king, that* ***the king believed all his words.***
> *41 And he began to cry unto the Lord, saying:* ***O Lord, have mercy;*** *according to thy abundant mercy which thou hast had upon the people of Nephi, have* ***upon me, and my people.***
> *42 And now, when he had said this, he fell unto the earth, as if he were dead.*
> *43 And it came to pass that his servants took him and carried him in unto his wife, and laid him upon a bed; and he lay as if he were dead for the space of two days and two nights; and* ***his wife, and his sons, and his daughters mourned over him,*** *after the manner of the Lamanites, greatly lamenting his loss.*

THE KING BELIEVED ALL HIS WORDS; O LORD, HAVE MERCY UPON ME, AND MY PEOPLE; HIS WIFE, AND HIS SONS, AND HIS DAUGHTERS MOURNED OVER HIM

Lamoni prays unto the Lord for mercy. He is rendered incapacitated and brought before his wife and family. They assume he is dead. He lies in that condition for two days and nights.

CHAPTER 19

OVERVIEW

When the king remains lifeless for two days and nights, his wife sends for Ammon, who discerns that "the light of the glory of God . . . the light of everlasting life [is] lit up in his soul" (verse 6). Ammon tells the queen that her husband "sleepeth in God" (verse 8) and will arise on the morrow. She believes him and he extols her great faith. The king arises the next day and bears witness of the Atonement. All three—king, queen, and Ammon—are then overpowered by the Spirit and fall to the ground. A Lamanite woman named Abish sounds the news of the extraordinary happenings. A crowd assembles and debates the implications. One individual tries to slay Ammon but is struck dead by the power of God. Abish takes the queen by the hand and she arises and bears witness of Jesus. The queen takes the king by the hand and he arises and comforts and teaches the people. The gospel message is spread throughout the land and many are baptized. The Church is established. Thus commences the work of the Lord among the Lamanites.

> *1 AND it came to pass that after two days and two nights they were about to take his body and lay it in a sepulchre, which they had made for the purpose of burying their dead.*
> *2 Now the* ***queen*** *having heard of the fame of Ammon, therefore she sent and desired that he should come in unto her.*

Queen of the Lamanites: Wife of Lamoni

The wife of King Lamoni is one of the most exemplary women depicted in the Book of Mormon. The account of her conversion is brief, and she remains unnamed in the record. However, her superlative faith is extolled by Ammon, and her example of coming unto Christ and following in the footsteps of her husband is instrumental in bringing many of the Lamanite people into the fold.

3–5 Ammon comes before the queen, who tells him that the servants have made it known to her "that thou art a prophet of a holy God, and that thou hast power to do many mighty works in his name" (verse 4). She requests that Ammon go to her husband, whom she refuses to give up for dead.

> *6 Now, this was what Ammon desired, for he knew that King Lamoni was under the power of God; he knew that the dark veil of unbelief was being cast away from his mind, and the light which did light up his mind, which was* ***the light of the glory of God,*** *which was a marvelous light of his goodness—yea, this light had infused such joy into his soul, the cloud of darkness having been dispelled, and that* ***the light of everlasting life was lit up in his soul,*** *yea, he knew that this had overcome his natural frame, and he was carried away in God—*

The light of the glory of God, the light of everlasting life was lit up in his soul

This well-known passage describes with exceptional precision the experience of one who is under the influence of the Holy Ghost. It is a moving demonstration of the Savior's words: "I am the light of the world: he that followeth me shall not walk in darkness, but shall have the light of life" (John 8:12; compare Mosiah 16:9; 3 Nephi 9:18).

7–9 The seed of faith demonstrated by the queen is welcomed by Ammon, who assures her that her husband is not dead but he "sleepeth in God" (verse 8) and will rise on the morrow. When she confirms her belief in his words—"I believe that it shall be according as thou hast said" (verse 9)—Ammon makes a statement concerning her character that is among the most glorious expressions of praise to a woman in all of the Book of Mormon.

wife of King Lamoni

> *10 And Ammon said unto her: Blessed art thou because of thy exceeding faith; I say unto thee, woman, there has not been such* ***great faith*** *among all the people of the Nephites.*

Great faith

Consider the implications of what has occurred. A stranger has come onto the scene whom the queen has never seen before. He is respected and even held in awe by the servants—but the queen has not been an eyewitness to his miraculous power. Her husband, under the administration of this man, is now comatose and considered dead by many. And yet she believes the words of Ammon. That is the power of her "great faith." That is evidence of the operation of the Spirit in this situation. The queen's commitment and support will be an important part of the foundation being laid for the work of the gospel among the Lamanites.

11–15 Throughout the night the queen watches over her husband as she awaits the hour of his restoration. In accordance with Ammon's word, the king arises the next day—reaching out his hand to his wife as he blesses the name of God and blesses the faithful queen also. He bears testimony of having seen the Redeemer in vision and also invokes a reference to the mother of Jesus who should bring Him into the world. So great is the joy of the king and queen that they both are overpowered by the Spirit and fall to the ground. Ammon, too, having given thanks to God for the remarkable manifestation of the Spirit, collapses in joy. Seeing this, the servants begin to pray, for the fear of the Lord had come upon them.

> *16 And it came to pass that they [the servants] did call on the name of the Lord, in their might, even until they had all fallen to the earth, save it were one of the Lamanitish women, whose name was* ***Abish,*** *she having been converted unto the Lord for many years, on account of a remarkable vision of her father—*

Abish

This woman (whose name is pronounced AY-bish) has been converted unto the Lord many years previous because of a remarkable vision of her father, the details of which we are not told. She has kept this fact a secret among her Lamanite colleagues, but now, observing the remarkable manifestation of the Spirit upon her mistress the queen, as well as upon the king and his servants and the Nephite visitor named Ammon—all of whom have fallen to the ground in a kind of spiritual rapture—she deems it prudent to inform the people of this good news. Being touched with the spirit of missionary work, she desires to share the warm feelings of her heart with her neighbors and associates in the city.

17–28 Abish runs forth from house to house, making the happenings known unto the people. However, the outcome is rather different from what she expects, for the gathering throng soon begins to advocate widely divergent views concerning the state of those who lie prostrate upon the ground. Some claim that the Nephite visitor has brought destructive influences upon their royal leadership. Others are angry at Ammon for having slain some of their companions who scattered the king's flocks. One of this latter group attempts to slay Ammon but is himself rendered lifeless by the intercession of the Lord. Concerning this event, Mormon adds the editorial comment: "Now we see that Ammon could not be slain, for the Lord had said unto Mosiah, his father: I will spare him, and it shall be unto him according to thy faith—therefore, Mosiah **trusted him unto the Lord**" (verse 23). Still others proclaim that Ammon is "the Great Spirit" or that he had been sent "by the Great Spirit" on account of the iniquities of the Lamanites. Seeing the dissension and chaos that she has introduced by assembling the people, Abish, full of sorrow, takes action that triggers a series of positive events.

Trusted him unto the Lord

This story instills in us the motivation to increase our faith and trust in the Lord. All missionary parents who send their sons and daughters into the mission field understand the feelings of faith and trust that accompany such a sacrifice. We can assume that King Mosiah was given to constant prayer on behalf of his four sons who were laboring such a long time in dangerous territory—but his prayers would have been prayers of faith and hope, for the Lord had promised that his sons would be preserved in safety.

29 And it came to pass that she went and took the queen by the hand, that perhaps she
might raise her from the ground; and as soon as she touched her hand she arose and
stood upon her feet, and cried with a loud voice, saying: ***O blessed Jesus,*** *who has*
saved me from an awful hell! O blessed God, ***have mercy on this people!***
30 And when she had said this, she clasped her hands, being filled with joy, speaking
many words which were not understood; and when she had done this, she took the
king, Lamoni, by the hand, and behold he arose and stood upon his feet.

O blessed Jesus, have mercy on this people!

The nature of the queen's spiritual experience clearly is centered on the Savior and His Atonement. She has gone through the mighty change of heart. Perhaps she's been instructed during her visionary experience to administer to the needs of her husband, for she reaches out and takes him by the hand and he arises. The entire scene is an anticipatory reenactment of the process of overcoming the second death, of coming forth as a new person, liberated from darkness and sin under the redeeming power of God—precisely the nature of the ordinance of the baptismal covenant that the king and queen will shortly experience.

31–35 Immediately thereafter, the king administers to the people, pacifying them and proclaiming to them the gospel message he has received through Ammon. Ammon and the servants of the king confirm these truths, with the result that many who have been summoned to the royal court by Abish join the Church. They spread the word of salvation among the people of the land: "and they did all declare unto the people the selfsame thing—that **their hearts had been changed;** that they had no more desire to do evil" (verse 33). Many are baptized and become a righteous people.

Their hearts had been changed

There is power in the word of God. There is a transformative influence that comes through bearing testimony of the truth of the gospel. When we receive the word with a willing heart, the desire to do evil will recede and vanish. A mighty change of heart is the result of truly being born again, with no disposition to do evil but to do good continually (see Mosiah 5:2). A changed heart brings about a changed life. Are our hearts changed? Do we have a strong desire to do good? Have we found strength through the Spirit to say, with the Savior, "Get thee behind me Satan" (Luke 4:8)?

> *36 And thus* ***the work of the Lord did commence among the Lamanites;*** *thus the Lord did begin to pour out his Spirit upon them; and we see that* ***his arm is extended to all people*** *who will repent and believe on his name.*

THE WORK OF THE LORD DID COMMENCE AMONG THE LAMANITES; HIS ARM IS EXTENDED TO ALL PEOPLE

When we believe and repent, we are blessed with the Spirit. It can happen to an individual. It can happen to a family. It can happen to an entire community. The Lord extends His Spirit to all.

CHAPTER 20

OVERVIEW

The Lord directs Ammon to go to the land of Middoni to free Aaron and his companions from prison. En route, Lamoni and Ammon encounter Lamoni's father, who tries to take Ammon's life. Ammon subdues the father and spares his life in exchange for the release of Aaron and his companions. The father is touched by Ammon's love for his son and agrees to grant Lamoni independence to run the affairs of Lamoni's kingdom. Ammon and Lamoni arrive in Middoni. With the help of the local king, they are able to secure the release of Aaron and his companions.

1–3 Ammon's mission in the land of Ishmael having been completed, Lamoni wishes to take him to the land of Nephi to introduce him to his father. But the Lord constrains Ammon for reasons of safety and commands him instead to go to the land of Middoni to liberate Aaron and his companions from prison.

> *4 Now Lamoni said unto Ammon: I know,* ***in the strength of the Lord thou canst do all things.*** *But behold, I will go with thee to the land of Middoni; for the king of the land of Middoni, whose name is Antiomno, is a friend unto me; therefore I go to the land of Middoni, that I may flatter the king of the land, and he will cast thy brethren out of prison. Now Lamoni said unto him: Who told thee that thy brethren were in prison?*
>
> *5 And Ammon said unto him:* ***No one hath told me, save it be God;*** *and he said unto me—Go and deliver thy brethren, for they are in prison in the land of Middoni.*

In the strength of the Lord thou canst do all things; no one hath told me, save it be God

This famous statement from Lamoni—"in the strength of the Lord thou canst do all things"—shows the king's unshakable faith in Ammon and in the power of the Lord. But it also shows that the king is a practical and resourceful person. He conceives a strategy to help liberate Ammon's brethren by using his political clout in appealing to his friend at Middoni, the king of the land, for help in accomplishing the objective. Thus "the strength of the Lord" also encompasses all we can do through our own best efforts. We can pray for and depend upon the strength of the Lord, but at the same time we must do all in our power to reach our objectives. It is the Lord who directs Ammon to Middoni. It will be the Lord who blesses the process of liberation. And it will be Lamoni who contributes his best talents and connections to ensure that the job is done.

6–8 On the way to Middoni, Ammon and Lamoni encounter the **father of Lamoni,** the king over all the Lamanite territories.

Father of Lamoni, King of the Lamanites

The king over all the Lamanite territories at the time of the fourteen-year mission of the sons of Mosiah remains unnamed in the text of the Book of Mormon. He is referred to simply as "the father of Lamoni." As we have seen, Lamoni is the lesser Lamanite king who has been converted, along with his wife and his court, through the devoted labors of Ammon (see Alma 17–19). The "chance" encounter between the father of Lamoni and his son, who is en route to Middoni with Ammon, sets the stage for the father's eventual conversion through the ministry of Aaron. It will be through the proclamation of the great king that the Church can be established throughout the Lamanite country. The father of Lamoni is an example of a man of courage who is willing to respond to the Spirit of the Lord in altogether relinquishing the misguided traditions of his fathers and embracing an entirely new way of life.

9–27 The father of Lamoni questions his son on the latter's failure to appear at the feast he has sponsored for his sons. He also questions him concerning his association with a Nephite, "one of the children of a liar" (verse 10). During the ensuing dialogue, the father orders his son to slay Ammon. Lamoni refuses to do so, saying that Ammon and his companions "are just men and holy prophets of the true God" (verse 15). Then the father becomes angry with Ammon, whom he views as an interloper, and tries to take his life. But Ammon is able to overpower the king, sparing his life in exchange for allowing Aaron and his companions to be freed from prison and allowing Lamoni the independence to conduct the affairs of his kingdom. The father's heart is softened through "**the great love [Ammon has] for his son**" (verse 26). In this way, the stage is set for the father's later conversion through the teachings of Aaron, who is soon "led by the Spirit to the land of Nephi, even to the house of the king which was over all the land" (Alma 22:1).

THE GREAT LOVE [AMMON HAD] FOR HIS SON

When our love is expressed and felt, it becomes the true motivator for righteousness. This is especially true of the pure love of Christ. It has power. It is the motivating energy within every righteous act. When love is felt, lives are changed. Gratitude is realized, leading to action, as was in the case of Lamoni's father.

28–30 Ammon and Lamoni arrive in the land of Middoni, where Lamoni finds favor in the eyes of the local king. Ammon and his brethren are freed from prison, having suffered severe mistreatment but having shown great patience in all of their travail.

> *An account of the preaching of Aaron, and Muloki, and their brethren, to the Lamanites.* [Note: This preamble was included in the original edition of the Book of Mormon published in 1830.]

CHAPTER 21

OVERVIEW

Aaron meets with strong resistance as he teaches the Amalekites and Amulonites at Jerusalem concerning the Atonement of Christ. He and his companions go to Middoni where their enemies imprison them and cause them much suffering. They are freed by Ammon and Lamoni and thereafter achieve much missionary success, being "led by the Spirit of the Lord" (verse 16). Ammon and Lamoni return to the land of Ishmael where they nurture and teach the Saints in an atmosphere of liberty and joy.

> *1 NOW when Ammon and his brethren separated themselves in the borders of the land of the Lamanites, behold* ***Aaron*** *took his journey toward the land which was called by the Lamanites, Jerusalem, calling it after the land of their fathers' nativity; and it was away joining the borders of Mormon.*

Aaron, Messenger of Hope

Aaron is another among the faithful missionary figures of the Book of Mormon. Like the other sons of King Mosiah, he is initially "numbered among the unbelievers" (Mosiah 27:8). But the Lord has an important calling for these young men and sends a heavenly messenger to intervene and bring about their spiritual transformation (Mosiah 27:11–18). After that, they go about "preaching the word of God in much tribulation" (see Mosiah 27:32), confirming their newly found faith, and bringing about much good in their own land and later among the Lamanites.

Following their miraculous conversion, Aaron and his brethren are filled with an overwhelming motivation to carry the gospel message to the Lamanites: "Now they were desirous that salvation should be declared to every creature, for they could not bear that any human soul should perish; yea, even the very thoughts that any soul should endure endless torment did cause them to quake and tremble" (see Mosiah 28:3). Thus, rather than accept the voice of the people as first choice to succeed his father as king (Mosiah 29:2–3), Aaron embarks on a missionary journey of service and hope that lasts fourteen years (approx. 90 B.C. to 77 B.C.; see Alma 17:4).

2–15 Aaron preaches in Jerusalem to the Amalekites and Amulonites, Nephite dissenters and apostates who have helped the Lamanites build the city. Aaron's message is unequivocally rejected by these callous people. As practitioners of the philosophy of the Nehors, they believe that all mankind will be saved and that there is no need for a Messiah and Redeemer. (The Amulonites are followers and descendants of the priests of wicked King Noah.) Aaron substantiates his witness of the Savior through the scriptures—but his audience remains unmoved. Aaron leaves and joins his companions, Muloki and Ammah, in a neighboring village. Having no success there, they go to Middoni where they are cast into prison and subjected to severe mistreatment until freed by Ammon and Lamoni.

> *16 And they went forth whithersoever* ***they were led by the Spirit of the Lord,*** *preaching the word of God in every synagogue of the Amalekites, or in every assembly of the Lamanites where they could be admitted.*
> *17 And it came to pass that the Lord began to bless them, insomuch that* ***they brought many to the knowledge of the truth;*** *yea, they did convince many of their sins, and of the traditions of their fathers, which were not correct.*

They were led by the Spirit of the Lord; they brought many to the knowledge of the truth

Aaron and his companions respond to the guidance of the Spirit and are blessed with a harvest of willing souls. Missionaries throughout the world pray for the Spirit to direct them to the honest in heart. Parents plead for the Spirit to help them raise their children in righteousness. Teachers pray with faith so they can teach by the Spirit (see D&C 42:14). We can be assured that the Spirit will lead us to do good, to do justly, to walk humbly, to judge righteously, and enlighten our souls and fill us with joy (see D&C 11:12–13). The Spirit is the key to a righteous life. Are we led by the Holy Spirit?

18–22 Ammon and Lamoni return to the land of Ishmael. Lamoni causes synagogues to be built throughout the land as places of assembly and worship. He teaches the people many things and grants them freedom of worship.

> *23 And Ammon did preach unto the people of King Lamoni; and it came to pass that he did teach them all things concerning things pertaining to righteousness. And* ***he did exhort them daily, with all diligence;*** *and they gave heed unto his word, and they were zealous for keeping the commandments of God.*

He did exhort them daily, with all diligence

Ammon teaches the people all they need to know about salvation and righteousness. He exerts a powerful influence on them, and they hearken to his counsel and obey the laws of God. His example reminds us that we can also magnify our stewardships before the Lord by counseling with diligence and regularly contacting all those we are called upon to teach. Our success will be increased through the blessings of the Lord.

CHAPTER 22

OVERVIEW

Using the scriptures, Aaron teaches the father of Lamoni about the Creation, the Fall, and the plan of redemption through the Atonement of Jesus Christ. The king agrees to "give away" all his sins to know God (verse 18). He prays and falls into a spiritual stupor. The queen concludes that Aaron has slain her husband, and she orders Aaron to be slain. Aaron revives the king, who ministers to his household and makes a proclamation throughout the land allowing the preaching of the gospel. The Nephites organize their boundaries to be more secure from the unconverted Lamanites.

> *1 NOW, as Ammon was thus teaching the people of Lamoni continually, we will return to the account of Aaron and his brethren; for after he departed from the land of Middoni* ***he was led by the Spirit*** *to the land of Nephi, even to the house of the king which was over all the land save it were the land of Ishmael; and he was the father of Lamoni.*

He was led by the Spirit

Aaron is a noble servant of the Lord who is worthy of the guidance of the Spirit, having searched diligently and prayed and fasted continually (see Alma 17:2–3). We can emulate his example in all that we do, knowing that the blessings of spiritual guidance will surely follow.

2–14 Aaron teaches the father of King Lamoni the principles of the gospel and bears witness to the reality of God. The king is receptive to all that is taught him. Aaron unfolds the plan of redemption through the scriptures, beginning from the Creation and the Fall, and establishing the verity of the Atonement of Christ. The faithful and obedient will have eternal life.

> *15 And it came to pass that after Aaron had expounded these things unto him, the king said:* ***What shall I do that I may have this eternal life*** *of which thou hast spoken? Yea, what shall I do that I may be born of God, having this wicked spirit rooted out of my breast, and receive his Spirit, that I may be filled with joy, that I may not be cast off at the last day? Behold, said he, I will give up all that I possess, yea, I will forsake my kingdom, that I may receive this great joy.*
> *16 But Aaron said unto him: If thou desirest this thing, if thou wilt bow down before God, yea, if thou wilt repent of all thy sins, and will* ***bow down before God, and call on his name in faith, believing that ye shall receive,*** *then shalt thou receive the hope which thou desirest.*

What shall I do that I may have this eternal life; bow down before God, and call on his name in faith, believing that ye shall receive

Aaron gives the king the formula for having the blessings and power of hope and salvation. We can have hope of eternal life as we repent and act in faith.

The goal of happiness and eternal life is achieved by keeping the commandments and enduring cheerfully to the end. The sins of commission and omission that so easily beset us are to be turned into acts of righteousness. We are to abstain from sin and give up things that have no eternal value. We are to be about our Father's business and not about the things of life that have no lasting value. What will we do to have the joy of eternal life? What will we give up that we might have the blessings of heaven?

> *17 And it came to pass that when Aaron had said these words, the king did bow down before the Lord, upon his knees; yea, even he did prostrate himself upon the earth, and cried mightily, saying:*
> *18 O God, Aaron hath told me that there is a God; and if there is a God, and if thou art God, wilt thou make thyself known unto me, and* ***I will give away all my sins to know thee,*** *and that I may be raised from the dead, and be saved at the last day. And now when the king had said these words,* ***he was struck as if he were dead.***
> *19 And it came to pass that* ***his servants ran and told the queen*** *all that had happened unto the king. And she came in unto the king; and when she saw him lay as if he were dead, and also Aaron and his brethren standing as though they had been the cause of his fall, she was angry with them, and commanded that her servants, or the servants of the king, should take them and slay them.*

I WILL GIVE AWAY ALL MY SINS TO KNOW THEE; HE WAS STRUCK AS IF HE WERE DEAD
The king utters a sentence that conveys the pure essence of the gospel of Jesus Christ, i.e., that we are to give away all our sins to know God. In his new state of mind, so different from his previous attitudes and desires, the king falls into a state of rapture that is misinterpreted by the queen as a sign of death. In fact, he is overpowered by the Spirit as he makes the inner commitment to change his life for good. We will know God if we are willing to "give away all [our] sins."

HIS SERVANTS RAN AND TOLD THE QUEEN—WIFE OF THE FATHER OF LAMONI
The king's heart has already been softened by the love that Aaron's brother, Ammon, has shown his son, King Lamoni (see Alma 20:26). Therefore, the king is receptive to Aaron's message and is overcome by the Spirit. However, the queen mistakes this spiritual rapture for death and orders her servants to slay Aaron and his companions as murderers. As it turns out, she too is reconciled to the mighty changes taking place in her family circle and soon becomes a central part of the movement. The queen's people will be the parents of the future courageous stripling warriors of

Helaman, who will report: "Yea, and they [the stripling warriors] did obey and observe to perform every word of command with exactness; yea, and even according to their faith it was done unto them; and I did remember the words which they said unto me that their mothers had taught them" (Alma 57:21).

20–35 Knowing the truth of the situation, the servants refuse to follow the queen's order to slay Aaron, fearing for their own safety before this messenger of the Lord. When she observes the panic of her servants, "she also [begins] to fear exceedingly, lest there should some evil come upon her." She commands her servants that they should go and call the people that they might slay Aaron and his brethren (verse 21). At this point, Aaron, knowing the suspicious mindset of the citizens of the land, raises the king from his spiritual slumber, much to the astonishment and relief of the queen and her entourage. The king ministers to them all, and "his whole household [is] converted unto the Lord" (Alma 22:23). By proclamation of the king, missionary work is then permitted throughout the land, resulting in the conversion of many thousands of Lamanites. Eventually, these people, soon to be called "Anti-Nephi-Lehies" (Alma 23:17), will forever renounce the use of their former weapons of war and are given a protectorate among the Nephites. The sons of these people—also known as the "people of Ammon"—become the 2,000 (later 2,060) stripling warriors who serve with honor in preserving the liberty of the people under the direction of Helaman. The Nephites organize their boundaries to be more secure from the unconverted Lamanites.

CHAPTER 23

OVERVIEW

The converted king of the Lamanites declares religious freedom throughout the realm. Aaron and his associates establish churches in all parts of the land. The missionary harvest is great, with Lamanites in seven cities coming into the fold of Christ. The Amalekites and Amulonites remain hard-hearted and reject the word of God. The converted Lamanites change their name to Anti-Nephi-Lehies. They prosper and become a righteous and peaceful people.

1–3 The king of the Lamanites sends out a proclamation that Ammon and his brethren are authorized to preach throughout the realm without restriction—"that the word of God might have no obstruction, but that it might go forth **throughout all the land**" (verse 3).

Throughout all the land

When we teach one, we teach many. Ammon's initial outreach is to King Lamoni. Aaron's initial outreach is to the father of King Lamoni. But there is enormous potential in their missionary activity, because these two royal students of the gospel open the floodgates of opportunity to reach thousands of others.

Missionary work can be a wonderful leveraging enterprise: when we bless the life of one person by bringing him or her into the fold of the Savior, that person, in turn, might bring many more into the fold over time. Thus our efforts can be magnified and multiplied in an endless process of enlarging the circles of spiritual influence, like the proverbial pebble in the pond causing increasing and ever-expanding ripples.

Within these passages of the Book of Mormon we see manifested the joy of helping people come unto Christ. Surely the sons of Mosiah and Alma experience the uplifting feelings described in the Doctrine and Covenants:

> Remember the worth of souls is great in the sight of God; . . .
>
> Wherefore, you are called to cry repentance unto this people.
>
> And if it so be that you should labor all your days in crying repentance unto this people, and bring, save it be one soul unto me, how great shall be your joy with him in the kingdom of my Father!
>
> And now, if your joy will be great with one soul that you have brought unto me into the kingdom of my Father, how great will be your joy if you should bring many souls unto me! (18:10,14–16)

The sons of Mosiah give their all to the Lord. They exemplify the valor and commitment called for by President Ezra Taft Benson: "In a word, we dedicate our all to the work of the Lord—the establishment and growth of his kingdom and the spread of righteousness. This is a major responsibility. We accept gratefully the challenge and pray ever for the Lord's sustaining power as we go forward. This great work is divine—directed by the Lord Jesus Christ through his church, The Church of Jesus Christ of Latter-day Saints" (*God, Family, Country: Our Three Great Loyalties* [Salt Lake City: Deseret Book, 1974], 50).

Memories: Be Bold in Proclaiming the Gospel

The account of how Ammon and Aaron established the Church among the Lamanites, beginning with the ruling royal families, illustrates the effective partnership between valiant missionaries and the Spirit of our Father in Heaven. When the Lord sends us to deliver the truth, we must do it in faith, boldly, fearing nothing. As Paul confirmed: "For whosoever shall call upon the name of the Lord shall be saved. How then shall they call on him in whom they have not believed? and how shall they believe in him of whom they have not heard? And how shall they hear without a preacher? And how shall they preach, except they be sent?" (Romans 10:13–15).

In our latter days there is ample opportunity to exhibit boldness on behalf of the kingdom of God. On December 1, 1831, in Hiram, Ohio, Joseph Smith and Sidney Rigdon received what is now Doctrine and Covenants Section 71, a commandment to set aside for a season their translation of the Bible and instead preach the gospel in the communities round about. The purpose for this new campaign was to use the truth to counteract the negative publicity being engendered at the time by anti-Mormon articles being published by defector Ezra Booth (see *HC* 1:215–217, 238–239): "Wherefore, confound your enemies; call upon them to meet you both in public and in private; and inasmuch as ye are faithful their shame shall be made manifest. Wherefore, let them bring forth their strong reasons against the Lord. Verily, thus saith the Lord unto you—there is no weapon that is formed against you shall prosper" (D&C 71:7–9). Joseph and Sidney were required to tap deeply into their spiritual faith to trust in the Lord for victory. And victory they obtained. For the next five or six weeks they labored diligently, "setting forth the truth, vindicating the cause of our Redeemer; showing that the day of vengeance was coming upon this generation like a thief in the night" (*HC* 1:241). Thus we see that the truth, delivered in the boldness of the Spirit, establishes the Lord's kingdom. Truth is an irrepressible weapon against folly, lies, bigotry, and darkness.

I recall from my experiences as a missionary in Germany many years ago an incident that happened in the city of Kassel. One of our missionaries serving in that city became aware of a series of anti-Mormon lectures being given by the minister of one of the large local congregations. This missionary and his companion therefore decided to attend the next lecture. For a time they listened silently from a bench in the rear of the large cathedral as the minister blasphemed the Church from his elevated pulpit before a receptive congregation of over a thousand. After a while, the young elder became more and more restless at the waves of lies and falsehoods emanating from the pulpit. As he later described it, he felt as though he were being lifted to his feet by an unseen force and propelled down the center aisle of the church to a position directly below the pulpit. He proceeded immediately to proclaim the words given to him by the Spirit of the Lord, as he described it, in order to refute every falsehood being proclaimed in the name of truth. He then bore fervent witness of the truth of the restored gospel, after which he and his companion distributed hundreds of tracts to the astounded parishioners leaving the building afterwards. This incident of courage and humble guidance by the Spirit opened many doors in that city to missionary work. (Richard J. Allen)

4–5 Aaron and his brethren establish churches throughout the land. Thousands come into the fold of Christ and are nourished through the holy scriptures.

> *6 And as sure as the Lord liveth, so sure* ***as many as believed,*** *or as many as were brought to the knowledge of the truth, through the preaching of Ammon and his brethren, according to the spirit of revelation and of prophecy, and the power of God working miracles in them—yea, I say unto you, as the Lord liveth, as many of the Lamanites as believed in their preaching, and were converted unto the Lord,* ***never did fall away.***

As many as believed never did fall away

So remarkable was the spiritual transformation among the Lamanites that Mormon, the compiler and abridger of the sacred record, is impressed to declare that they remained true throughout their lives, never falling away. What does it take to ensure that one never falls away? It takes commitment like that of the Lamanite converts. They are zealous in keeping the commandments. They are passionate and devoted to their covenants. They are honest and upright in all things. They are firm in their faith and endure to the end. Conversion to the Lord through the Spirit is a transforming and magnifying experience, leading to inner peace and a commitment to follow the commandments and endure to the end. It is the Spirit that converts. President Brigham Young taught:

Brigham Young

> *The Spirit, Not Logic or Debate, Makes Converts*—Let one go forth who is careful to prove logically all he says by numerous quotations from the revelations, and let another travel with him who can say, by the power of the Holy Ghost, Thus saith the Lord, and tell what the people should believe—what they should do—how they should live, and teach them to yield to the principles of salvation,—though he may not be capable of producing a single logical argument, though he may tremble under a sense of his weakness, cleaving to the Lord for strength, as such men generally do, you will invariably find that the man who testifies by the power of the Holy Ghost will convince and gather many more of the honest and upright than will the merely logical reasoner. (*Discourses of Brigham Young,* comp. John A. Widtsoe [Salt Lake City: Deseret Book, 1954], 330)

7–15 As a result of the adoption of a policy of religious freedom by the reigning king of the realm, many thousands of Lamanites are converted through the efforts of the sons of Mosiah.

They become "**a righteous people**" (verse 7), God-fearing and industrious, with a hope toward the future and a faith in their Lord and Savior, Jesus Christ. In contrast, the Amalekites universally refuse to respond to the gospel invitation—"save only one" (verse 14); the Amulonites follow suit and do not reform their ways.

A RIGHTEOUS PEOPLE

The converted Lamanites rise in majesty to embrace their heritage as a remnant of the house of Israel, with all the privileges and blessings accorded the righteous by a merciful God. In contrast, the Nephite dissenters—the Amalekites and Amulonites—remain in spiritual darkness.

In their capacity as messengers of the good news of redemption, the sons of Mosiah contribute to the harvest of the Abrahamic covenant by means of which the word of truth is dispensed to the honest at heart. This divine process continues today. President Ezra Taft Benson declared:

> The missionary force brought a harvest of converts from all over the world. Seeds planted abroad as missions became stakes. Truly Zion had put on her beautiful garments; her borders had become enlarged. When Joseph Fielding Smith, son of President Joseph F. Smith, became president of the Church, he declared: "We are coming of age as a Church and as a people. We have attained the stature and strength that is enabling us to fulfill the commission given us by God through the Prophet Joseph Smith that we should carry the glad tidings of the restoration to every nation and to all people." (*Come unto Christ* [Salt Lake City: Deseret Book, 1983], 82)

President Benson also declared: "The sweetest work in all the world is the work in which we are engaged in helping to save and exalt the souls of the children of men. There isn't anything so important, so precious, so enjoyable, so soul-satisfying" (*The Teachings of Ezra Taft Benson* [Salt Lake City: Bookcraft, 1988], 189).

YOU ALWAYS HAVE FIVE MINUTES

> "Do you have five minutes?" The question struck a responsive chord. And although I didn't have time to talk to those missionaries, I remembered that a friend once said that "if you have any time for your fellowmen, you must have time to listen to those who tell others of their beliefs. You always have five minutes." So I invited them in.

Their message was interesting, and after their second visit a feeling began to grow inside me that maybe their words were true. However, my husband would have none of it. After I had visited with them four or five times, my husband became so angry that he threatened to leave me and the children if I didn't put an end to their visits.

We vacationed in Austria that summer, and I tried to forget about religion, but I had such mixed feelings that after we came home to Denmark I told my husband that I must earnestly pray to know whether or not the message of the missionaries was true. He replied, "That's a good idea, and when you have done that, we won't talk about it any more."

For three days I kept the Word of Wisdom and sought the Lord in prayer, but my prayers seemed empty words to me. Still, I persisted, and finally I found myself offering a sincere prayer with faith in Christ. I knew when I arose from my knees that if I didn't get an answer, I wouldn't pray any more. An hour later the doorbell rang. It was the missionaries.

When they walked into our living room, a strange feeling came over me. It started in my head and went completely through me, and I knew that my prayers had been answered. I went into the bedroom to thank the Lord and I laughed and cried and prayed, all at the same time.

When I returned to the living room, the elders told me they had been teaching a lady that day when they suddenly had nothing more to say to her. This had never happened to them before, but they made another appointment with her and left. On their way to the next appointment, they found themselves outside our apartment building, and our little boy ran up to them and asked if they were going to visit his mother. Since they had been rejected there before, they debated the matter, but one of them said the Spirit strongly impressed him to call. Ten days later, I was baptized.

There is a lovely conclusion to my story. At this time one of the General Authorities of the Church was visiting in Denmark and the missionaries took me to see him. He told me that if I would follow the counsel of Church leaders, it wouldn't be long before my husband was baptized. Surely he has made a mistake, I thought. My husband will never join the Church. That same evening my branch president asked me what I thought of the Church and I answered, "I have found so much love here." Then he said to me, "That same love you feel here you must take home to your husband."

Great Missionary Story

I was a little angry. I loved my husband and thought such counsel unnecessary. But on the long drive home, I realized that I must speak kindly to my husband about the Church. My change of attitude made him curious, and when the children came home from church with sparkling eyes, he really began to investigate. Three months later my husband and our eight-year-old boy were baptized. It was truly one of the happiest days of my life. (Eika Olsen, in *Remarkable Stories from the Lives of Latter-day Saint Women,* comp. Leon R. Hartshorn [Salt Lake City: Deseret Book, 1973], 2:194–195)

16 And now it came to pass that the king and those who were converted were desirous that they might have a name, that thereby they might be distinguished from their brethren; therefore the king consulted with Aaron and many of their priests, concerning the name that they should take upon them, that they might be distinguished.
17 And it came to pass that they called their names ***Anti-Nephi-Lehies;*** *and they were called by this name and were no more called Lamanites.*
18 And they began to be a very industrious people; yea, and they were friendly with the Nephites; therefore, they did open a correspondence with them, and the curse of God did no more follow them.

Anti-Nephi-Lehies

The missionary labors of the sons of Mosiah—Ammon, Aaron, Omner, and Himni—take place approximately 90 B.C. to 77 B.C. (see Alma 17:4). It is at the end of this period that the father of Lamoni, the great king over all the Lamanite territories, sees the wisdom of separating his enlightened followers from the traditionalists who remain hard-hearted. Therefore, he and his fellow converts decide, in counsel with Ammon and the priests, to take upon themselves a name that will thereafter distinguish them from their brethren. By consensus, the name chosen is **"Anti-Nephi-Lehies"** (Alma 23:16), superseding the name of Lamanites. So firm is their resolve to place their bloody past deeds behind them and start a new life in Christ that they forever abandon their weapons of war and make an oath never to take them up again (see Alma 24:15–18).

EVIDENCE: Anti-Nephi-Lehies

The possible meaning of the name Anti-Nephi-Lehies is considered by scholar Daniel H. Ludlow:

Alma 23:18

> The Lamanites converted by the four sons of Mosiah and their missionary companions took upon themselves the name of "Anti-Nephi-Lehies." (Alma 23:17; Alma 24:1–5.) The "Nephi-Lehi" part of the title probably had reference to the lands of Nephi and Lehi (or the people then living in those lands) rather than to the descendants of Nephi or Lehi. However, Dr. Hugh Nibley has found "a Semitic and common Indo-European root corresponding to anti that means 'in the face of' or 'facing,' as of one facing a mirror, and by extension either 'one who opposes' or 'one who imitates.'" (Quoted in Eldin Ricks, *Book of Mormon Study Guide*, 63.) Thus the term "Anti-Nephi-Lehies" might refer to those who imitate the teachings of the descendants of Nephi and Lehi" (*A Companion to Your Study of the Book of Mormon* [Salt Lake City: Deseret Book, 1976], 209).

CONCLUDING THOUGHTS

Effective missionaries, like the sons of Mosiah, prepare themselves to be instruments in the hands of the Lord. This takes a strong desire, devoted gleaning of saving knowledge, cultivating a testimony of the gospel, exhibiting faith in the Lord Jesus Christ, and living worthy of the Spirit. Above all, missionary service requires that we have charity for all. This is our role as disciples of Christ in this the dispensation of the fulness of times. We are all missionaries. We learn that effective missionaries are first servants, and then teachers, and that by teaching the one, we teach the many. Truly the Book of Mormon is our divine companion to missionary work in the latter days.

CHAPTER 24

OVERVIEW

The Lamanites threaten to come up against the Anti-Nephi-Lehies. Before he dies, the aging king confers the kingdom upon one of his sons, whom he names Anti-Nephi-Lehi. Ammon confers with Lamoni and Anti-Nephi-Lehi on how to respond to the imminent attacks of their enemies. The king and his people give thanks to the Lord for His mercy in forgiving them of their sins, and they covenant to forsake any form of aggression. They bury their weapons and prostrate themselves in prayer before the attacking forces. Many of the attackers—more than those slain among the peacemakers—desist and repent of their sins, joining themselves to the people of the Lord. However, none of the Amalekites or Amulonites repent.

1–2 The Amalekites and Amulonites incite the unconverted Lamanites to rebel against the king of the Anti-Nephi-Lehi people.

> *3 Now the king conferred the kingdom upon his son, and he called his name* ***Anti-Nephi-Lehi.***

Anti-Nephi-Lehi—King of the Covenant

Through the blessings of the Lord, the sons of Mosiah experience a remarkable missionary harvest among the Lamanites, including Lamoni, king in the land of Ishmael, and his father, king over all the land. Just prior to his death, the aging father of Lamoni confers the kingdom upon another of his sons, whom he names Anti-Lehi-Nephi (see Alma 24:3–4). Concerning the life of this new king we know very little. Mormon has preserved for us the stirring speech he delivers to his people to sharpen their resolve in honoring the covenant they have made to forsake their former warlike lifestyle and embrace the gospel with total commitment. Here are the circumstances leading up to the delivery of his speech:

4–6 The aging king dies amidst the sounds of war. Ammon and his colleagues meet with King Lamoni and his brother, Anti-Nephi-Lehi, to discuss how the people should respond to the threats being made against them. The converts follow the counsel of their king and unanimously oppose taking up arms or even making any preparations for war.

> *7 Now, these are the words which he said unto the people concerning the matter:* ***I thank my God,*** *my beloved people, that our great God has in goodness sent these our brethren, the Nephites, unto us to preach unto us, and to convince us of the traditions of our wicked fathers.*
> *8 And behold,* ***I thank my great God*** *that he has given us a portion of his Spirit to soften our hearts, that we have opened a correspondence with these brethren, the Nephites.*
> *9 And behold,* ***I also thank my God,*** *that by opening this correspondence we have been convinced of our sins, and of the many murders which we have committed.*
> *10* ***And I also thank my God,*** *yea, my great God, that he hath granted unto us* ***that we might repent*** *of these things, and also that he hath forgiven us of those our many sins and murders which we have committed, and taken away the guilt from our hearts, through the merits of his Son.*

I THANK MY GOD THAT WE MIGHT REPENT

The king expresses his gratitude to God for the opportunity to repent. These royal converts have been forgiven of their sins; their guilt has been taken away through the Savior. We should never forget the blessing of the principle of repentance—a gift from God through our Savior Jesus Christ. When we repent, we receive joy, but we also bring joy to the Lord (see D&C 18:13).

11–13 The king admonishes his people to avoid staining their swords anymore with the blood of their brethren, lest the Atonement of Christ might not be able to cleanse them again.

EVIDENCE: EXEMPTION FROM MILITARY SERVICE (Alma 24:11–13; 27:23–24)

In the Book of Mormon, the only individuals exempted from active military duty were Ammon's converts, who had repented of their previous shedding of blood and sworn an oath never to take up arms again. These righteous Lamanites, who joined the Saints in Zarahemla, were not subject to military service if they would help supply their Nephite protectors with provisions. In ancient times, every able-bodied man was obligated by law to defend his nation or tribe; this was the case in Nephite society as well. However, certain exceptions were allowed under the law of Moses. One provision of the law stated that the duty of military service applied only in fighting an enemy, not in fighting against one's brethren. In the Nephite army, Ammon's people would have been forced to slay their own brethren, the Lamanites. Another portion of the law offered humanitarian exemptions from the military for those who had recently married, built a new house, or planted a new vineyard, and those who felt "fearful and fainthearted" (see Deuteronomy 20:5–9; 24:5). Certainly the Ammonites were fearful and fainthearted at the thought of breaking an oath with God by taking up arms. Lastly, according to a provision of the Mosaic law, men remaining at home were required to continue to provide behind-the-lines support, which often meant—as it did in Alma 27:24—providing food and other supplies for the armies. (See *Echoes,* 357–361.)

> *14 And **the great God has had mercy on us,** and made these things known unto us that we might not perish; yea, and he has made these things known unto us beforehand, because he loveth our souls as well as he loveth our children; therefore, in his mercy he doth visit us by his angels, that the plan of salvation might be made known unto us as well as unto future generations.*
> *15 **Oh, how merciful is our God!** And now behold, since it has been as much as we could do to get our stains taken away from us, and our swords are made bright, let us*

hide them away that they may be kept bright, as ***a testimony to our God*** *at the last day, or at the day that we shall be brought to stand before him to be judged, that we have not stained our swords in the blood of our brethren since he imparted his word unto us and has made us clean thereby.*
16 And now, my brethren, if our brethren seek to destroy us, behold, we will hide away our swords, yea, even we will bury them deep in the earth, that they may be kept bright, ***as a testimony*** *that we have never used them, at the last day; and if our brethren destroy us, behold,* ***we shall go to our God and shall be saved.***

The great God has had mercy on us; Oh, how merciful is our God! A testimony to our God; we shall go to our God and shall be saved

The Anti-Nephi-Lehies are prepared to follow the exhortation of their king and honor a covenant of peace by refusing to take up arms against their brethren. The framework of the covenant is to be the mercy of the Lord. His mercy has lifted from their shoulders the burdens of sin, and His mercy will in turn lift them up unto Him in the event they should lose their lives in honoring their covenant. Thus they bear testimony to their commitment by burying their swords deep in the earth. In our day, what is our own testimony before the Lord? Are we willing to live up to our covenant commitments? How do we witness our sincere commitment before Him?

17–27 The people unitedly bury their weapons of war in the earth, thus "vouching and covenanting with God, that rather than shed the blood of their brethren they [will] give up their own lives" (verse 18). When the Lamanites begin to attack, the people prostrate themselves before them and begin to pray. Many are slain before the miraculous moment comes in which the bloodthirsty assailants, amazed at such behavior, desist their attack, "for **they repented** of the things which they had done" (verse 24). As a result, over a thousand also abjure the use of force and join the people of Anti-Nephi-Lehi—more than the number of those who have been lost in the attack. "Thus we see," Mormon reminds us, "that the Lord worketh in many ways to the salvation of his people" (verse 27).

They repented

Many of the attacking individuals are transformed in their hearts to see the courage and commitment of their victims. They immediately abandon their objective to exact revenge and to kill. They are brought to the point of making a covenant of peace witnessing their willingness to repent. "By this ye may know if a man repenteth of his sins—behold, he will confess them and forsake them" (D&C 58:43). In the wake of continuing battles with the Nephites, other Lamanites will in the future, also come to a realization of the error of their ways and join with the Anti-Nephi-Lehies (see Alma 25:13). Just as these converted Lamanites who have entered into a covenant of peace abstain from their former bloodthirsty practices, followers of Christ repent of their sinful ways and forever abandon those practices that are contrary to the teachings of the Savior. President Howard W. Hunter taught these stimulating truths:

> How can men of conscience ignore the teachings of the Master in their daily affairs, in business, or in government? We stand by and wink at many things because we fear to do anything about them. We may be against crime or communism, but what do we do about it? We may be against corruption in government or against juvenile delinquency, but what do we do about it? We may have a belief in the gospel of Jesus Christ, but what are we doing about it? We need to push fear into the background and come forward with a definite, positive declaration, and assume responsibility.
>
> Can we stand on the sidelines and merely observe? This is a day for action. This is the time for decision, not tomorrow, not next week. This is the time to make our covenant with the Lord. Now is the time for those who have been non-committal or who have had a halfhearted interest to come out boldly and declare belief in Christ and be willing to demonstrate faith by works. (*The Teachings of Howard W. Hunter,* ed. Clyde J. Williams [Salt Lake City: Bookcraft, 1997], 46)

Memories: Commitment to Our Covenants

As missionaries, and as future parents in Zion, we must remember that we don't change any faster than we make and keep commitments. The Lord calls them covenants. Our exaltation is determined by how well we have kept our baptismal, our priesthood, and our temple covenants. And when we keep those covenants, the promises and blessings are ours. I have learned that when covenants are deepened because our commitment is strong, our lives are different. If in your lives—either at this moment as elders and sisters, or later—you find yourselves vacillating, look deep into your souls and check your level of commitment to your covenants. And when your level of commitment to your covenants has deepened to where you feel that it is life eternal to keep them, you will be a missionary for life. You will help many souls come unto Christ. When you make covenants with the Lord at that altar in the temple, and you become a mother or father, and find yourselves missionaries of a whole different sort, you will find that you'll never be totally converted until you learn to make and keep covenants by committing yourselves to the Lord.

Our blessings here and hereafter are dependent upon keeping the covenants we make with God. We re-covenant each week. This is how Heavenly Father helps us—by continually reminding us of our commitments to His law and His covenants. The Spirit will help us keep those covenants, and keeping those covenants will exalt us." (Ed J. Pinegar, *The Ultimate Missionary Companion* [American Fork, UT: Covenant Communications, 2001], 143–144.)

28–29 Most of those who slay the prostrated people of Anti-Nephi-Lehi are Amalekites and Amulonites—adherents, for the most part, to the order of Nehors. None of these are among the group who desist their aggression and join the people of God. Those who convert at this point are actual descendants of Laman and Lemuel.

> *30 And thus we can plainly discern, that **after a people have been once enlightened** by the Spirit of God, and have had great knowledge of things pertaining to righteousness, **and then have fallen away** into sin and transgression, **they become more hardened,** and thus their state becomes worse than though they had never known these things.*

After a people have been once enlightened and then have fallen away they become more hardened

Here is a sad commentary on human nature in the context of spiritual matters. Apostates become more hardened still. Aaron has attempted to preach the gospel to the Amulonites around 90 B.C. but with no success because of the hardness of their hearts (see Alma 23:14). The Amulonites stir up their Lamanite colleagues against the Anti-Nephi-Lehies—the converts of Ammon and Aaron and their colleagues (see Alma 24:1–2). The Amulonites participate in the slaying of the believers who have laid down their arms and are prepared to suffer death at the hands of the enemy. The attackers who are Lamanites by lineage are softened in their hearts when they see the devotion of the fallen converts, their brethren; however, the Amulonites and Amalekites are the last to desist. There is scarcely any manifestation of the hardness of hearts that exceeds that as demonstrated by apostates to the faith. The examples of the Amulonites and the Amalekites confirm this troubling fact. Eventually the Amulonites turn against their Lamanite allies and are subsequently hunted down and slain (Alma 25:8–12).

CHAPTER 25

OVERVIEW

The Lamanites destroy the city of Ammonihah, thus fulfilling the prophecy of Alma to that effect. The renegade priests of Noah (the seed of Amulon) kill many convert Lamanites by fire, thus fulfilling the prophecy of Abinadi. The Lamanites hunt and destroy the seed of Amulon, again fulfilling the prophecy of Abinadi. Many of the Lamanites join the people of Anti-Nephi-Lehi and become righteous, keep the law of Moses, and look forward to the coming of Christ. The sons of Mosiah rejoice in their missionary success.

1–12 In the ebb and flow of people and their interrelationships during this period of time, there is confirmation of the fulfillment of prophecy. Many of the Lamanites who have turned away from slaying the Anti-Nephi-Lehies now act on their antipathy toward the Nephites by crossing into the land of Zarahemla and destroying the city of Ammonihah and its inhabitants. This fulfills the prophecy of Alma (see Alma 8:16) concerning the ultimate outcome if the people failed to repent—and it repeats the report of the downfall of Ammonihah given earlier (see Alma 16:9–10). In subsequent battles with the Lamanites, the Nephites slay virtually all of the seed of Amulon and his brethren, the renegade priests of Noah. The Amulonites who survive flee into the east wilderness, usurping power and authority over the Lamanites and causing many of the converts among the people to be martyred by fire. This action so angers the Lamanites that they begin to hunt the remaining seed of Amulon and slay those who do not flee: "And behold they are hunted at this day by the Lamanites" (verse 9). These actions confirm the prophecy of Abinadi before the court of King Noah when he said: "But this much I tell you, what you do with me, after this, shall be as a type and a shadow of things which are to come" (Mosiah 13:10; compare Mosiah 17:15). Just as Abinadi has been killed by fire, the future Lamanite converts are also killed by fire at the hands of the seed of Amulon—the surviving element of King Noah's circle of priests. At the same time, Abinadi prophesies to his tormentors at King Noah's court: "Yea, and ye shall be smitten on every hand, and shall be driven and scattered to and fro, even as a wild flock is driven by wild and ferocious beasts. And in that day ye shall be hunted, and ye shall be taken by the hand of your enemies, and then ye shall suffer, as I suffer, the pains of death by fire" (Mosiah 17:17–18).

Noah himself is put to death by fire (see Mosiah 19:20) and the remnant of his priests are indeed smitten and hunted down—just as Abinadi predicted. In this complex series of events we see confirmed the words of Alma that "the word of God must be fulfilled" (Alma 5:58).

13–14 Many of the Lamanites return to their own land and join with the people of God, the Anti-Nephi-Lehies. They bury their weapons of war and become a righteous people.

> *15 Yea, and they did keep **the law of Moses;** for it was expedient that they should keep **the law of Moses** as yet, for it was not all fulfilled. But notwithstanding **the law of Moses,** they did look forward to the coming of Christ, considering that **the law of Moses** was a type of his coming, and believing that they must keep those outward performances until the time that he should be revealed unto them.*
> *16 Now they did not suppose that salvation came by the law of Moses; but **the law of Moses** did serve to **strengthen their faith in Christ;** and thus they did retain a hope through faith, unto eternal salvation, relying upon the spirit of prophecy, which spake of those things to come.*

The law of Moses; strengthen their faith in Christ

The Israelites had been a stiffnecked people and the law was designed to help them to look to Christ as if He had already come (see Mosiah 3:13–15). The law of Moses was a schoolmaster to bring people to Christ and to strengthen their faith (see Galatians 3:24–25; Alma 25:15–16). It was to help them to look forward to the coming of Christ (see Jacob 4:5; Jarom 1:11). Salvation did not come by the law but through the Atonement of Christ (see Mosiah 13:27–28). It was taught merely as a shadow of things to come (see Mosiah 16:14–15). The law of Moses was fulfilled through and in the Lord Jesus Christ (see 3 Nephi 9:17; 15:4–8).

> *17 And now behold, Ammon, and Aaron, and Omner, and Himni, and their brethren did rejoice exceedingly, for the success which they had had among the Lamanites, seeing that the Lord had granted unto them according to their prayers, and that he had also **verified his word unto them in every particular.***

Verified his word unto them in every particular

The sons of Mosiah come to the end of their fourteen-year mission among the Lamanites. Their missionary harvest has been great. They know that the Lord has answered their prayers "in every particular" (verse 17)—and they are full of joy because of it. As we look back upon our own lives, to what extent can we discern the hand of the Lord in our successes? With an eye of faith and a disposition to pray always, we will, like the sons of Mosiah, be able to see that the Lord has verified His word unto us "in every particular."

CHAPTER 26

OVERVIEW

Ammon glories in the blessings the Lord has granted him and his brethren in bringing thousands of souls unto Christ. Their many converts "are in the hands of the Lord of the harvest, and they are his; and he will raise them up at the last day" (verse 10). Aaron counsels Ammon not to boast, but Ammon asserts that he does not boast in himself but in God, "for in his strength I can do all things" (Alma 26:12). The faithful and penitent can know the mysteries of God and rejoice in the light and glory of the Lord, who loves all people.

> 1 *AND now, these are the words of Ammon to his brethren, which say thus: My brothers and my brethren, behold I say unto you,* ***how great reason have we to rejoice;*** *for could we have supposed when we started from the land of Zarahemla that God would have granted unto us such great blessings?*

How great reason have we to rejoice

We cannot praise the Lord enough or thank Him too profusely for His bounteous blessings to us. In an uncommonly expressive outpouring of emotion, Ammon recounts before his brethren the trials and blessings of their missionary labors and rejoices in the triumphs of conversion presided over by "the Lord of the harvest" (Alma 26:7). President Ezra Taft Benson discusses the trials, challenges, blessings, and joys of missionary work:

> We must not allow ourselves to become discouraged. Missionary work brings joy, optimism, and happiness. We must not give Satan an opportunity to discourage us. Here again, work is the answer. The Lord has given us a key by which we can overcome discouragement: "Come unto me, all ye that labour and are heavy laden, and I will give you rest. Take my yoke upon you, and learn of me; for I am meek and lowly in heart; and ye shall find rest unto your souls. For my yoke is easy, and my burden is light." (Matthew 11:28–30.)
>
> In the Savior's time the purpose of a yoke was to get oxen pulling together in a united effort. Our Savior has a great cause to move forward. He has asked all of us to be equally yoked together to move His cause forward. It requires not only a united effort; it requires also complete dependence on Him. As He said to His early apostles, "Without me ye can do nothing." (John 15:5.)

Our work will be light and easy to bear if we will be dependent on the Lord and work.

We must not worry about being successful. We *will* be successful—there is no doubt about it. The Lord has sent us to the earth at the time of harvest. He does not expect us to fail. He has called no one to this work to fail. He expects us to succeed. The Prophet Joseph Smith said, "After all that has been said, the greatest and most important duty is to preach the Gospel." (*HC* 2:478.)

We are engaged in missionary service to testify of the greatest event that has transpired in this world since the resurrection of the Master: the coming of God the Father and His Son, Jesus Christ, to the boy-prophet, Joseph Smith. We are sent out to testify of a new volume of scripture, a new witness for Christ.

Missionary work provides us the happiest years of our lives. I know whereof I speak. I have tasted the joy of missionary work. There is no work in all the world that can bring an individual greater joy and happiness. (*Come unto Christ* [Salt Lake City: Deseret Book, 1983], 95)

Memories: The Joy in a Converted Soul

It was about 1969 when a young girl named Susan Gerszewski came to see me. "Bishop, you've got to take my name off the records of the Church."

I said, "Oh Susan, what's wrong?"

"My brothers think I'm a dork for being here at BYU, and I can't stand the pressure when I go home and my parents are wondering what's gone wrong with me."

And then all of a sudden, the Lord stepped in and words came out of my mouth like this: "Susan, I promise you that if you stay faithful, your brothers will join the Church and your parents' hearts will soften." Now how could I say that? I couldn't. Only the Lord could.

She said, " Oh I just don't know, Bishop, I just don't know."

I said, "Well Susan, is the Book of Mormon true?"

"Well, of course it is, Bishop."

"Do you love the Savior and do you believe in Heavenly Father?"

"Yes I do."

"Is the Prophet the head of the Church today?"

"Of course."

"Is this the true Church?"

"Of course it is. But I just can't stand the pressure."

I said, "Susan, will you be willing to try? Because the Lord just gave you a promise."

She said, "Well, I guess I can try." That year she moved out of the ward and I lost track of her.

Well, at BYU in 1972 I volunteered to teach another religion class, besides the Book of Mormon, before going to my dental office. It was the Gospel Principles and Practices class. There were about sixty students in the class. Life was going merrily along when on the last day to drop the class, a student came up to me and said, "I've got to drop your class."

I asked, "How come?"

He said, "Well I'm on scholarship, and if I don't get a B or a B+ I could lose my scholarship; and I got a C+ on the test, and besides, I'm not a Mormon."

I looked at his little information sheet I had him fill out before class, and I'd missed it. He'd checked "nonmember" so close to the "member" that I'd missed it.

I said, "Well, Jim, you mean you're just afraid you won't get a B?"

He said, "Well, how can I? I'm not a member and I just can't risk it."

I said, "Jim, I've got an idea. Do you normally study once a week for this class?"

He answered, "Yes."

I said, "Jim, I've got it. Would you mind studying with me Tuesday nights before class on Wednesday, for an hour?"

He said, "Okay, but what will that do?"

I continued, "Well, Jim, you want a B, right? Do you know who makes out the grade?" He answered, "Well, you do."

I smiled. "That's right, Jim, I'm guaranteeing you a B or a B+."

"You mean you'll guaran . . ."

"I guarantee it. Look, I'm going to teach you extra Tuesday nights. If you're in my house for an hour, well, I'll make up the test, too. I'll even help you prepare for the test. Jim I'm guaranteeing you this."

Jim said, "Well that's a deal, I'm going to study with you."

So Jim came up to my house to study. This went on for a couple of weeks, and then one day he asked, "Hey, Brother Ed, could I bring my brother and my roommate up? I mean, we have banana splits and root beer floats and doughnuts every study night; we might as well have parties when you teach."

And so I said, "You bet, you bring them up." So we went along for four more weeks. Then one night when they came up, they were kidding around a lot. I said, "You guys are sure having a hoot tonight. What's up around here?"

They looked at each other as if to say, "Okay, who's going to tell him?" Then Jim finally said, "Brother Ed, we've been thinking, and we talked to our bishop, and we all want to be baptized, and will you baptize us and confirm us members of the Church next week?"

As I floated down from the ceiling I said, "Yes, Jim. I will, I will, I will." Well, his name was Jim Gerszewski. Jim was Susan's brother; Susan was at the baptism, and all of us felt intense joy that day.

Now you tell me that God our Father and Jesus Christ are not in charge of everything on this earth. How could those words come out of my mouth: "Your brothers will join the Church"? How, two years later, could one of those brothers be in my class? There were 20,000 students at BYU. Don't tell me that the Lord's hand isn't in all things that are good. All three boys served missions. All three were married in the temple.

So as I learned again that year, the Spirit "will show unto you all things what ye should do" (2 Nephi 32:5). Why is this so important? Because the vision in missionary work is that you must prepare people to feel the Spirit. Their needs are individual—so you must be in tune to what they need. Then, once they feel the Spirit, you can invite them to make a commitment. Once you've invited them to make a commitment, you must follow up with them to help them keep that commitment. (Ed J. Pinegar)

No Finer Missionary Guide

Over the years I have found great satisfaction in plumbing the spiritual depths of the Book of Mormon with students in Sunday School, priesthood, and institute classes in a quest to learn the essence of missionary work. The missionary experiences of the sons of Mosiah, for example, offer a unique and powerful blueprint of what it takes to be an effective missionary (see especially Mosiah 27–28, Alma 17–26). There is no finer missionary guide than what one finds in the scriptures. Looking back over their chronicle of courage in the face of affliction and triumph in the face of overwhelming odds provides a remarkably comprehensive portrait of the ideal and noble missionary. The following chart summarizes the salient points and gives the scriptural references for review:

Item	Key point	Key scriptural phrases	Reference
A. Are we prepared?			
1.	repentance	"And they traveled throughout all the land of Zarahemla . . . zealously striving to repair all the injuries which they had done to the church"	Mosiah 27:35

Item	Key point	Key scriptural phrases	Reference
2.	desire	"For they could not bear that any human soul should perish"	Mosiah 28:3; see D&C 4:3
3.	spiritual priorities	"Having refused the kingdom which their father was desirous to confer upon them"	Alma 17:6
4.	scripture study	"They had searched the scriptures diligently"	Alma 17:2
5.	fasting and prayer	"They had given themselves to much prayer, and fasting"	Alma 17:3; see also 17:9
B. Are we called of the Lord?			
6.	divine approval	"And the Lord said unto Mosiah: Let them go up, for many shall believe on their words"	Mosiah 28:7
7.	empowered	"He [Ammon] departed from them, after having blessed them according to their several stations"	Alma 17:18; and see 17:3
C. Do we have the right purpose at heart?			
8.	service	"That they might be an instrument in the hands of God to bring . . . their brethren . . . to the knowledge of the truth"	Alma 17:9; also 17:16
9.	great cause	"For they supposed that great was the work which they had undertaken"	Alma 17:13
D. Do we have the essential missionary qualities?			
10.	patience and long-suffering	"Yet ye shall be patient in long-suffering and afflictions, that ye may show forth good examples unto them in me"	Alma 17:11
11.	courage	"The hearts of the sons of Mosiah . . . took courage to go forth unto the Lamanites"	Alma 17:12
12.	trust	"They separated themselves and departed one from another, trusting in the Lord"	Alma 17:13

Item	Key point	Key scriptural phrases	Reference
13.	persistence	"And they had been teaching the word of God for the space of fourteen years"	Alma 17:4
14.	humility	"Yea, I know that I am nothing; as to my strength I am weak . . . in his strength I can do all things"	Alma 26:12; and see 18:35
15.	wisdom and innocence	"Now Ammon, being wise, yet harmless . . ."	Alma 18:22; see Matt. 10:16; D&C 111:11
E. Have we sought the appropriate missionary gifts?			
16.	prophecy and revelation	"Therefore they had the spirit of prophecy and revelation"	Alma 17:3
17.	power and authority	"And when they taught, they taught with power and authority"	Alma 17:3
18.	discernment	"Ammon, being filled with the Spirit of God, therefore he perceived the thoughts of the king"	Alma 18:16; and see 18:18
F. Do we proceed according to a careful plan?			
19.	follow the Spirit	"And they went forth whithersoever they were led by the Spirit of the Lord"	Alma 21:16; and see 20:2; 11:21–22
20.	leverage your time	"The king of the Lamanites sent a proclamation . . . that the word of God might have no obstruction" i.e. the missionaries sought out leaders of influence to spread the gospel to many	Alma 23:1–3; and see Alma 21:22
21.	be a servant	Ammon to King Lamoni: "I will be thy servant"	Alma 17:25; and see 18:8–10; 14, 17; 19:3
22.	be a friend	"We know that he is a friend to the king"	Alma 18:3
23.	appeal to the deepest values	". . . that I may win the hearts of these my fellow servants" [i.e., by saving their lives]	Alma 17:29; and see 19:7; 20:26

Item	Key point	Key scriptural phrases	Reference
24.	apply talents	"They began to be astonished at his power"	Alma 17:36
25.	show leadership and initiative	"And they did follow Ammon . . . they did as Ammon commanded them"	Alma 17:32, 34
26.	be positive	"Be of good cheer"	Alma 17:31
27.	commit people to action	"Wilt thou hearken unto my words, if I tell thee by what power I do these things?"	Alma 18:22
28.	be bold when appropriate	"And Ammon began to speak unto him with boldness"	Alma 18:24
29.	use questions effectively	"Believest thou that there is a God?"	Alma 18:24; 19:9
30.	teach only fundamentals	"But the sufferings and death of Christ atone for their sins, through faith and repentance . . ."	Alma 22:14
31.	teach from the scriptures	"And [they] laid before him the records and the holy scriptures"	Alma 18:36; see also Alma 22:12
32.	bear testimony	"This is God . . . and he knows all the thoughts and intents of the heart . . . I am called by his Holy Spirit to teach these things"	Alma 18:28, 32, 34
33.	teach prayer	"If thou wilt bow down before God . . . then shalt thou receive the hope which thou desirest"	Alma 22:16
34.	confirm the workings of the Spirit	"Now, this was what Ammon desired, for he knew that King Lamoni was under the power of God . . ."	Alma 19:6, 10
35.	use multiple witnesses	"And they did all declare unto the people the selfsame thing"	Alma 19:33

Item	Key point	Key scriptural phrases	Reference
G. Do we follow through?			
36.	give thanks	"He fell upon his knees, and began to pour out his soul in prayer and thanksgiving to God"	Alma 19:14; and see 26:16
37.	perform ordinances	"And as many as did believe were baptized"	Alma 19:35
38.	fellowshipping	"And they became a righteous people, and they did establish a church among them"	Alma 19:35
39.	ongoing teaching	"And he did exhort them daily, with all diligence"	Alma 21:23
40.	offer protection	"Let us gather together this people of the Lord"	Alma 27:5

(Richard J. Allen)

2–9 Ammon summarizes the Lord's blessings unto them as instruments in His service to harvest an abundant group of souls strong in the faith: "But behold, they are in the hands of the Lord of the harvest, and they are his; and he will raise them up at the last day" (verse 7).

> *10 And it came to pass that when Ammon had said these words, his brother Aaron rebuked him, saying: Ammon, I fear that thy joy doth carry thee away unto boasting.*
> *11 But Ammon said unto him:* ***I do not boast in my own strength,*** *nor in my own wisdom; but behold, my joy is full, yea, my heart is brim with joy, and I will rejoice in my God.*
> *12 Yea, I know that I am nothing; as to my strength I am weak; therefore I will not boast of myself,* ***but I will boast of my God, for in his strength I can do all things;*** *yea, behold, many mighty miracles we have wrought in this land, for which we will praise his name forever.*

I do not boast in my own strength but I will boast of my God, for in his strength I can do all things

Ammon employs essential elements of missionary work—devotion, knowledge of saving truths, openness to the directions of the Spirit, forceful action, and love—in order to further the cause of the Lord with great success. When his brother Aaron reproves him for what appears to be a boastful attitude following their mission to the Lamanites, Ammon responds that he is not boasting of himself, but only of His God. Let us be strong in our humility and trust in the Lord; we can then truly do all things "in his strength" (verse 12).

13–15 Ammon continues to recount the matchless blessings of the Lord in liberating so many of the Lamanites from their sinful ways and in bringing them into the everlasting light of salvation.

> *16 Therefore, let us glory, yea, we will* ***glory in the Lord;*** *yea, we will rejoice, for our joy is full; yea, we will praise our God forever. Behold, who can glory too much in the Lord? Yea, who can say too much of his great power, and of his mercy, and of his long-suffering toward the children of men? Behold, I say unto you, I cannot say the smallest part which I feel.*

Glory in the Lord

Following the example of Ammon, let us recognize and remember the power, mercy, and long-suffering of God—and glory in His goodness. Let us always give credit to the Lord in what we do. He is our strength. He is our support. All things are done in and through the Lord Jesus Christ.

17–20 Ammon recounts how he and his brothers, in their youthful state of rebellion, "went forth even in wrath, with mighty threatenings to destroy his church" (verse 18). But the Lord reached out and touched them with the Spirit of forgiveness and love.

> *21 And now behold, my brethren, what natural man is there that knoweth these things? I say unto you,* ***there is none that knoweth these things, save it be the penitent.***
> *22 Yea, he that repenteth and exerciseth faith, and bringeth forth good works, and prayeth continually without ceasing—****unto such it is given to know the mysteries of God;*** *yea, unto such it shall be given to reveal things which never have been revealed; yea, and it shall be given unto such to bring thousands of souls to repentance, even as it has been given unto us to bring these our brethren to repentance.*

THERE IS NONE THAT KNOWETH THESE THINGS, SAVE IT BE THE PENITENT; UNTO SUCH IT IS GIVEN TO KNOW THE MYSTERIES OF GOD

The mysteries of God include the doctrines, principles, and knowledge of God and His plan of exaltation, which man cannot know save by revelation. The mysteries of God are made known as we repent, exercise faith, pray, bring forth good works, and diligently give heed to the word of God (see Alma 12:8–12). We must seek that the mysteries of God be unfolded to us (see D&C 6:5–7) by the power of the Holy Ghost (see 1 Nephi 10:17–22). We must remember that the mysteries of God are found in the word of God (see Mosiah 1:3; 2:9). If we follow the example of Ammon and his brothers, we can know the mysteries of God.

23–26 When they first declare their desire to do missionary work among the Lamanites, the sons of Mosiah are scorned by their colleagues in Zarahemla. The prevailing opinion at the time is to take up arms and destroy the Lamanites. But the sons of Mosiah travel abroad among the Lamanites, not with the intention to destroy, but to save.

> *27 Now when our hearts were depressed, and we were about to turn back, behold, the Lord comforted us, and said: Go amongst thy brethren, the Lamanites, and bear with* ***patience*** *thine afflictions, and* ***I will give unto you success.***

PATIENCE; I WILL GIVE UNTO YOU SUCCESS

The lesson inherent in Ammon's statement is this: Never give up. As we learn patience and as we trust in the Lord, He will give us success.

28–29 Ammon recounts his many experiences of teaching the people in various venues—and the afflictions and challenges the missionaries have had to face, testifying that "through the power and wisdom of God **we have been delivered again**" (verse 29).

WE HAVE BEEN DELIVERED AGAIN

The sons of Mosiah endure their trials with patience and courage. They have not held back. They have gone wherever the people could be found. They have taught the gospel by precept and example—everywhere. We, too, can be missionaries every day of our life, in all circumstances. We can open our mouths and find that they will be filled with words of truth and salvation.

> *30 And we have suffered all manner of afflictions, and all this, that perhaps we might be the means of* ***saving some soul;*** *and we supposed that our joy would be full if perhaps we could be the means of saving some.*

Saving some soul

The worth of souls in great in the eyes of the Lord (see D&C 18:10). Like the sons of Mosiah, we should be willing to suffer all things to build up the kingdom of God and bring souls unto Christ.

> *31 Now behold, we can look forth and see the fruits of our labors; and are they few? I say unto you, Nay, they are many; yea, and we can witness of their sincerity, because of their* ***love toward their brethren*** *and also toward us.*

Love toward their brethren

The sons of Mosiah witness a miraculous change in their Lamanite associates. Where there has been bloodthirsty malice, there is now peaceful charity; where there has been the darkness of sin and evil, there is now the light of the Lord. The results of true conversion are love and light—without measure. When we are truly converted as disciples of Christ (see John 13:34–35), we will love our fellowmen and have the desire to bring them under the illuminating influence of the Savior.

32–34 Ammon remembers with admiration and rejoicing the covenant of peace entered into by their Lamanite converts—even their being willing to lay down their lives rather than take the lives of their brethren.

> *35 Now have we not* ***reason to rejoice?*** *Yea, I say unto you, there never were men that had so great reason to rejoice as we, since the world began; yea, and my joy is carried away, even unto boasting in my God; for he has all power, all wisdom, and all understanding; he comprehendeth all things, and he is a merciful Being, even unto salvation, to those who will repent and believe on his name.*
>
> *36 Now if this is boasting, even so will I boast; for* ***this is my life and my light, my joy and my salvation, and my redemption from everlasting wo.*** *Yea, blessed is the name of my God, who has been mindful of this people, who are a branch of the tree of Israel, and has been lost from its body in a strange land; yea, I say, blessed be the name of my God, who has been mindful of us, wanderers in a strange land.*

Reason to rejoice; this is my life and my light, my joy and my salvation, and my redemption from everlasting wo

Ammon's edifying words serve as the capstone of his testimony of his Savior. As an instrument in the Lord's hands, we, too, can assist in the work. From our devoted service flows the joy of beholding the power and goodness of God at work in the process of the Restoration and the fulfillment of the Abrahamic covenant.

> *37 Now my brethren, we see that* ***God is mindful of every people,*** *whatsoever land they may be in; yea, he numbereth his people, and his bowels of mercy are over all the earth. Now this is my joy, and my great thanksgiving; yea, and I will give thanks unto my God forever. Amen.*

God is mindful of every people

God loves all people, everywhere. They are His children. We should seek to emulate His love and concern for all mankind. This is the essence of the witness of Ammon and his brethren—some of the greatest missionaries ever to labor in the Lord's vineyard.

CHAPTER 27

OVERVIEW

Ammon and the king consult concerning the safety of the people of Anti-Nephi-Lehi, now coming increasingly under Lamanite attack. Ammon consults the Lord, who commands that the people be moved to safety in the land of Zarahemla. En route to Zarahemla, Ammon and his brethren encounter Alma and rejoice. The people of Zarahemla provide the land of Jershon as a protectorate to the immigrant converts, who are known henceforth as the people of Ammon. They are "a highly favored people of the Lord" (verse 30).

1–11 The Amalekites incite violence upon the people of Anti-Nephi-Lehi. Ammon counsels the king to move his people to a place of safety in the land of Zarahemla. The king demurs, fearing retribution from the Nephites for previous misdeeds. He suggests his people become slaves to the Nephites in exchange for protection, but Ammon informs him that such inequality is a violation of Nephite law. Ammon inquires of the Lord for guidance, who commands as follows:

12 Get this people out of this land, that they perish not; for Satan has great hold on the hearts of the Amalekites, who do stir up the Lamanites to anger against their brethren to slay them; therefore get thee out of this land; and blessed are this people in this generation, for ***I will preserve them.***

I WILL PRESERVE THEM

The Lord commands the Anti-Nephi-Lehi people to flee for safety. In all ages, the Lord has instructed the Saints: "Behold, it is my will, that all they who call on my name, and worship me according to mine everlasting gospel, should gather together, and stand in holy places" (D&C 101:22; compare 45:32). There is refuge and safety in gathering together in circles of Zion where strength comes through affinity with like-minded groups and congregations. For this reason, the Lord instructs Ammon to take the Anti-Nephi-Lehies out of the region of their origin and closer to the center place of the realm where they can be granted safety and protection. As it turns out, the sons of Mosiah will meet Alma on their journey back to Zarahemla (see Alma 27:16-17, compare Alma 17:1–4). The Saints will welcome them in full fellowship and give them the land of Jershon as their inheritance.

This is a stirring example of how the Saints can gather and stand in holy places. In this context, President James E. Faust has asked:

> "Who shall stand in his holy place?" May there be extended a helping hand to those who have wavered in their faith or who have transgressed, to bring them back. After fully repenting, they will have a special need for the redemptive portion of the endowment. May they know that their sins will no more be remembered.
>
> As we recall the commandment to stand in holy places, we should remember that beyond the temple, the most sacred and holy places in all the world should be our own dwelling places. Our homes should be committed and dedicated only to holy purposes. In our homes all of the security, the strengthening love, and the sympathetic understanding that we all so desperately need should be found.
>
> "Who shall ascend into the hill of the Lord? or who shall stand in his holy place?
>
> "He that hath clean hands, and a pure heart; who hath not lifted up his soul unto vanity, nor sworn deceitfully" (Ps. 24:3–4). For "holiness becometh thine house, O Lord, for ever" (Ps. 93:5). (Who Shall Ascend Into the Hill of the Lord?" *Ensign*, Aug. 2001, 4–5)

He Knew My Need

Fellowshipping thousands of new Saints, as in the case of the Anti-Nephi-Lehies, may not be an opportunity in every ward and stake—but everywhere someone needs to be loved and to be fellowshipped into the fold. The following story beautifully teaches the principle of loving fellowship:

> It was a lovely Sunday morning, but clouds of despair and discouragement had gathered within me. For weeks, I had felt increasingly unable to cope with numerous personal commitments and still give my family the quality time they needed. The harder I tried to foster a spirit of love and harmony, the more contention increased.
>
> My challenges seemed insurmountably great, and it was with a heavy heart that I sat through the opening exercises of Relief Society. The lesson was on fellowshipping members—the new sister, the inactive sister, the active sister. "Remember," read the manual, "the worth of souls is great in the sight of God." (D&C 18:10.) I thought of the few sisters in our small community, many of them inactive. Once I had felt close to all of them, but after recent rebuffs by two or three sisters, I felt estranged from all of them—even those who were once close friends. I felt drained, empty. Why should I press my friendship on those who didn't want it?
>
> "Right now," I thought bleakly, "*I'm* one of those active sisters who needs fellowship. I can't even cope with my own family. What makes me think I have anything to offer anybody else?"
>
> When the teacher challenged us to fellowship one sister during the week, I dutifully wrote down a name. "How can I expect the Lord to help me," I thought, "if I'm not doing my share?" But a wave of hopelessness and guilt washed over me as I stuffed the name into my purse. "I know I'm not going to do anything with this. I have nothing to give. Who would want anything from me, anyway?"
>
> Then the lesson was over. Before I could slip silently out the door, a sister from a neighboring community walked back and sat beside me. "Hey, I know this may sound crazy," she smiled, "but I've had the strongest feeling lately that I need to get better acquainted with you. How about getting together one day this week?"
>
> Before I could answer, a second sister, one from my own community, was at my side. "Are you feeling okay, Kathy?"

> I looked at her through rapidly brimming eyes. She put her hand on mine. The tears I had fought back all morning now began to fall, but my spirit soared, and I nodded in answer to her question.
>
> I had not felt able to cope, nor worthy to ask the Lord for help. Yet he had known my anguish, and these sisters had answered his call. How could I *not* cope, I realized, with him on my side! (Kathleen Pederson Whitworth, "He Knew My Need," in "Sharing," *Ensign* March 1985, 14)

13–15 Ammon and the king gather all of the people and move them to the borders of the land of Zarahemla. Ammon and his brethren then journey to the capital city to make arrangements for the safety of their convert people.

> *16 And it came to pass that as Ammon was going forth into the land, that* ***he and his brethren met Alma,*** *over in the place of which has been spoken; and behold, this was a joyful meeting.*
> *17 Now the joy of Ammon was so great even that he was full; yea,* ***he was swallowed up in the joy of his God,*** *even to the exhausting of his strength; and he fell again to the earth.*
> *18 Now was not this exceeding joy? Behold, this is joy which none receiveth save it be the truly penitent and humble seeker of happiness.*

He and his brethren met Alma; he was swallowed up in the joy of his God

The joy of encountering former companions in missionary service is a unique experience not fully comprehended by the world. Upon meeting Alma—whom he had not seen for fourteen years—Ammon collapses with joy. The joy of bringing souls unto Christ and sharing this joy with others is truly a highlight of the mortal experience (see Alma 29:9–10; 36:24). Such joy is received and felt by all those who are penitent and humbly seek happiness. We can receive joy and happiness as we aspire to help people come unto Christ.

19–26 Alma accompanies his brethren back to Zarahemla to his own home. They then consult with the chief judge concerning the people of Anti-Nephi-Lehi. The chief judge conducts a vote among the people, who agree to provide the immigrants the land of Jershon (south of Bountiful and east by the sea) as an inheritance and place of refuge. The Nephites agree to protect the people, providing they contribute resources to support the army. Alma and Ammon return to the Anti-

Nephi-Lehies to report the development. The people rejoice and receive the land with thanksgiving. They call themselves the people of Ammon from that time forth. It will be the valiant sons of these converts who serve as the 2,000 stripling warriors under Helaman—those faithful and fearless youth who will be the decisive factor in protecting the people from Lamanite attacks several decades later, around 64 B.C. to 62 B.C.

> *27 And they were among the people of Nephi, and also numbered among the people who were of the church of God. And they were also distinguished for their* ***zeal toward God, and also toward men;*** *for they were perfectly honest and upright in all things; and they were* ***firm in the faith of Christ, even unto the end.***
> *28 And they did look upon shedding the blood of their brethren with the greatest abhorrence; and they never could be prevailed upon to take up arms against their brethren; and they never did look upon death with any degree of terror, for their hope and views of Christ and the resurrection; therefore,* ***death was swallowed up to them by the victory of Christ over it.***
> *29 Therefore, they would suffer death in the most aggravating and distressing manner which could be inflicted by their brethren, before they would take the sword or cimeter to smite them.*
> *30 And thus they were a zealous and beloved people,* ***a highly favored people of the Lord.***

Zeal toward God, and also toward men; firm in the faith of Christ, even unto the end; death was swallowed up to them by the victory of Christ over it; a highly favored people of the Lord

How do we become a people highly favored of the Lord? The pattern is exemplified by the people of Ammon, who exhibit the following qualities: zeal (i.e., charitable fervor) toward God and others, honesty, faith in Christ, a peaceable disposition, a certainty of hope in the victory over death through Christ, and being beloved of all. Do we have these qualities in our own character?

EVIDENCE: Asylum (Alma 23–27)

As part of the law of Moses, a person who committed inadvertent manslaughter would seek asylum, which involved escaping to a city of refuge. Moses established at least six cities of refuge where persons guilty of inadvertent manslaughter could live until the death of the current high priest. By residing in such a place of asylum, the person—if found innocent of murder by a council of elders—could escape the blood vengeance of the victim's family. The Nephites, aware of the seriousness of premeditated murder (see 2 Nephi 9:35), would have been aware of the provisions in the law of Moses that dealt with inadvertent manslaughter. Many scholars consider Jershon—the Nephite land given to the Anti-Nephi-Lehies—a city of refuge. While we do not know if it falls into this category, Jershon could definitely be classified as a place of asylum. As converted Lamanites, the Anti-Nephi-Lehies were judged by the Zarahemla congregation and then given the land of Jershon, that they might seek refuge from the Lamanites. The Nephites then protected the Anti-Nephi-Lehies with their armies, thus fulfilling another provision of the law of Moses in regard to asylum. (See *Echoes,* 425–430.)

CHAPTER 28

OVERVIEW

Mormon gives a summary statement of the first fifteen years of the history of the people under the rule of the judges. Many thousands have been slain, while many thousands have come into the fold of Christ. Evil leads to misery and eternal wo; goodness leads to a salvation and "never-ending happiness" (verse 12).

1–11 The prophet-scriptorian Mormon provides a summary perspective on the first fifteen years of history from the time Alma first becomes chief judge and high priest in the land. It is a time of both sorrow and rejoicing. Tens of thousands have fallen among the Lamanites and Nephites during the horrendous battles. At the same time, thousands have come unto the fold of Christ to be nourished by the bread of life and salvation.

> *12 While many thousands of others* ***truly mourn*** *for the loss of their kindred,* ***yet they rejoice and exult in the hope,*** *and even know, according to the promises of the Lord, that they are raised to dwell at the right hand of God, in a state of never-ending happiness.*
> *13 And thus we see how great the inequality of man is because of sin and transgression, and the power of the devil, which comes by the cunning plans which he hath devised to ensnare the hearts of men.*
> *14 And thus we see* ***the great call of diligence of men to labor in the vineyards of the Lord;*** *and thus we see the great reason of sorrow, and also of rejoicing—****sorrow***

because of death and destruction among men, and joy because of the light of Christ unto life.

TRULY MOURN, YET THEY REJOICE AND EXULT IN THE HOPE; THE GREAT CALL OF DILIGENCE OF MEN TO LABOR IN THE VINEYARDS OF THE LORD; SORROW BECAUSE OF DEATH AND DESTRUCTION AMONG MEN, AND JOY BECAUSE OF THE LIGHT OF CHRIST UNTO LIFE

Consider the devoted labors and heartfelt concern of Mormon. Under the inspiration of God he scours the records of the people and extracts the wisdom and truth that will recapture the essence of God's message for future readers. He observes with sorrow the sufferings of both the wicked and the innocent. He notes the transcendent joy of those who experience the mighty change of heart and come unto Christ. He wants his readers to learn the lessons of faith, repentance, obedience, humility, and a willingness to press forward in the strength of the Lord. Mormon writes at a time when the Nephite nation is in the throes of extinction. Although his heart must be filled with anguish over the fate of his own people, he nevertheless bears solemn witness to us—his readers of the latter days—that iniquity leads to misery and destruction and that righteousness leads to happiness: "And thus we see the great call of diligence of men to labor in the vineyards of the Lord; and thus we see the great reason of sorrow, and also of rejoicing—sorrow because of death and destruction among men, and joy because of the light of Christ unto life" (verse 14). Are we ready to accept Mormon's message and conduct our lives in accordance with the truths of the gospel of Jesus Christ?

CHAPTER 29

OVERVIEW

Alma expresses an overpowering desire to be an instrument in bringing people unto the Lord. "O that I were an angel" (verse 1) is his initial outpouring of exuberance—but he tempers his wish to conform with the calling given him according to his abilities and talents. God knows best. He is all-wise in deciding how truth is dispensed to all nations. Alma glories in the success of his brethren and invokes a blessing upon them and their converts.

1 ***O THAT I were an angel,*** *and could have the wish of mine heart, that I might go forth and speak with the trump of God, with a voice to shake the earth, and cry repentance unto every people!*

2 Yea, ***I would declare unto every soul,*** *as with the voice of thunder,* ***repentance and the plan of redemption,*** *that they should repent and come unto our God, that there might not be more sorrow upon all the face of the earth.*

O THAT I WERE AN ANGEL; I WOULD DECLARE UNTO EVERY SOUL REPENTANCE AND THE PLAN OF REDEMPTION

There is great joy in being an instrument in the hands of God. Great satisfaction comes from investing our gifts and talents in full measure to the building up of the kingdom of God. Mormon preserves for us Alma's intimate expressions as he processes his spiritual feelings of being a valiant and committed missionary servant of the Lord. Alma has a great desire to preach the gospel to the whole world, and thus allows himself for a moment to wish for extramortal powers to reach others with overwhelming impact and effectiveness: "O that I were an angel. . . ." (verse 1).

3 But behold, I am a man, and do sin in my wish; for ***I ought to be content*** *with the things which the Lord hath allotted unto me.*

I OUGHT TO BE CONTENT

Alma repents of his overreaching zeal and glories in being a mere mortal (albeit one of great prophetic gifts). He confirms his gratitude before the Lord just to be able to do his job to the best of his ability. Missionary work is his joy and glory. He also feels joy in the success of others.

4–7 Alma knows that by God's decree men may choose salvation or destruction according to their desires. Why then should he desire more than to perform the work to which he is called?

8 For behold, ***the Lord doth grant unto all nations,*** *of their own nation and tongue, to teach his word, yea, in wisdom, all that he seeth fit that they should have; therefore we see that the Lord doth counsel in wisdom, according to that which is just and true.*
9 I know that which the Lord hath commanded me, and I glory in it. I do not glory of myself, but I glory in that which the Lord hath commanded me; yea, and ***this is my glory, that perhaps I may be an instrument in the hands of God*** *to bring some soul to repentance; and this is my joy.*

THE LORD DOTH GRANT UNTO ALL NATIONS; THIS IS MY GLORY, THAT PERHAPS I MAY BE AN INSTRUMENT IN THE HANDS OF GOD; I REMEMBER

The Lord is in charge. According to His infinite wisdom, He determines the measure of truth dispensed to each nation. It is our opportunity in life to serve as instruments in His hands to bring people unto Him. The Prophet Joseph Smith was specifically called to be an instrument in the hands of God:

> This messenger [Moroni] proclaimed himself to be an angel of God, sent to bring the joyful tidings that the covenant which God made with ancient Israel was at hand to be fulfilled, that the preparatory work for the second coming of the Messiah was speedily to commence; that the time was at hand for the Gospel in all its fullness to be preached in power, unto all nations that a people might be prepared for the Millennial reign. I was informed that I was chosen to be an instrument in the hands of God to bring about some of His purposes in this glorious dispensation. (*HC,* 4:536–537).

When we function worthily as instruments in the hands of God and observe the fruit of our labors—seeing His children come into His fold as a result of our service—then we remember His goodness to us. Elder Joseph B. Wirthlin reminds us that in our service toward building the kingdom of God we act as conduits for the blessings of the Spirit:

> Each of us has the sacred responsibility to proclaim the gospel. The Savior's commandment applies to all members of the Church, not just to full-time missionaries or to returned missionaries. We each have the responsibility to follow the Spirit when it prompts us to share the gospel so that others can come to follow the Savior.
>
> We must act when the Spirit speaks! When I hearkened to the Spirit, the young man from Germany responded positively to my message. But it wasn't really *my* message. It was God's message, brought to my mind by the Spirit of the Lord. I was but an instrument in the Lord's hands, led by his Spirit to open my mouth and proclaim the message of the Restoration. In opening my mouth, I became, as the Lord promises, "even as Nephi of old." (D&C 33:8.) Father Lehi gives this explanation of why his son was so adamant in proclaiming the gospel: "Behold, it was not [Nephi], but it was the Spirit of the Lord

> which was in him, which opened his mouth to utterance that he could not shut it." (2 Nephi 1:27.) (*Finding Peace in Our Lives* [Salt Lake City: Deseret Book, 1995], 241)

An instrument in the hands of God

Let us seek to be an instrument in the hands of God to help people repent—for this is our glory and joy. Our opportunity is to help people come unto Christ. This is the thing of most worth unto us (see D&C 15:6).

President Hugh B. Brown confirms this in a story of his mission days in England:

> When I think of missionary work—and incidentally it is my first love—I remember the words of Alma, "I know that which the Lord hath commanded me, and I glory in it. I do not glory of myself, but I glory in that which the Lord hath commanded me; yea, and this is my glory, that perhaps I might be an instrument in the hands of God to bring some soul to repentance; and this is my joy." (Alma 29:9.)
>
> When I think back on early missionary experiences, there comes to mind one incident which I shall never forget. Fifty-six years ago I was in Norwich, England, on a mission. I had been tracting, and in those days we went three times to every door regardless of the reception. On this occasion I came to a door where I remembered the woman had been particularly antagonistic, and I knocked on the door with the big brass knocker. I knocked as a mature missionary knocks, for I had been there nearly two years. New missionaries, as you know, sometimes knock rather carefully hoping they won't be heard, but I knocked vigorously and had no response. I looked through the window and saw a woman sitting in the front room knitting. I recognized her, for she had given me a tongue lashing before, and I knew she wasn't deaf nor dumb. She wouldn't respond so I went around to the back door. In those days we carried a walking stick. We had those long Prince Albert coats and derby hats. I took my walking stick and knocked on the door so hard that she came out like a setting hen comes off the nest in response to a troublesome boy. I think for several minutes she gave me the worst Scotch blessing I have ever had. But she had an impediment of speech; she had to stop every fifteen minutes to draw her breath, and when she did stop I said, "My dear lady, I apologize for having annoyed you, but our Heavenly Father sent me

6,000 miles to bring you a message and inasmuch as he sent me I can't go home until I give you that message." She said, "Do you mean the Lord sent a message to me?" I said, "I mean just that. He sent it because he loves you." She said, "Tell me the message." And I told her as best I could the Joseph Smith story. She listened intently, apparently impressed. And then I again apologized for having been rude enough to insist on her coming out and then I added, "Sister, when you and I meet again, and we will meet again, you are going to say 'thank you, and thank God that you came to my back door and insisted on speaking to me.'"

That was in 1906. Ten years later, in 1916, I was in England again, this time in uniform. President George F. Richards was the president of the mission. He had the flu, and he called me at the military camp and asked if it was possible to get a leave and go down to Norwich and hold a conference for him. I, of course, was very glad to visit my old mission field. At the close of the morning session a woman and four grown daughters came down the aisle.

I was shaking hands with old friends, and as I took her by the hand she bowed her head and kissed my hand and wet it with her tears. She said, "I do thank God that you came to my door ten years ago. When you left that day I thought about what you had said, I couldn't get it out of my mind. I was fighting it, but I couldn't sleep that night. I kept thinking, 'God has sent a message to me. But,' she said, 'I fought it for three days. I tried to find the missionaries from the address on the tract, and when I found them, you had returned to Canada. We continued to investigate until my daughters and I joined the Church, and next month we are leaving for Utah.' I cite that as a word of encouragement to you, my brothers and sisters. The joy that comes into the heart of a man or woman who has been instrumental in the hands of God in carrying the message of life and salvation to some soul, be it only one, is a joy beyond anything that men in the world can know. I am sure I need not emphasize that to you for you know it from experience. (*Continuing the Quest* [Salt Lake City: Deseret Book, 1961], 61–63)

*10 And behold, when I see many of my brethren truly penitent, and coming to the Lord their God, then is my soul filled with joy; then do **I remember** what the Lord has done for me, yea, even that he hath heard my prayer; yea, then do **I remember** his merciful arm which he extended toward me.*

*11 Yea, and **I also remember** the captivity of my fathers; for I surely do know that the*
Lord did deliver them out of bondage, and by this did establish his church; yea, the
Lord God, the God of Abraham, the God of Isaac, and the God of Jacob, did deliver
them out of bondage.
*12 Yea, **I have always remembered** the captivity of my fathers; and that same God who*
delivered them out of the hands of the Egyptians did deliver them out of bondage.
13 Yea, and that same God did establish his church among them; yea, and that same
God hath called me by a holy calling, to preach the word unto this people, and hath
given me much success, in the which my joy is full.

I remember; I also remember; I have always remembered

Missionary work is an exercise in remembering. All too frequently we come to take our blessings for granted—we tend to forget the goodness and mercy of God when left on our own. But when we reach out and teach others the plan of redemption and watch them go through the mighty change, we are revitalized in our convictions. We remember what it was like to become a new person in the Lord. We recall His matchless blessings unto us. Watching converts being lifted up through the Spirit reinvigorates our memory of having gone through the same thing. Alma brings this powerful thought into our minds and helps us to remember our blessings and discern the hand of the Lord at work in our lives today, just as it was from the beginning of our conversion. Do we remember always the blessings of the Lord?

*14 But I do not joy in my own success alone, but **my joy is more full because of the***
***success of my brethren,** who have been up to the land of Nephi.*
15 Behold, they have labored exceedingly, and have brought forth much fruit; and how
great shall be their reward!
16 Now, when I think of the success of these my brethren my soul is carried away, even
to the separation of it from the body, as it were, so great is my joy.
*17 And now **may God grant** unto these, my brethren, that they may sit down in the*
kingdom of God; yea, and also all those who are the fruit of their labors that they may
go no more out, but that they may praise him forever. And may God grant that it may
be done according to my words, even as I have spoken. Amen.

My joy is more full because of the success of my brethren; may God grant

A sure sign of a disciple of Christ is that he or she has learned how to rejoice in the progress of others.

It is not only joy in ourselves that constitutes spiritual maturity, but more importantly having joy in the successes of others. John the Beloved stated: "I have no greater joy than to hear that my children walk in truth" (3 John 1:4). Emissaries of the Lord have no greater joy than to see those they teach walk in truth. Church leaders have no greater joy than to see their congregants and students walk in truth.

CONCLUDING THOUGHTS

To look in upon these famous scenes from the Book of Mormon is to see the unfolding stories of conversion to the Lord, of making a covenant of peace, of rejoicing in the blessings of the gospel, of seeking and finding refuge among the Saints, and of experiencing the profound joy and enduring glory in being an instrument in the hands of God.

Alma and the sons of Mosiah stand as beacons of light, examples to all of the blessings of missionary work. They were truly instruments in the hands of God. They were ready to be used, they had a strong desire to serve, they were clean and pure, they knew their purpose, and they trusted in the Lord. They worked with all their heart, might, mind, and strength. They thrust in their sickles and saved thousands of souls. We too can be instruments in the hands of God—in our homes as we bless each family member, and at school and work where we can be a friend to the lonely or just a smile to lift their spirits. In everything we do, every day of our lives, we can ask the question, "Whom can I bless? How can I serve?"

TOPICAL INDEX